RAMSEY ZARIFEH was born in Kent but has spent most of his working life outside the UK. After graduating from Magdalene College, Cambridge, with a degree in English, he spent two years in Japan on the JET scheme. Following a spell at Reuters in London he returned to Japan to research this guide. He has worked as a journalist and editor for a variety of radio and television stations and websites. He returns to Japan as often as possible and files reports about the country several times a year for travel magazines and radio programmes.

Japan by Rail
First edition: 2002; this second edition 2007

Publisher
Trailblazer Publications
The Old Manse, Tower Rd, Hindhead, Surrey, GU26 6SU, UK
Fax (+44) 01428-607571, info@trailblazer-guides.com
www.trailblazer-guides.com

British Library Cataloguing in Publication Data
A catalogue record for this book is available from the British Library

ISBN 978-1-873756-97-3

Maps © Trailblazer 2002, 2007
Colour photographs © as credited
B&W photographs © Kazuo Udagawa

The haiku at the start of each chapter in this book is reproduced with permission of:
Tohta Kaneko: p9; Minako Kaneko: p416; Kazuko Konagai: p73; Professor Makoto Ueda
and University of Toronto Press (*Modern Japanese Haiku – An Anthology*): p36 & p371

Editor: Anna Jacomb-Hood
Series editor: Patricia Major
Layout: Anna Jacomb-Hood
Japanese proof-reader: Kazuo Udagawa
Cartography: Nick Hill
Cover design: Richard Mayneord
Index: Jane Thomas

Every effort has been made by the author and publisher to ensure that the information
contained herein is as accurate and up to date as possible. However, they are unable to
accept responsibility for any inconvenience, loss or injury sustained by anyone as a
result of the advice and information given in this guide.

Printed on chlorine-free paper by
D2Print (☎ +65-6295 5598), Singapore

JAPAN
BY RAIL

RAMSEY ZARIFEH

TRAILBLAZER PUBLICATIONS

Acknowledgements

Thanks are due to the Central Japan Railway Company (JR-Tokai), without whose generous support the first edition of this book would never have been written. Takao Hashimoto and Naoyuki Ueno of JR-Tokai's London office provided assistance with the second edition. My thanks also go to the Japan National Tourist Organization (JNTO) and to Noboru Okabe, General Manager of Swiss International Air Lines in Tokyo.

I am also grateful to: Mari Watanabe in Sapporo, Nicholas Sebel and Nicola Jones in Matsue, Yoshiko Minami in Nara, Keiji and Hiromi Shimizu in Kyoto, Yuji Nakayama in Osaka, Kenichi Anazawa in Tokyo, and Deirdre Gough in the UK.

Special thanks to Anthony Robins in Nagoya for continuing to answer all my rail-related questions and for helping to update the Takayama city guide. I am grateful to Richard Brasher and Alistair Logan for taking some of the photos, and to everyone else I met along the way for giving me advice and telling me about their own experiences of travelling in Japan.

Renewed thanks to Anna Jacomb-Hood for her meticulous editing, to Kazuo Udagawa for language help and for some of the photos and to Kenichi Udagawa for tackling the timetables.

For the haiku (poems) at the start of each chapter I should like to thank: the President of the Modern Haiku Association (Japan), Tohta Kaneko; the President of the British Haiku Society, David Cobb, whose introductions, haiku suggestions and general advice were invaluable; Kazuko Konagai for supplying and translating a wide range of appropriate haiku; and series editor Patricia Major for liaising with everyone above and for making the final selection.

My thanks are also due to Ichie Uchiyama for providing the calligraphy for the book title, to Nick Hill for drawing the maps, Jane Thomas for the index, and also to the publisher, Bryn Thomas. Thanks also to my parents and to my brothers, Alex and Andrew.

A request

The author and publisher have tried to ensure that this guide is as accurate and up to date as possible. Nevertheless things change. If you notice any changes or omissions that should be included in the next edition of this book, please write to Ramsey Zarifeh at Trailblazer (address on p2) or email him at ramsey.zarifeh@trailblazer-guides.com. A free copy of the next edition will be sent to persons making a significant contribution.

www.japanbyrail.com

For interviews with the author and for more photos and web links, see Ramsey Zarifeh's website: 🖳 www.japanbyrail.com.

Updated information will shortly be available at
www.trailblazer-guides.com

Front cover: Mt Fuji (3776m/12,388ft; see p130) in spring;
snow covers the peak for most of the year. (Photo © JNTO).

CONTENTS

PART 7: KYUSHU

PART 8: SHIKOKU

APPENDICES

INTRODUCTION

Think of Japan and one of the first images you're likely to conjure up is that of the bullet train speeding past snow-capped Mt Fuji. For many, what lies beyond the frame of this image is a mystery. But step inside the picture, hop on board that train and you'll quickly discover the true scope and variety of what the country has to offer.

The fascination of Japan lies in its diversity: remote mountain villages contrast with huge neon-lit cities that never sleep; the vast natural landscape of unspoilt forests, volcanoes and hot springs more than compensate for the occasional man-made eyesore; the silent oasis of a Shinto shrine or a Buddhist temple is not far from the deafening noise of a virtual-reality games arcade. Nowhere else in the world do past and present co-exist in such close proximity as in this relatively small country.

The ideal way of seeing it all is by rail, whether it's on one of the world-famous bullet trains (*shinkansen*) or on the wide network of local or express trains, or even on one of the many steam trains. An early 20th-century guide-book advised visitors to 'make travel plans as simple as possible. The conditions of travel in this country do not lend themselves to intricate arrangements'. Today, however, nothing could be further from the truth. Trains run not just to the minute but to the second, so itineraries can be as complicated or minutely timetabled as you wish. Or you can simply turn up at the station and plan your journey as you go. Most Japanese travel by train, so it's the ideal way to meet the people and find out what life is really like for at least some of the 127 million who live here.

The real secret to touring the country is the Japan Rail Pass, deservedly recognized as the 'bargain of the century'. Rail-pass holders can travel easily almost anywhere on the four main islands over a network that stretches for 20,000km. Take advantage of the freedom it confers to explore on and off the beaten track beyond the Tokyo metropolis and the tourist capital of Kyoto.

Japan need not be too expensive as, apart from your rail pass, you can cut costs by staying in youth hostels, *minshuku* (Japanese-style B&Bs) or business hotels (Western or Japanese style). For those with a larger budget staying in *ryokan* (upmarket B&Bs) can be an amazing experience, but if you prefer there are world-class five-star hotels throughout the country.

Unexpected pleasures also await the traveller: where else are you greeted by a conductor wearing white gloves who bows and doffs his cap as you hurtle along at 190mph (300kph) on a shinkansen? Where else can you buy cans of hot coffee from a vending machine at the top of a mountain or take a crash course in Zen meditation in a temple? It's said that no *gaijin* (outsider) can ever fully know Japan but only by visiting and seeing for yourself can you discover what the country is really like: somewhere between the images of traditional past and hi-tech future which flicker worldwide on the small screen.

Routes and costs

ROUTE OPTIONS

So you know you're going to Japan: the next step is to work out what you want to see and how much ground you want to cover once you've arrived. This guide shows you how travelling around Japan by rail is the best way of seeing as much as possible in a short space of time. Travelling by air may be quicker but only by rail can you see the country close up and in full colour. And there are few places in the world where the trains virtually always run on time, travelling at speeds of up to 190mph (300kph); where smartly dressed conductors doff their caps and bow to the whole carriage before checking tickets, and where it really can be as much fun to travel as it is to arrive. Welcome to Japan by rail.

Japan Rail (JR) boasts that its network covers every corner of the four major Japanese islands. If you looked at the maps in JR's timetable you'd see what appears to be a close approximation to a bowl of spaghetti. The choice of routes is, if not infinite, at the very least overwhelming.

To simplify travel planning and to reassure the first-time visitor that a qualification in orienteering is not needed to negotiate your way round the country, this guide splits Japan into: Central Honshu (see pp125-92); Western Honshu (pp233-78); Northern Honshu/Tohoku (pp278-326); the Kansai region (pp192-232) which includes the cities of Kyoto, Nara and Osaka; Hokkaido (pp327-70); Kyushu (pp371-415); and Shikoku (pp416-48). To help plan a trip, sample itineraries are provided (see pp21-7) as well as information on using the route guides (see p449).

COSTS

Contrary to popular belief, a visit to Japan doesn't have to be expensive but it is important to plan your budget as it is an easy country to spend money in.

Package tours which include travel by rail (see pp17-20) rarely offer better value than organizing an independent trip. From the UK you'd be unlikely to pay anything less than £1700 for a 14-day tour including return flights, rail travel, accommodation in basic Japanese inns, some meals and the services of a tour guide. This may be an option if you prefer to let someone else do all the planning and route selecting but given the price of a 14-day rail pass

きよお！と喚いてこの汽車はゆく新緑の夜中

*Kyoh! screaming aloud
this train runs into
the fresh green midnight*
(Tohta Kaneko)

(£187/US$371) it would certainly be more cost effective (as well as more fun!) to organize your own trip.

Though the initial cost of a Japan Rail pass (see box p13) may seem a lot, bear in mind that a return ticket on the shinkansen between Tokyo and Kyoto costs ¥26,840; since a one-week rail pass costs ¥28,300 the pass almost pays for itself from this one trip. Take just one additional journey and the pass really begins to save you money. The return fare from Tokyo to Hiroshima by shinkansen is ¥36,500, well over the cost of a one-week pass. A return journey to Sapporo in Hokkaido from Tokyo by a combination of shinkansen and limited express works out at ¥46,360, more than the cost of a two-week pass.

So, a rail pass turns travelling around the country into a real bargain but what about all the other costs? One couple boast on the web that they live in Japan on ¥500 (£2/$4) a day, though their tips for survival include 'pot noodle', 'hide in the toilets on long-distance trains' to avoid buying a ticket, and for accommodation 'cardboard boxes and newspaper make really good insulation'. This is definitely not recommended. For a better idea of what you're likely to be spending per day, see the box below. Alternatively, check 🖳 www.price checktokyo.com, where you'll find lists of up-to-date prices for everything from beer to butter, toothpaste to toilet paper in Tokyo, though the prices seem applicable for the country as a whole.

❏ **SAMPLE DAILY BUDGETS**

Note: The budgets below do not include travel costs because they assume you have a Japan Rail Pass. The exchange rates are rounded up/down for convenience.

Low

Accommodation	¥2600 (£10/US$21) hostel without meals
Breakfast	¥500 (£2/US$4) coffee and toast
Lunch	¥500 (£2/US$4) sandwich or convenience-store snack
Dinner	¥1100 (£5/US$9) noodles/pasta or a hostel meal
Sightseeing	¥1700 (£7/US$14) less if you only visit free attractions
Total	**¥6400 (£26/US$52)**

Mid-range

Accommodation	¥5300 (£22/US$43) basic business hotel (no meals) or ¥7000 (£29/US$57) minshuku with two meals
Breakfast	¥890 (£4/US$7) egg, ham, toast and coffee
Lunch	¥1100 (£5/US$9) lunch deal in a café/restaurant
Dinner	¥1600 (£7/US$14) set evening meal at a restaurant
Sightseeing	¥1700 (£7/US$14) more if you visit lots of galleries/museums
Total	**¥10,590 (£45/US$87), or ¥9800 (£41/US$80)**

High

Accommodation	¥16,000 (£67/US$131) ryokan/upmarket hotel
Breakfast	¥2140 (£9/US$18) buffet breakfast
Lunch	¥3570 (£15/US$30) three courses
Dinner	¥6250+ (£26+/US$52+) à la carte
Sightseeing	¥9000+ (£37+/US$74+) guided city tours and entry fees
Total	**¥36,960+ (£154+/US$305+)**

When to go

In general, Japan has a mild climate, though it's difficult to talk at all generally about a country which stretches for some 3000km north to south. It can be below freezing and snowing in Hokkaido, while southern Kyushu is enjoying sunshine and mild temperatures. April and May are often considered the best months to visit, when the worst of the Hokkaido winter is over and the rest of Japan is not yet sweltering in humidity. Cherry-blossom viewing takes place March to May.

The rainy season in June/July (with occasional typhoons) marks the change from spring to summer but the squalls and showers soon dry up to be replaced by heat and humidity. Humidity is high

TOKYO

**MAX / MIN TEMPERATURE CHARTS (°F / °C)
AND AVERAGE RAINFALL (MM / INCH)**

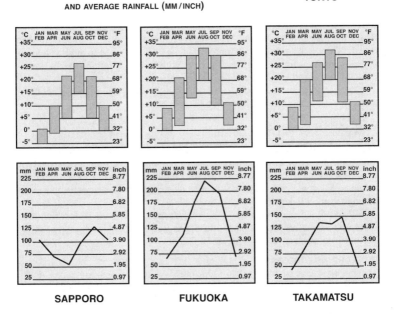

SAPPORO   FUKUOKA   TAKAMATSU

throughout the summer months so carry bottled water if you are planning long days of sightseeing at this, the hottest, time of the year. Hokkaido is by far the coolest and least humid place in summer but this also makes it one of the busiest. The high temperatures and – particularly in the south – sweltering heat can last well into September and often there is a lot of rain then but things usually cool down and dry up by the beginning of October.

Autumn is another pleasant season, though October/November are the 'leaves' viewing' months, when people flock to see temple grounds covered in fallen leaves. The main areas for skiing are central Japan and Hokkaido. If you don't mind the cold, late autumn/early winter can be a peaceful time to visit.

Try to avoid Japan's national holidays, in particular **Golden Week** (April 29th-May 5th), when it seems as if the entire country is on the move; hotels and trains are booked out and prices rise to meet demand. The school holiday season in August is another busy time, particularly around mid-August during the **obon** festival when people head back to their home towns.

For further information visit the Japan Meteorological Agency's website 🖥 www.jma.go.jp/jma/indexe.html.

Rail passes

The original and still the best-value rail pass available to visitors is the Japan Rail Pass, which covers the whole country. Most regional JR companies have their own pass(es) which compliment the national pass; see opposite for further details. These are a cheaper alternative and may be of interest to anyone intending to focus their travel on a specific area. With some exceptions the JR passes must be purchased before arrival in Japan (for full details, see p20).

Travel by rail becomes much more expensive without the rail pass, but there are still some discounts and bargain tickets to be had (see p84).

THE JAPAN RAIL PASS

The Japan Rail Pass is truly the bargain of the century. It entitles the pass holder to travel freely on almost all JR services, including most shinkansen (the bullet train). The only exceptions are the *Nozomi* shinkansen and some overnight services. Having a rail pass means you can travel almost everywhere without having to buy a ticket.

JR has a dedicated website (🖥 www.japanrail.com) in English which provides up-to-date information about the Japan Rail Pass and all regional passes. For more details, see 🖥 www.japanrailpass.net.

Who can use the pass?

The rail pass can be used by any non-Japanese tourists visiting Japan under 'temporary visitor' status. Some Japanese nationals not residing in Japan can

❑ **JAPAN RAIL PASS – COSTS**

Days	Ordinary Class	Green Class
7 days	¥28,300 (£117/US$233)	¥37,800 (£156/US$311)
14 days	¥45,100 (£187/US$371)	¥61,200 (£254/US$504)
21 days	¥57,700 (£239/US$475)	¥79,600 (£330/US$655)

Children aged 5 and under travel free providing they do not occupy a seat; those aged 6-11 pay half. Prices are fixed in yen, but the charge is payable in local currency. The prices in brackets are for rough guidance only. The exact cost depends on the exchange rate in your home country at the time of purchase. It's worth shopping around as travel agencies apply different exchange rates.

use a rail pass but all other Japanese cannot. The pass cannot be used by anybody arriving in Japan for employment.

Buying the pass

The most important rule concerning use of the rail pass is that it **cannot** be purchased in Japan. It is sold, in the form of an exchange order, at authorized agents (see pp17-20) outside Japan. Before contacting an agent, work out what kind of pass you will need. First decide whether you would like a **7-day**, **14-day** or **21-day** pass. The pass runs on consecutive days from the date you first use it but there is no limit to the number of passes you can buy.

Once you've decided the length of pass you want, the next step is to decide what class you'd like to travel in. There are two types of rail pass: the **Ordinary Pass** is valid for standard-class rail travel, which is likely to be more than adequate for most people. Seats in ordinary class are very comfortable and on some trains are as good as first-class rail travel elsewhere in the world. For those used to luxury and wishing to travel in a bit more style, the **Green Pass** is the one to get. Green-class carriages (known as 'Green Cars') offer much wider seats, more legroom, and often include extras such as slippers, personal TVs, laptop power points and free tea/coffee.

Local trains in Japan have standard class only but most limited expresses and shinkansen convey Green cars – the main exceptions are the Hikari Rail Star (Okayama to Hakata) and the Kyushu shinkansen.

REGIONAL JAPAN RAIL PASSES

In addition to the pass for nationwide travel, most companies in the JR Group offer their own range of regional passes; these are a cheaper alternative if you're planning to restrict your travel to specific areas. None of the regional passes includes travel on the bullet train between Tokyo and Kyoto so you need to buy the national pass if planning to take this route or be prepared to pay the cost of the ticket.

Regional rail passes can be purchased before arrival in Japan, or at Narita, Kansai and Nagoya airports, and at selected mainline stations.

❑ JR EAST RAIL PASS

Days	Class	Adult	Youth (12-25)
5-day	Ordinary	¥20,000 (£83/US$164)	¥16,000 (£66/US$131)
	Green	¥28,000 (£116/US$230)	n/a
10-day	Ordinary	¥32,000 (£132/US$263)	¥25,000 (£103/US$205)
	Green	¥44,800 (£185/US$368)	n/a
Flexible 4-day	Ordinary	¥20,000 (£83/US$164)	¥16,000 (£66/US$131)
	Green	¥28,000 (£116/US$230)	n/a

Children aged 5 and under travel free providing they do not occupy a seat; those aged 6-11 pay half the ordinary/green adult rate.

JR East Rail Pass

Valid for travel on the JR East network, which extends east of Tokyo and includes the route around Tohoku (see pp278-308) as far as the northern tip of Honshu, but does not include Hokkaido. The pass is also valid for travel from Tokyo into the Japanese Alps, as far as Nagano (see p168) and Matsumoto (see p174). It also includes travel on the Tohoku, Nagano and Joetsu shinkansen, the Narita Express train from Narita Airport to downtown Tokyo, and JR services in the Tokyo metropolitan area (including the hot-spring resort of Atami, see p128). Passes are available in 5- and 10-day varieties, or the flexible 4-day ticket is valid for any four days within one month from the first date of use. The pass is an especially good deal if you're aged between 12 and 25 because there is a youth rate. For more details see 🖳 www.jreast.co.jp.

JR West Rail Pass

There are two types of JR West Rail Pass: the Sanyo Area Pass and Kansai Area Pass. Both are available in ordinary class only. These passes are the exception to the rule and can be purchased in Japan as well as overseas but you still need to show your passport with 'temporary visitor' stamp.

The Sanyo Area Pass is valid only for stops on the Sanyo line between Shin-Osaka and Hakata (Kyushu). The pass permits travel on: all shinkansen services on this route (including the Nozomi) as well as local trains, the JR ferry

❑ JR WEST RAIL PASS

Sanyo Area Pass		Kansai Area Pass	
Days	Adult	Days	Adult
4-day	¥20,000 (£83/US$164)	1-day	¥2000 (£8.30/US$16)
8-day	¥30,000 (£124/US$247)	2-day	¥4000 (£16.60/US$32)
		3-day	¥5000 (£21/US$41)
		4-day	¥6000 (£25/US$49)

Children aged 5 and under travel free providing they do not occupy a seat; those aged 6-11 pay half the adult rate.

service to Miyajima (see p268), and the journey from Kansai Airport to Osaka. It is **not** valid for journeys to Kyoto. To buy this pass (4-day or 8-day) visit a JR travel service centre at any main station between Shin-Osaka and Hakata.

The **Kansai Area Pass** is useful if you're spending only a few days in and around Kyoto and plan to make a couple of short excursions. It covers travel on local trains only between Kyoto, Osaka, Kobe, Nara, Himeji and Kansai Airport. It is also valid for non-reserved seats on the Haruka LEX to Kansai Airport. The pass is available for **one day** or **four days**. To buy this pass, visit a JR travel centre at either Kansai Airport, Kyoto or Shin-Osaka station. For more details see 🖳 www.westjr.co.jp.

JR Kyushu Rail Pass
Valid for travel on all JR Kyushu lines including the Kyushu shinkansen, so the pass is useful for the Kyushu route guide (see pp371-88). However, this pass cannot be used on the Sanyo shinkansen linking the Kyushu capital of Fukuoka/Hakata (see p389) with mainland Honshu.

The **5-day pass** costs ¥16,000 (£66/US$131) and the **3-day pass** costs ¥13,000 (£54/US$107). Children aged 6-11 travel for half price and 5 and under travel free providing they do not occupy a seat. The pass can be purchased prior to arrival in Japan as well as at the following JR stations in Kyushu: Kokura, Hakata, Nagasaki, Kumamoto, Kagoshima, Oita and Miyazaki. For more details see 🖳 www.jrkyushu.co.jp.

JR Hokkaido Rail Pass
JR Hokkaido offers two types of rail pass, both of which are valid on all JR Hokkaido trains, but not for the journey from Honshu to Hokkaido. The **5-day pass** costs ¥18,000 (£74/US$148) in standard class and ¥25,000 (£103/US$205) for first class (Green Car). A **3-day pass** costs ¥14,000 (£58/US$115) in standard class and ¥20,000 (£83/US$164) for first class.

JR Hokkaido offers a special service which allows you to 'reserve' your rail pass online in advance of your arrival in Japan, saving you time and cutting out the need to fill in forms when you get there. Reserved passes can be collected at the JR Hokkaido Visitors Information Desk (see p359) inside Sapporo station or, if you are flying into Sapporo, from New Chitose Airport station.

As an alternative to the two rail passes, JR Hokkaido also sells a **7-day Hokkaido Round Tour Pass** (Hokkaido Furii Passu), which costs ¥23,400 (£97/US$193) in standard class and ¥34,500 (£143/US$284) for first class. The ticket – which, unlike the other rail passes, can be purchased by anyone – offers 7-day unlimited rides in the unreserved carriages of both express and limited expresses as well as on some JR Hokkaido buses. You can make up to six free seat reservations (in either standard or first-class carriages, depending on which ticket you have bought) during the validity of the ticket. However, the pass cannot be used during peak holiday seasons: Golden Week, Obon, and New Year (see p67).

Finally, the **One-day Sapporo-Otaru Welcome Pass, which** costs ¥1500 (£6/US$12), is available only to tourists from abroad and allows unlimited rides

Overcoming the language barrier

One of the biggest worries for first-time visitors to Japan is the language barrier. How easy is it to make yourself understood and navigate your way around the country? The answer is that it's surprisingly easy; most Japanese can understand some English, even if not everybody speaks it.

You don't need to be able to read Japanese characters to find your way around; station (place) names are written in English on every platform, and on-board announcements are made in English on all shinkansen and some limited express trains; the vast majority of hotels and ryokan have their names written in English outside, and in most towns and cities, road signs and street names are in both Japanese and English. However, it's always useful to have the name of the place you're heading for written on a piece of paper, so you can show it to taxi drivers or passers-by when asking for directions. Ask hotel reception or tourist information staff to write

down in Japanese all the places you're planning to visit during the day.

For more details about English on the railways see p87 and for some useful words and phrases see pp452-5.

on JR Hokkaido trains between Sapporo and the port city of Otaru, as well as on all subway lines in Sapporo itself. This pass comes with a handy leaflet on how to use the ticket and a sightseeing map of Otaru. Rail fans might consider purchasing this pass if they are planning a day trip to the transport museum in Otaru (see p364).

For more details on the above see 🖳 www2.jrhokkaido.co.jp/global/eng lish/railpass/index.html.

GETTING A RAIL PASS

The majority of rail passes have to be bought outside Japan. The full list of agents authorized to sell these passes is available on 🖳 www.japanrailpass.net. Authorized agents include: JTB (🖳 www.jtbusa.com/enhome/groupinfo.asp), Nippon Travel Agency (NTA; 🖳 www.nta.co.jp/english/rail/agents.htm), Kintetsu International (🖳 www.knt.co.jp/kokusai/global/index.html), Toptour Corporation (🖳 www.toptour.co.jp), Japan Airlines (JAL; 🖳 www.jal.com/en/travel/jr_pass), All Nippon Airways (ANA: see box p28) and JALPAK (🖳 www.jalpak.com).

The agencies listed below are all authorized to sell the Japan Rail Pass; most also book flights and accommodation, and can organize itineraries. Enquire also about tailor-made package tours.

The list below includes the main agents; where there are several branches of a particular agency in one country full contact details have not been given but these are available on the relevant company's website.

From the UK and Ireland

Japan Travel Centre (☎ 0870-890 0360, 🖥 www.japantravel.co.uk, 212 Piccadilly, London WIJ 9HX) The travel centre (and a very useful book store) are upstairs and there's an excellent Japanese restaurant (both counter and table service) on ground level as well as a small Japanese food section in the basement.

Access Japan/Sunrise Tours (☎ 020-7808 3160, 🖥 www.accessjapan.co.uk, Dorland House, 14-20 Regent St, London SW1Y 4PH).

JTB (☎ 020-8237 1601, 🖥 www.jtbuk.com, Horatio House, 79-85 Fulham Palace Rd, London W6 8JA).

ANA Tours (☎ 020-8846 0200, 🖥 www.anatours.co.uk/eng/index.htm, 4th Floor, Hythe House, 200 Shepherds Bush Rd, London W6 7NY).

AWL Travel (🖥 www.alt.com) has branches in London (☎ 020-7222 1144, 1 Artillery Row, SW1P 1RH) and in Dublin (☎ 01-679 5340, 2nd Fl, 42 Dawson St, Dublin 2).

Emerald Global Ltd (☎ 020-7312 1700, 🖥 www.etours-online.com, 15-16 New Burlington St, London W1X 1FF).

Ffestiniog Travel (☎ 01766-512400, 🖥 www.festtravel.co.uk, Harbour Station, Porthmadog, Gwynedd LL49 9NF).

Trailfinders (☎ 0845-058 5858, 🖥 www.trailfinders.com) has branches throughout Britain and in Ireland; check their website for details of your closest office.

Reliance Tours (☎ 020-7437 0503, 🖥 www.reliance-tours.co.uk, Astoria House, 62 Shaftesbury Ave, London W1D 6LT).

RailChoice (☎ 0870-165 7300, 🖥 www.railchoice.co.uk, 15 Colman House, Empire Square High St, London SE20 7EX).

InsideJapan Tours (☎ 0870-120 5600, 🖥 www.insidejapantours.com, Lewins House, Lewins Meads, Bristol, BS1 2NN) offers both self-guided adventures and and small group tours.

Gendai Travel Ltd (☎ 0870-033 9577, 🖥 www.gendai.co.uk/en, Bloomsbury Bldg, 6 Southampton Place, London WC1A 2DB).

H.I.S. Europe Ltd (☎ 0870-873 7880, 🖥 www.his-euro.co.uk, 14 Charles II St, London SW1Y 4QU).

Top Tour Europe (☎ 20-7493 2173, 🖥 www.tteuk.com/japan-rail-pass, 2nd Floor, 295 Regent St, London W1B 2HL).

Euro Creative Tours/Jaltour (☎ 0870-111 8830, 🖥 www.jaltour.co.uk, 2F Dorland House, 14-16 Regent St, London SW1Y 4PH).

Audley Travel (☎ 01993 838 100, 🖥 www.audleytravel.com, New Mill, New Mill Lane, Witney, Oxon OX29 9SX).

Into Japan Specialist Tours (☎ 01865-841443, 🖥 www.intojapan.co.uk, 80 Fernhill Rd, Begbroke, Kidlington OX5 1RR) offer both scheduled tours, which coincide with major festivals, and tailor-made tours which come with a rail pass.

From continental Europe

● **Austria** Net Travel Service (☎ 01-71609, Operngasse 6/2/2, 1010 Vienna); **Verkehrsburo-Ruefa Reisen GmbH** (☎ 01-588 0545, Friedrichstrasse 7, A-1010 Vienna); **H.I.S. Travel** (☎ 01-587 1073, Opernrlng 1/R/503-506, 1010

Vienna); **Jalpak International** (☎ 01-512 7580, ▣ cta.vie.jalpak@aon.at, Kaerntnerstrasse, 11/Weihburggasse 2, 4th Floor, A-1010, Vienna).

● **Belgium**   **Nippon Travel Agency** (▣ www.nta.co.jp/english/rail/agents .htm) has two authorized agents in Belgium: Ictam (☎ 02-512 3813, 62-4 rue de la Montagne, 1000 Brussels) and Japan P.I. Travel (☎ 02-512 0107, 100 rue de Stassart, 1050 Brussels); **Euro Express Travel Service** (☎ 02-627 1818, ▣ www.eurex.be, 311 Ave Louise, 1050 Brussels); **Jalpak International** (☎ 02-639 0910, ▣ www.jalpak.be, 283 Ave Louise, Box 17, 1050 Brussels).

● **Denmark**   NET **Travel Service** (☎ 3345 4000, ▣ www.netravel.dk, Vester Voldgade 94, DK 1552, Copenhagen).

● **France**   Universal Netlink (☎ 01.53.45.93.30, ▣ www.jtb-uni.com, 18 rue des Pyramides, 75001 Paris), part of the JTB Group; **H.I.S. International Tours** (☎ 01.53.06.34.00, ▣ www.his-tours.fr, 14 rue Gaillon, 76002 Paris); **Nippon Travel Agency** (▣ www.nta.co.jp/english/rail/agents.htm) has three authorized agents: Voyageurs au Japon (☎ 01.42.61.60.83, 45 rue Saint-Anne, 75001 Paris); Miki Travel (☎ 01.3.98.50.50, 9 rue Scrive, 75009 Paris) and NTA (☎ 01.44.50.10.10, 4 rue Ventadour, Paris 75001); **Destination Japon** (☎ 01.42.96.09.32, ▣ www.des tinationjapon.fr, 11 rue Villedo, 75001 Paris); **JCT International** (☎ 01.44 .55.15.30, ▣ www.jalpak.fr, 4 rue Ventadour, 75001 Paris).

● **Germany**   JTB has offices in: Frankfurt (☎ 069-2998 7823, Weissfrauenstr 12-16, 60311 Frankfurt-am-Main) and Munich (☎ 089-594671, Schwanthalerstr 22, 80326 Munich); **Nichidoku Fernost Reisen** (☎ 0221-400 8330, ▣ www. nichidoku.com, Duerenerstr 89, 50931 Cologne); **H.I.S.** (▣ www.his-ger many.de) has offices in Frankfurt, Dusseldorf and Munich; **Jalpak International GmbH** (☎ 069-9218 7710, 069-2972 9516, ▣ www.jaltour.de, Rossmarkt 15, 60311, Frankfurt-am-Main); Jalpak also has branches in Munich, Hamburg and Dusseldorf.

● **Italy**   JTB (☎ 06-4890 4745, ▣ www.jtbitaly.com, Piazza San Bernardo 105, 00187 Rome); **Jalpak International** (▣ www.jalpak.it) has branches in Rome (☎ 06-481 9417, Via L Bissolati 76, 00187) and Milan (☎ 02-7255 3333, Piazza Bertarelli 1, 20122).

● **The Netherlands**   Tozai Travel (☎ 020-626 2272, ▣ www.japansewinkelt je.nl/, NZ Voorburgwal 175-177, 1012 RK Amsterdam); **Jalpak International** (☎ 020-570 9870, ▣ jaltour@creativetours.nl, Jozef Israelskade 48C, 1072SB, Amsterdam).

● **Spain**   Kintetsu International Express (☎ 91-559 1284, Planta 13, Oficina 7, Torre de Madrid Plaza de Espana, 18, 28008 Madrid); **JALTour** (▣ www.jal tour.com) has branches in Madrid (☎ 91-593 3819, C/Luchana 23-6-1A, 28010) and Barcelona (☎ 93-487 6349, Paseo de Gracia 53-2, 08007).

● **Sweden**   Net **Travel Service** (☎ 08-5662 4516, ▣ www.japanspecialis ten.nu, Lojthantsgatan 25, 115 50 Stockholm).

• **Switzerland Harry Kolb Travel** (☎ 044-715 3636, 🖳 www.harrykolb.ch, Pilgerweg 4, CH-8802 Kilchberg, Zurich); **Tourasia** (☎ 043-233 3090, 🖳 www .tourasia.ch, Grindelstrasse 5, CH-8304 Wallisellen); **Jalpak International** (🖳 www.jaltour.ch) has branches in Geneva (☎ 022-732 2525, 44 rue de Lausanne, 1201) and Zurich (☎ 01-212 477, 3rd Fl, Sihlstrasse 55, 8001).

From the USA
JTB USA (🖳 www.jtbusa.com/enhome) has branches in Los Angeles, San Francisco, Chicago, New York, New Jersey and San Jose.
East & West Travel Corporation (☎ 1-415-398-5777, 210 Post St, Suite 810, San Francisco, CA 94108).
Nippon Travel Agency (🖳 www.nta.co.jp/english/rail/agents.htm#america) has branches in San Francisco, Los Angeles, New Jersey and Honolulu.
Jalpak International USA (🖳 www.jalpak.com) has branches in Los Angeles, New York, San Francisco, Miami, Chicago, Washington DC, Atlanta, Seattle, Houston, Detroit and Honolulu.
IACE Travel (🖳 www.iace-usa.com) has branches in New York, Boston, Washington, Atlanta, Dallas, Orlando, Chicago, Columbus, Detroit, Seattle, Las Vegas, Los Angeles, San Jose, San Diego, and Honolulu.
Kintetsu International Express (🖳 www.kintetsu.com) has branches in New York, New Jersey, Chicago, Los Angeles, San Jose and Honolulu.
Toptour Corporation (🖳 www.streamlines.jp; 🖳 www.ttasfo.com) has branches in New York, San Francisco and Los Angeles.
Tokyu Travel America (☎ 650-593-1285, tollfree ☎ 1-800-852-0109, 🖳 www .ttasfo.com/, 1301 Shoreway Rd, Suite 170, Belmont, CA 94002-4158).
Amnet (🖳 www.amnet-usa.comjpn/kakuyasu-rail-pass-english.asp) has offices in New York, Boston, Chicago and Los Angeles.

From Canada
JTB International (☎ 416-367-5824, 🖳 www.jtbi.ca/en, sales@jtbcnd.com, Carlton Tower Suite 1510, 2 Carlton St., Toronto, Ontario M5B 1J3).
Kintetsu International Express (🖳 www.knt.co.jp/kokusai/global/index .html) has branches in Toronto, Vancouver and Banff.
Nippon Travel Agency (☎ 604-662-8002, 🖳 www.nta.co.jp/english/rail/agents .htm, Suite 310, 1100 Melville St, Vancouver, BC V6E 4A6).
IACE Travel (🖳 www.iace-usa.com) has branches in Vancouver and Toronto
Tokyo Tours Ltd (☎ 416-504-5111, tollfree 1-877-896-8687, 🖳 www.tokyo tours.ca, 436 Adelaide St, West Toronto, Ontario M5V 1S7).

From Asia
• **Malaysia Jalpak** (☎ 03-2161-0922, 🖳 www.jalpak.com.my, Suite 20, 01A, Level 20, Menara Citi Bank 165, Jalan Ampang, 50450 Kuala Lumpur).

• **Singapore JTB** (☎ 6320-5310, 🖳 www.jtb.com.sg, 77 Robinson Rd, #10-02A, Singapore 068896); **Creative Tours** (☎ 6222 8465, 🖳 www.creative tours.com.sg, 16 Raffles Quay, #01-01 Hong Leong Bldg, Singapore 048581).

From South Africa
AWL Travel (☎ 011-268 0614, 1F, North Block Sanlam Park, 9 Fredman Drive, Sandton, PO Box 650540, Benmore 2010).

From Australia
JTB Australia (🖳 www.japantravel.com.au) has branches in Sydney, Melbourne and Surfers Paradise.

AWL Pitt Travel (☎ 02-9264 7384, 🖳 www.japanpackage.com.au, Shop RP 1.09, The Galeries Victoria, 500 George St, Sydney, NSW 2000).

Kintetsu International Express (🖳 www.kintetsu.com.au) has branches in Sydney, Melbourne, Surfers Paradise and Perth.

H.I.S. (🖳 www.traveljapan.com.au) has branches in Sydney, Cairns, Gold Coast, Perth, Melbourne and Adelaide.

Sachi Tours/Nippon Travel Agency (☎ 02-9223 3833, 🖳 www.nta.com.au, Level 9, Bank of America Centre, 135 King St, Sydney, NSW 2000).

Jalpak International (🖳 www.jalpak.com.au/travel_info/jrpass.htm) has branches in Sydney, Adelaide, Brisbane, Gold Coast and Melbourne.

Rail Plus Australia (☎ 03-9642 8644, 🖳 www.railplus.com.au, Level 4, 10-16 Queen St. Melbourne).

From New Zealand
JTB (🖳 www.jtbcorp.jp/en/company/overseas_operations.asp) has branches in Auckland, Christchurch and Queenstown.

Jalpak (☎ 09-303 2887, 🖳 aklssp.jal@jalpak.co.nz, 12th Floor, Westpac Trust Tower, 120 Albert St, Auckland).

H.I.S. (☎ 09-336 1336, 🖳 www.traveljapan.co.nz, Cnr Swanson St & Mills Lane, Auckland).

Rail Plus (☎ 09-377 5415, 🖳 www.railplus.com.au, Level 1, 149 Parnell Rd, Parnell, Auckland).

EXCHANGE ORDERS

For the national rail pass (and any regional pass purchased before you travel to Japan), what you actually buy before departure is not the pass itself but an Exchange Order; you can turn this in for the real thing once in Japan. Exchange orders are valid for three months from the date of issue, so only purchase one less than three months before you plan to start travelling by rail. When purchasing the exchange order, you should also receive a guide to using the pass and a timetable in English of main rail services in Japan. If not, see p85 for further information about timetables.

How and where to turn in the exchange order
Once in Japan, take your exchange order to any **JR Travel Service Center** authorized to handle the Japan Rail Pass. The most obvious ones are at the JR stations in Narita (Tokyo) and Kansai (Osaka) airports. Major JR stations such as Tokyo, Nagoya, Kyoto, Osaka, Shin-Osaka, Sapporo and Hakata have travel service centres, but it's often easiest to sort your pass out at the airport offices,

even if you're not going to start travelling immediately. Staff there are used to handling rail-pass requests and are extremely efficient.

At the time of exchange JR staff will ask to see your passport to check that you have been admitted on 'temporary visitor' status. You'll also be asked to specify the day you want to start using the pass; this can be any day within one month of the day you turn in the exchange order. Once a date has been stamped on the rail pass it cannot be changed. JR will not replace lost passes.

HOW TO USE THE RAIL PASS

Once you've received the pass, all you do is show it whenever you pass a ticket barrier and JR staff will wave you through. Since the pass is not computerized it cannot be fed through automatic wickets but this is not a problem as there is always a staff member around.

Unless you are boarding a train which contains reserved carriages only (as is the case with the Hayate shinkansen which runs between Tokyo and Hachinohe, see p294), seat reservations are not necessary as you can just turn up for any train and sit in the unreserved carriages. However, on some trains, and at certain times of the year (see p67), it's a good idea to make a reservation in order to guarantee a seat if the unreserved carriages are full. Since rail-pass holders can make any number of seat reservations for free (see p86 for details) it's worth doing so in any case.

A few JR trains run on sections of track owned by private companies. Rail-pass holders are supposed to pay a supplement for the section of journey over non-JR track. In practice, you will only have to pay if a conductor is checking tickets at the time the train is running along the non-JR track. Any instances where this occurs are referenced in the route guide.

For details of other rail passes/special tickets see p84.

Suggested itineraries

With such a vast network of rail services, one of the hardest tasks in planning a trip to Japan is working out how much you can fit in. **One week** is really too short to attempt anything more than a quick shuttle between Kyoto and Tokyo, with perhaps a day trip to Nara (see p224) or Hiroshima (see p261). To get anything like a sense of what the country is really about, and to give yourself time to get over jet lag and/or culture shock, plan for at least **two** or **three** weeks.

The following itineraries are neither prescriptive nor are they intended to be the last word on rail travel in Japan. Their purpose is to give a flavour of what can be accomplished. Unless otherwise stated, the routes suggested below assume arrival in and departure from Tokyo and do not include days before/after the rail pass is used.

GENERAL ITINERARIES

One-week itinerary

Day 1 Take the shinkansen from Tokyo (p90) to Kyoto (p206); afternoon and overnight in Kyoto.

Day 2 Spend day in Kyoto and consider a half-day trip to Nara (p224), then back to Kyoto for second overnight stay.

Day 3 Pick up the shinkansen to Hiroshima (p261), perhaps stopping along the way for half a day in Okayama (p256). Overnight in Hiroshima.

Day 4 Spend day in Hiroshima and second overnight.

Day 5 Board a Sanyo line train from Hiroshima for Miyajima-guchi and transfer to the JR ferry to Miyajima Island (p268). Spend the rest of the day touring the island and overnight here.

Day 6 Take ferry back to Miyajima-guchi, return to Hiroshima and transfer on to shinkansen back towards Tokyo. Stop off along the way at Shizuoka (p154), from where you can make a side trip to Kunozan Toshogu Shrine.

Day 7 Morning in Shizuoka, then board a shinkansen for the last part of the journey back to Tokyo.

Two-week itinerary: into the mountains and along the coast

Day 1 Take the Asama shinkansen from Tokyo (p90) to Nagano (p168); spend the rest of the day and the night there.

Day 2 After a dawn visit to Zenko-ji temple (p168), take the Shinano LEX to Matsumoto (p174), a city which is home to one of Japan's best-preserved castles. Overnight here.

Day 3 Picking up the Shinano once more, continue further south to Shiojiri and change to a local train to reach the old post town of Narai (p138). By late afternoon, pick up the train and continue as far as Nagiso (p140), from where it's a short bus ride to Tsumago, another post town where a number of traditional inns offer the weary (rail) traveller a chance to rest.

Day 4 After an early morning wander around Tsumago (before the tour buses arrive!), return to Nagiso and continue south to the terminus of the Shinano in Nagoya (p159). Afternoon and overnight here.

Day 5 Head west along the Tokaido shinkansen line to Kyoto (p206), Japan's ancient capital. Take in a couple of the city's famous sights or follow one of the half-day side trips by rail described on p220-4.

Day 6 Spend a second day in Kyoto or take the train to nearby Nara (p224). Overnight in Kyoto or Nara.

Day 7 From Kyoto, it's a brief hop on the shinkansen to Osaka (p115). Though a city of commerce rather than tourism, Osaka is worth a half-day stop; theme park enthusiasts will want to head to Universal Studios Japan (p117). Overnight here or in Kobe (p250), one stop along on the shinkansen line.

Day 8 Spend a couple of hours in Kobe or press on to nearby Himeji (p235), fêted for its picture-postcard castle, one of the country's most visited tourist attractions. Pick up the shinkansen again and continue on to Okayama (p256) in time for an overnight stay.

⛩ An itinerary for the enthusiast

Rail enthusiasts and anyone else wanting to get maximum use out of the rail pass might consider the following one-week itinerary, a non-stop tour of the country from Sapporo in Hokkaido to Kagoshima on the southern tip of Kyushu. Take a deep breath and watch the kilometres clock up from the comfort of your train seat!

Day 1 (479km) Starting in Sapporo (see p356), take a Super Hokuto LEX to Hakodate and then the (Super) Hakucho LEX to Aomori. Spend the night in Aomori.

Day 2 (1040km) An early start from Aomori, as you take the Inaho LEX leaving at 06:07, arriving in Niigata (see p320) at 12:59. Either rush to get the 13:02 Hokuetsu LEX to Kanazawa (arr 16:40) and then the 16:52 Thunderbird to Osaka arr 19:37. Alternatively, spend time in Niigata before boarding the 15:36 Hokuetsu which arrives in Kanazawa at 19:15 and then the 19:40 Raicho arriving in Osaka at 22:33.

Day 3 (447km) Enjoy a (brief) lie-in after the marathon journey of day two, before boarding a westbound shinkansen from Shin-Osaka to Okayama, where you could stretch your legs in the gardens of Korakuen (see p256). Head next for Shikoku by taking a train across the Inland Sea from Okayama to Takamatsu (see p430). Visit your second garden of the day at Ritsurin-koen (see p431) or take a side trip to nearby Yashima (see p436). As evening falls, take a westbound limited express from Takamatsu to Matsuyama (see p442).

Day 4 (408km) Get up early, take a short tram ride from Matsuyama to nearby Dogo Onsen (see p447) for an early morning bath, before boarding the limited express back to Okayama. From here transfer to the shinkansen and continue west to Hiroshima. Before dusk, take a local train west to Miyajima-guchi and cross via the JR ferry to Miyajima Island (see p268). You should just have time to see the island before crashing out for the night.

Day 5 (458km) Backtrack to Hiroshima, transfer to the shinkansen and travel all the way to the Hakata terminus, on the tip of Kyushu. Fukuoka/Hakata has enough shops and museums to keep most people happy for an afternoon. As evening falls, board a limited express for Nagasaki.

Day 6 (414km) Spend the morning in Nagasaki (see p396) before taking a limited express back towards Hakata, transferring in Tosu for the final part of the journey south to Kagoshima (see p409). If feeling particularly ambitious, you could stop off in Kumamoto (see p404) for a couple of hours to take in the city's castle.

Day 7 Take a ferry to Sakurajima (see p415). Rent a cycle or car and head for the hot springs at Furusato Kanko Hotel which overlook the sea. Take a long hot soak in the outdoor tub, stare out over the water, contemplate your 3246km journey.

Day 9 Early morning is the best time to visit Okayama's stroll garden and castle. In the afternoon pick up a westbound shinkansen and alight in Hiroshima (p261). Overnight here.

Day 10 Spend day in Hiroshima and second overnight.

Day 11 Take a Sanyo line train to Miyajima-guchi, then transfer to the JR ferry to reach Miyajima Island (p268).

Day 12 Opportunity for an early morning hike up Mt Misen (see box p270) before taking the ferry back to the mainland, retracing your steps to Hiroshima and picking up a westbound shinkansen to Fukuoka/Hakata (p389) in Kyushu.

Day 13 Spend day in Fukuoka/Hakata or (if feeling ambitious) take an early train and pack in a day trip to Nagasaki (p396).

Day 14 Finally retrace your steps by riding the shinkansen all the way back to Tokyo (you'll have to change along the way at Okayama or Shin-Osaka, covering a distance of 1175km in just over six hours.

If you prefer to have more time in Tokyo it might be best to cut out the trip to Fukuoka/Hakata in Kyushu.

Three-week itinerary

Make the most of a three-week rail pass by combining the two-week itinerary outlined above with a week focusing on one of the regions described below.

The two-week itinerary ends in Fukuoka/Hakata (p389), capital of Kyushu, so you're perfectly placed to continue with a third week of travel around the island. If you prefer to spend the extra week exploring Shikoku (pp416-48), the starting point is Okayama (reached on day 9 of the two-week itinerary). Another option would be to explore the less developed side of Western Honshu (pp242-9) away from the Sanyo coastline. In this case, follow the two-week itinerary as far as day 12, then the Western Honshu regional itinerary.

REGIONAL ITINERARIES

Regional itineraries assume use of a one-week rail pass. If you have the luxury of more time to focus on a particular region, one week can easily become two or three by slowing down the pace and including a number of side trips along the way. For more details about each region, see the introduction to the individual route guides.

Central Honshu   (see pp125-92)

Day 1 Board a Tokaido shinkansen from Tokyo station and ride as far as Shizuoka (p154), perhaps stopping along the way for a short pilgrimage to the grave of poor Toby (see box p129). Spend the afternoon in Shizuoka visiting the hill-top Kunozan Toshogu Shrine. Alternatively go to the Fuji/Hakone area (see p113) by taking the shinkansen to either Odawara (p128) or Mishima (p130).

Day 2 After an overnight stay in Shizuoka (or Odawara or Mishima), pick up a Kodama shinkansen as far as Kakegawa. From here, backtrack two stops along the conventional JR Tokaido line to Kanaya, starting point for a side trip on the Oigawa steam railway (p131). Finally return to Kakegawa, connect up once again with the shinkansen and continue to Nagoya (p159) for the night.

Day 3 At least two side trips can easily be made from Nagoya; both affording excellent views of the surrounding countryside. The Shinano LEX runs on the JR Chuo line to Nagano (p168), with stops along the way at the traditional post towns of Narai (p138) and Tsumago (p140) as well as the castle town of Matsumoto (p174). Alternatively the Hida LEX runs along the JR Takayama line to picturesque Takayama (p179). Either side trip can be made at a push in a day, but it would be more relaxing to stay overnight somewhere along the way.

Day 4 Return to Nagoya and spend the day seeing some of the city sights or take a short side trip by private Meitetsu Railway to nearby Inuyama (p167).

Day 5 From Nagoya board the Mie rapid train which heads around Ise Bay to Ise (p198), spiritual centre of Japan's indigenous religion, Shinto.

Day 6 After an overnight stay in Ise, pick up the Mie rapid train heading back towards Nagoya but get off at Taki (p198), from where you can transfer on to the Wide View Nanki LEX which heads south towards the Kii Peninsula. By getting off at Shingu (p200), it's possible to take a side trip by JR bus inland to Doro-Kyo Gorge. Overnight in Shingu.

Day 7 From Shingu pick up the Ocean Arrow LEX which follows a coastal route all the way to Shin-Osaka, from where you can begin a rail tour of western Honshu (pp233-78), or visit Kyoto (p206). Jumping on an eastbound Tokaido shinkansen from Shin-Osaka or Kyoto will deposit you back in Tokyo.

Western Honshu (see pp233-78)

Day 1 Starting in Osaka (Shin-Osaka) take a westbound shinkansen as far as Hiroshima (p261). Overnight here.

Day 2 Spend day in Hiroshima before picking up the shinkansen and continuing west to Shin-Yamaguchi (p240), access point for an excursion across Honshu. Overnight in Shin-Yamaguchi.

Day 3 In the morning, take the Super-Oki LEX (at weekends and in summer a steam locomotive operates on this route, see p241) which runs inland along the Yamaguchi line to Yamaguchi (p242). Overnight here.

Day 4 Make an early start by taking the JR bus to the limestone cave at Akiyoshi-do (p243). Return to Yamaguchi, pick up the Super-Oki and continue north to the picturesque town of Tsuwano (p244), where you'll find plenty of inexpensive *minshuku* and *ryokan*.

Day 5 Spend day in Tsuwano before picking up the Super-Oki once again. From here, the train heads east following the San-in coast to Matsue (p271), known as the 'city of water'. Two possible places to stop en route are the aquarium in Hashi (p247) and Nima (p248), home to the unusual Sand Museum. Overnight in Matsue.

Day 6 Spend day visiting Matsue Castle and the old haunts of Irish writer Lafcadio Hearn before taking a leisurely sunset cruise around Lake Shinji (p276). Spend a second night in Matsue.

Day 7 From Matsue, pick up the Super-Yakumo LEX which cuts across Honshu to Okayama (p256) on the Sanyo coast. There should be enough time to visit the city's stroll garden before taking the shinkansen back to Osaka.

Northern Honshu (see pp278-326)

Day 1 From Tokyo, take a Tohoku shinkansen north to Sendai (p308), from where you could take a side trip to Matsushima Bay (p286), considered one of the top three scenic spots in Japan. Return to Sendai for the night.

Day 2 Pick up the shinkansen and travel the short distance to Ichinoseki (p288), from where local trains run along the Tohoku line to the temple town of Hiraizumi (p289). Stay overnight in a temple with the option in the summer months of taking part in an early morning session of *zazen* (Zen meditation).

Day 3 Retrace your steps to Ichinoseki and continue on the shinkansen to the terminus in Hachinohe (p294). Change trains here and pick up the Super-Hakucho LEX to Aomori (p316), Honshu's northernmost city.

Day 4 Spend day in Aomori and include a side trip to nearby Nebuta no Sato (see box p320), a vast exhibition space which displays some of the colourful floats used during the city's Nebuta Festival in August.

Day 5 From Aomori, board the JR bus south to Lake Towada (box p298), formed from a volcanic crater. Spend the afternoon by the lake before picking up another JR bus to Towada-Minami station. From here pick up a local westbound train on the Hanawa line to Odate (p301). Transfer to the Ou line and head south towards Akita (p302), a useful overnight base.

Day 6 From Akita, pick up the Inaho LEX which runs south to Niigata (p320). Possible stops along the way include Sakata (p305), home to an art museum and traditional Japanese garden, and Tsuruoka (p306), access point for the Dewa-Sanzan mountain chain. Overnight in Niigata.

Day 7 Spend the morning in Niigata before completing the rail loop around northern Japan by picking up a Joetsu shinkansen back to Tokyo.

Hokkaido (see pp327-78)

Day 1 Starting from Aomori, on the northern tip of Honshu, take the Super-Hakucho LEX and head through the Seikan tunnel to the port city of Hakodate (p350); spend the night here.

Day 2 From Hakodate, take the Super-Hokuto LEX to Sapporo (p356), perhaps stopping for a couple of hours at Onuma-koen (p331) to visit the lakes which overlook Mt Komagatake. Overnight in Sapporo.

Day 3 Spend day visiting the island's capital and find out what the city was like in the 19th century by taking a side trip by JR bus to the Historical Village of Hokkaido (p364). By evening take the Super White Arrow LEX along the Hakodate line to Asahikawa (p365) and overnight here.

Day 4 Take the bus from Asahikawa to the foot of Mt Asahi (p370). A ropeway (cable car) runs part of the way up the mountain or you could take one of the hiking trails to the top. Overnight in the village at the foot of the mountain.

Day 5 Return by bus to Asahikawa and transfer to a local Furano line train to Furano (p348), known in Japan for its fields of lavender in summer and thick blankets of snow in winter. Overnight here or in nearby Bibaushi (p349).

Day 6 Spend day in Furano before returning to Asahikawa and boarding the Super White Arrow back to Sapporo in time for a final overnight stay.

Day 7 From Sapporo pick up the Super-Hokuto, return to Hakodate, transfer to the Super-Hakucho to Hachinohe (see p396) and board a shinkansen to Tokyo.

Kyushu (see pp371-415)

Day 1 Starting from the capital, Fukuoka/Hakata (p389), take the Kamome LEX west to Nagasaki (p396). Spend day and overnight here.

Day 2 Spend the morning in Nagasaki and then return in the direction of Fukuoka/Hakata as far as Tosu (p379), from where you can transfer to the Relay-Tsubame LEX which heads down the west side of the island. Continue as far as the city of Kumamoto (p404), where there should be time to pay a visit to the city's castle before finding somewhere to stay overnight.

Day 3 Take a side trip from Kumamoto inland to the Aso tableland (p387). It's a three-hour journey to Aso, from where a bus and ropeway whisk you up to the Nakadake crater. Peer over the side of this active volcano before deciding whether you want to stay overnight in Aso or return in time to stay a second night in Kumamoto.

Day 4 Spend day at leisure in Kumamoto before picking up the Relay-Tsubame to Shin-Yatsushiro (p380), from where the Kyushu shinkansen runs south to the terminus in Kagoshima (p409), Kyushu's southernmost city.

Day 5 Spend day and second overnight in Kagoshima.

Day 6 Take the ferry to Sakurajima Island (p415), rent a cycle and spend the day biking around the brooding Sakurajima volcano. Overnight here or take the ferry back to Kagoshima.

Day 7 Retrace your steps by taking a combination of Kyushu shinkansen and Relay-Tsubame LEX back to Fukuoka/Hakata, from where you can connect up with a shinkansen back to Honshu.

Shikoku   (see pp416-48)

Day 1 Starting from Okayama on Honshu, board the Marine Liner rapid train which crosses the Inland Sea before heading to Takamatsu (p430). Visit Ritsurin Park or take a side trip by rail to the nearby roof-top plateau of Yashima (p436) before spending the night in Takamatsu.

Day 2 From Takamatsu pick up the Shimanto LEX and continue south along the Dosan line to Kochi (p437), stopping along the way to visit the mountain-top shrine at Kotohira (p420) and/or Oboke Gorge (p421). Overnight in Kochi.

Day 3 Spend the morning in Kochi before picking up the Nanpu LEX which continues along the Dosan line to Kubokawa. Connect up here with a local Yodo line train which chugs slowly west to the bull-fighting city of Uwajima (p424).

Day 4 Spend day and second overnight in Uwajima.

Day 5 From Uwajima take a limited express north along the Uchiko line to Matsuyama (p442), perhaps stopping off briefly in the small town of Uchiko (p426), which contains a well-preserved historical quarter and small Noh theatre. Spend the rest of the day and the night in Matsuyama.

Day 6 Take a side trip by tram from Matsuyama to the hot springs at Dogo Onsen (p447) and relax in the 100-year-old bath house.

Day 7 From Matsuyama board a Shiokaze LEX heading back to Okayama, from where the Tokaido shinkansen heads east to Tokyo and west towards Fukuoka/Hakata on the island of Kyushu.

Getting to Japan

There are several ways to book a flight to Japan. Either direct through an airline (see box p28); through a travel agency (see pp17-20), on the internet through a company selling discounted tickets (see pp28-31) or as a courier. Courier flights

⛩ **Airlines flying to Japan**

Airlines that fly to more than one destination in Japan offer the possibility of flying into eg Narita (Tokyo) and out of Kansai (Osaka) so it is worth asking about fares on those airlines. Some of the airlines below also fly to Hiroshima, Sendai and Fukuoka and other destinations.

Airlines with flights to Japan include: **Aeroflot** (NRT; 🖳 www.aeroflot.com); **Air China** (NRT, NGO; 🖳 www.airchina.com.cn); **Air Canada** (NRT, KIX; 🖳 www.aircanada.com); **Air France** (NRT, KIX, NGO; 🖳 www.airfrance.com); **Air India** (NRT, KIX; 🖳 www.airindia.com); **Air New Zealand** (NRT, KIX; 🖳 www.airnewzealand.com); **Alitalia** (NRT, KIX; 🖳 www.alitalia.com); **All Nippon Airways** (NRT, KIX, NGO; 🖳 www.anaskyweb.com); **American Airlines** (NRT, KIX, NGO; 🖳 www.aa.com); **Austrian Airlines** (NRT; 🖳 www.aua.com); **British Airways** (NRT; 🖳 www.britishairways.com); **Cathay Pacific** (NRT, KIX, NGO; 🖳 www.cathaypacific.com); **Continental** (NRT, KIX, NGO; 🖳 www.continental.com); **Delta** (NRT, KIX, NGO; 🖳 www.delta.com); **Dragonair** (NRT; 🖳 www.dragonair.com); **Egypt Air** (NRT, KIX; 🖳 www.egyptair.com.eg); **Emirates** (KIX, NGO; 🖳 www.emirates.com); **Eva Air** (NRT, KIX, NGO; 🖳 www.evaair.com); **Finnair** (NRT, KIX, NGO; 🖳 www.finnair.com); **Japan Airlines/JAL** (NRT, KIX, NGO; 🖳 www.jal.com); KLM (NRT, KIX; 🖳 www.klm.com); **Korean Air** (NRT, KIX, NGO; 🖳 www.koreanair.com); **Lufthansa** (NRT, KIX, NGO; 🖳 www.lufthansa.com); **Malaysia Airlines** (NRT, KIX, NGO; 🖳 www.malaysiaairlines.com); **Northwest Airlines** (NRT, KIX, NGO; 🖳 www.nwa.com); **Qantas** (NRT, KIX, NGO; 🖳 www.qantas.com); **Qatar Airways** (KIX; 🖳 www.qatarairways.com); **Scandinavian Airlines System** (NRT; 🖳 www.flysas.com); **Singapore Airlines** (NRT, KIX, NGO; 🖳 www.singaporeair.com); **Swiss International Air Lines** (NRT; 🖳 www.swiss.com); **Thai Airways International** (NRT, KIX, NGO; 🖳 www.thaiair.com); **United** (NRT, KIX, NGO; 🖳 www.united.com); **US Air** (NRT, KIX; 🖳 www.usairways.com); **Virgin Atlantic Airways** (NRT; 🖳 www.virgin-atlantic.com).

* NRT = Narita International Airport (Tokyo), KIX = Kansai International Airport (Osaka); NGO = Central Japan International Airport (Nagoya)

are possibly the cheapest way to get a direct flight to Japan though they are not possible from every destination, or indeed through every airline. For further information see 🖳 www.courier.org.

FROM THE UK AND IRELAND

All Nippon Airways (☎ 0870-837 8866), **Japan Airlines** (☎ 0845-774 7700, Dublin ☎ 01-408 3757), **Virgin Atlantic** (☎ 0870-380 2007) and **British Airways** (☎ 0870-850 9850) operate daily direct flights from London Heathrow. There are no direct flights from Ireland. Fares from the UK to Japan start at around £600 return but do depend on the season and the airline; the cheapest fares are on indirect routes. Flights are offered through most of the agencies listed on p17. See box above for website details for the airlines listed.

Websites such as Opodo (🖳 www.opodo.co.uk), Expedia (🖳 www.expedia.co.uk) and Ebookers (🖳 www.ebookers.com) are also worth investigating.

FROM CONTINENTAL EUROPE

Apart from **All Nippon Airways** and **JAL** (see website for relevant phone contact details), **Lufthansa** (Germany ☎ 0180-583 8426), **KLM** (Netherlands ☎ 0204-747747) and **Swiss International Air Lines** (Switzerland) are major carriers to Japan. Swiss flies the modern Airbus A340 on the Zurich–Tokyo route, has award-winning service and good-value connecting flights across Europe

Flights can be booked through most of the agencies listed on p17. Websites such as 🖳 www.opodo.de, 🖳 www.opodo.fr, 🖳 www.opodo.es, 🖳 www.opodo.it, 🖳 www.travellink.se, 🖳 www.travellink.dk, 🖳 www.opodo.at) are also worth checking.

FROM NORTH AMERICA

All Nippon Airways (☎ 1-800-235-9262) and **Japan Airlines** (☎ 1-800-525-3663) have connections from all over North America to Japan. Other carriers include **United** (☎ 1-800-538-2929), **Delta** (☎ 1-800-241-4141), **American** (☎ 1-800-433-7300) and **Air Canada** (toll-free ☎ 1-800-247-2262).

Flights can be booked through most of the companies listed on p19. Discounted fares are also offered through: Travel CUTS (US ☎ 1-800-592-2887, Canada ☎ 1-866-246-9762, 🖳 www.travelcuts.com); Airbrokers International (🖳 www.airbrokers.com); Travelbag (☎ 0800 082 5000, 🖳 www.travelbag.co.uk), and Flight centre (🖳 www.flightcentre.com). Websites worth looking at include Expedia (🖳 www.expedia.com) and Cheap Flights (🖳 www.cheapflights.com).

FROM ASIA

Singapore Airlines (Singapore ☎ 65-223 8888) operates flights to Tokyo, Osaka, Nagoya, Hiroshima and Fukuoka and has connections with cities around the world from its hub in Singapore. **Cathay Pacific** (Hong Kong ☎ 2747-1888) flies from Hong Kong to Tokyo, Osaka and Fukuoka, while subsidiary **Dragon Air** (Hong Kong ☎ 3193-3888) serves Hiroshima and Sendai.

FROM SOUTH AFRICA

South African Airways (☎ 0861-359 722, 🖳 www.flysaa.com) operates code-share flights with a number of airlines from Johannesburg to Hong Kong, from where onward connections can be made to Japan. Apart from through AWL (see p20) flights can be booked through Flight Centre (🖳 www.flightcentre.co.za).

FROM AUSTRALASIA

Qantas (Australia ☎ 13 13 13) operates flights from Cairns, Brisbane, Sydney, Melbourne and Perth. **Air New Zealand** (☎ 0800-737 000) operates flights from Auckland and Christchurch.

Flights can be booked through most of the agencies listed on p20 and through: Trailfinders (🖳 www.trailfinders.com.au); Flight Centre (🖳 www

PLANNING YOUR TRIP

❑ Embassies and consulates

The full list of embassies and consulates can be found at 🖳 www.mofa.go.jp/about/emb_cons/mofaserv.html.

● **Australia** (☎ 02-6273 3244, 🖳 www.japan.org.au), 112 Empire Circuit, Yarralumla, Canberra ACT 2600. There are consulate-general offices in Sydney, Melbourne, Brisbane and Perth.

● **Austria** (☎ 01-531920, 🖳 www.at.emb-japan.go.jp), Hessgasse 6, 1010 Wien.

● **Belgium** (☎ 02-513 2340, 🖳 www.be.emb-japan.go.jp), 6th Floor, ave des Arts 58, 1000 Bruxelles.

● **Canada** (☎ 613-241 8541, 🖳 www.ca.emb-japan.go.jp), 255 Sussex Drive, Ottawa, Ontario K1N 9E6. There are consulate offices in Calgary, Montreal, Toronto and Vancouver.

● **Denmark** (☎ 3311-3344, 🖳 www.dk.emb-japan.go.jp), Pilestraede 61, 1112 Copenhagen K.

● **France** (☎ 01.48.88.62.00, 🖳 www.fr.emb-japan.go.jp), 7 ave Hoche, 75008 Paris; there are consulate offices in Marseille and Strasbourg.

● **Germany** (☎ 030-210940, 🖳 www.de.emb-japan.go.jp), Hiroshimastrasse 6, 10785 Berlin; consulate offices in Dusseldorf, Frankfurt, Hamburg and Munich.

● **Hong Kong** Consulate-General (☎ 2522-1184, 🖳 www.hk.emb-japan.go.jp), One Exchange Square, 8 Connaught Place, Central, Hong Kong.

● **Ireland** (☎ 01-202 8300, 🖳 www.ie.emb-japan.go.jp), Nutley Building, Merrion Centre, Nutley Lane, Dublin 4.

● **Italy** (☎ 06-487991, 🖳 www.it.emb-japan.go.jp), Via Quintino Sella, 60 00187 Rome; consulate office in Milan.

● **Malaysia** (☎ 03-242 7044, 🖳 www.my.emb-japan.go.jp), 11 Pesiaran Stonor, 50450 Kuala Lumpur; consulate office in Penang.

● **Netherlands** (☎ 070-346 9544, 🖳 www.nl.emb-japan.go.jp), Tobias Asserlaan 2, 2517 KC, The Hague.

● **New Zealand** (☎ 04-473 1540, 🖳 www.nz.emb-japan.go.jp), Level 18, Majestic Centre, 100 Willis St, Wellington 1; consulate offices in Auckland and Christchurch.

● **Singapore** (☎ 65-235 8855, 🖳 www.sg.emb-japan.go.jp), 16 Nassim Rd, Singapore, 258390.

● **South Korea** (☎ 02-765 3011-13, 🖳 www.kr.emb-japan.go.jp), 114-8 Unni-Dong Jongno-gu, Seoul 110-350, Jongro-1Ka, Jongro-ku, Seoul.

● **South Africa** (☎ 012-452 1500, 🖳 www.japan.org.za), 259 Baines St, c/o Frans Oerde St, Groenkloof, Pretoria 0181.

● **Spain** (☎ 91-590 7600, 🖳 www.es.emb-japan.go.jp), Calle Serrano 109, 28006 Madrid.

● **Sweden** (☎ 08-579 35300, 🖳 www.japansamb.se), Gärdesgatan 10, 11527, Stockholm.

● **Switzerland** (☎ 031-300 2222, 🖳 www.ch.emb-japan.go.jp), Engestrasse 53, 3026 Berne; consulate office in Geneva.

● **UK** (☎ 020-7465 6565, 🖳 www.uk.emb-japan.go.jp), 101-104 Piccadilly, London W1J 7JT. A Consulate-General (☎ 0131-225 4777, 🖳 www.edinburgh.emb-japan.go.jp) is at 2 Melville Crescent, Edinburgh EH3 7HW.

● **USA** (☎ 202-238-6700, 🖳 www.us.emb-japan.go.jp), 2520 Massachusetts Ave NW, Washington DC 20008-2869. There are Consulate-General offices all over the States, including Chicago (☎ 312-280-0400), Los Angeles (☎ 213-617 6700), Miami (☎ 305-530-9090), New York (☎ 212-371-8222), San Francisco (☎ 415-777-3533) and Seattle (☎ 206-682-9107).

Japan National Tourist Organization (JNTO)
The best source of tourist information prior to arrival in Japan is the **Japan National Tourist Organization**. Branches around the world are well stocked with leaflets and staff can answer almost any question you have about Japan on the spot. The offices are information centres only; they do not sell any tickets or rail passes. Their website, ☐ **www.jnto.go.jp**, has regular travel updates; alternatively contact the main overseas offices:

● **UK** (☎ 020-7734 9638, ☐ www.seejapan.co.uk, info@jnto.co.uk), 1st floor, Heathcoat House, 20 Savile Row, London W1X 1AE.
● **France** (☎ 01.42.96.20.29, ☐ www.tourisme-japon/fr), 4 rue de Ventadour, 75001 Paris.
● **Germany** (☎ 069-20353, ☐ www.jnto.go.jp/deu) Kaiserstrasse 11, 60311 Frankfurt am Main.
● **USA** (☎ 212-757-5640, ☐ www.japantravelinfo.com), One Rockefeller Plaza, Suite 1250, **New York**, NY 10020; and (☎ 213-623-1952), 515 South Figueroa St, Suite 1470, **Los Angeles**, CA 90071.
● **Canada** (☎ 416-366-7140, ☐ www.japantravelinfo.com), 165 University Ave, Toronto, Ontario M5H 3B8.
● **Australia** (☎ 02-9251 3024, ☐ www.jnto.go.jp/syd), Level 18, Australia Square Tower, 264 George St, Sydney, NSW 2000.
● **Singapore** (☎ 6223-8205, ☐ www.jnto.go.jp/sin), 16 Raffles Quay, #15-09 Hong Leong Bldg, Singapore 048581.
● **Thailand** (☎ 02-233 5108, ☐ www.jnto.go.jp/bkk), 19th Fl, Ramaland Bldg, No 952 Rama 4 Rd, Bangrak District, Bangkok 10500.
● **Hong Kong** (☎ 2968-5688, ☐ www.jnto.go.jp/chc), Suite 3704-05, 37/F, Dorset House, Taikoo Place, Quarry Bay.

.flightcentre.com.au and ☐ www.flightcentre.com.nz) and STA Travel (Australia ☎ 134 STA, ☐ www.statravel.com.au; NZ ☐ 0800-474400, ☐ www .statravel.com.nz).

Before you go

PASSPORTS AND VISAS

All visitors to Japan must be in possession of a valid passport. Japan has signed agreements with over 50 countries exempting their citizens from applying for a visa if they are visiting for the purposes of tourism. Amongst other countries, citizens of the UK, Austria, Belgium, France, Germany, Ireland, Italy, Netherlands, Singapore, Spain, Switzerland, the USA, Canada, Australia and New Zealand can enter Japan for a period of up to 90 days under the 'reciprocal visa exemption' scheme. Citizens of the UK, Austria, Germany, Ireland and Switzerland can apply for a further 90-day extension while in Japan.

Citizens of all other countries, including Hong Kong and Malaysia, need to apply for a tourist visa from the Japanese embassy or consulate in their home country (see box p30).

Visa requirements change periodically, so before making travel arrangements check with the Japanese embassy in your home country.

HEALTH AND INSURANCE

No vaccinations or health certificates are required to enter the country and there's no need to worry about diseases such as malaria, which are not endemic in Japan. Tap water is safe to drink even in big cities like Tokyo, but bottled water is readily available in convenience stores (sparkling water is harder to find than still) and from vending machines.

Don't arrive in Japan without a comprehensive travel insurance policy. Japanese hospitals invariably offer high standards of care and most doctors speak English, but diagnosis, treatment and prescriptions can be prohibitively expensive.

If you're on medication, bring a copy of your prescription. This may be needed if Customs inspect your bags but will also be useful if you need a repeat prescription. Note that many international drugs are sold under different brand names in Japan.

WHAT TO TAKE

The best advice is to pack as little as possible. Travelling light makes getting around much easier, especially if you are getting on and off lots of trains; it also means you'll have no problem fitting your luggage into a coin locker (see p88) at the station. Lifts and/or escalators are available at most stations, though you may find that access to/from the platforms at some smaller stops is only via stairs, in which case compact luggage is an advantage.

If planning to stay mostly in Japanese-style accommodation it's worth bringing slip-on shoes as you're expected to take your shoes off in the entrance hall (*genkan*). Guests walk around either in the slippers provided or, if these are too small, just in socks (pack a few pairs without holes!). Guests in Japanese-style accommodation are also usually provided with a small towel which doubles as a flannel; if you prefer a large towel it might be better to bring one.

Nightwear is not essential as guests in most forms of accommodation, apart from hostels, are provided with a *yukata* (a cotton robe tied with a belt) that can be worn in bed and which is used as a dressing gown to go between your room and the bathroom. Yukata (and Japanese-style towels) can often be rented or purchased from the front desk if they are not provided.

Pack according to the season and the region in which you're likely to be travelling (see p11). As a general rule, shorts and T-shirts are fine in the summer, though you'll probably need a sweater or two in the spring and autumn. Take warm clothes for the winter, especially if travelling in northern Japan.

At any time of the year, it's worth packing a few smart clothes – older Japanese in particular are generally well-dressed (even when on holiday themselves) and smart clothes could be useful if you expect to socialize with any Japanese. If you forget anything, clothes and shoes are relatively cheap as long as you avoid the designer-label boutiques, but it's not always easy to find large sizes.

Don't bother packing an umbrella as disposable ones are readily and cheaply available in convenience stores. Tourist attractions which involve walking around outside usually have a supply of umbrellas for visitors to borrow.

If you want an unusual souvenir of your trip, take a notebook (see box p48).

MONEY – see also p63

Japan is a cash-based economy so when travelling around it's best to ensure you always have a supply of cash. The most convenient way of getting hold of cash is to use one of the thousands of post office ATMs around the country, all of which accept foreign-issued cards (including Maestro and Visa) and have instructions in English. ATMs operated by Tokyo-based Seven Bank, located in 11,700 7-Eleven and Ito Yokado stores in 31 prefectures across Japan, accept US-issued Visa, MasterCard, American Express and Cirrus cards. The ATMs dispense information and printed receipts in English, Korean, Chinese and Portuguese.

Travellers' cheques (in ¥ or US$ only) are a useful way to take money but ensure you cash them before heading off the beaten track. Also be prepared for a long wait when you go to a bank to exchange them.

Credit cards are accepted in most major tourist places but don't rely on this. Upmarket hotels tend to accept credit cards but cash is the preferred currency in youth hostels, minshuku, budget ryokan and business hotels.

SUGGESTED READING

History

A History of Japan: From Stone Age to Superpower Kenneth Henshall (Macmillan, 1999) A scholarly but very readable book.

A Traveller's History of Japan Richard Tames (Windrush Press, 1993) A great, pocket-sized book that's ideal to dip into as you travel around.

Embracing Defeat: Japan in the Aftermath of World War II John Dower (Penguin, 1999).

Shogun James Clavell (Flame, 1999) Billed as an epic tale of 17th-century Japan, Clavell's novel is based on the story of Will Adams, the first Englishman to arrive in Japan. Hard going at first but worth the effort.

Hiroshima John Hersey (Penguin, 1986) Originally written in the 1960s this remains one of the most authoritative accounts of the A-Bomb's devastation of Hiroshima. The narrative is told from the point of view of different survivors in the moments before, and minutes, hours, days and years after the explosion.

Travel narratives

Hokkaido Highway Blues Will Ferguson (Canongate, 2000) Ferguson travels from southern Kyushu north to Hokkaido following the path of the cherry blossom; an irreverent account of life on the open road.

Japan: True stories of life on the road Edited by Donald George and Amy Carlson (Travelers' Tales, 1999) A superb selection of travel narratives; perfect for dipping into on long train journeys.

The Roads to Sata Alan Booth (Kodansha, 1985) The late Alan Booth walked the length of Japan, from Hokkaido to Kyushu, looking for beer. Equally absorbing is his *Looking for the Lost: Journeys Through a Vanishing Japan* (Kodansha, 1995), a series of travel narratives taking in parts of Japan that most foreigners never see.

Dave Barry Does Japan Dave Barry (Ballantine Books, 1992) Humourist Dave Barry takes a family holiday in Japan, all expenses paid by his publisher.

A Ride in the Neon Sun Josie Dew (Warner Books 2000) Josie Dew pedals around Japan and writes entertainingly about her encounters and experiences.

Rediscovering the old Tokaido: In the footsteps of Hiroshige Patrick Carey (Global Oriental, 2000) The story of a nostalgic journey on foot along what remains of the road that linked Edo and Kyoto in the days before the Tokaido railway line.

Life in Japan

Kokoro: Hints and Echoes of Japanese Inner Life Lafcadio Hearn (Tuttle, 1972) The best introduction to Irish writer Lafcadio Hearn's experiences of life in Meiji-era Japan (see p39).

The Blue-eyed Salaryman Niall Murtagh (Profile Books, 2005) Amusing insight into what office life is like for a foreigner working in Japan.

Fresh Fruits Shoichi Aoki (Phaidon Press, 2005) Photographer Shoichi Aoki's celebrated collection of photographs of the changing street fashions of Tokyo teenagers. See also the original *Fruits* (Phaidon Press, 2001).

Number 9 Dream David Mitchell (Sceptre, 2001) The British novelist who taught English in Hiroshima for eight years presents an extraordinary post-*Blade Runner* Japanese world which has been variously described as terrifying and exhilarating.

In the Miso Soup Ryu Murakami (Bloomsbury, 2006) A gritty, frightening tale of life in the backstreets of Tokyo.

Angry White Pyjamas: An Oxford Poet Trains With The Tokyo Riot Police Robert Twigger (Indigo, 1997) Brit Robert Twigger abandons an English-teaching career going nowhere fast in Tokyo and takes up *aikido*.

Xenophobe's Guide to the Japanese Sahoko Kaji, Noriko Hama and Jonathan Rice (Oval Books, 2004) A pocket-sized humorous guide to what makes the Japanese tick.

The Big Bento Box of Unuseless Japanese Inventions Kenji Kawakami (WW Norton & Co, 2005) Kawakami is the wacky inventor of *chindogu*, bizarre gadgets such as the 'cockroach swatting slippers' and 'umbrella head belt'. Hilarious and pointless. Or more accurately: pointless, therefore hilarious.

Memoirs of a Geisha Arthur Golden (Random House, 1997) Golden's novel about a trainee *geisha*'s life has become a modern classic and a Hollywood blockbuster. Sayuri is born in a fishing village but she is sold to a Kyoto geisha house from where she rises to become one of the city's most famous and sought-after geisha.

The Tale of Murasaki Liza Dalby (Vintage, 2001) Dalby claims to be the only Westerner to have become a geisha and was a consultant on the film adaptation of *Memoirs of a Geisha*. This novel is an imagined diary of 11th-century Japanese court lady Murasaki Shikibu, author of *The Tale of Genji*.

Geisha Lesley Downer (Headline, 2000) This is a personal account of the months Downer spent in the Gion tea houses, befriending the *mama-san* who hold the purse strings and manage the careers of trainee geisha. She gets closer than any commentator to a revelation of life behind the enigmatic smiles and painted faces of geisha in Kyoto.

Reading Zen In The Rocks: The Japanese Landscape Garden François Berthier (University of Chicago, 2000, translated by Graham Parkes).

Japanese abroad

The Thames and I: A Memoir of Two Years at Oxford Crown Prince Naruhito (Global Oriental, 2005, translated by Sir Hugh Cortazzi) A unique insight into Prince Naruhito's student days at Oxford. Find out what the prince made of Brussels sprouts, fish and chips and having to do his own laundry. Particularly poignant is his description of the moment he boarded the plane to return to Japan: 'I realised that an important chapter in my life was over. A new page was opening, but I felt a large void in my heart and as I stared out of the windows of the plane I felt a lump in my throat.'

Japanamerica: How Japanese Pop Culture Has Invaded the US Roland Kelts (Palgrave, Macmillan, 2006) One of the few accounts in English of how influential anime, manga and Japanese pop culture as a whole have been in the United States.

The railway

Japanese Railways in the Meiji Period 1868-1912 Tom Richards and Charles Rudd (Brunel, 1991) The authors provide a detailed account of the railway's early days.

Shinkansen: From Bullet Train to Symbol of Modern Japan Christopher Hood (Routledge, 2006) A comprehensive and readable account of the history of the world-famous bullet train. See also 🖳 www.hood-online.co.uk/shinkansen.

High Speed in Japan Peter Semmens (Platform 5, 2000) A thorough and engaging account of the shinkansen age.

Guidebooks

Lonely Planet's *Japan* is one of the most comprehensive general guides to the country. *The Rough Guide to Japan* (Rough Guides) and *Japan* (Eyewitness Travel Guides, Dorling Kindersley) are also good.

Facts about the country

GEOGRAPHY

Japan is made up of over 3000 islands, a total land mass almost as large as the state of California. The four main islands are **Honshu**, the largest, followed by **Hokkaido**, the most northern and also the least populated, then **Kyushu**, the southernmost, and **Shikoku**. Stretching 3000km from north to south, the northernmost regions of Japan are subarctic, while the extreme south is subtropical.

Four-fifths of the land surface is mountainous and rural; most of the 127 million people who live on the four main islands are packed into the coastal plains. This has led to so-called 'urban corridors', the longest of which, and perhaps the most densely inhabited in the world, is the Tokaido belt which runs between Tokyo and Osaka.

HISTORY

Space permits only a condensed 'bullet points' history of Japan. For recommended books on the history of Japan, see p33.

Birth of a nation: myth and reality

Nobody knows exactly when Japan was first inhabited by humans but estimates range from between 500,000 and 100,000 years ago. The **Jomon period**, named after a rope pattern found on the oldest form of pottery in the world, began around 10,000BC but the country was not unified until the 4th century, when the Yamato dynasty was established and the title of Emperor first used.

A capital is established: 710-794

Up until the 7th century, tradition dictated that the capital was changed every time a new Emperor ascended to the throne. But in 710, the Imperial Court decided to settle in Nara (see p224), a city still proud that it was the capital of Japan and the home of seven Emperors in just 77 years before the court was moved to Kyoto in 794. The **Nara period** was marked by influences from China and the growing popularity of its imported religion, Buddhism. The main Chinese influence is visible today in Todai-ji (see p225), the largest wooden building in the world which contains the biggest statue of Buddha in Japan, a bronze image cast in 752. Religious riches and treasure aside,

蝶
の
空
七
堂
伽
藍
さ
か
し
ま
に

To the butterfly in the sky
all buildings on the temple ground
are upside down
(BOSHA KAWABATA)

hunger and poverty were commonplace outside the Imperial Court, though there was worse to come in later centuries.

Flourishing of the arts but rivalry outside the court: 794-1192

Nara was soon over-run with Buddhist temples and Shinto shrines, and Emperor Kammu could no longer bear being closeted there. So, a new capital was established, in 794, in Heian (present-day Kyoto) where it was to remain until 1868. A symbolic fresh start was assured by a complete reconstruction of the city on a grid layout.

Japan's most famous literary work, *The Tale of Genji* by Murasaki Shikibu, was written during this period (the **Heian period**), as was *The Pillow Book*, a revealing account of life at the Imperial court by a woman very much on the inside, Lady-in-Waiting Sei Shonagon. It was not just literature that flourished, but painting, sculpture and poetry; the Emperor hosted outdoor parties where guests would be invited to compose haiku over cups of saké.

Outside the walls of the Imperial Court, far from the parties and poetry gatherings, a new warrior class was emerging: the samurai. The bloodiest military campaign of all for national supremacy raged between the rival Minamoto (also known as Genji) and Taira (also known as Heike) clans. The epic war, now steeped in as much legend as historical fact, swung between the two clans, before a decisive sea battle in 1185 routed the Tairas. But peace was short-lived and the feudal era had begun.

The first shogun: 1185-1333

The bloody corpses of the defeated Taira had hardly washed away before Minamoto no Yoritomo, victorious leader of the Minamoto clan, moved the capital to Kamakura and was sworn in as the country's first shogun. The Imperial Court remained in Kyoto but real power had shifted geographically and politically to the samurai. Government of the country remained in the hands of successive shoguns for the next 700 years, until the Meiji Restoration of 1868.

The popularity of Buddhism grew during the **Kamakura period**. The Zen sect in particular, with its emphasis on a life of simplicity and austerity, appealed to the warrior class who had always been ill at ease with the effete world of culture and arts during the Heian period. Instead of ushering in a new era, Yoritomo's death in 1199 prompted his widow and her family to assume control. The political capital remained in Kamakura until 1333, when Emperor Go-Daigo succeeded in overthrowing the shogunate.

Eruption of civil war, West and East meet: 1336-1575

The Emperor's moment of triumph turned out to be unexpectedly brief. He was soon booted out of Kyoto by Takauji Ashikaga, the military turncoat who had defected from the Kamakura court in time to become the Emperor's right-hand military man and assist in the rebellion against the Kamakura shogunate. Rightly or wrongly expecting credit for this assistance and anticipating the title of shogun as due reward, Ashikaga was aggrieved when Go-Daigo completely overlooked him. Seeking revenge, Ashikaga forced Go-Daigo into mountain exile and appointed a new Emperor who was gracious enough to name him

JAPAN

shogun. From his hideaway, Go-Daigo made another attempt to retain direct rule but he died soon after, in 1339, and the rival Imperial Court he established was never a serious threat to the Kyoto government.

The Golden and Silver pavilions, two of Kyoto's major tourist draws, were constructed as villas for the shoguns during this period. As in the Heian period, culture and arts took centre stage, with Noh theatre, the tea ceremony and flower arranging all being established in the latter half of the **Muromachi period**. But war was also becoming commonplace as rival feudal lords clashed over territory and isolated skirmishes spiralled into full-scale civil war.

As the nation fought with itself, Christianity made its first appearance in Japan when the missionary Francis Xavier sailed into Kagoshima in 1549, carrying with him enormous ambition: to convert Emperor and shogun alike. He failed, but relations with the West developed further in Nagasaki, where the port was opened to trade with the Portuguese.

Reunification: 1575-1600
The long road to reunification began in 1568 when Nobunaga Oda descended on Kyoto. Nobunaga soon cemented his authority by building the first castle stronghold and, unknowingly, setting a trend to be repeated by feudal lords all over Japan. Castles, each one grander and its defences safer than the last, became a must-have for every lord needing to prove his power over the people he ruled. Sadly, in the centuries since, most of the castles have been destroyed by war and fire. Only a few original examples, such as the castles of Himeji (see p235) and Matsumoto (see p174), remain intact today.

Nobunaga hardly had time to settle into his own castle before he was assassinated in 1582. His successor, Hideyoshi Toyotomi, picked up where Nobunaga had left off and continued with efforts to reunite the country, a task largely completed by 1590. Flushed with success at home, Hideyoshi rebranded himself as an international warrior during two ill-fated attempts to capture Korea. After his death, his son and heir, Hideyori, was swept aside by the warlord Tokugawa Ieyasu, who went on to establish his own government in Edo (present-day Tokyo).

Closing down on the outside world: 1600-1853
Ieyasu knew that the lessons of history were there to be learnt. The Kamakura shogunate had shown itself open to attack from rival clans but Ieyasu and his successors tolerated no intruders. Some 300 feudal clans across Japan were forced to travel to Edo for regular audiences with the shogun. The expense and length of such journeys, nearly three centuries before the rail network would shuttle anyone to Tokyo within a day, ensured that feudal lords were never able to build up the power or finances to mount a challenge to the Tokugawa shogunate.

Strict laws of personal conduct were enforced and a social hierarchy developed with the shogun at the top and peasants and merchants at the bottom. Sandwiched in between were the samurai, though they too were restricted in movement and activity by their own code of conduct. In 1639, Japan suddenly closed all its ports to international trade, with the exception of a tiny Dutch enclave in Nagasaki. The policy of self-seclusion also prohibited all Japanese from leaving the country. Despite, or perhaps because of, the 'no vacancies' sign held up to the outside world, the **Edo period** was one of the most peaceful in Japanese history. Once again, the arts flourished, kabuki theatres opened and merchants traded in lacquerware and silk. But peace and prosperity at the price of national isolation could not last forever; by the middle of the 19th century, the feudal system was looking increasingly outdated. Not for much longer could the shogun keep the outside world at bay.

The era of modernization: 1853 to the present

Commodore Perry's arrival in 1853 accompanied by the 'Black Ships' of the US Navy was to alter the course of Japan's history for ever. The ships were laden with gifts but Perry's visit was anything but a social call. The Americans demanded that the ports be opened to trade and it became increasingly clear that the authorities would not be able to resist the influx of technology from the outside world. The Tokugawa shogunate clung desperately to power for another decade but was finally overthrown in 1867. In the following year, Emperor Meiji was restored to the throne, though he remained politically powerless. Edo, by now renamed Tokyo, became the official capital and Japan embarked on its long period of modernization. One of the most notable achievements was the building of a national railway, an account of which begins on p73.

As the country began to catch up with the rest of the world, the last remnants of the ancien régime were cast away. The land owned by feudal lords was carved up into prefectures which still exist today. Swordless samurai were deprived of their status and forced to find work elsewhere – even their trademark top-knot hairstyle had to go. A new, Western-style, constitution was instituted in 1889 and compulsory education introduced. Wealthy Japanese parents sent their children to Oxford or Cambridge university, while engineers from the West were drafted in to provide the initial technology which would one day turn Japan into an economic superpower.

However, by the end of the first decade of the 20th century, British and other foreign engineers had all but disappeared (the Japanese learned the skills, then learned how to do better themselves). An increasingly confident Japan sought to gain a foothold in Asia; by the time of Emperor Meiji's death in 1912, the country had already engaged in wars with China and Russia. Elsewhere in the world, Japan was keen to promote its culture and traditions; for six months in 1910, the new international face of Japan was displayed to an intrigued British public at White City in west London, on the site occupied today by BBC Television Centre. Over 8,000,000 visitors caught a glimpse of a country in transition. There were demonstrations of judo, kendo, karate and sumo. A tea house, replica Japanese gardens and Ainu village were constructed. But the star attraction was a white-knuckle ride which gave visitors a bird's eye view of London:

To amuse the masses, the exhibition devised and operated a contraption called the 'Flip-Flap', the sight and sound of which … caused a terrifying impact on my childhood mind: a pair of great mobile steel towers arranged scissor-like each with an observation cage swinging from its peak … passengers were loaded into the cages and then, with loud clang-

ing sounds of the steam engine that worked the towers, they slowly rose to what seemed to be a tremendous height, then criss-crossed and eventually the passengers in each cage were lowered to the ground at the opposite side. It seems that always, down to the days of the inauguration of Tokyo Tower, promoters have never failed to make money by simply hauling groups of the populace by mechanical means to points of observation at unaccustomed altitudes. (Ian Mutsu, *Japan Times Weekly*, October 2nd 1971)

The end of the first half of the 20th century was dominated by Japan's involvement in WWII, culminating in the devastating atomic bomb attacks on the cities of Hiroshima and Nagasaki in August 1945. Shortly afterwards, Emperor Hirohito, who had ascended to the throne in 1926, announced Japan's surrender.

Under American occupation after the war, the country embarked upon another period of sweeping reform. By the time the Tokyo Olympics opened in 1964, and the bullet train was speeding between Tokyo and Osaka, Japan's rise to economic superpower was complete.

Over the next two decades, the rest of the world could only watch in amazement as the country that had been closed to outsiders for more than two centuries became the fastest growing economy in the world.

The economic downturn of the late 1990s worried the Japanese and put pressure on the ruling Liberal Democratic Party to produce a magic formula and wipe away the lingering recession in an instant. But anybody who bet in the early years of the 21st century that the days of Japan Inc were over would by now be sorely disappointed.

In this new century Japan faces different challenges, not least of which is how to compete with the increasing economic might of China. Japan may no

Imperial politics

The death of Emperor Hirohito in January 1989 was a pivotal moment in Japan's modern history. Once exalted as the divine leader of the nation and later reinvented as a constitutional monarch following American occupation after WWII, Hirohito's death marked the end of an era. His successor and the current Emperor, Akihito, seemed to breathe new life into a monarchy which had ruled for at least 1600 years. Ever since Akihito's son, Crown Prince Naruhito, married a career woman and Oxford graduate, Masako Owada, the media had periodically indulged in some light relief from the economic doom and gloom by speculating on when the couple would produce a child.

When Masako gave birth to a girl, Princess Aiko, in 2001, the media frenzy shifted gear and attention focused on a potential succession crisis: no males had been born into the Imperial family since the crown prince's younger brother, Akishino, in 1965. Under Japanese law, only a male child is eligible to inherit the throne.

But talk of changing the law to allow female succession quickly evaporated in 2006 after Princess Kiko (Prince Akishino's wife) gave birth to Prince Hisahito. Hisahito is third in line to the throne, behind Naruhito and his father Akishino.

Some politicians, while welcoming Hisahito's birth, quietly expressed disappointment that the talked-about reforms were being put on ice. A woman last sat on the Japanese throne over 1300 years ago. Today the thought of a female emperor is as far away as ever.

⛩ **Political factions**
Though the LDP appears to be a single, united political force, just beneath the surface lie a number of rival factions, each with its own power base and supporters. Whenever an LDP leadership election is announced, the party's political machine cranks up as each faction vies to put forward the successful candidate. With so much attention focused by the press on the political machinations of the LDP, you'd be forgiven for thinking that politics in Japan is a one-horse race. But there are a number of opposition parties, including the Socialists, who briefly came to power in 1993 as part of an eight-party anti-LDP coalition before joining with the LDP to form an alliance in 1994.

longer rule the world when it comes to consumer electronics, computer games or cars, but it will not give up its economic supremacy in Asia without a fight. The competition has only just begun.

POLITICS

For over 50 years Japanese politics has been dominated by the ruling Liberal Democratic Party (LDP), founded in 1955 and still in power today. Though the LDP has been widely credited for Japan's economic success, it has also been dogged by accusations of cronyism and corruption.

Kakuei Tanaka, prime minister in the 1970s, was dubbed the LDP 'kingmaker' and the country's political powerbroker. Few would argue he was also one of the most corrupt politicians of modern times; his greatest achievement, having a shinkansen line built from Tokyo to Niigata solely because Niigata (see pp320-6) was his constituency, bankrupted the entire national railway.

By the 1990s, as the country was searching for a way out of the economic doldrums, the LDP still showed no signs of reforming itself. When Prime Minister Keizo Obuchi (unflatteringly dubbed 'Cold Pizza' by the media) died in office in 2000, he was replaced by the gaffe-prone Yoshiro Mori, who rapidly became one of Japan's most unpopular prime ministers. Mori was barely out of the headlines for the 11 months he was in office, though for all the wrong reasons. One of his most notable gaffes, for which he was forced to make an embarrassing public apology, came when he described Japan as a 'divine country' with the Emperor at its centre. He caused another public outcry shortly before an election when he suggested that wavering voters should 'stay in bed' rather than vote against him on polling day.

Mori was succeeded in 2001 by the maverick Junichiro Koizumi, Japan's 11th prime minister in just 13 years. Koizumi caused a stir after his election when he appointed five women to his cabinet. Considered an outsider and someone who would not shy away from taking genuine economic reform, voters seemed just as impressed by his appearance. The Japanese media seemed to speculate more on how Koizumi gained his 'distinctive silvery mane' than on his political manifesto. His first foreign minister, Makiko Tanaka (daughter of

---

⛩ King Koizumi

Koizumi retired from the top job in Japanese politics in 2006, but he will not be easily forgotten. Koizumi shares his birthday with Elvis Presley and in 2001 released a limited-edition charity compilation album of his favourite Elvis songs entitled 'Junichiro Koizumi Presents: My Favourite Elvis Songs'.

As health minister in 1998, Koizumi was asked which was more pressing: approving Viagra or reducing toxic dioxin emissions. He replied: 'Personally, Viagra'.

As prime minister he frequently invited Hollywood stars to his official residence. He famously danced with Richard Gere in front of the cameras and sang karaoke with Tom Cruise. He once serenaded Australian Foreign Minister Alexander Downer with a karaoke rendition of 'I Can't Help Falling in Love with You'.

---

former prime minister Kakuei Tanaka), was less complimentary, famously dubbing Koizumi 'a weirdo with a hair cut from the *Lion King*'.

Throughout his time in office Koizumi remained popular with voters for his maverick style and reformist agenda. But he also made enemies within his own ranks. A party which had enjoyed almost uninterrupted power for so long did not always appreciate Koizumi's rhetoric and manner. When MPs from within his own ranks voted against his plans to reform the country's postal system in 2005 he lost no time in holding them to account by calling a snap election which he turned into a referendum on his reforms. The gamble paid off: Koizumi secured a landslide victory, ousted many of his most outspoken critics, and pressed ahead with his plans.

Koizumi remained a colourful character to the end: just weeks before he stepped down in 2006, he embarked on a farewell tour of the United States, the highlight of which – for him, if not for his American hosts – was a trip to Elvis's home in Graceland. Pictures of Koizumi, a lifelong Elvis fan, crooning 'Love Me Tender' while wearing Elvis glasses next to a bemused George W Bush flashed around the world.

Koizumi was always going to be a hard act to follow and the man chosen to do so was the conservative Shinzo Abe, who became Japan's youngest prime minister since WWII when he took office in 2006 aged 52. Abe's tenure marked a return to the more traditional, grey-suited Japanese political leader, but he pledged to press on with Koizumi's economic reforms. Whatever else he does, Abe is certainly keeping the job in the family: both his grandfather and great uncle were prime ministers and his father was foreign minister.

ECONOMY

When Japan's bubble economy finally burst in the early 1990s, the nation and world reeled in shock. Throughout the previous decade the country's economy had seemed unstoppable. At 2.5%, interest rates were the lowest in the world, making money easy to borrow. Banks assisted in pumping up the bubble by offering loans to virtually anybody with little or no scrutiny of their personal finances. As a piece of real estate, Japan was worth the whole of the US seven times over. The value of land was pushed artificially high and companies staked their livelihood solely on the soaring price of the square feet they owned. This made them profitable on paper but bankrupt the moment the bottom fell out of the property market. The gloomy economic outlook extended well into the 21st century, but by the middle of the first decade there were signs of cautious optimism and a renewed sense that Japan was finally back in business. The unemployment rate – a barometer for the state of the economy – has been falling steadily while consumer prices are on the rise. Perhaps most significantly of all, average land prices in Japan's three biggest cities – Tokyo, Osaka and Nagoya – rose in 2006 for the first time since 1990, suggesting that the economic rebound from 15 years in the doldrums is not just another false dawn.

If more proof were needed that things were beginning to look up, consider the case of Toyota, which in 2007 is set to overtake US-based General Motors (GM) as the world's largest car manufacturer. The Japanese firm sold its first car, the A1, in 1936. In 2007, it was expected to produce a record 9.42 million vehicles. Toyota's stock-market value is more than seven times the market value of GM and Ford combined.

RELIGION

The two main religions in Japan are **Buddhism**, imported from China, and **Shinto** (literally, 'the way of the gods'), Japan's indigenous religion. Shinto's origins extend as far back as Japanese mythology, to the belief that all aspects of nature (water, rocks, trees and wind, for example) have their own god. Shinto was the official state religion until 1945, up to which time the Emperor himself was considered to be a divine being.

Buddhist places of worship are temples, the names of which in Japanese always end with the suffix –*ji*. In Shinto, places of worship are shrines and are much plainer in design than the often brightly coloured temples. Shinto shrines are most obviously distinguished from temples by the red *torii* (gate) which marks the entrance to the shrine precinct. Despite numerous attempts by foreign missionaries over the centuries, **Christianity** has made few inroads into Japan, though the Western white wedding is considered a fashionable way to tie the knot. For a good introduction to religion in Japan, see the relevant chapter in Ninian Smart's *The World's Religions* (Cambridge University Press, 1989).

Hi-tech fiasco

Japan may be the envy of much of the rest of the world when it comes to computer games and hi-tech technology, but that doesn't mean it always gets things right. In 2006 the government was forced into an embarrassing U-turn on a disastrous ¥2 billion scheme allowing people to apply for passports online.

The project was quietly ditched after it was revealed that of the 3.75 million passports issued in 2005, just 103 applications had been made online – which worked out at a staggering cost of around ¥16 million per online applicant, as opposed to ¥4000 for a traditional passport application.

⛩ **Longevity record**
  Japanese women are the world's longest lived – and have been for the past 20 years. They enjoy an average life expectancy of 85.59 years, while Japanese men can expect to live 78.64 years, second only to their Icelandic counterparts, who average 78.8 years.
  The health ministry puts the impressive longevity record down to a healthy diet, which tends to be rich in vegetables and fish products, and relatively low in animal fats. But it's not all good news: long life expectancies combined with a falling birth rate could be storing up problems for the future in a country where one in four of the population is expected to be over 65 within the next decade.

THE PEOPLE

Of the 127 million people living in Japan, the vast majority are born Japanese. Commentators liken Japan to an exclusive club; only rarely is anyone from outside the circle given the much sought-after membership card – a Japanese passport. History disputes the much-touted fact that the Japanese are an entirely homogenous people since the country is said to have been first settled by migrants from various parts of mainland Asia. The Ainu, an ethnic minority who are culturally and physically distinct from the Japanese, are further proof that Japan is much more multicultural than it may at first seem. Believed to have inhabited northern Honshu and Hokkaido since the 7th century, the number of Ainu began to dwindle as the Japanese colonized the north of the country. For more on the Ainu, their cultural heritage and battle for survival, see box p366.

It would be wrong to assume that the 'closed shop' nature of Japanese nationality means the people are unwelcoming. On the contrary, it would be hard to find a more friendly and welcoming country. The traditional image of the polite but formal, hard-working Japanese is only partially accurate. Indeed, any generalizations about the Japanese as a whole are unfair. Even the briefest (rail!) journey here proves that the people are as diverse as the landscape is varied.

SPORT

Traditional sports

Perhaps the best-known traditional Japanese sport is **sumo wrestling**. Two wrestlers (who usually weigh between 90kg and 160kg each) attempt to push each other out of a 4.55m-diameter clay circle; the winner is decided when any part of a wrestler's body apart from the soles of his feet touches the ground, or if he steps or is pushed out of the ring. Sumo wrestlers are divided into six divisions, the highest rank being that of *yokozuna* (grand champion). There are six sumo tournaments (known as *basho*) every year and each lasts for 15 days. Tickets for ringside seats are expensive and usually sell out weeks in advance but the public broadcaster NHK provides live coverage of the tournaments. Basho are held in Tokyo (January, May and September), Osaka (March), Nagoya (July) and Fukuoka (November). See also box opposite.

Of all the martial arts, **aikido** is perhaps the one most steeped in religion. Created in Japan by Morihei Ueshiba (1883-1969; see p203), aikido combines the disciplines of judo, karate and kendo. Practitioners of aikido attempt to harness an opponent's 'ki' (spiritual power) which in turn is said to enable them to throw him or her to the ground with little effort. **Judo** follows a similar principle though the techniques are very different. Much of the basic judo training involves throwing your opponent to the floor and holding him or her down. Judo has been a regular Olympic event since the Tokyo Olympic Games in 1964 and is now practised worldwide. There are ten ranks, called *dan*, which are internationally recognized.

Karate originated in China and only reached mainland Japan in the early 1920s; today it exists in many different styles. **Kendo** (literally, 'the way of the sword') is sometimes known as Japanese fencing. Opponents wear protective masks, chest gear and gloves while using a bamboo stick *(shinai)* or metal sword *(katana)* to strike each other. **Kyudo**, or Japanese archery, is one of the oldest martial arts and can be performed on the ground as well as on horseback, when it is known as **yabusame**.

JNTO (see box p31) publishes a *Traditional Sports* leaflet which has details of where and when it's possible to observe practice sessions for the sports mentioned above, as well as information on how to apply for sumo tournament tickets.

Modern sports
Baseball is taken as seriously as it is in the USA, with professional teams divided into Central and Pacific leagues. All major cities have a professional team but the sport also attracts large numbers of students at school and university clubs. **Rugby** has a smaller following but is growing in popularity as the country makes its mark on the international stage. Japan narrowly missed out on the chance of hosting the 2011 Rugby World Cup, when it was pipped at the post by New Zealand.

Soccer has taken off in a big way since the launch of the J-League in 1993. A measure of the sport's success came when Japan successfully co-hosted the 2002 World Cup with South Korea.

⛩ Shorts? No thanks
Should sumo wrestlers be allowed to wear shorts when competing in the ring? Japan's amateur sumo association turned more than a few heads when it suggested a switch from the traditional *mawashi* (wrapped cloth) to shorts, in a bid to encourage more schoolchildren to take up the sport. 'Kids are not going to want to take part if they don't look cool,' said the amateur association, worried about the decline in popularity of sumo at a grassroots level.

But the response from the professional association of sumo wrestlers was swift and unequivocal: they would never support the introduction of shorts and vowed to bar anyone wearing them from taking part in youth tournaments: 'We have no intention of allowing children in shorts into the ring.'

CULTURE

Japan is known as much for its ancient traditions as its futuristic technology. The following is a brief guide to the country's highly distinctive culture.

Traditional culture

Ikebana Perhaps the most celebrated of Japan's ancient cultural traditions is ikebana, or the art of flower arranging. Ikebana was once synonymous with the formality of the tea ceremony, when participants would contemplate the beauty and careful positioning of the flowers decorating the tea room. Just as there are different schools of judo and karate, so too there are a number of officially recognized schools of ikebana in Japan. Both men and women practise ikebana; indeed, it was even considered an appropriate pastime for the samurai. Foreign visitors interested in attending an introductory class can contact Ikebana International in Tokyo (☎ 03-3293 8188, 💻 www.ikebanahq.org, office@ike banahq.org).

Chanoyu Commonly known as the tea ceremony, chanoyu is one of the country's most highly regarded aesthetic pursuits. Considered to be a form of mental training as well as a means of learning elegant manners and etiquette, *sado* ('the way of the tea') is much more than just an elaborate way of pouring a cup of tea. While the powdered green tea is whipped up with boiling water using a special bamboo whisk and poured into the serving bowl, guests are offered a small cake or sweetmeat to prepare themselves for the bitter taste of the tea. The ceremony, which can last up to a couple of hours, is held in a simple tatami-mat room decorated with hanging scrolls and discretely positioned flowers. Some top-end hotels in cities such as Tokyo and Kyoto offer tea-ceremony demonstrations and even provide stools for guests who aren't used to sitting on their knees for long.

Kabuki, Bunraku and Noh Probably the most accessible of traditional dramatic forms in Japan is **kabuki**, a theatrical art which dates back to the 17th century. A knowledge of Japanese is not necessary to enjoy the colourful performances, where men dress as women, the make-up is as bright as the costumes are lavish, and members of the audience frequently shout out their appreciation when actors take to the stage, strike a dramatic pose or deliver a famous line. The kabuki theatre comes equipped with a *seridashi*, a trap door in the floor which allows actors to enter the stage from below, as well as a gangway through the audience which lets the actors make a dramatic, sweeping entrance, their silk costumes rustling behind them as they step gracefully towards the stage. It would be hard to find a more lively or entertaining theatrical experience in Japan. The best place to sample a performance is at the Kabuki-za theatre (see p101) in Tokyo.

Also originating in the 17th century and closely related to kabuki is **bunraku** (puppet play). Puppets up to two-thirds the size of humans are dressed in costumes which are just as elaborate as those worn by actors on the kabuki stage. The puppets are operated by three stage hands while a fourth narrates the

⛩ **Geisha in the 21st century**
Maiko, apprentice geisha, train for up to six years for the right to be called a geisha. During this time the maiko-san will learn how to play traditional instruments, such as the shamisen and koto (see below), how to dance and how to dress in a kimono. Above all the trainee is required to become skilled in the manners and comportment associated with the geisha world, since every one of them will be judged by the customers to whom they are sent in the evenings to entertain.

In the 1920s there were about 80,000 geisha and a steady flow of new applicants. Today, one estimate suggests that there are probably no more than 4-5000 throughout Japan. Given the long hours and difficult working conditions it's not surprising that there are few new applicants. However, a new breed of geisha is shunning the long training programme and opting for a fast-track approach to the profession. More and more young professional women, dressed in platform heels and forever chatting on their mobile phones by day, are now moonlighting as geisha after only the briefest crash course in technique. Customers unwilling or unable to pay for an evening with a traditional geisha can opt instead for one of the new breed who charge a fraction of the price.

story to the tune of the traditional *shamisen* (wood instrument covered in cat skin with three strings made of silk).

Less immediately accessible than kabuki is **Noh**, a classical form of theatre which dates back more than 600 years. Performances of Noh are a combination of music and dance, but the style of movement is much more formalized than kabuki, while the dancing is choreographed to represent actions such as crying and laughing and is accompanied by flutes and drums. Most of the actors wear stylized masks which depict a wide range of facial expressions and emotions. Performances, on a special raised stage with a roof and a sparse set, often take place by firelight during the summer months in the precincts of Shinto shrines.

Shamisen, koto and taiko Proficiency on traditional Japanese instruments such as the **shamisen** (see above) and the **koto** (Japanese harp) was once as much a test of a geisha's talent as her ability to dance. Partly because of the cost of purchasing and maintaining such instruments, their popularity has faded. But one traditional instrument that remains popular for its infectious rhythm is the **taiko** drum. Bare-chested taiko drummers beating a furious rhythm while drenching themselves and their instruments in sweat are a staple sight and sound at most Japanese festivals, where the noise is the perfect accompaniment to a summer parade through the streets. Shaped like a cylinder, the body of the taiko drum is hollow and covered at both ends with leather. Smaller hand drums, known as *tsuzumi*, are often used in Noh and kabuki.

Popular culture
Manga Comic books (manga) are big business in Japan, with an annual turnover of nearly ¥570 billion. Look out for everyone from schoolchildren to businessmen reading them on the train or subway. Live animation on television has been no less successful.

Stamping around Japan

Stamp collecting is a popular pastime in Japan, though the most popular stamps are not of the postage kind. Virtually every tourist attraction here has its own stamp and ink pad at the entrance. Some towns organize seasonal 'stamp rallies', when tourists are invited to follow a trail from one attraction to another, collecting stamps as they go. Small souvenir prizes are sometimes doled out to those who completely fill their 'stamp cards' (a gesture of thanks for contributing to the local tourism industry). In Japan, it's almost as if you only know you've really been somewhere when you can bring back the stamp to prove it.

Stamps are particularly popular on the railway. Even the tiniest rural station will more than likely have a stamp in the waiting room or by the ticket desk. Pack a blank notebook in your luggage, try to forget your image of the nerdy stamp collector, and by collecting stamps as you go you'll have an instant souvenir of your rail trip around Japan, as well as a useful record of your personal itinerary.

Famous cartoon characters who have achieved recognition beyond Japan's borders include **Pokemon, Hello Kitty**, the cat with no mouth, **Doraemon**, a blue robot from the 21st century, and **Miffy the rabbit**. The secret to their longevity is a successful career beyond the media for which they were originally created: one manufacturer launched a limited edition Hello Kitty car, complete with Kitty steering wheel, seat covers and paintwork.

Pachinko and video games Another popular form of entertainment is a trip to the **pachinko parlour**. Players sit in front of upright pinball machines and feed them with tiny silver ball bearings. The machines then rattle a lot and, with luck (little skill seems to be involved), more silver balls pour out through the slot into a tray; these can be exchanged for prizes like washing powder and tins of ham. These unglamorous prizes are then traded in for cash at a semi-hidden booth outside. It's illegal to play for cash in the pachinko parlours so owners get around the law by allowing customers to exchange the prizes for money off the premises.

In big cities you're never far from a **video game arcade**; the best ones are the Sega Joypolis. Here you'll find the latest virtual-reality games and hi-tech simulators, as well as more unusual slot machines. One game yet to become a hit outside Japan is the Sub Marine Catcher; instead of trying to manoeuvre an electronic arm to grab a prize such as a teddy bear, this version has a tank full of live lobsters. If the player is successful, the arm picks up the lobster and it falls through the slot and straight into his/her hands (plastic bags are provided to carry your winnings home).

Television Japanese television is known for its weird game shows, such as the now defunct *Endurance* which, at its most extreme, challenged contestants to plunge into scorpion pits or sit for as long as possible in tanks of ice. The trend continues with shows such as *Muscle Ranking* and *Super Human Coliseum*.

Travel documentaries are popular, even more so if they are dressed up as game shows. *Experience the World* sends a celebrity to a far-flung corner of the globe to complete a series of challenges, while yet more celebrities compete to

＃ **Celebrity spotting in the commercial break**
Ever since Roger Moore, the suave, sophisticated TV *Saint*, came over to Japan to become the face for Lark Cigarettes (slogan: 'Speak Lark'), there's been no shortage of foreign celebrities happy to be flown here first class to lend their name to a range of products – in exchange for a handsome fee and an assurance that their endorsements would not be seen outside Japan.

In recent years, celebrities drafted in to give that glamorous edge to household products include Kiefer Sutherland (advertising healthy snack CalorieMate), Tiger Woods (Wonda Coffee, slogan: 'It's wonderful Wonda'), Brad Pitt (Levi's 501 jeans), and Richard Gere (men's beauty spa Dandy House).

To see the latest crop of celebrities selling their credibility in the name of a cheap buck, check out ⌨ www.japander.com, a great online resource which includes clips of some of the best (and worst) adverts. Many are also available at ⌨ www.you tube.com.

answer questions about the tasks back in the studio. Cookery programmes, drama serials and love stories are also a mainstay of TV schedules.

Music   There is no greater music phenomenon in Japan than **J-Pop**. Most pop artists disappear as quickly as they rise to fame; longevity is counted in months not years. Those who have survived longer than most include the kings of pop, Tsuyoshi and Koichi Dohmoto, better known as the Kinki Kids, and the boy bands SMAP, V6 and Arashi.

Girl-band Morning Musume ('Morning Daughters'), known simply as MoMusu, was formed when producer Tsunku trawled round search-for-a-star contests, literally picking out losers as he went. The group quickly proved that lack of talent was no impediment to commercial success. Whenever one member of the group faded in the popularity stakes she was simply replaced by another person from the bottomless talent pool. Artists with staying power include R&B pop sensation Utada Hikaru, known in Japan as 'Hikki', and rock band L'Arc en Ciel, who have sold over 25 million singles and albums.

If you're in Japan on New Year's Eve, NHK broadcasts its *Red and White Song Contest*, where the biggest music stars from the last year perform live in a competition between male and female artists.

＃ **Small-screen sensation**
Japanese television host Norio Minorikawa – known universally as Minomonta – is officially the world's busiest person on television. In 2006 he became a Guinness World Record Holder for the most number of hours on television. He spends on average a total of 21 hours and 42 minutes every week on live television, appearing on 11 shows. He hosts a variety of news programmes, chat shows, wildlife programmes and game shows, including the Japanese version of 'Who Wants to Be a Millionaire?'. This does not include an additional five pre-recorded programmes including 'Millionaire', the wildlife show 'Amazing Animals' and 'Full Throttle TV', a programme in which he dispenses lifestyle, health and relationship advice.

Practical information for the visitor

ARRIVING IN JAPAN

Japan has two major international gateways, Narita Airport, east of Tokyo, and Kansai Airport, built on a man-made island off the coast in Osaka Bay. Immigration and Customs are efficient at both but don't expect to rush through the formalities.

If you can choose to fly into either Narita or Kansai opt for the latter, since the airport is more modern and offers a wider range of facilities. If you're planning to travel around the Kansai region (which includes Kyoto) it makes sense anyway to fly into Kansai rather than Narita. Both airports offer ample facilities for changing money and both are connected to the Japan Rail network, so you can exchange your rail pass and begin your journey soon after touching down.

Japan's newest major international airport opened in 2005 near Nagoya (see box p160). It handles far fewer international flights than Narita and Kansai, and is not linked directly to the JR network, but could still be useful if planning a tour around Central Japan.

Tokyo

Narita International Airport (☎ 0476-34 5000, 🖳 www.narita-airport.jp), is Japan's major international gateway. It's almost 70km outside Tokyo but is linked directly to the centre of the city by rail. With landing slots filled to capacity, Narita is a busy and congested airport, but arrival (and departure) procedures are typically efficient. Tokyo's second airport is **Haneda** (☎ 03-5757 8111, 🖳 www.tokyo-airport-bldg.co.jp) but you'll only pass through here if you're taking a domestic flight or if you're on a China Airlines (🖳 www.china-airlines.com) flight to/from Taiwan. Haneda is closer to the centre of Tokyo than Narita and is accessible via a monorail which runs from Hamamatsucho station (see p94) on the JR Yamanote line.

Narita has **two terminals** connected by a free shuttle bus. The South Wing of Terminal 1 reopened in 2006 as a new state-of-the-art facility for Star Alliance airlines (🖳 www.staralliance.com), which includes All Nippon Airways. Most airlines belonging to the rival Oneworld alliance (🖳 www.oneworld.com), which includes Japan Airlines, operate from Terminal 2.

In the arrivals lobby of both terminals is a **tourist information desk** (☎ 0476-34 6251 or 30 3383, daily, 8am-8pm), where accommodation bookings can be made through the **Welcome Inn Reservation Center** (🖳 www.itcj.jp, daily, 8am-7:30pm). The **money exchange counter** (daily, 6:30am-11pm) is a good place to change travellers' cheques or foreign currency, particularly at the weekend when banks are closed.

Japan Rail and the private Keisei Railway have ticket desks in the arrival lobbies but to convert an exchange order you have to go to the rail station level

⛩ **Sausage sniffers**
   Look out when you arrive at Tokyo's Narita airport for Cleo and Candy. They are Japan's first meat-sniffing dogs, a pair of beagles trained to hunt out banned meat products – including ham or sausage that does not come with a certificate of inspection from the country of origin. During their first six months on active duty, the dogs found a total of 1625kg of illegally imported meat. One man was caught red-handed attempting to smuggle in hundreds of sausages hidden in the bottom of his bag.

on B1 (one floor below the arrivals hall). **Rail-pass exchange orders** can be converted to the relevant pass at the View Plaza travel agency (11:30am-7pm), or at the normal JR ticket office outside these times. Seat reservations can also be made if you've already planned your itinerary.

See p105 for notes about getting to Tokyo from Narita.

Osaka

International flights land at **Kansai Airport** (☎ 0724-55 2500, 🖥 www.kansai airport.or.jp). Kansai Airport (opened in 1994) is a more impressive gateway to Japan than Narita but has its own share of problems. Conceived before Japan's economic bubble burst, the airport is now hugely in debt; airlines object to the exorbitant landing fees and the island it's built on has been sinking at such an alarming rate that a moat is to be built around it. In a bid to relieve congestion and allow for more flights, a second runway was due to open in 2007.

International arrivals are on the first floor and departures are on the fourth. Staff at **Kansai TIC** (☎ 0724-56 6025, daily, 8:30am-8:30pm Apr-Oct, 9am-9pm Nov-Mar), in the arrivals lobby, can advise on travel throughout the Kansai region and will book accommodation anywhere in Japan through the Welcome Inn reservation network (see box p55). The office is not usually busy and staff are only too pleased to help anyone who can find them. Changing money or cashing travellers' cheques is easy as there are branches of nine banks; at least one is open between 6am and 11pm. There are also ATMs in the arrivals lobby which accept foreign-issued credit cards. If you're looking for somewhere to eat, check out the north side restaurant area on the second floor.

Rail pass exchange orders can be converted either at the small JR West Information Counter (daily, 9:30am-7pm) in the arrivals lobby, or at the JR Travel Center (daily, 10am-6pm) or ticket office (daily, 5:30am-11pm) at Kansai Airport station. Most people don't notice the information counter and go straight to the station but you might save time by stopping here first.

See p121 for notes about getting to Osaka/Kyoto from Kansai airport.

TOURIST INFORMATION

The staff in the main **tourist information centres (TICs)** at Narita and Kansai and in Tokyo and Kyoto (see the relevant city guides for details) speak English and can provide information on onward travel throughout Japan. Most towns and cities have a tourist information office (look for the 'i' logo). Though staff

---

❑ **Tourist information**

If you're stuck anywhere in Japan and need assistance in English, call the Japan National Tourist Organization information line (☎ 03-3201 3331, daily 9am-5pm). Operators are very knowledgeable and will help with any travel or tourism enquiry.

---

at the smaller offices do not always speak English they can usually provide maps and town guides in English.

A network of **goodwill guides** operates in a number of towns and cities. These are English-speaking volunteers who guide foreign tourists around local sights. They can usually be contacted via the local tourist information office or search the online database at 🖳 www.guidesearch.jp.

GETTING AROUND

By rail (see pp79-89)

By air

Japan's two major airlines operate a comprehensive network of domestic flights. All Nippon Airways (ANA, ☎ 0120-029 709, 🖳 www.ana.co.jp) and Japan Airlines (JAL, ☎ 0120-25 5971, 🖳 www.jal.co.jp) operate flights to/from most destinations across the country. A number of smaller airlines operate selected routes: Hokkaido International Airlines (ADO, known as Air Do, ☎ 0120-057 333, 🖳 www.airdo.jp) flies between Tokyo and Sapporo, Hakodate and Asahikawa in Hokkaido; Skymark Airlines (SKY, ☎ 03-3433 7670, 🖳 www.sky mark.co.jp) operates between Tokyo and Fukuoka, Kobe, Sapporo and Naha (Okinawa). Starflyer (🖳 www.starflyer.jp) is a recent addition to the domestic-aviation scene, flying between Tokyo and Kitakyushu airport on the island of Kyushu; the airline plans to extend its network to include Nagoya, Seoul and Shanghai. Reservations are only accepted online and all seats on the planes offer internet access. Nice touches include personal video screens, coat hooks, cup holders and retractable foot rests – Japanese luxury at an economy price!

If you're pushed for time and are planning to travel long distances it can make sense to combine use of the rail pass with a domestic flight. However, do a bit of research because it may work out quicker to take a shinkansen if you add on the time it takes to get to/from the airports.

In recent years the price of domestic flights has fallen as a result of more competition, but it still pays to book ahead for the best deals. Both ANA and

---

❑ **Cable cars and ropeways**

An important point to note is that a **cable car** in Japan is a funicular/mountain railway and a **ropeway** is what many others consider a cable car (ie carriages suspended from a cable).

⛩ **Welcome cards**
   Welcome cards are free and they entitle non-Japanese to discounts, small gifts or special services in a number of hotels, restaurants, museums and tourist attractions in certain parts of Japan. They are available either from the tourist information offices in these areas or the main TIC (see p106) in Tokyo. However, the Tokyo Museum Guide, Mt Fuji, Tokai and Kagawa cards (and the relevant discount information) can be downloaded and printed from the websites given below:

● **Tokyo Museum Guide** (🖳 www.tcvb.or.jp/en/index_en.htm) A printout from this website entitles the holder to discounts at a number of art galleries and museums in Tokyo.

● **Tokyo Handy Guide/Map** The card/map offers discounts at 37 museums, parks and gardens in Tokyo.

● **Mt Fuji** (🖳 www.mtfuji-welcomecard.jp/) This card is only available as a website printout and it is welcome at 202 places in the Fuji, Hakone and Izu region.

● **Tokai** (🖳 www.j-heartland.com) This Welcome Card offers discounts in 235 places in Aichi, Gifu, Mie and Shizuoka prefectures.

● **Kobe** The booklet card entitles the holder to discounts at 101 facilities in the city including on the City Loop bus.

● **Northern Tohoku** (🖳 www.northern-tohoku.gr.jp/welcome/english/index.html) The card offers discounts in 187 places in Aomori, Iwate and Akita prefectures.

● **Kagawa** (🖳 www.21kagawa.com/visitor/kanko/e-index0.htm) This card is valid around Takamatsu, Shikoku and offers discounts at 150 sites and facilities.

● **Fukuoka** (🖳 www.city.fukuoka.jp/info/welcome/main-e.htm) This guidebook card is valid at 73 places in Fukuoka City.

● **Kitakyushu** The card offers discounts, free drinks or small gifts at 79 sites/facilities in Kokura and Kitakyushu City, Kyushu.

   You may have to show your passport (with a 'temporary visitor' stamp in) when you apply for the card if in a tourist information office and/or when you use it.

JAL offer discount 'air passes' for foreign visitors. These are worth considering if you are planning to take two or more domestic flights.

By bus or tram

The **bus** service in Japan is almost as efficient as the rail service; a novel experience for anyone who comes from a country where bus timetables are largely fictional. On most intra-urban buses, you enter at the back and take a ticket from the machine by the door. To work out how much the fare is, just before your stop, match the number on the ticket with the fare underneath the corresponding number on the board at the front of the bus. Leave the bus at the front, throwing the exact fare (notes are accepted) and your ticket into the box by the driver; if you don't have the correct money you can change a note to coins by using the change machine nearby. However, some intra-urban buses are operated by JR so check in advance if you have a JR pass as that will give you free travel..

   Several cities and large towns still have a **tram** service. On most trams fares are collected in the same way as on buses. However, it is often possible to get a one-day bus/tram pass which makes life easier and is often good value.

   For information about JR's inter-urban bus services, see box p54.

> **JR bus/ferry services**
> In addition to its rail services, JR also operates some **Highway Bus** routes, though they hardly compete with the trains in terms of speed and are prone to getting snarled up in traffic. They are also less user-friendly than the trains since announcements are usually in Japanese only. The main JR Highway Bus route, for which rail passes are valid, runs from Tokyo railway station to Nagoya, Kyoto and Osaka railway stations. Seats for this service should be booked in advance at the JR bus ticket office at the relevant train station. Further details are not included because it's faster and more convenient to travel by train. However, JR bus services to places of interest not accessible by rail are included in the route guides.
>
> Rail passes are also valid for the JR **ferry service** which operates between Miyajima-guchi (near Hiroshima) and Miyajima Island (see p268).

By taxi

Taxis are usually available outside even the tiniest of stations but it's also fine to flag one down in the street if the red light in the lower right-hand corner of the windscreen is on. The starting fare is around ¥650 for the first 2km plus ¥100 for each additional 500m thereafter; a surcharge (up to 30%) is added between 11pm and 5am. Thus, taxis are not cheap but you pay for the service. The drivers wear white gloves and peaked caps, and you don't even have to open the door yourself because the driver operates the rear passenger doors from the front.

By bicycle

It is possible to rent a bike at many stations; details are given where relevant.

ACCOMMODATION

There is a wide range of possibilities and accommodation is almost always of a high standard. Unless stated otherwise, rates quoted are generally the lowest you should expect to pay. For most accommodation **check-in** starts **from 4pm** and **check-out** is **by 11am**. In most business hotels, guests are asked to vacate their rooms by 10am. Most ryokan (see p57) and minshuku (see p56) prefer, and some insist, that you reserve a room before you arrive, especially if you want meals.

Accessible Japan (www.wakakoma.org/aj) is a useful website for information on hotels which offer specially adapted rooms for the disabled.

Hostels/temples

The cheapest places tend to be **youth hostels**, which get crowded out with young Japanese during Golden Week (see p67) and in the summer. These are great place to stay if you want to meet and socialize with other travellers as many of the hostels organize a programme of events, evening sing-songs and the like. Some of the most atmospheric hostels are found in rural areas; Hokkaido in particular has a number of excellent hostels.

There are two kinds of hostel: a small number are operated by local authorities but the majority are privately run and belong to the Association of Japan Youth Hostels (JYH; www.jyh.or.jp); JYH is part of Hostelling International/

YHA (⌨ www.hihostels.com). Two rates are generally offered: the lower one is for YH(HI) members (bring a YH/HI card) while non-members pay about ¥1000 extra; both rates are quoted where relevant. A few hostels will only accept YH(HI) members but you should be able to buy a membership card on the spot. Municipal hostels tend to be marginally cheaper though both charge around ¥3000-3500 per person.

All hostels provide dormitory accommodation while some also offer private rooms (ideal for families travelling together) for an additional charge. At most hostels breakfast and dinner are offered for an additional charge. Some hostels have communal kitchen facilities. It's wise to call ahead and make a booking since managers may not appreciate it if you turn up unannounced.

A few hostels, such as the ones in Takayama (see p184) and Nagano (see p172), are attached to, or in, **temples**. At these places it may be possible (if you ask!) to join early-morning prayers or participate in a session of zazen with resident monks. A few temples which are not hostels also open their doors to paying guests; these too are an excellent opportunity to experience a part of Japanese culture close up. Two places worth seeking out are Koya-san (see pp230-2), deep in the mountains in Kansai, and Motsu-ji (see p289) in Hiraizumi.

⛩ **Booking accommodation**

It's wise though not essential to book your first couple of nights' accommodation before you arrive in Japan. If booking directly from overseas it's best to do so either through the relevant hotel/ryokan website or by email, clearly stating dates and specific requests. Communicating your request on the phone may be complicated and hoteliers much prefer to have written confirmation. If booking online make sure you receive written confirmation and take a print-out with you to show at check-in.

If you do turn up without a place to stay, most tourist information offices can assist with accommodation reservations. Before you leave for Japan, ask JNTO (see box p31) for information on/copies of the following:

● *Directory of Welcome Inns* – a directory of budget to mid-range hostels, hotels and ryokan which can be booked free of charge through the Welcome Inn Reservation Center (WIRC) at ⌨ www.itcj.jp. A full list of participating hotels is available online. The staff at JNTO offices cannot book accommodation but, in Japan, bookings are accepted if you go in person to the WIRC counters at the tourist information offices in Tokyo, Kyoto, and at Kansai and Narita airports.
● *Youth Hostels Map of Japan* – includes contact numbers for hostels across Japan.
● *Japanese Inn Group* – a nationwide directory of ryokan (not a chain of inns) which are used to dealing with foreign guests. Traditionally, ryokan rates in Japan include two meals but Japanese Inn Group members also offer room-only rates. Some of the inns in the group can be booked on-line and most accept credit cards. See the directory for a booking form and for details of each member inn, or check ⌨ www.jpinn.com.

The number of general **hotel-reservation websites** continues to rise. They include: ⌨ http://hotel.jp-guide.net, ⌨ www.japanhotel.net, ⌨ www.e-stay.jp, ⌨ www.j-reserve.com, ⌨ www.e-japanhotels.com and ⌨ www.cheaphostelsjapan.com. All include pictures and descriptions of properties. Whenever booking online, make sure you take a print-out of your email confirmation with you and present it at check-in.

Camping

JNTO publishes a leaflet, *Camping in Japan*, with a region-by-region guide to some of the most popular camp-sites in the country, access details and overnight charges. A drawback for rail travellers is that nearly all camp-sites are a long way from stations.

Minshuku

Minshuku are small, family-run inns where the rates usually include supper and breakfast; expect to pay around ¥6000 per person; rates are usually reduced for children. However, room-only rates are available in some minshuku. JNTO publishes a useful booklet, *Minshukus in Japan*, listing over 250 minshuku nationwide.

Urban minshuku are usually fine but are often less personal and character-ful than rural ones which might be in old farmhouses and thus offer a great experience of being in a traditional Japanese home. Rooms are Japanese style (tatami mats and futons); see box p58. There are no private bathrooms and you may not be provided with a towel or yukata, but most have a TV in the room.

Meals are eaten at set times (usually 6 or 6.30pm for supper and about 7.30am for breakfast), occasionally with the family. Invariably the food is Japanese, so be prepared for (raw) egg, fish and miso soup at breakfast!

Pensions

Pensions are the Western-style equivalent of minshuku and are becoming increasingly popular with Japanese. Like minshuku, pensions are usually small, family-run affairs but they offer beds rather than futons. Rates start from around ¥6000 and usually include a Western breakfast but not dinner.

Business hotels

A little more expensive but with less character are business hotels, used as the name suggests by businessmen looking for a place to crash. Business hotels are not to be confused with Japan's infamous capsule hotels, since you get a prop-er room rather than a sleeping compartment. Most rooms are Western style and are singles, though virtually all business hotels have some twins and doubles. Facilities include a café where you can get evening meals and breakfast (increasingly this is now included in the room rate) and vending machines (soft drinks, beer, saké, and perhaps pot noodle and ice cream). Rooms are clean but tidy, with cramped toilet/bath units and rarely much space to hang your clothes.

⛩ The JR Hotel group

Japan Rail pass-holders will receive a list of JR-run hotels which offer small discounts (usually around 10% off the rack rate). The hotels are all Western style and are convenient since they're nearly always right outside the station (or in some cases, above the station). They range from standard business to top-class luxury hotels. They're rarely the cheapest overnight option but may be useful as an overnight base if planning an early rail journey the next day. See the city guides for individual hotel details or check the website 🖥 www.jrhotelgroup.com.

⛩ **Budget hotel chains**
Gone are the days when a night in a Japanese business hotel meant a smoke-filled shoebox, peeling wallpaper and narrow single bed. More and more chains are opening up offering a cut-price but altogether more pleasant overnight stay, with rates including free breakfast and in-room internet access if you bring your laptop.

The majority of the chains listed below offer both single and twin rooms, while some also have doubles. Not all chains are present in all parts of the country, so you'll need to check the websites (though some are Japanese only) and shop around. Also, some hotels accept cash only.

● **Toyoko Inn** (🖥 www.toyoko-inn.com) One of the best budget hotel chains in Japan, where virtually all the staff (including management) are women and where the aim is to replicate the welcome of a traditional ryokan in a modern hotel setting. A Japanese breakfast is available at all hotels, while some branches also offer a free curry-rice evening meal. For ¥500 you can become an 'International' Toyoko Inn Club member, collect points for overnight stays and receive a voucher for a free one-night stay for every ten nights you stay at Toyoko Inns. As a Club member you also get to check in one hour early (3pm instead of 4pm).
● **Roynet Hotel** (🖥 http://roynet.co.jp/e) Automated check-in. They are also aiming to be as environmentally friendly as possible.
● **R&B Hotel** (🖥 www.randb.jp) R&B is short for 'Room and Breakfast'; they offer freshly baked croissants, orange juice and coffee for breakfast.
● **Comfort Inn** (🖥 www.choicehotels.com) An expanding chain also offering a continental breakfast.
● **Super Hotel** (🖥 www.superhotel.co.jp) Now well established with branches across the country. Continental breakfast.
● **Route Inn** (www.route-inn.co.jp) Has hotels in most parts of the country.

Rates vary from around ¥4000 for the most basic singles up to ¥9000 for a room with slightly more breathing space. A towel, yukata, TV, and Japanese tea are usually provided.

There is invariably a cluster of business hotels outside main stations. Some of the newer ones offer a no-smoking floor and a few have women-only floors. The newest even boast an automatic check-in where you feed your money into a slot and receive an electronic key card in return. Many business hotel chains operate nationwide; for more details, see the box above.

Ryokan

Ryokan are more upmarket and have better amenities than minshuku and you really should plan to stay at least one night in one. In luxury ryokan particularly, where per person rates start from around ¥20,000, every guest is a VIP. From the moment you arrive you're waited on by your own kimono-clad maid who will pour tea as you settle in, serve you meals (usually in your room) and lay out your futon. You may also have en suite facilities and your own Japanese bath. But you don't have to stay in a luxury property to enjoy first-class service. Many ryokan charge more affordable rates averaging ¥9000-12,000 per person including two meals. Rooms are more spacious than those found in business

⛩ **Ryokan and minshuku etiquette**

A stay in a Japanese inn is a wonderful experience and thoroughly recommended, but it's worth bearing the following in mind: you'll find a row of **slippers** waiting in the entrance hall; this is where you're expected to leave your outdoor shoes. The slippers can be worn anywhere except on the tatami floor of your room and in the toilet/bathroom (see below). If you're heading out for a stroll around the local area, *geta* (wooden clogs) are usually provided as an alternative to putting on your outdoor shoes.

Before you enter the toilet or bathroom make sure you take off the house slippers because toilets in particular have their own (plastic) slippers. These are hard to miss as they usually come in bright blue or pink and have 'toilet' written on them. Don't forget to switch back to your other slippers when you leave.

The **bedding** is stored in cupboards in the rooms; at most ryokan, staff lay your futon out each night and put it away in the morning (usually while you are having breakfast/supper), while at minshuku you're expected to do it yourself. Don't be surprised to find that the pillow is very hard – traditionally pillows are filled with rice husks – and, in winter, that a blanket is put below the duvet part of the futon. Also in the room you'll find a hand towel and a yukata (a dressing gown/pyjama combo). Remember to cross the yukata left over right (the opposite way is for the deceased).

The **golden rules for having a bath** are: wash outside the tub, only climb in once you're clean, and never let the bathwater out! When you enter the bathroom you will find bowls, stools and taps; pick up a bowl and a stool and sit in front of a tap. Soap and shampoo are usually provided; use your small towel (if provided) as a flannel and scrub as hard as you can! Expect the water in the bath to be fairly hot. Bathrooms are nearly always communal but this doesn't necessarily mean you have to share your bath time with complete strangers. In the majority of places used to foreign guests the bathroom can be locked from the inside. The bath is often large enough to accommodate two or three and may be made of cedar-wood and the water scented with pine or mint.

Tipping is not encouraged but if you've enjoyed exceptional service you might want to leave a small amount of money (notes only) in an envelope or wrapped in tissue paper in your room.

If you have **breakfast** in a ryokan or minshuku the meal is likely to be Japanese (miso soup, grilled fish, pickles, some kind of egg, and rice). If you see a bowl with an egg in its shell it is almost definitely a raw egg. The Japanese break that into their rice bowl and mix it with soy sauce and then eat it.

hotels and may include *shoji* (sliding paper screens) and an alcove or two containing a Japanese fan, vase or scroll.

Most ryokan have a garden and some have their own hot spring which may or may not include a *rotemburo* (hot outdoor bath), the perfect place to unwind after a hard day's sightseeing.

Meals are nearly always Japanese and the dishes are prepared so that they are as much a visual treat as a gastronomic one and often feature local produce/specialities. A typical meal might include some tempura, sashimi/sushi, a meat dish, vegetable dishes and pickles, and will always include miso soup and rice; dessert is likely to be slices of fresh fruit. All this can be washed down with beer, saké and/or Japanese tea. Some ryokan offer a choice of Japanese- or Western-style breakfast.

Other accommodation options

Also at the top end of the market are luxury **Western hotels**, including international chains such as the Hyatt, Hilton and Marriott, where rates start from around ¥20,000 for a standard twin.

If all else fails and you're stuck for accommodation in a city, find out the location of the nearest **capsule hotel**, good for a one-off novelty but not recommended for claustrophobics. The majority of capsule hotels are for men only.

A final option might be a night in a Japanese **love hotel** where, during the day, rooms are available at an hourly rate for a euphemistic 'stay', but in the evening (from around 10pm) can be booked for an overnight stay. Rates are about the same as, or slightly cheaper than, business hotels. Like capsule hotels you'll find love hotels in big cities and primarily in areas around mainline stations. They're easy to spot because the exteriors are usually bright and garish. The over-the-top design continues inside with a variety of themed rooms which sometimes contain bizarre optional extras such as rotating beds, tropical plants and waterfalls. The service in these places, by contrast, tends to be very discrete and you are unlikely ever to see a staff member. A display board at the entrance lights up to inform guests what rooms are available. You then go to pay at a counter after which a mysterious hand passes you the key to your room. The whole experience is not as seedy as it might sound; the arrival process is designed to protect the customers' anonymity and a night here is just as much an experience of Japan as is a stay in a traditional ryokan.

WHERE TO EAT

Eating out in Japan can seem a daunting prospect but with so much on offer it's also a great opportunity to try a variety of cuisines.

Japanese restaurants tend to specialize in a particular kind of food, so it's more common to find a *sushi* restaurant or *soba* shop than a generic 'Japanese restaurant'. It's also worth bearing in mind that many restaurants close early, often by 10pm. For late-night eating try bars or *izakaya* (see p62).

Japanese food

For details of Japanese food and drink, see pp450-1.

A quick and cheap breakfast is served in **coffee shops** advertising 'morning service' or 'morning set' – usually coffee, toast and a boiled/fried egg. Two chains to look out for are Pronto and Doutor; Starbucks continues to spread inexorably across Japan. There also seem to be branches of Mister Donut everywhere – the doughnuts are good but of more interest is the bottomless coffee cup.

To save time and money for lunch, **convenience stores** (known as *conbini*) are a good bet; all stock sandwiches, rolls, noodles and the like, and nearly all are open 24 hours and have microwave ovens so food can be heated up if required. Major convenience-store chains include Lawson, 7-Eleven and Family Mart; in Hokkaido, look out for Seicomart. Other good places for snack-style food are bakeries (every large station has at least one) and the food halls, usually in the basement, of department stores. Here, as well as in stations, you'll

⛩ **Vegetarians**
Vegetarians are rare in Japan so foreign visitors need to make their dietary requirements clear to restaurant staff. It may be assumed, for example, that as a vegetarian you eat fish or even chicken. To avoid being given something you don't want, it's far better to explain exactly what you can eat rather than simply say you're a vegetarian. The best place for a truly vegetarian meal is a Buddhist temple. The superbly crafted *shojin ryori* prepared by monks can be tried in some places, such as the temple town of Koya-san (see box pp230-2).

find take-out lunch boxes which are cheaper than eating at a restaurant. For details on the *ekiben* (rail station lunch box), see box p89.

The cheapest sit-down meals are at counter-service **ramen**, **soba** and **udon shops**. A bowl of ramen costs about ¥400. Alternatively, try a **shokudo**, a restaurant which serves a variety of economical dishes. Shokudo, popular with young people and students, always have plastic models of food outside and there are usually several in and around station areas. Other cheap places to eat include the nationwide chains of *gyudon* restaurants, including Yoshinoya and Nakau. Bowls of rice and beef start from ¥300.

Two other places to consider when eating on the cheap are **canteens** on university campuses (if you can find them) and in city halls. The latter are probably the easiest to locate. Canteens in city halls are subsidized and meant for the staff but are open to anyone. They're often on the top floor which means you get a cheap meal and a decent view thrown in to the bargain.

Look out for **stalls** in the evenings and at festivals which sell snacks such as *yakitori*, *yaki-imo*, *takoyaki*, as well as hearty bowls of noodles and steaming hot plates of *yakisoba*.

Japan's best known culinary export is sushi; the cheapest **sushi restaurants** are *kaiten-zushiya*, where you sit around a revolving counter and help yourself to plates of sushi (different colour plates denote different price bands). At the end of the meal the restaurant staff count how many plates you've taken and tell you how much to pay. It's usually possible to eat your fill for less than ¥1500. Restaurants specializing in *tonkatsu* are also a culinary mainstay; there are usually one or two in large stations. *Tempura* restaurants tend to be a bit more expensive than sushi places.

⛩ **Vending machines**
Vending machines (*jidohan-baiki*) are on every street corner, as well as in unexpected places such as mountain tops, temple precincts and remote villages. Few sell food, except ice cream, but many sell a bewildering choice of hot and cold drinks. Hot, and cold, cans of tea and coffee come in a variety of formats. Check that fruit juices say '100% juice' or you might get a sweet syrupy concoction. Beer and saké vending machines close at 11pm.

丹 **Eating out and how to order**
　　Most restaurants hang a *noren* (split curtain) at the entrance whenever they are open. In the evenings, bars show they are open by hanging or illuminating a red lantern outside. Before entering the restaurant take a look at the food display in the window outside. Here you'll find plastic models of the dishes on offer; make a mental note of what you think looks good before heading inside.

　　As you go in, don't be alarmed by the loud greeting that is often shouted not just by the waiter or waitress but by the entire kitchen staff. After the chorus of 'Irasshaimase' ('Welcome') dies down you'll be taken to a table and handed the menu along with hot towels and glasses of ice cold water or Japanese tea (all part of the service). If you're lucky, the menu will contain pictures of what's on offer. If not, your earlier preparation will pay off. Staff are usually more than happy to come outside with you to see what 'model' you want rather than risk bringing something you didn't order or can't eat.

　　At some (noodle) places you choose what you want from a list on a machine at the entrance, buy a ticket, hand it to the person behind the counter and then take a seat.

All **department stores** have at least one 'restaurant floor' where you'll find a variety of Western and Japanese eateries; most offer a daily set lunch which can be very good value. Restaurant floors tend to stay open until 10pm, though the department stores themselves close earlier.

Other foods

In major cities you'll rarely be far from restaurants serving ethnic cuisine, the most popular being Chinese, Indian, Italian and French. Italian places tend to be cheap but bland, while Indian restaurants serve relatively authentic curries. Cheap Japanese restaurants often serve their own version of the Indian dish, a comfort food known as *kare raisu* (curry rice; see p450).

　　French food is considered classy and therefore is expensive. Luxury hotels invariably have at least one French restaurant, where a bottle of imported Perrier costs nearly as many yen as it has bubbles. Malaysian and Thai restaurants are popular, though the spiciness you might expect is often toned down to suit the Japanese palate.

　　For fast food, McDonald's is everywhere, but look out too for the Japanese chain Mos Burger. In big cities you'll find branches of Pizza Hut, Wendy's, Lotteria and KFC. Don't reject out of hand the large number of so-called '**family restaurants**' that seem to be everywhere. The menu at these places is a mix of Western and Japanese eg spaghetti, steaks, pizza, noodles, tonkatsu and curry rice. Some places also offer a salad bar and all-you-can-drink soft drinks bar. Popular family restaurant chains include Royal Host, Jonathan's, Gusto, Ringer Hut and others which are found only in specific regions. An advantage of family restaurants is that they have picture menus which makes ordering easy. You may have to sign in at busy times to ensure that queuing diners are assigned tables in the correct order; there are usually seats to sit on while waiting. At your table you will often find a bell to ring when you are ready to order.

NIGHTLIFE AND ENTERTAINMENT

Japan has its fair share of clubs, discos and bars. Some are ultra-exclusive and expect you to part with a wad of cash in the form of a cover charge before you even see the drinks menu but many more offer good value for money. Every town and city has its own entertainment district which often radiates out from the area around the main railway station. To find the nightlife look for the large numbers of businessmen staggering about at dusk in search of their favourite karaoke bar or izakaya. For details of traditional Japanese entertainment see p46.

Karaoke bars Some people have never forgiven Japan for inventing karaoke but its presence in every town and city is unavoidable. You'll know you've stumbled into a karaoke bar if you see television screens strategically placed around the room and rows of whiskey bottles stacked up behind the bar (most bars operate a 'bottle keep' system for regulars). If you do visit a karaoke bar, sooner or later you'll be invited to sing. Protest in these situations is futile and it's at least reassuring to know that virtually all karaoke machines have some English songs programmed into them (usually a mixture of The Beatles, the Carpenters, Bob Dylan and *We are the world*).

Izakaya and robotayaki **Izakaya** are small atmospheric Japanese-style pubs. They are often filled with locals who go along after work for a few beers and an evening meal. A typical izakaya consists of seating along a counter, with tables squeezed into any other space available. The menu changes according to what the owner (known as the 'master') has bought in from the market but there's nearly always a choice of fresh fish and meat. Everything is served in snack-size portions so it is a good chance to try a variety of things; dishes usually cost ¥300-600 each.

Don't worry about not being able to read Japanese as you can always point to what's in the chilled cabinet on the counter or look at what the others are eating. Izakaya are great places to meet people and it will probably not be long before someone strikes up a conversation with you. These places don't tend to open much before 6pm and close around 1am or even later; to find them, look for the tell-tale red lanterns hanging outside.

Robotayaki offer similar food and drink; the main difference is that the food is cooked in front of you.

Beer gardens The name is a bit of a misnomer because beer gardens are almost always on the roof of department stores and large hotels rather than on the ground. For a fixed price (around ¥4000) most places offer an all-you-can-eat-and-drink beer-and-buffet deal for a set time (90-120 minutes).

Beer gardens are open only from the end of May to early September and are highly recommended as places from which to escape the summer humidity.

Cinema The multiplex rules in Japan so you're rarely more than a short walk from a cinema. The good news is that films are shown in their original language and subtitled in Japanese. The downside is that tickets tend to be expensive.

Avoid the high prices by going in the afternoon or early evening or try showing a student card. Most cinemas also offer reduced prices once a month on 'movie day' and women can take advantage of half-price tickets on the weekly 'ladies day' (often a Wednesday).

MEDIA

Four English-language daily **newspapers** are published in Japan but the best are the *Japan Times* and the *Daily Yomiuri* – you can find copies at kiosks in most large stations. Outside the Tokyo metropolitan and Kansai areas, they're usually a day late.

The main national broadcaster of **television** programmes is NHK (Nippon Hoso Kyokai), the Japanese equivalent of the BBC. NHK operates two analogue channels, NHK-G (the main channel) and NHK-E, which broadcasts mainly educational programmes. The nightly news programme on NHK-G at 7pm is simultaneously broadcast in English and Japanese but you can pick up the English only if the TV in your hotel has a 'bilingual' button. Private broadcasters such as TBS, Fuji and TV Asahi fill the rest of the airwaves with unashamedly ratings-driven shows (see Popular culture, p47). Both the *Daily Yomiuri* and *Japan Times* carry TV listings in English.

Radio is not as popular as TV and most programmes are broadcast only in Japanese. A few cities produce selected pop music shows in English.

ELECTRICITY

The electric current in Japan is 100 volts AC, but there are two different cycles: 50Mhz in eastern Japan (including Tokyo) and 60Mhz in western Japan. Plugs in Japan are of the two-pin variety.

TIME

Japan is GMT + 9 so at 9pm in Tokyo it is 12 noon in London, 7am in New York, 4am in California and 11pm in Sydney (all same-day times, not taking summer daylight-saving times into account).

BANKS AND MONEY MATTERS

The unit of currency is the Japanese yen (¥). Bank notes are issued in denominations of ¥10,000, ¥5000, ¥2000 and ¥1000. Coins are ¥500, ¥100, ¥50, ¥10, ¥5 and ¥1; ¥50 and ¥5 coins have a hole in the middle.

For such a sophisticated economy banking practices remain somewhat archaic. Banks are open Monday to Friday from 9am to 3pm only. The section dealing with currency exchange (travellers' cheques) often operates even more limited hours.

❏ Exchange rates	
£1	¥223
€1	¥153
US$1	¥116
Can$1	¥99
Aus$1	¥90
NZ$1	¥80

To get the latest rates of exchange check:
💻 www.oanda.com/convert/classic or www.xe.com/currency

⛩ **Taxes and tipping**
A **5% consumption tax** (called *shohizei*) is levied on nearly all goods and services in Japan, but you won't necessarily notice it in shops because the tax is already included on price tags. Hotel rate-cards will usually show room charges both before and after tax – the latter is the only one you need to worry about. As a rule, hotel charges quoted throughout this guide refer to the room rate after tax.

Additionally, upmarket hotels levy a **service tax** of between 10 and 20% in addition to the 5% consumption tax. Room rates quoted in this guide are mostly on a per room basis and do not include taxes unless otherwise stated.

The good news is that there is no culture of **tipping** in Japan but see box p58.

Always take a passport along and expect to wait at least 30 minutes for the transaction to be completed.

Japan has always been a cash-based society and although things are changing credit cards are nothing like as popular as they are in many other countries so check that any hotel, restaurant or shop accepts credit cards before you go in.

Many ATMs inside (or even outside!) banks do not accept foreign-issued cards. The good news is that all 26,000 Post Office ATMs across the country (including small branch offices) accept Visa, MasterCard, Diners Club, American Express, Cirrus, Plus and Maestro cards issued outside Japan. On-screen instructions are available in English. When you get to the machine, press the button next to 'English Guide' on the right side of the screen.

With very few exceptions, ATMs in Japan are not open 24 hours. The normal hours for post office ATMs are 9am-7pm on weekdays and 9am-5pm on Saturday and to noon on Sunday (some ATMs are closed on Sunday).

For more details check 🖥 www.yu-cho.japanpost.jp/e_index.htm; then click on 'Need cash'.

POST AND TELECOMMUNICATIONS

Post

Post offices open Monday to Friday 9am-5pm; main branches also offer a limited service in the evening and at weekends. Post offices in Japan are identifiable by a red T sign outside.

Japan's postal service is fast and very efficient but not all that cheap. Postcards cost ¥70 to send abroad and ¥50 within Japan. Aerograms cost ¥90 anywhere in the world. For airmail letters the price depends on the destination; letters up to 25g cost ¥90 within Asia, ¥110 to North America, Oceania, Europe and the Middle East and ¥130 to Africa and South America. For letters up to 50g, the prices increase to ¥160, ¥190 and ¥230 respectively.

The location of the main post office in a particular city is marked on the relevant city map but details, such as specific opening hours, are not provided in the text.

Internet

Wireless internet access was slow to take off but has exploded in Japan in recent years. If you are bringing your laptop to Japan, you'll be able to surf the web in many hotels (including all Toyoko Inn hotels, see 🖥 www.toyoko-inn.com), cafés, railway stations and public buildings. McDonald's, for example, offers (for a fee!) wireless internet access in all its outlets.

In every city and town it won't take you long to find an internet café, where the going rate is around ¥400 per hour. This often includes free soft drinks and snacks – so you shouldn't ever have to pay for a drink while surfing the web!

Some places require you to become a member by paying an additional charge (¥100 or ¥200) and by showing proof of identity such as a passport (a copy of the relevant pages is usually accepted), but plenty of places don't require registration. Staff will often help you get set up if the operating system is Japanese.

Phone

Mobile phones are the ultimate everyday accessory in Japan as around the world. Unfortunately you won't be able to use your own phone while in Japan because the mobile network is not compatible with that of any other country.

If you're only visiting Japan but want to stay in touch it might be worth renting a mobile and inserting your own SIM card, or alternatively renting a Japanese mobile. You rent the handset at a daily rate (expect to pay around ¥500 per day) and your credit/debit card is billed for calls made. You'll need to provide proof of identity and an address at the time of purchase.

Phone company SoftBank (☎ 03-3560 7730, 🖥 www.softbank-rental.jp) has counters at both Narita and Kansai airports, and branches throughout the country, where you can rent or buy a mobile. If you call/email them in advance, you can reserve a phone number and give it to friends/relatives before you arrive in Japan. A similar service is provided by both NTT DoCoMo (☎ 044-210 5109, 🖥 http://roaming.nttdocomo.co.jp/index.html) and PuPuRu (🖥 www.pupuru.com) so it is worth comparing prices.

マナーモードに
設定の上、通話は
ご遠慮ください。

Please set your mobile phone to silent mode
and refrain from talking on the phone.

On almost every rail line in Japan mobile phones must be on silent mode; if you really need to talk to someone you need to go to the area between carriages.

The proliferation of mobile phones has not yet led to a decrease in the number of **public telephones**. Public telephones are also installed on all shinkansen and some limited express services, though a surcharge is levied and you may get cut off if the train heads into a tunnel. Green phones and the newer grey boxes (for both national and international calls) accept both ¥10 and ¥100 coins and/or telephone cards (see below). It's best to use only ¥10 coins for local calls since no change is given in return for partially used ¥100 coins. Local calls cost ¥10 per minute.

Prepaid telephone cards (¥1000) can be bought from a shop or kiosk, or from the vending machine inside the phone box. Many cities and individual tourist attractions sell their own souvenir phone cards which are great to collect as well as use. Both green and grey phones accept the cards.

Making a call When calling **city-to-city** in Japan dial the area code first (all telephone numbers in this guide include the area code). The area code can be omitted if calling a local number (for example, if you call a Tokyo number from within Tokyo omit the 03). Numbers starting 0120 or 0088 are toll free.

Three telecoms operators provide **international services**. Though the three compete with each other their rates do not vary a great deal. The companies and their respective access codes are SoftBank Telecom (0061-010), NTT (0033-010) and KDDI (001-010). To make an international call, dial any of the three access codes, followed by the country code, area code (minus the initial '0') and telephone number. Making overseas calls is cheaper at night and at weekends and on public holidays. International calls can be made from the grey phones.

Two alternative but expensive options are to place a direct-dial call from your hotel room or to look for one of the public phones in major cities which accept credit cards.

MUSEUMS AND TOURIST ATTRACTIONS

Most museums and tourist attractions are open on Sunday and national holidays but closed on Monday. If a public holiday falls on a Monday, museums are closed on Tuesday instead. Typical opening hours are 9:30am-5pm but last admission is usually 30 minutes before the official closing time.

Admission prices quoted in this guide are for standard adult tickets. The child rate (up to age 16) is usually 50% of the adult rate. University students sometimes qualify for small savings so it's worth showing an ISIC card at the entrance to find out if a discount is available.

FESTIVALS

Japan is truly a land of festivals; hardly a day goes by when there is not a celebration taking place somewhere. These can be huge, rowdy events attracting thousands of visitors, such as Sapporo's Ice Festival (see p362), Aomori's Nebuta Festival (see p320) or Kyoto's Gion Festival (see p217), or local festivals in small towns and villages which are little known outside the area.

Parades of large floats, street processions to the tune of taiko drummers, firework displays, and colourful costumes are all part of the festival experience. Eating while walking around in public is generally frowned upon but this rule is broken at festival time; street stalls serve yakisoba, takoyaki, kakigori (crushed ice served with different fruit flavours, similar to Slush Puppy), candy floss, beer and cups of hot saké.

For information on specific festivals, see the relevant city guides. JNTO (see box p31) publishes a comprehensive list which is useful if you want to plan your itinerary to include one or more.

NATIONAL HOLIDAYS

Japan observes 15 national holidays, when all banks, offices and post offices, and most shops are closed. Museums and tourist attractions are usually open. Nearly everything, apart from public transport and larger shops, closes for the New Year holiday, from December 31st to January 3rd. The period from 29th April to 5th May is called Golden week and is a prime holiday time, as is Obon (mid-August) even though there is no national holiday then. If a holiday falls on a Sunday, the following day is treated as a holiday.

LANGUAGE

Japanese is one of the most difficult languages to learn to read/write, mixing as it does

❑ **National Holidays**
● **January 1st** New Year's Day – traditionally people visit a shrine; many women dress up in kimonos
● **2nd Monday in January** Coming of Age Day – girls who have reached the age of majority (20) mark the occasion by dressing up in gorgeous kimono and visiting their local shrine
● **February 11th** National Foundation Day – commemoration of the legendary enthronement of Japan's first Emperor (Jimmu)
● **March 20th** Vernal Equinox Day
● **April 29th** Greenery Day (the late Emperor Hirohito's birthday)
● **May 3rd/4th** Constitution Memorial Day and an additional day
● **May 5th** Children's Day – kite-flying events are held all over the country
● **July 20th** Maritime Day
● **September 15th** Respect-for-the-aged Day
● **September 23rd** Autumnal Equinox Day
● **2nd Monday in October** Sports Day
● **November 3rd** Culture Day
● **November 23rd** Labour Thanksgiving Day
● **December 23rd** The Emperor's Birthday

Chinese characters, known as *kanji*, with two different syllabaries, *hiragana* and *katakana* (the latter is used exclusively for writing words which the Japanese have borrowed from other languages); see pp452-5.

That said, basic greetings and phrases are not difficult to remember and any efforts to speak Japanese will be welcome. The Japanese always seem amazed and impressed that foreigners can speak their language, especially given the various levels and subtle nuances that need to be used in certain situations. Foreigners are not expected to know the intricacies of the language so there's no need to worry about making a linguistic faux-pas. Basic phrases such as those listed on pp452-5 should help.

A misunderstanding sometimes arises over the meaning of the Japanese word 'hai' which is translated into English as 'yes'. Anyone who has had contact with the Japanese business world knows that the Japanese do not like to commit immediately to a straightforward 'yes' or 'no' answer to a proposal, at least during a first meeting. Thus, 'hai' often means 'yes, I am listening' (this also applies when talking on the phone) rather than 'yes, I agree'.

⛩ **English or Japlish?**
'English' is everywhere you look in Japan, on vending machines, advertising hoardings and in shops, though it doesn't take long to realize that this is not the English you may know. The Japanese use of English to sell products or simply look trendy has been dubbed 'Japlish'. Here is a selection of signs I spotted around the country:

● Outside a pachinko parlour in Sapporo: 'The heart of the people here is burning hotly. It is for holding a chance. I am praying your fortune. This is the space filled with joy and excitement.'
● Outside a funeral parlour in Nagoya: 'Your good times are only just beginning.'
● Sign outside a curry restaurant in Shizuoka: 'Why is the curry very black? The curry by France Tei is a very black, painful taste. Another cannot eat this taste. This dish is being liked by a lot of people.'
● Sign inside a clothes shop in Kobe: 'We support your socks life. Our socks are knitted with a workman's spirit.'
● A shop sign in Kyoto: 'We sell ladies used furniture.'
● On a vending machine in Shizuoka: 'When you have felt thirst in your heart, you are in need of an oasis for quench your thirst. Your heart are thirsting for a good feeling of place.'
● Inside a restaurant in Kyoto advertising its 'Steak rice in summer' dish: 'This is so hearty that you will not spend without summer lethargy. Tomato sauce must tempt the taste buds of you. This one is a full volume dish.'

Although nearly everyone in Japan learns English at school, this does not mean they can speak it. Despite efforts to bring more native English speakers into Japanese schools as 'assistant language teachers', the classroom emphasis continues to be on written English and grammar, rather than spoken skills. If you need help, try talking to school or university students. If you can't make yourself understood, try writing your question down; many Japanese find reading English much easier than listening to, or speaking, it.

ASSISTANCE

Even if you don't immediately find someone who speaks English, it's unlikely you'll find anyone unwilling to help if you ask. I once asked for directions to an ATM; instead of just being pointed the right way I was accompanied on the 20-minute journey to the cashpoint. This is not an exception to the rule; you'll almost certainly find that the Japanese are delighted to go out of their way to help you.

Though few police officers outside cities speak English, all will be polite and helpful. In even the smallest village you're likely to find a street corner *koban* (police box), where officers are only too pleased to give you directions if you're lost.

❑ **Emergency numbers**
Police (emergencies) ☎ 110
Police (general information) ☎ 03-3501 0110 or 03-3503 8484
Fire/Ambulance ☎ 119
Hospital information ☎ 03-5285 8181
Tokyo English Life Line (free, anonymous phone counselling, daily, 9am-11pm) ☎ 03-5774 0992, 🖥 www.telljp.com)

⛩ **Female travellers**
     Japan is one of the safest countries in the world and it's unlikely females travelling alone will have any problems. If someone does approach you in the dark the chances are that all he wants to do is practise his English. However, in crowded commuter trains women might find themselves being groped. The best thing to do is shout out – the offender will be embarrassed – or try to move away. However, in Tokyo some subway lines have women-only carriages (see box p107).
     The best advice for safe travel is the same as for anywhere else in the world: don't take unnecessary risks, know where you're going if someone invites you out, and always arrange to meet in a public place.

Pharmacies are everywhere and can be recognized by the green cross outside the store. Few pharmacists speak much English but gestures will generally do the trick.

SHOPPING

Department stores open daily from 10am to around 7 or 8pm, but are closed one day a month (usually Wednesday or Thursday but rarely Sunday).

If you arrive when the store opens dozens of eager staff members will be standing in position to greet and bow to you. The bowing and welcoming does not stop when you step inside as dozens more staff wait at the foot and top of each escalator (and in the lifts) to welcome you personally to each floor.

If you can negotiate your way through the hordes of staff (realizing as you go that this is how Japan achieves its low unemployment figures) you'll eventually find departments that sell everything from furniture to food, from digital cameras to kimonos. The sheer variety of goods can be overwhelming but if you have the time department stores are a great place to explore and discover Japan's latest fashions and craziest inventions. Souvenir hunters will certainly not be disappointed: watches, silks, bamboo and lacquerware, pottery, woodblock prints, Japanese fans, dolls, kimonos, chopsticks and the ubiquitous *tamagochi* can all be found under one roof. As if selling goods were not enough, department stores also stage exhibitions of art or ikebana and sometimes even fashion shows. Some have playgrounds and amusement arcades; these are often on the roof.

If you prefer to stay on ground level Japan also boasts a wide range of **speciality shops** and stores. Every town or city has its own shopping area often

❑ **Floor confusion**
Finding your way around a department store is not always easy because many are made up of several buildings and annexes all of which interconnect. Also, a point of confusion, particularly for the British, is the way floors are numbered. '1F' means the ground floor, and is not the same as the 'first floor' (which is really the second floor). 'BF' indicates the basement. Some of the larger stores produce their own guide books to help visitors get around.

identified by plastic flowers, the colour of which varies according to the season, suspended from lamp posts; many such areas are pedestrianized and provide covered walkways. Shopaholics will not be disappointed.

Another great shopping experience are the many **open-air markets** which sell locally made goods, traditional handicraft and fresh produce. Tourist information offices can provide details of the market day(s) in a particular town or city. Fresh fruit and vegetables are inevitably good buys; melons, for example, are one of the most expensive kinds of fruit in Japan, but you'll often be able to buy one

JAPAN

⛩ Cultural tips

Perhaps the most important piece of advice to remember when visiting Japan is that foreigners are not expected to know the conventions that dictate how the Japanese behave in public. Nobody's going to care, for example, if you haven't mastered the art of bowing. Indeed, people would probably be more concerned if you did know exactly how low to bow on every occasion since it might suggest you know more about the culture than the Japanese themselves (which is a far greater sin). There are a few cultural tips worth knowing about, though the best advice if in doubt is to copy what everyone else around you is doing.

● The Japanese prefer consensus over disagreement and rarely show strong emotions. Flaring into a temper if your hotel room is not ready, for example, would be considered inappropriate behaviour and people might not know how to react.

● Avoid blowing your nose in public as this is considered rude; sniffing, however, is seen as a demonstration of your ability to resist temptation.

● It's understood that foreigners are unable to sit on their knees for long periods of time so if you have to sit on the floor it's fine to sit cross-legged, but don't point your legs towards anyone.

● Take your shoes off as you enter a minshuku, ryokan, temple, or someone's home; shoes and slippers are never worn on tatami mats.

● Chopstick etiquette is important to the Japanese. Pitfalls to avoid include 'spearing' food with chopsticks or using them to rummage through dishes. Avoid passing food between pairs of chopsticks and never stick them upright in a bowl of rice as these actions are associated with death.

● Slurping noodles is supposed to improve the flavour and is encouraged; it's also common to bring the bowl up to your mouth to ensure you don't spill the liquid.

● If drinking beer or saké with a group it's polite to pour someone else's glass and wait for yours to be filled.

● Except at a festival it's not customary to eat while walking along the street, though at most you might receive a few bemused stares.

● Punctuality is sacred; the Japanese seem to abide by the 'five minutes early' rule for meetings and appointments.

● Business cards (known as *meishi*) are also sacred. Though tourists are not expected to carry a supply it's a good idea to bring some if you have any; at the very least it will save you writing out your details every time anyone asks for your address. If you are offered a business card, it's considered very bad form to put it straight in your pocket and even worse if you get out a pen and scrawl notes on it. It's best to look at it for a while before putting it away.

● If you're expecting to visit someone's home bring a souvenir from your home country as a gift; otherwise bottles of whiskey, chocolates, flowers or tea towels are perfect.

For details of etiquette in a ryokan/minshuku, see the box on p58.

⛩ **Hi-tech attention to the call of nature**
　　Most toilets in Japan are Western style, though on some older trains and in public loos you'll still find Asian squat toilets. Toilet paper is rarely found in public loos.
　　Big hotels constantly try to outdo their rivals by fitting guest rooms with futuristic lavatories. The facilities on some top-class models include a choice of background music (to hide your own natural noises), heated seats with adjustable temperature gauge, a built-in bidet and a device that measures your blood pressure while you wait. On even the most basic models there are at least two buttons to press: one is for the flush and the other activates a vertical hot water jet – you really don't want to get these two mixed up. On some toilets there are two levels of flush though the effect of using the wrong one is not so dramatic.
　　Don't be surprised if you catch sight in the evening of drunk businessmen relieving themselves in the street or on station platforms – a reminder, perhaps, that however hi-tech the Japanese make their toilets, there are never enough of them.

for a quarter of the price you'd pay in a department store (though you have to forego the fancy wrapping paper, beautifully packaged box and gold ribbons).

ACTIVITIES

Hiking

Since four-fifths of Japan is mountainous there are some excellent hiking opportunities; routes and paths are nearly always well signposted and almost always well trodden. The Japanese Alps (Central Honshu, see pp125-92) and Hokkaido (see pp327-70) are the places to head for the most spectacular hiking. For more information on the great outdoors, see the regularly updated 🖳 www .outdoorjapan.com.

Skiing

It's worth trying skiing in Japan, if only for half a day – where else in the world can you get bowed off a chair lift?
　　There are skiing opportunities throughout the Japanese Alps. For the latest snow reports in English, resort reviews and even information on how to find an English-speaking ski instructor and where to buy the most fashionable snowboard, check 🖳 www.snowjapan.com. JNTO publishes a mini-guide called *Skiing in Japan* which provides details of the best ski resorts in the country.

Relaxing in a hot spring

Hot springs, known as *onsen*, are hugely popular among Japanese who consider the chance to relax in a hot tub the perfect escape from the stress of life. Hokkaido, in particular, is full of natural hot springs where the water is often pumped direct from a bubbling pool of volcanic rock. Diehard onsen lovers travel the country in search of the perfect hot spring. Open-air baths in rural areas are often the least accessible since they're usually high in the mountains. They also lack facilities such as changing areas and are rarely segregated,

⛩ **Volcanoes, earthquakes and typhoons**
Japan is a hotbed of **volcanic activity**; even world-famous Mt Fuji, which last erupted in 1707, has in recent years shown renewed signs of life. Hokkaido in particular has several active volcanoes but there's no need to panic as the island's hiking routes and paths are always closed at the first sign of smoke.

Earthquakes of course are not seasonal, nor can they be accurately predicted. They are, however, a fact of life in Japan and most cities have an earthquake centre equipped with a simulator room where Japanese can prepare for any eventuality by experiencing the full force of the Richter scale. Minor quakes/tremors are very common but unless you're particularly sensitive you'll probably only hear about them the next day. In the very unlikely event you find yourself waking up to a sizeable quake, the best thing to do is to get under something solid, such as a table. Major quakes are extremely rare and not worth becoming paranoid about.

Typhoons (*tsunami*) strike coastal regions, particularly in Shikoku and Kyushu, in late summer. Fortunately these are usually predicted a day or two before they hit the coast so it's unlikely you will be taken unawares.

though they are nearly always free of charge. At the other extreme are Japan's infamously gaudy onsen resorts, such as Beppu (see p383) in Kyushu, where luxury hotels operate themed bath houses and the water is really only a sideshow. Somewhere in between these two extremes are public bath houses and small-scale hot springs. These generally include several indoor baths of varying temperatures, a sauna, plunge pool and at least one outdoor bath called a rotemburo. If you're lucky with the location, the outdoor bath will afford sweeping views of the mountains and surrounding countryside.

The usual procedure at any bath house after buying a ticket at the entrance (from the counter or from a vending machine) is to head directly for the changing rooms. To avoid stumbling into the wrong room, memorize the Japanese characters for male and female (see p455). As when taking a bath in a minshuku or ryokan, you're expected to wash before entering the water (see box on p58). Swimming costumes are not worn but small towels are provided to protect your modesty when walking around. The onsen experience does not end the moment you step out of the bath. Changing rooms are often equipped with exercise bikes, massage chairs, weighing machines, combs, brushes, aftershaves, scents, industrial-size fans to help you dry off, and vending machines.

With so many hot springs scattered around Japan, it's hard to know where to start, though JNTO's leaflet *Japanese Hot Springs* contains a useful region-by-region guide to the country's best-known onsen.

A place on Shikoku that is definitely worth considering, because it is both traditional and easily accessible, is Dogo Onsen (see p447). For an unusual bathing experience in a holy hot spring by the ocean, take a trip to the island of Sakurajima (see p415) on Kyushu. Rail enthusiasts might prefer to head for the Kansai area where, in Nachi, there's a chance to soak in a tub which affords views of a railway track (see p202).

Railway history

When Commodore Perry appeared off the coast of Japan in 1853 with the US Navy's 'Black Ships' (see p39), the country, like many others, had no railway whatsoever. In the years since the end of Japan's policy of self-isolation, its rail network has become the envy of the world. This transformation, given the country's natural topography and history of devastating earthquakes, is nothing short of extraordinary.

PIONEERING EARLY DAYS

One of Perry's gifts on his second trip to Japan in 1854 was a quarter-size steam locomotive and accompanying track. However astonishing the sight of this miniature railway set up on the beach must have been, it would be a mistake to believe that the Tokugawa shogunate was entirely ignorant of technological developments outside Japan. From the tiny Dutch enclave in Nagasaki, the only point of contact with the outside world in 265 years of self-imposed isolation, the Shogun had received an annual report on developments in the rest of the world. But it was not until the Meiji Restoration of 1868 (see p39) that the idea of constructing a railway in Japan began to take root.

蒸気機関車マリゴールドの野を過ぎる

Given the lamentable state of Britain's railways today, it comes as something of a surprise to discover that the Japanese government employed a number of British engineers and pioneering railwaymen to assist in the development of the country's rail network, notably Edmund Morel (1841-71); Morel was appointed chief engineer but died a year before the opening of Japan's first railway line, between Tokyo and Yokohama, on 12th October 1872. Ninety-two years before the inauguration of the Tokaido shinkansen between Tokyo and Osaka, Emperor Meiji and his entourage set off on the country's first official train ride, a 30-km journey from Shimbashi, in Tokyo, to Yokohama. The driver for this historic journey was British and the coach the Emperor rode in was made in Birmingham. Some Japanese guests, it is reported, kept to tradition (see box p70) by taking off their shoes before boarding and so travelled to Yokohama in their socks.

The use of foreign engineers was not without its complications, not least of which was the language barrier. British railwaymen accustomed to grey skies and drizzle also found it hard to adapt to Japan's hot and humid climate.

The steaming locomotive passing across the field full of marigold at night
(KAZUKO KONAGAI)

> ### ❑ The Golden Age of steam?
> The JR network may now be the envy of the rest of the world but it would appear from Kelly and Walsh's *Handbook of the Japanese Language* (Yokohama, 1898) that rail travel in Japan used to be far from trouble-free. The following phrases appear (together with their Japanese equivalent) in a section entitled 'A Journey By Railway' and are a useful gauge of the state of the nation's railway in its early days:
>
> *When will the train start?*
>   *Immediately, Sir.*
> *Didn't you tell me 'immediately' half an hour ago?*
>
> *The Railroad Department seems to be asleep!*
> *The whole railroad system is disorganised and upset.*
> *The Railroad Department doesn't seem to care the least for the convenience of the Public.*
>
> *They don't yet realise the value of time.*
> *Are we not behind time?*
>   *That is the usual thing in Japan.*
>
> *We are now at last at our destination.*
> *We are three hours late.*

Edmund Holtham, writing about his time as a railway engineer, describes how the summer heat made work 'rather a burden … in spite of running down to Kobe for a game of cricket and a plunge in the sea, I fell out of condition' (*Eight Years in Japan*, 1883).

A significant turning point came in the spring of 1879 when Japanese drivers were allowed to operate the trains between Tokyo and Yokohama – though on about one-sixth of the salary. It wasn't long before the Japanese were taking over from the British and other Western engineers. By 1904, as the last British railwayman set off for home, the country had embarked on an unprecedented expansion of the railway network.

NATIONALIZATION AND EXPANSION

As the railway expanded, people began to move around at previously unimaginable speeds. The old Tokaido road, for centuries the only way of getting between Edo (Tokyo) and Kyoto, was quickly abandoned after the opening of the Tokaido line in July 1889. A journey which had taken 12 or 13 days could now be completed in just 20 hours. By 1906, when a 'super express' was introduced, the journey time was cut still further to 13 hours 40 minutes. The year 1906 was significant in another way; 8000km (5000 miles) of track had been laid in just 34 years, though the majority of this was in the hands of private rail companies. Under pressure from the military, who were finding it increasingly difficult to move around the country at any speed when they had to wait for connections between the private railways, the government passed the 1906 Railway Nationalization Act, giving itself the authority to purchase the 'trunk' lines, while allowing private railways to own local lines. The railway was to remain a nationalized industry until 1987.

ARRIVAL OF THE 'BULLET TRAIN'

Electrification

A nationwide network of trunk lines was well on its way to completion by 1910 but major electrification of the railway had to wait until after WWII, during which many lines sustained severe damage from bombing raids. In the early 1950s the journey by train between Tokyo and Osaka took most of a day and there was an observation car at the back with armchairs for passengers to enjoy the view down the line. The Tokaido line, running through what had become Japan's major industrial corridor, was electrified in 1956. It was also in the mid-1950s that the idea began to surface for a new, high-speed link between Tokyo and Osaka. The proposal was not just for an upgrade of the existing Tokaido line but for a completely new railway that would allow a top speed of 250kph. Crucially, businessmen in Tokyo and Osaka would be able to commute between each city and return home the same day.

Picking up speed

There is no more instantly recognizable symbol of modern Japan than the *shinkansen* (literally 'new main line'), known throughout the world as the bullet train. When the government finally gave its approval for the project in 1958, Japan National Railways (JNR) had six years to prepare the line in time for the opening ceremony of the 1964 Tokyo Olympics. The deadline was made and the ribbon cut at precisely 6am on October 1st 1964, but the construction bill had spiralled from an original estimate of ¥200 billion to ¥380 billion. Initial design faults also meant passengers experienced ear pain whenever the train darted into a tunnel and, more alarmingly, gusts of wind blowing up through the toilets.

The foreign press corps was taken for a test run, however, and appeared suitably thrilled. A *Times* journalist gushed on cue to his readers, remarking that the shinkansen fully lived up to the boast of a 'new dimension in train travel': 'In the airliner-style seats one groped subconsciously, but in vain, for the safety belt as the train hummed out of Tokyo, rather like a jet taking off in a narrow street. Bridges, tunnels, even passing trains flash by, thanks to the air-tight doors, as in a silent film. It is uncannily smooth…So much tends to the vulgar in modern Japan that it is pleasant to report the superb fittings and finishing in this train…Ablution facilities dazzle, with winged mirrors, and three lavatories per car set, one of them Western-style…' (*The Times*, September 28th 1964).

Two services began operation in 1964, the *Hikari* ('light'), which initially took four hours and stopped only in Nagoya and Kyoto, and the stopping *Kodama* ('echo'), which took five hours. The new line was an instant success and tickets sold out weeks in advance; Queen Elizabeth II and Prince Philip went for a ride during their 1975 state visit to Japan – though only after a railway strike was called off at the last minute. The construction deficit was overturned and the line was soon extended west to Okayama (in 1972), and on to Hakata (in 1975). Expansion east of Tokyo on the Tohoku shinkansen quickly followed.

Out of control

As the shinkansen spread further and sped faster, JNR's debt loomed larger. Though the Tokaido shinkansen was a financial success, the rest of the network was in meltdown. The railway's total deficit year on year throughout the 1970s and 80s spiralled into thousands of billions of yen. Fares became daylight rob-

THE RAIL NETWORK

bery, particularly in comparison with those offered by private railways, the network was grossly over-staffed, labour relations were poor and morale low. Some pointed the finger at greedy politicians. Such was the glamour of the shinkansen, reported *The Times* in January 1987 (23 years after it had enjoyed that free test ride), that 'every politician of note feels he needs a shinkansen station in his district': 'Over the years, promises of shinkansen services have brought in innumerable votes for the ruling Liberal Democratic Party. And with every new shinkansen put on to a marginal or loss-making line, JNR's deficit has increased.'

At midnight on April 1st 1987, the whistle was finally and literally blown on all this by the president of JNR, who rode a steam locomotive back and forth near Shimbashi in Tokyo (the starting point for Japan's first railway in 1872) on a symbolic last journey for the nationalized industry. JNR, undeniably the ultimate political pork barrel in Japan, had not made money for 20 years. Its liabilities on that April Fool's Day stood at ¥37 trillion (£160 billion), more than the combined debts of Brazil and Mexico, and £12 billion more than the US budget deficit of the previous year.

Privatization of the railway was achieved by carving up the network into six regional passenger railway companies and one nationwide freight company, to be known collectively as the JR Group. In a bid to reduce some of the debt, unprofitable lines were closed, railway land was sold and staffing levels reduced. No longer constricted by the rules governing a nationalized company, the JR companies have since diversified into everything from department stores to hotels, hospitals and helicopters.

In the 21st century, expansion of the shinkansen continues apace: construction of the Tohoku shinkansen line north from the current terminus in Hachinohe to Aomori and from there on towards Hokkaido will one day make it possible to ride the bullet train all the way from Tokyo to Sapporo – a high-speed journey unimaginable just two decades ago. The Kyushu shinkansen is also expanding, and plans are underway to open a line from Nagano (see p168) to Kanazawa (see p185).

The first of the next-generation shinkansen, the N700, went into service in 2007 as Nozomi trains on the Tokaido/Sanyo shinkansen line. On-board fea-

⛩ Rail museums

Rail museums of varying size and interest are spread throughout the country but space does not permit a nationwide listing. Three of the best-known are the **Transportation Museum** in Omiya (see p281), the **Modern Transportation Museum** in Osaka (see p117) and the **Umekoji Steam Locomotive Museum** in Kyoto (see p212). See the appropriate city guides for full details.

Keen rail buffs should also consider heading for Hokkaido. The island boasts some of Japan's most scenic railway lines and is also home to an excellent open-air transport museum in the port city of Otaru. Although not included in the route guide around Hokkaido, Otaru is easily reached in 30 minutes by rapid train along the Hakodate line from Sapporo (see p364 for further information and details of a special rail pass for day trips from Sapporo to Otaru). **Otaru Transportation Museum** (☎ 0134-33 2523, 🖳 www.otarukoutsukinenkan,com; daily, ¥940, 9am-6pm, Apr 10th to Nov 3rd, ¥470 9am-5pm, Nov 4th to Apr 9th) is built on the site of Hokkaido's first railway station and is filled with locomotives and carriages. There's even the chance to take a 400m ride on a steam locomotive from one end of the ground to the other. To reach the museum take a bus from stop No 6 outside Otaru station and get off at 'Kotsu kinenkan mae'.

Elsewhere in Japan, the outdoor **Sakuma Rail Park** (see p134) in central Honshu is worth visiting as much for the train journey out to it along the rural Iida line as for the museum itself. And if you're heading towards Nagano by shinkansen from Tokyo stop off at **Karuizawa** (see p135). Next to the sleek new shinkansen station is the former JR station now restored to its former glory and open to the public as a reminder of the railway's heyday.

There's another good **railway museum** in Yokokawa, accessible by local train on the JR Shin-etsu line from Takasaki (see p135). This line used to continue beyond Yokokawa to the mountain resort of Karuizawa, but when the Hokuriku shinkansen to Nagano was completed the route between Yokokawa and Karuizawa was closed since it was expensive to operate. The museum (🖳 www.usuitouge.com/bunkamura, Wed-Mon, 9am-4/4:30pm, ¥500) is built on the site of the old Yokokawa depot and has a good collection of rolling stock. A small discount is available if you buy a ticket from the JR counter in Yokokawa station rather than at the museum's ticket office. The museum is a short walk from the station (ask the station staff to point you in the right direction).

tures include laptop power points, leg warmers for first-class passengers who 'feel a chill to the legs' and, from spring 2009, wireless internet access. The N700 is, for now at least, the last word in high speed and comfort.

MAGLEV: THE FUTURE?

The future of the railway is brighter and its operating companies healthier than could ever have been imagined prior to 1987 but fierce competition from an airline industry reaping the benefits of increased deregulation has put pressure on the rail companies to answer back with discounts and value for money. But in fast-paced Japan, where nobody ever waits for a train, there will always be demand for yet more speed.

That demand is now being met with test runs of the Maglev, or the 'superconducting magnetically levitated linear motor car'. The Maglev, it is hoped,

THE RAIL NETWORK

will one day travel at over 500kph along an as yet unconstructed Chuo shinkansen line, bringing Tokyo and Osaka to within 60 minutes of each other. But arguments persist over funding for the project amid fears that it could become the biggest white elephant in railway history. The cost of construction of the new line alone is estimated at ¥17-18 billion per kilometre. If it does see the light of day, the Chuo shinkansen will easily become the most expensive transport project in the world.

STEAM RAILWAYS

In 1936 around 8700 steam locomotives were in operation across Japan. Complaints about the emission of black smoke and technological advances brought about the demise of the commercial steam railway, as more efficient diesel and electric trains were brought into service after the war. By 1976, steam had all but disappeared.

For years, many steam locomotives (known in Japan as SLs) were left to rust away in museums, or were shunted into corners of public parks and quietly forgotten. Perhaps because the Japanese now have the psychological room to look back on the nation's history of modernization, restored SLs have made a comeback.

In the late 1980s and '90s, with the vocal and financial support of nostalgic rail fans and local authorities, steam trains began to reappear as tourist attrac-

---

⛩ **Steam locomotive (SL) operations**
    The following is a list of major preserved steam operations in Japan. Listings show the name, type of engine, operating route, and railway company. Rail passes are valid for SL journeys on JR Group lines but seats should be reserved in advance. Schedules change annually but as a rule of thumb trains run at the weekend between March and November and daily during the summer season. For up-to-date information in English, contact JR's information line (☎ 050-2016 1603).
● **Oigawa Railway** Kanaya to Senzu on the Oigawa line. Operated by the private Oigawa Railway (see p131; ☎ 0547-45 4113, 🖥 www.oigawa-railway.co.jp; rail passes not valid), this is one of the busiest preserved steam operations in the country, with services throughout the year. Several locomotives, including the C12 164, which was restored thanks to a ¥50 million funding initiative by the Japan National Trust, are used.
● **SL Hakodate Onuma (C11 171)** runs on an 80-minute journey between Hakodate and Mori on the Hakodate line. You can even rent a period conductor's uniform. This service typically runs during Golden Week (see p67) and at weekends in July and August. For further information and to make seat reservations enquire at the JR ticket office in either Hakodate or Mori station; see also p332.
● **SL Banetsu-Monogatari (C57 180)** Niitsu to Aizu-Wakamatsu on the Banetsu-Sei line. See p308 for further information.
● **SL Kita-Biwako (C56 160)** Maibara to Kinomoto on the Hokuriku line. For more information see p195. The dates for this service are very limited; typically just a few days around Golden Week (29th April to 5th May).
● **SL Yamaguchi (C571; nickname Lady of Rank)** This train runs from Shin-Yamaguchi to Tsuwano on the Yamaguchi line. See p241 for details.

Train punctuality
In the UK a train is judged to be on time if it leaves roughly according to the timetable – and most passengers are just grateful it is leaving it all. Things are very different in Japan where trains are officially late if they are more than one minute off the published schedule. On some lines they are meant to stay within 15 seconds of the schedule and drivers assiduously check the time and any deviation from the schedule as they pass each station. Most services have a window built in to their schedule so that any lost time can be made up along the way.

tions on rural lines. No longer the exclusive preserve of *tetsudo maniaku* (rail enthusiasts), of which there are thousands in Japan, preserved steam operations now cater to the tourist trade. But some experts warn that the current nostalgia boom will be short-lived. Railway-equipment manufacturers are no longer geared up to supply spare parts for old locomotives and it may only be a matter of time before the SLs are once again shunted away into the sidings, for ever.

The railway

JAPAN RAIL TODAY

The railway in Japan is widely considered to be one of the most efficient in the world and reaches nearly all parts of the four main islands. Private railways provide additional coverage but the bulk of the railway network is operated by six regional companies known collectively as the JR Group (hereafter known as JR). For the Japan Rail pass-holder, the six companies can be considered one national company because the pass is valid on virtually all trains across the entire JR network.

Every day, 26,000 JR trains travel on a network which stretches for 20,000km. These range from some of the fastest trains in the world shuttling businessmen from one meeting to another, to one-carriage diesel trains on remote rural lines. JR well deserves its reputation for punctuality and efficiency on all its lines; it is extremely rare for services to run late. In more than 20 trips to Japan I have been on a late-running train just twice, but even these delays were never more than a few minutes and staff made frequent apologies.

Rail information in English
For information in English on all JR services once you're in Japan, call the JR-East Infoline (☎ 050-2016 1603, daily except New Year's Day, 10am-6pm). Operators can provide information on timetables and fares, and advise on routes. Seat reservations are not accepted by phone. This service is provided by JR East, but information is available for all services operated by the JR Group.

THE RAIL NETWORK

The only time when there is a risk of major disruption is after a serious earthquake or in the event of really extreme weather conditions. Warm water is sprayed on to the tracks on the Tohoku shinkansen east of Tokyo to ensure that snow does not disrupt service, but in northern Honshu and Hokkaido severe snow in winter occasionally causes disruption.

Rail companies around the world must envy JR's track record: not a single fatality on the shinkansen since services began in 1964. The only time a shinkansen has ever derailed was in 2004 following a major earthquake near Niigata, but there were no passenger injuries or deaths.

After midnight, when the shinkansen closes down for the night, a small army of engineers inspect and repair the track on a special shinkansen nick-named the 'Dr Yellow'. They have only six hours each night to carry out essential track maintenance.

Not only is JR the most efficient rail network in the world, the trains are also some of the best maintained. It's worth turning up early for your shinkansen to see the army of uniformed cleaning staff who have only a few minutes to ensure the carriages are swept, the toilets cleaned, and all the seats turned around to face the correct way. At stations, platforms are always spotless, floors are constantly

No smoking

JR trains are no longer the paradise for smokers they once were. The trend in recent years has been to reduce the number of smoking carriages on shinkansen and limited-express services.

All shinkansen and limited-express trains operated by JR East became non-smoking in 2007. However, smoking is still allowed on sleeper services. Dedicated smoking areas at stations and on platforms have been expanded, giving smokers the opportunity for a last puff. A few trains such as overnight sleepers and special-event services will still allow some smoking.

The new N700 operating on the Tokaido/Sanyo shinkansen line is all non-smoking. However, there is a smoking area on the deck of carriage No 4.

JR West has a no-smoking policy on limited-express trains travelling less than 300 kilometres between originating and terminating stations. This policy excludes overnight sleeper trains. More non-smoking carriages have been introduced on trains travelling more than 300 kilometres. On most Yakumo LEX trains between Okayama and Izumo-shi (via Yonago and Matsue) all seating is completely no smoking; smoking is only permitted in a special smoking alcove. On Thunderbird LEX trains operating between Osaka and Toyama (via Kyoto and Kanazawa) the number of non-smoking cars has been increased. JR West-operated shinkansen trains retain some smoking carriages.

JR Hokkaido was the first JR company to ban smoking entirely on its services when it removed all smoking carriages as well as smoking corners at the ends of carriages in 2006.

JR Kyushu limited-express services became entirely non-smoking, including both seating areas and boarding-deck areas, in 2007, with the exception of a few trains (particularly between Hakata and Miyazaki) that run for longer than two hours, which retain at least one smoking carriage. The Kyushu shinkansen has been entirely non-smoking since it began operations in 2004.

❏ **Japan by rail on the web**
Useful websites include:
🖳 **www.hyperdia.com/cgi-english/hyperWeb.cgi** and 🖳 **www.jorudan.co.jp/eng lish/norikae** Input your origin and destination points for anywhere on Japan's rail network and these sites will come up with an itinerary, including transfers, journey time and fare.
🖳 **www.geocities.com/TheTropics/Cove/5750/tips.html** Run by a rail enthusiast with information on rail travel in Japan with maps and travel advice pages.
🖳 **www.h2.dion.ne.jp/~dajf/byunbyun/index.htm** Anything you could ever want to know about the shinkansen, written by a rail enthusiast.
🖳 **www.jnto.go.jp/eng/arrange/transportation/index.html** JNTO's page devoted to rail and air travel around Japan includes an on-line train timetable
🖳 **www.seat61.com/Japan/htm** General information about all aspects of train travel in Japan, including the rail passes (which can also be bought through the website)

All the companies in the JR Group (except for JR Shikoku) have websites in English:
JR Hokkaido 🖳 www2.jrhokkaido.co.jp/global/index.html; **JR East** 🖳 www.jreast .co.jp/e/index.html; **JR Central** 🖳 http://jr-central.co.jp/english.nsf/index; **JR West** 🖳 www.westjr.co.jp/english/global.html; **JR Shikoku**: 🖳 www.jr-shikoku.co.jp; **JR Kyushu:** 🖳 www.jrkyushu.co.jp/english/index.html. These websites have details of the rail passes, tickets and package tours available to foreign tourists for their area.
The **JR Group** website (🖳 www.japanrail.com) is maintained by the JR East New York office, representing the JR Group. The office (US ☎ 212-332-8686, One Rockefeller Plaza, Suite 1410, New York, NY 10020, Mon-Fri 9am-5pm) provides rail-related information but does not sell tickets/rail passes.

swept, wiped and disinfected, dustbins emptied before they are ever full and escalator rails wiped (staff seem to be employed exclusively for this task).

THE TRAINS

Shinkansen

JR's flagship trains are, of course, the shinkansen, better known as the bullet train. All shinkansen can be used with the rail pass except for the Nozomi ('Hope'), which runs on the Tokaido and Sanyo shinkansen lines between Tokyo and Hakata and is the fastest of all the bullet trains. Nozomi services now have both reserved and unreserved cars. If you take a Nozomi you'll have to pay the full fare, including the super express supplement, so make sure that if you're travelling west of Tokyo to Kyoto/Osaka, you take only a Hikari or Kodama shinkansen. At the time of writing the N700 (see p76) is the latest version of the shinkansen.

The shinkansen offers what is almost certainly the smoothest train ride in the world, as the train appears to glide effortlessly along the line; all shinkansen run on special tracks. The seating configuration is usually 3x2 and, as with all shinkansen and limited express services, seats can be turned around so that a group travelling together can face each other. Facilities on board include telephones, Japanese- and Western-style toilets, and a nappy-changing room which

THE RAIL NETWORK

can be used as a 'sick bay' by anyone who is not feeling well – the key is available from the train conductor. Mini-shops and trolley services selling sandwiches, bentos, pastries and hot/cold drinks are found on most services though Nozomi trains have vending machines only. Whichever train you take, it's far cheaper to stock up at a station kiosk or convenience store before you travel. There are no dining cars on bullet trains. Dining cars remain on only a few of the luxury overnight sleeper services, notably the Cassiopeia (between Ueno, in Tokyo, and Sapporo) and the Twilight Express (between Osaka and Sapporo). However, the rail pass is not valid on either of these services.

Limited expresses

Next step down are limited expresses (LEX; called *tokkyu*), which run on the same tracks as the ordinary trains (see below) but stop only at major stations. The standard of comfort and range of facilities on board varies considerably. Most limited expresses are modern and offer almost as smooth a ride as the shinkansen but a few (mainly diesel-powered ones) are not quite as glamorous or hi-tech.

The JR companies constantly try to outdo each other by rolling out ever more space-age-style interiors whenever they upgrade their limited express services. Many trains have on-board vending machines and telephones (though expect to pay a premium rate).

The seating configuration varies but is very often 2x2 and as is common in Japan all seats can be turned around to face the other way. Refreshments trolleys are usually available but as with the shinkansen it is worth buying food and drink in advance as the trolleys have a limited selection. There is generally a mixture of Japanese and Western-style toilets.

Express, rapid and local trains

Despite their names, **express** (*kyuko*) and **rapid** trains (*kaisoku*), are much slower than limited expresses and boast few facilities; they are also increasingly rare. Seating is usually 2x2 though on some local trains there are long rows of bench-style seats on either side of the train which leaves plenty of standing room in the middle. There is usually no trolley service but most of these trains have at least one toilet, though (particularly on local trains) this is likely to be Japanese style.

Slowest of all are the **local trains** (*futsu*) which stop at every station. The smallest trains with just a single carriage are called 'one-man cars'. A few lines

---

Luggage space
On all shinkansen and most limited express trains there are luggage racks at either end of each compartment which are wide enough to store rucksacks and suitcases. On some of the more modern trains you'll also find airline-style overhead storage bins. Local trains do not have dedicated storage areas but as long as you're not travelling during the rush hour, there's always space to leave your luggage by the door, on a seat or in the aisle.

in rural areas, particularly in Hokkaido, are served by local trains only. I. other places the only reason for taking the local train is if you plan to stop at a station not served by limited express.

One of the pleasures of a ride on a local train is the chance to stand right at the front next to the driver's compartment; here you'll see close-up how and why the Japanese rail network is so efficient. Wearing a suit, cap and regulation white gloves the driver of the smallest local train seems just as meticulous as the driver of a 16-carriage shinkansen. Before the train pulls away from each stop the driver points at the clock as if to confirm the train is indeed leaving on time, then points ahead to check the signals have given him (or her) the all clear to go.

Sleeper trains

In addition to the trains mentioned above, JR operates a (dwindling) number of sleeper services. On services which are all berths and do not have a reserved seat section, rail-pass holders have to pay both the limited express charge and a hefty supplement for use of a berth. This can be anything from ¥6300 for a bed in a compartment to ¥20,000 or more for a bed on one of the luxury sleeper services such as the Twilight Express (see box below); supplements vary according to the distance travelled.

❑ **Major sleeper services**

Name of train	To/from	To/from
Fuji	Tokyo	Oita (Kyushu)
Ginga	Tokyo	Osaka (Kansai, Honshu)
*Hayabusa	Tokyo	Kumamoto (Kyushu)
*Moonlight Nagara	Tokyo	Ogaki (near Nagoya, Honshu)
**Sunrise-Izumo	Tokyo	Izumo-shi (Western Honshu)
**Sunrise-Seto	Tokyo	Takamatsu (Shikoku)
*Moonlight Echigo	Shinjuku (Tokyo)	Niigata (Honshu)
*Akebono	Ueno (Tokyo)	Aomori (Tohoku, Honshu)
Cassiopeia	Ueno	Sapporo (Hokkaido)
Hokuriku	Ueno	Kanazawa (Honshu)
Hokutosei	Ueno	Sapporo (Hokkaido)
* Noto	Ueno	Kanazawa (Honshu)
Kitakuni	Osaka (Kansai, Honshu)	Niigata (Honshu)
Nihonkai	Osaka	Aomori (Tohoku, Honshu)
Twilight Express	Osaka	Sapporo (Hokkaido)
*Akatsuki	Kyoto (Kansai, Honshu)	Nagasaki (Kyushu)
*Naha	Kyoto	Kumamoto (Kyushu)
*Hamanasu	Aomori (Tohoku)	Sapporo (Hokkaido)
*Marimo	Sapporo (Hokkaido)	Kushiro (Hokkaido)
*Rishiri	Sapporo	Wakkanai (Hokkaido)
*Dream Nichirin	Hakata (Kyushu)	Miyazaki (Kyushu)

* Reserved seating is available to rail-pass holders without supplement.
** Reserved carpet space (called *nobi-nobi zaseki*) is available to rail-pass holders without supplement.

❑ **Collecting rubbish**
For security reasons rubbish bins on JR East trains are locked shut. Rubbish collectors pass through the carriages frequently and there are people standing at the exits as you get off with plastic bags (not that they check what you are throwing in their bag!).

The type of berth available varies from train to train so check when making a reservation what the accommodation choice is. A reserved seat is the cheapest option though some trains are 'all bed' (couchette or semi/private compartment). The de luxe sleepers (Cassiopeia and Twilight Express) which run between Osaka/Tokyo and Hakodate/Sapporo have luxuries such as on-board showers and dining cars, but don't expect great facilities on other services. Slippers and a yukata are often provided but, surprisingly, buffet cars/vending machines are rare. The best advice is to pick up some snacks and drink before you set off.

Other overnight services have either reclining seats or carpet space where you can lie down on the floor; these are free to rail-pass holders but places should be reserved in advance.

ALTERNATIVES TO A JAPAN RAIL PASS

If you arrive in Japan without a rail pass there are a few other ticket options, though none is quite such a good deal.

The **Full Moon Green Pass** is a discount ticket for married couples with a combined age of at least 88. This 'double ticket' can be bought anytime from September 1-May 31 for use from October 1-June 30. It is not valid during peak travel periods in late Dec/early Jan, late March/early April, and Golden Week (late April/early May).

The pass allows unlimited travel on all JR trains in first-class carriages (Green cars) and is valid for two people for either five days (¥80,500), seven days (¥99,900) or twelve days (¥124,400) days. The pass includes the use of B-class sleeping berths on overnight rail services but does not include the Nozomi shinkansen. For foreign visitors to Japan the standard Green Japan Rail Pass is as a rule better value than the Full Moon Pass (two 7-day Green Japan Rail Passes cost ¥75,600 and two 14-day Green Passes ¥122,400) but it is worth considering if you have not bought, or are not eligible for, the former. To purchase a Full Moon Green Pass, from major stations or travel agents in Japan, you need to show proof of age and marriage in the form of a health-insurance card or passport.

The **Kansai Thru Pass** allows unlimited travel between Kyoto, Nara, Osaka, Himeji, Koya-san, Kobe, and Kansai International Airport. The pass (2 days, ¥3800; 3 days, ¥5000) is valid on 32 private rail and bus companies but travel on JR services is not permitted.

For further information check 🖳 www.surutto.com. Also check the website for an up-to-date list of locations where you can buy the pass; points of sale include Kansai International Airport and Kyoto station.

JR East sells a one-day **Holiday Pass** (¥2300), offering unlimited use of local JR trains in the Greater Tokyo area, including Yokohama (see p110) and Kamakura (see p112), on weekends and during holidays.

The JR group companies offer **seasonal excursion tickets** which allow unlimited travel in selected areas over a set number of days. The validity and type of these tickets changes regularly so enquire at any tourist information centre or JR ticket office for details. Probably the best buy is the near-legendary **Seishin Juhachi Kippu** ('Youth 18 ticket'); this is a seasonal ticket aimed at young people travelling around in holiday time, but there is no upper age limit. The ticket costs ¥11,500 and what you receive is actually a set of five tickets which can be used for travel on local trains only. The five tickets can be used by five people travelling together on one day (which works out at ¥2300 per person), or by one person travelling on any five days within the period of validity. The ticket can be purchased from any JR ticket office between July 1st and August 31st and is valid for travel between July 20th and September 10th. It is also sold during the following periods: February 20th to March 31st, for travel between March 1st and April 10th, and December 1st to January 10th for travel between December 10th and January 20th.

TIMETABLES

This guide contains timetables (see pp456-71) for the main routes described. JR publishes a condensed timetable (Railway Timetable) in English which contains details of the major shinkansen and limited express services. If you are intending to stick only to main rail routes, this is all the information you will need and if you have bought a Japan Rail pass you should have been given one of these but not all authorized agents do so. Bear in mind, however, that timetables change so you should not rely on either of these sources. Double-check through the English infoline (see box p79), or at a rail station before you travel.

Alternatively, if you can read Japanese, or even if you can't but are up for the challenge, get a copy of the Japanese timetable (Jikokuhyo/¥1050). The huge volume, which lists everything that moves in Japan (trains, buses, ropeways, cable cars, ferry services, chair lifts) is published monthly. You'll find a well-thumbed copy in every JR ticket office. Much easier to carry around is the pocket-sized version (Pocket Jikokuhyo/¥500), also published monthly; this condensed volume still contains much more information than JR's Railway Timetable in English or the timetables in this guide. Both versions of the Japanese timetable are available from any bookstore in Japan.

For a guide to using the Japanese timetable see p456.

BUYING A TICKET

This is the most expensive way of travelling and is not really recommended if you can purchase a rail pass. The fare structure in Japan is straightforward. First there is a basic fare which corresponds to the kilometre distance you travel. This ticket is valid only on local and rapid trains. Supplements have to be paid if

❏ Sample single fares from Tokyo		Supple-
To	Fare	ment
Aomori (739km)	¥10,190	¥6700*
Hakata (1176km)	¥13,440	¥8480
Hiroshima (894km)	¥11,340	¥6910
Kyoto (514km)	¥7980	¥5440
Nagano (222km)	¥3890	¥4280
Nagasaki (1330km)	¥14,810	¥9570*
Sapporo (1212km)	¥14,070	¥9110*
Takayama (533km)	¥8510	¥6090*

* Includes both the shinkansen and limited express surcharge
All sample fares shown include the seat reservation charge (¥510)

using any other train. The fare for a return trip by rail is discounted by 20% if the one-way distance exceeds 600km.

Tickets can be purchased from ticket machines or at JR ticket offices. If buying from a machine and unsure of the fare to your destination, the best advice is to buy the cheapest ticket and then pay the difference to the train conductor or at a 'fare-adjustment machine' at your arrival station. Most ticket machines have an option to purchase several tickets for the same journey in one go; this is useful if travelling in a group – push the buttons which indicate the number of adults and children in the group. Some ticket counters at Tokyo station accept credit cards issued overseas but in most other places you'll need to pay in cash. Tables of the basic per kilometre fares and limited express/shinkansen supplements are printed in the condensed English-language timetable; a few sample fares are provided in the box above.

MAKING SEAT RESERVATIONS

Seat reservations can be made up to one month before the date of travel but only in Japan. To make a reservation either find the ticket office, known as 'Midori no Madoguchi', at any JR station or if there are long queues, try a Travel Service Center (TSC). TSCs are JR-run travel agencies which also handle seat reservations; they are found in larger stations – look for the racks of holiday brochures outside. The regional JR companies call their TSCs by different names but they all offer the same service. The names to look out for are JR Tokai Tours (in the JR Central area), View Plaza (JR East), Travel Information Satellite (TiS) (JR West), Warp Navi (JR Shikoku), Joyroad (JR Kyushu) and Twinkle Plaza (JR Hokkaido).

Midori no Madoguchi
(Green Window)
reservation office

Seat reservations can be made on shinkansen, limited express and express services, but rapid and local trains are all non-reserved. Seat reservations on all shinkansen (except the Nozomi) and limited express trains cost nothing if you have a rail pass so it's always worth making a reservation, particularly if travelling at peak times. (All other passengers have to pay a supplement for a reserved seat). Remember that if you board a train without a seat reservation and sit in a reserved carriage, the conductor will charge you the appropriate supplement for the distance you're travelling, even if you have a rail pass. Pass holders, however, are not penalized for not using a seat reser-

⛩️ **The Japanese calendar**
Traditionally the Japanese have named and counted their years by the length of an Emperor's reign. The count starts with each new Emperor. The year 2006, for example, was known as Heisei 18; Heisei being the name that refers to the current Emperor's era, and 18 being the number of years that have elapsed since he ascended to the throne; the year 2007 is Heisei 19. While the Western system of counting years is widely used, the Japanese system is often found on official documentation (eg train and seat reservation tickets).

vation, so it doesn't matter if you miss the train (see box below) or change your plans – just cancel your reservation by handing in your seat reservation ticket and then make another one.

At the time of reservation you can usually choose on which side of the train you want to sit. For the classic view of Mt Fuji from the shinkansen, ask for a seat on the right side coming from Tokyo, and on the left side from Kyoto. You can also choose if you want to be in a smoking or non-smoking car, but very few trains now have smoking carriages; see box p80 for details. Note that on most limited expresses there is only one Green Car and it is usually non-smoking. Smoking is not permitted on any local trains.

In all ticket offices you'll find reservation request forms that are supposed to be filled out before going to the ticket desk. Almost always, however, staff are happy to issue seat reservations without a form, so just head to the desk and tell them where and when you want to go (or at least write the basic information down on a piece of paper). Even if the staff do want you to complete a form it is not difficult as some forms have English on them.

❏ **Last-minute booking**
Thanks to JR's computerized seat-reservation system, you can book seats up to the very last minute and even as the train is waiting in the station. Only at peak travel times, such as the Golden Week holiday (see p67), are seats booked weeks in advance.

All JR seat-reservation tickets can be printed in English, but unless you specifically ask for this they may be printed in Japanese. For details of how to read your seat reservation ticket if it is in Japanese, see the sample on p455.

RAILWAY STAFF

JR staff are always impeccably dressed in company uniforms which differ slightly in design from one region to another. Suits are the norm but short-sleeve shirts are worn in summer. JR Central's conductors on the shinkansen are given a new tie once a month. The female staff who serve refreshments on board JR Hokkaido trains wear badges announcing themselves as 'Twinkle Ladies'.

Don't expect all JR staff to speak English, though basic questions concerning platform and destination are usually no problem. At the ticket offices in major stations (such as Tokyo and Kyoto), you'll find someone who speaks

THE RAIL NETWORK

⛩ **Standing in line**

The British may be known for queuing but the Japanese have turned standing in line into an art form. At mainline stations, including all shinkansen stops, locator maps of trains are found on each platform. These show the layout and configuration of your train and indicate precisely where you should wait on the platform. Look out along the edge of the platform for numbered signs which indicate the stopping point for each carriage. You can be sure that the train will stop where it should and the doors of each carriage will open opposite the appropriate platform markers.

At busy stations there are often a bewildering number of signs telling you where to stand for particular trains. If you've got a seat reservation ticket you could show it to someone on the platform and ask them to point you in the direction of the right queue. But don't get unduly stressed about standing in the right line: all the carriages are interconnected and you can easily find the way to the right compartment once you're on board.

English. Some train conductors on the bullet train also speak some English. All carry pocket timetables and can advise on connection times and even tell you from which platform your next train will be departing.

STATION FACILITIES

All large stations and most smaller stations have **coin lockers** which range in price from ¥300 to ¥600; ¥300 lockers are big enough for day packs only, while all but the biggest ruck sacks should fit comfortably into a ¥500 locker. Lockers take ¥100 coins, so if you need change ask at a station kiosk. Some lockers do not have a key but dispense a password/number which you will need to key into the locker to retrieve your luggage. The fee is charged on a midnight to midnight basis, so if you store your luggage at 6pm and leave it there until the following morning or afternoon, you have to pay the same fee again to retrieve it.

Though check-in time in Japan is not usually until late afternoon, the majority of hotels, ryokan and hostels are happy to keep your luggage for free during the day before you check in, so you don't have to fork out for coin lockers every time you arrive somewhere.

Food

The cheapest places to look for food are in station bakeries and coffee shops, open from around 7am to 9pm. If you just want to pick up a snack or a drink, look either for a convenience store outside the station or for kiosks inside the station. Stations of all sizes have at least one noodle stall where you can get a filling bowl of udon or soba for around ¥300-400.

THE RAIL NETWORK

⛩ **Railway fare**
Crucial to the success of an ekiben (station lunch box) is the shape of the box and whether the contents are pleasing to the eye as the the lid is uncovered. Most are priced at around ¥1000 but Kanazawa station has a ¥10,000 bento box, shaped like a chest of drawers – you pull out each drawer to reveal another layer or course of your meal.

Like all institutions, the press delights in reporting on the ekiben's imminent demise (why pay for a fancy lunch box when you can grab a cheap burger?). Statistics suggest that sales of ekiben are nearly half what they were a decade ago. This is partly because of faster train services (by the time you've unwrapped the box, you're nearly at your destination) but also an indication that people prefer to buy – or make their own – sandwiches rather than splash out on an on-board ekiben.

The most popular railway food is the ekiben (see box above), or station lunch box. 'Bento' is a generic term for a packed lunch, but the ekiben is a cut above the rest. There's an ekiben stall (or several) in every station; the boxes feature local ingredients which give you a taste of the place you are passing through. The boxes are also sold on shinkansen and limited express trains, but it's much cheaper to buy one at the station before you leave.

Facilities for the disabled
In large stations there are adequate facilities for disabled passengers, including elevators, ramps or stair lifts from platform to concourse level. Unfortunately, in many smaller stations there are no special facilities and often only stairs and overhead walkways. The good news is that the situation is changing; new stations with improved facilities are being built but don't expect your image of hitech Japan to ring true in terms of wheelchair accessibility.

Where there are no special facilities, JR staff are happy to provide assistance to disabled passengers. Enquire at the JR ticket office at least 30 minutes before the departure of your train. Train conductors and/or station staff will also help with boarding and exiting carriages. On older trains, aisles are narrow and not designed for wheelchair use. Unless facilities are specifically referred to in the route and city guides, seek assistance from station staff.

Accessible Japan (💻 www.wakakoma.org/aj) is a useful website for information on trains with space for wheelchairs and railway stations with special access.

BICYCLES

JR does not generally allow cycles to be carried on trains unless they can be folded up or dismantled and carried in a special bag. Cycles, however, can be rented from many JR stations (details are given in the relevant city guides); rates are about ¥200 per hour or ¥1000 for the day.

THE RAIL NETWORK

PART 4: TOKYO AND OSAKA

Tokyo

INTRODUCTION

It will come as no surprise to first-time visitors that Tokyo is the most populous city in the world; 12.5 million people are packed into the city. There's no denying this makes Tokyo seriously overcrowded. Rumours that staff are employed at some stations to push people on to trains are true, at least during peak rush-hour times. But if you avoid the morning and evening rush hours, it's possible to travel around Tokyo in comfort. And whatever the time of day, the trains run according to the timetable.

More surprising than the mass of people is the fact that Tokyo became Japan's official capital only in 1868, when Emperor Meiji was restored to the throne (see p39). For centuries before, it was an undiscovered back-water and might have remained so had Tokugawa Ieyasu not decided to settle there.

In 1603 Ieyasu chose Edo (called Tokyo since 1868) as the seat of government for the Tokugawa shogunate. Right up until the collapse of the shogunate in 1867, Japan's official capital remained Kyoto but the Emperor who resided there exercised no real power.

In the years since Edo was renamed Tokyo and snatched the capital prize from Kyoto, the small town has become a thriving city of commerce, industry, entertainment and luxury. Little of the old Tokyo remains but one area worth seeking out for its atmosphere is Asakusa (see p103), home to one of Japan's most vibrant temples and packed with narrow streets which are a world and at least a century away from the skyscrapers of Shinjuku (see p95) and the city-within-a-city in Roppongi (see p103).

Some arrive in Tokyo and never leave, captivated by the neon, designer stores and relentless energy of the place. Others arrive and never leave their hotel rooms, terrified of the noise and sheer number of people who fill the streets day and night.

The answer is somewhere between these two extremes. Stay just long enough to get a feel for the city but get out in time to make full use of the rail pass and discover how much lies beyond this metropolis.

さまざまの事おもひ出す櫻かな

Ah! what memories!
Myriad thoughts evoked
by those cherry trees!
(MATSUO BASHO)

WHAT TO SEE AND DO

JR's Yamanote line runs in a loop around Tokyo; the text below suggests stopping-off points both on and off the line. The route begins and ends at

⛩ **Tokyo on the net**
There are dozens of websites dedicated to life in Tokyo. A few worth check-ing out for everything from restaurant to art-gallery reviews are: 🖳 http://metropo lis.co.jp, 🖳 www.planettokyo.com, 🖳 www.digi-promotion.com and 🖳 www.tokyo q.com. The official website of the Tokyo Metropolitan Government is 🖳 www.met ro.tokyo.jp.

Tokyo station, the main arrival/departure point by shinkansen. Yamanote line trains have on-board colour screens above the doors telling you what the next stop is, how long it will take to get there and even which side of the train the exit is going to be, so it's easy to navigate your way around.

A full circuit of the Yamanote line takes about an hour and is recommend-ed as a way to orientate yourself and get a sense of the different sides to Tokyo, the range of architecture, and the mishmash of old and new.

On the Yamanote line

Tokyo The Marunouchi side of Tokyo station is the old half and has a tradi-tional red-brick frontage which is currently the subject of major redevelopment. The landmark Tokyo Station Hotel, centrepiece of a multi-billion-yen project to restore this side of the station to its early 20th-century heyday, is due to reopen in 2011. Until then you can expect building work and scaffolding to obscure much of the outside facade.

A short walk north-west from the Marunouchi exit brings you to the impos-ing **Imperial Palace**, surrounded by a stone-wall moat. Home to the Emperor and his family, this is a quiet oasis of green but is mostly off-limits to the pub-lic except on two days of the year (December 23rd and January 2nd), when the Emperor, his wife, and other family members wave from the balcony to thou-sands of enthusiastic flag-waving patriots and tourists. The **East Gardens** (Higashi Gyoen) are open to the public (9am-3pm Dec-Feb, 9am-4pm Mar-Nov, daily except Mon/Fri, free), as is **Hibiya Park**, adjacent to Palace Plaza.

Yurakucho Alight here for the **tourist information centre** (see p106). **Tokyo International Forum** (🖳 www.t-i-forum.co.jp), the glass building on the other side of the station, mainly hosts conventions so is unlikely to be of interest but the building itself is worth a look for its magnificent architecture.

Shimbashi In the square outside the station is – to quote one rail fan – a 'rather sad, stuffed and mounted' steam locomotive (C11 292), built by Nippon Sharyo in 1945. For another rail-related sight in the area, see the box on p92.

Shimbashi was the birthplace of the railway in Japan and it remains a cen-tre of rail innovation as the starting point for the Tokyo Waterfront New Transit Line, a monorail better known as the **Yurikamome** (see p92). The driverless and computer-controlled Yurikamome whisks passengers to **Odaiba**, an island of reclaimed land in Tokyo Bay.

⛩ **Shiodome**

Shiodome, by Shimbashi, was a former railroad area which has recently undergone redevelopment and is now a futuristic office and leisure space. But the district's railway heritage has not been entirely forgotten: in 2003 JR-East opened **Old Shimbashi Station** (☎ 03-3572 1872), a replica of Japan's first station building, which stands today on the site of the birthplace of the country's railway. The building houses a small Railway Exhibition Hall which traces the history of the railway station and of railways in Japan (there are signs in English). The station is open Tue-Sun 11am-6pm and admission is free.

The original building, which served as the terminus for Japan's first 29km rail line from Tokyo to Yokohama in 1872 (see p73), burnt to the ground in the Great Kanto Earthquake of 1923. But Shimbashi, later renamed Shiodome station, rose from the ashes and continued to serve as an important railway junction in various guises – latterly as Tokyo's main freight terminal – until 1986, when it was finally abandoned.

The 22-hectare site was later sold to private investors and has now become what it is today: a huge business, shopping and residential complex known as **Shiodome Sio-site** (🖥 www.sio-site.or.jp).

The replica station building is next to **Shiodome City Center building** (🖥 www.shiodome.st). Shiodome is directly connected to Shimbashi station on the JR Yamanote Line.

The Yurikamame monorail to Odaiba

The chance to see Tokyo from another angle makes a trip from Shimbashi to Odaiba worthwhile in itself, but the monorail calls at plenty of tourist attractions along the way. Sit in the front, or right at the back, for the best views. As you leave Shimbashi look to the right for views down onto the shinkansen.

A one-way journey from Shimbashi to the terminus at Toyosu (¥370) takes around 30 minutes. A one-day pass for the Yurikamome (🖥 www.yuri kamome.co.jp.eng lish/index.php) costs ¥800, valid for unlimited travel between Shimbashi and the terminus at Toyosu. A ¥900 pass includes unlimited monorail and water-bus services; however, the latter are not frequent. For waterbus timetables see 🖥 www.suijobus.co.uk/english. Buy a ticket or pass from one of the machines and look out for a map of the area (in English) from one of the stalls at stations en route.

From Shimbashi trains stop at **Shiodome** (see box above), **Takeshiba**, **Hinode** (a stop on the water-bus route; see box p103), **Shibaura-futo** after which the train does a loop and crosses the spectacular Rainbow Bridge.

Odaiba-kaihin-koen Stop here to visit a seaside park with a man-made beach and **Decks Tokyo Beach**, a vast retail space which includes the Tokyo Joypolis games arcade and Little Hong Kong, a dozen restaurants set in a themed area and spread across the 6th and 7th floors.

This is also the nearest stop for **Fuji Television,** which has its studios on Odaiba (look for the space-age metallic building with a sphere suspended in the middle). There is no charge to visit the studios (10am-8pm) but you have to pay to go in the spherical observatory (🖥 www.fujitv.co.jp/en, Tue-Sun, 10am-8pm; ¥500).

Daiba Get off at this station for **Aqua City Odaiba**, a shopping centre, and **Mediage**, a cinema complex, both with views of the Rainbow Bridge and Fuji Television Building.

Fune-no-kagakukan Nearest stop for the **Museum of Maritime Science** (🖥 www.funenokagakukan.or.jp/index_e.html, Tue-Sun, 10am-5/6pm; ¥700), built in the shape of a cruise ship, which sounds dull but is well designed, entertaining and informative. Also **Miraikan** (Museum of Emerging Science and Innovation; ☎ 03-3570 9151, 🖥 www.miraikan.jst.go.jp; daily July-Aug 10am-5pm, Wed-Mon the rest of the year; ¥500), in Tokyo Academic Park, where you can discover the latest in robot technology or just lie back and watch the earth revolve with displays of the sea-surface temperature and projections of future global warning and a global chemical weather-forecasting system.

Telecom Center Alight here for **Telecom Tower**, which resembles the Grande Arche de la Défense in Paris. Inside is an observation deck (Tue-Fri 15:00-21:00, Sat/Sun 11:00-21:00, ¥500/¥400 with a Yurikamome day pass) which offers views of the city. This is also the stop for **Oedo Onsen Monogatari** (☎ 03-5500 1126, 🖥 www.ooedoonsen.jp, daily, 11am-8am (no entry 2-5am); ¥2827 or ¥1987 if you enter after 6pm), an enormous hot-spring theme park set in the Edo period with more baths than you'll be able to visit in a day. The hot water used to fill the tubs is pumped up from a natural source 1400m below ground. Massages and other spa treatments are available at additional cost. If you're not planning on visiting another spa resort in Japan, or you just want to escape the humidity of Tokyo in the summer, this is the place to come to experience why the Japanese take the art of bathing so seriously.

Aomi From here you can visit **Palette Town**, an entertainment complex which includes the **Mega Web** theme park (🖥 www.megaweb.gr.jp/English, daily 11am-9pm, occasional closed days), a showcase for Toyota with paid attractions such as a 3D motion theatre and the 'E-com Ride' where you can go for a spin in a car which drives itself. Palette Town also includes **Venus Fort**, a shopping centre geared to women and Italian in feel with plazas and fountains. Also here is the tallest (115m-high) **ferris wheel** (10am-10pm, ¥900) in Japan, though the one in Sakuragicho (see p111) is not much smaller.

Kokusai-tenjijo-seimon This is the stop for **Tokyo Big Sight International Exhibition Center** (🖥 www.bigsight.co.jp/english). The Conference Tower is probably architecturally the most unusual building in this area as it is based on an inverted pyramid.

Ariake If you haven't visited the Sony Building (see p101) in Ginza get off here for the **Panasonic Center** (🖥 http://panasonic.co.jp/center/tokyo/en/access/index.html) where their latest products are displayed.

The Yurikamome extension from Ariake to Toyosu opened in 2006. After Ariake trains stop at **Ariake-Tennis-no-Mori**. There is a good view of Tokyo Tower from **Shijo-mae**. The next stop is Shin-Toyosu and the terminus is at **Toyosu**, future site of Tokyo's fish market (see p102) and home to the Lalaport shopping centre. Toyosu links up with the Yurakucho subway line – useful if you bought a one-way ticket from Shimbashi and don't want to return to Tokyo the same way you came.

As an alternative route back to Tokyo, get off at **Hinode**, and walk a couple of minutes to the passenger ferry terminal. From here you can catch a ferry (daily, 9am-6pm, dep every 40 mins, approx 40 mins; ¥760) up Sumida-gawa to **Asakusa** (see p103). This is another great way of seeing Tokyo; an on-board commentary is provided in English and Japanese.

Hamamatsucho The Tokyo Monorail to **Haneda Airport** (p50) starts here.

Shinagawa A shinkansen station opened here in 2003 (see p127).

Meguro Meguro is an upmarket area that's home to some of Japan's TV celebrities since it's convenient for Shibuya (home to NHK, the Japanese equivalent of the BBC) and Akasaka (home to the more commercial and ratings-driven TBS).

Ebisu From the station follow the signs for Yebisu Garden Palace, accessed via a series of moving walkways. Here you'll find shops, a cinema, restaurants, a hotel and **Beer Museum Yebisu** (Tue-Sun, 10am-6pm; free). Located behind Mitsukoshi department store, the museum was opened by Sapporo Breweries and is dedicated to the 'history, science and culture of the beloved beverage'. No beer is brewed here but there is a chance to tour a 'virtual brewery'. There is a tasting lounge at the end (¥400 to taste four different beers). A leaflet in English is provided at the entrance but the signs are mostly in Japanese. This museum is worth a look if you're not visiting Sapporo, where you can tour a working brewery (see p356).

Shibuya Follow the signs for the Hachiko Exit (see box p301), which will lead you to the main shopping area. The zebra crossing in front of the station is always packed with people making a beeline for the big names and high-street retailers crammed into this area. Head up Koen-dori (the road goes to the right of Starbucks) away from the station to find Tower Records (foreign books are on the seventh floor), Häagen Dazs, and all the top fashion department stores. The road to the left of Starbucks leads to a pedestrianized area which is quieter and has a branch of HMV on the right, as well as plenty of other shops and restaurants.

One place worth visiting for an evening meal or drink while in Shibuya is the intriguing ***Pink Cow*** (☎ 03-3406 5597, 🖳 www.thepinkcow.com, Tues to Sun, 5pm-late), Villa Moderuna B1F, a restaurant/bar which doubles as a gallery and venue for special events. They do a great all-you-can-eat buffet on Friday and Saturday (7-10pm) for ¥2625 per person.

To find the Pink Cow, turn right at the Tower Records corner, go straight, walking under a bridge and across Meji-dori. Keep going straight, passing two more sets of traffic lights and turn left. The Pink Cow is on the right, directly across from Aoyama Park Tower.

Harajuku Opposite Harajuku station is Yoyogi Park, home to **Meiji Jingu**, Tokyo's best-known shrine. Dedicated to Emperor Meiji and his consort, the shrine is divided into Outer and Inner gardens. Busy throughout the year, the shrine is invaded by thousands at New Year. Harajuku is just as hip as nearby

Shibuya and there are plenty of restaurants, cafés and trendy (read: retro/alternative) clothes and music stores in the streets around the station.

Yoyogi   The huge skyscraper you can see looming over Yoyogi station is Nippon Telecom's DoCoMo Tower.

Shinjuku   Probably the busiest station in the world, Shinjuku is home not only to JR but also to the private Odakyu and Keio railways.

   If you were to follow any of the mass of commuters (taking the west exit) between 6 and 8.30am, you would probably end up heading directly for the **Tokyo Metropolitan Government Building**, completed in 1991 and the workplace of 13,000 bureaucrats. The best reason for visiting here is the free, bird's eye, view of Tokyo. Take the direct elevator inside the No 1 Building (go down the steps outside so that you enter the building at basement level; before entering the lift you will have to pass through a security check) up to one of two 202m-high observatories (Tue-Sun, 9:30am-5pm, longer in summer) on the 45th floor. The cafés on the 45th floor are overpriced but there's a cheap cafeteria on the 32nd floor; it's meant for government employees but is open to anybody – take one of the ordinary lifts to reach this floor. The NS Building (on the right just before you reach the Metropolitan Government Building) has an exterior lift – go to the basement to access it. It's good for a free view of the Metropolitan Building. The NS Building has restaurants and there's an aerial walkway within the building.

   Shinjuku Gyoen (🖳 www.shinjukugyoen.go.jp, Tue-Sun 9am-4:30pm, ¥200) is a complete surprise in amongst Shinjuku's skyscrapers. Built in 1906 as an Imperial Garden, all 58.3 hectares are open to the public and the site includes an English landscape garden, French garden and traditional Japanese garden. A couple of traditional tea houses serve green tea and Japanese sweetmeats for ¥700. People come here to escape the busy city that surrounds the park; though you never quite feel you've left the metropolis, this is a pleasant temporary escape. Take the east exit from Shinjuku station and walk south-east for about 10 minutes.

   For somewhere to eat, head for one of the 28 restaurants on the 12th-14th floors of Takashimaya department store in **Times Square**, on the south side of Shinjuku station (it's connected to the station by a walkway). Times Square also contains an I-MAX cinema, a huge branch of Kinokuniya Books (foreign books are on the sixth floor) and the entertainment arcade, Shinjuku Joypolis.

   There's a certain Jekyll and Hyde character to Shinjuku. While the west side of the station is a sea of grey suits and immaculately turned-out businessmen, conformity is abandoned over on the east side. The streets around **Kabukicho**, a few minutes walk north of the east exit, fill up as the sun sets and the neon is switched on. Cinemas, clubs, restaurants, pubs and hostess bars compete for business and cater for all tastes.

Shin-Okubo   Years before the Bankside Globe opened in London, the Japanese had built their own reproduction of Shakespeare's playhouse, the

Tokyo Globe (🖥 www.tglobe.net). Most of the performances are in Japanese, though the RSC sometimes performs here when touring in Asia. Turn left out of the station and then right at the first junction (look for a McDonald's). Continue straight along this street for 5-10 minutes until you reach the Globe. On the adjacent 'Shakespeare Alley' is the *Globe Tavern*, serving evening meals and beer on tap for an authentic Elizabethan experience.

Takadanobaba Bus No 2 runs from outside this station to Waseda University campus, home to the **Tsubouchi Memorial Theatre Museum** (🖥 www.waseda.jp/enpaku/index-e.html, Mon, Wed, Thur, Sat, Sun 10am-5pm, Tue and Fri 10am-7pm, closed during university holidays; free). The museum is right in the middle of the campus and is dedicated to Shoyo Tsubouchi (1859-1935), founder of Waseda's Department of Literature and the first person to translate the complete works of Shakespeare into Japanese. The museum was built in 1928 and is modelled on the 17th-century Fortune Theatre, which once stood in London.

Pick up the excellent pamphlet, from the library on the ground floor, and then explore the three floors dedicated to the performing arts, with exhibitions on Shakespeare, Noh (try on a Noh mask and have a go at walking like a Noh actor) and Kabuki. If you get lost on your way to the museum, ask any student for 'Waseda-daigaku Tsubouchi-kinenkan Engeki-hakubutsukan' – it's easier to find than it is to say.

Ikebukuro On either side of Ikebukuro station are two enormous department stores; **Seibu** is on the east side and its rival **Tobu** is on the west. An underground passageway links both sides of the station. Both Seibu and Tobu have restaurant floors and food halls.

Otsuka Transfer here for the **Arakawa tram line** (see p103).

Nippori Nippori is a point of transfer for the private Keisei Railway line to Narita Airport (see p105).

Uguisudani Up until WWII, Uguisudani was a popular geisha quarter but it is now better known as a night-time pleasure area full of love hotels.

Ueno A major rail junction and the second stop after Tokyo for shinkansen services to the north. Ueno is an access point for Asakusa (see p103) as it is the nearest stop for transferring from the Yamanote line to the Ginza subway line.

Right outside the station is **Ueno Park**, Japan's oldest public park and the largest in Tokyo. During the cherry-blossom season in April, thousands of Tokyo residents descend on Ueno Park armed with portable karaoke machines, picnic hampers and crates of beer.

The park is home to a number of big museums, including: **Tokyo National Museum** (🖥 www.tnm.go.jp, Tue-Sun 9:30am-5pm, ¥600), the country's largest museum with exhibits on the history and fine arts of Japan, China and India; and the **National Museum of Western Art** (🖥 www.nm wa.go.jp, Tue-Sun 9:30am-

5pm, Fri to 8pm; ¥420), which displays masterpieces collected by a Japanese business magnate while travelling around Europe in the early 1900s, and **Ueno Zoo** (Tue-Sun 9:30am-5pm, ¥600), which opened in 1882 and is known in particular for its giant panda.

Shitamachi (literal translation: 'downtown') **Museum** (Tue-Sun 9:30am-4:30pm, ¥300, English-language guide/leaflet ¥500) is a small museum with recreated shops and homes from the Edo period and is worth a visit to see what much of Tokyo/Japan would have looked like then. It is on the south-eastern side of Ueno Park near Shinobazunoike pond.

Another reason for visiting Ueno is to wander around **Ameyoko Market**. Take the Shinobazu exit at Ueno station and head for Ameya-dori, a long shopping arcade that extends out beneath the elevated rail tracks. Stallholders call out loudly to passers-by and this is one of the few places in Japan where you are expected to haggle. You can buy almost anything here, including (fake?) Prada handbags, Rolex watches, clothes, fresh fish, meat, fruit and vegetables.

Okachi-machi Okachi-machi is known for its cheap jewellery stores.

Akihabara Akihabara is the discount electrical goods district of Tokyo and is worth visiting if you want a chance to see the latest gadgets months before they hit the worldwide market. Digital cameras, TVs, CDs, DVDs, PCs and other abbreviations that will soon be part of the global electronic vocabulary are all on display and available for purchase. If you're planning to buy, check first whether the guarantee is valid overseas and if the equipment is compatible with the electrical current in your home country.

One of the best stores is **Yodobashi Camera** (daily, 9:30am-10pm) accessed from Exit 1. The shop is on the opposite side of the main area (for which you need to take the Electric Town exit). Yodobashi Camera has seven floors of every kind of electronic product – if you get overwhelmed with all the noise and find it impossible to decide what to get head for the sixth floor (Household products) and the massage chairs. Even though all the instructions are in Japanese someone will probably be willing to show you what to press. However, do not expect to stay longer than 10-15 minutes.

While Akihabara has been traditionally associated with cutting-edge technology, the district is increasingly becoming a centre for animation and manga (comics) and is home to **Tokyo Anime Center** (💻 www.animecenter.jp; daily 11am-7pm, free) on the 4th Floor of the UDX Building. Follow the signs to the Electric Town exit, turn right out of the station, cross the plaza and go up the escalator.

The Anime Center is a short walk along on the left-hand side. The centre is geared to children but is worth visiting for anyone interested in animation especially as, unlike Studio Ghibli (see box p101), there is a lot of explanation in English, and indeed Chinese and Korean as well. There is a 3D Theater which screens new works as well as other anime-related events.

Tokyo This completes the loop around the Yamanote line.

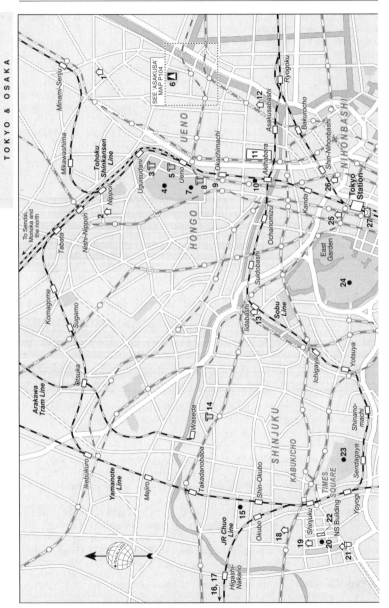

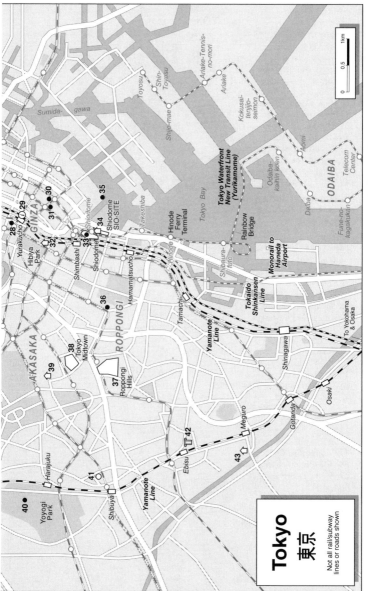

TOKYO & OSAKA

Tokyo
東京

Not all rail/subway
lines or roads shown

TOKYO　東京

Where to stay

1	Andon Ryokan	1	行燈旅館
2	Annex Katsutaro Ryokan	2	アネックス勝太郎旅館
12	Tokyo Sumidagawa Youth Hostel	12	東京隅田川ユースホステル
13	Tokyo International Hostel	13	東京国際ホステル
18	Nishitetsu Inn Shinjuku	18	西鉄イン新宿
19	Hotel Century Hyatt	19	ホテルセンチュリーハイアット
21	Park Hyatt Tokyo	21	パーク ハイアット 東京
25	Four Seasons Tokyo Marunouchi	25	フォーシーズンズホテル丸の内東京
26	Mandarin Oriental	26	マンダリン オリエンタル ホテル
32	Peninsula Hotel Tokyo	32	ペニンシュラホテル東京
34	Conrad Tokyo	34	コンラッド東京
39	Hotel Asia Center of Japan	39	ホテルアジア会館
43	Hotel Claska	43	ホテルクラスカ

Where to eat and drink

21	New York Bar	21	ニューヨーク バー
41	Pink Cow	41	ピンクカウ

Other

3	Tokyo National Museum	3	東京国立博物館
4	Ueno Park	4	上野公園
5	National Museum of Western Art	5	国立西洋美術館
6	Senso-ji	6	浅草寺
7	Ueno Zoo	7	上野動物園
8	Shitamachi Museum	8	下町風俗資料館
9	Ameyokocho Market	9	アメ横町
10	Tokyo Anime Center	10	東京アニメセンター
11	Yodobashi Camera	11	ヨドバシカメラ
14	Tsubouchi Memorial Theatre Museum	14	早稲田大学演劇博物館
15	Tokyo Globe	15	東京グローブ
16	Suginami Animation Museum	16	杉並アニメーションミュージアム
17	Ghibli Museum	17	ジブリ美術館
20	Tokyo Metropolitan Govt Bldg	20	東京都庁
22	NS Building	22	NSビル
23	Shinjuku Gyoen	23	新宿御苑
24	Imperial Palace	24	皇居
27	Central Post Office	27	中央郵便局
28	Tokyo International Forum	28	東京国際フォーラム
29	Tourist Information Centre	29	観光案内汐留
30	Kabuki-za	30	歌舞伎座
31	Sony Building	31	ソニービル
33	Shiodome City Center Building; Old Shimbashi Station	33	汐留シテセンタービル；旧新橋駅展示室
35	Tsukiji Market	35	築地市場
36	Tokyo Tower	36	東京タワー
37	Roppongi Hills	37	六本木ヒルズ
38	Tokyo Midtown	38	東京ミッドタウン
40	Meiji Jingu (Yoyogi Park)	40	代々木公園 (明治神宮)
42	Beer Museum Yebisu	42	恵比寿麦酒記念館

⛩ Animation museums

If Tokyo Anime Center in Akihabara (see p97) has whet your appetite for the cartoon world, there are a couple of other places just outside the city centre you might like to consider visiting: **Suginami Animation Museum** (☎ 03-3396 1510, 🖥 www .sam.or.jp; Tue-Sun 10am-6pm, free) hosts special exhibitions and has displays on every aspect of animation as well as a theatre showing some anime classics. Take the JR Chuo line to Ogikubo station, follow signs for the North exit, take a Kanto bus from either Stop No 0 or No 1 and get off at Ogikubo Keisatsusho-mae (Ogikubo Police station), a five-minute journey.

Studio Ghibli Museum (☎ 0422-40 2233, 🖥 www.ghibli-museum.jp; Wed-Mon 10am-6pm; ¥1000), a celebration of the work of leading Japanese animator Hayao Miyazaki, famous for – among many others – his 2001 film, *Spirited Away*. The museum is popular with children but is worth visiting if you are interested in animation. However, explanations are only in Japanese. Many of Miyazaki's original drawings are on display and the entry price includes a screening (approx 20 mins) of one of his short films. The nearest station to the museum is Mitaka on the JR Chuo line from Shinjuku; 20 mins. To get to the museum take the community bus from outside the South Exit of the station (round trip ¥300); the bus is small so you may have to queue at busy times. Alternatively it is a 15-minute walk.

It is **essential** to get **tickets in advance** – either from a JTB office in your home country (see pp17-20) or from the Travel View travel agency near Mitaka station – ask at the station. The main reason is that entry is limited and the museum is very popular. However, as long as the foreigner allocation of tickets has not been sold for that day you should get in – but do not go to the museum until you have a ticket.

On arrival your advance ticket is swapped for a genuine piece of film which you can keep as a souvenir. If you make the effort to go out there it is worth a stroll around Mitaka Inokashira Park – if nothing else for some peace and quiet after the noise from all the excited Japanese children in the museum!

Off the Yamanote line

Ginza One stop on the Marunouchi subway line from Tokyo, Ginza is billed in tourist literature as the 'most fashionable shopping paradise in Japan'; the main thoroughfare, Chuo-dori, is lined with upmarket department stores and designer label boutiques.

Apart from shopping, Ginza's best-known entertainment is kabuki (see p46); performances are staged at **Kabuki-za**, 10 minutes south-east of central Ginza on a corner of Harumi-dori. Tickets for most performances range from ¥2500 to ¥10,000 but if you don't want to sit through a whole performance (four to five hours), tickets for the fourth floor (around ¥1000; unreserved seats) are valid for one hour but are only available half an hour before the performance. Headphones for an English translation can be rented for the first, second and third floors. The programme changes every month; schedules are available from the tourist information centre (see p106) or from Kabuki-za (☎ 03-3541 3131, 🖥 www.kabuki-za.co.jp, 🖥 www.shochiku.co.jp/play/kabukiza/theater).

If you fancy jumping from traditional theatre to a hi-tech vision of the future, make a beeline from Kabuki-za to the **Sony Building** (🖥 www.sony building.jp; daily 11am-7pm, free), which hosts a number of shops and restaurants but most interesting are the Sony Showrooms on the 1st-4th floors. It's best to take the lift to the top and walk down touching, seeing and hearing the latest technology as you go. Take Exit B9 from the subway; alternatively it is a five-minute walk from the Ginza exit of JR Yurakucho station (on the Yamanote line).

Tsukiji Tsukiji (⌨ www.tsukiji-market.or.jp), two stops from Ginza on the Hibiya subway line, is Japan's biggest fish market (90% of all fish sold in Tokyo comes from here). The market kicks into life at 5am with the fish auction (you can get a cheap sushi breakfast if you wake up early enough) and runs through until 12 noon. The market is closed on Sunday, national holidays and the second and fourth Wednesday of the month. One veteran Tsukiji fish wholesaler once famously compared a 'good tuna' to a sumo wrestler: 'A sumo wrestler eats a lot, but because he exercises, the fat is smooth and has lots of muscle. It's the same for a tuna.'

The market is always very busy so traders would certainly appreciate it if you keep out of their way as much as possible. Plans are afoot to move Tsukiji

---

⛩ **Roppongi in the 21st century**

For a glimpse of 21st-century urban life, it's worth paying a visit to at least one of the cities-within-a-city that are Roppongi Hills (⌨ www.roppongihills.com) and Tokyo Midtown (⌨ www.tokyo-midtown.com). Both offer multi-billion-dollar cityscape visions of the future where shops, cinemas, restaurants, galleries, museums and offices all converge on one space. Both Roppongi Hill and Tokyo Midtown can be accessed directly from Roppongi station on the Hibiya subway line.

Roppongi Hills Roppongi Hills was the brainchild of construction tycoon Minoru Mori, one of the world's richest men. Crowds of well-heeled Japanese flock to the upmarket design stores and restaurants, but there's something here to please visitors of all budgets. An English 'Gourmet Guide' lists all the restaurants and cafés, many of which will not break the bank. Once you've shopped and eaten to your heart's content, don't leave Roppongi Hills without visiting the landmark **Mori Tower**, inside which you'll find: **Mori Art Museum** (⌨ www.mori.art.museum, Wed-Mon 10am-10pm, Tues 10am-5pm), a great contemporary art space on the 53rd floor; the 50th floor **Mori Urban Institute for the Future** (Mon-Thur 10am-8pm, Fri-Sun 10am-10pm), which contains, among many other things, magnificent scale models of New York and Tokyo; and the 52nd floor **Tokyo City View** (⌨ www.tokyocityview.com, daily 9am-1am), an observation platform which affords a spectacular 360-degree panorama of the city down below. Entrance to Tokyo City View costs ¥1500 and the ticket is also valid for the Art Museum and Urban Institute.

Tokyo Midtown Apart from shops, restaurants, offices and residences the Tokyo Midtown site includes: a *Ritz Carlton Hotel* (☎ 03-5474 5311, ⌨ www.ritzcarlton.com/hotels/tokyo/), on the top nine floors of **Midtown Tower**, a 53-storey skyscraper, the tallest building in Tokyo; a new **Suntory Museum of Art** (⌨ www.suntory.com/culture-sports.sma/museum) where the theme is art in life; **21_21 Design Sight** (⌨ www.21 21designsight.jp) which hosts design and art events/exhibitions, and the **National Arts Centre** (⌨ www.nact.jp; Wed-Mon 10am-6pm, to 8pm on Friday; entry charge depends on the exhibition), which is unusual in that it has no permanent exhibition.

❑ **Japan by rail on the web**
Useful websites include:
🖳 **www.hyperdia.com/cgi-english/hyperWeb.cgi** and 🖳 **www.jorudan.co.jp/eng lish/norikae** Input your origin and destination points for anywhere on Japan's rail network and these sites will come up with an itinerary, including transfers, journey time and fare.
🖳 **www.geocities.com/TheTropics/Cove/5750/tips.html** Run by a rail enthusiast with information on rail travel in Japan with maps and travel advice pages.
🖳 **www.h2.dion.ne.jp/~dajf/byunbyun/index.htm** Anything you could ever want to know about the shinkansen, written by a rail enthusiast.
🖳 **www.jnto.go.jp/eng/arrange/transportation/index.html** JNTO's page devoted to rail and air travel around Japan includes an on-line train timetable
🖳 **www.seat61.com/Japan/htm** General information about all aspects of train travel in Japan, including the rail passes (which can also be bought through the website)

All the companies in the JR Group (except for JR Shikoku) have websites in English: **JR Hokkaido** 🖳 www2.jrhokkaido.co.jp/global/index.html; **JR East** 🖳 www.jreast .co.jp/e/index.html; **JR Central** 🖳 http://jr-central.co.jp/english.nsf/index; **JR West** 🖳 www.westjr.co.jp/english/global.html; **JR Shikoku**: 🖳 www.jr-shikoku.co.jp; **JR Kyushu**: 🖳 www.jrkyushu.co.jp/english/index.html. These websites have details of the rail passes, tickets and package tours available to foreign tourists for their area.
    The **JR Group** website (🖳 www.japanrail.com) is maintained by the JR East New York office, representing the JR Group. The office (US ☎ 212-332-8686, One Rockefeller Plaza, Suite 1410, New York, NY 10020, Mon-Fri 9am-5pm) provides rail-related information but does not sell tickets/rail passes.

swept, wiped and disinfected, dustbins emptied before they are ever full and escalator rails wiped (staff seem to be employed exclusively for this task).

THE TRAINS

Shinkansen
JR's flagship trains are, of course, the shinkansen, better known as the bullet train. All shinkansen can be used with the rail pass except for the Nozomi ('Hope'), which runs on the Tokaido and Sanyo shinkansen lines between Tokyo and Hakata and is the fastest of all the bullet trains. Nozomi services now have both reserved and unreserved cars. If you take a Nozomi you'll have to pay the full fare, including the super express supplement, so make sure that if you're travelling west of Tokyo to Kyoto/Osaka, you take only a Hikari or Kodama shinkansen. At the time of writing the N700 (see p76) is the latest version of the shinkansen.

The shinkansen offers what is almost certainly the smoothest train ride in the world, as the train appears to glide effortlessly along the line; all shinkansen run on special tracks. The seating configuration is usually 3x2 and, as with all shinkansen and limited express services, seats can be turned around so that a group travelling together can face each other. Facilities on board include telephones, Japanese- and Western-style toilets, and a nappy-changing room which

THE RAIL NETWORK

can be used as a 'sick bay' by anyone who is not feeling well – the key is available from the train conductor. Mini-shops and trolley services selling sandwiches, bentos, pastries and hot/cold drinks are found on most services though Nozomi trains have vending machines only. Whichever train you take, it's far cheaper to stock up at a station kiosk or convenience store before you travel. There are no dining cars on bullet trains. Dining cars remain on only a few of the luxury overnight sleeper services, notably the Cassiopeia (between Ueno, in Tokyo, and Sapporo) and the Twilight Express (between Osaka and Sapporo). However, the rail pass is not valid on either of these services.

Limited expresses

Next step down are limited expresses (LEX; called *tokkyu*), which run on the same tracks as the ordinary trains (see below) but stop only at major stations. The standard of comfort and range of facilities on board varies considerably. Most limited expresses are modern and offer almost as smooth a ride as the shinkansen but a few (mainly diesel-powered ones) are not quite as glamorous or hi-tech.

The JR companies constantly try to outdo each other by rolling out ever more space-age-style interiors whenever they upgrade their limited express services. Many trains have on-board vending machines and telephones (though expect to pay a premium rate).

The seating configuration varies but is very often 2x2 and as is common in Japan all seats can be turned around to face the other way. Refreshments trolleys are usually available but as with the shinkansen it is worth buying food and drink in advance as the trolleys have a limited selection. There is generally a mixture of Japanese and Western-style toilets.

Express, rapid and local trains

Despite their names, **express** (*kyuko*) and **rapid** trains (*kaisoku*), are much slower than limited expresses and boast few facilities; they are also increasingly rare. Seating is usually 2x2 though on some local trains there are long rows of bench-style seats on either side of the train which leaves plenty of standing room in the middle. There is usually no trolley service but most of these trains have at least one toilet, though (particularly on local trains) this is likely to be Japanese style.

Slowest of all are the **local trains** (*futsu*) which stop at every station. The smallest trains with just a single carriage are called 'one-man cars'. A few lines

---

Luggage space
On all shinkansen and most limited express trains there are luggage racks at either end of each compartment which are wide enough to store rucksacks and suitcases. On some of the more modern trains you'll also find airline-style overhead storage bins. Local trains do not have dedicated storage areas but as long as you're not travelling during the rush hour, there's always space to leave your luggage by the door, on a seat or in the aisle.

in rural areas, particularly in Hokkaido, are served by local trains only. In all other places the only reason for taking the local train is if you plan to stop at a station not served by limited express.

One of the pleasures of a ride on a local train is the chance to stand right at the front next to the driver's compartment; here you'll see close-up how and why the Japanese rail network is so efficient. Wearing a suit, cap and regulation white gloves the driver of the smallest local train seems just as meticulous as the driver of a 16-carriage shinkansen. Before the train pulls away from each stop the driver points at the clock as if to confirm the train is indeed leaving on time, then points ahead to check the signals have given him (or her) the all clear to go.

Sleeper trains

In addition to the trains mentioned above, JR operates a (dwindling) number of sleeper services. On services which are all berths and do not have a reserved seat section, rail-pass holders have to pay both the limited express charge and a hefty supplement for use of a berth. This can be anything from ¥6300 for a bed in a compartment to ¥20,000 or more for a bed on one of the luxury sleeper services such as the Twilight Express (see box below); supplements vary according to the distance travelled.

❏ Major sleeper services

Name of train	To/from	To/from
Fuji	Tokyo	Oita (Kyushu)
Ginga	Tokyo	Osaka (Kansai, Honshu)
*Hayabusa	Tokyo	Kumamoto (Kyushu)
*Moonlight Nagara	Tokyo	Ogaki (near Nagoya, Honshu)
**Sunrise-Izumo	Tokyo	Izumo-shi (Western Honshu)
**Sunrise-Seto	Tokyo	Takamatsu (Shikoku)
*Moonlight Echigo	Shinjuku (Tokyo)	Niigata (Honshu)
*Akebono	Ueno (Tokyo)	Aomori (Tohoku, Honshu)
Cassiopeia	Ueno	Sapporo (Hokkaido)
Hokuriku	Ueno	Kanazawa (Honshu)
Hokutosei	Ueno	Sapporo (Hokkaido)
* Noto	Ueno	Kanazawa (Honshu)
Kitakuni	Osaka (Kansai, Honshu)	Niigata (Honshu)
Nihonkai	Osaka	Aomori (Tohoku, Honshu)
Twilight Express	Osaka	Sapporo (Hokkaido)
*Akatsuki	Kyoto (Kansai, Honshu)	Nagasaki (Kyushu)
*Naha	Kyoto	Kumamoto (Kyushu)
*Hamanasu	Aomori (Tohoku)	Sapporo (Hokkaido)
*Marimo	Sapporo (Hokkaido)	Kushiro (Hokkaido)
*Rishiri	Sapporo	Wakkanai (Hokkaido)
*Dream Nichirin	Hakata (Kyushu)	Miyazaki (Kyushu)

* Reserved seating is available to rail-pass holders without supplement.
** Reserved carpet space (called *nobi-nobi zaseki*) is available to rail-pass holders without supplement.

❑ **Collecting rubbish**

For security reasons rubbish bins on JR East trains are locked shut. Rubbish collectors pass through the carriages frequently and there are people standing at the exits as you get off with plastic bags (not that they check what you are throwing in their bag!).

The type of berth available varies from train to train so check when making a reservation what the accommodation choice is. A reserved seat is the cheapest option though some trains are 'all bed' (couchette or semi/private compartment). The de luxe sleepers (Cassiopeia and Twilight Express) which run between Osaka/Tokyo and Hakodate/Sapporo have luxuries such as on-board showers and dining cars, but don't expect great facilities on other services. Slippers and a yukata are often provided but, surprisingly, buffet cars/vending machines are rare. The best advice is to pick up some snacks and drink before you set off.

Other overnight services have either reclining seats or carpet space where you can lie down on the floor; these are free to rail-pass holders but places should be reserved in advance.

ALTERNATIVES TO A JAPAN RAIL PASS

If you arrive in Japan without a rail pass there are a few other ticket options, though none is quite such a good deal.

The **Full Moon Green Pass** is a discount ticket for married couples with a combined age of at least 88. This 'double ticket' can be bought anytime from September 1-May 31 for use from October 1-June 30. It is not valid during peak travel periods in late Dec/early Jan, late March/early April, and Golden Week (late April/early May).

The pass allows unlimited travel on all JR trains in first-class carriages (Green cars) and is valid for two people for either five days (¥80,500), seven days (¥99,900) or twelve days (¥124,400) days. The pass includes the use of B-class sleeping berths on overnight rail services but does not include the Nozomi shinkansen. For foreign visitors to Japan the standard Green Japan Rail Pass is as a rule better value than the Full Moon Pass (two 7-day Green Japan Rail Passes cost ¥75,600 and two 14-day Green Passes ¥122,400) but it is worth considering if you have not bought, or are not eligible for, the former. To purchase a Full Moon Green Pass, from major stations or travel agents in Japan, you need to show proof of age and marriage in the form of a health-insurance card or passport.

The **Kansai Thru Pass** allows unlimited travel between Kyoto, Nara, Osaka, Himeji, Koya-san, Kobe, and Kansai International Airport. The pass (2 days, ¥3800; 3 days, ¥5000) is valid on 32 private rail and bus companies but travel on JR services is not permitted.

For further information check 🖥 www.surutto.com. Also check the website for an up-to-date list of locations where you can buy the pass; points of sale include Kansai International Airport and Kyoto station.

🏯 Separation of the sexes

In 2000, Keio Electric Railway, a private rail company which operates in the Tokyo metropolitan area, introduced women-only carriages on late-night trains in a bid to counter the threat of male gropers. At first introduced only for a trial period, the carriages proved so popular that the service has expanded to other Keio lines. JR East has also introduced a similar service on Saikyo, Rinkai, Chuo, Ome, Hachiko and Joban/Chiyoda line trains (all in the Tokyo area).

Service hours vary; on some lines there are women-only carriages on inbound trains in the morning rush hour whilst others just include them in the evening.

tram line and on JR trains in the metropolitan area. Alternatively the Toei and Tokyo Metro 'Common One-day Ticket' (¥1000) offers unlimited use of all Toei Tokyo Metro lines for one day. If in Tokyo for a month or more, consider the one-month Tokyo Metro All-Line Pass (¥16,820), valid on all Tokyo Metro lines.

If you prefer a guided tour of the city, **Sky Bus** (☎ 03-3215 0008, 🖥 www.sky bus.jp) operates a one-hour, open-top red double-decker bus tour, taking in the area around the Imperial Palace (see p91) and Ginza (see p101). The ticket counter for same-day reservations is on the first floor of the Mitsubishi Building, across from the Marunouchi South entrance of Tokyo station. The bus leaves (hourly departures, 10am-6pm, ¥1200) from in front of the Mitsubishi Building.

Hato Bus (🖥 www.hatobus.com/tour) offers a variety of half- and full-day bus tours in and around Tokyo. Check the website for details.

Internet

There are hundreds if not thousands of internet cafés around the city, though the turnover rate is high. Tokyo TIC publishes an as up-to-date list as possible of internet cafés.

Where to stay

Accommodation is available all over Tokyo but this guide recommends the Asakusa district. Apart from being a very atmospheric area to stay, there are places to suit all budgets and the location is good for exploring the city. From Tokyo station, take the Yamanote line to Ueno, change to the Ginza subway line and get off at Asakusa (the last stop).

Accommodation in Asakusa (see map p104) *Taito Ryokan* (☎ 03-3843 2822, 🖥 www.libertyhouse.gr.jp) has only a few tatami rooms (with common bath) in an old building but it is centrally located. The manager is extremely friendly and will help

🏯 Comprehensive railway map

If you plan to travel extensively around Tokyo look out in larger bookstores for a very useful map (¥250) called **Railways of the Tokyo Metropolitan District**, showing all the rail lines (JR, private and subway) in and around Tokyo, Yokohama (see p110) and Kamakura (see p112). One side is in English and the other Japanese.

you get the most out of your stay in Tokyo. A nightly rate of ¥3000 (no meals) makes this one of Tokyo's real bargains. Single guests may be asked to share rooms. *Tokyo Ryokan* (☎ 090-8879 3599, 🖳 www.tokyo ryokan.com, tokyoryokan@ruby.dti.ne.jp) is a very characterful place in a somewhat delapidated-looking building offering similar hospitality to and at exactly the same rate as Taito Ryokan.

Ryokan Shigetsu (☎ 03-3843 2345, 🖳 www.shigestsu.com) is a great place just off the arcade which leads up to Senso-ji. The top-floor public bath has a view of the temple's five-storey pagoda. Western singles go from ¥7665, with tatami rooms for two at ¥15,750 (no meals).

If you're looking for a Western-style hotel, *Hotel Skycourt Asakusa* (☎ 03-3875 4411, 🖳 www.skyc.jp/hotel-e.htm, asakusa @skyc.jp; ¥8085/S, ¥15,015/Tw) has unremarkable boxy singles and twins. Take bus No 42 from outside Matsuya department store and get off at 'Asakusa 7-chome', right outside the hotel. At the luxury end of the market is *Asakusa View Hotel* (☎ 03-3847 1111, 🖳 www.viewhotels.co.jp/asa kusa; ¥15,000/S, ¥28,000/D).

Finally, for an authentic Edo experience try *Sukeroku no Yado Sadachiyo Ryokan* (☎ 03-3842 6431, 🖳 www.sada chiyo.co.jp). The ryokan is everything you imagine a Japanese inn to be. Tatami rooms have attached bath and toilet and are decorated with antiques from the Edo period. Prices are per person, with two people paying a minimum of ¥9500 each for a standard room; add another ¥8500/pp for two meals. Look for the rickshaw parked outside.

Not far from Asakusa is the 40-bed *Tokyo Sumida-gawa Youth Hostel* (☎ 03-3851 1121, 🖳 www.jyh.or.jp/english/kan to/sumida/index.html, 🖳 tokyo.yh@vesta .ocn.ne.jp; ¥3000/4000); meals are not served at this hostel. Take the east exit of JR Asakusabashi (one stop from JR Akhibara station on the JR Sobu line; see map p98).

Accommodation in Shinjuku (see map p98)
Shinjuku has several world-class hotels. One of the best value is *Hotel Century Hyatt* (☎ 03-3349 0111, 🖳 www

.hyatt.com; rooms from ¥21,400, check website for packages), nine minutes on foot from the west exit of Shinjuku station. A free shuttle bus operates between the hotel and the west exit of the station. Rooms are spacious and facilities include several restaurants and a top-floor pool. A sleek alternative is the *Park Hyatt Tokyo* (☎ 03-5322 1234, 🖳 www.parkhyatttokyo.com; from ¥46,800/Tw, check website for packages), used as the location for Sofia Coppola's critically acclaimed film, *Lost In Translation*. Closest to Nishi-Shinjuku station on the Marunouchi subway line but in walking distance of Shinjuku station is *Nishitetsu Inn Shinjuku* (☎ 03-3367 5454, 🖳 www.n-inn.jp/info/shinjuku; ¥10,300/S, ¥15,300/Tw), a relatively new place offering standard, clean business hotel rooms.

Accommodation around Tokyo station (see map pp98-9)
One of Tokyo's most stylish hotels is *Four Seasons Tokyo Marunouchi* (☎ 03-5222 7222, 🖳 www .fourseasons.com/marunouchi; ¥55,000/S, ¥60,000/D, check website for packages). Adjacent to the station, this 57-room boutique hotel is an ideal base for rail travellers looking for a quiet haven in the heart of the capital. Facilities include a spa and fitness studio. Style guru Tyler Brûlé calls the Four Seasons a 'benchmark among boutique-size business hotels'. Newest kid on the top-end block is the elegant *Peninsula Hotel Tokyo* (☎ 03-6270 2888, 🖳 www.pen insula.com), opened in late 2007 in **Yurakucho** opposite the Imperial Palace. The *Mandarin Oriental Tokyo* (☎ 03-3270 8800, 🖳 www.mandarin-oriental.com/ tokyo), in **Nihonbashi**, has huge rooms, impressive spa facilities, five-star service and nightly rates from around ¥45,000. Check the website for special offers.

Tokyo Station Hotel (🖳 www.tshl.co .jp), built in 1914 using 8.9 million pieces of red brick, is closed, as part of the extensive renovations of Tokyo Station, until 2011. When it reopens it will be the perfect place for rail fans to spend the night.

Accommodation in other areas (see map pp98-9)
For an unusual overnight stay

❑ Metropolitan area accommodation tax

There is a special accommodation tax in the Tokyo metropolitan area. The tax is only levied on guests who stay at hotels or inns in Tokyo where room rates are ¥10,000 or more. The tax is ¥100 for rooms costing from ¥10,000 to ¥14,999 per person per night; ¥200 for rooms costing ¥15,000 or more.

you could do worse than try *Hotel Claska* (☎ 03-3719 8121, 💻 www.claska.com; ¥10,500/S, ¥18,900/D), a five-minute taxi ride from **Meguro** station (see p94) on the JR Yamanote line. It's a small place where no two rooms are the same with a funky first-floor café-cum-DJ-lounge space. The hotel even boasts its own 'DogMan' dog-grooming salon. Pack your pooch. Weekly, monthly and long-term stay rates (for the hotel, not the salon!) are available.

The stunning *Conrad Tokyo* (☎ 03-6388 8000, 💻 www.conradhotels.com; from ¥45,000/D/Tw, check website for packages) in **Shiodome** (see box p92), is a luxury hotel; the star attraction is a Gordon Ramsay restaurant.

Tokyo International Hostel (☎ 03-3235 1107, 💻 www.tokyo-ih.jp; ¥3860/pp), on the 18th and 19th floors of Iidabashi Central Plaza, right outside the west exit of **Iidabashi** station on the JR Sobu line (transfer from Yoyogi or Akihabara on the Yamanote line), has mostly bunk-bed dorms. Breakfast costs ¥450 and dinner ¥900.

Andon Ryokan (☎ 03-3873 8611, 💻 www.andon.co.jp; ¥8190/S/D/Tw) is an upmarket but still terrific-value modern designer ryokan inn. It lies just outside downtown Asakusa. Take the JR Yamanote line to Akihabara station, change onto the Hibiya subway line to **Minowa** station, from where the ryokan is a five-minute walk. The website has a handy map.

Hotel Asia Center of Japan (☎ 03-3402 6111, 💻 www.asiacenter.or.jp) in **Akasaka** (not to be confused with Asakusa) has moderately priced Western rooms. Singles/twins cost ¥7665/11,130. Facilities include a coin laundry and an inexpensive restaurant. A buffet breakfast (¥945) is served from 7am to 10am. Take Exit No 2

of **Nogizaka** station on the Chiyoda subway line.

Several readers have recommended *Annex Katsutaro Ryokan* (☎ 03-3828 2500, 💻 www.katsutaro.com; ¥6300/S, ¥10,500/D), **Yanaka**, for its 'spacious rooms, good price, great neighbourhood, washing-machine and dryer, and internet access'. There are plenty of Japanese restaurants to choose from (unagi, okonomiyaki) near by as well as a typically Japanese shopping street. Take the Yamanote line to Nippori station; it is a 7-minute walk from the west exit of the station.

Accommodation around Narita Airport

There's no shortage of hotels in the airport vicinity, though most are overpriced. One of the best deals is *Hotel Skycourt Narita* (☎ 0478-73 6211, 💻 www.skyc.jp/narita-e.htm; ¥4300/S (Fri-Sun), ¥4700 (Mon-Thurs), ¥7200/Tw). It's a business hotel, so all rooms are private with attached bath. A free shuttle bus operates to and from Narita. Though this hotel is near the airport, there are no amenities in its immediate vicinity, so bring food with you if arriving late.

If you prefer to stay in a hotel actually on site, your only choice is *Narita Airport Rest House* (☎ 0476-32 1212, 💻 www.apo-resthouse.com, yoyaku@apo-resthouse.com; ¥7455/S, ¥10,290/Tw), a somewhat down-at-heel establishment which only has its proximity to the airport going for it. It's rather like walking into a hotel circa 1977, but the management's philosophy seems to be that they have a captive audience so there's no need to renovate. Aviation fans may like to note that the hotel is run by an in-flight catering service company, TFK. Some rooms have views of parked aircraft.

Where to eat

There are so many good places to eat at all over Tokyo that it is hard to recommend anywhere in particular. Tokyo, Shinjuku and Ikebukuro stations have attached department stores with restaurant floors which are usually open until 10pm. Ginza, Harajuku and Shibuya are good areas to wander around in search of cafés and restaurants. Tokyo also has some of the best and most expensive restaurants in Japan, many of which are in the top hotels.

If you're staying in Asakusa (see p103), there are plenty of small, atmospheric, ramen restaurants and bars that serve yakitori, fried fish and draught beer. Finally, it's hard to look anywhere in Tokyo without seeing a branch of a fast-food chain, such as McDonald's, KFC, Mos Burger and Mister Donut.

Nightlife

Tokyo is very much a 24-hour city, though there are certain areas which really only come alive after dark. You'll never be far from a bar or club in downtown Roppongi (see p103), or in Kabukicho (see p95). In the summer many hotels and department stores open rooftop beer gardens which offer two-hour all-you-can-eat-and-drink deals for around ¥3000.

If you fancy an end of holiday splurge, head for the *New York Bar* of the Park Hyatt Hotel in west Shinjuku (adjacent to the Tokyo Metropolitan Government Buildings, see p95). The gin and tonics don't come cheap but they have great live jazz and if you can secure a window table you'll get a breathtaking view of Tokyo by night and you can imagine you're Bill Murray or Scarlett Johansson from *Lost In Translation*.

Festivals and events

Senso-ji (see p103) has one of the busiest festival calendars in Japan. One of the more unusual events is the **Asakusa Samba Carnival** in late August/early September. The festival combines the Japanese culture of carrying *mikoshi* (portable shrines) with the rhythm of samba. Dancers from Brazil join in the street party.

Other festivals here are **Setsubun**, in February, when people throw soy beans around while shouting 'Oni wa soto! Fuku wa uchi' (Fortune in! Devils out!) to say goodbye to winter and welcome in spring and **Kiku Kuyo**, in October, when the temple area is filled with displays of chrysamthemums. **Sanja Matsuri** happens in the Asakusa area in mid-May; this is one of the biggest festivals in Tokyo and it features mikoshi processions.

Sumo tournaments (see p44) are held in Tokyo in January, May and September at Ryogokyu Kokugikan. The Emperor's Palace moat area is one of the main **cherry-blossom viewing** areas in March and the Sumida River is the location for Tokyo's biggest **firework display** (Hanabi Taikai) in late July.

SIDE TRIPS FROM TOKYO

Yokohama (see also p128)

Yokohama was a small fishing village in the Edo period but its place in history came when it was the location for the signing of the Japan-US Treaty of Peace and Amity in February 1854, less than a year after Commodore Perry (see p39) had arrived in the area demanding the Japanese open their ports to trade. Yokohama port was officially opened to foreign trade in 1859 and it was not long before representatives of other nationalities had also moved into the residential area designated for foreigners.

The more interesting areas to visit are Sakuragicho, for a taste of the 21st century, and Ishikawa-cho for a bit of history; both are on the JR Keihin-Tohoku/Negishi Line and are about 45 minutes from Tokyo. From Shin-

Yokohama take the JR Yokohama line to Sakuragicho but for Ishikawa-cho it is necessary to change at Higashi-Kanagawa and transfer to the JR Keihin-Tohoku/Negishi Line (about 25 mins in all).

The area around Yokohama Station is mostly department stores and offices. However, there is a **tourist information** office on the East–West walkway (daily 9am-7pm), as well as at Shin-Yokohama station (see p128), in the Minato Mirai Information centre (daily 9am-7pm) outside Sakuragicho station, and in the Sangyo Boeki Center (Mon-Fri 9am-5pm) near Yamashita-koen (see below). The tourist information offices have a number of leaflets and a very useful map of the area. Alternatively visit 🖳 www.welcome.city.yokohama.jp/eng.

Sakuragicho Home to Minato Mirai 21 (MM21), a city within a city featuring hotels, restaurants, shopping complexes and museums, this area all looks very different to how it must have been in 1872, when it opened as a terminus for Japan's first rail line between Tokyo and Yokohama. From Sakuragicho station it is an easy walk – a lot of it on a moving walkway – to the **Landmark Tower** where a lift (daily 10am-9pm, to 10pm on Saturdays and July-August, ¥1000) will whisk you in seconds to the Sky Garden Observatory (on the 69th floor). Also in the Minato Mirai 21 area is an amusement park, **Yokohama Cosmo World** (daily 11am-9pm Mar-Nov, weekends only Dec-Feb), with a 112.5m-high Ferris wheel, one of the tallest in Japan, but see p93.

Ishikawa-cho This is the best stop for **Chinatown**; turn left out of the station and follow the signs to Chinatown – this effectively means following the road around, over a bridge and then going straight on. Once in Chinatown proper the street is pedestrianized; you should then follow the signs to **Yamashita-koen** (Yamashita Park) which is also basically straight on; you'll know you're there when you see the sea. In total the walk should take 15-20 minutes.

Yamashita-koen-dori, the road running alongside the park, is interesting to stroll along. The main building of **Hotel New Grand** (see box below) is the only original hotel building left in Yokohama; the facade is virtually unchanged since it was built in 1927.

Beyond the hotel is **Toda Peace Memorial Hall**, which was originally English House No 7 and is the only foreign trading house remaining from before the Great Kanto earthquake. Josei Toda, a Buddhist and educationalist, wanted nuclear bombs abolished and the museum (daily 11am-7pm, free) here is operated by young people as a museum for peace and anti-war. **The Silk Museum** (Tue-Sun, 9am-4:30pm, ¥500) is in English House No 1, the former Jardine

---

⛩ **A Grand life**
In Yokohama, we decided to scrap any notion of being on a budget and treated ourselves to a stay at the **Hotel New Grand** (☎ 045-681 1841, 🖳 www.hotel-new-grand.co.jp; ¥20,000/Tw). It's right by Chinatown, with great views of Minato Mirai, the Landmark Tower, Yamashita Park and the *Hikawa Maru* ship. For the best Irish Coffee and the coolest, most original, bar in the world, go to *Takemi* in Chinatown.
Tina Hirschbühl, Switzerland

Matheson and Company building, where exhibits show the silk production process and everything else you need to know about the industry.

From here turn back and walk into the park itself. On the left is the **International Passenger Terminal**. The park is a very pleasant place for a rest, particularly watching the boats and cruise ships coming and going. The *Hikawu Maru* – a NYK Line passenger liner on the Yokohama to Seattle and Vancouver route – is moored permanently at the other end of the park to commemorate the centenary of the port. Not far away is the **Marine Tower** which has a 106m-high observatory floor. A combined ticket to visit both costs ¥1300; separately *Hikawu Maru* is ¥800 and the Marine Tower ¥700.

Soon after the Marine Tower you pass **Yokohama Doll Museum** (Tue-Sun 10am-5pm, ¥300) housing over 9000 dolls from around the world. From here follow signs to **Minato no Mieru Oka Koen** (Harbour View Park), which is on the other side of Hori-kawa (Hori River). Climb up the steps into the park and you will soon come to the ruins of the **French Consul's house**. The house was built in the 1860s but demolished in 1972. Keep walking through the park but head to the right and then out on to the road.

At the junction with the traffic lights turn right and head towards **Yokohama Foreigners Cemetery** (🖳 www.yfgc-japan.com; weekends and national holidays only, Mar-Dec 12-4pm). Over 4000 people from about 40 countries are buried here and even if it is not open it is worth going to look at the inscriptions on the graves you can see from the main entrance. From here it is an easy walk down through Motomachi and back to Ishikawa-cho station – just follow the signs.

Kamakura

Kamakura, a small town by the sea one hour south of Tokyo, is packed with temples and shrines and makes for a relaxed escape from the nearby city. It became the seat of feudal government in the 12th century after the struggle for power between the rival Taira and Minamoto clans was won by Minamoto Yoritomo (see p37).

Although its importance as a national power base faded many centuries ago, Kamakura is known for its **Great Buddha** (Daibutsu), an 11.4m-high bronze statue of the Buddha built in 1252, the second largest in Japan after the one in Nara (see p224). Kamakura's manageable size, open spaces, variety of temples and nearby beaches make it one of the best side trips from Tokyo.

To reach Kamakura by JR take a local train along the Yokosuka line from Tokyo station (4-5/hour; 53 mins; ¥890), however, a number of temples worth visiting are best accessed from Kita-Kamakura which is the last stop before Kamakura itself. The private Odakyu railway runs services from Shinjuku (see p95) to Fujisawa, where you change on to the Enoden line (see opposite) to reach Kamakura (¥715).

An alternative rail experience

An interesting round trip involves getting off the Yokosuka line at Ofuna (look out for the Kannon statue on the right as you enter the station) and transferring to the 6.6km long Shonan Monorail (follow the signs; 6/hr, 15 mins, ¥300).

The **Shonan Monorail** is unusual in that the train is suspended below the track so you get the experience of 'flying' but are actually only about 10 metres above ground level. For the best views try to sit at the front or back of the train. The line ends at Shonan-Enoshima; turn right at the bottom of the steps down from the platform and then left out of the station. Walk straight down until you see Enoshima Enoden station on your left.

The **Enoden line**, a single-track railway opened in 1902, runs between Fujisawa and Kamakura (about 10km). Both old-fashioned and modern train-sets are used so it is pot luck what you get but even so the journey is a pleasant one along the coast – at times the track passes so close to houses it almost feels intrusive. If planning to visit the Great Buddha (see opposite) it is best to get off at Hase (Enoshima to Hase ¥250, 20 mins 5/hr) from where the Buddha is a 10-minute walk, otherwise stay on till Kamakura, another five minutes. Enoden Kamakura station is adjacent to JR Kamakura from where you can take the Yokosuka line back to Ofuna and Tokyo.

Tokyo Disney Resort

Only a short journey by train from Tokyo station, but a world away from the commuter belt which surrounds it, is Tokyo Disney Resort. The main attraction, Tokyo Disneyland, opened in 1983 as an almost exact copy of the original in Anaheim, California, which opened in 1955. A one-day passport costs ¥5800 (12-17 years ¥5000, 4-11 ¥3900). The After 6 Passport (¥3100) offers reduced price entry on week nights after 6pm and the Starlight Passport (¥4700, 12-17 years ¥4100, 4-11 ¥3200) is available at weekends/holidays for admission after 5pm.

Tokyo DisneySea (theme: the myths and legends of the sea) followed in 2001 as the second resort theme park, the highlight of which – at least for white-knuckle junkies – is the Tower of Terror ride. Ticket prices for DisneySea are the same as for Disneyland. A two-day combined passport, which allows entry to both parks, costs ¥10,000 (12-17 years ¥8800, 4-11 ¥6900).

The nearest train station is Maihama on the JR Keiyo line (take the train direct from Tokyo station). For opening hours call ☎ 0473-54 0001, or check the website ▣ www.tokyodisneyresort.co.jp.

Hakone

The private Odakyu Railway (▣ www.odakyu.jp/english) runs services from Odakyu Shinjuku station (connected to JR Shinjuku) to Hakone, an area of lakes, trees and mountains 90km west of Tokyo, between Mt Fuji and the Izu Peninsula. Rail tickets, accommodation and one-/two-day package tours of the region can be booked at the Odakyu Sightseeing Service Center (☎ 03-5321 7887, ▣ welcome@odakyu-dentetsu.co.jp, daily, 8am-6pm), on the ground floor concourse by the west exit of Odakyu Shinjuku station. This centre is designed for foreign visitors to Japan and staff speak English. Best value is the **Hakone Free Pass**, a package ticket which includes return rail travel from Shinjuku to Hakone. The pass is valid for three days and for a variety of modes of transport in Hakone. The trip doesn't have to be particularly strenuous since you get to make a loop of the area via a mountain railway, funicular and rope-way (see box p52), from which there are excellent views of Mt Fuji if the weather cooperates.

Apart from the scenery, one of the highlights is a trip on board one of the kitsch but fun **Hakone Sightseeing Ships** (⌨ www.hakone-kankosen.co.jp), which convey you around Lake Ashi; a lake formed by the eruption of a volcano. Replica 17th-century pirate ships do the full circuit (¥1780; about 100 mins) and a Mississippi side-wheeler steamboat does a trip round the southern half of the lake (¥1220; about 40 minutes); boats leave daily every 40 minutes between 9.30am and 5pm Apr to Nov, every 50 mins and to 4pm Nov to Apr. It's just about possible to do all this in a day if you make an early start from Shinjuku but an overnight stay would be more relaxing.

From Shinjuku the Hakone Free Pass costs ¥5500 (children ¥2750). Rail-pass holders can save over ¥1000 by taking a shinkansen from Tokyo west along the Tokaido line as far as Odawara (see p128) and then transferring to the Odakyu railway for the rest of the journey to Hakone. The pass includes the journey by regular Odakyu trains from Shinjuku to Hakone-Yumoto (change trains in Odawara) but for an ¥870 supplement each way you can take the more luxurious Romance Car LEX which is slightly faster, runs direct to Hakone-Yumoto and is well worth the additional expense.

From Odawara the pass costs ¥4130 (children ¥2070). It's even cheaper if you travel between Monday and Friday, though in this case the pass is only valid for two days (from Shinjuku: adults ¥4700, children ¥2350; from Odawara: adults ¥3410, children ¥1700). The weekday pass is not sold during peak holiday times (Mar 19th-Apr 10th, Apr 28th-May 5th, Jul 19th-Aug 31st, Dec 29th-Jan 3rd).

If you're staying/travelling for any length of time in the Hakone area, it's worth getting hold of the **Mt Fuji Welcome Card** (see box p53) which gives discounts on some attractions in the area.

Nikko

Some 150km by rail north of Tokyo lies the temple and shrine town of Nikko, where the star attraction is the grand **Toshogu Shrine**, originally built in 1616 as a mausoleum for Tokugawa Ieyasu, founder of the Tokugawa shogunate. The first shrine was rebuilt a few years later in 1636 on the orders of Ieyasu's grandson, Iemitsu, who wanted an even more grand and everlasting memorial to his grandfather. As much as the colourful opulence of the shrine complex, it's Nikko's location, in the mountains and surrounded by lakes and waterfalls, which attracts the crowds, particularly in the autumn and for the shrine's main festival in mid-October.

By JR (and for rail-pass holders) the best way of reaching Nikko is to take a Tohoku shinkansen as far as Utsunomiya (see p281) and then transfer to a local, Nikko-line train for the 50-minute journey to Nikko (at least one service an hour). Without a rail pass, the best way of reaching Nikko is by private Tobu Railway (⌨ www.tobuland.com/foreign for ticket reservations) direct from Asakusa station to Tobu Nikko station (two hours by rapid train, ¥1320; or 1 hour 50 minutes by LEX, ¥2620).

The best deal is the **All Nikko Pass** (¥4400) which can be bought at the Tobu Sightseeing Service Center (daily, 8am-2:30pm) at Tobu Asakusa station.

The pass is valid for four consecutive days, allows rail travel between Asakusa and Nikko, and unlimited travel on Tobu-operated buses in and around Nikko ; it also gives some discounts on attractions. Check the Tobu website for details. This special ticket is available only to foreign visitors and is a good investment if you don't have a rail pass.

A third way of getting to Nikko from Tokyo is by limited express from JR Shinjuku station (see p95) to Tobu Nikko station. This service is jointly operated by JR and Tobu, takes two hours and costs ¥3900. The **JR Tobu Nikko Kinugawa Free Kippu** (¥7800) is a joint JR/Tobu ticket which includes a round trip to Nikko by limited express from Shinjuku and unlimited travel on buses in Nikko and nearby Kinugawa. The pass is valid on three consecutive days. The route from Shinjuku is not an attractive option since services are infrequent and the journey is more expensive than from Asakusa. Rail-pass holders can travel some of the way for free but will have to pay the fare for the part of the rail line that is operated by Tobu.

Even though it is possible to visit Nikko in a day it is worth considering spending a night there, particularly if you are visiting in the autumn as the colour of the leaves is spectacular. However, Nikko's main drawback is its proximity to Tokyo which means it attracts large crowds year-round.

Osaka

INTRODUCTION

Osaka is the commercial and industrial centre of western Japan; as such it is of more appeal to the businessman than the tourist. Also, with the ancient capitals of Kyoto (see p206) and Nara (see p224) so close, there's no great incentive to stay in Osaka for very long. But with an international airport close by, Japan's third largest city (after Tokyo and Yokohama) functions as a useful gateway to the Kansai area and is less than three hours by shinkansen from the nation's capital.

The city's big historical draw is Osaka Castle but as a modern reconstruction it's nowhere near as impressive as nearby Himeji (see p235). But even a commercial city like Osaka has some surprises for the visitor willing to make the effort: an open-air museum of traditional farm houses (see p116) perfectly captures the tranquility of life well before the industrial revolution, while the city's spectacular aquarium (see p120), the best of its kind in Japan, affords a truly breathtaking view of life in the depths of the ocean. And while Tokyo is home to Disneyland, Osaka plays host to a more modern thrills-and-spills theme park: Universal Studios Japan (see p117) on Osaka Bay.

Two good online resources for tourism in Osaka are 🖳 www.tourism .city.osaka.jp and 🖳 www.octb.jp.

⛩ **Osaka Unlimited Pass**
  If you're going to spend even just a short time in Osaka, it's worth investing in the Osaka Unlimited Pass (¥2000), which – as its name suggests! – provides unlimited use of private train lines (Hankyu, Hanshin, Nankai, Keihan and Kintetsu Railways, but not JR), subway lines and buses within Osaka city for one day as well as free admission to 25 tourist attractions in and around the city, including Osaka Castle, the Floating Garden Observatory and Osaka Museum of Housing and Living.

  It also offers discount admission to a number of other attractions, including Osaka Aquarium and the Modern Transportation Museum, and reductions at selected restaurants, shops and hotels.

  The pass can be purchased from all the tourist information offices listed on p121 and from some hotels in the city. For more details see 🖳 www.lmaga-kansai.com/en. Free admission to the 25 attractions is valid only on the same day that you use the pass for transportation.

WHAT TO SEE AND DO

Open-Air Museum of Old Japanese Farm Houses

The Open-Air Museum of Old Japanese Farm Houses (Tue-Sun 10am-5pm Mar-Oct, 10am-4:30pm Nov-Feb, ¥500) is three stops north of Shin-Osaka by subway. You can walk around this quiet wooded area and look inside 11 farmhouses collected and reassembled from all over Japan. In the houses are displays of craft and farm implements; there are bilingual signs but it's worth picking up a pamphlet at the entrance. This is a great opportunity to see something of rural Japan without having to leave the sprawling metropolis of Osaka. It's an amazingly peaceful retreat – from inside the grounds of the museum it's hard to tell you're less than ten minutes from the city. Take the Midosuji subway line from Shin-Osaka to Ryokuchi-koen station and head for the west exit which leads into Ryokuchi-koen (park). The museum is on the north side of the park, about 15 minutes on foot from the station (follow the signs).

Osaka Castle

This castle (daily, 9am-5pm, ¥600) was originally built in 1586 by Toyotomi Hideyoshi but was destroyed by fire only a few years later in 1615. It was completely reconstructed in 1629, only for the main tower to be struck by lightning and once again burnt to the ground. A further reconstruction in the 1930s suffered aerial bombardment during WWII. The *donjon* has been fully restored and is worth climbing for the views of Osaka but the displays inside are less impressive. The castle is a short walk from Osakajo-koen station on the Osaka Loop line. Taking the central exit, you'll see the castle in front of you in the distance. Extensive renovation work was carried out in 1997 and the castle tower has an elevator for wheelchair access.

Osaka Museum of Housing and Living

Osaka Museum of Housing and Living (daily except Tues/3rd Mon of month, 10am-5pm, ¥600) sounds dull but is a worth a look if you want to step back in time and see what the city was like in the Edo period (see p39). An English audio guide is available. The museum entrance is on the 8th floor of Osaka Municipal Housing Information Center, which is close to, and signposted from, Tenjinbashisuji 6-chome station on the Tanimachi and Sakai-suji subway lines.

Osaka Human Rights Museum/Liberty Osaka

Osaka Human Rights Museum (🖳 www.liberty.or.jp, daily except Mon/4th Fri of month, 10am-5pm, ¥250), also known as Liberty Osaka, focuses on people who have faced discrimination in Japan, including the country's Korean population and the Ainu (see p366). One exhibit focuses on people living with HIV/Aids. The museum is ten minutes on foot south of Ashiharabashi station on the JR Osaka Loop Line.

National Museum of Art

The National Museum of Art (🖳 www.nmao.go.jp, Tue-Sun, 10am-5pm, ¥420) is housed in a swish, modern underground facility in Osaka's Nakanoshima district. Check the website for details of special exhibitions. Take the Yotsubashi subway line to Higobashi, Exit No 2 and walk west for about ten minutes.

Modern Transportation Museum

The Modern Transportation Museum (🖳 www.mtm.or.jp, Tue-Sun, 10am-5:30pm, ¥400) is underneath Bentencho station on the Osaka Loop line. It's one of the best-organized transport museums in Japan with exhibits on the history of the railway from the steam age to the future. Boats, planes, buses and cars are given a little space, but the focus is on rail. A huge model railway periodically bursts into life, while outside there's a collection of full-size locomotives and passenger carriages. Ask for the excellent English brochure at the entrance, since nearly all the signs are in Japanese only.

Umeda Sky Building

JR Osaka station is in the Umeda area of the city. There is little here in the way of sights but it's a great place to shop and eat. Umeda Sky Building behind the station is one of Japan's most imaginative skyscrapers, with a 'Floating Garden Observatory', which affords a panoramic view of the city (daily 10am-10:30pm, ¥700).

Universal Studios Japan

One of Osaka's biggest draws is Universal Studios Japan, opened in 2001 on a 54-hectare site in Osaka Bay. Modelled on the original Universal Studios theme park in Florida, visitors are offered a similar mix of attractions and can expect long queues (though you can buy a 'Universal Express Pass Booklet' which allows you to avoid the queues for major attractions). The park has a working TV studio, and backstage production tours let visitors see behind the scenes at Japanese drama and variety shows.

A one-day passport costs ¥5800 and a two-day passport is ¥10,000. Tickets can be purchased at the park entrance but also in advance at JR ticket offices, Lawson convenience stores, and online (see p120). Park operating hours vary depending on the season (extended opening hours in summer) (cont'd on p120)

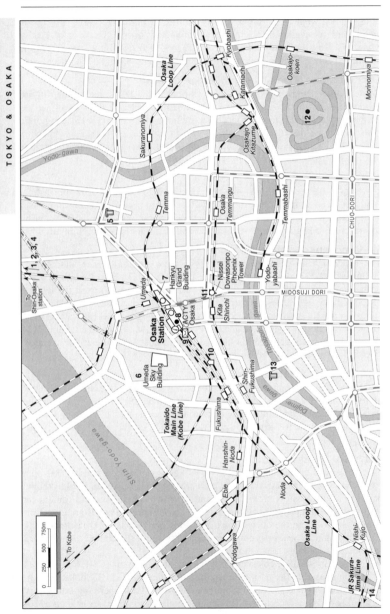

Osaka Loop Line

Kyobashi

Katamachi

Osakajo-koen

Morinomiya

Sakuranomiya

Osakajo Kitazume

12

Temma

Yodo-gawa

Osaka Temmangu

Temmabashi

CHUO-DORI

5

To Shin-Osaka station

1, 2, 3, 4

Umeda

Hankyu Grand Building

7

Nissei Dowasompo Phoenix Tower

11

Kita Shinchi

Yodo-yabashi

MIDOSUJI DORI

Osaka Station

8

ACTY Osaka

9

10

Shin-Fukushima

13

Umeda Sky Building

6

Tokaido Main Line (Kobe Line)

Fukushima

Hanshin-Noda

Ebie

Noda

Osaka Loop Line

Dojima-gawa

Tosabori-gawa

Shin Yodo-gawa

To Kobe

Yodogawa

Nishi-Kujo

JR Sakura-Jima Line

14

0 250 500 750m

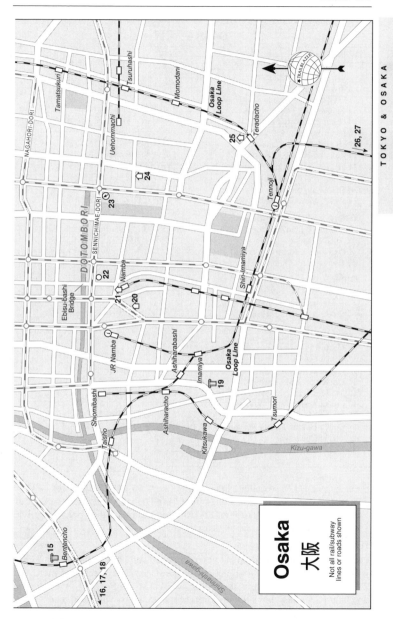

Osaka
大阪

Not all rail/subway
lines or roads shown

OSAKA 大阪

Where to stay

2	Toyoko Inn Shin-Osaka Chuo-guchi Shinkan	2	東横イン新大阪中央口新館
3	Toyoko Inn Shin-Osaka Chuo-guchi Honkan	3	東横イン新大阪中央口本館
4	Shin-Osaka Youth Hostel	4	新大阪ユースホステル
10	Hotel Monterey Osaka	10	ホテルモントレ大阪
16	Hyatt Regency Osaka	16	ハイアットリージェンシーオーサカ
20	Hotel Il Cuore Namba	20	ホテルイルクオーレなんば
21	Swissotel Nankai Osaka	21	スイスホテル南海大阪
24	Osaka International House Hotel	24	大阪国際交流センターホテル
25	Hotel 1-2-3 Tennoji	25	ホテル１－２－３天王寺
26	Osaka International YH	26	大阪国際ユースホステル
27	Osaka Municipal Nagai YH	27	大阪市立長居ユースホステル

Where to eat and drink

7	Hankyu Grand Building	7	阪急グランドビル
8	ACTY Osaka	8	アクティ大阪
11	Dynamic Kitchen & Bar Sun	11	ダイナミック キッチン＆バー 燦
22	Doutonbori Gokuraku Shoutengai	22	道頓堀極楽商店街

Other

1	Open Air Museum of old Japanese Farm Houses	1	日本民家集落博物館
5	Osaka Museum of Housing & Living	5	大阪市立住まいのミュージアム
6	Umeda Sky Building	6	梅田スカイビル
9	Central Post Office	9	中央郵便局
12	Osaka Castle	12	大阪城
13	National Museum of Art	13	国立国際美術館
14	Universal Studios Japan	14	ユニーバーサルスタジオジャパン
15	Modern Transportation Museum	15	交通科学博物館
17	Osaka Aquarium	17	海遊館
18	Osaka Maritime Museum	18	なにわの海の時空館
19	Osaka Human Rights Museum/ Liberty Osaka	19	大阪人権博物館 / リバティおおさか
23	Bean's B:t Café	23	ビーンズビットカフェエ

(cont'd from p117), so call the information line ☎ 06-6465 3000 or see 🖥 www .usj.co.jp. The park is about 250m on foot from Universal City station on the JR Sakurajima line, which starts from Nishi-Kujo station on the Osaka Loop line. The journey from Osaka station takes 15 minutes.

Bayside Osaka

Osaka Aquarium Kaiyukan (🖥 www.kaiyukan.com, daily, 10am-8pm, ¥2000) is one of the most popular attractions in the Kansai area, receiving more than 2.5 million visitors a year. After riding an escalator to the top of the building, you begin a journey down to the depths of the ocean, passing every conceivable fish along the way. Some visitors seem to take more interest in the scuba-diving cleaning staff who scrub the inside of the tanks, but the real stars are the sharks, crabs, dolphins and penguins. A particular highlight is the main 'Pacific Ocean' tank which extends down several floors, but there's also a surprise right at the end with the tanks of fluorescent floating jelly fish – this is one attraction that's worth the expense. From Bentencho on the Osaka Loop line, transfer to the Chuo subway line and get off at Osaka-ko station.

The aquatic theme continues at **Osaka Maritime Museum** (💻 www.jik ukan.or.jp, Tue-Sun, 10am-5pm, ¥600), in a huge glass dome and accessed through a tunnel under Osaka Port. The museum shows how ships and ports developed in Osaka and around the world – a celebration of man's triumph on the high seas. The museum centrepiece is a full-scale reproduction of the *Naniwamaru*, an Edo-period cargo vessel. Four floors of exhibits are built around the 30m-long ship; one of the most popular attractions is a virtual Venetian gondola ride. Take the Chuo subway to Osaka-ko then transfer to the OTS line and go one stop to Cosmosquare.

PRACTICAL INFORMATION
Arrival and departure
Getting to and from Kansai Airport

The fastest way of accessing Osaka (and Kyoto) is **by rail**; Kansai Airport station is directly connected to the terminal building. The blue half of the station is run by Japan Rail; the red half by the private Nankai Railway. JR's Haruka LEX (see Table 2, p457) takes 75 minutes to Kyoto (¥3290) and stops on the way at Tennoji (¥2070, 33 mins) and Shin-Osaka (¥2780, 50 mins). Fares listed are for reserved seats. A 'rapid' service (slower than the Haruka) also operates to Osaka station (¥1160, 65 mins). Nankai operates the limited express 'rapi:t' train from Kansai to Osaka Namba station (¥1390, 29 mins) where you can transfer to the subway. Rail passes are not valid on the rapi:t.

Limousine **bus services** (💻 www.kate .co.jp/pc/english/english.html) run between the airport and various destinations in the Kansai region, including Osaka, Kyoto and Nara. Bus stops are located outside International Arrivals and tickets can be purchased from vending machines outside the terminal building.

Tourist information

There are tourist information desks – known as 'Osaka Visitors' Information Centers' – at Shin-Osaka (☎ 06-6305 3311, 8am-8pm), Osaka (☎ 06-6345 2189, 8am-8pm), Tennoji (☎ 06-6774 3077, 8am-8pm), JR Namba (☎ 06-6643 2125, 8am-8pm) and JR Universal City (☎ 06-4804 3824, 9am-8pm). The office at JR Osaka station is hard to find; it's in a booth outside Midosuji exit, close to Hankyu department store. All the tourist offices are staffed by English speakers who can provide you with a city map and subway plan. If you need information on travel outside Osaka, it's better to visit Kansai TIC at the airport.

Getting around

The main railway junctions are **Shin-Osaka**, the shinkansen station to the north of the city, **Osaka**, further south in Umeda, and **Tennoji**. Osaka and Tennoji stations are both on the Osaka Loop line. The **Osaka Loop line** (orange colour trains; departures from platforms 1 and 2 at JR Osaka station) is the most useful means of getting around the city with a rail pass.

The **subway** is convenient for reaching places off the Loop line. A one-day pass costs ¥850; it allows unlimited use of the subway and city buses. On the 20th of every month (the following day if the 20th is a Sunday or public holiday) as well as every Friday you can purchase a 'No My Car Day Pass' for ¥600 (same validity as the ¥850 pass).

If you arrive at Shin-Osaka by shinkansen, transfer to a local train for the short ride to Osaka station. Osaka station is large and confusing but there are plenty of coin lockers in the main concourse areas and a JR information desk by the main ticket barrier. The platforms are as follows: 1 and 2 for the Osaka Loop Line; 5 and 6 for Sannomiya (Kobe) and Himeji; 7 and 8 for Shin-Osaka and Kyoto; 11 for Fukui, Kanazawa and Toyama.

Internet
There are several internet cafés in the vicinity of JR Osaka station. Ask for a list at the tourist information office (see p121).

Convenient if you are staying at Osaka International House Hotel (see column opposite) is **Bean's B:t Café** (☎ 06-6766 3566, 🖳 www.interfarm.co.jp/cafe, daily except 1st/3rd Sun, 10am-9pm), in Tennoji charges foreign visitors ¥250 for 30 minutes' surfing. They also have a good selection of drinks and set breakfast/lunch deals. The nearest station is Tanimachi 9-chome on the Tanimachi subway line.

Where to stay
For luxury accommodation, try **Hyatt Regency Osaka** (☎ 06-6612 1234, 🖳 www .hyatt.com) on Osaka Bay. It has all the facilities you would expect: indoor and outdoor pools, a state-of-the-art health/fitness centre and a choice of restaurants. Rates for twin rooms start at ¥11,700. The Hyatt Regency is an official Universal Studios Japan hotel and packages including overnight accommodation/entrance to the theme park are available. A limousine bus for Kansai Airport (¥1300) stops right outside the hotel. Or from Bentencho on the Osaka Loop line, take the Chuo subway line to Osaka-ko and transfer to the New Tram line to Nakafuto, from where the hotel is a two-minute walk.

Swissotel Nankai Osaka (☎ 06-6646 1111, 🖳 www.swissotel.com), directly above Namba station, is a haven of luxury where twins go from ¥17,000. Check the website for details of special packages, some of which include treatments at the hotel's top-end Amrita Spa facility.

Hotel Monterey Osaka (☎ 06-6458 7111, 🖳 www.hotelmonterey.co.jp/osaka;

¥15,015/S, ¥27,720/Tw) is an upmarket European-style hotel close to JR Osaka station. There is a choice of Italian, French, Chinese and Japanese restaurants; rooms are spacious with tiled or wooden floors.

Toyoko Inn Shin-Osaka Chuo-guchi Shinkan (☎ 06-6303 1045, 🖳 www.toyo ko-inn.com; ¥6510/S, ¥8610/D/ Tw) is part of the popular nationwide chain where the rates include breakfast. It's five minutes on foot from the main exit of JR Shin-Osaka station. **Toyoko Inn Shin-Osaka Chuo-guchi Honkan** (☎ 06-6305 1045, 🖳 www. toyoko-inn.com) has the same rates as its sister hotel next door.

Osaka International House Hotel (☎ 06-6773 8181, 🖳 www.inter-hotel.jp/new/ index.html, i-house@inter-hotel.jp) has good-value, spacious singles for ¥6500 and twins for ¥12,000 with attached bath, aircon and bilingual TV. There's a restaurant, and an information centre staffed by English speakers. The hotel is a 10-minute walk south from Tanimachi 9-chome station on the Tanimachi subway line.

A good budget choice is **Hotel 1-2-3 Tennoji** (☎ 06-6770 2345, 🖳 www.hotel 123.co.jp/english/tennouji.html), which has clean, compact singles with attached bath for ¥5145. The rate for two adults sharing a room is ¥6195, and two adults plus one child is ¥7245. All rates include breakfast. Take the Osaka Loop line to Teradacho. Leave the station, cross to the other side of the road (McDonald's is opposite the exit) and turn left. The hotel is a minute's walk up the road, on the third street on your right.

Hotel Il Cuore Namba (☎ 06-6647 1900, 🖳 www.ilcuore.info, ilcuore@hot wire.co.jp; ¥8500/S, ¥13,000/D, ¥15,000/ Tw) is conveniently located for Nankai's Namba station, with plenty of economical eating places nearby. Its design has a bit more flair than your average business hotel. The 11th floor is for ladies only. Book online for discounts on the published room rates. Breakfast is ¥1000. Coin laundry available.

Osaka International Youth Hostel (☎ 0722-65 8539, 🖳 www.osaka-yha.com/ osakakokusai) is on the south side of

> ❏ **Business-hotel accommodation**
> A useful website if you're looking for business-hotel accommodation in and around Osaka is 🖳 www.hotwire.jp, an online reservation service which is regularly updated with the best deals and special packages.

Hamadera Park, south of Osaka city. It's a large, modern hostel with excellent facilities and charges ¥3300/4300 for dormitory accommodation, with breakfast at ¥630 and dinner at ¥1050. Internet access is available (¥100/15 mins). Take the Loop line to Tennoji and transfer to the JR Hanwa line to Otori. From here, transfer to the Higashi-Hagoromo line and go one stop to the terminus at Higashi-Hagoromo. From here, walk towards Hamadera Park and follow the signs to the hostel.

Shin-Osaka Youth Hostel (☎ 06-6370 5427, 🖳 www.osaka-yha.com/shin-osaka, shin-osaka@jyh.or.jp) has 126 beds and costs ¥3300; supper is ¥1050 and breakfast ¥480 (¥300 for YH/HI members and foreign guests). Reception is on the 10th floor of the Koko Plaza Building, a short walk from the east exit of Shin-Osaka station. The hostel website has a useful map showing the route on foot from the station.

Osaka Municipal Nagai Youth Hostel (☎ 06-6699 5631, 🖳 www.nagaiyh.com/english) is in Nagai Park south of the city. It's a modern hostel (100 beds), built on the side of Nagai Stadium, home to Osaka's J-League soccer team. The nightly rate for dormitory accommodation is ¥2500 or a private room is ¥3000. Breakfast costs ¥420 and dinner ¥735. The hostel closes occasionally, so call ahead. From Shin-Osaka, take the Midosuji subway line to Nagai (exit No 1). Alternatively, take the JR Hanwa line to Nagai station. Head for the stadium and walk around it until you reach the hostel entrance.

If you need to stay near Kansai Airport, *Kanku Hineno Station Hotel* (☎ 0724-60 1911, 🖳 www.hotwire.co.jp/hineno; ¥6800/S, ¥9500/D, and ¥10,000/Tw) is right outside JR Hineno station, ten minutes by local train from the airport. It has comfortable rooms that include bilingual TV. A free hotel shuttle bus runs to the airport.

Alternatively, if you prefer to stay at the airport itself, *Hotel Nikko Kansai Airport* (☎ 0724-55 1111, 🖳 www.nikkokix.com; from ¥9500/S, ¥14,000/Tw) is an upmarket place less than a stone's throw from the terminal building. Book online and as far as possible in advance for the cheapest deals.

Where to eat
There's endless choice in the area around JR Osaka station in Umeda, particularly for lunch-time deals. The best place to hunt around is **ACTY Osaka** (🖳 www.acty-osaka.co.jp), in the same building as Daimaru department store in front of the Midosuji side of Osaka station. The **Sky Restaurant Floor** (the 27th floor) has a choice of restaurants and (free) views of Osaka. On the 16th is the **World Restaurant Floor**, with a wide variety of places to eat including Russian, Chinese, Japanese, Mexican and Italian. Hankyu Grand Building, also close to Osaka station, has two floors of **restaurants** (28th and 29th floors).

In the same area, and affording great city-by-night views from its 27th-floor location in the Nissei Dowasonpo Phoenix Tower building, is *Dynamic Kitchen & Bar Sun* (🖳 www.dynac-japan.com/sun, daily 11:30am-3pm, 5-11pm), with a huge selection of meat, fish and vegetarian dishes from ¥800. An English menu is available. It's a popular place for locals to meet friends and unwind after work.

Nightlife
The **Kita area**, around JR Osaka station, is busy after dark and packed with restaurants and bars. However, the main centre for nightlife is **Dotombori**, on the southern side of Dotombori Canal in the Minami (southern) district of the city. A useful point of reference and a good place to start a

⛩ **Pot noodle**

Osaka is the undisputed instant-noodle capital of Japan, if not the world. The city's association with the global phenomenon that is pot noodle can be traced back to 1958, when Osaka inventor and businessman Momofuku Ando (1910-2007) launched Chicken Ramen, the world's first instant noodle dish. Generations of students around the world have Ando to thank for inventing the Cup Noodle in 1971, a mass-market product in a polystyrene pot which remains today one of the world's most instantly recognizable supermarket-shelf items. Nissin, the company Ando founded in 1948, has grown to become one of Japan's largest and most successful companies, selling in excess of 85 billion instant-noodle products in 70 countries each year.

In 1999 Ando opened the **Momofuku Ando Instant Ramen Museum** (💻 www .nissin-noodles.com) in his home city of Ikeda, near Osaka, where noodle fans can wallow shamelessly in chicken-ramen nostalgia. As if to prove in his old age that Ando was anything but living on past success, in 2005 his company made history when it developed Space Ram, a vacuum-packed Cup Noodle given to Japanese astronaut Soichi Noguchi as an in-flight meal on board the US space shuttle *Discovery*.

night out is Ebisu-bashi, a bridge which spans Dotombori Canal. From here, the canal is brightly lit up by competing neon signs and the streets surrounding it are packed with cinemas, cheap eateries, clubs and bars. A great place to head at the end of a day of sightseeing is *Doutonbori Gokuraku Shoutengai* (💻 www.douton bori-gokuraku.com, daily 11am-11pm; ¥315), a food, drink, shopping and entertainment theme park which recreates Taisho-era Osaka (1912-26) on several floors of a building near Ebisu-bashi bridge. Here you can find everything from takoyaki to okonomiyaki. After paying the ¥315 entry fee, you are given a swipe card to use at all the restaurants and shops and then pay at the end.

Festivals

The biggest event in Osaka's busy festival calendar is the **Tenjin Matsuri** which takes place from July 24th to 25th. The highlight is a procession of more than 100 brightly coloured boats down Dojima-gawa on the evening of the 25th. Also, performances of traditional dance and music are staged on a boat lit by lanterns and moored in the middle of the river.

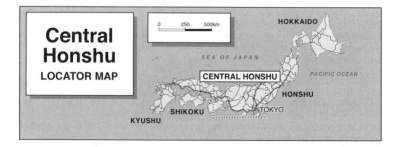

Central Honshu

LOCATOR MAP

0   250   500km

HOKKAIDO

SEA OF JAPAN

CENTRAL HONSHU

PACIFIC OCEAN

HONSHU

KYUSHU

SHIKOKU

TOKYO

Central Honshu – route guide

INTRODUCTION

Culturally rich and geographically diverse, central Honshu is a vast land area stretching from the Pacific Ocean in the south to the Sea of Japan in the north. If this region is Japan's beating heart, the Tokaido line which runs along the southern coast is the country's transportation artery. It is above all a functional rail line – perhaps the most functional in the world, transporting thousands of passengers every day between the business and industrial hubs of Tokyo, Nagoya and Osaka.

But it would be a great shame to restrict your travel by rail only to the Tokaido shinkansen. Much of the area along the Tokaido line is heavily built up and polluted by factories and heavy industry so, in its own way, a journey along this line offers a real taste of Japan; concrete proof that nature has indeed been spectacularly sacrificed for the industrial revolution. For many visitors who only just have the time to rush between Tokyo and Kyoto, this is all they see of the country. But just a short distance from the industrialized southern coast lie the majestic Japanese Alps. The easiest way of reaching the region and the Alps is to take a shinkansen from Tokyo to Nagano. The Central Japan rail network is fast, efficient and even in the winter months of heavy snowfall almost invariably on time.

Highlights of a tour around this region include **Takayama** (see p179), a mini-Kyoto in the mountains, the preserved Edo-period 'post towns' of **Narai** (see p137) and **Tsumago** (see p140), and **Kanazawa** (see p185), a city on the Japan Sea coast which is home to one of Japan's most celebrated gardens.

> ❑ **Welcome cards**
> Welcome cards (see box p53) for this area include the Tokai card and the Mt Fuji card.

Finally, between April and November, the **Tateyama-Kurobe Alpine Route** (see p145) offers a unique opportunity to appreciate the region's astonishing beauty in a day-long journey from the Japan Sea coast to the Japanese Alps, involving as it does a variety of modes of transport.

A one-week tour would be enough to see a couple of the highlights; two or three weeks would give you time to take in the views and explore more of what the region has to offer.

霧雨や富士を見ぬ日ぞ面白き

Foggy drizzle!
Intriguing is the day
we can't see Mt Fuji
(MATSUO BASHO)

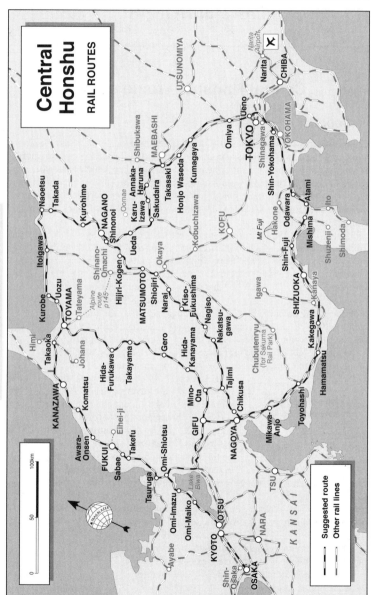

Central Honshu
RAIL ROUTES

HONSHU

Narita Airport

UTSUNOMIYA

Narita
CHIBA

Shibukawa

MAEBASHI

Omiya
Ueno
TOKYO
Shinagawa
YOKOHAMA
Shin-Yokohama

Naoetsu
Takada
Kurohime

Karu-
izawa
Annaka-
Haruna
Sakudaira
Takasaki
Honjo Waseda
Kumagaya

Hakone
Odawara
Shin-Odawara
Atami
Ito

Itoigawa
Uozu
Kurobe

NAGANO
Shinonoi
Oomae

Ueda

Kobuchizawa

KOFU
Mt Fuji
Mishima
Shuzenji
Shimoda

Shinano-
Omachi
Alpine
route p145
Tateyama

Hijiri-Kogen

Okaya

Shin-Fuji

Himi
Takaoka
TOYAMA

MATSUMOTO
Shiojiri
Narai
Kiso-
Fukushima
Nagiso
Nakatsu-
gawa

Igawa

SHIZUOKA
Kanaya

Kakegawa

Johana

Hida-
Furukawa
Takayama

Gero
Hida-
Kanayama

Chubutenryu
(for Sakuma
Rail Park)

KANAZAWA
Komatsu

Mino-
Ota
Tajimi
Chikusa

Hamamatsu

Awara-
Onsen
Eihei-ji
Sabae
Takefu

Omi-Shiotsu

GIFU

NAGOYA
Mikawa-
Anjo
Toyohashi

FUKUI
Tsuruga

Omi-Imazu
Omi-Maiko

OTSU

TSU

Ayabe

Lake
Biwa

KYOTO
NARA

KANSAI

Shin-
Osaka
OSAKA

100km
50
0

Suggested route
Other rail lines

TOKYO TO NAGOYA BY SHINKANSEN
[Table 3, pp458-60]

Distances by Hikari shinkansen from Tokyo. Fastest journey time: 2 hours.

Tokyo to Atami   [Map 1]
Tokyo   [see pp90-115]

Take a Hikari shinkansen from Tokyo west towards Nagoya, Kyoto, Osaka and Okayama. If you are travelling further west you will need to change trains at Shin-Osaka or Okayama. The only shinkansen which run all the way from Tokyo to Hakata (see p389) are the Nozomi services, for which rail passes are not valid. Rail passes are valid for Kodama shinkansen from Tokyo, but these should be avoided if possible because they stop at every station and are thus much slower.

Shinagawa (7km) Approximately half the Hikari and Nozomi services and all kodama trains call here. A few of the new N700 shinkansen services (see box p458) start/finish here instead of Tokyo station – to relieve congestion at the latter. The downside is that there is no connection with northbound Tohoku shinkansen services from here. All Tohoku bullet trains (operated by JR East) depart from Tokyo station.

If you are transferring in Tokyo onto the local JR Yamanote line, it makes sense to change here rather than at the crowded Tokyo station, since Shinagawa is smaller, easier to

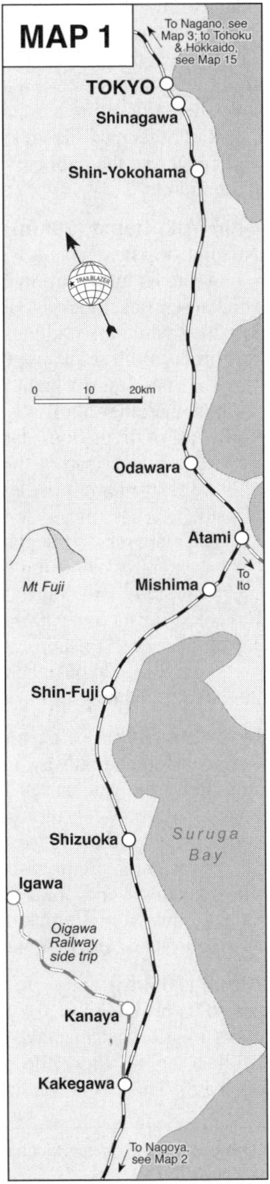

MAP 1

To Nagano, see Map 3; to Tohoku & Hokkaido, see Map 15

TOKYO
Shinagawa
Shin-Yokohama
Odawara
Atami
Mishima   To Ito
Mt Fuji
Shin-Fuji
Shizuoka   Suruga Bay
Igawa
Oigawa Railway side trip
Kanaya
Kakegawa
To Nagoya, see Map 2

0   10   20km

HONSHU

❑ **Railway robot**
To celebrate the opening of the sleek, modern Shinagawa station (the first new station on the Tokaido shinkansen in 15 years) in 2003, Sony (whose headquarters are in the Shinagawa area) sent one of its robots along to take a ride on the first bullet train to stop here. The robot, called QRIO, boarded the train, handed a ticket to the conductor and waved its hands. In doing so it became the world's first (and perhaps last?) robot passenger to travel on the bullet train.

manage and the shinkansen/conventional line platforms are closer together. Yamanote line services depart from platforms 1 and 2. There are coin lockers (all sizes) at the back of the platform side of the main JR concourse. You'll also find a selection of eateries, including a revolving sushi restaurant, as well as toilets where tips are requested though not necessarily given.

Rail buffs may like to know that a train station was first built in Shinagawa and opened to the public on May 7, 1872. Nothing remains today of the original building.

Shin-Yokohama (29km) The third station after Tokyo but not all Hikari or Nozomi stop here so check schedules before setting off.

A **tourist information office** (daily 10am-6pm, closed 1-2pm) is behind the shinkansen ticket barrier. However, the office will be closed Oct 2007 to mid-Jan 2008 while the station is redeveloped. **Coin lockers** (¥300-600) are next to this office. Both shinkansen and ordinary train lines run from this station.

The main tourist sight is the unusual **Ramen Museum** (🖳 www.raumen .co.jp/home/index.html, Wed-Mon 11am-11pm, ¥300), five minutes on foot north-east of the station – take the exit by the tourist information office (but first pick up a sketch map of the route from the office). The ground floor museum tells the story of how noodles rose from a humble beginning to embrace the global market.

The main reason the place gets packed out is the re-created ramen village in the basement; a collection of traditional ramen shops from around Japan. The most popular are ones from Sapporo (see p363) in Hokkaido and Fukuoka/Hakata (see p395) in Kyushu, the two best-known centres for ramen in Japan. The souvenir shop could be the place to pick up a few unusual mementos.

From Shin-Yokohama take a JR Yokohama line train (from platform 5; about 20 mins) to Sakuragicho (see p111) for a taste of 21st-century life in Japan.

Odawara (84km) Several Hikari stop here. In March 1886, the Zuso Jinsha Railway ('human railway') was opened between Odawara and Atami (the next stop along the shinkansen line), a distance of 25km. It took more than four hours to go between the two towns. The eight-seater coach, carried by three people, was used for 12 years until the introduction of steam locomotives.

Once an important castle town, Odawara is now a major junction on both the shinkansen and Tokaido mainlines, as well as a terminus for the private Odakyu line from Shinjuku. It's also the main gateway to **Hakone** (see p113), an area of lakes and mountains accessible as a day trip from Tokyo.

Atami (105km) Only a few Hikari stop here. Atami is a famous spa town but, due to its proximity to Tokyo, it often gets unpleasantly crowded. British travellers might want to make a pilgrimage here to the grave of 'poor Toby', a Scottish terrier whose life was tragically cut short after a visit here (see box opposite). There is no tourist information office as such but you can pick up a

---

(Opposite) The Great Buddha of Kamakura (see p112), an 11.4m-high bronze statue. (Photo © JNTO)

⛩ **Sir Rutherford Alcock and 'Poor Toby'**
Sir Rutherford Alcock, a British minister, visited Japan in 1859 and the following year climbed Mt Fuji. Clearly not a man used to modesty, Alcock stopped in Atami on his return from Fuji and had a monument built here with the inscription: 'I am the first non-Japanese to have climbed Mt Fuji and visited Atami'. It stands next to the Oyu geyser, alongside a monument to Alcock's faithful Scottish terrier Toby. Having survived the journey from Britain, Toby suffered the misfortune of standing on the piece of ground from where the geyser used to periodically erupt. The inevitable happened; the unsuspecting dog was blasted into the air by the force of the boiling water shooting out from the earth.

A distraught Alcock organized a funeral for his pet in Atami, an event which was almost certainly the origin of Britain's reputation in Japan as a nation of eccentrics. Toby was buried beside the geyser, perhaps as a warning to other mad dogs and Englishmen to beware of the danger that lurks close by. His tombstone reads simply: 'Poor Toby, 23 September 1860'. If the sign at the geyser is to be believed, the dog did not die in vain. 'At that time, Japan had a bad impression of the British people,' reads the sign. Alcock reported back to Britain that the Japanese had been very kind to him during his period of mourning and advised his country that they should not look upon Japan as an enemy. 'Thanks to his report and advice,' continues the sign, 'Great Britain's public opinion towards Japan turned favourable'.

In Toby's day the spring gushed hot water and steam six times a day, 'shaking the earth with its vigorous blasts'. During the 100 years since Alcock's visit to Atami the geyser gradually gave up and died. In 1962 it was given a new lease of (artificial) life and now goes off for three minutes at four-minute intervals.

map which lists the main sightseeing points at the View Plaza travel agency in the station. Coin lockers (¥300) are available.

Hot springs abound, with a choice of seven spas; you can pick up a stamp card (see box p48) and trek around the town visiting them all. A well-known sightseeing spot is **Oyu geyser** (see box above), which claims to be one of the three largest geysers in the world, along with the Great Caesar in Iceland and the Old Faithful in Yellowstone National Park, USA. The other main tourist draw is **MOA Museum of Art** (💻 www.moaart.or.jp, Fri-Wed, 9:30am-4:30pm, ¥1600), on a hillside overlooking Atami; accessible by bus (10 mins) from the station. It contains a large collection of woodblock prints, ceramics and gold and silver lacquerware. Tickets are slightly cheaper (¥1300) if purchased in advance from any 7-Eleven, Family Mart, or Lawson convenience store or at the View Plaza travel agency at Atami station.

In 1604, the shogun Tokugawa Ieyasu visited Atami to bathe in the hot springs. From that time on, hot spring water was dedicated to the shoguns and transported annually from Atami to Edo Castle, Chiyoda-ku, Tokyo. Celebrations are still held in commemoration of this on February 10th and October 10th.

(Opposite) Kaminarimon Gate (see p103), the main entrance to Senso-ji in Asakusa, Tokyo, marks the start of a long parade of stalls towards the main temple compound. (Photo © JNTO/© Y Shimizu)

Side trip – Atami to Shimoda

Atami is the starting point for the Ito line to **Ito**, where William Adams, the first Englishman to set foot in Japan, spent much of his life after a shipwreck off the coast of Kyushu in 1600. He became known as Anjin-san and his arrival is celebrated during the Anjin Matsuri in August. Beyond Ito, the line continues to **Shimoda** but this section of track is operated by the private Izukyu Railway so rail passes are not valid. Shimoda is the place to gaze out over the sea and imagine what it must have been like to behold Commodore Perry's 'Black Ships' in 1854 (see p39). Shimoda is the southernmost town on the Izu Peninsula; apart from Commodore Perry, it is known for its beaches and surfing.

Limited expresses depart Atami at 10:23am, 10:56am, 11:24am, 11:54am, 12:20pm, 1:23pm, 2:22pm and 4:46pm, arriving in Ito 20 minutes later and in Shimoda approximately 80 minutes after leaving Ito. From Shimoda to Atami, limited expresses depart at 9am, 9:53am, 12pm, 12:27pm, 2pm, 3pm and 4pm.

Local trains run roughly half-hourly from 5:03am to 11:04pm between Atami and Shimoda, thought some of these require a change in Ito. Local trains take 24 minutes from Atami to Ito and 60 minutes from Ito to Shimoda.

Atami to Nagoya   [Map 1, p127; Map 2, p132]

Mishima (121km) A few Hikari stop here. Mishima is an access point for the Hakone region (Lake Ashi) and Mt Fuji as well as to Shuzenji (see below). To get to **Ashino-ko** (Lake Ashi) take a Numazu Tozan Tokai bus (hourly, ¥1000, 50 mins) from bus stand 5, outside the South Exit of the station, to Moto-Hakone. From there you could take one of the sightseeing boats (see p113), or walk to Hakone-machi through part of the Ancient Cedar Avenue (cedars were planted to provide shade for travellers on the old Tokaido Highway) to the Hakone Checkpoint/Exhibition and then take a bus from bus stand 4 (by Hakone-machi pier) back to Mishima.

If intending to **climb Mt Fuji** (3776m/12,388ft), change here for a local JR train to Numazu (one stop along the Tokaido mainline towards Kyoto). Change at Numazu for the Gotemba line to Gotemba (30 mins), from where you can pick up a Fuji-kyu bus (¥1080; 45 mins) to the fifth station on Mt Fuji. It's then $6^{1}/_{2}$ hours on foot to the summit. This bus runs only during the official climbing season (Jul 1st-Aug 31st). For information on climbing Mt Fuji, see the JNTO leaflet *Mt Fuji and Fuji Five Lakes*.

A 35-minute side trip by rail can be made on the private Izu-Hakone line (¥500, rail passes not accepted) which runs some 20km south of Mishima to **Shuzenji**, another popular hot-spring town. The star attraction here is the temple, Shuzen-ji, founded in 807 by Kobo Daishi, the Buddhist monk who now lies in eternal meditation on Koya-san (see pp230-2).

Shin-Fuji (146km) Only Kodama stop here. There are hideous smoke stacks everywhere you look as you pass through Shin-Fuji, which is a shame since you expect a place with this name to afford picture-postcard views of Japan's most famous natural wonder.

Around here start looking out for views of Mt Fuji; on the right side of the train (from Tokyo) or on the left side (to Tokyo).

Shizuoka (180km) [see pp154-9]

One hikari an hour stops here. It's worth including a brief stop in Shizuoka on your itinerary.

Kakegawa (229km) Only Kodama stop here, the nearest point of access for Oigawa (see below), home to one of Japan's most spectacular steam railway lines.

Side trip to Oigawa Steam Railway [see Map 1, p127]

The Oigawa Railway began operations in 1927 to transport timber, freight and tea from the mountains along Oigawa River. During the 1960s revenue from freight began to fall as did the number of people living in the mountainous areas, so the railway turned to tourism for revenue. The preserved steam operation (top speed 65kph) runs at least once a day (more departures in high season) from Shin-Kanaya to the terminus at Senzu. Taking the steam train really is like stepping back in time. The train conductor sings old railway songs over the loudspeaker as you pass through the Oigawa tea fields. Sit on the right for views of the river.

To reach the start point for the Oigawa Railway (☎ 0547-45 4113, 🖳 www .oigawa-railway.co.jp), take a local JR train from Kakegawa two stops east to **Kanaya**; there are coin lockers (¥300) in the station. The entrance to Oigawa Kanaya station is on your right as you leave JR Kanaya station. Purchase tickets for the steam railway from here, board the train and go one stop along the Oigawa line to Shin-Kanaya station, where you transfer on to the steam locomotive for the journey to Senzu.

With time to kill waiting for the SL departure at **Shin-Kanaya**, there's a small steam museum (9am-5pm) with a few model railways, as well as a gift shop selling Oigawa tea. There's another small rail museum (10am-4pm, ¥100) at the Senzu terminus. Opposite Shin-Kanaya station is a café called *Warau Neko* (daily, 10am-8pm), easy to find as it's the only place full of good luck pottery cats, which according to the owner are supposed to bring in customers – if you're there, it's clearly worked. Alternatively, *ekiben* – in the shape of a steam train, of course – are sold before you get on the train.

At the end of the main rail line (40km) is a light railway that travels higher up into the mountains (25km) to the very end of the line at **Igawa**. Only a few families live along the light railway line (the average number of people who get on and off each stop is 0.5). Domoto station is named after the tea-producing family who live there. When a dam was constructed over 20 years ago in the area the train passes through, around 100 residents were forced to move away as villages were flooded.

Steam trains depart Kanaya at 10:02am, 11:48am and 12:47pm (they go first to Shin-Kanaya, where the journey proper commences) and arrive in Senzu at 11:25am, 1:12pm and 2:15pm. Trains depart Senzu at 2:58pm and 3:23pm and arrive in Kanaya at 4:25pm and 4:46pm. However, these times are subject to change. Kanaya to Senzu costs ¥1810 one-way (¥560 supplement to ride in the steam locomotive); Senzu to Igawa (light railway) is ¥1280 one-way.

Hamamatsu (257km) Some Hikari stop here. Located almost halfway between Tokyo and Osaka, and home to such world-famous companies as Yamaha, Suzuki and Honda. Hamamatsu is known as the 'music city', partly because of Yamaha's presence (it's said that every piano made in Japan is

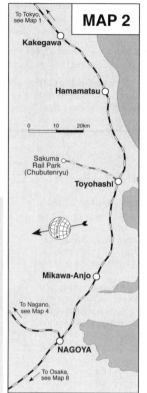

MAP 2

To Tokyo,
see Map 1

Kakegawa

Hamamatsu

0   10   20km

Sakuma
Rail Park
(Chubutenryu)

Toyohashi

Mikawa-Anjo

To Nagano,
see Map 4

NAGOYA

To Osaka,
see Map 8

built here) but also because of the number of music festivals/concerts staged here. The biggest annual festival is the Hamamatsu Matsuri (May 3rd-5th).

The **tourist information centre** (☎ 053-452 1634, 💻 http://hamamatsu-daisuki.net, daily 9am-7pm) is on the right-hand side as you exit the shinkansen side of the station. Here you'll also find **coin lockers** of all sizes. Immediately above the station is the May One shopping complex with **restaurants** on the 7th floor.

For even more dining options, head for the 8th floor of Entetsu department store, to the left as you take the Act City station exit.

The best place to get your bearings lies almost directly in front of the Act City exit of Hamamatsu station and is hard to miss: standing 212 metres high, the vast **Act City** complex is home to both the quirky **Museum of Musical Instruments** (💻 www.gakkihaku.jp, daily except 2nd Wed of the month; ¥400), which boasts a collection of more than 2000 instruments of all shapes and sizes from around the world, as well as the 45th-floor **Observation Gallery** (daily, 10am-9pm, ¥500). This is well worth the admission fee for the chance to take in the surrounding area and – if the weather is cooperating – the spectacular snow-capped cone of Mt Fuji.

Keep an eye out, too, for the imposing black and white façade of **Hamamatsu-jo** (daily, 8:30am-4:30pm, ¥150), a castle first built over 400 years ago by Japan's most celebrated warlord, Tokugawa Ieyasu (see p38). Anyone hoping for promotion at work could do worse than head straight for the castle as soon as they rejoin firm ground. According to legend, Hamamatsu-jo gained its nickname 'castle of promotion' by virtue of the fact that every feudal lord who lived inside it later went on to enjoy even higher office. There's no proof that 21st-century visitors to the castle will reap the same reward once bestowed upon its erstwhile occupants, but a trip here might just pay off after you return home.

Yamaha (☎ 053-460 2901) offers guided tours of its piano-manufacturing facilities and **Honda** (☎ 053-439 2011, 💻 www.world.honda.com/hamamatsu factory) does the same for its motorcycles.

All tours must be booked well in advance of arrival in Hamamatsu. Honda requires a minimum of 10 people.

If you need to stay in Hamamatsu, the best place is ***Hotel Okura Act City*** (☎ 053-459 0111, 🖳 http://hamamatsu.okura.com; ¥12,075/S, ¥21,000/Tw), right outside the station. The rooms are on the 32nd floor or higher, so you're guaranteed a good view. The hotel plays on the city's musical theme: everything from the yukata in your room with a musical-instrument design to the musical motif on the bathroom walls and the up/down lift signs shaped like grand pianos! The hotel has a good all-you-can-eat buffet deal for ¥2000 in the 2nd-floor Figaro coffee shop.

Hamamatsu delicacies include eel and *suppon* (soft-shelled snapping turtle), which is usually served as sashimi, in a soup or deep-fried. Local tourist literature even suggests 'brave souls should try turtle's blood mixed with saké'. But you'd probably be even braver if you tried another local specialty, eel cookies, 'made with fresh butter and crushed eel bones, eel extract or garlic mixed in. It's the most popular souvenir from Hamamatsu'.

Side trips by bus from Hamamatsu

To escape from the city, jump on a bus from the terminal outside Hamamatsu station and head 40 minutes west to **Hamana-ko**, a lagoon as famous for its stunning sunset vistas as for the variety of hot springs built around the eastern shore. Hamana-ko – open to the sea since a tidal wave ripped open the mouth of the lake in the 16th century – is celebrated in Japan as a centre for the cultivation of *unagi* (eel). Look out too for swallows which nest in and around the lake area: considered a symbol of Hamamatsu, locals say this particular bird resembles a conductor wearing a tuxedo, an appropriate symbol for Japan's city of music.

Only 15 minutes by bus (No 4 from stop No 6, ¥250) are the **Nakatajima Sand Dunes**, a conservation area for loggerhead turtles, which come to lay their eggs from early summer to autumn. The entrance to the dunes is in front of you as you leave the bus (the stop is called 'Nakatajima Sakyu'). For even more extensive sand dunes, visit Tottori (see p249).

The view as the train heads towards Toyohashi may discourage you from stopping there but it has a few attractions and – for rail enthusiasts – connects with the Iida line that runs out to Sakuma Rail Park (see p134) where old rolling stock is displayed.

Toyohashi (294km) Some hikari (about 8/day) stop here. Take the east exit for the main part of the city and the tram line. The station is equipped with elevators from platform to concourse and street level. Toyohashi Information Plaza (daily, 9am-7pm) on the main concourse has maps which include sightseeing details and corresponding tram stops. Close to the tourist information counter are coin lockers (up to ¥600).

A single tram line runs through the city (¥150 flat fare) and out to **Toyohashi Park**, where you'll find the reconstructed Yoshida Castle, City Art Museum, Sannomaru Tea Ceremony Hall (where you can try a bowl of green tea for ¥350), and a small Russian Orthodox church.

Toyotetsu Terminal Hotel (☎ 0532-56 1100, 🖳 www.toyotetsu.com/hotel; ¥5460/S, ¥10,500/D, ¥11,550/Tw) is outside the station's east exit. The rooms

⛩ **Exporting Eton**
Japan is known for its theme-park fantasy lands, such as Huis ten Bosch (see p403), a clogs-and-all Holland in Kyushu. But Japanese car manufacturer Toyota, in partnership with the Central Japan Railway Company and other major corporate names, has gone even further by opening a male-only boarding school near Toyohashi which is closely modelled on Britain's Eton College – even down to the appointment of house masters who are responsible for pastoral care.

The real Eton in Windsor, Berks, played an unofficial advisory role in the setting up of the 130,000-square-metre educational facility, but all the teachers and the financial backing come from Japan.

are small but clean. Facilities include a coin laundry and a top floor restaurant which serves set meals in the evening. *Flying Mug Café* in the station does morning sets. A couple of minutes from the east exit is a *Vie de France* bakery with a café on the second floor.

Side trip to Sakuma Rail Park

This is not the largest or most convenient open-air railway museum in Japan as it's way out along the JR Iida line but it has enough exhibits, including the driver's cab of a first series shinkansen and a simulator for a local train, to impress the enthusiast. The journey here, through some of the most rural parts of Honshu, is an enjoyable diversion from the Tokaido mainline.

Sakuma Rail Park (☎ 0539-65 0003, 10am-4pm Sat/Sun and daily during Golden Week and August, ¥140) is at Chubutenryu station, some 62km along the Iida line from Toyohashi. It takes just under two hours by local train but twice a day (dep 09:08am arr 10:17am and dep 1:08pm arr 2:16pm) there's a more comfortable limited express (Inaji LEX) that takes just over an hour. Limited express services depart from Chubutenryu at 3:01pm (arr Toyohashi 4:10pm) and 5:05pm (arr 6:11pm).

After Toyohashi, Kodama call at **Mikawa-Anjo (336km)** but all other services run non stop to Nagoya. If hotel rooms are booked up in Nagoya – and since it's a major business hub and conference city, they often are – consider staying at Mikawa-Anjo, where there's a reasonably priced *Toyoko Inn* (☎ 0566-72 1045, 🖳 www.toyoko-inn.com; ¥5880/S, ¥7980/D/Tw) outside the station.

Nagoya (366km)   [see pp159-68]

All shinkansen services stop here. If continuing to Kyoto, stay on the shinkansen and connect with the route guide starting on p194.

TOKYO TO NAGANO BY SHINKANSEN   [Table 4, p460]

Distances from Tokyo. Fastest journey time: 1 hour 21 minutes.

Tokyo to Nagano   [Map 3 opposite]
Tokyo (0km)   [see pp90-115]

The Asama shinkansen, for Nagano, departs from platforms 20-24. The Asama has only six carriages and fills up quickly, so reserve a seat if possible.

There are luggage storage areas between the carriages. Smoking is not permitted in any carriage.

Ueno (3.6km) Most trains make a brief stop here, though reserve a seat in advance if you're joining the train at Ueno – unreserved cars can fill up before the train leaves Tokyo station.

Omiya (30km) After Omiya a few shinkansen call at **Kumagaya (65km)** and **Honjo-Waseda (86km)**.

Takasaki (105km) Takasaki is the point at which the Joetsu shinkansen to Niigata and the Nagano shinkansen lines divide. The only reason to get out here (when the far more attractive surroundings of the Japan Alps are so close) is to visit the small rail museum in Yokokawa (see box p77).

Takasaki is an important production centre for Daruma dolls, modelled on the founder of Zen Buddhism in China and popular as lucky charms. The idea is that the purchaser of a Daruma paints in one of the eyes at the time of buying it but paints in the other eye only if his/her wish comes true. Daruma craftsmen receive a rush on orders for the dolls during general election campaigns from candidates trying to buy themselves some luck.

After Takasaki, a few shinkansen call at **Annaka-Haruna (124km)** but the majority stop next at Karuizawa. This section includes a number of tunnels and you start to feel as if you are going uphill, proof enough that this is now mountain territory, as the train heads towards its namesake, Mt Asama.

Karuizawa (147km)

Mary Crawford Fraser (1851-1922; see box p136), wife of a former British ambassador to Tokyo, would probably be amazed by Karuizawa's transformation; it is now a thriving mountain resort with top-notch hotels, golf courses and villas for diplomats and celebrities.

Once also a favourite haunt of John Lennon (see p281) and Yoko Ono, more international

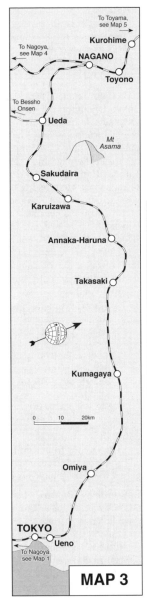

MAP 3

> ❑ 'Poor old Karuizawa was a grand place once…now only mountain pilgrims and crazy foreigners like ourselves go near it. The place has become so poor that it has not even a public bath!' **Mary Crawford Fraser**, *A Diplomat's Wife in Japan: Sketches at the turn of the century*, edited by Sir Hugh Cortazzi, Weatherhill, 1982.

recognition came when Karuizawa hosted an equestrian event at the 1964 Tokyo Olympics and the inaugural curling event at the 1998 Nagano Winter Olympics; in fact, Karuizawa station was rebuilt for the Nagano Olympics. The original station, dating from 1910, has been fully restored and is open to the public (Tue-Sun, 9am-5pm, ¥200). It's to the left as you leave the station.

From the platforms, follow signs for the north exit to find the **Visitors' Information Office** (☎ 0267-42 2491, daily 9am-5pm) on the right after the ticket barrier. **Coin lockers** are available on the ground floor (mostly ¥300 but a limited number of ¥500 ones).

The resort is not much more than a tacky array of gift shops selling mountain honey, jam and pot pourri, and places to eat with names such as the 'Domestic Sausage Restaurant'.

Unless you're on a budget-free trip, don't even think about staying the night in Karuizawa. The rich and/or famous stay at *Mampei Hotel* (☎ 0267-42 1234, 🖳 www.mampei.co.jp), where backpacks will not impress the concierge and where if you have to ask the price you should be looking elsewhere.

Side trip to Onioshidashi-en

The main reason for stopping in Karuizawa is to take a bus ride 21km north to Onioshidashi-en, an area of volcanic rock on the northern side of Mt Asama (2560m), a still active volcano.

Onioshidashi-en (daily, 7am-6pm May-Sep, 8am-5pm Oct-Apr, ¥400) was formed after Mt Asama erupted spectacularly on August 5th 1783, spewing out enough lava to fill Tokyo Dome 161 times. Lava on the north slope cooled and solidified to become an eerie but magnificent place to walk around. Heavy snowfall means that some of the paths are closed in winter. Take a bus (¥1180 one-way; 35 mins) from stop No 1 outside the station. Services are infrequent, so check at the information office in the station.

The journey from Karuizawa to Sakudaira is mostly in tunnels or the views are obscured by steep sides or trees but once you reach Sakudaira you start to get views of the mountains in the distance.

Sakudaira (164km) The town of Saku is a case study for the legacy left by the Olympic Games. With the opening of the Nagano shinkansen, the small town boomed. Before, it took over 3½ hours to Tokyo. Now the journey is 80-90 minutes, turning Saku into a satellite commuter town for the capital.

If there's no room at the inn in nearby Nagano (see pp169-72), *Toyoko Inn Sakudaira Ekimae* (☎ 0267-66 1045; 🖳 www.toyoko-inn.com; ¥6090/S and ¥8190/D/Tw) is outside the Asama exit of the station.

Ueda (189km) Last stop before the Nagano terminus, Ueda is a former castle town. English maps are available at the ground-floor **tourist information counter** (daily, 9am-6pm). Go straight as you leave the shinkansen ticket barrier and it's at the end of the concourse, next to a branch of the Doutor coffee shop. The **JR ticket office** (5:30am-10pm) and View Plaza travel agency (Mon to Sat 10am-6pm, Sun 10am-5pm) are close to the shinkansen ticket barrier. There are **coin lockers** (including a few ¥500 ones) to the left as you exit the station (it closes overnight from 11pm to 6am).

The only thing left of **Ueda Castle** is three turrets, located inside a park about ten minutes on foot north of the station. The castle was completed in 1585 and twice saw off attacks by the Tokugawa clan (see p38). According to a sign inside the park, 'there were many other castles in feudal Japan. But no castle was attacked twice in this way and none was so brilliantly defended as Ueda Castle', before revealing – almost as an afterthought – that the castle was indeed 'later destroyed by the Tokugawa troops'. Though there's not much left to see, the park is a pleasant place to stroll and for rail buffs there's a great vantage point from the turrets which overlook the elevated shinkansen track – perfect for spotting and photographing the Asama shinkansen as it glides towards/away from Ueda station. The only other attraction worth seeing is another 15 minutes north-east of the park: **Yanagimachi** is a carefully preserved street of Edo-period houses, where you'll find a couple of atmospheric tea houses/coffee shops and a saké store.

If you need a place to stay, the new *Toyoko Inn Ueda Eki-mae* (☎ 0268-29 1045, 🖳 www.toyoko-inn.com, ¥6090/S, ¥8190/D/Tw) is to the left as you leave the station.

Side trip by rail to Bessho Onsen
Ueda is a point of transfer for two private lines: Shinano Tetsudo (a commuter line) and the Ueda Dentetsu Bessho Line. To reach the platforms for both, head up the stairs by the tourist information office.

Bessho Onsen, a hot-spring resort, is just under half an hour away by local train along the Bessho line (¥570 one-way; no rail passes). This is a good place to head if you're looking to soak in a hot tub since the baths here are said to have healing properties which make the skin smooth. There are several bath houses in town, but the only one with a rotemburo (outside bath) is O-yu (6am-10pm, ¥150).

The TIC at Ueda station can provide English maps of Bessho Onsen as well as details of train times to/from Ueda.

Look out on your right as you leave Ueda station for the three remaining turrets of what was once Ueda Castle, on a hill overlooking the shinkansen track. Soon afterwards, the train darts into a long series of tunnels as it begins the final stretch of the journey to Nagano.

Nagano (222km)   [see pp168-73]
Terminus of the shinkansen line, Nagano is a major gateway to the Japanese Alps.

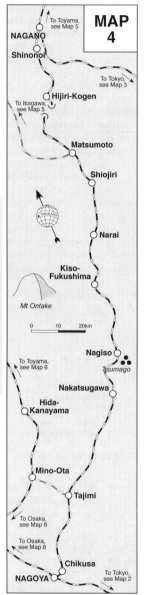

MAP 4

To Toyama, see Map 5
NAGANO
Shinonoi
To Tokyo, see Map 3
Hijiri-Kogen
To Itoigawa, see Map 5
Matsumoto
Shiojiri
TRAILBLAZER
Narai
Kiso-Fukushima
Mt Ontake
0   10   20km
Nagiso
To Toyama, see Map 6
Tsumago
Nakatsugawa
Hida-Kanayama
Mino-Ota
Tajimi
To Osaka, see Map 8
To Osaka, see Map 8
Chikusa
NAGOYA
To Tokyo, see Map 2

NAGANO TO NAGOYA VIA MATSUMOTO
[Table 5, p460]

Distances by JR from Nagano. Fastest journey time: 3 hours.

Nagano to Nagoya [Map 4]

Nagano (0km) From Nagano, pick up the Wide View Shinano LEX which runs along the Shinonoi line towards Nagoya. The Shinano is a modern train with large panoramic windows, hence the name 'Wide View'.

Shinonoi (9km) The first stop after Nagano by limited express, this is the nearest train station to the Nagano Olympic Stadium, 15 minutes away by taxi (no bus).

From here, the Shinonoi line becomes the Chuo line, though there's no need to change trains as limited expresses run direct to Nagoya.

After Shinonoi there are views, to the left, of the valley and towns below the rail line. A few limited expresses call at **Hijiri-Kogen (31km)**. There's one very long tunnel shortly before arriving in Matsumoto.

Matsumoto (63km) [see pp174-9]
To return **to Tokyo** from Matsumoto, pick up the Azusa LEX which takes just under three hours to the capital. Matsumoto is also a terminus for the JR Oito line to Itoigawa (see p143) via the ski resort of Hakuba (see p178).

Shiojiri (76km) If planning to visit Narai (see below), you'll need to change from a limited express to a local train here. The line is now running through the beautiful Kiso Valley, surrounded by the Central Alps to the east and the Northern Alps to the west.

♦ **Narai (97km)** Narai is the first in a series of 'post towns' along this route that were once used as stepping stones on the journey to Edo (Tokyo). In the days before the railway, a total of 69 post stations lined the Nakasendo highway, a trunk road connecting Edo with Kyoto. Not all the post towns have survived but a handful, including the one here in Narai and two more further down the line, have been preserved. Here you'll find a 1km stretch of road lined with Edo-period houses. Narai was 34th of the 69 towns on the highway and the most prosperous in the Kiso Valley. Steep slopes and thick forest made this section of the highway the most challenging (it took three days to cross the valley), so Narai became an important stop for weary travellers to rest and stock up on supplies.

There are no coin lockers at Narai station though it seems safe enough to leave luggage here for a couple of hours. The old wooden station sets the tone for what to expect along the main road. Even the benches in the waiting room are fitted with mini tatami mats. More unusually, the station is run not by JR staff but by a local senior citizens' club – members take it in turns to be at the station to meet trains.

Turn left out of the station and the main street is straight in front of you. Look out for the odd saké shop (a hangover from the drinking houses that provided travellers with some liquid relief on their journey to/from Edo) and craft shops, many of which sell locally made *nurigushi* (lacquered combs).

Several of the old buildings contain small restaurants serving soba. One is immediately on your left as you leave the station. Alternatively, walk down the street for about five minutes and look out on the right for a shop displaying an ice-cream sign. Go in here and at the back are a few tables and a small tatami area where soba is served. Ask for the ¥1400 'osusume menu' (recommended menu), which is huge and includes mountain potatoes and pickles.

The local train service from Shiojiri to Narai (20 mins) and then to Kiso-Fukushima (20 mins), from where it's possible to rejoin the limited express, operates irregularly but approximately once an hour. There is one very long tunnel just after leaving Narai station.

Kiso-Fukushima (118km) Kiso-Fukushima was once a checkpoint on the highway between Edo and Kyoto and has a few sights scattered around including a temple and rock garden, and the former residence of a local governor who managed the checkpoint in the Edo period. It's also the main rail access point for a visit to Mt Ontake, a 3067m volcano, popular with hikers in summer and skiers in winter.

The station here is small and has no coin lockers. Exit the station and turn to the left for the **tourist information counter** (☎ 0264-22 4144, daily, 9am-5pm), which can supply basic maps of the area around the station. Cycles can be rented (up to four hours ¥500, one day ¥1000) from the JR ticket office in the station. Buses to Mt Ontake (¥1360 one-way) take just over 50 minutes but only run three times a day (check with the information counter for departure times). The bus drops you at Ontake Ropeway, from where gondolas climb to 2150m (daily, 8:45am-5:30pm, ¥2400 return). It's then a 3¹/₂-hour hike to the summit. A combined ropeway and bus return ticket costs ¥3800. The ticket office is across the street from Kiso-Fukushima station.

This is the nearest station to *Kiso Ryojoan Youth Hostel* (☎ 0264-23 7716, 🖳 www.jyh.or.jp/english/index.html, ryojyouan@oct.zaq.ne.jp; ¥3100/4100; 41 beds), an atmospheric hostel in an old wooden building. Breakfast costs

---

⛩ **Edo highlights in two days**
A possible **two-day itinerary**, starting in Matsumoto and ending in Nagoya, might be as follows: on the first day, leave Matsumoto and travel by train to Narai. Spend the morning in Narai before picking up the train to Nagiso. Take the bus to nearby Tsumago and overnight at a minshuku. Next day, leave Tsumago early and begin the hike to Magome. Spend some time in Magome, then pick up the bus to Nakatsugawa, from where you can connect with the train to Nagoya.

¥450 and dinner ¥1000. If you haven't made a booking, ask at the tourist office to call ahead and see if there's space. To reach the hostel, take a bus from right outside the station to Ohara, the last stop (20 mins).

Nagiso (152km) Not all limited expresses stop here, the nearest station to the post town of **Tsumago** (see box below). Buses run from outside the station to Tsumago (10:10am, 12:20pm and 2:20pm, 7 mins, ¥270) or take a taxi (¥1100). Luggage can be left for the day at the station for ¥410 per item (ask JR staff). Cycles can be rented (up to 4 hours/¥500) from the JR ticket office. In the station is a tourist information counter (daily, 8:30am-5pm), with guides to Tsumago.

Buses from Nagiso station pull in at the terminal just below Tsumago's main street, from where you head up a path to a side entrance as if walking onto an Edo-period film set. Most of the houses are now craft shops, inns and restaurants. This doesn't mean that the area is tacky or full of souvenir kitsch but it does feel more commercial than nearby Narai (see p138).

A great way to fully experience post-town life is to do what those who once travelled the road between Edo and Kyoto did – stay overnight. In the early evening, once the day crowds have gone, Tsumago feels much less like a Universal Studios Edo theme park. All the minshuku offer the same rates (¥7500 inc two meals); ask at the tourist office (☎ 0264-57 3123, 🖳 www.nagiso-town.ne.jp, info@town.nagiso.nagano.jp, daily, 9am-5pm) along the main street about which have vacancies.

Tsumago is at one end of a popular hiking route through the Kiso Valley to the southernmost post town, **Magome**. The three-hour walk between the two is

---

⛩ **Tsumago – a ghost town comes back to life**
The opening of the Chuo railway line in 1911 along Kiso-gawa effectively robbed the post towns of their purpose, as the old highway was abandoned in favour of the locomotive. For decades in the last century, Tsumago stood forgotten, left behind by the age of the train. But in 1968, a century after the beginning of the Meiji era, a renovation programme began on Tsumago's houses which had by then fallen into a state of disrepair.

Now the old post town has been reconstructed and survives, as it did before, thanks to a steady influx of visitors. It's ironic, therefore, that the train – the modern invention that killed off the post towns – now brings visitors to spend money here and keeps the tourism industry alive.

not particularly strenuous, though you'd need proper hiking boots in winter when snow can be half a metre deep. A luggage delivery service (daily Jul 20th-Aug 31st, Sat/Sun Apr 1st-Jul 19th and Sep 1st-Nov 23rd, ¥500 per piece) is available at the tourist information offices in both Tsumago and Magome. Drop off your luggage by 9am in either town and it will be waiting for you at the other end. To rejoin the rail route after the hike, take a bus from Magome to Nakatsugawa, the next limited express stop along the Chuo line to Nagoya (see below).

Nakatsugawa (171km) Nakatsugawa is only 10 minutes down the line by limited express from Nagiso but it feels much further away. Business hotels, concrete, the odd factory smoke stack ... here are the realities of post-Edo life, an unpleasant warning that you are less than an hour from the industrial heartland of Nagoya. The only reason for stopping here is to take a bus to the post town of Magome (see above).

A **tourist information counter** (daily, 9am-5pm) is on the left as you leave the station, as are **coin lockers** (mostly ¥300 but one ¥600). **Buses to Magome** (¥540) depart from stop No 3 outside the station (operated daily by Nohi Bus; services are irregular but approximately 1/hr).

Tajimi (215km) Tajimi is a terminus for the local Taita line that takes 30 minutes (2/hour) to reach Mino-Ota station on the Takayama line. If planning to visit Takayama (see pp179-84), instead of going all the way to Nagoya to change lines, cross via the Taita line here to Mino-Ota and pick up the route to Takayama from p147.

The Japanese Alps are by now a distant memory, replaced by chimney stacks and pachinko parlours for the last 20 minutes into Nagoya. **Chikusa (244km)** is the final stop on the limited express, just a few minutes out of Nagoya.

Nagoya (251km) [see pp159-68]
From Nagoya, connect up with the Kansai route guide beginning on p194.

NAGANO TO NAGOYA VIA TOYAMA AND TAKAYAMA
[Tables 6 & 7, p461]

Distances by JR from Nagano. Fastest journey time: $6^1/4$ hours.

Nagano to Naoetsu [Map 5, p143; Table 6a/d, p461]
Nagano (0km) [see pp168-73]
Pick up a local train along the Shin-etsu line heading for Naoetsu. Trains operate irregularly but approximately hourly; the journey to Naoetsu takes about 90 minutes. Not all stops are mentioned in the route below.

Toyono (11km) A couple of local trains terminate here so you may have to change here for another local train. After Toyono, the limited express also calls at **Kurohime (29km)**.

Myoko-Kogen (37km) A few local trains from Nagano terminate here. After Myoko most services stop at **Sekiyama (44km)**.

Nihongi (52km) On either side of the train there are spectacular views of the surrounding mountains. On leaving Nihongi station, the train reverses first before continuing along the line.

Arai (58km) By the time you leave this station, the mountain scenery is beginning to recede. As the line heads towards the coast you can see the height of the mountains gradually drop.

Takada (68km) The old castle town of Takada merged with the port town of Naoetsu in 1971 to become, for administrative purposes, Joetsu City. Joetsu has been named 'the birthplace of modern skiing in Japan' after an Austrian officer, Major Theodor Von Lerch (1869-1945), was posted to Japan and asked to teach skiing to the Takada 58th Infantry Regiment. Joetsu's history books record that January 12th 1911 was the day skiing was taught in Japan for the first time. Lerch used only one stick while skiing; his technique is demonstrated every year at the Lerch Festival in early February, when a local ski group takes to the slopes with a pair of wooden skis and a long bamboo stick.

Takada Castle was originally built as a stronghold to maintain peace throughout east and west Japan. A **Lotus Festival** is held in the first half of August along the moats of Takada Park, the former site of Takada Castle. During the festival, tea ceremony parties and haiku poetry gatherings are held in the park, and the moats are completely covered in thick, green lotus leaves. It takes 15-20 minutes on foot to reach Takada Park.

Naoetsu (75km) Fittingly for a place where land meets the sea Naoetsu station is a replica of a cruiser ship with round portholes for windows. There is no tourist information office but there's a decent hotel, *Hotel Century Ikaya* (☎ 0255-45 3111, 🖥 www.ikaya.co.jp; ¥6825/S, ¥13,650/D, ¥12,600/Tw), opposite the main station exit.

In December 1942 an old salt warehouse here became a prisoner-of-war camp for 300 Australian soldiers, many of whom died from sickness or the cold. In 1995, a Peace Memorial Park was constructed on the site of the old PoW camp, which is now home to **Naoetsu Peace Memorial Museum**. To visit the museum (admission free), contact Mr Hosaka (☎ 0255-45 4878). To reach the park, go straight out of the station and take the road on the left of the taxi office. It bears right but keep following it. Go over the bridge and then turn left. Go straight ahead and the park is on your left, just before another bridge. If you keep going straight without turning into the park, you will see Naoetsu port.

There is a **ferry service** to Sado Island (2-4/day; 2¹/₂ hours, ¥2920). Overnight ferries also run year-round between Naoetsu and Fukuoka/Hakata in Kyushu (¥11,260 one-way), and Muroran in Hokkaido (¥5250 one-way). For information, contact Joetsu International Network Office (☎ 0255-26 5446).

▲ From here, you can pick up the Hokuetsu LEX which runs east along the coast towards Niigata (see pp320-6). To follow the route below, change trains

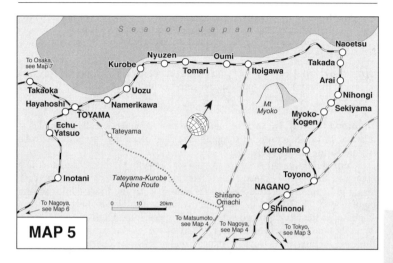

here and join either the Hakutaka LEX or Hokuetsu LEX, both of which run west along the Hokuriku line towards Toyama (and from there onto Kanazawa, see pp185-92).

Naoetsu marks the end of JR East territory. The line and stations west of here are run by JR West (a subtle change in colour of the JR logo from green to blue). JR East passes are not valid for the journey west from Naoetsu.

Don't expect views of the coastline as you hurtle through a series of tunnels. There are occasional sightings of the Japan Sea on the right but mostly the track runs slightly inland past buildings that obscure the coastline.

Naoetsu to Toyama   [Map 5, above; Table 6b/c, p461]
Itoigawa (114km) A terminus for the Oito line from Matsumoto (see p138). After Itoigawa some trains stop at **Oumi (121km)**, **Tomari (139km)** and **Nyuzen (144km)**.

Kurobe (161km) Most limited expresses stop here from where there's a possible side trip by private railway to **Kurobe Gorge**.

Side trip through Kurobe Gorge
Next to JR Kurobe is a station on the private Toyama Chiho Railway line to **Unazuki-Onsen** (30 mins, irregular service but roughly hourly). A five-minute walk from here (follow the crowds) takes you to Unazaki station, starting point for the private Kurobe Kyokoku Railway line. A **'torocco' train** with open-air carriages pulled by a tramcar runs on the 75-minute journey through the gorge to the terminus at Keyaki-Daira (¥1440 one-way).

Anyone into Japan's *onsen* culture should consider taking this side trip as the line passes a number of open-air hot springs. For rail enthusiasts, this is a chance to travel on a narrow-gauge railway which affords sweeping views of the northern Japanese Alps. The Kurobe Kyokoku Railway runs daily, approximately twice an hour between 8am and 4pm, from late April to late November and is very busy during the summer and in late October for autumn leaves' viewing.

Uozu (167km) Uozu is also a stop on the private Toyama Chiho Railway (see opposite) linking Kurobe and Unazuki-Onsen with Toyama.

After Uozu, some limited expresses also call at **Namerikawa (176km)**.

Toyama (193km) Toyama is a major business city and not really a tourist destination. The main reason for stopping here is to begin the **Tateyama-Kurobe Alpine Route** (see opposite).

Coin lockers of all sizes are to your left as you exit the station, next to a branch of the Vie de France bakery. You can also **rent cycles** from the desk inside the coin-locker area. Take the central exit for the **tourist information booth** (☎ 0764-32 9751, 🖥 www.tic-toyama.or.jp; daily 8:30am-8pm), in a small hut to the left as you go out. The staff speak some English.

A 24-hour **internet café**, Wip (¥250/30 mins), is in the basement of the CIC Building (connected to Toyama Excel Hotel Tokyu) directly across the street from the station.

The best place for a view of the area is the observation platform at the top of **Toyama City Hall**. It's free – just take the lift to the top. This is also a good place to head for a cheap lunch in the ground-floor canteen, where all the city-hall workers congregate on weekdays. City Hall is on the left side, ten minutes on foot up the main street which leads away from the station.

To the left as you exit the JR station is the private Toyama Chiho Railway station, from where services depart to Tateyama (for the start of the Alpine Route) and to Unazuki-Onsen (see p143). Toyama Airport (☎ 0764-95 31010, 🖥 www.toyama-airport.co.jp) handles domestic flights and a few international routes to Seoul, Taipei, and Vladivostok (for connection with the Trans-Siberian Railway).

If beginning the Alpine Route early in the morning it may be necessary to overnight in Toyama. Across the street and to your left as you exit the station is

---

⛩ **A light railway experiment**

Rail buffs might like to consider riding the private Toyama Light Rail line from Toyama (entrance is from the north exit of JR Toyama station) up to the coast at Iwasehama, a journey of 7.6 kilometres.

This short stretch of line – served by a light-rail vehicle called 'Portram' – is unique in Japan since it marks the first time that a conventional rail track has been discontinued and converted for use by a light-rail operator. The Toyamako line previously operated by JR West was shut down in March 2006 and reopened a month later in its new guise as a light railway. For further information see 🖥 www.lightrailnow.org.

Other rail operators currently serving loss-making local lines are keeping a close eye on the experiment in Toyama: if the light railway here is a success, the idea is likely to catch on elsewhere.

Toyoko Inn Jr Toyama Eki-mae (☎ 076-405 1045, 🖳 www.toyoko-inn.com; ¥4830/S, ¥7350/D/Tw) and close by is the more upmarket *Toyama Excel Hotel Tokyu* (☎ 076-441 0109, 🖳 www.tokyuhotels.co.jp), where singles start at ¥9817 and twins go from ¥20,790.

Tateyama-Kurobe Alpine Route   [see map below]

Toyama is a gateway for the 90km Tateyama-Kurobe Alpine Route (☎ 076-432 2819, 🖳 www.alpen-route.com), a five-hour journey from Toyama on the coast through the Japanese Alps to Omachi. More than a million people every year follow this route, which involves a combination of train, cable car, bus, ropeway and a bit of legwork. The route is accessed by taking a train on the private **Toyama Chiho Railway** from Toyama to the cable car station at Tateyama; services operate roughly hourly throughout the day though not at regular times.

First opened in 1971, the highest point on the route is 2450m but the most spectacular part is the 23km bus journey from Bijodaira to Murodo; in April/May this usually means going through a corridor of ice. It takes nearly two months of bulldozing to carve out this corridor and remove around 20m of snow.

If any journey in Japan is proof of the Japanese desire to conquer the elements, it must be this one. The route is impassable in winter, when Siberian winds sweep south across the Japan Sea, dumping snow in blizzards across the Tateyama mountain range that doesn't melt away until well into July. The only section of the entire route which requires any footwork is the 20-minute walk across Kurobe Dam, completed in 1963. The route ends with a bus journey to Shinano-Omachi, from where you can pick up a limited express (35 mins) or local train (65 mins) on the JR Oito line to Matsumoto (see p138).

The route is open from around mid-April to the end of November (heavy snowfall can delay the opening). The journey can be completed in either direction and a **one-way package ticket** covering all stages between Toyama and Shinano-Omachi costs ¥10,560. The return fare is ¥17,730. Check the website for the latest fares/timetable. Allow a full day (6-8 hours) to complete the journey; when you buy the ticket the travel agent should provide you with an itinerary showing connection times for the different modes of transport on the route – if not, ask for one.

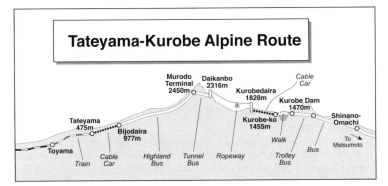

Toyama to Nagoya [Map 5, p143; Map 6, opposite; Table 7, p461]

For the next part of the journey, distances quoted are from Toyama.

Toyama (0km) Take the Wide View Hida LEX (4/day; Takayama Line). Green Car passengers (¥290) can rent headphones on board for the in-seat audio channels. The panoramic windows are great for the views though, because of the mountainous terrain, tunnels frequently block out the scenery. All the same, the line to Takayama remains one of the great rail journeys in Japan, as the train runs south from the coast deep into the Hida mountain range.

However, at the time of writing the railway line between Toyama and Takayama was being repaired and is scheduled to reopen in autumn 2007. A replacement bus service operates while the rail service is suspended. For timetable information call the JR East Info Line (☎ 050-2016 1603).

The train then calls at **Hayahoshi (8km)**, **Echu-Yatsuo (17km)** and **Inotani (37km)** but there's nothing to stop off for until Hida-Furukawa, around 80 minutes after Toyama.

Hida-Furukawa (75km)

If nearby Takayama is a miniature Kyoto, Furukawa is an even smaller version of Takayama and is certainly less crowded. Pick up a map and guide from the **tourist information booth** (daily, 9am-5:30pm; no English spoken) outside the station. **Cycles** can be rented (4 hours, ¥500) from the JR ticket office in the station, though the town is manageable on foot.

Every year on April 19th-20th the peace of Furukawa is shattered by the town's annual festival, the highlight of which is a parade of floats and a big drum, carried by a team of men dressed in white loincloths. Throughout the year, a few of the floats are on display in the centre of town (10 mins west of the station) at **Hida-Furukawa Festival Hall** (daily, 9am-5pm, to 4.30pm in winter, ¥800), where you can also watch a 3D film of the festival parade. Across the street is **Hida-no-takumi Bunkakan** (daily 9am-5pm in summer, Wed-Mon 9am-4.30pm in winter, ¥200), a new heritage centre which displays techniques and tools used by Furukawa craftsmen. To visit both places, buy the ¥900 combination ticket.

Hida Furukawa Youth Hostel (☎/🖹 0577-75 2979, 🖳 www.jyh.or.jp/eng lish/toukaihidafuru, hidafyh@rapid.ocn.ne.jp; 22 beds) is in a modern wood building and charges ¥3300/4300) plus ¥1000 for dinner and ¥500 for breakfast. The hostel is actually closer to **Hida-Hosoe (70km)**, two stops back by local train towards Toyama. It's a 15-minute walk west of the station, opposite Shinrin Park. Alternatively, take a bus from Hida-Furukawa station (15 mins) and get off at 'Shinrin-Koen guchi'. It's a good idea to reserve here as the hostel only sleeps 22. It is closed March 30th-April 10th.

Takayama (89km) [see pp179-84]

From Takayama, the line continues to follow roughly the course of Hida-gawa. The best part of the journey is the next 50km to Gero, with stunning river and mountain scenery on both sides of the track.

Some of the Wide View Hida services that start in Takayama also stop at **Kuguno (103km)**, **Hida-Osaka (117km)**, and **Hida-Hagiwara (129km)**.

Gero (138km) Gero is one of the best-known spa towns in Japan. This onsen resort dates back over 1000 years and is mainly popular with elderly Japanese holidaymakers. The town is also known for its tomato juice, considered to be a healthy tonic after a day wallowing in a hot tub.

After Gero, a few limited expresses call at **Hida-Kanayama (159km)** and **Shirakawa-guchi (193km)**.

Mino-Ota (199km) Situated on Kiso-gawa, Mino-Ota is a terminus for the local Taita line that takes 30 minutes to reach Tajimi on the Chuo line. If planning to visit Matsumoto (see p138), instead of going all the way to Nagoya to change lines, cross via the Taita line here to Tajimi and pick up the route to Matsumoto from p141 (though it is described in reverse).

Unuma (209km) A few limited expresses stop here, the nearest JR station to Inuyama (see p167), a popular side trip from Nagoya. Local trains to Inuyama can be caught from the private Meitetsu Railway's Shin-Unuma station on the other side of Kiso-gawa, across the bridge.

Gifu (226km) Gifu is more of a political and administrative centre than a tourist destination. The city suffered heavy air raids during WWII. A couple of attractions which remain are cormorant fishing on Nagara-gawa (Nagara River), and Gifu Castle, a 1956 reconstruction and therefore not a high priority.

Gifu station is a terminus for the Takayama line and a stop on the Tokaido mainline. There are two sides to the station but the main exit is the Nagara side, outside which the main road heads north towards Nagara-gawa. There are a few **coin lockers** in a corner of the ticket barrier level but not as many as you would expect in

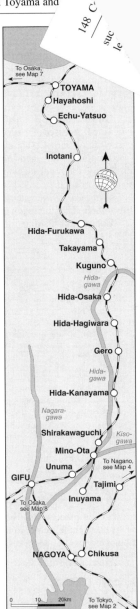

To Osaka, see Map 7
TOYAMA
Hayahoshi
Echu-Yatsuo
Inotani
Hida-Furukawa
Takayama
Kuguno
Hida-gawa
Hida-Osaka
Hida-Hagiwara
Gero
Hida-gawa
Hida-Kanayama
Nagara-gawa
Shirakawaguchi *Kiso-gawa*
Mino-Ota
To Nagano, see Map 4
Unuma
GIFU
Tajimi
To Osaka, see Map 8
Inuyama
NAGOYA — Chikusa
0   10   20km
To Tokyo, see Map 2

HONSHU

a large station. A lift for wheelchair users operates from arrival to street el. There aren't many places to eat in the station but at basement level you'll ind a branch of the *Vie de France* bakery which includes a café. Gifu City **tourist information centre** (☎ 058-262 4415, 🖳 www.kankou-gifu.jp, daily, 9am-7pm, to 6pm in winter) is on the same (2nd) floor as the ticket barrier. Maps are available and staff will help book accommodation. For further information see 🖳 www.gifucvb.or.jp/en.

Gifu Castle is perched on top of Mt Kinka (329m) overlooking Nagaragawa and accessed via ropeway from Gifu Park. The concrete reconstructed castle (daily, 9am-4:30/5:30pm, ¥200) has little to recommend inside – a video of cormorant fishing and some photos of other castles in Japan. The best part of the visit is the ropeway, which on a clear day affords views of the city and the river. To reach the castle from the station (east exit), take a City Bus from stop No 11 marked 'Nagarasagiyama-mawari' and get off at the Gifukoen-mae stop. From there, take the ropeway (3 mins, ¥1050 return) to the castle.

Cormorant fishing (nightly at approx 7:30pm, May 11th-October 15th, ¥3300), known in Japanese as *ukai*, takes place on Nagara-gawa, 2km north of the station. Fishermen dressed in traditional costume of straw skirt, sandals and black kimono use cormorant birds to fish for *ayu* (sweetfish). The birds, tied to reins and steered by fishermen standing inside the boats, dive down and catch the fish in their beaks. The rein around each bird's neck prevents it from swallowing any of the catch. Today, the event is geared towards the tourist trade, but when the river is lit up by fire and the cormorants set to work, it's an impressive sight. If you don't want to pay to watch from a boat, there's no charge for standing along the river bank.

For fishing schedules and ticket information, contact the tourist information office in Gifu station or the boat office (☎ 058-262 0104) by Nagara-gawa.

> ❑ **Chaplin and Basho**
>
> It's little known but often cited by tourism officials in Gifu that silent comedian Charlie Chaplin was a fan of cormorant fishing and was apparently 'so enchanted that he came to Gifu to witness the sight a second time'. Locals recall with pride that Chaplin described the activity as 'the greatest art Japan has to offer'.
>
> He was not alone in admiring the skills of the fishermen. The celebrated Japanese poet Matsuo Basho (see p286) even composed a haiku on the subject:
>
> 'Cormorant boat, where
> Before long, what looks like fun
> Perhaps ends in sorrow.'

A good place to stay the night is *Comfort Hotel Gifu* (☎ 058-267 1311, 🖳 www.choicehotels.com; ¥6090/S, ¥11,550/Tw), across the street from the station. Smart rooms and a continental breakfast is included.

After Gifu, some services stop at **Owari-Ichinomiya (239km)**.

Nagoya (256km) [see pp159-68]
To link with the Kansai route guide, see p194 or p196.

NAGANO TO NAGOYA VIA TOYAMA AND KANAZAWA

From **Nagano (0km)**, follow the route guide starting on p141 as far as **Toyama (193km)**, then pick up the route below.

Distances by JR from Toyama. Fastest journey time: (to Nagoya) 3 hours 35 minutes; (to Osaka) 3 hours 10 minutes.

Toyama to Fukui   [Map 7, below; Table 8, p462]

Toyama (0km) From Toyama, continue along the Hokuriku line towards Kanazawa. The Thunderbird LEX runs from here to Kyoto/Osaka via Kanazawa. This train has vending machines and all Green Car seats are fitted with TV (a choice of three satellite stations as well as music and radio pro-grammes). Even those roughing it in the ordi-nary seats can tune in to the music channels if carrying their own portable radio; FM frequen-cies are displayed on the screen at the front of each car. The older Shirasagi LEX runs to Nagoya via Kanazawa. The Hakutaka LEX and Hokuetsu LEX both terminate at Kanazawa.

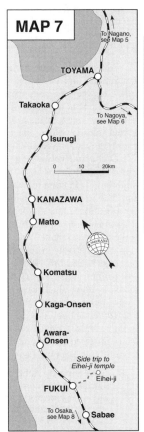

Takaoka (19km) Takaoka feels quiet and uncosmopolitan after Toyama but it does have a ferry connection with Vladivostok in Russia (see box, p150). It also has the distinction of being the smallest city in Japan to boast its own tram line! A **tourist information booth** (daily 9:30am-5:30pm) is in the station; maps are available and the staff speak a little English. A few ¥600 large **coin lockers** are on your left as you go out of the station. For assistance in English, **Takaoka International Exchange Center** (☎ 0766-27 1855, Mon-Sat, 10am-7pm) on the 7th floor of the Daiwa department store, ten minutes on foot up the main street with the tram line which runs away from the station. On the same floor are a branch **post office** (with **ATM**) and several restaurants.

Takaoka is known as a centre for bronze production; the biggest bit of bronze in town is the **Daibutsu**, a 15.85m-high Buddha statue weighing 65 tonnes, the third largest in Japan. The statue is five minutes on foot from the sta-tion's north exit; turn right on to the main road (Sakurababa-dori), go straight to the fourth road on your left (Daibutsu-dori), turn left and go straight until you reach the Daibutsu.

⛩ **Takaoka to Vladivostok**
The frequency of sailings between Fushiki Port in Takaoka and Vladivostok changes every year but there is generally one a week from Mid-May to December, departing on Thursday (40-45 hours). One-way tickets cost from ¥30,800 to ¥97,900 including meals and the port tax at Vladivostok, with 10% off some fares for students.

For up-to-date schedules and fares, contact **FKK Air Service** (☎ 0766-22 2212, 🖷 22 7456, 🖳 http://fkk-air.toyama-net.com/rus_sennai.html (Japanese), fkk-air@toyama-net.com), Duo Bldg, Shimonoseki-machi 4-56, Takaoka-shi, Toyama 933-0021. FKK can also book flights to Vladivostok.

Alternatively try **United Orient Shipping & Agency Co** (Tokyo Kyodo Kaiun; ☎ 03-5640 3901, 🖷 03-5640 1633, 🖳 www.bisintour.com, 🖳 k-yoshida@uniori ent.co.jp), Tomare Nihonbashi-Hamacho 9F, 3-2-3 Chuo-ku, Tokyo 103-0007. If writing an email in English put 'Vladivostok Ferry Reservation' as the subject so they know the email is not spam.

To reach Fushiki Port, take a local train from Takaoka three stops on the Himi line to Fushiki.

Also worth a look is **Zuiryu-ji** (daily, 9am-4:30pm, ¥500), a large temple ten minutes on foot south of the station. Originally built 360 years ago, the roof of the temple was made of lead – a rarity in Japan – so that it could be used to make bullets in the event of war. In mid-January, a **Nabe Festival** is held here. The nabe, a stew made with cod, crab and other winter seafood, is cooked in a giant cauldron with a capacity of 1200 litres – enough to serve 3000 people. The cauldron is displayed at Takaoka station.

Daibutsu Ryokan (Daibutsu-machi 75, ☎ 0766-21 0075, 🖷 22 0075, 🖳 bud dha@pl.coral net.or.jp) is almost opposite the Daibutsu and has spacious if slightly faded tatami rooms. Rates are ¥4600 for one, ¥9000 for two or ¥13,200 for three people sharing a room; breakfast is ¥800 and dinner ¥1600. If you prefer a bed to a futon, try *Manten Hotel Takaoka Eki-mae* (☎ 0766-27 0100, 🖳 www.manten-hotel.com; ¥6500/S, ¥11,000/Tw), right outside the station's central exit. It's a relatively new place with comfortable rooms and a smart restaurant. Alternatively, *Super Hotel Takaoka* (☎ 0766-28 9000, 🖳 www.superho tel.co.jp; ¥4980/S, ¥6980/Tw/D) is five minutes on foot from the south exit (the exit for Zuiryu-ji). *APA Hotel Takaoka Marunouchi* (☎ 0766-27 2111, 🖳 www .apahotel.com, ahtakaoka@apa.co.jp; ¥6000/S, ¥8500/D, ¥11,000/Tw) is four stops on the tram from the station. Get off at Hirokoji.

Tontei (11am-2pm and 5pm-12 midnight) is on the second floor of the building on the right-hand corner of the main road with the tram line which leads off from the station. It serves excellent tonkatsu, prepared and fried in front of you. Set meals cost ¥900-1000.

Side trips by rail from Takaoka

Takaoka is a terminus for two local JR lines; both offer possible side trips by rail, though neither is a top priority.

On the **Johana line**, two-car, one-man trains run on a 29.9km journey through vast rice paddies dotted with houses which are surrounded by trees to block the wind. The service started in 1897 as the Chuetsu Railway and in 1912 was extended beyond Takaoka station to Himi, on the coast of the Japan Sea. The line was cut down to its current stretch after the Himi line was laid between Takaoka and Himi stations. In the country where even taxi doors are automated, it's a novelty to discover that passengers on Johana line trains have to open and close the doors themselves.

The **Himi line** extends only 16.5km up the coast but there are good (if brief) views of Toyama Bay out to the right. Close to the Himi terminus you'll find Himi Fisherman's Wharf (Thur-Tue, 7am-6pm), where you can see the early morning catch of fish before having a sushi breakfast.

After Takaoka a few services stop at **Isurugi (35km)**.

Kanazawa (60km) [see pp185-92]

After Kanazawa a few services stop at **Matto (69km)**.

Komatsu (88km) Some Thunderbird LEXs do not stop here. Komatsu is not really a sightseeing destination, but since the town is midway between Kanazawa and Fukui it would make a convenient base for visiting both places. Also, it has a hotel whose location right opposite the station is perfect for rail travellers: *Hyper Hotel Komatsu* (☎ 0761-23 3000, 🖳 www.hyper-komatsu.co.jp; ¥5040/S, ¥7140/Tw); breakfast is included in the rate. Even if you don't stay here, it's worth visiting the Japanese restaurant on the second floor. *Kamado* is a modern izakaya mixing traditional Japanese service with a stylish, modern décor. The menu is only in Japanese but don't let this put you off. As well as fresh fish, there are steaks, cheese fondues, salads and garlic bread. Count on spending ¥2000-4000 per person. Mugs of beer are ¥450.

Kaga-Onsen (102km) Not all limited express trains stop here. Look up to the right just before the train pulls into this station (10 mins after leaving Komatsu) and you'll see a giant gold Kannon statue looking down on the station.

After Kaga-Onsen, some limited expresses stop at **Awara-Onsen (119km)**.

Fukui (136km) History has not been kind to Fukui; the city has been completely destroyed twice, once by war and soon after by an earthquake. The main reason for stopping here is to take a side trip to nearby Eihei-ji (see p152).

The **tourist information booth** (☎ 0776-63 3102, daily, 8:30am-5pm) is to the left of the central ticket barrier; the staff there can provide maps and general information. **Coin lockers** (all sizes) are in a room to your right immediately after going through the ticket barrier.

Buses go from in front of the station to **Daianzen-ji** (Wed-Mon, 9am-5pm), founded in 1658. The main attraction here is an 11-faced statue of the Bodhisattva of compassion. The image is celebrated for its matchmaking powers. The best place to sit – where the love vibes are strongest – is immediately under the large, sparkling gold lamp shade. Say a prayer here, it is said, and you may not be walking alone for much longer. Zazen training sessions are held here twice a month on Friday evenings (6:30-9pm). The Head Priest is said to be a humorous raconteur. The sessions (¥400) offer a gentle introduction to Zen meditation. Foreign visitors are welcome but reservations (☎ 0776-59 1014, 🖳 www.daianzenji.jp) are required. From the station, take Keifuku bus No 16 (¥400) from stop No 7 bound for Kawanishi and get off at the Daianzen-ji Monzen stop.

Hotel Riverge Akebono (3-10-12 Chuo, ☎ 0776-22 1000, 🖳 www.riverge .com) has good-value rooms, a coin laundry, decent restaurant and a hot spring. In the main building, singles cost ¥6200, twins ¥11,000 and doubles ¥12,000. In the newer annex, twins go from ¥14,000 and doubles from ¥16,000. Across the street, the hotel also operates **Akebono Bekkan**, an old Japanese inn with tatami rooms (¥4000 per person). The hotel is a 10-minute walk from the station's central exit. Go straight up Ekimae-dori, turn left at the fourth intersection and walk for 50m up this road to the hotel.

Side trip to Eihei-ji

Eihei-ji, built onto a mountainside to the east of Fukui, was founded in 1244 by the Buddhist priest Dogen as a centre for Zen training. The name means 'temple of eternal peace', though with so many tour groups piling through it's best to arrive as early as possible to appreciate the tranquillity.

The most sacred building inside the compound is the Joyoden (Founder's Hall), in which Dogen's ashes are kept along with those of his successors. Just as impressive as the fine buildings and beautiful setting is the feeling of how busy and alive the temple remains over 750 years after its foundation. As you walk around you'll almost certainly see priests at work, perhaps practising how to move sacred objects, or a trainee priest reciting a sutra.

Eihei-ji is open daily from dawn except on certain festival days and when there are private ceremonies. Buy a ticket (¥400) from the vending machine at the main entrance. A booklet is available in the temple (not at the ticket booth).

Rail services towards Eihei-ji start from the private Echizen Railway station outside the east exit of JR Fukui station. From Fukui, ride the train until Eiheiji-guchi (30 mins, ¥440; no rail passes), where you change to a Keifuku bus to Eihei-ji (15 mins, ¥410).

Cheaper and more practical but less frequent is the direct Keifuku bus from Fukui station to Eihei-ji, which takes 33 minutes and costs ¥720. Buses for Eihei-ji leave Fukui at 10am, 11:50am, 1:30pm and 3:30pm.

Fukui to Tsuruga   [Map 8, opposite; Table 8, p462]

The route from Fukui heading south towards Kansai has a number of tunnels.

Sabae (150km)   Some limited expresses make a brief stop at Sabae. Spectacle-wearers should spare a thought for Sabae as the train passes by: the city is known for making frames for glasses and claims to have cornered 90% of the domestic market and 20% of the world market. The mayor of Sabae boasts proudly that his city is the 'uncontested eyeglass-frames capital of Japan'. Who would dare wrestle that title away?

After Sabae, some trains also call at **Takefu (155km)**. There's one very long tunnel that lasts around 10 minutes shortly before Tsuruga, just north of Lake Biwa, the largest lake in Japan.

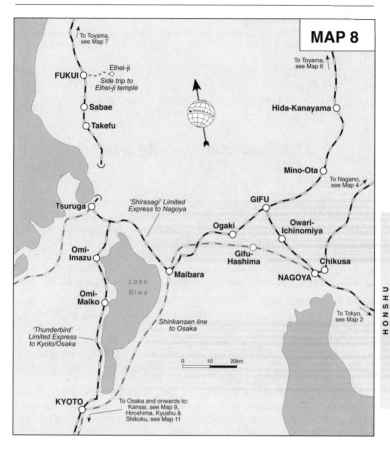

Tsuruga (190km) Tsuruga is one of the largest ports on the Japan Sea coast (Shin Nihonkai Ferry Company, ☎ 0770-23 2222, 🖳 www.snf.co.jp, operates regular scheduled services to Tomakomai in Hokkaido) and is also a major rail junction, marking the end of the Hokuriku line. This is the last chance to change between the Shirasagi LEX for Nagoya and the Thunderbird LEX for Osaka/Kyoto.

The Thunderbird does not always stop at Tsuruga. Fifteen kilometres after Tsuruga the track divides into two lines which run down either side of Lake Biwa. There are better views of the lake (on the left) on the journey to Kyoto/Osaka but even so trees and tunnels often block the view.

Moving on from Tsuruga   **[Map 8, p153]**

The Thunderbird LEX heads down the west side of the lake, before joining the Tokaido line westbound to Kyoto (284km; p206), Shin-Osaka (323km) and Osaka (327km; p116).

The Shirasagi LEX runs down the east side of the lake to Maibara (236km; p195), then joins the Tokaido line eastbound to Ogaki (272km), Gifu (286km; p147), Owari-Ichinomiya (299km) and Nagoya (316km; p159).

Central Honshu – city guides

SHIZUOKA

Often overlooked as being too soon after Tokyo to make it a destination in its own right, Shizuoka has a couple of attractions that make an overnight stay worthwhile. Capital of Shizuoka prefecture, a well-known tea-producing area, the city was chosen by the first Tokugawa shogun, Ieyasu, as his retirement home. There's an excellent selection of restaurants and the place feels much more manageable than Tokyo. It's also a good staging post for a visit to the Oigawa Railway (see p131), just a little further down the Tokaido Line.

What to see and do

Don't be put off by signs for the 'incineration plant' and 'sewage plant' marked on the map to Shizuoka available from the tourist office. The two main sights you could pack into one day are the Prefectural Art Museum, which has a superb annex filled with reproductions of Rodin's sculptures, and Kunozan Toshogu Shrine, the journey to which via a winding bus route and ropeway is as impressive as the shrine complex itself.

Before setting off to visit these places, get a bird's eye view of the city and surrounding area by walking over to the **Prefectural Office**, about 10 minutes on foot north of the station. The office is made up of several buildings but the one you want is the tall building to the right as you face the Prefectural Office complex. This is the East Building, connected to the *Bekkan* (annex building). From the second floor take the passageway through to the Bekkan where you can ride the elevator up to the 21st floor observation platform. There's a small tea room here. On a (rare) clear day you can see Mt Fuji.

Immediately behind the offices is **Sumpu Park** (daily, 6am-10pm). There's little left of Sumpu Castle, where Tokugawa Ieyasu (see boxopposite) spent the last 11 years of his life until his death in 1616, but at least the park is an open space. The reconstructed south-east tower is open to the public (Tue-Sun, 9am-4:30pm, ¥200). In a corner of Sumpu Park is **Momijiyama Garden** (Tue-Sun, 9am-4:30pm, ¥150), with its immaculately kept grounds and paths leading to an exquisite Japanese tea pavilion.

Top of the visitor's list should be the excellent **Prefectural Art Museum** (🖳 www.spmoa.shizuoka.shizuoka.jp; Tue-Sun 9:30am-5pm, until 7:30pm on

┌───┐

⛩ **Tokugawa Ieyasu – where does he lie?**
If you ask most people where Tokugawa Ieyasu is buried you will almost certainly be told that his mausoleum is in Nikko (see p114), the famous temple and shrine
town north of Tokyo. But anybody from Shizuoka will tell you that the man is in
Kunozan Toshogu Shrine, just outside their city. Once pressed a little, however, the typical citizen of Shizuoka will cave in and admit that his body was actually moved to
Nikko – though they'll point out that Kunozan Toshogu was the original mausoleum.

└───┘

Fri, May-Sep); a combined temporary/permanent exhibition ticket costs around
¥1000 but it depends on the exhibition). Find out what the temporary exhibition
is, but the real reason for coming is to check out the Rodin Wing. This part of
the museum is spacious, well organized and boasts an impressive collection of
bronze Rodin casts, including his famous *Thinker* and the *Gates of Hell*. A
handset can be rented for an informative and amusing commentary in English
on all the sculptures. Outside, a promenade offers excellent views of the mountains – it's hard to believe you're only an hour away from Tokyo by shinkansen.
To get here, take bus No 44 (¥350) from stop No 13, which is across the road
from Shizuoka station (take the north exit and cross the road by Hotel Associa
Shizuoka). The bus takes 25 minutes and is marked 'Kenritsu Bijutsukan'.

On the third floor of the Southpot building outside the station's south exit
is **Shizuoka Art Gallery** (Tue-Sun, entrance fee depends on exhibition), which
hosts a variety of temporary exhibitions.

Consider fitting in a visit to **Kunozan Toshogu Shrine**, way out of the city
centre but accessible via a scenic road and ropeway. The shrine is a mausoleum
to Tokugawa Ieyasu, who spent the last years of his life in Shizuoka. To reach
Nihondaira Ropeway station from Shizuoka station, take bus No 42 (35 mins;
¥580) from stop No 13 and get off at 'Nihondaira' (the last stop). The short ride
by ropeway (daily, 9:10am-4pm, ¥550 one-way, ¥1000 return) terminates by the
entrance to the shrine. Buy the combination ticket here (¥650) that allows
entrance to the shrine and the small museum that contains a number of
Tokugawa Ieyasu's personal artefacts.

Behind the main shrine, surprisingly ornate and colourful and looking more
like a Buddhist temple than an austere Shinto shrine, is the simple mausoleum,
surrounded by trees. The reason for the mix of Buddhism and Shinto, evident
when you see the main shrine, is that Kunozan Toshogu was originally built as
a blend of the two. This coexistence was brought to an end when the then
Emperor prohibited simultaneous worship of the two religions. Buddhist decoration was torn down. The Bell Tower became the rather more solemn Drum
Tower and a five-storey pagoda that once stood here was bulldozed. By contrast, the small museum is a colourful treasure trove of Tokugawa Ieyasu's possessions. A collection of glittering swords, hanging scrolls, samurai armour and
an antique table clock from Madrid make this a fascinating diversion and alone
worth the visit to the shrine.

There are two ways back to the shrine from Shizuoka. One way is to take the ropeway back to Nihondaira and then pick up the bus back to the station. A combined return ropeway, shrine and museum ticket (available only at the top ropeway station) costs ¥1550; this represents the best value if you intend to return to Shizuoka city by bus from Nihondaira.

The alternative is to walk down the 1159 steps from the shrine to the coast and pick up a bus from there. The steps, the traditional entry point to the shrine, are much more manageable going down so it's better to do it this way round. There's the added attraction of a number of strawberry farms at the bottom. Even if you're not here in the strawberry season, there are shops at the foot of the steps where strawberries are big business year-round – strawberry juice, ice cream and jam are there in abundance. Turn left when you reach the foot of the steps (don't go as far as the main road in front of you) and walk 150 metres to the bus stop, where you can pick up a bus (No 14; ¥470) back to Shizuoka station. If you really want to climb the 1159 steps up to the shrine you can catch this bus from stop No 4 outside Shizuoka station.

PRACTICAL INFORMATION
Station guide
Shizuoka has both north and south sides but the main exit for the city (where all the buses arrive and depart) is the north side. In the middle of the station concourse is the entrance to ASTY, a **restaurant complex** with a variety of reasonably priced if rather unexciting options; see also p158.

For **coin lockers** (up to ¥600) look down the passageways that run off from the main concourse.

Tourist information
There is normally an English speaker on hand at the tourist information office (☎ 054-252 4247, daily 8:30am-6pm), along a passageway behind the JR ticket gate. The guide to the city bus service tells you how to get to the main sights, what bus to catch, how much the fare is, how long it will take and which bus stop to wait at. Maps are also available. A useful online resource for travel plans in and around Shizuoka is 🖳 www .shizuoka-guide.com.

Getting around
To get a feel for the city, jump on the Shizuoka sightseeing bus that, for a flat fare of ¥100, does a 40-minute loop of the city. The old-fashioned retro bus departs from stop No 1 outside the north exit and calls at Sumpu Park.

Internet
Free Internet access is available on the second floor of the **Prefectural Office East Building**. Head for the Kenmin Service

---

SHIZUOKA 静岡

Where to stay
6 Hotel ECC Shizuoka
9 Hotel Associa Shizuoka Terminal
12 Hotel Century Shizuoka
14 Hotel Privé Shizuoka Station
15 Ryokan Kagetsu

6　ホテルエックスシズオカ
9　ホテルアソシア静岡ターミナル
12　ホテルセンチュリー静岡
14　ホテルプリヴェ静岡ステーション
15　旅館花月

Where to eat and drink
2 Prefectural Office Bldg
3 Café Ciccio

2　県庁
3　カフェチッチョ

Where to eat and drink *(cont'd from opposite)*

4	Kushiko	4	串幸
5	El Pollito	5	エルポッリト
9	Hotel Associa Beer Garden	9	ホテルアソシアビアガーデン
12	La Fleur	12	ラ フルール

Other

1	Momijiyama Garden (Sumpu Park)	1	紅葉山庭園
2	Prefectural Office East Building	2	県庁東館
7	Airs Café	7	エアーズカフェ
8	Central Post Office	8	中央郵便局
10	Prefectural Art Museum	10	県立美術館
11	Kunozan Toshogu Shrine	11	久能山東照宮
13	Shizuoka Art Gallery (Southpot)	13	静岡アートギャラリー (サウスポット)

⛩ Shizuoka's white elephant?

Shizuoka is set to get its own international airport, to be called Mt Fuji Shizuoka Airport, in 2009, with flights planned to major cities in Japan and other Asian destinations, including Bangkok. Construction of the ¥90-billion airport has been dogged by controversy and accusations that it will be a white elephant and that it is unnecessary given the city's proximity to Tokyo (and Nagoya, see box p161). If the urban planners get their way, however, the idea is to build a new Tokaido shinkansen station at the airport (the Tokaido shinkansen line runs just below the planned location for the airport terminal) between Shizuoka and Kakegawa shinkansen stations. It would mark the first time that a shinkansen station is directly connected to an airport.

Center (Mon-Fri, 8:30am-5pm). Sign your name at the desk and you'll be told which computer to use; a maximum of 30-60 minutes, depending on how busy it is.

Alternatively, surf the web at **Airs Cafe**, which is below street level just before you reach Seibu department store. You'll need to become a member (¥105) so bring photo ID. The first hour is ¥105. Packages are available for two-, three- and four-hour periods.

Where to stay

The most convenient place is *Hotel Associa Shizuoka Terminal* (☎ 054-254 4141, 💻 www.associa.com/sth; ¥11,200/S, ¥16,500/D, ¥19,900/Tw), immediately on your right as you take the north exit from Shizuoka station. The reception staff speak English and the rooms are bright and furnished with a minibar and bilingual TV. Rail pass-holders are entitled to a small discount.

Even more luxurious, but not much more expensive is *Hotel Century Shizuoka* (☎ 054-284 0111, 💻 www.centuryshizuoka .co.jp; ¥11,500/S, ¥17,000/D, ¥18,000/Tw), outside the south exit of Shizuoka station. It has smart, well-appointed rooms, including an executive floor. There are several restaurants to choose from.

If you're looking for a night in a Japanese inn, *Ryokan Kagetsu* (☎ 054-281 0034, 🖷 281 0759, 💻 kagetsu@mail.wbs .ne.jp; ¥5500/pp) has modern tatami rooms and there's a large communal bath. Breakfast (¥800) and dinner (¥1500) are extra. Staff are friendly and speak a little English. It's a seven-minute walk from the

south exit of Shizuoka station. Take the main road in front of you until you come to a road that leads off diagonally to the right. Go up this road to the end, then bear left and carry on straight until you come to a small driveway on the right, at the end of which is the ryokan. If you get to a petrol station on your left, you've gone too far.

Also on the south side of the station, just a couple of minutes from the exit, is *Hotel Privé Shizuoka Station* (☎ 054-281 7300, 💻 www.hotel-prive.com; ¥6825/S, ¥12,600/Tw/D). Good value, smart rooms and the usual small bathrooms but bilingual TV is a surprise in this category. The hotel has a faux-European atmosphere, including the somewhat chintzy exterior.

Over on the north side of the city, a bit further from the station, is *Hotel ECC Shizuoka* (☎ 054-251 1741, 💻 www.hot elecc.co.jp) with small but clean rooms and free coffee/bread for breakfast. Singles are ¥6700 (or squeeze two people in for ¥9000) and twins ¥12,000.

Where to eat and drink

There are plenty of casual dining and take-out choices in the station: *Soup Stock Tokyo* serves delicious warm hearty soups from ¥610 and *Café Denmark* has pizza slices, cakes and other baked goodies, along with a range of hot and cold drinks to eat in or takeaway. By the south exit is a branch of *Haagen Dazs*. In Parche department store, outside the station's north exit, is a **conveyor-belt sushi restaurant** (*kait-en-zushiya*) that is often packed out since it's cheap and the sushi is fresh and delicious. Also here is a branch of **Baskin-Robbins** ice cream.

La Fleur (daily, 11am-2pm, 5-8pm), on the ground floor (1st Floor) of Hotel Century Shizuoka, is a good bet if you're feeling more than a bit peckish. The all-you-can-eat lunch (including dessert) is ¥2200 (¥2800 at weekends). The evening dinner buffet is ¥3200 (¥3700 at weekends).

For budget food, head for the **Prefectural Office**. In a corridor inside the main building (the old building in the centre as you stand facing the prefectural office complex) is a highly recommended *onigiri stall* (Mon-Fri, 9am-12pm). They sell over 100 types of onigiri (from ¥900; the onigiri are so popular that they're usually sold out by 11:30am. Stock up here and have lunch in adjacent Sunpu Park.

There's a good choice of bars and restaurants in Shizuoka. A good place for lunch is **Café Ciccio**, an Italian café that opens out on to the street. It's open all day but the best time to stop here is 11am-3pm when they do a panini lunch-set with your choice of filling, including a salad and coffee from ¥525.

El Pollito is a small place serving authentic Mexican food. There's a menu in English and a selection of Mexican beers (not just Corona) from ¥600.

Fun to try in the evening is **Kushiko**, a robatayaki place where you sit at the counter and order huge chunks of meat on big metal sticks (like giant kebabs). The friendly owners have an unusual speciality house drink called *shochu-ochaiwari* – a mix of green tea and shochu.

In summer, **Hotel Associa Beer Garden** is a good place to head in the evening for an all you can eat/drink deal during a set time.

NAGOYA

Just over a century ago, Nagoya had a population of 157,000. Today, over two million people live in what has become the fourth largest city in Japan. Much of the city was flattened by WWII air raids, and in 1959 a typhoon struck the southern part of Nagoya flooding the entire area and destroying over 100,000 buildings. But the city has bounced back to become a major industrial centre with the headquarters and production plants of Toyota, Honda and Mitsubishi all in the area.

Though not an attractive city, Nagoya functions as a rail gateway to the Japanese Alps and to Kansai, which means that most rail travellers will pass through at some stage. Osaka and Tokyo may be better known but Nagoya feels more relaxed and easier to manage than either of them.

What to see and do

For a bird's eye view of Nagoya, take the express elevator from the 2nd floor of Nagoya station to the 15th, the entrance to Marriott Associa Hotel. What you'll see is a sprawling city, most spectacular when lit up at night. Don't bother with the Panorama House (Tue-Sun, 10am-10pm, ¥700), a viewing platform accessed from the 12th floor.

Nagoya Castle (daily, 9am-4:30pm, ¥500) was built in 1612 on the orders of Tokugawa Ieyasu to be a secure base along the main Tokaido Highway. The castle was razed to the ground during a WWII air raid and only three corner towers and gates survived. The donjon was reconstructed in 1959 and is known for the pair of gold dolphins (*kinshachi*) on the roof (which very occasionally are brought down and put on display). Though hard to tell from the ground, the

---

🏮 Central Japan International Airport

Central Japan International Airport, known as Centrair (🖳 www.centrair.jp), opened in 2005 on a manmade island off the coast of Tokoname, a suburb of Nagoya. International carriers such as Lufthansa (from Frankfurt) and Air France (from Paris) operate flights to Centrair; check the website for up-to-date flight schedules.

If the airport's PR machine is to be believed this is not just a place to catch a flight but an 'entertainment centre which inspires awe and happiness in all who visit'. Centrair's main practical claim to fame is that it is the only airport in Japan (possibly even the world) with its own **hot-spring baths**, which are open daily to passengers and anyone else who fancies a terminal dip. Plane spotters will be in something approximating heaven since guests are invited to 'look out at airplanes flying all over the world and think about distant foreign countries, while you relax in the bath'.

The unusual spa facilities meant that when it first opened Centrair became a destination in itself. Genuine ticket-carrying passengers regularly complained that they couldn't find a table at any of the restaurants or use the hot spring because the place was full of tourists enjoying a day out at the airport.

Access to/from the airport is by train or shuttle bus. The private Meitetsu railway (no rail passes) operates a direct service (28 mins, ¥1200) between the airport and Meitetsu Nagoya station (next to the JR station). JR operates a shuttle bus (☎ 052-354 3811, 🖳 www.jrtbinm.co.jp; 1/hr between 6.30am and 5pm, ¥1000 one-way, ¥1900 return valid for two weeks; no rail passes) between JR Nagoya station and the airport terminal. The bus departs from outside the Taiko-dori exit (shinkansen side) of Nagoya station. Tickets can be purchased at the bus stop or from the JR ticket offices in Nagoya station.

If you're catching an early-morning flight and need to stay the night at Centrair, your best bet is the on-site *Comfort Hotel Central International Airport* (☎ 0569-38 7211, 🖳 www.choicehotels.com; ¥9500/S, ¥13,000/Tw), which is linked directly with the terminal building.

---

dolphin on the north side is male and the one on the south side is female. It's worth climbing up the tower to reach the seventh floor observatory. To reach the castle take the Meijo subway line to Shiyakusho. After visiting the castle, look in on the 630-seat **Nagoya Noh Theater** (same times as castle; free), built in 1997. It's open to the public when there are no performances.

Tokugawa Art Museum (🖳 www.tokugawa-art-museum.jp.english; Tue-Sun, 10am-5pm, ¥1200) exhibits treasures that belonged to the Owari branch of the ruling Tokugawa family as well as sections of a 12th-century illustrated scroll of *The Tale of Genji* – though the pieces are too fragile to be kept on permanent display. The gorgeous contents of the museum are matched by an equally extravagant entry fee. Take a local train from JR Nagoya station along the Chuo line four stops to Ozone station. The museum is 10 minutes on foot from the south exit.

(Opposite) Osaka's Umeda Sky Building (see p117). Impressive from the outside, it's also worth taking the lift inside up to the Floating Garden Observatory. (Photo © Ramsey Zarifeh).

In the former headquarters of the Toyoda Spinning & Weaving Company is the **Toyota Commemorative Museum of Industry and Technology** (☎ 052-551 6115, 🖳 www.tcmit.org/english; Tue-Sun 9:30am-5pm, ¥500), much more interesting than it sounds. The Toyota Group was founded by Sakichi Toyoda, inventor of the automatic loom. Automobiles were only added later, by Kiichiro, Sakichi's eldest son. In the museum, the Textile and Automobile Pavilions are interactive in parts, and exhibits are informative about how prototype ideas are turned into reality. The name 'Toyoda', incidentally, didn't change to 'Toyota' until 1935, when it was used as a brand name for export cars. It was thought that Toyota would be easier for foreigners to pronounce. The new spelling also brought the number of katakana strokes in the word to eight, which is considered lucky in Japan; Toyoda had 10 strokes. The museum is a 15-minute walk north from the Sakura-dori exit of JR Nagoya station. Glance up as you leave the station: the skyscraper across the street from the Sakura-dori exit is **Midland Square**, the new headquarters (opened in 2007) for Toyota and the *Mainichi Shimbun* newspaper. The building is just under two metres higher than the JR Central Towers (246.9m vs 245m) which loom above the station itself.

Just before the Toyota Museum, on the same side of the road, is **Noritake Garden**, free-to-enter open-plan grounds which are home to **Noritake Craft Center** (Tue-Sun, 10am-5pm, ¥500). This world-renowned porcelain company gives visitors the opportunity to follow the manufacturing process from creation and decoration to final inspection. There's also a museum where some of the company's special-order vases, many with price tags of up to ¥10 million, are on display. If those are out of your price range, there are several shops where mere mortals can purchase more affordable pieces of porcelain.

Sakae area The beating heart of the city may be shifting ever more towards the JR station area, but that doesn't mean that downtown Sakae is giving up without a fight. Aside from the many shops, bars and restaurants, it's also home to the 180-metre **Nagoya TV Tower**. Now dwarfed by the JR Towers and Toyota headquarters, the tower was a skyscraper when it was built in 1954 as the first television tower in Japan. It's worth climbing the 435 steps to the 100-metre 'Sky Balcony' (daily, 10am-9pm, ¥600) if you want a panoramic view of life from the centre of city.

If you're a fan of Japanese technology, you won't want to miss a visit to the **Robot Museum** (☎ 052-957 1640, 🖳 www.robot-museum.net, Mon-Fri 11am-7pm, Sat-Sun 10am-8pm; ¥1300), which opened in 2006. The country's first museum dedicated to robots and the history of robotics (it traces the history of robotic technology from early wind-up dolls to the latest in walking-and-talking lifelike androids) is located in a renovated car showroom. *(cont'd on p164)*

(Opposite) Top: It may not be the Sahara but Tottori's sand dunes (see p249) are the closest thing to a desert in Japan. **Middle**: Covered in snow in winter, Biei's sunflower fields turn bright yellow as summer approaches (see p349). **Bottom**: Even in a predominantly industrial city such as Niigata, there are hidden surprises such as this lotus pond in Hakusan Park (see p320). (Photos © Ramsey Zarifeh).

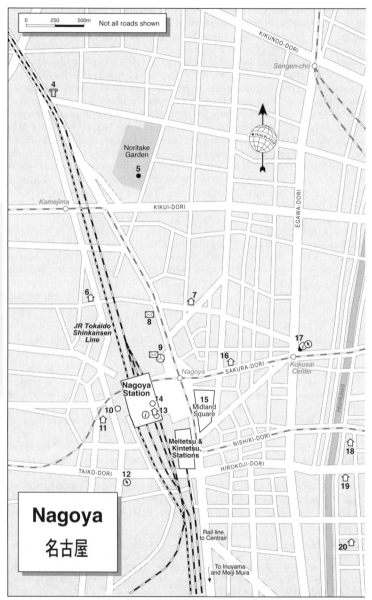

0   250   500m   Not all roads shown

KIKUNOO-DORI

Sengen-cho

4

Noritake
Garden

5

Kamejima

KIKUI-DORI

EGAWA-DORI

6

7

8

JR Tokaido
Shinkansen
Line

9

17

16

SAKURA-DORI

Kokusai
Center

Nagoya

Nagoya
Station

14

15
Midland
Square

Honkawa

10

13

11

12

Meitetsu &
Kintetsu
Stations

NISHIKI-DORI

18

TAIKO-DORI

HIROKOJI-DORI

19

Nagoya
名古屋

Rail line
to Centrair

20

To Inuyama
and Meiji Mura

HONSHU

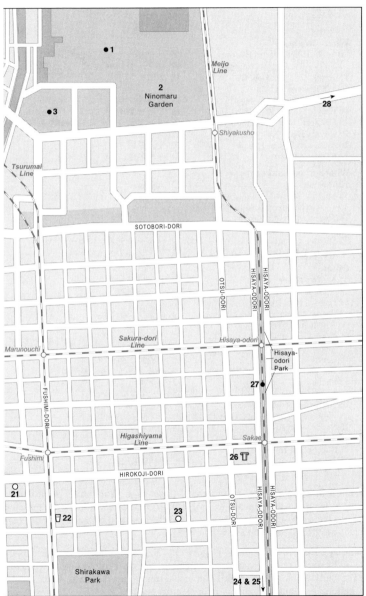

●1

2
Ninomaru
Garden

●3

*Meijo
Line*

28

○*Shiyakusho*

*Tsurumai
Line*

SOTOBORI-DORI

OTSU-DORI

HISAYA-ODORI

HISAYA-ODORI

*Sakura-dori
Line*

Marunouchi ○

Hisaya-odori ○

Hisaya-
odori
Park

27 ●

FUSHIMI-DORI

*Higashiyama
Line*

Sakae ○

Fushimi ○

26 🍶

HIROKOJI-DORI

○
21

🍶 **22**

23
○

OTSU-DORI

HISAYA-ODORI

HISAYA-ODORI

Shirakawa
Park

24 & 25
↓

HONSHU

NAGOYA　名古屋

Where to stay

6	Super Hotel Nagoya Ekimae	6	スーパーホテル名古屋駅前
7	Sofitel The Cypress Nagoya	7	ソフィテル ザ サイプレス 名古屋
11	Toyoko Inn Nagoya-eki Shinkansen-guchi	11	東横イン 名古屋駅新幹線口
13	Nagoya Marriott Associa Hotel	13	名古屋マリオットアソシアホテル
16	Fitness Hotel 330 Nagoya	16	フィトネスホテル３３０名古屋
18	Comfort Hotel Nagoya Chiyoda	18	コンフォートホテル名古屋 チヨダ
19	Roynet Hotel Nagoya	19	ロイネットホテル名古屋
20	Aichi-ken Seinen Kaikan	20	愛知県青年会館
24	Ryokan Meiryu	24	旅館名龍

Where to eat and drink

10	Yabaton	10	矢場とん
13	Mikuni Nagoya, La Jolla, Ka-Un (Nagoya Marriott Associa Hotel)	13	ミクニナゴヤ, ラホヤ、華雲
14	Towers Plaza (JR-Takashimaya)	14	タワープラザ (高島屋)
21	Hard Rock Café	21	ハードロックカフェ
22	Shooter's Sports Bar	22	シューターズ　スポーツバー
23	Buttsu Trick Bar	23	ブッツトリックバー

Other

1	Nagoya Castle	1	名古屋城
2	Ninomaru Garden	2	二之丸庭園
3	Nagoya Noh Theater	3	名古屋
4	Toyota Commemorative Museum of Industry and Technology	4	産業技術記念館
5	Noritake Craft Center (Noritake Garden)	5	ノリタケクラフトセンタ (ノリタケの森)
8	Central Post Office	8	中央郵便局
9	Bus terminal and post office	9	バスターミナル; 郵便局
12	Manboo	12	マンボー
15	Midland Square	15	ミッドランドスクエア
17	Tourist Information; internet (Nagoya International Center)	17	観光案内; インターネット (名古屋国際センター)
25	Nagoya Port Area	25	名古屋港
26	Robot Museum	26	ロボットミュージアム
27	Nagoya TV Tower	27	名古屋テレビ塔
28	Tokugawa Art Museum	28	徳川美術館

(cont'd from p161) The museum café is set in a 'near future' environment where the aim is that 'humans and robots will coexist peacefully'. The museum boasts the world's largest store for robot-related toys and items; it is located outside exit 9 of Sakae subway station.

Nagoya Port area South of Nagoya city, Nagoya Port has been redeveloped as a 'Leisure Zone'. Some of the attractions are the **Fuji Antarctic Museum** (Tue-Sun, 9:30am-5pm, ¥300), on board the *Fuji*. *Fuji* was used for 18 Antarctic expeditions until its retirement to Nagoya Port in 1983. Inside are crew quarters, including kitchen, dentist surgery and barber shop, as well as operation rooms. On the top deck is a small museum about the Antarctic expeditions. The Antarctic theme continues at **Nagoya Public Aquarium** (Tue-Sun 9:30am-5:30pm, to 5pm in winter, ¥2000), where the penguin tank recreates extreme weather conditions to make the birds feel at home. Next to the aquarium is a stadium for shark and dolphin shows.

Least interesting is the **Nagoya Port Building**, which contains a **Maritime Museum** (Tue-Sun, 9:30am-5pm, ¥300) and **observation platform** (daily except 3rd Mon, 9:30am-9pm, ¥300). A combination ticket for all the above costs ¥2000.

To save a few yen on the subway fare to Nagoya Port, first take a local train from JR Nagoya station one stop on the Chuo line to Kanayama station, from where you can connect up with the Meijo subway line to the terminus at Nagoyako (Nagoya Port; ¥230).

PRACTICAL INFORMATION
Station guide
Nagoya station's Towers are a city landmark and home to the city's top hotel and the JR-Takashimaya department store. The station has two main sides but for the city centre take the Sakura-dori exit. Sakura-dori is the main road heading away from the station towards Sakae. Within the station, there are plenty of **coin lockers** (up to ¥600).

On the main concourse you'll find a JR ticket office and branch of the JR Tokai Tours travel agency. To exchange your railpass voucher for the real thing, or to get any other rail-related information in English, head for the **JR Information Center** (daily 10am-6pm), a booth in the middle of the concourse on the Taiko-dori side of the station. Nagoya City also operates a Tourist Information Office (see column opposite).

There is a small branch **post office** with **ATM** in the station, close to the entrance to the bus terminal. Ask the tourist-information office to point you in the right direction.

JR lines running through or terminating at Nagoya are the **Tokaido line** (platforms 1-6) which heads east to Toyohashi and west to Gifu the **Chuo line** (platforms 7-10) for Nakatsugawa and Matsumoto and the **Kansai line** (platforms 11-13) for Matsusaka. The shinkansen tracks (platforms 14-17) have a separate entrance near the Taiko-dori side of the station.

Nagoya is also a junction for two private railways, the Meitetsu and Kintetsu.

The stations (first Meitetsu, then Kintetsu) are a couple of minutes' walk from the Sakura-dori side of JR Nagoya. Head out of the station and turn right.

Tourist information
A **tourist information office** (☎ 052-541 4301, 💻 www.ncvb.or.jp; daily, 9am-7pm) is on the first floor concourse of the Sakura-dori side of the station. The English-speaking staff can provide city maps and accommodation lists but can't make bookings. Ask for a copy of the English 'JR Nagoya Station Guide' which lists all the shops and restaurants in the vast station complex.

For more information, **Nagoya International Center** (NIC; ☎ 052-581 0100, 💻 www.nic-nagoya.or.jp; Tue-Sat 9am-8:30pm, Sun 9am-5pm) is a 10-minute walk east from the station along Sakura-dori. The centre has newspapers, magazines, satellite TV, a library and internet access (30 mins/¥250). If you'd like to visit a Japanese home for the afternoon ask here; bring your passport. This service is free but transport costs must be paid by the visitor. NIC publishes the monthly *Nagoya Calendar*, which contains listings of city-wide events. *Chubu Weekly* has more articles about the area but also contains film and concert details. Finally, *Nagoya Avenues* is a bi-monthly magazine with features on the city and surrounding area. You can find all of these at NIC and some may be available from the tourist information counter at the station.

HONSHU

Getting around

Nagoya has an efficient subway system with six lines: Higashiyama (yellow), Meijo (purple), Tsurumai (blue) and Sakura-dori (red), Meiko (white/purple) and Kamiida (pink). Nagoya station is connected with the Higashiyama and Sakura-dori lines.

A one-day subway pass costs ¥740, or subway plus bus pass is ¥850. On the 8th of every month, the price of the subway plus bus pass is reduced to ¥620.

The best deal for visitors is the **Ikomai Pass**, billed as 'ecological and economical'. Available from subway ticket offices, this costs ¥1300, allows unlimited travel on the subway for one day and includes free entry on that day to a number of attractions, including Nagoya Castle (see p159). The pass also gives discounts at other sights, including Tokugawa Art Museum, Toyota Commemorative Museum of Industry and Technology, and Fuji Antarctic Museum. These discounts are valid for one year, so there's no rush to see the lot in one day.

Internet

As well as the computer facilities at NIC (see p165), a 24-hour internet café, **Manboo** (🖳 www.manboo.co.jp; ¥400 for first hour, price drops for subsequent hours), is close to the Taiko-dori exit of Nagoya station. The price includes a soft drink.

Festivals

The biggest festival of the year is **Nagoya Matsuri**, a three-day event in mid-October.

Where to stay

Towering immediately above JR Takashimaya in the station, is the elegant 780-room *Nagoya Marriott Associa Hotel* (☎ 052-584 1111, 🖳 www.associa.com/english). Japan's newest world-class hotel certainly can't be beaten for location – from the station concourse, a sky shuttle whisks you up the twin towers to the gleaming 15th-floor lobby.

The rooms are beautifully furnished and have spacious bathrooms. Facilities include 24-hour room service, a dedicated concierge floor and a fitness club with an indoor pool and state-of-the-art gym. Rates vary according to the season but start from around ¥20,000 for a standard room. It's worth asking if there are any special deals or packages.

Another good upscale choice close to the station is *Sofitel The Cypress Nagoya* (☎ 052-571 0111, 🖳 www.sofitelthecypress.com) with room rates from ¥16,250.

A more affordable option is *Roynet Hotel Nagoya* (☎ 052-212 1055, 🖳 www.roynet.jp; ¥7800/S, ¥10,800/D), close to Fushimi subway station. Nearby is the reliable *Comfort Hotel Nagoya Chiyoda* (☎ 052-221 6711, 🖳 www.choicehotels.com) with singles from ¥5880 and doubles from ¥7980 including a continental breakfast.

If you prefer to be in the station area, a good bet is *Toyoko Inn Nagoya-eki Shinkansen-guchi* (☎ 052-453 1047, 🖳 www.toyoko-inn.com; ¥6090/S, ¥7560/D, ¥8610/Tw). Take the Taiko-dori exit (shinkansen side of the station) and walk up the main road which leads off from there (look for a shop called Bik Camera). The hotel is on the first road on your left after Bik Camera. Also near the station, on the shinkansen side, is *Super Hotel Nagoya Ekimae* (☎ 052-451 9000, 🖳 www.superhotel.co.jp; ¥5980/S, ¥7980/D) which has the usual functional rooms; the rate includes breakfast.

A five-minute walk up Sakura-dori from the station is *Fitness Hotel 330 Nagoya* (☎ 052-562 0330, 🖳 www.hotel330.co.jp), which according to its publicity operates on 'the concept of 'fitness=health' aiming at the life toward the next century'. There's no fitness centre but you do get a grey tracksuit instead of a *nemaki* (dressing gown) in your room. Compact but modern singles go from ¥7500 and doubles from ¥12,000. *Aichi Ken Seinen Kaikan* (☎ 052-221 6001, 🖹 204 3508) offers bargain dormitory-style accommodation (¥2992/pp for YH/HI members) and has a few private rooms. It's south-east of the station across Hori-gawa. Dinner is an extra ¥945.

Finally, *Ryokan Meiryu* (☎ 052-331 8686, 🖳 www.japan-net.ne.jp/~meiryu, 🖳 meiryu@japan-net.ne.jp) is a homely Japanese inn with tatami rooms (none en suite). Rates are ¥5250 for one person, ¥8400 for two and ¥11,025 for three. Optional breakfast is ¥630 and dinner ¥2310 per person. Services include free internet access and coin-operated laundry. The ryokan is a three-minute walk southeast of Kamimaezu station (exit 3) on the Meijo subway line.

Where to eat and drink

Inside the station, head for **Towers Plaza** on the 12th and 13th floors of the JR-Takashimaya department store, where you'll find nearly every kind of Japanese food as well as others including Italian, Chinese and a branch of *Starbucks*. The two basement floors are also crammed with food and freshly made lunch boxes to take out. For more upmarket dining, Nagoya Marriott Associa Hotel (see opposite) has a wide range of restaurants including: *Mikuni Nagoya*, a top-class French restaurant on the 52nd floor with views over the city; *La Jolla*, a California Grill on the 15th floor, also offering panoramic views and inventive cuisine; and *Ka-Un*, the hotel's best Japanese restaurant with sushi and tempura bars, as well as table and tatami seating.

Yabaton, a Nagoya-based restaurant chain famous for its misokatsu (deep-fried pork cutlet dipped in a delicious miso-based sauce), has several branches around the city (and there's now even one in Tokyo!). Downtown branches often have long queues – a better bet is to head for the Nagoya station branch (daily, 11am-9pm) in the basement of the Esca shopping mall, the entrance to which is down an escalator right outside the Taiko-dori exit. Seating is at counters and tables.

After dark, the best place for entertainment is the Sakae district east of Nagoya station across Hori-gawa. *Buttsu Trick Bar* in Sakae is worth a look if only for its giant Buddha but it also does good Asian food and a range of cocktails. It's on the eighth floor of a building very close to the Princess Garden Hotel and is open evenings only from 6pm.

In the Fushimi district just west of Sakae is a branch of *Hard Rock Café*, serving the usual burgers and fries to a young crowd (daily 11am to late; happy hour Mon-Thu 4-6:30pm). Look for it next to the Hilton Hotel. Also in Fushimi and popular with foreign residents is *Shooter's Sports Bar*, which has draught beer, pool tables, and a lunch menu from ¥790.

Side trips by rail from Nagoya

A popular side trip is to nearby **Inuyama**, known for its **castle** (daily, 9am-5pm, ¥5300), perched on a hill overlooking Kiso-gawa. Built in 1537, it was partly destroyed during the division of Japan into prefectures at the beginning of the Meiji era in 1871 and after an earthquake in 1891. Four years later, what was left of the castle was handed back to the Naruse family who had originally owned it – this act of charity was, however, tempered by a condition: the castle had to be repaired. Restoration work on the donjon was completed in 1965.

The other big sight is **Meiji Mura** (⌨ www.meijimura.com, daily 9:30am-5pm Mar-Oct, 9:30am-4pm Nov-Feb, ¥1600), an open-air collection of Western-style buildings from the Meiji era, including the 1898 Sapporo Telephone Exchange, St John's Church from Kyoto, and a steam locomotive that chugs the short distance between 'Tokyo' and 'Nagoya' stations.

Inuyama can be accessed along the private Meitetsu Inuyama line from Meitetsu Railway's Shin-Nagoya station (¥540, 30 mins), next to the Sakura-dori exit of JR Nagoya. From Inuyama station, a bus service runs to Meiji Mura (¥410, 20 mins). For Inuyama Castle, continue on to Inuyama-Yuen station, one stop after Inuyama.

If you want to save money and use the rail pass, the closest JR station to Inuyama is Unuma (see p147) on the Takayama line. From Nagoya, take a

Hida LEX bound for Takayama and change at Unuma (30 mins), where you transfer to Meitetsu's Shin-Unuma station, from where local trains (3 mins; ¥160) run to Inuyama.

Not all Hida LEX services bound for Takayama stop at Unuma; check at the JR ticket office in Nagoya before boarding the train.

NAGANO

Situated in the centre of Honshu, Nagano is the junction of the northern, central and southern Japanese Alps, and is often referred to as the 'roof of Japan'. The city has expanded from its original site around Zenko-ji. However, the temple, a 20- to 30-minute walk north of the station, remains the focal point of the city. The extension of the shinkansen from Tokyo to Nagano in time for the 1998 Winter Olympics reduced the fastest journey time from the capital to just 85 minutes.

What to see and do

The 1998 Winter Olympics officially began with the ringing of the bell at **Zenko-ji**. The temple is said to have been founded in the 7th century as a place to house the golden triad, a sacred image of the Buddha. It is never displayed in public but every seven years an exact copy is brought out as part of the Gokaicho ceremony – the next will be in 2009. Inside the main hall, people gather around the statue of Binzuru, considered to be Buddha's most intelligent follower; by rubbing the statue, they hope their own aches and pains will be rubbed away. Access to the pitch-black passage containing the 'key to paradise' is by ticket from vending machines (daily 9am-4:30pm, ¥500) inside the main hall. Anyone who touches the key is assured eternal salvation. Anyone who doesn't can buy another ticket and try again. Don't go in if you're claustrophobic or afraid of the dark.

To avoid the crowds, arrive in the early evening or better still at dawn, when the high priest and priestess make an appearance to pray for the salvation of visiting pilgrims. The starting time of this daily ceremony depends on the season – in the summer it's as early as 5:30am, in December at 7am; check the exact times with the tourist office. You can buy a guide for ¥50 at the information office on the left side of the approach to the temple.

Though it's possible to take a bus to the temple from the station (bus No 6, from stop No 1 outside the Zenko-ji exit, ¥100) runs between the station and the entrance to Zenko-ji, it's easy to walk the 30 minutes north up Chuo-dori. Heading up the main street lined with shops and department stores, look out on the right for **Saiko-ji**, a small temple founded in 1199; a leaflet is available. You'll know you've reached the start of the main path towards the temple, because it's lined with shops, soba restaurants and stalls line the street leading up to the Zenko-ji main gate.

To relive the Olympics, visit the **M-Wave Arena**, speed-skating venue during the Games and now home to the **Nagano Olympic Museum** (Wed-Mon, 10am-4pm, ¥700). The museum is occasionally closed when the M-Wave building is used for speed-skating events so check with the tourist information office before setting out. On display are Olympic medals, pictures and a digital video database of clips from previous Games. Pride of place is given to Hiroyasu Shimizu's skates. Shimizu became a national hero when he took gold in the 500m speed-skating event and bronze in the 1000m in the M-Wave Arena. A 3D-video theatre shows highlights of the Games, including the opening ceremony and Shimizu's moment of triumph. While you're here take a look in the vast arena – its suspended wooden roof is supposed to resemble ocean waves. In summer, the arena is used for a variety of events including a sumo tournament. The skating rink is open from October to March (daily, 10am-6pm).

To reach the M-Wave Arena, take a Nagaden bus (¥300, 20 mins) bound for Yashima from bus stop No 1 on the ground floor of the station's east exit and get out at 'M-Wave-mae'.

PRACTICAL INFORMATION
Station guide
Rebuilt for the Olympics, Nagano station has two sides, East and Zenko-ji. Take the latter for the city centre and Zenko-ji itself. Coin lockers (up to ¥500) are near both exits. Shinkansen services depart from platforms 11-14 and have a separate entrance to other JR lines. There are lifts between the main concourse and street level and toilets behind the Welcome to Nagano sign on the shinkansen concourse. There is also a waiting room there with a tv screen and a branch of Newdays selling drinks and snacks. There are surprisingly few places to eat at in the station.

Tourist information
Nagano City TIC (☎ 026-226 5626, daily, 9am-6pm) is on the station concourse, opposite the shinkansen ticket barrier. English-speaking staff are available most days. Ask for leaflets in English as it's mostly only Japanese brochures on display. Staff will book accommodation for you (Nagano city only) and can advise on the best places to ski/hike. They have bus timetables and information on late-season skiing.

Getting around
The private Nagano Dentetsu Railway, known as 'Nagaden', operates in the Nagano area (see p173). The entrance is outside the Zenko-ji exit of JR Nagano station; the station itself is underground. The main bus terminal is at street level outside the Zenko-ji exit. Stop No 1 is for buses to Zenko-ji. Gururin-go bus operates on a circular route round the city every 20 minutes between 09:30 and 18:10; there is a flat fare of ¥100.

If you're considering the Tateyama–Kurobe Alpine Route (see p145), highway buses (¥2300 one-way, 100 mins) operate from April to November between Nagano station and Ogisawa, starting point for the Alpine Route west to Toyama.

Internet
Café Planet (💻 www.cafepla.net, ¥400/hour) is open 24 hours and is on a small side street just across from the Zenko-ji exit, next to Hotel Sunroute. Various package deals on offer, depending on the chair you sit in (massage or reclining cost more than the standard variety). Free drinks and shower facilities are available.

Where to stay
Mielparque Nagano (☎ 026-225 7800, 💻 www.mielparque.or.jp; ¥6300/S, ¥11,550/Tw) is less than five minutes on foot from the station's east exit. This hotel is in a sleek modern building where glass lifts whisk you from the lobby to your room. It is part of a chain run by the post office (there's a handy branch office on the ground floor with an ATM). The singles are nothing special, twins are roomy with larger bathrooms but best of all are the Japanese tatami rooms which can sleep up to five people. Breakfast (¥900) is extra.

The JR-operated *Hotel Metropolitan Nagano* (☎ 026-291 7000, 💻 www.metro-

HONSHU

n.co.jp; ¥9240/S, ¥18,480/Tw) is one of the most luxurious places in town, located to the left as you take the Zenko-ji exit.

Island Hotel (☎ 026-226 3388, 🖳 www.island-hotel.co.jp; ¥6000/S, ¥10,500/Tw) is a smart business hotel with free (basic) breakfast. All rooms are en suite, but there is also a hot spring-style common bath. Automated check-in, credit cards accepted. Free high-speed internet access in rooms (bring a laptop). There is a 'business booth' where you can surf the web for free. Twins are reasonably spacious with large (for this kind of hotel) bathrooms.

Comfort Hotel Nagano (☎ 026-268 1611, 🖳 www.choicehotels.com; ¥4830/S, ¥9870/Tw) has wireless internet access throughout the hotel. Compact rooms and free breakfast.

For something a little more upmarket try **Hotel JAL City Nagano** (☎ 026-225 1131, 🖳 www.nagano.jalcity.co.jp; ¥9933/S, ¥17,325/D/Tw), which is closer to Zenko-ji. Some rooms have wireless internet access – ask for one when reserving as they go fast.

A good business hotel is **Hotel Nagano Avenue** (☎ 026-223 1123, 🖳 www

---

NAGANO　長野

Where to stay

3	Matsuya Ryokan	3	松屋旅館
4	Zenko-ji Kyoju-in Youth Hostel	4	善光寺教授院ユースホステル
13	Hotel JAL City Nagano	13	ホテルＪＡＬシティ長野
16	Hotel Nagano Avenue	16	ホテルナガノアベニュー
17	Island Hotel	17	アイランドホテル
18	Holiday Inn Express Nagano	18	ホリデイインエクスプレス長野
19	Mielparque Nagano	19	メルパルク長野
20	Comfort Hotel Nagano	20	コンフォートホテル長野
24	Hotel Metropolitan Nagano	24	ホテルメトロポリタン長野

Where to eat and drink

5	Suyakame Miso	5	すやかめみそ
6	Daimaru	6	大丸
8	Fujikian	8	藤木庵
9	Rakucha Rengakan	9	楽茶レンガ館
10	Gotokutei	10	ごとく亭
12	Joy Guru	12	ジョイグル
15	Café Comme Ça	15	カフェコムサ
21	Tokyu department store	21	東急デパート
23	Heiando Café	23	平安堂
25	Capricciosa; Pronto; McDonald's	25	カプリシヨーザ；プロント；マクドナルド

Other

1	Zenko-ji	1	善光寺
2	Zenko-ji (Information)	2	善光寺案内所
7	Post office	7	郵便局
11	Central post office	11	中央郵便局
14	Saiko-ji	14	西光寺
19	Post office	19	郵便局
22	Café Planet	22	カフェプラネット
23	Heiando Books	23	平安堂
26	Bus terminal	26	バスターミナル

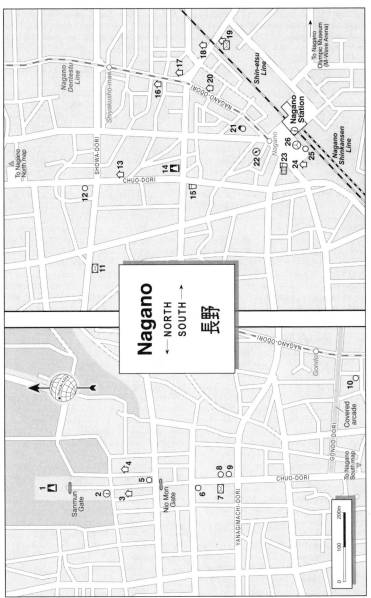

Nagano
長野

← NORTH
SOUTH →

HONSHU

Nagano Station

Nagano Shinkansen Line

Shin-etsu Line

Nagano Dentetsu Line

To Nagano Olympic Museum (M-Wave Arena)

Shiyakusho-mae

NAGANO-DORI

SHOWA-DORI

CHUO-DORI

To Nagano North map

Nagano

Gondo

NAGANO-DORI

GONDO-DORI

Covered arcade

To Nagano South map

CHUO-DORI

YANAGIMACHI-DORI

Sanmun Gate

Nio Mon Gate

0   100   200m

.avis.ne.jp/~avenue; ¥6300/S, ¥12,600/Tw). Facilities include a restaurant, coin laundry and sauna. Special rates which include breakfast are usually available by booking online.

Holiday Inn Express Nagano (☎ 026-264 6000, 🖳 www.holiday-inn-nagano .co.jp; ¥8800/S, ¥16,000/D, ¥17,000/Tw) has very comfortable rooms.

Zenko-ji Kyojuin Youth Hostel (☎/🖹 026-232 2768; ¥2900/3900, no meals) is just outside the main temple compound. Bags must be left in the entrance hall lockers so as not to damage the specially handmade tatami in all the dormitory rooms (the building is over 100 years old). It's 20 minutes on foot from the station up Chuo-dori.

If you're looking for Japanese-style accommodation, you can't beat *Matsuya Ryokan* (☎ 026-232 2811, 🖹 233 2047) for location, within the precinct which leads up to the main gate of Zenko-ji. It's a small traditional Japanese inn where an overnight stay with two meals will set you back around ¥10,000. Reservations for this and all other accommodation in Nagano can be made at the tourist information counter at the station.

Where to eat and drink

To the left as you take the Zenko-ji exit of Nagano station are a number of casual restaurants including pizza and pasta chain *Capricciosa* (daily, 11am-10pm), *Pronto* (which turns into a bar in the evenings but also serves pasta dishes during the day such as bacon and aubergine spaghetti for ¥680), *McDonald's*, and soba and ramen restaurants. Some of these are on the second floor (the same level as the station concourse). For take-out lunches, try the food hall in the basement of **Tokyu department store** outside the Zenko-ji exit.

Opposite the station is *Heiando Books and Café* (daily, 10am-9pm). The café is on the third floor and has fresh juices as well as coffee/cake sets.

Heading from the station up Chuo-dori, *Café comme Ca* is on the ground floor of the Again department store, shortly after the Howdy Seibu department store on the left-hand side. Good coffee and a wide selection of cakes are served in this gleaming white café. Further up Chuo-dori, *Joy Guru* (daily 11am-2:30pm, 5-10pm) is a no-frills Indian restaurant. Cheap curry sets and an all-you-can-eat buffet lunch for ¥850.

There are plenty of soba restaurants on the approach to Zenko-ji, including *Fujikian*, along Chuo-dori opposite a small branch post office. The name is written in kanji in grey letters above the front. Seating is on tatami or at wooden tables. The tempura and soba (from ¥1000) are delicious.

Rakucha Rengakan, next door to Fujikian (to the right as you face the entrance to Fujikian), is in a brick building with a small red awning above the door. They serve soba set meals (¥1150 for a meal with all the trimmings, including an ice-cream dessert) as well as Western-style meals such as pasta.

A little further up the same road (just before the final approach to Zenko-ji begins) and on the other side of the street is *Daimaru*, another soba restaurant with low wooden tables. Look out for the large shop-front window where you can see the owner preparing the noodles. It's a fraction cheaper than Fujikian. Most soba restaurants close around 6/7pm.

Suyakame Miso is easy to spot because it's on a corner as you approach the temple and they have a sign in English; it does grilled rice balls with miso (soybean paste) for ¥200 and miso-flavoured ice cream (¥250) – it sounds awful but tastes good. Also worth trying is the amazake (¥200), a sweet form of saké usually served warm.

Gotokutei (daily, 5-11pm) serves a range of Japanese dishes at reasonable prices (set meals from ¥1260 or splash out on the full 'Japanese dinner course' for ¥3150). They have an English menu and are used to dealing with foreign guests. A wide range of saké is available. It's on a side street which leads off from the Gondo covered arcade. The street is opposite Ito-Yokado department store.

Side trips by rail from Nagano

Possible trips by private Nagano Dentetsu Railway are to the small town of Obuse, or to the rail terminus at Yudanaka from where buses take 40 minutes to reach the vast skiing/hiking terrain of Shiga Kogen Heights. The Nagaden line starts underground but soon emerges to a very fertile part of Japan with peach and apple trees as well as grapevines on all sides, in addition to the usual rice fields so even though the train rocks and rolls a bit it is a pleasant journey.

Obuse (22/33 mins, ¥650/750 one-way by local/express train) was a stop on the old highway linking the Japan Sea with Edo (Tokyo) and now boasts a number of museums, temples and gardens. The biggest draw is **Ganshoin Temple** (daily, 9am-5pm Apr-Oct, 9:30am-4:30pm Nov-Mar; closed Wed Dec-Mar, ¥200), which belongs to the same Zen Buddhist sect as Eihei-ji (see p152). The temple is renowned for its ceiling painting of a phoenix 'staring in eight directions' by the artist Katsushika Hokusai (1760-1849). Pick up a map of Obuse from the tourist information office at Nagano station. The lockers (¥300) at Obuse station are suitable for day packs.

Yudanaka (50/60 mins, ¥1130/1230 one-way by local/express train from Nagano) is an onsen town which is a good base for a day trip to the Shiga Kogen Heights (see below). *Yurukuan* (☎ 0269-33 2117, 🖹 33 2119, 🖥 www .yurukuan.com; from ¥8000/13,300 S/Tw inc breakfast) is a large hotel with the original building on one side of the road and a more modern one on the other; a tunnel under the road links the two buildings. The hotel offers spacious Japanese- and Western-style rooms. The rooms are all en suite; those with a view cost an extra ¥1000. There are public baths as well as a rotemburo and a Jazuzzi – men can use the former in the morning and the latter in the evening; women at other times. Payment of the hot springs tax (¥150) entitles you to visit other baths in the town. Free internet access is available. Evening meals must be booked in advance (*kaiseki ryori* costs from ¥3000) but there are other places to eat in Yudanaka. If you can tell them what time you expect to arrive when you make a reservation they will meet you at the station.

Shiga Kogen Heights (☎ 0269-34 2323, 🖥 www.shigakogen.gr.jp) lies in the centre of Joshin-Etsu Kogen National Park. With mountain peaks of over 2000m and 21 ski resorts connected by chair lifts, this is the place to go for late-season skiing (usually until the end of the first week of May) on the slopes that hosted the downhill slalom courses during the Nagano Winter Olympics. A one-day lift pass costs ¥4500. A half-day ticket valid for the morning or afternoon is ¥3500. Check the website for the latest prices and ski season dates. Direct buses (70 mins, ¥1800 one-way) also operate during the ski season between Nagano station (east exit, stop No 3 or 4) and Shiga Kogen. In summer, in addition to the many hiking opportunities in the area, it is possible to buy a **Yamabiko course ticket** (¥1800).

The Yamabiko course includes a ropeway (cable car) trip from Shiga Kogen, then a ten-minute walk to a gondola which goes up to Higashi Tateyama (2030m) from where there are wonderful views of the surrounding mountains as well as an alpine garden. The return journey is by two different chair lifts to the top of the cable car. If in the area in August look out for groups of school children sent to the cooler hills to study in preparation for their high-school entry exams. A bus leaves Yudanaka hourly for Shiga Kogen (¥1000); the last bus back to Yudanaka leaves at 16:15.

MATSUMOTO

Surrounded by mountains, Matsumoto is an ancient castle town and a gateway to the north-western corner of Nagano prefecture. The 3000m peaks of the Japanese Alps form a backdrop to the west of the city. Locals like to think of Matsumoto as not the heart but the 'navel' of Japan – whichever it is, thousands visit the city every year to see one of the country's best-preserved castles.

What to see and do
Fifteen minutes on foot north of the station is **Matsumoto Castle**, considered to be one of the finest castles in Japan. A small fortress was first built here in 1504 but this was remodelled and expanded in 1593 to become what still stands today. It's a rare example of a Japanese castle which is not a 20th-century concrete reconstruction. The fortification once dominated the city skyline but the view is now obscured by office blocks and the castle remains invisible until the final approach. The five-storey donjon is known as 'crow castle' because the outside walls are mainly black. The design is unusual because the castle is built on a plain rather than a hill, but it still contains traditional defensive elements: the hidden floor, sunken passageways, specially constructed holes in the wall to drop stones on the enemy below and incredibly steep stairs to make an attack on the castle difficult for intruders. Tacked on to the side is the moon-viewing room, a later addition and the venue for 'moon-viewing parties', when invited guests could stare up at the moon while enjoying a cup or two of saké. Tickets (¥600) for the castle include admission to the nearby **Japan Folklore Museum**. Both are open daily, 8:30am-4:30pm.

Ten minutes on foot north of the castle is **Kaichi Gakko** (daily Mar-Nov but closed on Sun Dec-Feb, 8:30am-4:30pm, ¥300), a former elementary school built in 1876 which looks like something out of little England. The oldest Western-style school building in Japan, it remained open for 90 years. There's proof inside that, contrary to popular belief, the education system in Japan was not all work. The classrooms are open to the public and there's also a room dedicated to extra-curricular activities, which included ice-skating (note the 'geta-skates' that look uncomfortable and dangerous to wear). Upstairs, in the main hall, look out for the coil of rope used in *tsunahiki*, a tug-of-war tournament between classes that took place every year at the school athletics festival.

Matsumoto Timepiece Museum (Tue-Sun, 9am-5pm, ¥300) is by the river and there's a large pendulum clock (supposedly the biggest in Japan) outside. An English pamphlet is available. If possible, get here on the hour when you can see many of the clocks on display swing into action and chime. It's a small museum but watch- and clock-lovers will be in heaven. You'll find everything from tiny intricate pocket watches to enormous clocks – look out for the 19th-century cannon-shaped sundial from England. Inexplicably there is also a small selection of antique gramophones.

Finally, even if you're not staying at Marumo Ryokan (see p176), it's worth heading over to the **Nakamachi district** along the south side of Metoba-gawa, where you'll find old houses, craft shops and cafés.

PRACTICAL INFORMATION
Station guide
As trains pull into Matsumoto station, a female voice virtually sings the station's name to arriving passengers. From the platforms, follow signs to the Central Exit/Matsumoto Castle.

Passing through the ticket barrier, you arrive at the main concourse on the second floor, where you'll find a revolving model of Matsumoto Castle. Take the stairs down to the ground and turn left at the bottom for **coin lockers** (all sizes). There is an elevator from concourse to street level but assistance should first be sought from station staff. There are more (including ¥500/600 ones) in two other places: as you exit the ticket barrier go straight and walk through Midori department store. You'll find a row of lockers to your left as you leave the store. There are even more lockers just around the corner from the tourist-information booth on the ground floor.

The **bus terminal** is beneath Espa store across the street from the station.

Tourist information
The tourist information booth (☎ 0263-32 2814, daily April-Oct 9:30am-6pm, Nov-March 9am-5:30pm) is to the right of the station exit at street level. Friendly, English-speaking staff can assist with same-day reservations and will provide travel information.

Getting around
Matsumoto is compact enough to visit on foot, but if you really need it there is a 'Town Sneaker' bus (¥100 flat fare or ¥300 for a one-day ticket, which gives you reduced-price entry to Matsumoto Castle) which runs in a loop at regular intervals during the day.

The private Matsumoto Dentetsu line runs from Matsumoto station to Shin-Shimashima (see p178). Matsumoto Airport has connections with Osaka, Fukuoka, Sapporo and Matsuyama. A shuttle bus operates between the airport and the station.

Internet
You can surf the net at **People's** (🖳 www .peoples.jp, 1 hour; ¥200 + one drink), see

p178. Alternatively, free internet access is available inside the **M-Wing** building, five minutes on foot from the station, close to Parco department store. Once inside the building, head for 'Fureai International Information Center' (Mon to Fri 9am-10pm, Sat/Sun 9am-5pm) on the second floor. Sign in at the desk and you're supposed to limit computer use to half an hour. There's also a small selection of English newspapers and magazines.

Festivals
An outdoor performance of Noh is held in the grounds of Matsumoto Castle on the evening of August 8th. The performance is lit by bonfires with the brooding presence of the castle as a backdrop. On November 3rd, Matsumoto Castle Festival features a samurai parade and puppet shows.

Where to stay
Top of the range is *Hotel Buena Vista* (☎ 0263-37 0111, 🖳 www.buena-vista.co.jp), which is very plush and very expensive. Between July and October singles cost ¥12,000 and twins ¥21,000. Rates are reduced slightly outside this peak season.

Ace Inn Matsumoto (☎ 0263-35 1188, 🖳 http://ace.alpico.co.jp; ¥6700/S) is conveniently located right outside the station. It only has single rooms – all on the small side but they are good value since the rate includes breakfast. There's also a coin laundry and free internet access for hotel guests – ask at reception. Take the main station exit (for Matsumoto Castle) and it's on the corner on your right. A good alternative is *Toyoko Inn Matsumoto Ekimae Honmachi* (☎ 0263-36 1045, 🖳 www.toyoko-inn.com; ¥5460/S, ¥8190/D/Tw), opposite the Post Office in the centre of town.

Roynet Hotel Matsumoto (☎ 0263-37 5000, 🖳 www.roynet.co.jp, ¥10,000/S, ¥12,500/D, ¥17,000/Tw, ¥21,000/Tr) is just a few minutes on foot from the main station exit and next to Parco department store. It's a hyper-efficient place with automatic check-in, clean, compact rooms and a coin laundry. A more economical option is *Hotel New Station* (☎ 0263-35 3850, 🖳 www .hotel-ns.co.jp; ¥5800/S, ¥12,600/Tw), only two minutes on foot from the station. The rooms are basic but all have attached bath.

Just across the street is a newer business hotel, **Hotel Mor-Schein** (☎ 0263-32 0031, 🖳 www.mor-schein.co.jp; ¥7350/S, ¥11,550/D, ¥13,650/Tw). **Marumo Ryokan** (☎ 0263-32 0115, 🖹 35 2251; ¥5000/pp), a traditional inn in the Nakamachi district by Metoba-gawa, has tatami rooms (none en suite) with a fantastic wooden bath. Marumo Ryokan gets booked up fast – an alternative is the small and friendly **Nunoya Ryokan** (☎ 0263-32 0545, 🖳 nun oya@po.mcci.or.jp; from ¥5000 per person), one block back from the river. It's a small, traditional Japanese inn with the usual creaking wooden floors. The per person

rate (cheaper for double usage) is without meals. No en suite rooms but you can lock the communal bath for your own use. The owner speaks a little English and can recommend some of the local soba restaurants.

The nearest youth hostel is at **Asama-Onsen**. Take a bus from stop No 7 (from the terminal under Espa department store) bound for Asama-Onsen and get off at 'Matsumoto Dai-ichi Koko-mae' (20 mins). **Asama-Onsen Youth Hostel** (☎ 0263-46 1335; ¥3360/4360, no meals) is a bit grey and depressing.

Where to eat and drink
There's a good **coffee shop** on the station concourse opposite the JR ticket desk. Near

---

MATSUMOTO 松本

Where to stay

2	Asama Onsen Youth Hostel	2	浅間温泉ユースホステル
6	Marumo Ryokan	6	まるも旅館
7	Nunoya Ryokan	7	ぬのや旅館
10	Hotel Mor-Schein	10	ホテルモルシヤン
11	Hotel New Station	11	ホテルニューステーション
14	Roynet Hotel Matsumoto	14	ロイネットホテル松本
16	Toyoko Inn Matsumoto Ekimae Honmachi	16	東横イン 松本駅前本町
20	Ace Inn Matsumoto	20	エースイン松本
22	Hotel Buena Vista	22	ホテルブエナビスタ

Where to eat and drink

5	Kobayashi	5	こばやし
6	Kissa Marumo	6	喫茶まるも
12	Mister Donut	12	ミスタードーナッツ
13	Doutor	13	ドトール
14	Skylark	14	すかいらーく
18	Yoneyoshi	18	米芳
21	People's	21	ピープルズ

Other

1	Kaichi Gakko	1	開智学校
3	Matsumoto Castle	3	松本城
4	Japan Folklore Museum	4	日本民族資料館
8	Matsumoto Timepiece Museum	8	松本市時計博物館
9	M-Wing	9	Mウイング
15	Parco department store	15	パルコデパート
17	Post Office	17	郵便局
19	ESPA dept store; bus terminal	19	ESPAデパート; バスターミナル
21	Internet	21	インターネット

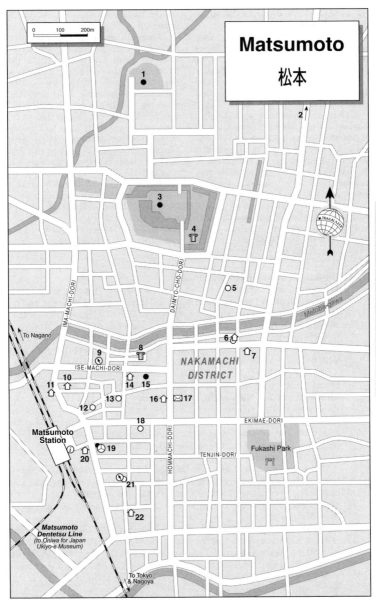

Matsumoto

松本

0   100   200m

1

2 ↑

3

4 ⊤

5 ○

6 ⌂

7 ⌂

DAIMYO-CHO-DORI

Metoba-gawa

To Nagano

NAKAMACHI
DISTRICT

IM-MACHI-DORI

8 ⊤

9

ISE-MACHI-DORI

10 ⌂

11 ⌂

14 ⌂

15 ●

12 ○

13 ○

16 ⌂   ⊠ 17

18 ○

EKIMAE-DORI

HOMMACHI-DORI

Matsumoto
Station

i

20 ⌂

19

TENJIN-DORI

Fukashi Park

21

22 ⌂

Matsumoto
Dentetsu Line
(to Oniwa for Japan
Ukiyo-e Museum)

To Tokyo
& Nagoya

HONSHU

the station you'll find branches of *Mister Donut* and *Doutor*.

Kobayashi serves delicious hand-made soba noodles. It's a quaint traditional place on a quiet street just set back from the river. Meals start at around ¥1000. There is a small display of plastic food outside. Look for the white hanging curtain and bench outside.

One of Matsumoto's specialities is *basashi*, raw horsemeat (it's also popular in Kumamoto, see box p408). A good place to try it is *Yoneyoshi*, less than five minutes from the station on the right-hand side of Ekimae-dori; look for the white hanging curtain and the glass cabinet outside that contains a bowl and vase with a horse painted on them. It's an izakaya-style place, with seats along the counter and at tables. If you're not sure what to have, go for one of the set meals (teishoku) such as the 'Yoneyoshi Teishoku' (¥1650). Teishoku

without basashi are also available. Lunch from ¥720.

In the evening, a good place to search out is *People's* (daily, 6pm-2/3am), across from the small park area opposite the Buena Vista Hotel. There's a menu in English, big portions of pasta and pizza, and prices are reasonable. This place sometimes has live music. It's on the second floor but look for the English sign on the street outside. *Skylark*, a 24-hour family restaurant on the first floor of Hotel Roynet Matsumoto, is open to anyone (not just hotel guests) in need of some late-night sustenance.

If you're in the Nakamachi area, it would be a crime to miss stopping at *Kissa Marumo* (daily, 8am-8pm), a café attached to Marumo Ryokan (see p176), which plays classical music and serves good coffee, ice cream and mouth-watering cakes.

Side trips by rail from Matsumoto

On the outskirts of Matsumoto is the **Japan Ukiyo-e Museum** (🖥 www.uk iyo-e.co.jp/jum-e) Tue-Sun, 10am-4:30pm, ¥1000), a private museum built by the Sakai Family which houses a collection of over 100,000 Japanese wood-block prints – only a fraction are on display at any one time.

To reach the museum take the private Matsumoto Dentetsu Railway from Matsumoto station to tiny Oniwa station. Ask at Oniwa ticket office for a map with directions to the museum; it is about a 15-minute walk from the station.

Continuing along Matsumoto Dentetsu Railway to the terminus at Shin-Shimashima (¥680) and transferring to a bus (65 mins; ¥1900) brings you to the hiking resort of **Kamikochi**, at an altitude of 1500m right in the centre of the Japanese Alps National Park. Japanese holidaymakers have flocked to Kamikochi ever since British missionary Walter Weston scaled the peaks at the end of the 19th century and popularized mountaineering. Kamikochi is open only from late April to early November, after which heavy snow shuts off road access for the winter.

In winter, the best **skiing** is in **Hakuba**, 60km north-west of Matsumoto. Local trains run along the JR Oito line to Hakuba in 90-110 minutes (you may have to change trains at Shinano-Omachi). Limited expresses (starting from either Shinjuku or Nagoya) stop in Matsumoto and then take 60 minutes to reach Hakuba.

From Hakuba station, buses take five minutes (¥180) to **Happo-One** ski resort, which has a network of fast gondolas and chair lifts up to peaks as high as 1900m – there's a mixture of runs suitable for all ski levels. Skis and boots can be hired from a number of shops in the resort. A one-day lift pass costs ¥4600 or half-day is ¥3300. The ski season lasts from December to April. The area is also popular in summer with hikers.

Instead of backtracking to Matsumoto, it's possible to continue north along the Oito line from Hakuba to the terminus on the Japan Sea coast at **Itoigawa**, a point of connection with the rail route west to Toyama and beyond (see p143). From Hakuba, trains run as far as Minami-Otari, where it's necessary to change trains for the last leg of the journey to Itoigawa.

TAKAYAMA

Deep in the mountains, in the region known traditionally as Hida, Takayama is deservedly one of the most popular destinations in central Honshu, combining as it does ancient traditions with a stunning natural location. Often referred to as 'little Kyoto', Takayama boasts temples, shrines, small museums, traditional shops and inns. As a result it gets very busy, particularly during the spring and autumn festivals, when 300,000 people come to watch the parade of floats.

The greatest pleasure, however, comes not from the museums or tourist sights but from the chance to wander round the old, narrow streets of wooden houses and discover a part of Japan that has been largely airbrushed out of the big cities. Set aside enough time to forget the 'sights' and enjoy the atmosphere; two or three days would be ideal. Takayama is also a good place to hunt around for souvenirs, particularly lacquerware, wood craft and pottery.

What to see and do

One of Takayama's many highlights is a visit to the daily **morning markets** (6/7am-12pm). One is right outside Takayama Jinya (see below), the other on the banks of Miya-gawa. Every morning, women from the surrounding area come here to sell vegetables, flowers and locally made crafts.

During the Edo period, **Takayama Jinya** (daily, 8:45am-5pm March to July/September, 8:45am-6pm in August, to 4:30pm the rest of the year; ¥420) was used as the government building for Gifu prefecture. It's now open to the

---

☖ **Sukyo Mahikari – a new religious movement**
Look out on the bus ride back to Takayama from the Folk Village (see p182) for the **Main World Shrine** (daily, 9:30am-4pm, free), along Highway 158 at the bottom of the hill and instantly recognizable from its elaborate gold roof with a red sphere perched on top.

You won't find this place on any official maps of Takayama because it is home to Sukyo Mahikari, one of Japan's 'new religions' that have sprung up in the post-war years. Mahikari is described as 'true light, a cleansing energy sent by the Creator God that both spiritually awakens and tunes the soul to its divine purpose'.

The movement began in 1960 when Yoshikazu Okada founded the 'Lucky and Healthy Sunshine Children'. In order to be taken more seriously the name was changed over the years until in 1974 it became Sukyo Mahikari, and Okada was replaced at the top by a woman called Keishu, who he proclaimed to be his daughter. Anyone is welcome to visit this bizarre shrine; the twin towers at the entrance look like minarets, an enormous fish tank stretches across the inside wall, there's a pipe organ that wouldn't be out of place in a cathedral, and a hall with a seating capacity of 4500. The sheer scale of the place is overwhelming.

public but most of the rooms are empty; tours are sometimes available in English (enquire at the main entrance). One or two of the rooms need little explanation; the torture room, for example, tells its own story. Look out for the old toilet in one of the rooms, with the helpful 'out of use' sign on it – it would be a desperate visitor who felt the need to relieve him/herself in front of crowds of sightseers.

If you're not here at festival time (see p183) you can see four of the large floats used during the festival at **Takayama Yatai Kaikan** (Float Exhibition Hall), open daily 8:30am-5pm, ¥820; the floats change three times a year, in March, July and November. Each float would cost the equivalent of $4 million to replace. A tape commentary in English is available. The attendant shows you a card stating this, rather than daring to tell you!

A short walk north of the river you'll find a street of **traditional shops** stretching along three blocks – suitable hunting ground for locally made sou-

---

TAKAYAMA 高山

Where to stay

3 Tenshoji Youth Hostel	3	天照寺ユースホステル
9 Takayama City Hotel Four Seasons	9	高山シティホテルフォーシーズン
11 Hida Hotel Plaza	11	ひだホテルプラザ
14 Country Hotel Takayama	14	カントリーホテル高山
18 Hida Takayama Washington Hotel Plaza	18	飛騨高山ワシントンホテルプラザ
21 Best Western Hotel Takayama	21	ベストウエスタンホテル高山
29 Hotel Associa Takayama Resort	29	ホテルアソシア高山リゾート
30 Minshuku Sosuke	30	民宿惣助

Where to eat and drink

5 Alice	5	アリス
6 Masakatsu Tonkatsu	6	政かつ　とんかつ
7 Kiyomian	7	清見庵
16 Black Sea Coffee	16	ブラックシーコーヒー
19 Myogaya	19	茗荷舎
22 Bistro Mieux	22	ビストロミヨー
23 Mieux's Bar	23	ミューズバー
24 Hida Komeya	24	飛騨米屋

Other

1 Takayama Yatai Kaikan	1	高山屋台会館
2 Yoshijima Heritage House	2	吉島家住宅
4 Higashiyama	4	東山
8 Morning Markets	8	朝市
11 Internet (Hida Hotel Plaza)	11	インターネット
12 Poppo Koen (park)	12	ポッポ公園
15 Hida-Takayama TIC; internet access	15	飛騨高山観光案内所; インターネット
17 Timely convenience store/ Rent a cycle	17	タイムリーコンビニエンスストア/ レンタサイクル

Takayama
高山

KOKUBUNJI-DORI

Takayama
Station

Takayama
Line

29, 30,
31 & 32

ROUTE 158

HIROKOJI-DORI

HACHIKENMACHI-DORI

Enako-gawa

Miya-gawa

Streets of
traditional
shops

3 & 4

HONSHU

Other *(key continued from opposite)*
20 Kamitsubo Rent a cycle
25 Central Post Office
26 Taguchi Rent a cycle
28 Takayama Jinya
31 Hida Folk Village; Teddy Bear Eco
   Village; Hida-Takayama
   Museum of Art
32 Kur Alp

20 上坪レンタサイクル
25 中央郵便局
26 田口レンタサイクル
28 高山陣屋
31 飛騨高山民族村; テディベアエコ
   ビレッジ; 飛騨高山美術館

32 クアアルプ

venirs. A good place to rest weary legs is at the nearby **Yoshijima Heritage House** (daily in summer, Wed-Mon in winter, 9am-4:30/5pm, ¥500), built in the Meiji period for a saké-brewing family. The entrance fee includes a cup of mushroom tea.

The main temple district is just east of Enako-gawa in **Higashiyama**, which is a little hilly but still a great area to explore on foot. The map available from the tourist information office has a suggested walking tour. The youth hostel (see p184) is part of Tensho-ji.

For a refreshing break try **Kur Alp** (see opposite; daily, 10am-10pm, ¥800), a hot-spring leisure complex with endless spas, pools and a water slide.

Hida Folk Village area Twenty minutes out of town along Highway 158, in the hills overlooking Takayama, is **Hida Folk Village** (daily 8:30am-5pm, ¥700). Over 30 traditional farmhouses and merchant cottages from rural areas have been moved here and restored. On a fine day it's a great mini-escape from the town below but since the village is all open air it's not so much fun in the rain. As well as the buildings, traditional crafts such as woodcarving and weaving have also been preserved and there are displays inside some of the houses. To reach the Folk Village take a bus from stop No 6 at the terminal outside the station. A ¥900 ticket available from the bus terminal includes return bus ride and entry to the village.

A short walk down the hill from the Folk Village, young children might like the **Teddy Bear Eco Village** (daily 10am-6pm, closed some days January to March, ¥600), a museum full of bears from all over the world, the oldest of which dates back to 1903. In the ecology corner there's a display of how real bears are suffering as a result of environmental destruction.

One university teacher in Japan wrote: "I was quite impressed with the number of artefacts and the relaxation room really was relaxing (but perhaps that reflects my escape from the usual rounds of university meetings). Also, the café was quite reasonable, had organic items and sold some fair-trade goods which is still something of a rarity in Japan."

Takayama Museum of Art (daily 9am-5pm, ¥1300) has a large collection of glassware from the 16th to 20th centuries. It's in a modern building two minutes further down the road from the Teddy Bear Eco Village.

A red double-decker London bus runs to the museum from Takayama station (departing 11:10am; 1:10pm; 3:10pm; 4:40pm, April 1-October 31).

冊 Railway relic

Rail fans may like to make a mini-pilgrimage to '**Poppo Koen**', just out to the west on the other side of the station. In this small park you'll find a well-preserved steam locomotive (No 19648, to be precise), built in 1917, as well as a 1934 vintage snow plough which – by the time it was taken out of service in 1980 – had clocked up enough miles to circumnavigate the globe twice.

PRACTICAL INFORMATION
Station guide
The small station gives a hint of the scale of Takayama itself. A **coin locker** room containing large ¥500 lockers is open daily, 7am-9pm. Turn right as you go out of the station and it's on the right.

Tourist information
Hida Takayama TIC (☎ 0577-32 5328, daily 8:30am-6:30pm, to 5pm Nov-Apr) is in a wooden booth outside the station. The English-speaking staff are very knowledgeable and will help book same-day accommodation.

Takayama isn't as shamelessly geared towards tourists as Karuizawa (see p135) but you will almost certainly not be alone here. The advantage of this is that there are plenty of signs in English.

Getting around
Takayama is best negotiated on foot or by **bike**: Rent A Cycle (daily, 10am-5pm, ¥200 per hour) is to the right as you leave the station. Look for the bikes outside a combined souvenir shop and convenience store called Timely.

You could also try Taguchi bike rental (daily, 8am-6pm, ¥300 for the first hour, ¥200 thereafter, six or more hours capped at ¥1300) or Kamitsubo (daily, 7:30am-7pm, ¥300 for first hour, ¥200 thereafter, ¥1200 per day). **Tourist rickshaws** are an emergency standby.

A year-round **bus service** operates between Takayama and Matsumoto (90 mins). There are also **highway buses** linking Takayama with Shinjuku in Tokyo, and Osaka. For schedules, enquire at the tourist office.

Internet
You can check email at the tourist information office (the door leading into the computer area has 'Staff only' written on it).

There is a coin-operated computer (¥100 for 10 mins) in the lobby of Hida Hotel Plaza. Turn left from the station, go past the bus terminal and it's on the right before City Hall.

Festivals
Takayama is known for its two annual **float festivals**, when 300-year-old floats are paraded through the streets. One is in spring (Apr 14th-15th) and the other in autumn (Oct 9th-10th). Look out around town for signs in English about the different floats. One sign reveals that a float puppet show was prohibited in 1892 because a scene involving an 'exotic woman's dance', during which 'a lion's head suddenly comes out of her mid-section' was deemed immoral. The scene was not reinstated until 1984.

Local records reveal that in 1697 Takayama was home to no fewer than 56 saké breweries. Over 300 years later, the number has shrunk to eight, though the popularity of the drink does not seem to have diminished. Every year in January and February, saké breweries in Takayama open their doors to the public and organize promotions where you can try their products for free – an excellent winter warmer. For further details, enquire at the tourist information office.

Where to stay
The JR-operated *Hotel Associa Takayama Resort* (☎ 0577-36 0001, 🖳 www.associa .com/tky, reservation-tky@associa.co.jp/ english) is the place to head for first-class luxury in the hills overlooking the town.

Expect spacious en-suite rooms, the hotel's own hot spring, two high-quality restaurants and impeccable service. Standard twins are ¥17,000, de luxe twins are ¥20,000 and triples are ¥28,500 (10% discount with rail pass).

The best reason for staying the night here is the chance to use the extensive in-house spa/hot-spring facilities (free except for hot-spring tax of ¥200 per person). The baths are on two separate floors – 5th and 7th – and each is open either to men or women on a daily rotating basis. If you stay the night you get the chance to use the baths on both floors over two days.

For yet more wallowing in water try Kur Alp (see opposite); it's connected to the hotel by an underground passage and hotel guests receive discounted entry. A free shuttle bus service runs between Takayama station and the hotel (a 10-minute journey). **Best Western Hotel Takayama** (☎ 0577-37 2000, 🖳 www.bestwestern.co.jp; ¥8900/S, ¥14,800/D, ¥15,750/Tw) is a five-minute walk east of the station and has rooms and facilities you would expect from an international chain. The standard twins are comfortable if not overly large and there's a good buffet breakfast. The daily curry/dessert buffet is ¥1260.

Apart from the clean and modern rooms, an additional selling point at **Takayama City Hotel Four Seasons** (☎ 0577-36 0088, 🖳 www.f-seasons.co.jp, fseasons@aioros.ocn.ne.jp; ¥6900/S, ¥16,200/Tw) is the hot spring-style bath. **Hida Takayama Washington Hotel Plaza** (☎ 0577-37 0410, 🖳 http://takayama.wh-at.com; ¥6700/S, ¥15,000/Tw) is convenient for the rail tracks: it's across the street from the station. Close by is **Country Hotel Takayama** (☎ 0577-35 3900, 🖳 www.country-hotel.jp), a relatively new place with mostly single rooms (¥5900) but a couple of twins/doubles (¥13,000) also.

Also worth considering is **Hida Hotel Plaza** (☎ 0577-33 4600, 🖳 www.hida-hotelplaza.co.jp; ¥6930/S, ¥16,110/D/Tw).

The best ryokan in Takayama can set you back up to ¥25,000 (inc two meals) but minshuku are a much more affordable option. **Sosuke** (☎ 0577-32 0818, 🖳 www.irori-sosuke.com), a short walk behind the station, is a homely 13-room minshuku which charges ¥7875 per person with two meals or ¥5040 without.

Cheapest of all and maybe the most atmospheric place to stay is **Tenshoji Youth Hostel** (☎ 0577-32 6345, 🖹 35 6392; 95 beds). Rates are ¥2940 for YH/HI members and ¥3940 for others; an extra ¥1000 will get you your own room. Breakfast is ¥525. Lights go out at 10pm in the dorms. Cycles can be rented here for ¥800 per day and a map of places to eat around the temple area is available from the front desk.

The hostel is 20 minutes on foot east from the station across the Miya-gawa and Enaka-gawa rivers, at Tensho-ji in Higashiyama.

Where to eat and drink

Masakatsu Tonkatsu (Wed-Mon, 11am-2pm, 5-8pm), on Yasugawa-dori, is a small place that serves large portions of melt-in-the-mouth tonkatsu. Seating is at a few tables or along the counter. This is a great place to go if you're hungry. Almost directly opposite is **Alice** (Thur-Tue, 11am-2pm, 4:30-8pm), which serves a variety of set meals for ¥1000-1800. The cheapest deal is the 'service lunch' for ¥850; the pasta set menu is ¥880.

Bistro Mieux (Thur-Tue, 11:30am-1:30pm and 5-9:30pm) is a five-minute walk from the station along Kokubunji St. Creative French food is presented with flair and there's a good selection of wines. Seating is at a high counter, or on tatami mats in the stylish back room, where they've thoughtfully provided space underneath the tables to put your legs. The dinner menu starts from ¥4200 but lunch menus are ¥1500-3500. The three-course ¥1575 set lunch is excellent value.

If Bistro Mieux sounds a bit pricey, head across the street to the newer **Mieux's Bar** (Thur-Tue, 12-2pm and 6-11pm), which has a cheaper menu with seating at a counter or at café-style tables. The tasty 'plate lunch' is ¥950.

Vegetarians will want to make a beeline for **Myogaya** (Wed-Mon, 8am-5pm), an organic restaurant serving brown rice and curries from ¥950.

Kiyomian (daily, 9am-5pm) serves a variety of noodles and Hida beef dishes. Try the Hida beef curry with the delicious soft slices of beef on top for ¥1500. An English menu is available.

Hida Komeya specializes in Hida beef and vegetables cooked with miso on a small stove. A meal here will set you back ¥2000.

If you're in search of a quick caffeine fix, try **Black Sea Coffee** (daily, 7am-5/6pm), a Starbucks clone across the street from the station. Look for the sign written in English.

HONSHU

KANAZAWA

Though somewhat isolated on the Japan Sea coast, the variety of sights in Kanazawa more than repays the effort of the journey.

In 1580 the Maedas, the second largest clan in feudal-era Japan, settled here. Peace and stability followed and Kanazawa quickly became a prosperous centre for the silk and gold lacquer industries. As its citizens became wealthy, Kanazawa's arts and culture scene began to flourish. Still today Kanazawa has a reputation for its patronage of 'high-class' arts such as Noh and the tea ceremony.

The city is also curiously proud of another claim to fame: it is allegedly one of the wettest places in the country, with an average of 178 rainy days per year. A local proverb translates as 'Even if you forget your packed lunch, don't forget your umbrella'.

Apart from the much-hyped Kenrokuen garden there are other surprises, such as well-preserved geisha and samurai districts and a working Noh theatre. The city also functions as a gateway to the Noto Peninsula, a knuckle of land that juts out into the Japan Sea north of the city. And just for good measure, a short train ride away is the intriguing UFO town of Hakui (see p191).

What to see and do

The first major stop on the bus from the city centre is at **Omicho**, a daily indoor market with around 170 stalls selling fresh fish, fruit and vegetables. A market is said to have existed here for more than 280 years. For the main shopping and eating district, **Katamachi**, stay on the bus until Korinbo. Most of the sights described below are within walking distance of Korinbo.

Kenrokuen and around Everyone visits Kanazawa to see **Kenrokuen** (daily Mar 1st-Oct 15th 7am-6pm, Oct 16th-Feb 28/29th, 8am-4:30 pm, ¥300), rated as one of the top three gardens in Japan. Inside, professional photographers wait around for the tour groups but if you can find some space away from the crowds, a couple of hours can easily be spent wandering round the grounds.

Constructed 200 years ago as the garden for Kanazawa Castle (of which just one gate remains), Kenrokuen is spread over 11.4 hectares and contains about 12,000 trees. The number six (roku) in the garden name refers to the six attributes of a perfect garden: vastness, seclusion, careful arrangement, antiquity, water and panoramic views. Water features in particular are everywhere – including the first fountain ever placed in a Japanese garden. Kenrokuen is in the city centre, 15 minutes by bus from the station. Maps are available at the entrance.

Close to Kenrokuen is **Ishikawa Prefectural Art Museum** (daily 9:30am-5pm, ¥350), full of hand-crafted lacquer cabinets, fancy cosmetic boxes, decorated plates, hanging scrolls and shoji screens. Across the street is **Ishikawa Prefectural Noh Theater** (Tue-Sun, 9am-5pm, free). Performances (some free) are held on many weekends throughout the year. If there are no performances, it's possible to take a look inside (enquire at the office).

The newest addition to this area and just a short walk from Kenrokuen is **Kanazawa 21st Century Museum of Contemporary Art** (Tue-Thur/Sun 10am-6pm, Fri/Sat 10am-8pm, 🖳 www.kanazawa21.jp; ¥350), opened in 2004 and billed as the 'world's most advanced art museum'. The design of the building – gleaming white, circular and set in its own landscaped gardens – threatens to overshadow the contents of the permanent collection, where you'll find an eclectic mix of Japanese and foreign contemporary art. Separate entry charges are levied for temporary exhibitions, which change every few months. The permanent collection is closed during the dismantling of/preparation for temporary exhibitions, so check the website or ask at the tourist information office before setting out. The building houses a well-stocked contemporary art library and is home to one of Kanazawa's swankiest **cafés** (Tue-Sun, 10am-10pm), just to the right of the main entrance. It's open until late, which makes this a good place to stop for a coffee, glass of wine and/or bite to eat while exploring the area.

Higashiyama district Across Asano-gawa is Higashiyama, Kanazawa's former **geisha quarter**, where you'll find a few streets lined with old geisha houses, instantly recognizable by their wooden latticed windows. Tea and coffee shops are now open in some of the houses but the area still retains a traditional charm and in the early evening there's the chance of spotting a geisha.

More than 90% of Japan's gold leaf is produced in Kanazawa and it's in Higashiyama that you'll find the **Sakuda Gold and Silver Leaf Shop** (open daily 9am-6pm), where the most expensive item for sale is a pair of gold-leaf screens for ¥3 million. At the other end of the scale are gold-leaf boiled sweets and telephone cards, but there's no charge at all for using the gold and platinum toilets on the second floor.

A JR bus heads out to the Higashiyama district (rail passes are accepted). Buses leave from the JR bus stop outside Kanazawa station's east exit. Get off just after crossing Asano-gawa.

Teramachi district

Temple lovers should head south of Sai-gawa to the Teramachi district. The most famous is **Myoryu-ji**, better known as **Ninja-dera** (daily, 9am-4/4:30pm, ¥800). A defensive stronghold as well as a temple, the rooms contain trick doors, false exits, secret tunnels and pits – no wonder you have to go on a guided tour (reservations required; call ☎ 076-241 0888). Tours are only in Japanese, so ask at the tourist office inside Kanazawa station for an English translation. To reach the temple, take a bus from the station to the Nomachi-Hirokoji stop.

If you're in Teramachi at 6pm on a Saturday, listen out for the sound of the bells of six temples ringing together. The resultant noise has been selected as one of the '100 best soundscapes in Japan'.

Nagamachi district

This district is an area of narrow, cobbled streets with a few preserved samurai houses. It's a pleasant surprise to stumble upon Nagamachi, a few minutes' walk west of the busy Katamachi shopping district. The Nomura family's **Samurai house** (daily, 8:30am-5:30pm; to 4.30pm Nov-Apr, ¥500) is open to the public and contains a shrine, samurai armour and a small but immaculate Japanese garden. For an extra ¥300, tea is served in a room overlooking the garden.

Station area **Ishikawa Prefectural Concert Hall** (🖥 www.ongakudo.pref.is hikawa.jp) is the large modern building to your right as you leave the station's east exit, next to the ANA Hotel. It's the home of Kanazawa Orchestra Ensemble but also attracts orchestras from across Japan and abroad. Ask for a performance schedule at the tourist information centre inside the station or check the website – with luck there will be something on while you're in town. The main hall seats 1500 and is a tremendous concert space. There's a run of the mill café, **Café Concerto**, on the second floor.

Kanazawa Yasue Gold Leaf Museum (☎ 076-233 1502, 🖥 kinpaku@city .kanazawa.ishikawa.jp; daily except last two days of month in Feb/May/ Aug/Nov, 9:30am-5pm, ¥300) is a hidden gem, just around the corner from Manten Hotel (see p190). It doesn't look like much from the outside, but this museum has a lot to offer. The first room you are ushered into shows in pictures and text the process of making gold leaf. All the signs are in Japanese – but don't worry, a member of staff will appear and start to tell you all about the display in English (reading from a manual!). After this you will be beckoned to a tatami area, where gold-leaf tea (including edible slivers of gold leaf) and biscuits await. You can sip your tea overlooking a small Japanese garden and stream with koi (carp). After this, you are given a demonstration of how gold leaf is made before you are invited upstairs to look at some of the objects that have been made using gold leaf – the gold-leaf screens and exquisite gold-leaf embroidered kimono are just two of the highlights. This museum really is a hidden gem which is well worth making time to visit. There's also a small shop selling gold-leaf products, including a cream which is said to do wonders for the skin.

PRACTICAL INFORMATION
Station guide
The station has a west and an east gate. Take the east gate for the city centre, bus terminal and Ishikawa Prefectural Concert Hall (see above). Look in the corridors off the main concourse for **coin lockers** (all sizes).

The east exit – with its enormous steel and glass dome – has become a symbolic gateway to the city. The dome is supposed to keep new arrivals from getting wet in notoriously rainy Kanazawa. According to the city authorities, it 'expresses the hospitality of the citizens of Kanazawa, who kindly greet and send off people who come to visit the rainy city, in the hope that they will not get wet when starting their journey'.

JR Highway Buses (rail passes accepted, reservations required) bound for Osaka (see p116) and Tokyo (see p90) leave from stop No 5 of the bus terminal outside the east exit.

Tourist information
The **tourist information centre** (☎ 0762-32 6200, 🖥 www.city.kanazawa.ishikawa.jp; daily 9am-7pm) is inside a shopping mall to the left of the station concourse as you face the main exit. An English-speaking volunteer will help with reservations and provide information on Kanazawa and the surrounding area. At the far end of the mall you'll find a small branch Post Office with ATM.

Ishikawa Foundation for International Exchange (☎ 0762-62 5931, Mon-Fri 9am-6pm, Sat/Sun to 5pm), on the third floor of the Rifare Building, about 10-minutes' walk south-east of the station, offers satellite TV, a library and free internet access. Also pick up from here or the tourist information centre the monthly *Ishikawa International Times* newsletter with local event details and film listings.

Finally, if you call the **Kanazawa Goodwill Guide Network** (☎ 076-232 3933, daily, 10am-6pm) two weeks ahead of your visit, they will arrange for a guide to accompany you to some of the sightseeing spots in and around the city.

Festivals

The Hyakumangoku Festival takes place every year around June 14th. The event celebrates the arrival of Lord Maeda into the city and begins at dusk with a procession of floating lanterns down Asano-gawa. Public tea ceremonies are also held in Kenrokuen (see p185) but the highlight of the day is a colourful parade through the streets which mixes acrobatics, horse-riding, period costume and even a 'Miss Hyakumangoku' beauty contest.

KANAZAWA 金沢

Where to stay

2	R&B Hotel Kanazawa Eki Nishi-guchi	2	R＆Bホテル金沢駅西口
3	Kanazawa Manten Hotel	3	金沢マンテンホテル
4	Kanazawa Central Hotel	4	金沢セントラルホテル
6	APA Hotel Kanazawa Eki-mae	6	アパホテル金沢駅前
8	Toyoko Inn Kanazawa Eki Higashi-guchi	8	東横イン 金沢駅東口
9	Hotel Nikko Kanazawa	9	ホテル日航金沢
13	Kanazawa Youth Hostel	13	金沢ユースホステル
14	Toyoko Inn Kanazawa Korinbo	14	東横イン 金沢香林坊
22	Ryokan Murataya	22	旅館村田屋
24	Matsui Youth Hostel	24	松井ユースホステル

Where to eat and drink

7	Café Concerto	7	カフェコンチェルト
11	Omicho Market	11	近江町市場
16	Hamano	16	浜の
17	Sayur	17	サユル
18	McDonald's	18	マクドナルド
20	Doutor Coffee	20	ドトールコヒ
21	Capricciosa	21	カプリシヨーザ
23	Ninnikuya	23	にんにくや

Other

1	Kanazawa Yasue Gold Leaf Museum	1	金沢市立安江金箔工芸館
5	Rent-a-Cycle	5	レンタサイクル
7	Ishikawa Prefectural Concert Hall	7	石川県立音楽堂
10	Ishikawa Foundation for International Exchange	10	石川県国際交流協会
11	Omicho Market	11	近江町市場
12	Sakuda Gold and Silver Leaf Shop	12	株式会社金銀箔工芸さくだ本社本店
15	Nomura Family Samurai House	15	武家屋敷野村家
19	Central Post Office	19	中央郵便局
20	Labbro Department Store	20	ラブロデパート
25	Myoryu-ji (Ninja-dera)	25	妙立寺
26	Kanazawa 21st Century Museum of Contemporary Art	26	金沢21世紀美術館
27	Ishikawa Prefectural Art Museum	27	石川県立美術館
28	Kenrokuen	28	兼六園
29	Ishikawa Prefectural Noh Theater	29	石川県立能楽堂

HONSHU

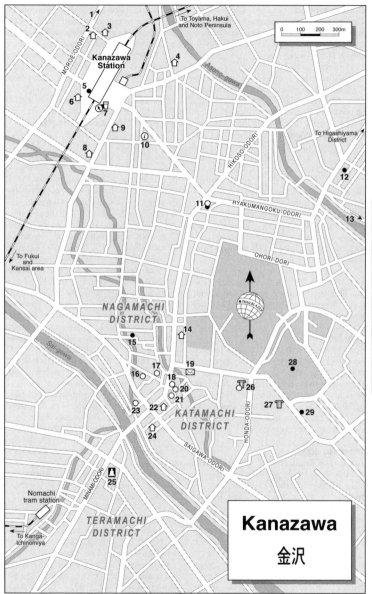

1
2
3
To Toyama, Hakui and Noto Peninsula

MOROE-ODORI

Kanazawa
Station

4

Asano-gawa

5
6
7
9
10
8

HIKOSO-ODORI

To Higashiyama
District

12

11
HYAKUMANGOKU-ODORI

13

To Fukui
and
Kansai area

OHORI-DORI

TRAILBLAZER

HONSHU

NAGAMACHI
DISTRICT

14
15

Sai-gawa

28

17
19
16
18
20
21
23 22
24

26

27
29

KATAMACHI
DISTRICT

HONDA-ODORI

SAIGAWA-ODORI

MINAMI-ODORI

25

Nomachi
tram station

To Kanga-
Ichinomiya

TERAMACHI
DISTRICT

Kanazawa

金沢

Getting around

The city centre is a 10-minute bus ride from the station. Buses leave from stops outside the east exit; take any bus from stop Nos 7, 8 or 9. There's a flat fare (¥200) within the city centre.

As its name suggests, the retro-style **Kanazawa Loop Bus** (daily, 8:30am-6pm, every 15 mins; ¥200 per ride or ¥500 for a one-day pass; purchased from the driver) does a circular tour of all the main city sights at regular intervals throughout the day. The one-day pass allows you to jump on and off as many times as you like. **Kanazawa Retro Bus** (daily, 8:30am-6pm, every 15 mins) runs in a loop around the city; ¥500 one-day passes can be bought at the tourist information office inside the station, at the bus ticket office outside the east exit or from bus drivers. This ticket can only be used on the Loop Bus, not on ordinary city buses. The Loop Bus leaves from stop No 10 at the bus terminal.

Rent A Cycle (daily, 8am-8:30pm; ¥800/4 hours) is along the side of the station building, to the left as you take the station's west exit and just past APA Hotel Kanazawa Eki-mae.

Internet

You can check email/surf the web for free (half-hour limit) at one of two internet terminals inside the Music Library (daily, 10am-6pm) on the basement level of Ishikawa Prefectural Concert Hall (see p187), right outside the station's east exit. Ask at the reception desk of the library and you'll be assigned a computer.

Where to stay

Toyoko Inn Kanazawa Eki Higashi-guchi (☎ 076-224 1045, 🖳 www.toyoko-inn .com; ¥6090/S, ¥8190/D/Tw) is very convenient for the station. An older branch, *Toyoko Inn Kanazawa Korinbo* (☎ 076-265 1045, 🖳 www.toyoko-inn.com; ¥5250/S, ¥7350/D/Tw) is in the Korinbo district, closer to the shopping, restaurants and bars.

R&B Kanazawa Eki Nishi-guchi (☎ 076-224 8080, 🖳 http://randb.jp; ¥5250/S) is a modern, single-room-only place where the rate includes a simple breakfast of cof-fee, orange juice and freshly baked crois-sants. Five to ten minutes on foot from the station's west exit, but it's a bit difficult to spot as there are no large signs on the roof.

A three-minute walk from the station's west exit is **Kanazawa Manten Hotel** (☎ 076-265 0100, 🖳 www.manten-hotel.com; ¥5800/S, ¥11,600/Tw). The rooms are small but well furnished and all single/twin rooms feature semi-double beds.

APA Hotel Kanazawa Eki-mae (☎ 076-231 8111, 🖳 www.apahotel.com, ahka eki@apa.co.jp; ¥8000/S, ¥12,500/D, ¥13,500/Tw), right outside the west exit, boasts that it is the closest hotel to the JR ticket barrier – it beats even Manten Hotel, only a stone's throw from the station, for location. It's an upmarket place with rea-sonable rooms and an 'Eki Spa Sauna' (daily, 6am-12am; ¥1000/3 hours, ¥2000/ day), a hot spring on the second floor which is free to hotel guests. There's also a branch of Seattle's Best Coffee on the ground floor.

For top-class luxury, head for **Hotel Nikko Kanazawa** (☎ 076-234 1111, 🖳 ww w.hnkanazawa.co.jp; ¥16,747/S, ¥28,875/D or Tw). It's outside the station's east exit and can hardly be beaten for its friendly staff and service. Less than a five-minute walk east of the east exit is **Kanazawa Central Hotel** (☎ 076-263 5311, 🖹 262 1444; ¥6800/S, ¥13,000/Tw, ¥18,000/Tr). It's a good standard business hotel with clean, comfortable rooms.

If you prefer Japanese-style accommo-dation, a great choice is **Ryokan Murataya** (☎ 076-263 0455, 🖳 www.spacelan.ne.jp/~ murataya; ¥4700/S, ¥9000/Tw, ¥12,600/ Tr). This traditional inn is just set back from the Katamachi district. Some of the rooms overlook a small garden and all are simply decorated with Japanese paper screens and hanging scrolls. Breakfast (¥500) is extra.

Kanazawa Youth Hostel (☎ 076-252 3414, 🖹 252 8590, 🖳 www.jyh.orj.jp; ¥3045/4045; 80 beds) is on a hill above Higashiyama. From the station, take bus No 90 bound for Utatsuyama and get off at Youth Hostel-mae, from where you have to walk the rest of the way uphill. Breakfast is ¥630 and dinner ¥1050. **Matsui Youth Hostel** (☎/🖹 076-221 0275, 🖳 www.jyh

.or.jp; ¥3255/4255, 15 beds) is more centrally located but there's a 10pm curfew, so anyone planning a night on the town might prefer to stay at a business hotel.

Where to eat and drink
A good place to stop for lunch is one of the sushi restaurants inside **Omicho market** as the fish is guaranteed to be fresh.

Plenty of restaurants line the streets of the Katamachi shopping district. Here you'll find branches of *McDonald's*, *Doutor* coffee shop and the Italian chain *Capricciosa*; the latter is open daily (11am-11pm, last orders 10pm) and has half-size meal deals including salad and a drink for ¥830. Vegetarians don't normally get much of a deal in Japan but *Sayur* is a popular vegetarian restaurant with a friendly manager.

Hamano is the place to head if you like fish; their speciality is local catches from the Noto Peninsula. Seating is along the main counter and there's plenty of saké and beer. Look for the name written outside in black kanji on white. *Ninnikuya* (daily, 5pm-12am) serves garlic in practically all its dishes and is very busy at weekends.

Side trips by rail from Kanazawa
A short side trip can be made by taking the private Hokuriku Railway 16km from Nomachi station (just south of the Teramachi district) to the terminus at **Kanga-Ichinomiya** (¥500, 35 mins). On the right across the street from the station is an old tofu shop, where tofu has been made in the traditional way for over 70 years. In front of the station is a road that leads up to Shirayama Shrine. There's no charge to enter the shrine which receives a large number of visitors on the first day of the New Year.

The area is very much off the beaten track and there's a real feeling of stepping back in time. The train ride itself, passing through tiny stations as it heads towards the countryside, is also fun. From Nomachi, roughly one train an hour goes to Kanga-Ichinomiya, usually at six minutes past the hour.

From Kanazawa Station, the JR Nanao line heads north towards the **Noto Peninsula**. An intriguing place to visit lies 40km along the line at **Hakui**, a self-proclaimed 'UFO town' (see box below). There's a tourist information desk (☎ 0767-22 7171, daily, 10am-6pm) in Hakui station, though they only have Japanese maps and the staff don't speak English. Cycles can be rented from the JR ticket office (2 hours/¥300, 4 hours/¥600).

⛩ **Little green men**
Hakui's connection with UFOs can be traced back to the discovery of a manuscript called 'Kashima Choshi', written before the Edo period; chapter 16 describes the sighting of a mysterious fireball in the sky – an ancient form of UFO? On the strength of this and other local tales a healthy tourism industry has built up; Cosmo Isle Hakui now attracts 70,000 visitors every year. It's all thanks to the museum's director (a former monk turned TV scriptwriter) who persuaded the Ministry of Home Affairs to pay half the construction bill for the dome. Even *Time* magazine picked up on the story of the UFO town on the Noto Peninsula, sending a reporter to ask 'why Hakui?' (Answer: 'The Japanese government is an easy touch for funds that might bring business to fading areas, and Hakui is near the constituency of former Prime Minister Yoshiro Mori'). Cynicism aside, the town revels in its UFO status and the boom has even spread to local restaurants, where 'UFO ramen' (noodles mixed with baby octopus, which in Japanese cartoons look like extra terrestrials) has become a hit on the menu. Get there before the aliens do.

HONSHU

Cosmo Isle Hakui (Wed-Mon, 9am-5pm, ¥800), an enormous dome containing a UFO museum, cost ¥5,260,000,000 to build when it opened in 1996.

On display are assorted space craft, astronaut suits and genuine moon dust. A few of the exhibits, including the Soviet Union's Vostok capsule and a NASA space suit with 24-carat gold helmet, are real. Just to prove the museum isn't all serious, there are items such as the prop box used by Tom Hanks to store his space suit during the filming of *Apollo 13*. Video booths show interviews with sober and eccentric professors and scientists connected with SETI (Search for Extra Terrestrial Intelligence) and there's also an extensive UFO database – conspiracy theorists can call up images of UFOs, and zoom in on each photo for a closer look. Cosmo Isle Hakui is 10 minutes on foot north of Hakui station. It's easy to spot as it's the only building with a 26m American rocket parked outside. Signs in the museum are in Japanese and English.

Kansai – route guide

INTRODUCTION

All roads lead to Kyoto, at least that's what most tourist brochures and travel documentaries on Japan let you assume. The ancient capital does indeed lie at the heart of the Kansai region but it would be a shame to restrict your travel solely to the well-beaten track. Japan's even more ancient capital, Nara, is less than an hour away by rail and it's easily worth staying a night or two there. Further south, the landscape becomes more rural, the crowds thin out and the views are worth seeking out. Kansai has one of the most extensive networks of rail lines in the country (operated by JR and private railways), which means you can go off the beaten track without the fear of leaving the big city far behind.

(Opposite) Top: Kinkaku-ji (see p213), Kyoto's famous Golden Temple, shines even on a grey day. (Photo © Kazuo Udagawa) **Bottom:** In their rush to visit Kyoto's Nijo Castle most people miss nearby Shinsen-en (see p220), a small, peaceful garden with an attractive red-lacquered bridge. (Photo © Richard Brasher).

(Overleaf) Geisha are renowned for their ability to entertain with music, dance, song and conversation. The women in these photos are maiko, trainee geisha (see box p47). (Photos top © Colin Sinclair, bottom © Alistair Logan).

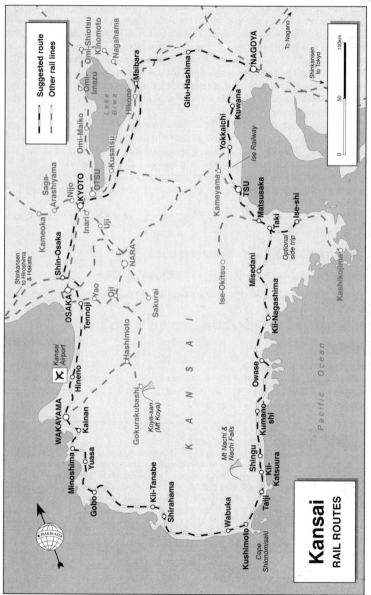

Suggested route
Other rail lines

Kansai
RAIL ROUTES

The first part of this route guide follows the shinkansen line **from Nagoya to Osaka** via Kyoto – there is relatively little to see en route but it's useful if you're in a hurry. With more time, consider a much longer route to Kyoto **via the rural Kii Peninsula**, easily accessed from Nagoya but very much off the traditional tourist trail. Limited expresses operate around the peninsula so the journey needn't be too time-consuming; the countryside and coastline certainly repay the effort. Taking this longer route also gives you the opportunity to go to **Ise** (see p198), home of the Grand Shrine and spiritual centre of Japan's indigenous religion, Shinto.

Finally, another spiritual centre, the mountain retreat of **Koya-san** (see pp230-2) offers a wholly unexpected change of pace. Koya-san can be accessed from Kyoto, Nara or Osaka, or as part of a longer journey around the Kii Peninsula and is ultimately reached by a hair-raising cable car.

If you've arrived in Japan without a rail pass, JR West, which operates services throughout the Kansai area, sells regional passes over the counter. For details, see p14.

For up-to-date information on events throughout the Kansai region, check 🖳 www.kansai.gr.jp.

NAGOYA TO OSAKA BY SHINKANSEN

For the route from Tokyo to Nagoya (366km) see pp127-34.

Distances from Tokyo. Fastest journey time: three hours (from Tokyo); one hour (from Nagoya).

Some Hikari and all Nozomi run non stop from Nagoya to Kyoto.

Nagoya   [see pp159-68]

Nagoya to Shin-Osaka   [Map 9, p197]
Gifu-Hashima (396km) Only Kodama stop here. Despite its name, this station is not close to Gifu city (see p147) at all, which is better reached on the route starting on p146.

⛩ **Alternative Kansai rail pass**
   If you're a tourist or Japanese national who lives abroad and don't have a JR pass, and are not interested in any of the regional rail passes sold by JR West (see p14) for the Kansai region, it's worth considering the **Kansai Thru Pass** (🖳 www.surut to.com). This pass (**2-day**/¥3800, **3-day**/¥5000). gives you unlimited access to most private railways (services other than JR), subways and buses throughout Kansai, including Osaka, Kobe, Kyoto, Nara, and Koya-san. It can also be used for the journey from Kansai International Airport to Osaka on the private Nankai railway (but you have to pay a supplement to ride Nankai's 'rapi:t' express service on this route). The ticket also offers discounts at 350 tourist facilities in the region (check the booklet given to you when purchasing the pass).

   The pass can be purchased before you leave for Japan (see pp17-20) or from a variety of locations in the Kansai region; for the full list check the JR West website.

> **⛩ Flying without wings**
> Every year in late July, the Birdman Contest is held at Matsubara Beach on Lake Biwa. The purpose of this fiercely competitive event is to see how far humans can fly before ditching into the water of Lake Biwa. A giant runway is built for the occasion and teams (individuals and groups) compete to 'fly' off the edge. This may be an eccentric sport but many of the teams are made up of engineering students who spend months designing and building the perfect, streamlined human craft ... only to crash seconds after take-off. Check with Hikone TIC (☎ 0749-22 2954) for exact dates. During the contest, free shuttle buses run between Hikone station and Matsubara beach.

Maibara (446km) Some Hikari and all Kodama stop here. Maibara is a major rail junction on the Tokaido line and Hokuriku line (to/from Kanazawa, see pp185-92) as well as the shinkansen. For a few days each year, typically around Golden Week (see p67), the 'SL Kita Biwako' runs 22km along Lake Biwa between Maibara and Kinomoto on the Hokuriku line. A ride on this steam locomotive is worthwhile if you stop along the way at Nagahama, where you'll find an old station building, dating back to the time when passengers changed to a ferry for the journey across Lake Biwa.

Maibara is one stop (approximately four trains per hour) from the castle town of **Hikone**, situated on the eastern shore of Lake Biwa, Japan's largest lake. Hikone is known for its castle (Hikone-jo), about a ten-minute walk up the main street, Ekimae Oshiro-dori, from the station. The castle is not quite as dramatic as the one further down the line at Himeji (see p235) but it benefits from the superb natural backdrop of Lake Biwa. **Genkyu-en**, a Japanese garden dating back to 1677, is at the foot of the castle. A ¥500 ticket gets you entry to both the castle and the garden (daily, 8:30am-5pm).

Five minutes by taxi from Hikone station (no bus) is **Matsubara Beach** on the shore of Lake Biwa, venue for the annual International Birdman Contest (see box above). Near the beach is **Hikone Port**, from where cruise boats make excursions to a couple of islands on the lake. A tourist information office (☎ 0749-22 2954, daily, 9am-6pm, English spoken) is to your left at the foot of the stairs leading down from Hikone station.

Hikone Volunteer Guides can organize free guided tours of Hikone, including a stop at the castle. Apply a week in advance to the tourist information office or Hikone Sightseeing Association (☎ 0749-23 0001, 🖥 info@hikoneshi.com).

From Hikone, either backtrack to Maibara and pick up the shinkansen to Kyoto/Osaka or continue directly along the Tokaido line from Hikone station (the fastest trains take 50 minutes to Kyoto).

Kyoto (514km)   [see pp206-24]

Nara lies off the shinkansen route but is accessible by JR Nara line from Kyoto (see p222). The Nara city guide begins on p224.

Shin-Osaka (553km)   [Osaka – see pp116-24]

NAGOYA TO OSAKA VIA THE KII PENINSULA

Fastest journey time from Nagoya to Osaka: 7 hours.

Nagoya to Owase   [Map 9, opposite; Table 9, p462]
Distances by JR from Nagoya.

Nagoya (0km)   [see pp159-68]
From Nagoya board a Wide View Nanki LEX or the slower Mie 'rapid' train
heading towards Tsu and Shingu. The Nanki has Western/Japanese toilets and a
trolley service. Green Car seats have an in-built audio system but there is a
charge for headphone rental.

If planning to visit the Grand Shrine at Ise (see p198) it's best to take the
Mie train; this is not as luxurious as the Nanki but does run direct from Nagoya
to Ise. Both the Nanki and the Mie have reserved and non-reserved cars.

The private Ise Railway also runs services from Nagoya to Ise; this would
be the most convenient route for those without a rail pass.

Kuwana (24km) The journey as far as Kuwana is not particularly scenic.

Yokkaichi (37km) After leaving Yokkaichi the industrial landscape starts to
clear. Some trains stop at **Suzuka**.

Tsu (44km) Tsu has little worth making a stop for.

Matsusaka (63km) Matsusaka is known for its locally bred cows and in particular for their unusual diet which is supposed to make them all the more
flavoursome when served up in strips on the table. 'If a cow should lose her
appetite', informs a local leaflet, 'she is given beer to drink as a tonic to activate her stomach, along with a gentle, full-body massage. Every cow receives
meticulous care'. Some sushi shops in Matsusaka even do a brisk sale in beef
sushi, though in restaurants the most popular dish is either steak or *shabu shabu*.

A guide map to Matsusaka is available from the tourist information office
(☎ 0598-23 7771, Tue-Sun, 9am-4pm), in the glass building next to the police
box *(koban)*, on the right as you leave the station. The staff here don't speak
English.

> **☖ Ise Railway supplement**
> A small section of the track between Nagoya and Tsu is owned by Ise
> Railway. If you have bought a ticket, the fare will include the supplement for the Ise
> section between Kawarada and Tsu. Rail-pass holders are supposed to pay the con-
> ductor on board the train. If travelling on the Nanki LEX this means paying both the
> standard fare (¥490) and limited express fare (¥310 yen) just for that section (what-
> ever your total journey is).
>
> On the Mie rapid train, only the standard charge (¥490) has to be paid. You could
> get away without paying the supplement if you are in a non-reserved seat and if the
> conductor checks tickets only when the train has left Tsu, since there is no way of
> telling from the rail pass where you joined the train.

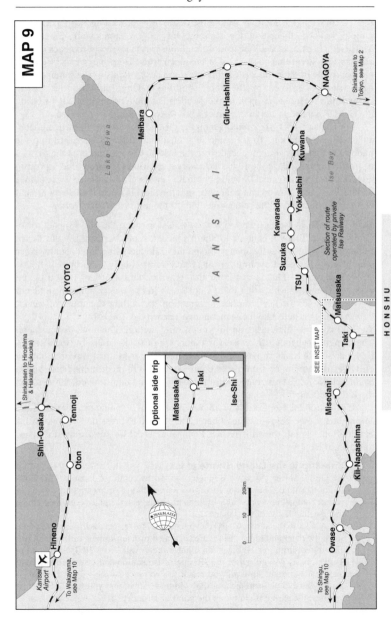

MAP 9

Shinkansen to Tokyo, see Map 2

NAGOYA

Kuwana

Yokkaichi

Kawarada

Suzuka

Ise Bay

Section of route operated by private Ise Railway

Gifu-Hashima

TSU

Matsusaka

Maibara

Taki

Lake Biwa

SEE INSET MAP

K A N S A I

KYOTO

Optional side trip

Matsusaka
Taki
Ise-Shi

HONSHU

Misedani

Kii-Nagashima

Shinkansen to Hiroshima & Hakata (Fukuoka)

Shin-Osaka

Tennoji

Oton

Hineno

Kansai Airport

To Wakayama, see Map 10

★TRAILBLAZER

20km

10

0

Owase

To Shingu, see Map 10

The main sights are in or around the castle ruins of **Matsusaka Park**, a ten-minute walk north-east of the station. Only a few stone walls are left of Matsusaka Castle, so walk instead through the park and go out the back to find a preserved street that looks as if it has been lifted from the set of a samurai movie. A few of the residents on this street are descendants of the samurai families who once lived in the same buildings. One building, the **Castle Guardman's House**, is open to the public (Tue-Sun 10am-4pm). It's first on the right as you walk down the street from the park; admission is free.

For a snack, try *Café comme ça* on the ground floor of the department store attached to the station. To try some of Matsusaka's famous beef, head up the main road that runs straight ahead from the station. On the corner at the first set of traffic lights, and on the right, is *Kameya*, a casual restaurant that serves up good-value beef set meals, including shabu-shabu. The entrance is next to a butcher's counter, so you can guarantee that the meat is fresh. It closes at around 6:30pm. Further along the same street but on the left is a *Mister Donut*.

Taki (71km) In the Edo Period, Taki was a stop along the pilgrim path to Ise Grand Shrine. Today it is home to Sharp's largest Liquid Crystal Display factory but tours are not usually open to the public. Taki has some quiet country lanes which make for good cycling terrain. Cycle rental (daily, 8am-6pm, 4 hours, ¥500; one day ¥1000) is available through the station office. If you do go cycling around here note that there's not much in the way of English signs but if you get stuck or need further information try calling the town office (☎ 05983-81117). There may be someone who can speak English.

▲ Taki is a tiny station but an important rail junction. The track divides here. The Sangu line goes off to Ise-shi (approx hourly, 20 mins by local train). Beyond Ise, JR trains run as far as **Toba**, famous for Mikimoto pearls, but the only way of moving on from Ise to continue the rail route described below is to backtrack to Taki. This route follows the Kisei line south towards Shingu and the Kii Peninsula.

If you took the Nanki LEX from Nagoya but are planning to visit the Grand Shrine at Ise (see below), change here. The limited express does not go to Ise but continues south towards the Kii Peninsula. The Mie rapid train does continue on to Ise.

Side trip to the Grand Shrine at Ise

Ise Grand Shrine (🖳 www.isejingu.or.jp) is the centre of Japan's indigenous religion, Shinto. The town receives over six million visitors annually, many of whom are making a once-in-a-lifetime pilgrimage to the place considered to be the spiritual home of the Japanese.

A visit to the shrine (daily, dawn to dusk, free) is necessarily in two parts, since the outer and inner shrines are separated by a ten-minute bus ride (¥410). The outer shrine, or **Geku**, is an eight-minute walk from JR Ise-shi station. Turn right as you go out of the JR side of Ise station and take the main road that heads straight up until you reach the entrance to the shrine. Devoid of gaudy decorations, and lacking the gold and red colours you find at Buddhist temples, the shrine is simple to the point of austerity.

From the Geku, retrace your steps to the entrance where a fleet of taxis waits to take pilgrims and visitors on to the **Naiku**, the Inner Shrine. Board a No 51 or 55 bus (¥410; 10 mins) for the Naiku. The sun goddess Amaterasu Omikami, the Imperial family's ancestral kami (deity), is enshrined here. A sacred mirror, symbol of the kami, is carefully wrapped up and hidden away in the inner sanctuary and never shown in public. Indeed, there's not a great deal to see at all, since the interior of both shrines is off limits. Both the outer and inner shrines, as well as Uji Bridge which you have to cross to reach the inner shrine, are completely rebuilt every 20 years. The last time was in 1993, so the next rebuilding will be in 2013.

Most coach parties rush off after a lightning tour of both shrines but with more time, and to make up for a lack of 'sights' at the shrines, it's worth visiting at least one of the three museums a short bus ride from the inner shrine. The obvious choice is **Jingu Chokokan Museum**. From the inner shrine, take bus No 51 (¥280) that goes to Uji-Yamada and Ise-shi stations via the Chokokan Museum. It's a Meiji-era building that houses a large-scale model of the inner shrine, allowing you to see all around the compound. This bird's eye view makes you realize how little of the shrine you see for real when standing at the outer gate. Also on display are some elaborate festival costumes, a selection of kagura masks, sacred treasures offered to the deities on the occasion of previous shrine renewals, and a few random paintings of Corsica. From the Chokokan, go down a flight of steps, and across the road is a modern building that is home to **Jingu Museum of Fine Arts**, opened in 1993 to commemorate the last rebuilding of the shrine. Inside are works of art offered to the shrine by Japanese artists; fortunately, instead of hiding them away in the inner shrine, they have been put on public display. Finally, back across on the other side of the road is **Jingu Agricultural Museum**. This is less interesting but does contain a photo of the current Emperor in wellington boots, getting down to a bit of manual labour in a field. After visiting the museums you can pick up the bus at the Chokokan stop and head back either to Ise-shi or Uji-Yamada stations.

Ticket deals for the three museums are as follows: ¥500 to visit just the Museum of Fine Arts, ¥300 to visit the Chokokan and Agricultural museums, or ¥700 for a package ticket to see all three. All three museums are open Tue-Sun (April-Oct 9am-4:30pm, Nov-Mar to 4pm).

Near the entrance to the outer shrine, and opposite the stop for buses going to the inner shrine, is Ise City TIC (daily, 9am-5pm) which has guide maps and a useful explanatory leaflet about the shrines. The latter is also available at the shrine offices by the entrance to both Geku and Naiku.

A good overnight choice is *Pearl Pier Hotel* (☎ 0596-26 1111, ▭ www .pearlpier.com; ¥6825-8400/S, ¥13,650/D, ¥16,800/Tw), a five-minute walk behind JR Ise station. A coin laundry is available. The hotel is easily recognizable – it's the building with a steel lifeboat hanging off one side. The hotel has a bakery/café called *Piccolo* (7am-5:30pm), a good place to create a packed lunch, and a more upscale Italian restaurant, *Il Mare* (5-9:30pm).

Leaving Taki sit on the left side of the train for the best views of the small mountain ranges and rivers that pass by, though the train sometimes dives into a tunnel. Some trains stop at **Misedani (96.5km)**.

HONSHU

Kii-Nagashima (127km) Until now the train has followed an inland course. From here, the track shadows the Pacific coast, albeit at a slight distance. A couple of minutes out of Kii-Nagashima is the small Nagashima Shipyard out to the left, followed by great views to the left of clusters of rock and small islands.

Owase (152km) A major junction on the line, but the area is not very attractive. A few minutes from here there are more glimpses of the coast but also a number of tunnels.

Owase to Shingu   [Map 10, opposite; Table 9, p462]
Distances by JR from Nagoya.

Kumano-Shi (186km) Five minutes by bus from here is **Onigajo**, a series of connecting caves along the shore which according to legend were once used by a pirate called Tagamaru as his secret den.

Shingu (209km) Shingu, in Wakayama, one of Japan's most rural and isolated prefectures, serves as a useful transport hub. The station is very small with a few coin lockers, an ekiben stand, Rent A Car office and a tourist information desk (Fri-Wed, 9am-5pm), where you can pick up maps and information about both Shingu and the surrounding area.

Two minutes away, just 100m to the east of Shingu station, a large Chinese gate marks the entrance to small **Jofuku Park**. Bikes can be rented for free (¥2000 deposit required) from the shop inside this park. One sight to head for is **Kamikura Shrine**, 20 minutes on foot over to the east side of town. On the evening of February 6th, there's a 'procession of fire' down the steps from the shrine as participants race to the bottom carrying burning torches.

A day excursion from Shingu can be made inland to **Doro-Kyo Gorge**. Package tickets including return bus and boat trip around the gorge are available but if you have a rail pass the best way of accessing the gorge is to take a JR bus from the bus terminal to the left as you leave Shingu station. The bus journey is 40 minutes to Shiko, from where boat cruises operate (¥3340). The tourist information office at Shingu station has bus timetables.

Shingu has a small number of cheap business hotels, one of which is *Sunshine Hotel* (☎ 0735-23 2580, 💻 www.sunshinenet.co.jp/hotel), seven minutes on foot from JR Shingu station. Go past the tourist office, turn left and walk over the railway track. Follow the road until you reach a set of traffic lights and turn left. Walk along this road until you see a small post office on the corner of a narrow road on the right. Turn on to this road and the hotel is on your right. It has very basic but spacious singles with attached bath at ¥5700 and twins at ¥10,500.

For food, try the local speciality, *meharizushi* – literally translated as 'goggle-eyed sushi', so called because each piece is so large that your eyes are supposed to open wide at the sight. *Mehariya*, a restaurant with both counter and tables, is a friendly place serving freshly made meharizushi with a bowl of soup for about ¥750. Look for it on the street beyond Sunshine Hotel.

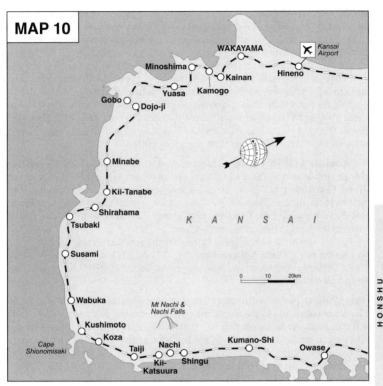

MAP 10

WAKAYAMA
Kansai Airport
Minoshima
Kainan
Hineno
Yuasa
Kamogo
Gobo
Dojo-ji
Minabe
Kii-Tanabe
Shirahama
Tsubaki
K A N S A I
Susami
0   10   20km
Wabuka
Mt Nachi &
Nachi Falls
Kushimoto
Koza
Kumano-Shi
Cape
Shionomisaki
Taiji
Nachi
Owase
Kii-
Shingu
Katsuura

H O N S H U

Shingu to Osaka/Kyoto [Map 10, above; Table 10, p463]
Distances by JR from Shingu.

Shingu (0km) From Shingu, continue along the JR Kisei line towards Tennoji in Osaka. Two limited expresses operate along this stretch of line. The most frequent is the Kuroshio, though the slightly faster Ocean Arrow has the bonus of a small lounge area with seats which face large, panorama windows. Lounge seats are non-reserved and are the best place to sit for views of the Pacific Ocean.

For the most part, the line from Shingu to Nachi follows the coast, though the view is occasionally obscured by trees.

♦ Nachi (13km) Limited expresses don't stop here, so take a local train from Shingu (20 mins); the service is irregular but operates approximately once an hour, except in the middle of the day. Buses run from outside the station (15 mins; ¥470) to **Nachi Falls**. Get off at the 'Taki-mae' bus stop, from where you walk under the torii (shrine gate) and down a flight of stone steps towards a 133m-high waterfall, where there's an altar at which visitors pray. The reason for the torii, usually found at the entrance to a shrine, is that this is believed to be a sacred waterfall. Legend has it that Emperor Jimmu arrived here (in the 7th century), after seeing the cascading water from the sea shore, and announced that it was the spiritual embodiment of a kami. A short walk uphill brings you to a Shinto shrine (Kumano Nachi) and adjacent Buddhist temple, Seiganto-ji.

Though very small, Nachi station does have the unique feature of its own **hot spring** on the second floor, a good place to head if you've got time to kill waiting for a bus to the falls. The onsen is called Nishiki no Yu (Tue-Sun, 10am-8pm, ¥600 and ¥200 towel rental); from the bath there are great views out over Nachi Bay and also of the train tracks below, so rail enthusiasts can enjoy the unusual experience of trainspotting from the comfort of a bathtub.

Kii-Katsuura (15km) Katsuura has a number of onsen, the best known is **Boki-do spa**, inside a cave, from where there are views out to sea. The cave is part of *Hotel Urashima* (☎ 0735-52 1011, 🖳 www.hotelurashima.co.jp). To reach it, first walk ten minutes from Kii-Katsuura station straight ahead to the boat terminal. From there, take the free ferry to the hotel. The entrance to the cave spa is through the hotel (¥1000, daily, 5am-11pm).

Check where the boat is going before boarding, as there's also a ferry service to another hotel, *Hotel Nakanoshima* (☎ 0735-52 1111, 🖳 www.kansai.ne.jp/shima), which rents out private indoor/open-air baths for ¥2100 for 50 minutes. Reservations are essential.

Taiji (20km) Some limited expresses stop here. Despite calls for a worldwide ban on whaling, whale meat still turns up on the menu around this part of the Kii Peninsula. At Shingu station (see p201), for example, you can buy a whale-meat lunch box and further down the line at Kushimoto (see below) one shop serves whale ramen. But it's Taiji that's famous for whaling and it has a number of whale-related attractions. From Taiji station, buses (¥200) run to **Taiji Whale Museum** (daily, 8:30am-5pm; ¥1050), where the focus seems to be more on celebrating man's 'triumph' over the whale than on the creature itself.

For the final part of the journey towards Kushimoto, the train heads inland. After Taiji, some trains stop at **Koza (35km)**.

Kushimoto (42km) Kushimoto station is the nearest stop to Cape Shionomisaki, a 15-minute bus ride away (¥600 return), and Oshima, an island off Honshu accessible by road via Kushimoto Ohashi bridge. There is no tourist information in Kushimoto but the bus stop is right outside the station. There's a small locker area in the station.

Cape Shionomisaki is the most southerly point on Honshu and there's a lookout tower (¥300) next to the last stop on the bus route. Nearby is a lighthouse that can be climbed (¥150) for further views of the cape. Besides these official lookout points, there is also an overgrown path at the cape that few people take, leading down to the rocks below. You might see fishermen down here doing battle with the waves.

If you fancy a night at Honshu's most southerly tip, try *Misaki Lodge Youth Hostel* (☎ 0735-62 1474, 📄 62 0529). It's best to phone ahead since if you arrive

---

🕊 Before the 'Black Ships'

Just off the Honshu coast close to Kushimoto, and linked to the mainland by a road bridge, is Oshima, a place which challenges the history books over the timing of the end to Japan's period of isolation from the rest of the world.

In April 1791, when the country's doors were still very firmly closed, two American merchant ships laid anchor at Oshima. The *Lady Washington*, commanded by Captain John Kendrick, and the *Grace,* commanded by Captain William Douglas, landed on Oshima to stock up on water and firewood. If this story is to be believed they predated Commodore Perry's better-known arrival in 1854 with a fleet of 'Black Ships' (see p39) by a full 63 years. A museum (daily, 9am-4pm, ¥250) on the island commemorates the visit of the *Lady Washington*. Only a few buses (¥590) each day run to Oshima from Kushimoto. Check the timetable at Kushimoto station.

---

in the middle of the day there may not be anybody around. They charge ¥3360 excluding meals for YH/HI members (¥4360 for non-members). To reach Misaki Lodge, take a bus from Kushimoto towards the cape, and get off at 'Kuroshiomae', one stop before the terminus at Shionomisaki.

◆ Wabuka (56km) You'll probably only notice this tiny station if on a local train but it's a good vantage point for views of the Pacific Ocean, with waves crashing over rocks. The latter half of the journey towards the next major stop at Shirahama is mostly inland.

All trains stop at **Susami** (73km) and some at **Tsubaki** (87km).

Shirahama (95km) Shirahama is a popular summer vacation destination. A fleet of taxis outside the station and regular buses (¥330, 15 mins) will speed you off to the main resort area. The tourist information desk (☎ 0739-42 2900) in the station is open daily, 8:30am-5pm, though there's only a skeleton staff on Thursdays.

Shirahama is not the place to come for deserted, unspoilt beaches. Resort hotels, hot springs, glass-bottom boat rides and a 'laser beam studded dance show' turn the bay area into a summer tourist mecca.

One of the closest attractions to the station is **Adventure World** (🖥 www.aws-s.com, daily, 9am-5pm, ¥3500). The park is divided into zones, including Safari World, Marine World and Panda Land. A giant panda male cub, Ko-hin, was born here in 2005.

In the summer, there are extended opening hours and additional attractions such as a night safari tour. This may be a good trip for a family with young children but the expense is a major drawback. A direct shuttle bus runs to Adventure World from Shirahama station in 10 minutes.

Kii-Tanabe (105km) Right in front of the station are love hotels, pachinko parlours and a whole street lined with bars and restaurants. However, there's more to Tanabe than this. The founder of aikido, Morihei Ueshiba (1883-1969), was born here; his statue stands close to the ocean on the other side of town. Tourist information (Japanese only) is available from an office to the right as you exit the station.

A good place if you wish to stay the night is ***Altier Hotel*** (☎ 0739-81 1111, 🖹 81 1112, 🖥 www.altierhotel.com; ¥5500/S, ¥11,000/Tw including a continental breakfast). The rooms are small but have attached bath and wide beds. It's on the right side, five minutes down the main street that runs away from the station.

About 10 minutes out of Kii-Tanabe, there are views of the Pacific as the train runs along an elevated track. Some trains stop at **Minabe (114km)**.

♦ **Dojo-ji (145km)** Only local trains stop here, from where it's a short walk to **Dojo-ji** temple. If on a limited express, the best plan is to get off at Gobo, the next station along from Dojo-ji, and then backtrack one stop on a local train. Services leave Gobo hourly (times vary) and take three minutes to Dojo-ji.

From the station, turn left on to the main road, go to the first junction and turn right. The temple is at the end of the street and is reached by a flight of steps at the end of a row of souvenir shops. Inside the temple is a three-storey pagoda, as well as the main hall. People come here to listen to the monks tell stories with the aid of long, painted scrolls. The best-known story, handed down by successive generations of priests, is about Kiyohime, a girl who falls hopelessly in love with Anchin, a pilgrim monk. It's a tragic tale of unrequited love with an unusual ending: Kiyohime turns into a serpent and burns the one she most desired to death. For the full story, as well as general information about the temple, ask for the *Brief Guide to Dojo-ji Buddhist Temple* at the office in the new building to the left as you enter the temple compound.

There are a couple of places to eat at along the road to the temple but back at the station is a good place that serves noodles and curry rice at reasonable prices. They also do breakfast sets until 11am. The interior is like a log cabin. Look for it on the right just as you leave the station.

Gobo (146km) Rail enthusiasts may want to take a ride on the Kishu Railway that runs the short distance (2.7km) between Gobo and Nishi-Gobo; some say that this is the shortest railway line in Japan. The journey takes eight minutes and costs ¥180. At Gobo station, you can board a Gobo Nankai Bus for **Amerika-Mura** (¥440, 20 mins), a small village of Japanese emigrés. To get you in the mood, platform speakers at Gobo play vaguely American-style music in between announcements. There's no tourist office at the station but ask JR staff for a local map.

Between Gobo and the next limited express stop at **Yuasa (164km)**, the train passes through a number of tunnels. After Yuasa, the scenery is just a line of identikit towns.

Minoshima (175km) Some limited expresses stop at Minoshima, part of Arida city, which is known for its oranges and for cormorant fishing on the Arida-gawa (1 June to early September). Shortly after leaving Minoshima, there's a large and ugly factory complex out to the left, so for once there's good reason to be grateful for the tunnel that follows soon after, blocking out the possibility of a lingering view.

Kainan (190km) Just before the train pulls in here there's a row of industrial plants out to the left, drawing a final line under the rural part of the peninsula.

Wakayama (201km) There's little to see in Wakayama apart from an average **castle** (¥350 to enter), from the top of which are views out over Kinokawa River. Originally constructed in 1585, the castle followed the fate of so many Japanese fortresses and was destroyed by fire. The present reconstruction dates from 1958. It's a ten-minute bus ride (¥220); buses leave from stop No 1 right outside the station.

The **tourist information desk** (☎ 0734-22 5831, daily, 9am-5pm) at Wakayama station is on the right as you exit the ticket barrier. An English guide to the city is available. To find **coin lockers** (all sizes), turn left out of the station and look for a room on the side of the station building.

The station area is a good place to hunt for food. Within the station building there are **restaurants** on the basement level of VIVO department store and a small bakery on ground level. Another good place to try is the fifth floor 'Gourmet Park' in Kintetsu department store, on your right as you leave the station. Also around the station area you'll find a *Mister Donut* and *McDonald's*.

If you need a place to stay, the JR-run *Hotel Granvia Wakayama* (☎ 073-425 3333, 🖳 www.granvia-wakayama.co.jp; ¥10,164/S, ¥17,902/D, ¥19,635/ Tw) is directly connected to the station. The usual discount is offered to rail-pass holders.

From Wakayama, trains continue along the JR Hanwa line towards Tennoji and Shin-Osaka. To reach Kansai International Airport, take a train on the Hanwa line and change at Hineno. The JR Wakayama line runs inland from here and goes part of the way to the mountain resort of Koya-san (see pp230-2).

Hineno (227km) Change here for the short journey on the Kansai Airport line to Kansai International Airport. The hotel (see p123) outside this station is useful if you need to stay close to the airport. A few trains stop at **Otori (247km)**.

Tennoji (262km) Tennoji is a station on the JR Osaka Loop line (see p121). Change here if going to Osaka station.

Shin-Osaka (277km)   [Osaka – see pp116-24]
Osaka's shinkansen station. Change here for the route around western Honshu (see p235). A few limited expresses continue on to **Kyoto** (316km; see pp206-24).

🎌 **Using the route guides**
The fastest point-to-point journey times are provided for each section of the route. Even though each route has been divided into different sections it may not be necessary to change trains as you go from one section to the next. Occasionally, however, it is essential to change train in order to complete the route described. Such instances are denoted by the following symbol ▲. Places which are served by local trains only are marked ♦. **(For more information see p449.)**

Kansai – city guides

KYOTO

Arriving in this sleek and bustling JR station, you'd be forgiven for thinking Kyoto was still the nation's capital. Kansai International Airport offers direct access to the ancient city and easily beats Tokyo's Narita Airport as an attractive gateway to Japan. Even if Kyoto ultimately lost its status as national capital and Imperial home in 1868 at the time of the Meiji Restoration (see p39), nobody could dispute its title of tourist capital. Here you'll find some of the most expensive hotels and luxurious ryokan, the grandest palaces and the most ornate temples.

Yet even in a city with more temples per square kilometre than anywhere on earth (at least that's what you're likely to conclude after a day or two here), Kyoto's ancient traditions and quiet back streets have to be sought out. Arriving by bullet train, the impression is more of a city like so many others: Kyoto has skyscrapers as well as shrines, *Starbucks* as well as wooden tea houses. There's no better way of seeing for real the pace of change in Kyoto than through its dwindling geisha population – nowadays you're more likely to see a Japanese (or a foreigner) who has paid to be dressed up as a geisha for a day than catch a glimpse of a real one (see box below). These days the genuine article – or what

---

Getting to know geisha

Perhaps the best way of discovering what a geisha (see box, p47) is like is to get yourself invited to an evening party at one of the Gion tea houses. This requires contacts in extremely high places (no amount of money will do unless you know someone) and is not an option for the majority of visitors.

The more likely option is to try and see one walking around but the chances of this depend very much on luck and whether you happen to be standing by the right doorway at the right moment. The best time and place to look for maiko-san (apprentice geisha) is around 5-6:30pm, along Hanami-koji in Gion.

Anyone with a lot of spare cash might consider dressing up as a maiko/geisha. A number of places around the city will daub you with make-up and transform you from bulky foreigner to petite maiko; the cheapest makeovers start at around ¥8000. Shop around, as some places include a free photo as well as the chance to walk/mince around outside. Kyoto Tourist Information Office (see p216) can provide you with a list of shops offering this service; most require reservations. One good option, with English-speaking staff, is **Studio Shiki** (☎ 075-531 2777, 🖥 www.maiko-henshin .com), which has two branches in Kyoto and also offers men the opportunity to dress up as a samurai swordsman. Reservations can be made online or by phone.

If all else fails, Peter MacIntosh (☎ 090-5169 1654, 🖥 www.kyotosightsand nights.com), a Canadian expat married to a former geisha, runs guided tours of Kyoto's geisha districts and can – for a price! – even organize parties attended by geisha.

⛩ **Bargain hunt**
Many visitors to Kyoto have at least one item on their souvenir-shopping list: a kimono. But with top-end garments selling for hundreds of thousands of yen, it's not an item of clothing that falls within most people's budgets.

A good tip for bargain-conscious shoppers is to pay a visit to a small store called **Tansuya**, in a corner of the first floor of the Avanti department store across the street from the shinkansen side of Kyoto station. This shop (which has other outlets in Kyoto and elsewhere in Japan, see 🖥 http://tansuya.jp) is one of the few kimono outlets in Kyoto which won't burn your credit card. You can pick up new and second-hand kimonos in a range of colours and fabrics from as little as ¥5000.

passes off for this – lives mainly on the small and big screen. Even the Hollywood blockbuster *Memoirs of a Geisha* was mainly shot on a ranch in California, a million miles from the narrow lanes of Kyoto's Gion district.

Despite fears that Kyoto's ancient traditions, wooden buildings and sacred precincts may one day be swamped by the 21st century demand for more space, it remains a grand and magnificent city. With a superb network of trains radiating out from here, Kyoto would make an excellent base for rail travel around Kansai and beyond – it's also the perfect place to return to, as there's always somewhere else waiting to be discovered.

What to see and do

After a day or two in Kyoto, it's easy to get 'templed out'. Quite apart from the fatigue of traipsing around endless numbers of temples and shrines, the cost can quickly add up. Entry to some shrines and temples is free but most charge ¥300-600, so a day of frantic temple ticking-off can easily add up to the cost of a night's accommodation. This applies even more from mid-October to the end of November, when the entrance fee to some temples is hiked up as people pour in to see the falling autumn leaves. A good idea is to home in on a few temples to get a flavour of Kyoto but also save time for a few of Kyoto's museums and other sights.

If you've already started your rail pass before arriving in Kyoto and are planning to stay in the city for more than a couple of days, you'll probably want to use it as much as possible rather than 'waste' days of rail travel you've paid for. With this in mind, the following is a brief description of the area around Kyoto station, a selection of city-wide must-sees, and a couple of suggestions for half-/full-day excursions by rail.

Kyoto station area The station area used to be much maligned as a disappointing gateway to the city but this view has changed since the opening of the new station building. Performances are held most weekends in the event space inside the station and the area outside; this means that the long flights of steps leading up the station atrium have become the place to hang out.

The top of the station is a good vantage point for views of the city, since it's free. **Kyoto Tower Observatory** (daily, 9am-9pm), the eyesore across the street, may be higher but it also costs ¥770 to take the lift up to the observation gallery. The only advantage to viewing Kyoto from inside Kyoto Tower is that it's the one building you can't see.

On the second floor of Theater 1200, attached to the station building, is **Tezuka Osamu Animation Theater** (Thur-Tue, 10am-7pm, ¥200). Tezuka Osamu was a famous Japanese animator who created the character Astro Boy. The theatre claims to be the 'only place on earth where you can see Tezuka original cartoon movies'.

A five-minute walk north of the station are two temples, Higashi Hongan-ji and Nishi Hongan-ji. These are not a bad place to start to get a feel for Kyoto's size and opulence. The scale of the buildings is unlike anywhere else in Japan and these are just a couple of many. **Higashi Hongan-ji** (daily, 5:30/6am-5/5:30pm, free) has an enormous Founder's Hall that boasts 175,967 roof tiles and contains 927 tatami mats. Look for the rope on display made of women's hair; 53 ropes of this kind were used to transport the enormous wooden beams of the two main halls to where they are today when they were rebuilt in 1895.

KYOTO – STATION AREA　　京都 – 駅周辺

Where to stay

2	Tour Club	2	旅倶楽部
5	Budget Inn	5	バジェット イン
11	Hotel Granvia Kyoto	11	ホテルグランビア京都
13	El Inn Kyoto	13	エルイン京都
18	Hotel Station Kyoto West	18	ホテルステーション京都西
19	Hotel Station Kyoto	19	ホテルステーション京都
20	Kyoka Ryokan	20	京花旅館
21	Murakamiya Ryokan	21	村上旅館
23	Matsubaya Ryokan	23	松葉屋旅館

Where to eat and drink

3	Second House	3	セカンドハウス
10	Eat Paradise (Isetan)	10	イートパラダイス (伊勢丹)

Other

1	Nishi-Hongan-ji	1	西本願寺
4	Coin Laundry	4	コインランドリー
6	Umekoji Steam Locomotive Museum	6	梅小路蒸気機関車館
7	Campus Plaza	7	キャンパスプラザ
8	Central Post Office	8	中央郵便局
9	Kyoto Prefecture International Center; Internet	9	京都府国際センター; インターネット
12	Tansuya (Avanti Dept Store)	12	たんす屋 (アバンティデパート)
14	Tezuka Osamu Animation Theater	14	手塚治虫アニメシアター
15	Bus information building (in front of JR Kyoto Station)	15	JR京都駅前バス総合案内所内
16	Bus stops	16	バスのりば
17	Kyoto Tower	17	京都タワー
22	Higashi-Hongan-ji	22	東本願寺
24	Shosei-en	24	渉成園

Kyoto – Station Area
京都―駅周辺

Keihan Main Line

Keihan-Shichijo

Kamo-gawa

KAWARAMACHI-DORI

24

ROKUJO-DORI

Karasuma Line

21
20
19
18
23

HIGASHI-NOTOIN-DORI

KARASUMA-DORI

17
16
15
14
13
12
11

22

Kyoto

Theater 1200

JR Nara Line to Uji & Nara

HONSHU

SHIOKOJI-DORI

Kyoto Station

SHINMACHI-DORI

8
9
10

Isetan dept store

NISHI-NOTOIN-DORI

SHICHIJO-DORI

3
7

2

ABURAKOJI-DORI

4

HORIKAWA-DORI

5

Kintetsu Kyoto Line

1

HACHIJO-DORI

JR Tokaido Main Line

JR Tokaido Shinkansen Line

6

200m
100
0

[See p212 for continuation of key]

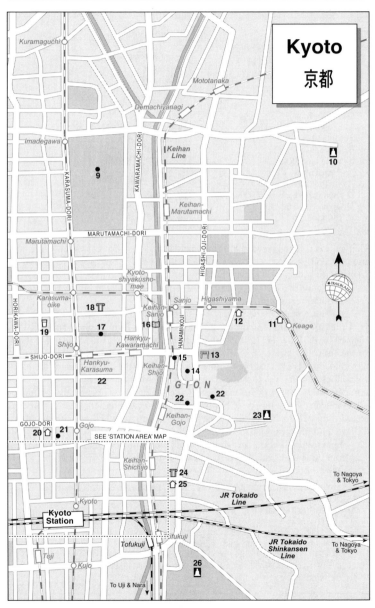

Kyoto

京都

Kuramaguchi

Mototanaka

Demachiyanagi

Imadegawa

Keihan
Line

● 9

10

KAWARAMACHI-DORI

Keihan-
Marutamachi

KARASUMA-DORI

MARUTAMACHI-DORI

HIGASHI-OJI-DORI

Marutamachi

Kyoto-
shiyakusho-
mae

Karasuma-
oike   18 🍴   Keihan-
                        Sanjo   Sanjo   Higashiyama

HORIKAWA-DORI

19 🍴   17 ●

Shijo   16 ▦   12   11 ⌂ Keage

SHIJO-DORI   Hankyu-
                               Kawaramachi   15 ●

Hankyu-
Karasuma
22   Keihan-
              Shijo   13 ▦

                              14 ●

              G I O N

              22 ●   22 ●

              23

GOJO-DORI   Gojo
20 ⌂ 21 ●

SEE 'STATION AREA' MAP

Keihan-
Shichijo

24 🍴
25 ⌂

Keihan-
Gojo

JR Tokaido
Line

To Nagoya
& Tokyo

Kyoto
Station   Kyoto

Tofukuji   Tofukuji   JR Tokaido
                                                    Shinkansen   To Nagoya
Toji   Kujo   Line   & Tokyo

              26

To Uji & Nara

HANAMI-KOJI

HONSHU

KYOTO　京都

Other *(key continued from p210)*

5	Toei Uzumasa MovieLand	5	東映太秦映画村
7	Nijo Castle	7	二条城
8	Shinsen-en	8	神泉苑
9	Kyoto Imperial Palace	9	京都御所
10	Ginkaku-ji	10	銀閣寺
13	Yasaka Jinja	13	八坂神社
14	Yasaka Hall (Gion Corner)	14	三条高倉 (ギオンコーナー)
15	Minami-za	15	南座
16	Junkudo	16	ジュンク堂
18	Museum of Kyoto	18	京都文化博物館
21	Hakusan-yu	21	白山湯
22	Studio Shiki	22	スタジオ四季
23	Kiyomizu-dera	23	清水寺
24	Kyoto National Museum	24	京都国立博物館
26	Tofuku-ji	26	東福寺

Conventional ropes were not strong enough for the task, so women's hair was used instead. A short walk east of Higashi Hongan-ji brings you to Shosei-en (daily, 9am-4pm, free), a garden belonging to the temple.

The Founder's Hall at nearby **Nishi Hongan-ji** (daily, 5:30/6am-5/5:30pm, free) is under restoration until 2008.

One more place in the station area that rail enthusiasts will want to seek out is **Umekoji Steam Locomotive Museum** (Tue-Sun 9:30am-5pm, ¥400), opened in 1972 on the 100th anniversary of Japan's first railway service. Fans of the railway's golden age will be in paradise as there are a large number of steam locomotives on display; some are in working condition. One of the locos runs along a specially constructed track (¥200 for a ride). This short run can't compete with the growing number of preserved steam locomotives running along real lines (see box p78) but is fun if you haven't had the chance to ride a steam train before. The journey lasts about ten minutes and operates at 11am, 1:30pm and 3:30pm.

The museum is about a 20-minute walk west of Kyoto station, or take a city bus from outside the station to 'Umekoji Koen-mae'. Pick up the leaflet available at the entrance.

⛩ Industrial clean

If you're in town in December, why not help out at Higashi-Hongan-ji's annual clean-up? Every year this event attracts hundreds of volunteers who attack the tatami flooring with bamboo sticks while others blow the dust away using giant fans.

A similar ceremony is held at Nishi-Hongan-ji, which has 650 tatami mats in its main hall. The ceremony dates back about 500 years and is supposed to spruce up the temple buildings ready for the New Year festival season.

Must sees Kiyomizu-dera (Kiyomizu Temple; daily, 6am-6pm, ¥300) is always packed with tour groups crowding the wooden observation platform which affords a spectacular view out over Kyoto. Every 33 years the crowds get even bigger when an 11-headed Kannon statue is put on display (the next is in 2033). Visit early in the day, or be prepared for the crowds.

From Kiyomizu-dera head north towards the Gion District, known as Kyoto's geisha quarter but also the home of **Yasaka Jinja** (free entry), a Shinto shrine dating back to 656. It becomes the focus of the city for the entire month of July during the Gion Festival (see p217).

Standing at the entrance to the shrine, Shijo-dori runs west towards the centre of **Gion**, while Higashioji-dori runs north and south. Head down Shijo-dori for the busy downtown shopping and entertainment district, but look out, just before Shijo Bridge, for **Minami-za**, Kyoto's famous kabuki theatre. There are no tours of the theatre building so to see inside you have to buy a ticket for a performance (see p219). The biggest annual event is in December when some of the country's best-known kabuki actors come here to perform.

Kinkaku-ji (daily, 9am-5pm, ¥400), better known as the **Golden Pavilion**, is perhaps Kyoto's most famous sight. The pavilion, its reflection glittering in Kyoko-chi, the Mirror Pond, is deservedly one of Japan's most-photographed buildings. The façade was regilded in 1987 and the roof restored in spring 2003 so the temple looks magnificent even on an overcast or rainy day. Bus loads of tourists make a stop here, so there's little else you can do but follow the crowds along the set path.

From Kinkaku-ji, it's a 15- to 20-minute walk south-west to Ryoan-ji. As you exit, turn right on to the street and go straight. Mid-way between the two temples, look out for a sign pointing towards the 'Museum for World Peace' – not an essential stop but interesting if you have time (see p214).

Ryoan-ji (daily, Mar-Dec 8am-5pm, Jan-Feb 8.30am-4.30pm, ¥500) provides a complete contrast to the showy opulence of the Golden Pavilion. Everyone comes here to sit and gaze out over Kyoto's (and probably the world's) best-known rock garden. Assembled sometime between 1499 and 1507 and measuring about 200 sq metres, the garden consists of white sand (raked) and 15 rocks, the latter divided into five groups. Visitors are asked to remain silent, though the peace and quiet is regularly interrupted by a recorded history of the temple. For an excellent account of Ryoan-ji's rock garden, and the different ways in which it might be interpreted, read François Berthier's *Reading Zen In The Rocks: The Japanese Landscape Garden* (see p35). The focus here is on the rock garden but a walk round the pond, Kyoyo-chi, and the rest of the grounds is recommended.

Ryoan-ji and Kinkaku-ji are in north-western Kyoto, some distance from the centre. The good news for rail-pass holders is that a JR bus service runs here roughly once an hour; the buses leave from the three JR bus stops right outside the main side of Kyoto station, before the main bank of city bus platforms; see p216 for details. Raku Bus (see p217) also operates to these temples.

See p220 for details of another must see – **Nijo Castle**.

Optional stops The **Museum of Kyoto** (daily except 3rd Wed, 10am-7:30pm, ¥500), on Sanjo-dori in central Kyoto, a three-minute walk from Karasuma-Oike subway station, traces the history of Kyoto, focusing on its glory days as the nation's capital and then moving on to the period of modernization after power shifted to Edo (Tokyo). There are good model displays that let you see what Kyoto once looked like but otherwise not much of a permanent collection. The redeeming factor is an excellent English volunteer guide service; this is very useful as most of the displays are only in Japanese. On the ground floor is a recreated Kyoto street from the Edo period with shops selling traditional crafts and a couple of restaurants.

Ritsumeikan University's **Museum for World Peace** (Tue-Sun, 9:30am-4:30pm, ¥400) is not widely publicized even though it is situated between Ryoan-ji and Kinkaku-ji (see p213). Perhaps because there are better known peace museums in Hiroshima (see p262) and Nagasaki (see p397), Kyoto's museum seems to attract few visitors but it really is worth fitting into your schedule. Built by Ritsumeikan University to promote the cause of peace, the museum tackles with astonishing candour the subject of Japan's military aggression during WWII and the country's 'unresolved war responsibilities'. It's unlikely you'd find anywhere else a picture of 'schoolchildren beating the portraits of Roosevelt and Churchill with large sticks in 1943'. The displays are well thought-out and informative, and include images of what Kyoto might have looked like had it suffered the fate of Hiroshima and Nagasaki. Originally on the list of possible A-Bomb targets – the planned epicentre was about 1km west of Kyoto station – Kyoto was later removed as a target for nuclear attack because the US Secretary of War knew it was the ancient capital of Japan, that it was very important for the Japanese, and that it was too beautiful to destroy. Pick up the excellent brochure at the entrance.

Kyoto Imperial Palace (Mon-Fri and 3rd Sat, tours at 10am and 2pm, free; over 20s only) can only be visited with an official guide; applications to join a tour must be made in advance to the Imperial Household Agency (see opposite). The palace grounds, which include some picture-postcard Japanese gardens, are interesting enough to make the effort of applying to join a tour worthwhile.

Rooms have to be viewed from a distance but it's just possible to make out the inside of the throne room. When the present Emperor was crowned in Tokyo, the thrones were taken from here and flown by helicopter to the capital. Even though the palace is no longer home to the Imperial Family, tight security remains; an official carrying a walkie-talkie follows the tour group around to make sure nobody sneaks away. The impression is not so much of grandeur but

---

❑ **Seeing red**
Some parts of Kyoto are considered to be of such historical importance that they are protected by laws which prohibit the use of brightly coloured signs. If they are too close to temples, signs for McDonald's and Coca Cola cannot be coloured red.

> ⛩ **Aching limbs**
> If your feet are exhausted after a day of trampling around Kyoto's temples, the best thing you can do for them is soak in a hot tub. **Hakusan-yu** (🖥 www.hakusan yu.com, Thur-Tue, 3-11pm, ¥370) is a bathhouse fairly near the station. It's considered one of the best in Kyoto and uses natural spring water pumped from beneath the ground. The baths are divided into men and women's sections – the latter includes a *rotemburo* (outside tub). Small towels can be rented (¥30). It's a wonderful place to soak the stress and pain away and mentally prepare for another day's sightseeing.

of how much the grounds feel like a prison – or must have done for the Emperor, who hardly ever left the palace.

To sign up for a tour, go with your passport to the Imperial Household Agency office, in the outer grounds of the palace, at least 20 minutes before the start of the tour (or the day before to be sure of a place). Applications for tours on the third Saturday of each month must be made by Friday. The Imperial Household Agency (☎ 075-211 1215) is open for enquiries/tour applications Mon-Fri, 8:45am-12pm and 1-4pm. To reach the Imperial Palace, take the subway from Kyoto station in the direction of Kokusai Kaikan and get off at Imadegawa station (the fifth stop). The entrance to the palace grounds is on Karasuma-dori.

Over on the east side of Kyoto lies **Ginkaku-ji** (daily, 8:30/9am-4:30/5pm, ¥500), better known as the Silver Pavilion. Originally modelled on its golden counterpart, don't be fooled by this temple's name. The idea was to cover its outer walls in silver; though the plans were never carried out, the name remained.

Kyoto National Museum (🖥 www.kyohaku.go.jp, Tue-Sun 9:30am-5pm, ¥420, additional charge for special exhibitions), opened in 1897, houses more than 12,000 works of art (not all on display at the same time!) and specializes in fine arts and handicraft, including rare examples of Heian-period pottery and lacquerware. The Fine Arts collection alone boasts more than 230 items designated as National Treasures or Important Cultural Properties. From bus stop No D2 outside Kyoto station, take City Bus No 206 or 208 to the 'Hakubutsukan Sanjusangendo-mae' bus stop, from where the museum is a one-minute walk.

PRACTICAL INFORMATION
Station guide
Kyoto station, rebuilt in 1997, is one of Japan's most eye-catching modern buildings. Japanese architect Hiroshi Hara suggests that the 27m-wide, 60m-high and 470m-long concourse lets you feel what it's like 'travelling down the side of a mountain into the valley basin'. Certainly it's an impressive sight either from the main concourse or up on the 12th floor Sky Garden, from where you can look down on to the station atrium and out over the city.

Isetan, the big in-station department store, stretches up both sides of the escalators that run up from the ground floor concourse. On the 7th floor is the 'Eki' museum with changing exhibitions. On the 11th is the 'Eat Paradise' restaurant floor where you'll find almost every kind of food. Some restaurants have tables either overlooking the station atrium or with window views of the city. See p219 for details of other places to eat in the station.

There are plenty of **coin lockers** (all sizes) around the station but if you need to keep bags in storage for more than three days, a baggage handling office (daily, 8am-8pm, ¥410/item/day) is on the basement floor.

The Haruka LEX to Kansai International Airport departs from platform 30. The shinkansen depart from platforms 11-14. Trains to Nara (see p224) leave from platforms 8, 9 or 10.

The World Currency Shop on the 8th floor of the Kyoto station building exchanges cash and travellers' cheques in most major currencies.

Tourist information

Kyoto City Tourist Information Office (daily, 8:30am-7pm) is on the second floor of the station building. The office is usually extremely busy so it's not a place to linger for lots of information, but they can provide you with a hotel/ryokan list.

Less well known, since it's over on the ground floor of the shinkansen side of the station, is the information desk (daily, 10am-4pm) staffed by volunteers. There's always an English speaker who will help with any tourism-related questions.

On the ninth floor of the Isetan department store inside the station (take the south elevator from the second floor of the store) is **Kyoto Prefecture International Center** (☎ 075-344 3300, daily except 2nd/4th Tues, 10am-6pm). The English-speaking staff can help with same-day accommodation bookings (☎ 075-343 4887) and also advise on travel in Kyoto and the surrounding area; pick up a copy of the useful *Tourist Map of Kyoto* here. This office is much more useful and geared up to for foreigners than the one on the second floor of the station. The centre also has foreign newspapers and magazines, and CNN on TV. Internet access is also available (see column opposite).

The best publication for listings and a guide to what's on in Kyoto is the monthly *Kyoto Visitor's Guide*, available free at all the tourist information counters listed above as well as at major hotels. *Kansai Time Out* is another useful monthly magazine with information on Kyoto, Osaka, Nara and Kobe. Its website, 🖥 www.kto

.co.jp, is also worth a look. JNTO publishes a handy guide to walking tours around Kyoto, which can be downloaded from 🖥 www.jnto.go.jp

An up-to-date online resource for finding out the entrance fees to temples in and around Tokyo is 🖥 www.templefees.com.

Books

The nearest store to Kyoto station with a selection of English books is on the third floor of the **Kyoto Tower building** opposite the downtown exit. Otherwise, the biggest bookstore in the downtown area, with English books on the 8th floor, is **Junkudo**, which also has a pleasant café called Morris, serving light pasta lunches, tea, and coffee and cake sets in the afternoon.

Internet

Kyoto Prefecture International Center (see column opposite) offers internet access at ¥100/15 mins. Alternatively, there is free internet access at **Campus Plaza** (Tue-Sun, 10am-9pm, last signing up for computer 8pm), less than five minutes on foot from the station downtown exit. On the ground-floor lobby area (which faces you as you enter the building) there is a bank of computers. When you sign up at the desk you'll be given a number which corresponds to a computer terminal. The free access is limited to one hour per session.

Getting around

Since Kyoto is so spread out, it's not really feasible to walk everywhere. The best plan is to take buses/subways to the different areas and then explore on foot. There's a flat rate of ¥220 on buses within the city but it's almost always worth investing in a bus pass. A **one-day city bus pass** (valid only within the city centre) costs ¥500. Pick up a transport map from any of the tourist offices which clearly shows how far you can go with the ¥500 pass; however, the pass is valid for buses to all the must-sees and optional sights, and some of the side trips mentioned in this guide.

Alternatively, a **combined subway/ city bus ticket** costs ¥1200, or a **two-day ticket** is ¥2000. Both passes are available from the **bus information building** in front of Kyoto station, near bus stop D1. Before taking any bus, pick up a copy of the *City Bus Sightseeing Map* from here or the tourist information office; this tells you how to get from the station and between the main sights by bus.

If you're following the familiar tourist trail, it's worth considering the special bus service called '**Raku Bus Kyoto Easy Sightseeing**' – look for the sign in English. Raku buses provide direct access to three tourist areas. A flat fare of ¥220 operates on all Raku bus services but the bus passes mentioned above are valid.

Raku Bus No 100 goes to Kyoto National Museum, Kiyomizu-dera, Gion and Ginkaku-ji; Ritsumeikan and Ryoan-ji are within walking distance of the bus stop for Ginkaku-ji. Raku Bus No 101 goes to Nijo Castle, Kitano Tenmangu Shrine and Kinkaku-ji; it also stops near the Museum of Kyoto. Raku Bus No 102 links the east side (Ginkaku-ji) to the Kinkaku-ji area. Stop announcements are made in English.

Bus No 100 leaves from bus stop D1 outside the main downtown station exit. Bus No 101 leaves from bus stop B2.

The JR bus for Kinkaku-ji and Ryoan-ji departs from JR Bus Stop No 3 (JR Bus Stop Nos 1 and 2 are for the long-distance JR Highway Buses). Don't confuse JR Bus Stop No 3 with any of the other stops outside the station for city buses. For Kinkaku-ji, get off at the 'Ritsumeikan Daigaku-mae' stop, from where it's a 15-minute walk to the temple. For Ryoan-ji, stay on the bus for another five minutes. The bus stop ('Ryoan-ji-mae') is right outside the entrance. However, not all JR buses from stop No 3 follow this route.

At the time of writing, buses which did follow the route left Kyoto station at 8:10am, 8:30am, 9am, 9:40am, 10:20am, 11am, 12:30pm, 1:30pm, 2:30pm, 3:30pm and 5pm. To check times, ask at the bus stop or pick up a copy of the *West Japan JR Bus Schedule*, available in English from the tourist information office at Kyoto International Center inside JR Kyoto station.

Hajime Hirooka, otherwise known as **Johnnie Hillwalker** (☎ 075-622 6803, ⌨ http://web.kyoto-inet.or.jp/people/h-s-love), conducts walking tours of Kyoto in English every Mon, Wed and Fri from Mar to Nov (regardless of the weather). The five-hour guided tour (¥2000) starts at 10:15am in front of Kyoto station and ends at 3:30pm near Kiyomizu-dera (see p213). Reservations are not required.

Festivals

In a city packed with temples there's nearly always a festival going on somewhere. Some are small and not widely publicized, others are known worldwide and attract thousands of visitors. For details of special events, enquire at any tourist office, or check the *Kyoto Visitor's Guide*.

One of the biggest festivals is **Jidai Matsuri**, which takes place in October (check the exact date with the tourist office). The highlight is a huge street procession which traces Kyoto's history from 1868 all the way back to 781, the date of the city's foundation. The festival began in 1895 to revive the city's fortunes after it lost its status as Japanese capital to Tokyo. It's one of the most colourful and vibrant events you'll find anywhere in Japan.

Another big festival is **Gion Matsuri**, which runs through the entire month of July and is the main annual celebration at Yasaka Jinja (see p213). The main events are between July 15th and 17th, when there's a huge procession of floats.

Where to stay

Station area Built into JR Kyoto station is *Hotel Granvia Kyoto* (☎ 075-344 8888, ⌨ www.granvia-kyoto.co.jp; ¥23,100/D, ¥25,410/Tw), where all the rooms are tastefully furnished, have large bathrooms and free wireless internet access (if you have a laptop). It's a luxurious haven from the noise of the station downstairs and an ideal base if you're travelling a lot by rail.

The indoor pool has excellent views of the station's atrium and there are a number of restaurants. Check the website for special offers, one of which includes the

HONSHU

opportunity to visit a famous Kyoto tea-house. The best bargain, and conveniently close to the station, is the friendly, spotless *Tour Club* (☎ 075-353 6968, 🖳 www .kyotojp.com), a small place with four-bed bunk dorms set around a small rock garden as well as a selection of well-maintained Western- and Japanese-style doubles and triples. The overnight charge is ¥2415. For a bit more privacy, opt for one of the Western-style double rooms (¥6982/room/ night) or triples (¥8880). *Budget Inn* (☎/🖹 075-344 1510, 🖳 www.budgetinnjp.com; ¥2500/night) is very close to and under the same management as Tour Club. Besides the dormitory accommodation, it also offers smart Japanese-style twins (¥8990) and triples (¥10,990), both with private bath/toilet. Both Tour Club and Budget Inn offer internet access (¥100/15 mins), cycle rental (¥630/day) and coin laundry.

Four minutes' walk from the station is *Hotel Station Kyoto* (🖳 www.kid97.co .jp/st-kyoto/). The hotel has two branches, both offering en suite Japanese- and Western-style accommodation from ¥5000 per person. *Hotel Station Kyoto West* (☎ 075-343 5000) is on Shichijodori and Hotel Station Kyoto (☎ 075 365 9000) is a minute's walk away on Higashi-Notoin-dori. Meals are not included in the rate but both branches have a café serving a limited selection of meals. Internet access is free for guests though the terminal is in the West branch.

Cheap Western-style accommodation is to be had at *El Inn Kyoto* (☎ 075-672 1100, 🖳 www.elinn-kyoto.com) just a couple of minutes on foot south-east of the shinkansen side of Kyoto station. Most rooms are singles (¥6800), though there are a few twins at ¥12,000. The hotel has wide beds, a coin laundry and a reasonable Western-style restaurant.

There are a number of good-value Japanese inns in the area: *Matsubaya Ryokan* (☎ 075-351 3727, 🖳 www.matsub ayainn.com), with very friendly owners, is five minutes east along the main road from the station. It has spacious tatami rooms, some of which overlook a small garden. Rates are ¥5460 for one, ¥9870 for two and

¥13,860 for three; add ¥525 per person for a room overlooking the Japanese garden.

Kyoka Ryokan (☎/🖹 075-371 2709, 🖳 kyoka@mbox.kyoto-inet.or.jp) is a bit faded but offers cheap rates of ¥4200 per person for a tatami room (no attached bath). There are also a couple of newer rooms with attached toilet/bath which go for ¥6300. Just around the corner is *Murakamiya Ryokan* (☎ 075-371 1260, 🖳 ryokanmurakamiya@par.odn.ne.jp), a rambling but efficiently run place that charges ¥4700 per person per night.

If none of the above ryokan has a vacancy, try the Kyoto Ryokan website (🖳 www.kyoto-ryokan.com) to check for availability elsewhere.

Other areas Traditionalists will shudder at the prospect of *Guest House Costa del Sol Kyoto* (see map pp210-11; ☎ 090-3998 1409, 🖳 www.costadelsol.co.jp), but luckily this is very far from being a Brits-in-Benidorm establishment. Clean dormitory accommodation on a tatami floor from ¥2000/night. Close to Gojo subway station on the Karasuma line, but within walking distance of Kyoto station. No credit cards.

A good luxury choice in the Higashiyama temple district is *Westin Miyako Hotel Kyoto* (☎ 075-771 7111, 🖳 www.westinmiyako-kyoto.com), which has a check-in/baggage drop facility (daily, 9am-6pm) at Kyoto station if you arrive early and want to do some sightseeing before heading to the hotel. They will deliver your luggage to your room. The check-in office is on the ground floor of the shinkansen side of the station and a shuttle bus to the hotel runs twice an hour. Standard double rooms go from ¥28,900. Also in Higashiyama is one of the city's newest hotels, *Hyatt Regency Kyoto* (☎ 075-541 1234, 🖳 http://kyoto.regency .hyatt.com), which looks very uninspiring from the outside and is minimalist inside but has everything you would expect of such a top-end hotel and prices to match. Standard doubles go from ¥31,500, but rates vary daily so it is always worth checking if there are any special offers.

YH/HI members might consider staying at *Higashiyama Youth Hostel* (☎ 075-761 8135, 🖳 www.syukuhaku.jp; ¥3360/¥4360, ¥4305/5305 with two meals) in eastern Kyoto. It has an institutional feel right down to the 10:30pm 'lights out' curfew. The hostel is reached by taking a No 5 city bus from Kyoto station (get off at Higashiyama-Sanjo).

More relaxed but less well located is *Kyoto Utano Youth Hostel* (☎ 075-462 2288, 🖳 utano-yh@mbox.kyoto-inet.or.jp). The nightly rate is ¥2500, with optional dinner at ¥850 and breakfast at ¥500. From Kyoto station, take No 26 City Bus and get off at 'Utano Youth Hostel Mae'. However, the Tour Club beats both of these hostels for friendliness and price.

Very close to Nijo station (see p220), so good for access to Nijo Castle, is *Kyoto Cheapest Inn* (☎ 075-821 3323, 🖳 http://kyotofashion.com/kyoto-inn; from ¥900/night). It's a pretty basic place with rock-bottom rates to match. Bring your own sleeping bag!

Where to eat and drink

At the station, the best place to head for is the 11th floor 'Eat Paradise' in **Isetan** department store. However, expect queues outside the majority of the restaurants, except the most expensive, at peak hours. *Tonkatsu Wako* has excellent tonkatsu; a hirekatsu set costs ¥1260. For take-out food, try the food hall in the basement.

For more upmarket dining, *Hotel Granvia Kyoto* has several restaurants, which tend to be less crowded than those elsewhere in the station. Don't forget the excellent *Vie de France* bakery on level B2 (central side), where you can eat in or take out a range of cakes, sandwiches and pastries.

Musashi (🖳 www.sushinomusashi .com, daily, 10am-10:30pm) is a revolving sushi restaurant on the ground floor of the shinkansen side of the station. The price policy is simple: all pieces of sushi are ¥120. Great value and delicious – the perfect place to grab a bite to eat while waiting for a train. There are plenty of other Japanese and Western cafés and restaurants in Gourmet Avenue in the basement **Porta** shopping mall. Take the escalators down from street level which are located outside the station downtown exit.

Second House (🖳 www.second house.co.jp), subtitled 'spaghetti and cake', serves great Italian food at reasonable prices. It's close to the station and offers free wireless internet access for laptop users.

The best place to hunt for restaurants is in the downtown area. *Nishiki Food Market* is a covered arcade known as 'Kyoto's kitchen'. It's a good place to wander round and pick up a bite to eat. Look out for the shop that sells tofu ice cream and doughnuts, and for the spices shop where you can buy freshly made spicy ice cream!

Canine lovers may like to visit Kyoto's *Dog Café* (Tue-Sun 11am-8pm), where the sign outside reads 'all good dogs welcome'. Humans are also allowed in (you don't have to be accompanied by a pet) to this old wooden building where there are good cakes and the coffee is freshly ground. There's also a range of doggie treats and you'll always find a couple of pups inside.

The café is on Takoyakushi-dori (look for the sign as it's slightly set back from the main street), so a stop here could be included in the excursion to Nijo described on p220.

Evening entertainment

Kabuki is sometimes staged at Minami-za in Gion, though it's not a cheap evening out as reserved seats start from ¥4200.

'Gion Corner' is a nightly performance of **traditional Japanese arts** catering to tourists. For ¥2800 you get to see a truncated version of the tea ceremony, ikebana (flower arranging), traditional dances as well as excerpts from kyogen (traditional comic plays) and bunraku (puppetry). Performances (🖳 www.kyoto-gion-corner .info) nightly (Mar 1-Nov 29 only) at 7:40 and 8:40pm on the first floor of Yasaka Jinja in Gion, close to Yasaka Jinja (see p213). Tickets can be booked in advance from major travel agencies.

Side trips by rail from Kyoto

The first of the two sample excursions described below can be done as a long day or, even better, an overnight trip, while the second (see p222) is convenient as part of a trip to Nara (see p224).

Along the JR Sagano line A trip along the Sagano line to Nijo or Toei and then to Saga-Arashiyama is a good way of making use of the rail pass but worth doing even if you don't have a pass.

Saga-Arashiyama, which is only 15 minutes away from Kyoto station, offers a complete change of pace and scenery. Further along the line an overnight stay at Hosen-ji temple (see p222) near Umahori station would make for a good spiritual retreat. Take a local train (from track Nos 31-34) to follow the route below (distances are from Kyoto station). Spend the morning (two hours would be fine) in Nijo Castle, before continuing on to the Arashiyama area. It would be difficult to include a visit to Toei MovieLand on the same day, so plan this as an additional day or to do on your return after a night in Arashiyama or Umahori. Pick up a map of the Arashiyama area from Kyoto Tourist Information (see p216) before you set off.

● **Nijo (4.2km)** The second stop along the line, Nijo, is the nearest rail station to **Nijo Castle** (daily except Tues in Dec, Jan, July and Aug, 8:45am-5pm, ¥600). Nijo station is a modern building with a large wooden roof (the original station building is preserved at Umekoji Steam Locomotive Museum, see p212). On the ground floor are a convenience store and a few coin lockers.

After leaving the station, head straight up the road in front of you. It takes about 15 minutes to reach **Shinsen-en**, a small Japanese garden that will be on your left. The garden is not well known but it's peaceful and features a red-lacquered bridge. Take the road that leads behind the garden to reach the outer perimeter of Nijo Castle. With the castle grounds in front of you, turn right and follow the perimeter round until you reach the main entrance gate.

The castle is one of Kyoto's best attractions and contains beautiful landscaped gardens in addition to Ninomaru Palace. Originally built in 1603 as an official residence of the first Tokugawa shogun, Ieyasu, it is well preserved and, unlike the former Imperial Palace (see p214), visitors are allowed inside. An unusual feature of Ninomaru Palace is the 'nightingale floor', so called because the floorboards that run along the side of the building 'squeak and creak' when you tread on them. Unfortunately, the squeaks are often drowned out by the recorded commentary or noisy chatter of tour groups hurrying through. On your way out through the gardens, look out for the koi (carp) in the central pond. Despite the tour groups, this castle should rank high on your list of places to see in Kyoto.

If you want to move from ancient to modern without leaving Nijo, one of the best cinemas in town is the new **Toho** multiplex right outside Nijo station. It shows all the latest Hollywood releases.

● **Hanozono (6.9km)** **Toei Uzumasa MovieLand** (☎ 075-864 7716, 🖳 www.eigamura30.com, daily 9am-5pm Mar-Nov, 9:30am-4pm Dec-Feb, closed Dec 21-Jan 1; ¥2200) is about 15 minutes on foot from the station. After a couple of days touring Kyoto's ancient temples, this very in-your-face thrills and spills entertainment park may be a good antidote. If you want to see actors running around dressed as samurai, or enjoy special effects such as collapsing mountains, this is the place to go. The park owners stress that MovieLand is a working film set, so there's a chance to see a real samurai film in production. It's not the most traditional of environments but it's possible to dress up as a maiko (trainee geisha), though it's not cheap at ¥11,000 (on top of the park entrance fee).

● **Saga-Arashiyama (10.3km)** You can tell if somewhere in Japan has sold out to tourists when you see (1) an Orgel Museum (antique music boxes), (2) *jinrishika* (rickshaws) lined up to ferry you about, and (3) a monkey park. Arashiyama has all of these but a lot more that is worth visiting as well – the scenery is particularly spectacular in the spring and autumn – so don't be put off by the outward signs of tourist tack. There are ¥300 coin lockers outside the station. The Torokko train station (see box p222) is to the right as you exit. There is no tourist office. Cycles can be rented from the shop opposite the Torokko station (daily Mar-Dec 9am-4:30pm, ¥500/2 hours).

Walk (or cycle) straight down the road from the station until you reach the river. Turn right and walk along, passing *Sunday's Sun*, a family restaurant with good views of the river and standard fare, until you reach **Togetsukyo-bashi** (Crossing Moon bridge), a traditional-style bridge first built in 836 though the current bridge dates from 1934. Togetsukyo is a famous spot for cherry-blossom and autumn leaves' viewing. Cross the bridge and at the end turn right and walk along the path by the river or take one of the **boat trips** (¥3900 for about two hours; daily 9am-3.30pm, 10am-2.30pm Dec to mid-Mar) down river to Kameoka; the boats seat up to 20 people and include three boatmen with poles and oars. Whether walking or in a boat it is not long before you escape the sights and sounds of the city. If in need of a rest from the walk there are a number of cafés by the river.

When you feel you have walked enough retrace your steps and if the thought of **Iwatayama monkey park** (daily 9am-5pm, to 4pm Nov to mid-Mar, ¥520) appeals follow the signs to it up the hill. Cross back over the bridge and head straight down the road opposite, which is lined with tourist shops and restaurants. Turn first left after passing Keifuku-Arashiyama station and follow the signs to Tenryu-ji. **Tenryu-ji**, originally built in 1255 as a palace with a view of Mt Arashiyama, was converted into a Zen temple in 1339 and is now a World Heritage site. The garden is open to the public (daily, 8:30am-5:30pm, to 5pm Nov to mid-Mar, ¥500). Near the entrance to the temple, look out for a sign that announces a secret supply of oysters buried underground. 'The function of the human body,' reads the sign, 'is activated by even a small amount of oyster extract…[in the event of an earthquake] this will keep you alive for three days without any help from others, while you wait for official assistance to come'.

Another good place for a wander in Arashiyama is through the **bamboo forest**, around the temple. Cool and shady in the summer, the forest also contains the small **Nonomiya Shrine**, where Imperial princesses underwent purification rites for three years as part of their training before being sent to the Grand Shrine at Ise (see pp198-9).

Go back to the main road and turn left. A ten-minute walk brings you to **Seiryo-ji**, once a country villa and a good place for lunch as there's a tiny restaurant called *Chikusen* (Fri-Wed, 10am-4:30pm) within the temple grounds. There are only a few low wooden tables but the service is excellent.

⛩ Riding the Romantic Train

Expensive but fun is a ride on the Torokko open-air carriage 'romantic train' which runs on a 25-minute journey along the scenic Hozu River. It gets completely booked out in the autumn when crowds descend on Arashiyama to see the leaves fall. It's wise to book tickets in advance (at JR ticket counters or from the TiS travel agency in Kyoto station; ¥600 one-way, ¥1200 return; 8-9/day); rail passes are not accepted. There are no services on Wednesday except in peak season (Apr 29th-May 5th, Jul 21st-Aug 31st, Oct 15th-Nov 30th) and the Torokko does not run between December 30th and the end of February. (For further details visit 💻 www.sagano-kanko.co.jp/eng/index.htm).

As an alternative to buying a return ticket, it's possible to take the train one way and then return to Arashiyama by boat. The course from the starting point in Kameoka (shuttle buses run between the Torokko station at Kameoka and the starting point for the boat rides) back down to Arashiyama is 16km and takes about two hours. Accept as hyperbole the description of the journey down the rapids as being the 'most exciting experience not only in Japan but also throughout the world'. It's not the Zambezi but the scenery is still spectacular and the ride makes for a good alternative to taking the train back. Departures are hourly between 9am and 3pm, March-November. Services are less frequent in winter but the boats are heated! Tickets cost ¥3900.

The ¥3500 lunch served on a tray is a real visual delight. Tea and a Japanese sweetmeat are also served (¥650). Just north-east of Seiryo-ji is **Daikaku-ji** (daily, 9am-4:30pm, ¥500), which has a viewing platform over adjacent Osawa Pond. Originally part of the country villa of Emperor Saga, the complex became a temple after his death in 876. To get there turn left out of Seiryo-ji, go straight over at the crossroads and walk along till you come to a petrol station on the left. Follow the signs to Daikaku-ji from here.

If you plan to spend the night in this area try *Umejirou* (☎ 075-871 5874, 💻 www5.ocn.ne.jp/~umejirou/; Japanese only), on the right-hand side a minute further along the main road. Umejirou has ten Japanese-style rooms; rates are from ¥5700 per person without meals or ¥7350 with two meals. The easiest way back to the station is to return to Seiryo-ji and then turn left down the main road and first left after crossing the tracks for the JR Sagano line.

Umahori (18.1km) This is the stopping-off point for **Hosen-ji** (☎ 0771-24 0378, 💻 www.zazen.or.jp, hosenji@zazen.or.jp), a temple which doubles as a centre for zazen meditation. Set on a quiet hillside, Hosen-ji is an ideal escape from the hurried pace of Kyoto.

It's possible to stay the night here (around ¥3000; monthly stay for ¥80,000) but reservations are essential and you'll need to be prepared to enter into the spirit of the occasion (the zazen-meditation classes are not optional).

Along the JR Nara line The fastest service to Nara by JR (rapid train) takes 45 minutes. Trains depart (from track Nos 8, 9 or 10 at Kyoto Station) roughly three times an hour though most services are local and take over an hour. If possible, time your departure to take one of the rapid trains which depart from Kyoto at 20 and 50 minutes past the hour and arrive in Nara at 3 and 33 minutes past. The first rapid train from Kyoto actually leaves at 9:09am, the sec-

ond at 9:50am; thereafter leaving at 20 and 50 minutes past th
regular service leaves at 5:20pm. In the opposite direction
leave Nara twice an hour, usually at 9 and 39 minutes past t
vary), arriving at 56 and 26 minutes past. The first rapic
Nara at 9:12am and the last at 4:39pm. If you're not in a hurry,
a local train, and consider stopping off along the way at one or mu.
places described below.

● **Tofuku-ji (1.1km)** Just one stop along the line and barely out of Kyoto station, it's a few minutes' walk south-east of the station to **Tofuku-ji**, one of
Kyoto's largest Zen monasteries and home to a famous five-storey pagoda.
Foreign visitors can try *zazen* (Zen meditation); sessions, led by the head of the
temple complex, are held once a month. Call in advance (☎ 075-561 0087) or
enquire at Kyoto TIC. Within the temple compound is an attractive garden
(daily, 9am-4pm, ¥300).

● **Inari (2.7km)** Next stop along the line; right outside this station is the first
orange-lacquered torii (shrine gate) which marks the entrance to **Fushimi-
Inari Shrine** (daily, dawn to dusk, free). The station itself is bright orange,
giving you a taste of what to expect in the shrine.

Fushimi-Inari is a huge complex and contained within the grounds is a long
series of tunnels of torii (orange shrine gates), about 10,000 in all, which you
might recognize from the film *Memoirs of a Geisha*. Pilgrims dressed in white
are a common sight here. It's only a short walk to the main shrine, behind which
paths lead off through the torii tunnels which snake up Mt Inari. Though the
walk is surrounded by trees and mostly in the shade, it's a step up from a gentle stroll, so wear trainers. There are a few tea houses along the way, where you
can sit on tatami mats by the window and enjoy views of the mountain on which
the shrine complex is built. You are rewarded for your effort when you reach an
observation point offering a great view of Kyoto, though from here it's a further walk up to the highest point of 233m (where there are no great views).

Before jumping back on the train, it's worth seeking out the small **Sekiho-
ji** (daily, 9am-5pm, ¥300), or more precisely the bamboo garden behind it.
Five to ten minutes on foot from Fushimi-Inari, but not easy to find, this small
temple has one of the most peaceful gardens in Kyoto. To head in the right
direction, turn right out of Inari station and go straight until you reach the rail
track. Don't cross the track but turn left up the road and walk up until you
reach an area of tombstones on your right. Turn right and go past the tomb
stones to find the temple entrance. It's well hidden but this means that few people bother to look for it. The secluded bamboo grove on the hillside behind the
main temple building is filled with stone statues of the Buddha and his disci-
ples. The images were created by artist Ito Jakuchu in the late 1700s and are
known for their comical facial expressions. The images are supposed to calm
the souls of the dead and help relieve the grief of those left behind.

● **Uji (14.9km)** Uji has been a well-known tea-producing area since the
Kamakura era (1185-1333) and also features in the last ten chapters of one of
Japan's most famous novels, *The Tale of Genji*. Uji Bridge, mentioned in some
of the chapter headings, was first built by a Buddhist priest in 646, though the
present construction dates from the 1990s. Heading towards Uji-gawa (turn
left as you leave the station and go straight), you'll first reach a small tourist

HONSHU

.formation booth, on the corner just before you cross the bridge. Staff can provide you with a map and point you in the right direction of Byodo-In, a five-minute walk south along the river.

Byodo-In (daily, 8:30am-5:30pm, ¥600) is a peaceful temple just set back from the west bank of Uji-gawa. It's known for its large Buddha statue in the main hall. The main building is known as Phoenix Hall since its shape, with two wings stretching either side of the main hall, 'resembles a phoenix spreading its wings'. After visiting the temple, a good place to take a rest is at the riverside **Taiho-an Tea House**, where green tea and Japanese cakes are served (daily 10am-4pm, ¥500, closed Dec 21st-Jan 31st; tickets from the adjacent tourist information office). Both the tea house and tourist information office are just outside the temple complex along Uji-gawa.

● **Uji to Nara (41.7km)** Rapid services from Kyoto stop at Uji, so you can pick the train up here and continue directly to Nara (journey time: 25 mins).

NARA

Some 40km south of Kyoto, Nara boasts a longer history than its nearby rival. Well before Kyoto rose to pre-eminence, Nara enjoyed the title of national capital. Nara became Japan's first permanent capital in 710 and, even though its time at the top was short-lived (the Imperial court had decamped to Kyoto by 794), the period was marked by the influence of Buddhism from mainland China. And the glory days have not been forgotten: Nara is already preparing for a party in 2010 to mark the city's 1300th anniversary.

Nara's tremendous collection of temples, particularly enormous Todai-ji, which houses Japan's largest statue of the Buddha, still stand today as proof of that influence, and of the great wealth that once poured into the city. Just outside the centre of Nara, Horyu-ji contains the world's oldest surviving wooden structures (an impressive fact, when you consider how frequently wooden temples burn to the ground in Japan).

Apart from its rich cultural heritage, Nara is known for the harmonious cohabitation of humans and deer. It won't be long before you spot one (they tend to wander in and around the shops along Sanjo-dori in search of food), and it's often not up to you how close you want to get to them. At least this means a picnic in Nara Park will never be lonely.

Nara's compact size makes it much more manageable than Kyoto and its vast park is more attractive than Kyoto's urban sprawl. A lightning-fast day excursion can be made from Kyoto but an overnight stay in Nara would allow you time to enjoy the sights at a more leisurely pace.

What to see and do

With just one day here, devote all your time to covering as much as possible in Nara Park. With more time you could also take in the Naramachi quarter, visit one or two of the museums, or make the short trip out to nearby Horyu-ji.

(Opposite) The autumn leaves blend well with the 28m-high five-storey pagoda, dating from the early 15th century, on Miyajima. (Photo © Bryn Thomas).

Approaching Nara Park from JR Nara station along Sanjo-dori, look out on your left for the three- and five-storeyed pagodas which belong to **Kofuku-ji**. Moved here in 710 when Nara became the capital, at the height of its prosperity, this temple boasted as many as 175 buildings but most of them have burnt down in the intervening 1300 years. The three-storeyed pagoda dates from 1143 and the five-storeyed one from 1426. The latter is at its most spectacular when lit up at night (summer only). The Tokondo (Eastern Main Hall; ¥300) and Treasure House (¥500) display a variety of Buddhist sculptures; both are open daily, 9am-5pm. Performances of Noh take place in the temple precincts in May; enquire at the tourist office for dates and times. The biggest draw in the park is **Todai-ji** (daily, 7:30/8am-4:30/5pm, ¥500 to visit the Daibutsuden). The main building is the world's largest wooden structure and it houses a 16.2m-high, 15-tonne bronze statue known as the 'Great Buddha of Nara'. Outside Kintetsu Nara station stands a statue of **Gyoki** (668-749), a famous priest who helped to build Todai-ji. A special service to mark the 1250th anniversary of his death was held at the temple in 1998 (even though 1999 was actually the 1250th anniversary).

Nara's most important shrine is **Kasuga Taisha**, the pathway to which is lined with lanterns (there are said to be 3000 in the precincts around the shrine). Founded in 768 at the foot of Mt Mikasa, this shrine of the Fujiwara family remained influential throughout the Heian Period (794-1185), after the capital had moved to Kyoto. Inside the shrine compound, fortune sticks are available in English for ¥200. The main shrine's annual festival is held on March 13th.

Nara National Museum (☎ 0742-22 7771, 🖥 www.narahaku.go.jp, Tue-Sun 9:30am-5pm, to 7pm on Fri from late April to late Oct, ¥500; extra charge for temporary special exhibitions), in the park, opened in 1895 as one of three Imperial museums (the other two were in Kyoto and Tokyo). It has now greatly expanded to include separate east and west wings as well as the original building. The permanent collection is entitled 'Masterpieces of Buddhist Art' and is vast (only a part of the museum's holdings can be displayed at one time). Nearly all exhibits have a brief explanation in English but it's difficult to get a perspective on the wealth of ceremonial objects, paintings, scrolls, statues and sutras on display without the help of an English-speaking guide. The permanent collection is located in the original building and the west wing. But the west and east wings are usually both used for special/temporary exhibitions. At these times, the permanent collection is limited to the original building, which houses the Japanese sculpture galleries. The museum has a pleasant *café* on the lower-level passageway between the old and new buildings which does coffee-and-cake sets in the afternoon.Though it's easy enough to tour Nara Park without a guide, it may well be worth organizing a guided tour of the museum with one of the volunteer guide groups mentioned on p228.

If you have time head to the **Naramachi** district, a very atmospheric old quarter with traditional houses, narrow streets, craft shops, mini museums and cafés.

(Opposite) A trip to the morning market is a highlight of a visit to Takayama (see p179). (Photo © Richard Brasher).

Some 12km south-west of Nara lies **Horyu-ji** (daily, 8am-4:30/5pm, ¥1000), founded in 607 and registered by UNESCO in 1993 as a World Heritage Site. The temple grounds are divided into two precincts, the western and eastern compounds. Highlights of the western compound are the Five-storeyed Pagoda and the Main Hall, believed to be the world's oldest surviving wooden structure. In the eastern compound, look out for the Hall of Dreams, built in 739 and housing a statue of the temple's founder, Prince Shotoku. Its octagonal shape is auspicious, since the number eight is considered lucky in Japan.

To reach Horyu-ji, take a local train on the Yamatoji line from JR Nara station (10 mins). Bus No 72 runs from outside Horyu-ji station to the temple (3/hour, 5 mins, ¥170). Get off at 'Horyujimon-mae'. Horyu-ji lies on the Kansai line between Nara and Osaka so could be visited en route to either city.

NARA 奈良

Where to stay
1 Nara Youth Hostel (YH)	1	奈良ユースホステル
2 Nara-ken Seishonen Kaikan YH	2	奈良青少年会館ユースホステル
5 Hotel Nikko Nara	5	ホテル日航奈良
8 Super Hotel JR Nara Eki-mae	8	スーパーホテルJR奈良駅前
9 Nara Washington Hotel Plaza	9	奈良ワシントンホテルプラザ
10 Hotel Fujita Nara	10	ホテルフジタ奈良
20 Ryokan Seikan-so	20	旅館静観荘
22 Nara Hotel	22	奈良ホテル
23 Kikusuiro	23	菊水楼
28 Nara Kasugano Youth Hostel	28	奈良かすが野ユースホステル

Where to eat and drink
7 Skylark	7	すかいらーく
12 Starbucks	12	スターバックス
14 Capricciosa	14	カプリチョーザ
15 Hiten	15	飛天
16 Ganko tonkatsu	16	とんかつがんこ
17 Okaru	17	おかる
18 Yamazakiya	18	山崎屋
21 Asuka	21	飛鳥
22 Hanagiku	22	花菊
24 Uma no me	24	馬の目

Other
3 Central Post Office	3	中央郵便局
4 Horyu-ji	4	法隆寺
6 Eki Rent-A-Car	6	駅レンタカー
7 Shalala	7	シャララ
11 Nara City Information Center	11	奈良市観光案内所
13 Kintetsu Rent-A-Cycle	13	近鉄レンタサイクル
19 Kofuku-ji	19	興福寺
25 Nara National Museum	25	奈良国立博物館
26 Todai-ji	26	東大寺
27 Kasuga Taisha	27	春日大社

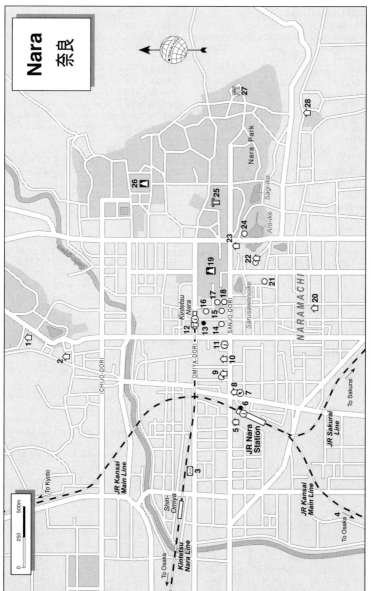

Nara 奈良

HONSHU

To Kyoto

JR Kansai Main Line

Shin-Omiya

Kintetsu Nara Line

To Osaka

JR Nara Station

JR Sakurai Line

To Sakurai

JR Kansai Main Line

To Osaka

Kintetsu Nara

OMIYA-DORI

SANJO-DORI

ICHJO-DORI

BAKUFO-DORI

NARAMACHI

Sarusawa-ike

Ara-ike

Sagi-ike

Nara Park

500m

250

0

PRACTICAL INFORMATION
Access
To reach Nara **from Kyoto** follow the route starting on p222. The private Kintetsu Railway also runs services from its station in Kyoto (inside the JR station) to Kintetsu Nara station. Coming **from Osaka**, take a JR Yamatoji line train direct to Nara. A limousine bus operates between Kansai International Airport (from stop No 9 outside Arrivals) and Nara Hotel (see column opposite) and JR/Kintetsu Nara stations (¥1800 one way; 85 mins).

Station guide
Rail-pass holders are likely to arrive at JR Nara station. The two principal JR lines are the Yamatoji line (to/from Horyuji, Tennoji and Osaka) and the Nara line (to/from Uji and Kyoto). JR Nara station has been rebuilt; the old station building, with a temple-style roof, is a listed building. It's to the left as you exit the new station.

To your right as you exit the station ticket barrier is the JR ticket office, branch of the Nippon Travel Agency and the tourist information counter (see below). Coin lockers of all sizes are in a building next to the station, to your left as you exit.

Tourist information
There are counters in both JR Nara (☎ 0742-22 9821, daily 9am-5pm) and Kintetsu Nara (☎ 0742-24 4858, daily 9am-5pm) stations. Both have English speakers and staff can assist with accommodation bookings. The main Nara City Information Center (☎ 0742-22 3900, daily 9am-9pm) is along Sanjo-dori, five minutes from JR Nara station.

JNTO (see box p31) produces a *Nara Walks* guide, downloadable from 🖳 www.jnto.go.jp. The tourist information counters in Nara have a pocket-size 'Nara Sightseeing Information' pamphlet which includes a handy restaurant guide (🖳 www.nara-restaurant.com).

Goodwill guides
Nara YMCA organizes free English-speaking guides for tours of Nara. Reservations are preferred (☎ 0742-45 5920, 🖳 eggnara

ymca@hotmail.com) or enquire at the tourist information counters in JR/Kintetsu Nara stations. A similar service is provided by Nara Student Guides (☎ 0742-26 4753).

Internet
Shalala (☎ 0742-27 5788, ¥390/hour, ¥750 /two hours) is a 24-hour internet café on the fifth floor of a building opposite JR Nara station. You'll need to fill out a registration form (in English) at the reception desk.

Getting around
The best way of seeing Nara is on foot, though renting a cycle is a good option if you're pressed for time.

Cycles can be rented for ¥300/day from the Eki Rent-A-Car booth (daily, 8am-8pm) to your right as you exit JR Nara station.

At weekends (all year) and daily (during peak holiday times) the **World Heritage Loop Line Bus** (☎ 0742-22 5263) runs – as its name suggests – in a loop around the city, including stops at all the main sights. An English audio commentary is available on board. A one-day loop line bus pass (¥800) allows you to jump on and off as many times as you like. Catch the bus (which will have either a yellow or purple design) from outside JR Nara station.

Festivals
As one of Japan's ancient capitals, Nara has many festivals, though one you may wish to avoid is the annual antler-cutting ceremony held for Nara deer in the autumn. July to October is the 'light up' season, when some of Nara's best-known sights, including Kofuku-ji and Todai-ji, are lit up nightly until 10pm.

Where to stay
By far the most atmospheric place to stay is *Nara Hotel* (☎ 0742-26 3300, 🖳 www.narahotel.co.jp), opened in 1909 and designed by the architect who was also responsible for the famous red-brick Tokyo Station Hotel (see p91). The old wing has enormous rooms with high roofs and spacious bathrooms. Rooms in the new wing may lack the history but are just as comfortable.

In the evening the bar is the perfect place to sip a gin and tonic after a hard day's sightseeing and maybe flick through the guest book. Members of the Imperial Family always stay here when visiting Nara (snapshots of their visits line a wall near reception). Singles cost ¥16,170 and twins start at ¥25,410 but a discount is offered to rail-pass holders. To live like a king, try the Imperial Suite: a snip at ¥346,500 a night!

The plushest modern place in town looms up behind JR Nara station. *Hotel Nikko Nara* (☎ 0742-35 8831, 🖳 www .nikkonara.jp; ¥9000/S, ¥17,000/D/Tw) is a haven of luxury with spacious rooms and a choice of places to eat, including a swish Chinese restaurant called Shuko. The buffet breakfast is ¥1600. Facilities include a karaoke room, hot-spring-style baths and cycle rental (¥500/day).

An excellent mid-range option is *Nara Washington Hotel Plaza* (☎ 0742-27 0410, 🖳 http://nara.wh-at.com; ¥6900/S, ¥12,000 /Tw/D), five minutes from JR Nara station along Sanjo-dori. Rates rise during April/May and October/November.

Hotel Fujita Nara (☎ 0742-23 8111, 🖳 www.fujita-nara.com; ¥7200/S, ¥10,200 /D, ¥12,200/Tw) is a little old-fashioned but OK for the price.

A cheaper option, just across the street from JR Nara, is *Super Hotel JR Nara Eki-mae* (☎ 0742-20 9000, 🖳 www.superho tel.co.jp; ¥4980/S, ¥6980/D), with the usual functional rooms and a free continental breakfast.

One of the most appealing areas to stay in is Naramachi, an old district full of small lanes and traditional houses. Here you'll find *Ryokan Seikan-so* (☎/🖷 0742-22 2670, 🖳 seikanso@chive.ocn.ne.jp; ¥4200/ pp, Western breakfast ¥472), an old inn built around a traditional Japanese garden. None of the tatami rooms has an attached bath but this is a popular, very reasonably priced place that fills up quickly. It's 15 minutes on foot south of Kintetsu Nara station (part of the way is along a covered arcade) or 25 minutes from JR Nara station.

You can't get more traditional than *Kikusuiro* (☎ 0742-23 2001, 🖷 23 2038), a ryokan with creaking wooden floorboards

and smart, kimono-clad staff who shuffle along the endless corridors. A one-night stay including two meals is worth the price at ¥40,000 per person.

The best bargain in town is at *Nara Kasugano Youth Hostel* (☎ 0742-23 5667, 🖳 kasugano@m3.kcn.ne.jp). It doesn't really look like a hostel as it's a small wooden house and takes only 11 people. The rate is ¥4410 including breakfast; dinner is ¥1050. From bus stop No 1 outside JR Nara station, take bus No 2 (city loop bus) and get off at Wara-ishi.

Nara Youth Hostel (☎ 0742-22 1334, 🖳 www.jyh.gr.jp/nara) has dormitory accommodation and a nightly rate of ¥3150/4150. Breakfast costs ¥630 and dinner ¥1050. Booking is possible online. From JR Nara station, take bus No 108, 109, 111, 115 or 130 from stop No 9 of the bus terminal outside the station and get off at 'Shieikujou' stop. Nearby *Naraken Seishonen-Kaikan Youth Hostel* (☎/🖷 0742-22 5540) is older but does have the advantage of offering single and twin occupancy rooms if they're not busy (additional charge). The basic nightly rate is ¥2650/3050, with breakfast at ¥330 and dinner an additional ¥900. To reach the hostel take bus No 12, 13, 131 or 140 from stop No 9 of the bus terminal outside JR Nara and get off at 'Ikuei Gakuen mae'.

Where to eat and drink
Deer is definitely not on the menu in Nara but there are plenty of fast-food choices along Sanjo-dori, including *McDonald's* and *Mos Burger*. A step up from these is *Capricciosa*, just off Sanjo-dori, serving huge helpings of pizza and pasta, and open daily 11am-10pm. Along Sanjo-dori, next to Washington Plaza Hotel, is *Skylark*, a cheap Western-style family restaurant with an all-you-can-drink soft-drinks bar. There is a branch of *Starbucks* in the basement of Kintetsu Nara station.

As well as fast food, Nara offers some excellent if expensive upmarket dining. If you're going to splurge on one good meal, Nara is a good place to do it. The tempura at *Asuka* (Tue-Sun, 11:30am-2:30pm and 5-9pm) is real melt-in-your-mouth stuff, with seating at the counter or tables. The cheapest lunch deal is the ¥1500 set meal that gives you a taste of everything, or opt for one of the tempura courses where you sit along the counter and the chef serves you direct. A menu in English is available for the counter courses, with set meal prices of ¥3500-5500. It's on an old, narrow street not far from Sarusawa-Ike.

Along a covered arcade off Sanjo-dori, **Hiten** (daily 11am-11pm, last order 10pm) serves a large range of Chinese dishes such as dim sum, spicy pork, chicken, shrimps and beef. The best time to go is for lunch when there are set meals from ¥850. A large set lunch for two would set you back ¥1800. It's still good value in the evening when individual dishes start from about ¥500.

Okaru (Thur-Tue, 11am-9pm) is a great okonomiyaki place with both tatami and table seating where you choose the ingredients for your pancakes which are then cooked and served on the griddle in front of you. From ¥680. Located in the covered arcade.

Ganko (daily, 11am-10pm), also in the covered arcade next to a branch of Mister Donut, serves delicious tonkatsu. Lunch sets cost from ¥1000 and an English menu is available. They also do take-outs from the counter at the front of the restaurant.

Yamazakiya (Tue-Sun, 11:15am-9pm), the entrance to which is behind a shop in the arcade selling pickled vegetables, is a traditional Japanese place where you can order from the plastic models of sample dishes outside. Lunch from ¥2000.

To really empty your pocket pay a visit to **Uma no Me**, close to Nara Hotel. This is about as traditional a Japanese place as you are likely to find. It's a very small restaurant decorated with Japanese *yakimono* (pottery), some of which dates from the early Meiji period. Seating is on tatami mats in the main part of the restaurant or in private rooms with a view over the garden. It's open for lunch (11:30am-3pm, from ¥3500), and for dinner (5:30-8:30pm, from ¥8000, reservation only); closed Thursdays. Finally, the Japanese restaurant in Nara Hotel, **Hanagiku**, serves skilfully prepared box-style lunches (*shokudo bento*) for ¥3696. It's open 11:30am-2pm and 5:30-9:30pm.

Side-trip to Koya-san

Three thousand feet (900 metres) above sea level, a religious centre was founded on Mt Koya in 816 by the Buddhist monk Kukai. Pilgrims and tourists have been flocking here ever since. Where once the monks of Koya-san earned an income by begging to visitors, today they do so by providing accommodation for them. A night spent in one of the temples, with a superb dinner and breakfast of shojin ryori and the chance to take part in early-morning prayers, should not be missed. Think of a visit to Koya-san as an experience in two phases, namely the journey there and the place itself.

The journey The private Nankai Railway operates services from Namba station in Osaka to Gokurakubashi station from where a cable car runs up to Koya-san. The journey to Gokurakubashi takes 100 minutes by express train or 90 minutes by limited express. The cable car takes five minutes. The whole journey, including the cable car, costs ¥1230 on the express and ¥1990 on the limited express. The best deal is Nankai's tourist-excursion ticket called 'Servic' which offers return travel, unlimited use of buses on Koya-san and reduced-price tickets on some attractions while you are there for ¥2780. For details of the Nankai timetable, see 🖳 www.nankai.co.jp.

Rail-pass holders can go part of the way to Koya-san by JR but have to transfer on to the Nankai line at Hashimoto station: **from Nara**, take a train on the JR Kansai line to Oji (14 mins) and then transfer on to the JR Wakayama line for Hashimoto; **from Kyoto**, take a train to Nara and then follow the route above; **from Osaka**, take a train from Tennoji station on the JR Yamatoji line to Oji (20 mins). From here, transfer to the Wakayama line and get off at Hashimoto (at least 60 mins); **from Wakayama** (see p205) there are two services an hour on the JR Wakayama line direct to Hashimoto (65 mins).

At **Hashimoto** cross via the overhead footbridge to the Nankai platforms and buy a ticket to Koya-san (45 mins, ¥810) from the booth on the platform. You might have to hang around a bit as connections between JR and Nankai are not always good. The final part of the route is quite possibly one of the finest rail journeys you can make in Japan. From Hashimoto, the train rattles and squeaks its way slowly upwards, until the track becomes surrounded by thick, pine-clad forests. As the train climbs (and your ears pop!), the temperature starts to drop. Here it's about 10° cooler (which makes it pleasant in the summer and freezing in the winter) than on the plains below. Inevitably, the train passes through a number of tunnels, though each time the train emerges into daylight, the scenery becomes more spectacular.

The train terminates at Gokurakubashi. The last part of the journey, one stop to Koya-san station, is a steep ascent by cable car. The five-minute 870m ride is included in the cost of the ticket from Hashimoto. From Koya-san station, buses take ten minutes to the centre (¥320); stop announcements are in English.

Koya-san Koya-san is small enough to get around on foot. About the only reason for using a bus is to shuttle between the centre and Koya-san station. One-day bus passes (¥800) are available but not worth the money unless you plan to bus everywhere. In the centre of town, **Koya-san Tourist Association** (☎ 0736-56 2616, ▤ 56 2889, ▣ www.shukubo.jp, daily, 8:30am-4:30pm) has maps and also sells a guide book (¥1000). Cycles can be rented from here (1 hour ¥400; 5 hours ¥1200). They can also rent you a portable audio guide (¥500) – useful if you want to listen to an informative English commentary as you walk around. If you are staying the night, audio guides can be returned the following day. Outside the office there are a few coin lockers suitable for day packs.

A combination ticket (¥1000) is available from the tourist office but is only worth buying if you intend to visit most of the sights charging admission. The main one to include is **Kongobu-ji** (daily, 8:30am-4:10pm, ¥350), the central monastery in Koya. This is the residence of the High Priest of Koya-san, responsible for around 3000 monasteries across the country that belong to the Shingon Buddhist sect. Next to the monastery is the 6 o'clock bell, rung by a monk every even hour between 6am and 10pm.

Sooner or later, everyone heads for **Okunoin**, part of an enormous cemetery where the body of Kukai is enshrined. According to tradition, on 21 March 835, Kukai entered into 'eternal meditation'. From that day, he has been known as Kobo Daishi; it is said he will not wake up until Miroku, the Buddha of the future, arrives. The cemetery is packed with tombs and gravestones of Kobo Daishi's followers. It's a good idea to visit early in the morning, when it's a long, peaceful walk from Ichinohashi Bridge on the edge of town through the cemetery towards the Hall of Lanterns, behind which is Kobo Daishi's mausoleum.

● **Where to stay and eat** It's a good idea to book accommodation on Koya-san in advance but tourist-office staff will ring around the temples to see what's available if you arrive without a reservation. Either book directly with the temples or send a fax to the tourist office (see above) stating dates and preferred accommodation at least two weeks before arrival. They will send confirmation by fax. Payment is in cash only. At all the temples, overnight guests are invited to attend morning prayers, which usually start at 6 or 6:30am. The cheapest rates are offered by **_Haryoin_** (☎ 0736-56 2702), also called a 'National Lodging House'; ¥6500 with two meals, or ¥3500 without. Haryoin is a small temple on the edge of town and one of the first stops coming from the cable car station. All rooms share a common bath.

Almost opposite Haryoin is the larger **_Rengejoin_** (☎ 0736-56 2233, 📄 56 4743) which has rates starting from around ¥10,000 including two meals. Rooms are larger and better appointed, and some have views over a beautiful rock garden. Common bath only.

One of my favourite places is **_Sekishoin_** (☎ 0736-56 2734, 📄 56 4429), founded in 923. The temple is next to Ichinohashi Bridge, which makes it very convenient for an early morning/evening visit to the Okunoin. Rooms in the new building are modern and more like a hotel than temple lodgings, rooms in the old temple building are more atmospheric; both kinds are available with/without bath. For two people sharing a room without bath the nightly rate (including two meals) is ¥16,000; add ¥8000 for a room with attached bath. To reach Sekishoin, take a bus heading for the Okunoin from Koya-san station and get off at Ichinohashi.

Two other good choices are **_Shojoshin-in_** (☎ 0736-56 2006, ¥9000-12,000/pp, with two meals), which also has easy access to the Okunoin, and **_Muryoko-in_** (☎ 0736-56 2104, 🖥 www.muryokoin.org; ¥10,500/pp, with two meals), where if you're lucky you'll bump into the temple's resident English-speaking Swiss monk (see box, below).

It may be worth knowing that most of the temples have beer vending machines so there's no problem having a drink in the evening. Also, if craving a bag of crisps or a bar of chocolate, there is one convenience store on Koya-san; **_Coco!_** is slightly hidden, on a back street behind the main road, on the opposite side to the tourist office.

🏯 A Swiss monk in Japan

'You want to meet Kurt?' asks the man at Koya-san's tourist office. 'That won't be difficult. He's more famous here than Arnold Schwarzenegger.' Kurt was born in Zurich, first visited Japan in 1980 and settled in Koya-san many years later with his Japanese wife. Today he goes by the name of Kurto Gensou and is one of the monks at Muryoko-in, a temple close to the centre of town.

Kurt greets me at his temple in English, Swiss-German and Japanese. 'Come on, I'll show you the local bar,' he says. Of all the images of Kurt I could have imagined, none was as a local sitting at the corner table of the only pub in town. But over a series of beers and cups of warm saké he explains that monks on Koya-san are not obliged or even expected to lead solitary existences. There is little time to learn more about Kurt's formative years as he has to return to his small room in the temple and prepare for an early start. 'I get up every day at 4am and the first thing I do is make a cup of green tea. In the silence of the morning, even the smallest sound of pouring tea into a cup becomes music,' he says. He then recites 'many hundreds or thousands' of different mantras before leading or joining in chanting and singing at the temple's early-morning ceremony.

Western Honshu – route guide

Many visitors to Japan take the shinkansen west along the Sanyo coast from Osaka to Hiroshima, perhaps en route to Kyushu. But western Honshu, also known as **Chugoku** (the 'middle lands'), has much more to offer than a hurried stop in Hiroshima. The Sanyo coast may have the fastest rail connections and the best-known sights but the less developed San-in coast provides a complete change of pace.

The journey from the Sanyo to the San-in coast offers yet another perspective, with spectacular mountain and river scenery and the chance to see a part of Japan that has not been bulldozed into the industrial revolution. The route along the San-in coast leads to Matsue (p271), justly famous for its splendid lake, Shinji-ko, and for being the former home of Irish writer, Lafcadio Hearn.

Two stations on this route are connection points for other rail journeys: Okayama (see p256) is the starting point for the Shikoku route guide and from Shin-Yamaguchi (see p240) it's only 20 minutes by shinkansen to Kokura, the starting point for the Kyushu route guide.

OSAKA (SHIN-OSAKA) TO SHIN-YAMAGUCHI BY SHINKANSEN

Distances from Shin-Osaka. Fastest journey time: $2^1/2$ hours.

The route below follows the shinkansen line; regular JR trains go on the Sanyo line which roughly parallels the route described but stops at more stations.

Taking the shinkansen try to use the Hikari Rail Star which runs between Shin-Osaka and Hakata (the entire length of this part of the route). Car No 4 has been designated the 'Silence Car', a rarity in Japan and a welcome haven from the usual non-stop on-board announcements. Even the staff who wheel the refreshments trolley through the carriage don't say a word. All seats in the silence car are reserved so you do have to plan ahead to guarantee a noise-free ride. Don't be put off if some staff at JR ticket offices try to dissuade you from reserving a seat in this car by saying that you might miss your stop because

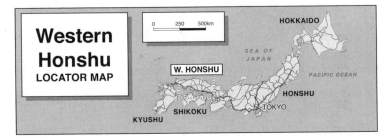

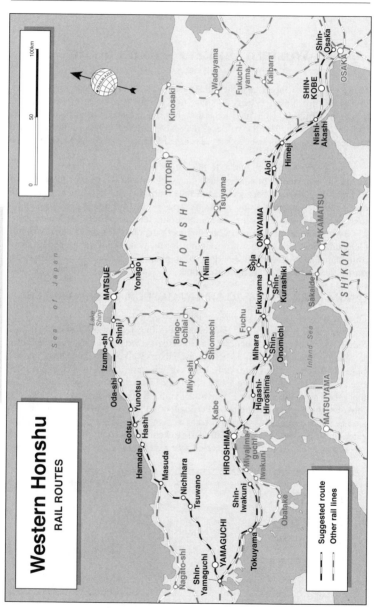

Western Honshu
RAIL ROUTES

Suggested route
Other rail lines

there are no announcements. If you have a Green Class Pass be aware that the Hikari Rail Star has no Green Car.

Standard Hikari services (ie not the Rail Star) only travel as far west as Okayama (see p256), after which you have to switch to the Rail Star. However, the standard Hikari do have Green Cars.

Osaka   [see pp116-24]

Shin-Osaka to Okayama
[Map 11, opposite; Table 3, pp458-60]

Shin-Kobe (37km)   [see pp250-5]
All trains stop here. To find coin lockers (all sizes) go straight ahead after the ticket barrier until you reach the end of the station building. The entrance to the subway (one stop to Sannomiya station for Kobe) is downstairs. On the main station concourse are a few cafés and stalls selling the city's best-known souvenir, Kobe beef.

Shinkansen fans should note that Shin-Kobe is a good place to view the bullet trains speeding past. The station is unusual in that it has only two tracks (no middle track for trains not stopping at the station), so the services that don't stop at Shin-Kobe shoot straight past along the platform edge. A barrier on the platform closes automatically whenever a through train is about to go past.

Only Kodama call at **Nishi-Akashi (60km)**, the next station along the line.

Himeji (92km) All Hikari stop here and some Nozomi. As the train pulls in, look out on the right and you'll see **Himeji Castle** on a hill in the distance.

Enquire at the tourist information desk (daily, 9am-5pm) on the concourse of Himeji's shinkansen station (to the left as you exit the central ticket barrier) about the availability of an English-speaking guide to show you around the castle. Usually staff will phone ahead and arrange for a guide to be waiting for you when you reach the castle entrance; alternatively take

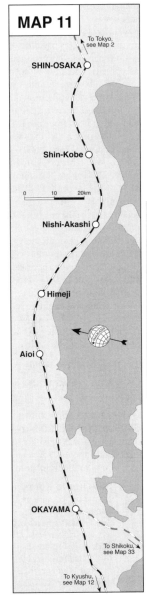

a chance on finding a guide when you get to the castle. All the guides are volunteers and their enthusiasm makes a visit to Himeji even more rewarding than a wander around the castle on your own.

If you fancy cycling to the castle, **Eki Rent A Cycle** (daily, 6:30am-11:30pm; ¥300/day) is outside the west exit of the station. To find it, turn right as you exit and walk alongside the station building.

From Himeji station, walk (or cycle) north for about 20 minutes up the tree-lined boulevard (Otemae-dori). About two-thirds of the way along, look out on the left for an udon restaurant, *Menme*, where you can get a filling bowl of noodles and a beer for around ¥1000.

Himeji Castle (🖳 www.himeji-castle.gr.jp, daily, Oct-May 9am-4pm, June-Sep 9am-5pm, ¥600) is truly one of the most picture-postcard buildings in Japan. What makes Himeji so special it that it has never been bombed or reduced to rubble. Originally a 14th-century fort, it was rebuilt in its present style at the beginning of the 17th century and has been on the World Heritage list since 1933. It is frequently used as a backdrop in samurai movies and even features in the James Bond film *You Only Live Twice* (see p431). It will take you a good two hours to explore the castle and the grounds.

Heading through the main gate, Sakura-Mon, you enter the garden where there are plenty of outer fortifications to explore. Inside the main tower, quickly pass through the lacklustre displays of weapons and wall-hangings, and at the end of a flight of very steep, ill-lit steps, you reach the top, from where there's a great view of Himeji city, the station and surrounding area.

A good overnight base in Himeji is *Toyoko Inn Himeji-eki Shinkansen-Minamiguchi* (☎ 0792-84 1045, 🖳 www.toyoko-inn.com; ¥5880/S, ¥7980/D /Tw), immediately to your left as you take the shinkansen exit of the station (the opposite side to the castle exit).

Only Kodama stop at **Aioi (112km)**.

Okayama (180km) [see pp256-61]
All trains stop here.

Okayama to Hiroshima [Map 12, p239; Table 3, pp458-60]
Shin-Kurashiki (206km) Only Kodama stop here. Shin-Kurashiki is not as convenient for Kurashiki itself as Kurashiki station is a nine-minute journey back along the JR Sanyo line (4/hour). Alternatively, get off at Okayama and take a regular JR train from there to Kurashiki station (14 mins).

Side trip to Kurashiki
It's worth going here to see the preserved **Bikan historical quarter** with its quaint old buildings, narrow lanes, small museums and canal. Theme-park junkies will approve of **Tivoli Park**, a local version of the Copenhagen original. From Kurashiki station, not Shin-Kurashiki, take the north exit for Tivoli Park and the south exit for the Bikan historical quarter and Eki Rent A Car/Cycle (on street level, to the right as you exit the station). Cycles cost ¥350 for four hours or ¥650 for the day. There are coin lockers to the right after the ticket barrier (all sizes). If these are full, there are more by the Eki Rent A Car

office at street level on the south side. Some staff at the **tourist information centre** (☎ 086-426 8681, daily Apr-Oct 9am-6pm, Nov-Mar 9am-5pm) on the station concourse near the ticket barrier speak English; they can help book accommodation and have a supply of maps (ask for the 'Stroll around Kurashiki' leaflet). Pick up a copy of the monthly *What's Up in Kurashiki*, which has events listings and occasionally restaurant reviews.

To see Kurashiki in a day, the best plan is to hire a bike and cycle out to Bikan, less than 1km south along Chuo-dori which leads away from the south exit of the station. There are a number of museums and galleries in the Bikan district. Places with names such as the 'I Love Candy Museum' can be avoided; instead top priority should be given to **Ohara Museum of Art** (🖳 www .ohara.or.jp; Tue-Sun 9am-5pm, ¥1000). The museum was established in 1930 by Keisaburo Ohara, the then president of Kurashiki Spinning Corporation, to display the works of Western art that his friend Kojima Torajiro had collected on a number of visits to Europe – all this decades before bubble-economy rich Japanese businessmen were snapping up world-famous Western art work from Christie's by telephone. Since then, the museum has expanded to house not only Western art but also a gallery of Asiatic art and a Craft Art gallery of ceramics and woodblock prints. But the biggest draw is its French Impressionist collection, as well as works by Picasso, Edvard Munch and Andy Warhol. An audio guide which introduces some of the works in the collection is available for hire (¥500).

If you're in the historical quarter, look out for the tourist information office, called **Kurashiki-Kan** (☎ 086-422 0542; daily Apr-Oct 9am-6pm, Nov-Mar 9am-5pm). It's on a corner by the canal and has an area where you can sit at tables and get a drink from vending machines.

Opened in 1997 outside the station's north exit, attractions at **Tivoli Park** (🖳 www.tivoli.co.jp) include a ferris wheel, roller coaster and log flume, as well as daily musical shows. The equivalent of Disneyland's Sleeping Beauty Castle is Tivoli Tower, a recreation of a medieval Danish castle. A day ticket is expensive (¥2000) and this doesn't even include entry to the paid attractions. If you're going to make a day of it, a one-day passport (¥4400), allowing unlimited use of all attractions, is the best deal. However, the best time to visit is after 5pm, when general admission tickets are reduced by 50% (¥1000). Opening times vary but are longest in the summer (check the website).

Check with tourist information about accommodation and rates at some of the small minshuku and ryokan in town. For proximity to the station, JR-run *Hotel Kurashiki* (☎ 086-426 6111, 🖳 www.hotels.westjr.co.jp/kurashiki; ¥7350/S, ¥14,700/D and ¥13,650/Tw) is the best choice. The rooms are above the station and some have views of Tivoli Park. Rail-pass holders receive 10% off advertised room rates.

Alternatively, *Toyoko Inn Kurashiki-eki Minami-guchi* (☎ 086-430 1045, 🖳 www.toyoko-inn.com; ¥5250/S, ¥6300/D) is on the left-hand side of Chuo-dori, next to a branch of the Lawson convenience store. It's three minutes on foot from the south exit of Kurashiki station.

Kurashiki Youth Hostel (☎ 086-422 7355, 🖳 kurashiki @jyh.gr.jp) has 60 dormitory bunks at ¥2940/3540; reservations are required. Take a bus from stop No 6 of the bus terminal outside the south exit and get off at 'Shiminkaikan-mae', from where you have to walk 15 minutes up the hill to the hostel. For ¥400 per bag (paid directly to the youth hostel), you can leave your luggage in the morning at the Rent A Cycle office (8:10am-4pm) by the south exit of the station, spend the day at leisure in Kurashiki, then pick up your bags (after 5pm) when you reach the hostel.

In summer, Hotel Kurashiki has a top-floor **beer garden**, with all-you-can-drink-and-eat deals (two-hour time limit) for ¥3000, or ¥3300 with a view of Tivoli Park lit up at night. In the station is a *McDonald's* and a branch of the tonkatsu chain *Saboten*, with a take-out counter.

Fukuyama (239km) All Hikari stop here as well as some Nozomi. As the train arrives look out on the right for a glimpse of Fukuyama Castle. This former castle town suffered extensive damage from WWII bombing raids. The view of concrete blocks as far as the eye can see is not an encouragement to linger but Fukuyama has a couple of quirky museums worth a half-day stop on the way to Hiroshima.

There are two sides to Fukuyama station. Take the north exit for the Castle Park, Prefectural Museum of History, and Fukuyama Automobile and Clock Museum. Coin lockers (including a few ¥600 ones) are outside and to the right as you take the north exit. Within the station is a shopping mall called 'Suntalk' with a few restaurants and a branch of *Andersen* which has a good selection of take-out sandwiches and cakes. Staff at the **tourist information counter** (☎ 0849-22 2869, daily, 8:30am-5pm) on the main concourse give out leaflets and maps but don't deal with hotel reservations.

Fukuyama Castle, built in 1619 and situated in a park by the north exit of the station, has a reconstructed castle tower and museum (Tue-Sun, 9am-5pm, ¥200) of no great interest. Much more fun is **Fukuyama Automobile and Clock Museum** (🖥 www.facm.net, daily, 9am-6pm, ¥900), a 15-minute walk north of the station. You're allowed to get in all the cars on display, including a 1954 Mercedes Benz and some original 1960s Mazdas. But it's much more than clocks and cars; there are also gramophones, early TV sets, electric organs, a horse-drawn carriage, light aircraft and waxworks of famous Americans. This is a place where you are encouraged to touch and feel, live and breathe, 1960s America.

If you need to stay in Fukuyama, one of the cheapest places is *Fukuyama Terminal Hotel* (☎ 0849-32 3311, 🖥 www.fukuyama-t-hotel.jp), five minutes west of the station. Single rooms at ¥5770 and twins at ¥10,270 with TV and aircon are not bad for the price.

Side trip to Matsunaga – The sole of Japan

Matsunaga, Japan's top production centre of traditional geta (wooden clogs), is between Fukuyama and the next shinkansen station at **Shin-Onomichi** (see p239). To reach here, take a local train two stops (approx 10 mins, approx 4/hr) from Fukuyama along the Sanyo line.

'As long as footwear continues to be made here,' says a travel brochure, 'Matsunaga will be the 'soul' of Japanese feet'. To prove it, the town is home to the unique **Japan Footwear Museum** (🖥 www.footandtoy.jp, daily, 9am-5pm, ¥1000). Laid out here in pairs is a sweeping history of footwear, from the earliest straw sandals to the latest in high-street fashion boots. Don't miss the glass cabinet that contains a few of the more quirky uses for shoes: a red, stiletto-heeled telephone, a geta-shaped ashtray and a large ceramic boot that doubles as a German beer mug. The coffee shop is a good place to put your feet up, but not for too long since museum staff might just snatch your footwear to add to the collection. Tickets are also valid for the adjacent **Japan Folk Toy and Doll Museum**. Most of the toys, dolls, kites and talismans on display are connected with religious festivals.

The Japan Footwear Museum is five minutes on foot (how else?) from the south exit (to the right as you pass through the ticket barrier) of Matsunaga station. Turn left on leaving the station, walk up to the junction, then turn right; the entrance is just up this road on the right.

From Matsunaga, rejoin the route by taking a train on the Sanyo line four stops to Mihara (approx 20 mins), on the shinkansen line.

Shin-Onomichi (259km) Only Kodama stop here.

Mihara (270km) Only Kodama stop here. Mihara is the nearest station to **Buttsu-ji**, a centre for training in Zen meditation, 40 minutes to the north by bus (4/day, ¥600). The temple is surrounded by cedar and maple trees, which attract visitors during the 'autumn leaves viewing' season (Oct-Nov), when admission costs ¥300. At other times entry is free and the temple is open daily, 8am-5pm.

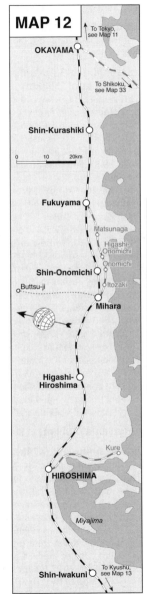

☐ **The Holy Grail**
Monty Python star turned globetrotter Michael Palin visited Buttsu-ji (see above) during his *Full Circle* travel documentary (episode 2, 14th Sept 1997) for BBC Television and attempted to interview the chief abbot:
'As I am only here for one night, what will I be able to learn in that time from being here, do you think?'
'You?'
'Yes.'
'But that is your problem. You must not ask me.'
'Oh well, interviewing never was a Zen activity.'

Higashi-Hiroshima (310km) Only Kodama stop here.

Hiroshima (342km)   **[see pp261-71]**
All trains stop here. For the island of **Miyajima** (see p268), transfer here to the Sanyo line.

Hiroshima to Shin-Yamaguchi   [Map 13, opposite; Table 3, pp459-60]
Shin-Iwakuni (383km) Only Kodama stop here. The first major stop after Hiroshima is the town of **Iwakuni**, known for the five-arched Kintaikyo Bridge which spans Nishiki-gawa. The scenery is certainly picturesque and there is the added attraction of a ride by ropeway up to Iwakuni Castle. However, a stop here shouldn't be considered a top priority, more a pleasant diversion if you have the time. A package ticket which includes the bridge, ropeway and castle costs ¥930. This ticket is sold up to 3:30pm, to give you time to get up and down by 5pm.

The tourist area is roughly equidistant between Shin-Iwakuni, the shinkansen station, and Iwakuni, which is on the Sanyo line, about a 15-minute bus ride away. **Buses** run between Shin-Iwakuni station, the bus terminal close to Kintaikyo Bridge and Iwakuni station (¥240 from Iwakuni and ¥280 from Shin-Iwakuni). **Tourist information** (Tue-Sun 9:30am-4:30pm) is available at both railway stations.

When the feudal lord of Iwakuni constructed **Kintaikyo Bridge** in 1673 his aim was to ensure that it could never be washed away, but it duly has been twice. A return walk across the bridge costs ¥300 when the toll booth is open. Over on the other side, you'll see the **ropeway** up to Iwakuni Castle (¥320 one-way, ¥540 return). Destroyed in 1615 at the time of the Tokugawa shogunate, **Iwakuni Castle** (¥260) was rebuilt in 1962 and moved to the top of a hill – not for reasons of military defence but to improve the view. There's little of interest inside (samurai armour you can see in any other castle in Japan and a model of Kintaikyo Bridge, which you can see for real down below), but the top-floor lookout commands excellent views in good weather of Nishiki-gawa, the bridge and the Inland Sea in the distance. In the summer it's a little cooler up here and there are some walking trails.

Tokuyama (430km) A stop for a few Hikari.

Shin-Yamaguchi (474km) Some Hikari stop here. Shin-Yamaguchi is the starting point for the JR Yamaguchi line which runs inland across western Honshu all the way up to the San-in coast. It is not an attractive city and functions only as a useful transport hub. Shin-Yamaguchi is a stop for both shinkansen and Sanyo line services. The JR ticket office is on the second floor of the shinkansen side, as is the tourist information office (daily, 8:30am-5pm).

An overnight stay in Shin-Yamaguchi may be necessary if planning to catch the morning steam train that runs along the Yamaguchi line to Tsuwano (see opposite). One of the best places in town is the smart but affordable boutique-style *Hotel Active! Yamaguchi* (☎ 083-976 0001, 🖳 www.hotel-active.com; ¥4980/S, ¥7980/Tw), right outside the station (shinkansen side). *Toyoko Inn*

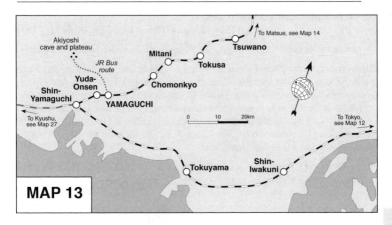

MAP 13

Shin-Yamaguchi Eki Shinkansen-guchi (☎ 083-973 1045, 🖥 www.toyoko-inn.com; ¥5040/S, ¥7140/D/Tw) is also outside the station (shinkansen side). It's relatively new and the rates include a free Japanese breakfast. For a quick snack there is a branch of the *Vie de France* bakery that includes a café on the ground floor of the station.

If heading for **Kyushu**, continue on the shinkansen from Shin-Yamaguchi to Kokura (23 mins) and pick up the route guide starting on p372.

The Lady of Rank – a grand steam experience

At weekends from March to November every year, the SL Yamaguchi (C571, nickname: 'Lady of Rank') runs between Shin-Yamaguchi and the picturesque rural town of Tsuwano (see p244). All seats on this 1937 steam-engine loco-motive are reserved but there are no additional charges for rail-pass holders. Without the pass, the fare from Shin-Yamaguchi to Tsuwano is ¥1620. The train leaves Shin-Yamaguchi in the morning (10:34am) and steams along on its 63km journey through the countryside, arriving in Tsuwano in time for lunch at 12:35pm. It then waits for around three hours before making the return jour-ney (leaving at 3:33pm and arriving back at Shin-Yamaguchi at 5:17pm). Rail fans might like to know that the Yamaguchi line was the first in Japan to wit-ness a steam renaissance, when JNR (see p75) introduced the SL Yamaguchi in 1979. Scheduled steam trains had been retired from the same stretch of rail-way line in 1973.

Apart from the steam locomotive itself, the highlight is a ride in one of the carefully preserved carriages, each designed to recall a different era of Japan's railway history. The best place to sit, however, is at the back of the train, where there's an observation car with (non-reserved) armchairs facing the window. Staff dress up in old railway uniforms and a huge crowd lines up to take pho-tographs as the train pulls out of the station. The train departs from the old-fashioned platform 1 at Shin-Yamaguchi station. There are daily services dur-ing Golden Week and most of August.

HONSHU

SHIN-YAMAGUCHI TO MASUDA
[Map 13, p241; Map 14, p245; Table 11, p463]

Distances by JR from Shin-Yamaguchi. Fastest journey time: 1 hour 35 minutes.

Shin-Yamaguchi (0km) Transfer to a Yamaguchi line train. It's mostly local trains on this line but three times a day the Super Oki LEX runs from Shin-Yamaguchi to the San-in coast. However, the Super Oki's noisy diesel engine (the railway line here is not electrified) makes it a rather unglamorous experience. Car No 1 is reserved and non-smoking, cars No 2 (smoking) and No 3 (non-smoking) are unreserved. The name 'Oki' comes from the Oki islands, a group of 180 islands in the Japan Sea.

Yuda-Onsen (10km) Just before the train reaches Yamaguchi, there's a brief stop at this small hot spring resort favoured by Japanese looking for a cure for arthritis and other aches and pains. According to legend, 600 years ago a wounded white fox bathed in the hot spring here and was miraculously healed. A large statue of the white fox stands in front of the station.

Yamaguchi (13km) Off the shinkansen track, if not quite off the beaten track, Yamaguchi must be one of the smallest prefectural capitals in Japan. The main reason for pausing here is to take a trip to **Akiyoshi Cave** (see opposite).

Yamaguchi Tourist Association (☎ 083-933 0090, daily, 9am-6pm) is on the second floor of Yamaguchi station. Staff will help book accommodation and can advise on travel throughout the area. A day or half day is good enough to see the main sights in Yamaguchi. Enquire at the bus ticket counter outside the station for **Rent A Cycle** (daily, 8am-5:30pm, 2 hours ¥320, each additional hour ¥100, or one day costs ¥840). If you rent a cycle, they'll store your luggage for free – considering it can cost up to ¥600 to use a large coin locker (some by the bus ticket counter), it can work out a lot cheaper to rent a cycle and leave your luggage there – even if you just leave the cycle round the corner.

The most unexpected sight in Yamaguchi is the modern **St Francis Xavier Memorial Church** at the top of Kameyama Park, 15 minutes on foot northwest from the station. The original church, built in 1952 to commemorate the 400th anniversary of Xavier's stay in Yamaguchi, burnt down in 1991. It was rebuilt in 1998 and now has a modern, pyramid design with two 53m-high square towers. Beyond the church, you'll really need a cycle to reach the **Five-Storey Pagoda** at Ruriko-ji. The temple grounds are part of Kozan Park, 1km north of Kameyama Park.

The cheapest lodgings are offered at *Yamaguchi Youth Hostel* (☎ 083-928 0057; 🖳 www.jyh.or.jp; ¥2730/3730, 30 beds); the English-speaking manager is helpful but the place is a little down-at-heel. Accommodation is in shared tatami rooms, with supper an additional ¥1050 and breakfast ¥525. To reach the hostel take a local train on the JR Yamaguchi line two stops to Miyano (6 mins; roughly twice an hour). Change to the bus which runs from outside Miyano station to Miyano-Onsen (10 mins); get off at the last stop. From here, follow the signs to the hostel (five minutes on foot. Apart from the usual business hotels in the station vicinity there is nothing in between the youth hostel and the upmarket *Hotel La Francesca* (☎ 083-934 1888, 🖳 www.xavier-cam.co.jp), at the foot of the road leading up to Xavier Memorial Church. It's a Tuscan-style villa with bright, spacious twins from ¥30,000 and even larger suites from ¥40,000.

If you leave the station and turn left on to the main road, the first large building you'll see on the left is **Pal-Lu Plaza**. Run by the post office, the building is part cinema, part restaurant and part conference hall. On the ground floor plaza is *Enchanté* (Tue-Sun, 11am-9pm), which does a buffet dinner.

For lunch, there are a variety of set meals (mainly Japanese) at reasonable prices. *Hotel La Francesca* (see above) has a classy Italian restaurant with the best deal at lunchtime when there are reasonably priced pasta lunches. It's open daily for lunch from 11am to 3pm, as a café from 3 to 5pm and for dinner from 5 to 9pm. Next to the hotel and under the same management is *Xavier Campana* (daily, 9am-8pm), a bakery which sells a range of cakes, sandwiches and salads. Look also for restaurants along the main street which leads up from the station towards a covered arcade, and along the arcade itself.

Less than a minute from the station, on the right side of the main street, is the Indian restaurant *Shiva* (daily, 11am-3pm, 5-9pm). The weekday lunchtime set menu (¥800) is a bargain, though the ¥1500 course menu is also good value. Following the main road up from the station, turn right onto the covered shopping arcade.

A few minutes' walk along on the right is **Chimakiya**, a department store with a basement food hall. Next door is a branch of *Mister Donut*.

Side trip to Akiyoshi cave and plateau

Though not accessible by rail, it's worth considering a trip to Akiyoshi cave and plateau since the route from Yamaguchi is operated by JR Bus so rail-pass holders can travel for free. The cave is 100m below Akiyoshi plateau and is the largest limestone cave either in Japan or in Asia – depending on who you talk to, or which leaflet you pick up.

After buying an entrance ticket (¥1200), you enter an area that resembles a rain forest; it's an unexpected scene, especially after the man-made shopping arcade just outside. The entrance to the cave is no less impressive. A crashing waterfall (almost) drowns out the noise of microphone-clutching, flag-waving tour guides, who appear to have no fear of wearing high heels inside a slippery limestone cave. The path is obvious so there's no danger of disappearing down a dark tunnel. For anyone wanting a bit more of an adventure, near the entrance there's a more off-the-beaten track that can be tried for an extra ¥300 (throw your money in the box and pick up a torch). The path winds its way past various rock formations, some of which have been given unusual names such as 'big mushroom' and 'crêpe rock'.

Though it's hard to gush quite as much as the publicity leaflet – 'the colours and shapes of stalactites, stalagmites, flowstones and limestone pools are so fantastic that you feel as if you are in an underground palace' – there's no denying that the interior is breathtaking. If visiting in the winter it's advisable to put on several layers as the temperature drops considerably inside the cave. In the summer, the temperature is a good reason for heading on in, to beat the humidity.

At the end of the trail inside the cave, an elevator whisks you up 80m to within an easy 300m walk of Akiyoshi plateau. The change of temperature hits you as you leave the lift and begin the short ascent towards the plateau, which spans the horizon in front of you as if part of an extravagant Scottish Highlands film set (the plateau even boasts its own 'Akiyoshi Thistle'). The size of the plateau varies according to what you read but the largest estimate suggests it covers an area of 130 sq km. The plateau dates back 300,000,000 years (the impressive figure is displayed on a board close to the viewing area) to the time when a coral reef formed in the sea; the rocks that exist today were once lumps of coral reef. Only 500,000 years ago, rhinoceros, giant deer and elephant roamed around the tree-covered plateau.

At the top, there's a lookout observatory, souvenir shop and a place to buy drinks and ice cream. To return to Akiyoshido bus centre, you can retrace your steps (¥100 to take the lift back down) and walk back through the cave; alternatively, you can walk, or catch a bus down from the plateau.

From Yamaguchi station, JR buses (¥1130 one way for non-pass-holders, 10/day) take around 55 minutes to reach Akiyoshi-do Bus Center close to the cave entrance. You can pick up a guide to the cave and plateau from the **tourist information desk** (☎ 08376-21620, daily, 8:30am-4:30pm) in the bus centre. From here, follow the signs to the cave entrance, which is a five-minute walk through a parade of shops.

♦ **Chomonkyo (32km)** This small station is popular with photographers looking for a suitable vantage point to snap the Yamaguchi steam train (see p241). Enthusiasts/photographers should make sure they are on a local train from Yamaguchi (about 30 mins) or Tsuwano (about 50 mins; see below) so that they can stop here. Services in either direction operate approximately hourly in the morning and evening and every 90 to 120 minutes during the day.

After Chomonkyo, the train passes through a succession of small stations before pulling in to Tsuwano. The final approach has some amazing views of the countryside. From the elevated track you can look down on villages of black-roofed houses – a rural side to Japan rarely seen and mostly forgotten. The limited express calls at **Mitani (39km)** and **Tokusa (50km)**.

Tsuwano (63km) Tsuwano is not the only town in Japan to hanker after the name 'little Kyoto' – Takayama (see p179) also claims that title, as do others – but it is certainly one of the most picturesque stops on a journey through western Honshu. A former castle town of samurai lodgings and small canals filled with plump koi (carp), Tsuwano can trace its foundation back over 700 years. During the Edo period (1600-1868), a number of persecuted Christians were banished to Tsuwano, a place presumed to be suitably out of the way for the troublemakers to be forgotten about.

The steam locomotive from Shin-Yamaguchi (see p241) terminates in Tsuwano. **Coin lockers** are on the left side of the station as you exit (a couple of large ¥600 lockers). A **tourist information office** (☎ 08567-21771, daily, 9am-5pm) is in a small building to the right as you leave the station; the best source of information is the bilingual English/Japanese booklet (¥200). It's updated every two years and contains detailed information about the key sights.

Rent A Cycle at the station charges ¥500 for two hours or ¥800 for one day.

The main sights are the ruins of **Tsuwano Castle**, the colourful **Taikodani Inari Shrine**, known for its tunnel of 1000 red gates, and **Washibari-Hachimangu Shrine**, venue for an annual display of *yabusame* (Japanese horseback archery) on the second Sunday in April.

Virtually all accommodation in Tsuwano is in a ryokan or minshuku. Staff at the tourist office will make bookings and provide directions to the places mentioned below. ***Wakasagi-no-yado*** (☎/📠 08567-21146, 💻 www.iwami .or.jp/tsuwanok/genki/wakasagi/sagi.htm) is a small, friendly minshuku where English is spoken. Rates (including two meals) are from ¥7000 per night. ***Tsuwano Youth Hostel*** (☎ 08567-20373; ¥3360 YH/HI mem, ¥4360 nonmem) is about ten minutes by bus from the station. The bus service is not that regular (tourist information has an up-to-date schedule), so it doesn't make for a very convenient base.

There is no shortage of places for lunch, with restaurants catering to the day tourist. ***Tsurube*** (Sat-Thur, 11am-7pm) serves excellent hand-made noodles in huge bowls for around ¥700-800. From the station, turn right on to the road in front of you, walk for about five minutes and look out for it on the right.

If you're looking for a snack, ***Talk Saloon Tsuwano*** (daily, 8:30am-5pm) shares a building with the telephone company NTT and does excellent all-day coffee-and-waffles sets. From the station, turn right and go straight down the main road. It's a five- to ten-minute walk down this road on the left. Most restaurants shut by 7pm, though this isn't really a problem since virtually all the ryokan/minshuku in Tsuwano include an evening meal in the nightly rate.

The 'Tsuwano Express Highway Bus' departs nightly (dep 9:40pm arr 6:23am; ¥9000 one way, ¥14,500 return) for Osaka (via Kobe, see p250) from in front of Tsuwano station. The 'Iwami Express Highway Bus' departs nightly (dep 6pm arr 7:50am, ¥13,100 one way,

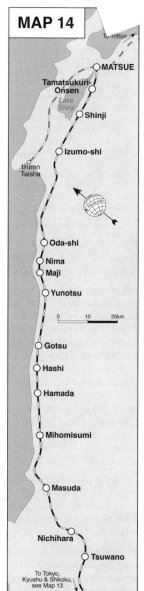

MAP 14

To Tottori

MATSUE

Tamatsukuri-Onsen

Lake Shinji

Shinji

Izumo-shi

Izumo Taisha

Oda-shi

Nima

Maji

Yunotsu

0   10   20km

Gotsu

Hashi

Hamada

Mihomisumi

Masuda

Nichihara

Tsuwano

To Tokyo, Kyushu & Shikoku, see Map 13

HONSHU

⛩ **Hidden Japan**

More than just rattling off the main sights, the real pleasure of Tsuwano is to wander around the old streets. With no obligation to tick off a list of must-see historical monuments, here is a luxury in waiting to watch time pass by slowly. No convenience stores, few cars, hardly any of that mind-numbing noise blaring out from shops, pachinko parlours and restaurants you find elsewhere in Japan. Not quite frozen in time, Tsuwano has at least decided not to follow slavishly the pace that other parts of Japan rush to keep. Armed with the excellent bilingual guide book, which contains a comprehensive list of all the town's sights, restaurants, lodgings and cafés, it is very tempting to spend several days here.

Being so picturesque, Tsuwano invites the crowds, but once they've departed after a frenetic day of sightseeing, in a puff of smoke as the steam locomotive heads back to ugly Shin-Yamaguchi, it's very gratifying to wander around the quiet roads and savour the atmosphere. Many visitors to Japan justifiably complain that travelling here is never relaxing. Tsuwano is one of the few places to challenge the perception of a fast-paced, hi-tech, can't-wait, non-stop country that, in its desperate rush to meet the future head on, rarely has time to dwell in the past.

¥23,800 return) for Shinjuku (see p95) in Tokyo. For details, contact Iwami Kotsu (☎ 0856-24 0085, 🖳 www.iwami-group.com, daily, 9am-6pm). Reservations are required for both services.

Nichihara (73km) After Tsuwano, the Super Oki LEX stops briefly at this town of astronomy. Nichihara's link with the stars is evident from the constellation design by the platform. There's no tourist office at the station but there is a 'plaza' with a small branch post office and souvenir stand. The staff are friendly but don't speak English.

Nichihara Astronomical Observatory (*Tenmondai* in Japanese) (🖳 www.sun-net.jp/~polaris/top.htm, ¥500, daily, 12-10pm; closed Jan-Mar) is a 50-minute walk uphill from the station. There is no bus service so the alternative to walking is an eight-minute taxi ride. During the day you can see the telescope inside the observatory and visit the small museum, but star gazing itself starts after dusk. *Pension Hokutosei* (☎ 08567-41010, 🖹 41647, 🖳 p-hokuto@sun-net.jp; ¥6300/pp with breakfast, ¥9450/pp with two meals), a Western-style pension next to the observatory (under the same management), is a good place to crash out after an evening gazing into deep space.

From Nichihara, the train continues north towards the San-in coast, roughly following Takatsu-gawa (Takatsu River) all the way out to the Japan Sea. If you've already travelled around Shikoku, you might notice the similarity of the landscape – lush and green, with rivers, forests and the occasional village and rice field.

Masuda (94km) A couple of minutes before arriving in Masuda, the scenery changes dramatically. After a slow journey through the rural spine of western Honshu, it's a rude awakening to emerge into a sea of smoke stacks and factory buildings. Masuda is an important railway junction, as it marks the end of the line from Shin-Yamaguchi and is the connecting point for lines running along the San-in coast.

There's no need to change trains here for the next part of the route if you're on the Super Oki LEX, which continues east along the San-in coast. However, it's worth noting that another LEX, the Super Matsukaze, starts at Masuda and continues along the same route as the Super Oki. Of the three daily Super Oki LEXs, two continue as far as Yonago (see p249), while one goes even further, to Tottori (see p249). All Super Matsukaze LEXs go as far as Tottori.

MASUDA TO MATSUE
[Map 14, p245; Table 11, p463]

Distances by JR from Masuda. Fastest journey time: 2 hours 40 minutes.

Masuda (0km) From Masuda, the Super Oki and Super Matsukaze LEXs head east along the San-in line. A few minutes out of Masuda, the train finally reaches the Japan Sea, dotted with rock formations. The sea here is rough and much less inviting than the calm water of the Inland Sea. For sea views, sit on the left side.

After Masuda some services stop at **Mihomisumi (22km)**.

Hamada (41km) This town is an unremarkable place.

From Hamada, the train heads a little inland, so views of the Japan Sea are less frequent.

Hashi (51km) This is the nearest stop to **AQUAS** (🖳 www.aquas.or.jp, Wed-Mon, 9am-5/6pm, ¥1500), a modern aquarium where you can see white beluga dolphins, seals, crabs, jelly fish and the like. Follow the signs to the aquarium from Hashi station.

Gotsu (60km) Change here to a local train if planning to visit Maji (see below) or Nima (see p248). Local/rapid trains leave approximately hourly though less frequently in the middle of the day and not all rapid services stop at Maji.

Yunotsu (77km) Not all limited expresses stop at Yunotsu, a spa town popular with elderly holidaymakers. Forest surrounds both sides of the track along this section of the route but you might catch the odd glimpse of the sea. The hot spring here is believed to have been established 1300 years ago by an injured raccoon. The healing waters are supposed to help rheumatism, neuralgia, gout, dermatitis and – of all things – whiplash.

♦ Maji (83km) Nearest station to the 'singing sand' beach of Kotogahama. The beach is named after Princess Koto, a member of the Heike clan who fled north to the San-in coast after the Heike were defeated by the rival Genji clan in the 12th century (see p37).

To thank the people who lived by the beach for offering her protection, she played the koto (Japanese zither) every day. According to legend, after her death the sand itself began to make a noise similar to that of the koto. To this day it's said that whoever walks along the beach will hear the sound of the sand 'singing' to them. But beware: tourist literature warns that 'even the slightest dirt will render the sand mute'.

To test this theory, leave Maji station and walk straight ahead to the beach. A volleyball tournament is held here annually at the end of July.

♦ **Nima (86km)** Just before the (local/rapid) train arrives at this small station, you might catch sight of an unusual glass pyramid building on the left which looks a bit like the entrance to the Louvre in Paris. This is **Nima Sand Museum** (🖳 www.nima-cho.ne.jp/museum, daily except 1st Wed of month, 9am-5pm, ¥700). Its main attraction is a giant egg timer which lasts for one year before needing to be turned over again. Passing by the self-playing piano by the entrance, there are various machines that revolve and pump sand round and round, displays of coloured sand, and jars of the stuff collected from beaches across Japan and around the world, including a sample from Waikiki Beach in Hawaii. The flow of sand in the egg timer, towering above the central atrium, is affected by outside temperature so the only way of ensuring that the year does not end too quickly is to use a computer which regulates the flow. Every year at midnight on 31st December, 108 people help to turn the hour-glass round and welcome in the new year; visitors are welcome to join in. It's an eight-minute walk to the Sand Museum – leave JR Nima station, cross the train tracks and head towards the glass pyramid building.

Oda-shi (97km) A commuter stop on the limited express but of little interest to the tourist. There are great views of the Japan Sea on the approach to Izumo-shi as the train runs on an elevated track. You might see the odd fishing boat out in the distance.

Izumo-shi (130km) Izumo-shi is the nearest JR station to **Izumo Taisha**, site of a well-known shrine and a popular side trip from Matsue (see p278). The shrine can be reached by private Ichibata Railway. From the north exit of the JR station, go straight and turn right on to the main road. Ichibata's station is just up this road on the right. It's a modern station with attached department store. From Ichibata Izumo-shi take a local train four stops to Kawato, where you change trains again for the final leg to Izumo-Taisha-mae.

For a speedy return to the Sanyo coast, the Yakumo LEX takes three hours to Okayama (see pp256-61).

Shinji (146km) This station is right on the edge of Lake Shinji but trees block all views until just before the train reaches Matsue.

Tamatsukuri-Onsen (156km) This popular hot spring resort, where it is claimed the gods once enjoyed bathing, is on the shore of Lake Shinji. The tourist information office in Matsue (see p274) can provide information on hotels and bath houses here.

During the last few minutes of the journey towards Matsue, there are views of Lake Shinji on the left.

Matsue (163km)   **[see pp271-8]**

Side trip to Tottori [Table 11, p463]

From Matsue (0km), the San-in line continues east towards the city of Tottori (122km); the fastest journey time is 85 minutes. The Super Matsukaze LEX runs direct to Tottori, stopping along the way at the industrial city of **Yonago** (29km). Yonago functions as a regional transport hub since it is a stop on the San-in line as well as a junction of the Hakubi line which runs south to Okayama (see pp256-61) just over two hours away by Yakumo LEX.

Tottori is known for its sand dunes which extend east to west along the coast for some 16km. The dunes are 20 minutes by city loop bus (¥200 per ride) which picks you up from outside Tottori station and drops you off at the main sand-dune area. It's hard to believe unless you actually make the effort to travel out here that Japan really does have its own mini desert. Just in case you forget where you are once you've arrived, non-native camels wait on the edge of the dunes for a classic Japanese photo opportunity (for a fee) or to take you for a ride. Horse-drawn carts are also on standby.

If you need somewhere to stay, ***Tottori Green Hotel Morris*** (☎ 0857-22 2331, 🖳 www.hotel-morris.co.jp/tottori) is a few minutes' walk north of Tottori station, just past Daimaru department store. Tiny singles go for ¥5250 while more spacious ones cost ¥5775. Twins are ¥10,290 and doubles ¥9240. A coin laundry is available. A newer addition to the business-hotel scene, with clean and compact rooms, is ***Toyoko Inn Tottori-eki Minami-Guchi*** (☎ 0857-36 1045, 🖳 www.toyoko-inn.com; ¥5460/S, ¥7560/D, ¥8190/Tw), one minute on foot from the south exit of Tottori station (the opposite side of the station to Daimaru department store).

For food, there's a *UCC coffee shop* on the second floor of the station and a variety of **ekiben** are sold on the main concourse; *Kanizushi* (strips of crab meat on a bed of rice) is the best known. Opposite the station is a ***Mister Donut***, and Daimaru department store has a basement food hall. More upmarket dining possibilities are to be had next door at ***Hotel New Otani Tottori*** (☎ 0857-23 1111, 🖳 www.newotani.co.jp). The names of the in-house restaurants and menus change every few years, but there's usually an all-you-can-eat buffet lunch for ¥1500 (11am-2pm). Staying the night at the New Otani is not such a good deal though, with singles from ¥9500 and doubles/twins at ¥18,000.

From Tottori, the Super Inaba LEX takes two hours to run south along the Inbi and Tsuyama lines to Okayama (see p256), while the Super Hakuto takes just over three hours to Kyoto (see p206).

Part of the track on the route between Tottori and Okayama/Kyoto (between Chizu and Kamigori) is operated by the private Chizu Kyuko railway, which means rail-pass holders must pay a ¥1260 supplement (payable on board) or ¥1770 if travelling on a limited express.

MATSUE BACK TO KYOTO/OSAKA

The fastest way back to the Sanyo coast is to take a Yakumo LEX along the Hakubi line to Okayama (see p256), a stop on the shinkansen. From Okayama, pick up a Hikari east to Shin-Osaka (for Osaka; see p116) or Kyoto (p206). The fastest journey time from Matsue to Okayama is 2 hours 20 minutes.

Western Honshu – city guides

KOBE

Short on sights for foreign tourists but big on food, shopping and entertainment, Kobe is a good place to break a journey along the Sanyo coast. Like Nagasaki (see p396), Kobe developed as an international port city and is today popular as a tourist spot for Japanese interested in seeing the foreign settlements and Western-style houses that lent the city an 'exotic' feel in the decades following the Meiji Restoration (see p39).

The biggest event of the more recent past took place at 5:46am on January 17th 1995 when Kobe was struck by the Great Hanshin Earthquake. Over 6000 people were killed, more than 100,000 buildings destroyed, and much of the city and surrounding area reduced to rubble. But, few outward signs of this tragedy remain.

For the latest information on sights and hotels in Kobe, see 🖳 www.feel-kobe.jp.

What to see

There's not a great deal to see in the area around **Shin-Kobe**, so if you've only got a little time it's best to catch a subway one stop to Sannomiya, the centre of downtown Kobe. That said, a short excursion can be made from Shin-Kobe by taking the **Ropeway**, a few minutes on foot from the station. Head towards Shin-Kobe Oriental Hotel just below the station and follow the signs to the ropeway entrance. The ropeway (return trip ¥1000) connects Shin-Kobe with 'Nunobiki Herb Park' on a hill behind the station. The herb park is a tourist trap and isn't worth bothering with on a cloudy day, but if the weather is co-operating it's possible to see as far as Kansai Airport.

To see for yourself what happened to Kobe in January 1995, head for the **Disaster Reduction and Human Renovation Institution**, a grand name for a new building which houses two museums: the Disaster Reduction Museum and Human Renovation Museum. Entry costs ¥500 for each (or ¥800 for both) and the building is open Tue-Sun 9:30am-5:30pm (July-Oct to 6pm). The Disaster Reduction Museum uses video, dioramas and interactive exhibits to great effect to remind visitors of the destruction wrought by the earthquake. The Human Renovation Museum, which takes as its theme the 'preciousness of life', is less effective and could easily be skipped. From JR Sannomiya station, take a local train one stop east to Nada station. The building is a ten-minute walk south from the south exit of the station.

Close by lies **Hyogo Prefectural Museum of Art** (🖳 www.artm .pref.hyogo.jp/eng/home.html; Tue-Sun, 10am-6pm; ¥500), opened in 2004 as part of a waterfront redevelopment known as HAT Kobe. Billed as the largest museum in Western Japan, the vast space houses an impressive collection of modern art.

North of Sannomiya station lies the **Kitano district**, with Western-style buildings such as an 'original Holland house' and 'Wien Austrian house', which are probably of more interest to the domestic tourist. Many of the buildings had to be reconstructed after the 1995 earthquake and aren't really worth seeking out. It is, however, worth visiting **Kitano Tenman Shrine** which also houses a youth hostel (see p255). The shrine dates from the late Heian period (794-1185) and is popular for the views it offers over the city. On a clear day this is the best place to take in Kobe's geography. By the entrance to the shrine is a small kiosk that sells cold drinks and ice cream. Just below here is a tourist information branch office.

Two stops west along the Sanyo line by local train from JR Sannomiya station is JR Kobe station, access point for **Harborland** and its shopping malls, department stores and small amusement park with ferris wheel. Head either underground as you exit the station or overground, walking under the elevated expressway towards the main shopping and entertainment area. A good walk can be made by following the bay around from Harborland all the way to **Meriken Park**, a popular place for young couples searching for a romantic bay view. **Kobe Maritime Museum** (Tue-Sun, 10am-4:30pm, ¥600), in Meriken Park, is more impressive from the outside than in.

Port Island and Rokko Island are man-made constructions off the coast and are accessible from the centre of Kobe via unmanned light transit railways. The larger **Port Island** is reached from JR Sannomiya via the Port Liner transit system. Caffeine addicts might be tempted to visit **UCC Coffee Museum** (🖳 www .ucc.co.jp/museum, Tue-Sun, 10am-5pm, ¥210), which traces the history of the popular beverage and houses an impressive collection of coffee cups. To visit the only museum in the country dedicated to coffee, take the Port Liner from Sannomiya to Minami-Koen station on Port Island.

The smaller **Rokko Island** is home to **Kobe Fashion Museum** (Thur-Tue 10am-6pm, ¥500). The permanent exhibition of costumes, from sleek evening dresses to flowing Imperial gowns, is housed in the fashion wing. Temporary exhibitions are staged in the art wing. To reach Rokko Island (🖳 www .ric.or.jp.english), take a train from JR Sannomiya along the Tokaido line two stops east to Sumiyoshi station, and transfer on to the Rokko Liner. For the museum, get off at Island Center station.

PRACTICAL INFORMATION
Station guide
The main JR stations in Kobe City are **Shin-Kobe** (for shinkansen) at the foot of Mt Rokko, **Sannomiya** in the city centre, and **Kobe**, a gateway to the city's Harborland shopping and entertainment area. Sannomiya is a major rail junction, with the Hanshin and Hankyu railways, subway and JR stations all crossing through here. This means that Sannomiya, far more than Shin-Kobe, is the centre for commerce, shopping and entertainment.

Tourist information
Kobe City Information Center (☎ 078-322 0220, daily, 10am-7pm, July-Aug to 8pm) is on street level by JR/Hankyu Sannomiya stations. There's also an **information counter** at Shin-Kobe station

HONSHU

(daily, 10am-6pm), though the staff here don't have as much information at their fingertips. On the 20th floor of Kobe International House in Sannomiya is **Kobe International Community Center** (☎ 078-291 8441, 🖳 www.kicc.jp, Mon-Sat, 9am-5pm), which has foreign newspapers, magazines and organizes monthly cultural events. Another reason for coming here is the free view of the Shin-Kobe area. Alternatively, there are great views from the observation point on the 24th floor of **Kobe City Hall** (daily, 10am-9pm; free) on Flower Rd.

Kobe Student Guides is a volunteer group of students from Kobe and Osaka. Volunteers are happy to guide foreign visi-

tors around sights in Kobe, Osaka (see p116) and around Himeji Castle (see p235). The only costs involved are the guide's transport, admission fees and lunch. Contact details for the group change from time to time, so pick up a leaflet from the tourist office or check 🖳 www.geocities.co.jp/CollegeLife/3136/.

Access to/from Kansai International Airport and Kobe Airport
For rail-pass holders, the best way of getting to Kansai Airport (see p51) is to take a shinkansen to Shin-Osaka, one stop along the line from Shin-Kobe, and from there to take the Haruka LEX. Alternatively a direct

KOBE 神戸

Where to stay, eat and drink

1 Kobe Kitano Youth Hostel	1 神戸北野ユースホステル
3 Shin-Kobe Oriental Hotel; Wakkoku (Shin-Kobe Oriental City)	3 新神戸オリエンタルホテル；和黒 (新神戸オリエンタルシティー)
4 Holiday Inn Express Shin-Kobe	4 ホリデイインエクスプレス新神戸
5 Super Hotel Kobe	5 スーパーホテル神戸
6 Hotel Monterey Amalie	6 ホテルモントレアマリー
7 Hotel Monterey Kobe	7 ホテルモントレア神戸
9 Toyoko Inn Sannomiya No 2	9 東横イン 神戸三ノ宮2
12 Kobe International House	12 神戸国際会館
15 Kobe Harbor Circus	15 神戸ハーバーサーカス
16 Mosaic	16 モザイク
18 Hotel Sunroute Sopra Kobe	18 ホテルサンルートソプラ神戸

Other

1 Kitano Tenman Shrine	1 北野天満神社
2 Shin-Kobe Ropeway	2 新神戸ロープウェイ
8 Kobe City Information Center	8 神戸市総合インフォメーションセンター
10 Disaster Reduction and Human Renovation Institution	10 人と防災未来センター
11 Hyogo Prefectural Museum of Art	11 兵庫県立美術館
12 Kobe International Community Center (Kobe International House)	12 神戸国際コミュニティセンター (神戸国際会館)
13 Kobe City Hall	13 神戸市役所
14 Post Office	14 郵便局
17 Kobe Maritime Museum (Meriken Park)	17 神戸海洋博物館 (メリケンパーク)
19 Kobe Fashion Museum (Rokko Island)	19 神戸ファッション美術館 (六甲アイランド)
20 UCC Coffee Museum (Port Island)	20 UCCコーヒー博物館 (ポートアイランド)

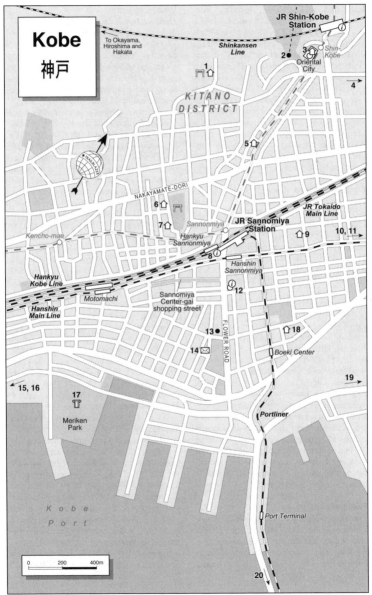

Kobe
神戸

To Okayama,
Hiroshima and
Hakata

Shinkansen
Line

JR Shin-Kobe
Station

2 ●

3 🏠
Oriental
City

Shin-
Kobe

4 →

KITANO
DISTRICT

1 ⛩🏠

5 🏠

NAKAYAMATE-DORI

6 🏠 ⛩

7 🏠

Sannonmiya

JR Sannomiya
Station

JR Tokaido
Main Line

Kencho-mae ○

Hankyu
Sannonmiya

8 ⓘ

9 🏠

10, 11

Hankyu
Kobe Line

Motomachi

Hanshin
Sannonmiya

ⓘ 12

Hanshin
Main Line

Sannomiya
Center-gai
shopping street

13 ●

14 ✉

FLOWER ROAD

🏠 18

Boeki Center

15, 16 ←

17
🍺

Meriken
Park

19 →

Portliner

Kobe
Port

0   200   400m

Port Terminal

20

HONSHU

limousine bus service operates from Sannomiya to the airport (65 mins, ¥1800).

Opened in 2006 at a cost of ¥314 billion on 2.72 sq km of reclaimed land off the coast, **Kobe Airport** serves domestic flights only. Skymark Airlines (🖳 www.sky mark.co.jp) operates several flights daily between Kobe and Tokyo's Haneda airport (see p50). Japan Airlines operates daily flights to and from Tokyo, Sapporo, Naha, Sendai, Kumamoto and Kagoshima. ANA serves Tokyo, Sapporo, Naha, Sendai, Niigata and Kagoshima. The airport is connected to downtown Sannomiya via the Port Liner; the journey time is 16 minutes.

Getting around

Kobe has a modern and efficient two-line subway. Arriving at Shin-Kobe, it's best to take the Seishin-Yamate subway line one stop to Sannomiya (¥200). The newer Kaigan line runs from Sannomiya to the city's main football stadium outside Misaki-koen station before looping back to connect with the Seishin-Yamate line at Shin-Nagata.

The one-day city bus and subway pass (¥1000) permits unlimited travel on the two subway lines and all Kobe city buses. The subway (like most in Japan) is very user-friendly, with signs in English and a button for an English translation on the ticket machines (look for the British flag).

The City Loop tourist bus service, which circles downtown Kobe in around 70 minutes, is another option. Individual rides cost ¥250 or a one-day pass is ¥650. Passes are available from the tourist information offices at Sannomiya or Shin-Kobe, or on the bus. Pick up a copy of the timetable and route guide when you buy the pass. Small discounts to some attractions are available to users of the one-day pass.

Festivals

The biggest annual event is **Kobe Matsuri**, which lasts for about 10 days towards the end of July. On the last weekend there's a big fireworks display and a parade of floats through the city. Check with the tourist office for exact dates/times.

Where to stay

Holiday Inn Express Shin Kobe (☎ 078-222 1212, 🖳 www.holidayinn.com; ¥8000/S, ¥13,000/D, ¥16,000/Tw) is in a quiet residential area five minutes on foot south-east of Shin-Kobe station. The rooms have neat touches such as Japanese screens across the windows and the rate includes continental breakfast.

A more upmarket place right outside Shin-Kobe station is the skyscraper *Shin-Kobe Oriental Hotel* (☎ 078-291 1121, 🖳 www.orientalhotel.co.jp; ¥15,015/S, ¥26,565/D/Tw), where the best rooms are on the Executive Floor. Facilities include an indoor swimming pool, several restaurants and high-speed internet access.

A cheaper option, midway between Sannomiya and Shin-Kobe, is *Super Hotel Kobe* (☎ 078-261 9000, 🖳 www.superhotel .co.jp; ¥5460/S inc continental breakfast). Part of an expanding national chain, this place has functional rooms that are fairly comfortable. All have aircon, TV, wide beds and attached bath but no telephone or fridge. Payment is in cash only, which you feed into a machine. Instead of keys, guests receive a receipt with a code number to unlock the door.

Another good budget choice is *Toyoko Inn Kobe Sannomiya No. 2* (☎ 078-232 1045, 🖳 www.toyoko-inn.com; ¥6720/S, ¥8820/D/Tw), five minutes south from the Sannomiya railway stations. Ten minutes south of Sannomiya is the more upscale *Hotel Sunroute Sopra Kobe* (☎ 078-222 7500, 🖳 www.sunroute.jp; ¥9240/S, ¥17,325/Tw, ¥19,425/D) with reasonably sized rooms and a pleasant coffee shop.

Just below the Kitano area, not far from Sannomiya, is *Hotel Monterey Kobe* (☎ 078-392 7111, 🖳 www.hotelmonterey .co.jp; ¥11,550/S, ¥21,945/Tw). The theme is Italy, with whitewashed walls, patio courtyards and fountains. The guest rooms are less ambitious but pleasant enough with wide beds and wooden floors. Still more intriguing is the annex, *Hotel Monterey Amalie* (☎ 078-334 1711, 🖳 www.hotel monterey.co.jp; ¥11,550/S, ¥21,945/Tw). The theme here is apparently nautical –

most striking are the extraordinary lifts, worth a look even if you're not staying here. There's a good French restaurant with a ¥1500 lunch menu.

Kobe Kitano Youth Hostel (☎ 078-221 4712, ✉ yh@kobe-kitano.net; ¥3200 YH/HI mem, ¥4200 non-mem, no meals), attached to Kitano Tenman Shrine (see p251), has modern four- and six-bed bunk dorms. Each bed can be curtained off for a bit more privacy and you even get an in-bed reading light! From the hostel meeting room, there's a fantastic view over Kobe. It's wise to book ahead in high season.

To get to the hostel, head for Tenman Shrine and go up the hill past the shrine entrance. The entrance is via a flight of stairs on the left side. Kitano is hilly, so be prepared for a bit of a slog if you've got a lot of luggage.

Where to eat and drink

There are plenty of restaurants where Kobe beef is on the menu. One of the best known is *Wakkoku*, on the third floor of **Shin-Kobe Oriental City** adjacent to Shin-Kobe station. An evening meal here doesn't come cheap, with course menus averaging ¥11,000 per head; it's better value at lunchtime, with the cheapest set course at ¥2500. There are many other restaurants and cafés at Shin-Kobe Oriental City, including places specializing in ramen, teppanyaki and tonkatsu.

The area in, around and underneath the railway station in Sannomiya is packed with places to eat. **Kobe International House**, along Flower Rd, has a concert hall and cinema as well as two basement floors of cafés and restaurants. The cinema is on the 11th floor, next to a café with a roof-top garden called 'Tooth tooth the dining garden: gastronome and sensuality'. It's a good place to relax and forget the bustle of city life.

The **Harborland** district around JR Kobe station also has countless dining possibilities. Two big shopping and restaurant complexes close to Kobe station are **Kobe Harbor Circus** and **Mosaic**. The latter is probably the busiest and also has a cinema complex.

Side trip from Kobe

Probably the most popular side trip from the city is to the **Rokko mountains** behind Shin-Kobe, considered the perfect escape from frenetic city life. As with many natural escapes that lie so close to densely populated areas in Japan, the Rokko area has its charms – gentle hikes and views of the Inland Sea – but also shameless tourist traps, such as a museum of music boxes, Mt Rokko pasture and a 'Kobe Cheese Castle'.

Before setting off pick up a copy of the excellent *Mountain Trails in Kobe* from the tourist information office; this has suggested routes and hiking courses. A trip on a cable car and ropeway into the mountains can be combined with a visit to **Arima-Onsen**, a hot spring resort on the other side of the mountain range. Arima-Onsen is one of the 'three ancient springs' in Japan, along with Kusatsu (accessible from Shibukawa in Central Honshu) and Dogo-Onsen (see p447), but the future has caught up with the past in the modern hotels that cater to tourists.

There are a number of possible approaches to Arima-Onsen; the best way for rail-pass holders is to take a local train from JR Sannomiya two stops east to JR Rokkomichi, then take a city bus (No 16) to Cable-Shita station, the starting point for a ten-minute cable car ride (¥1460 return) into the mountains. At the top of the cable car it's possible to connect with the Rokko Arima Ropeway which takes 30 minutes (¥2640 return) to reach the terminus at Arima station.

HONSHU

OKAYAMA

One of the largest cities in western Japan, Okayama faces the Inland Sea, enjoys a mild climate and is known for its large stroll garden called Korakuen. The city expanded politically and economically during the Edo period (1603-1867) but suffered a devastating air raid on 29th June 1945. The bombing of Okayama has been largely forgotten, even though an area of almost 8 sq km was razed to the ground, because it happened just a few weeks before the atomic bomb was dropped on Hiroshima. Over 25,000 buildings – including Okayama Castle – were destroyed and more than 1700 people lost their lives.

What to see

Korakuen, part of Okayama's 'culture zone', is the city's star attraction. The zone is on both sides of Asahi-gawa across town from the station. Take a tram from the terminus outside the station all the way down Momotaro-dori to Shiroshita (¥100). At this junction, turn left and walk north for a minute to find on the left side **Okayama Orient Museum** (🖥 www.city.okayama.okayama.jp/ orientmuseum.orient-e; Tue-Sun, 9am-5pm, ¥300), a recommended stop which houses a collection of ceramics and glassware mainly from Syria, Egypt and Iran. The displays are well lit and there is some English signage. A pamphlet is available at the entrance and there's a tearoom on the second floor. Just past the Orient Museum is **Okayama Prefectural Museum of Art** (Tue-Sun, 9am-5pm, ¥300), displaying the work of local artists. It's also a venue for temporary exhibitions.

Continue north until you see on your right a road leading across a bridge towards the entrance to Korakuen. The highlight of a stroll around the landscaped gardens of **Korakuen** (April-Sep 7:30am-6pm, Oct-Mar 8am-5pm, ¥350) is the 'borrowed' view – the black façade of Okayama Castle tower looming down from the hill above. The garden was constructed in 1700 by Tsunamasa Ikeda, feudal lord of Okayama, and it remained in the hands of the Ikeda family until 1871 when it was given to the prefecture. Built on an island on Asahi-gawa, Korakuen was the first garden in Japan to include grass lawns.

After strolling around, instead of backtracking to the main entrance, head for the smaller south exit (towards Okayama Castle). Straight in front of you as you go out is a small path that leads down to the river and a hut where rowing/paddle boats can be rented. Turning to the right after passing through the south exit, cross Tsukimi Bridge which leads to the castle entrance.

Okayama Castle (daily, 9am-5pm, ¥300) is known as *Ujo*, or 'crow castle', after its black exterior. The original 1597 donjon was destroyed during a heavy WWII air raid; the present reconstruction dates from 1966. Nevertheless, it's an impressive sight as you approach the donjon, with gold glittering from its roof. A volunteer guide service runs tours of the castle (from the booth to the

---

(Opposite) Top: The O-Torii gate (see p270) to Itsukushima Shrine, Miyajima, appears at high tide to be floating on the water but looks no less dramatic at low tide. (Photo © Alistair Logan). **Bottom**: Himeji Castle (see p236) is one of several World Heritage sites in Japan. (Photo © JNTO).

⛩ **Momotaro – the Peach Boy**
You can't wander around Okayama for long without noticing one of Japan's most celebrated folk heroes. The city is home to Momotaro, the legendary Peach Boy. A well-known fairy tale begins with an old woman washing her clothes in a river, when she discovers an enormous peach floating by. She fishes it out and drags it home to her husband. Salivating at the prospect of tucking into a juicy peach, the old man takes a knife and is about to cut it when the fruit suddenly breaks in half and a baby boy jumps out. The 'peach boy' grows up with superhuman strength and soon leaves his parents to sail off to the Demon's Isle where, in the best traditions of good against evil, he defeats the Demon King – with the help of a spotted dog, a monkey and a pheasant he picks up along the way.

Okayama claims the heroic figure of Momotaro for its own, partly because the prefecture is known for peaches but also because the legendary Demon's Isle is thought to be the island of Megishima, in the Inland Sea between Okayama and Shikoku. On the plaza, outside the east exit of Okayama station, is a statue of Momotaro and his entourage on their way to fight the demon. Momotaro's face appears on some of the city's manholes, on the Momotaro credit card and in most souvenir shops. The Okayama Momotaro Festival takes place in spring (usually on the third Saturday and Sunday of April). International mail sent from the central post office receives a peach boy stamp and there's even a naked peach boy statue (holding a peach) in Korakuen (see p256).

HONSHU

left of the entrance), but only in Japanese. On the fourth floor of the castle you'll find a selection of kimonos you can dress up in free of charge. One reader wrote: "It's not worth going inside Okayama Castle because the whole place is completely reconstructed. There are a couple of rooms on each floor with some exhibits but mostly it's a case of 'oh look, it's a tatami floor' or 'oh look, it's a gift shop' etc. Having said that, you do get a good view from the top."

Various combination tickets offer modest reductions on individual entrance fees; Korakuen plus the castle costs ¥520. If you don't want to visit the garden, you can buy a castle plus Oriental Art Museum ticket for ¥480.

The concert hall in **Okayama Symphony Hall** has a seating capacity of 2001; it's worth checking the event programme to see what's on. There are several shops inside the complex, including a Maruzen bookstore and Okayama Tourism and Products Center (daily, 10am-8pm), on the first floor; the latter sells a variety of locally made crafts.

Outside the west exit of Okayama station, and part of the same complex as ANA Hotel Okayama (see p260), are the regional offices and studios of national broadcaster NHK as well as the new **Okayama Digital Museum** (💻 www .okayama-digital-museum.jp, Tue-Sun, 10am-8pm; ¥300). Half of the exhibits are dedicated to primitive technology – mostly about technology developed in

---

(Opposite) **Top**: Hiroshima's A-bomb Dome (see p262), one of the few buildings to remain standing after the world's first atomic bomb was dropped on the city on 6 August 1945. (Photo © Richard Brasher). **Bottom**: A clock frozen at 8:15am, the time of the explosion, and saké cups fused together as a result of the intense heat. (Photos © Bryn Thomas).

Okayama – while the rest deals with the modern day. The entry ticket hangs around your neck and can be used to activate certain exhibits. It's not a big place and only worth going to if you have time to kill. Rail fans might like the *museum café* which affords views of the station; the café sells herbal juices, sandwiches and scones.

PRACTICAL INFORMATION
Station guide

Okayama station has two sides connected by an underground passage: The **east side** is the main exit for Momotaro-dori and Korakuen/Okayama Castle; the **west side** – being redeveloped at the time of writing– is the exit for ANA Hotel Okayama, Okayama Digital Museum, Okayama International Center, Matsunoki Ryokan and Okayama-ken Seinen Kaikan Youth Hostel. **Rent A Cycle** offices (4 hours/¥350; 1 day/¥650) are on both sides of the station (east side daily 7:30am-7:30pm, west side daily 7am-7:30pm). Most **coin lockers** (all sizes, including oversize ¥600 ones) are on the

OKAYAMA　岡山

Where to stay

1	Okayama-ken Seinen Kaikan YH	1	岡山県青年会館ユースホステル
2	Toyoko Inn Okayama-eki Nishiguchi-migi	2	東横イン岡山駅西口右
3	Okayama International Center	3	岡山国際交流センター
4	Matsunoki Ryokan	4	まつのき旅館
5	ANA Hotel Okayama	5	岡山全日空ホテル
6	Hotel Granvia Okayama	6	ホテルグランヴィア岡山
7	Mielparque	7	メルパルク
8	Okayama City Hotel	8	岡山シティーホテル
16	Comfort Hotel Okayama	16	コンフォートホテル岡山

Where to eat and drink

3	Café Fossette	3	カフェフォセット
5	Fukusa	5	福紗
9	Café Moni	9	カフェモニ
11	Skipper's	11	スキッパーズ
13	Ume no Hana (Cred Building)	13	梅の花 (クレド岡山ビル)
19	Bar Boccone	19	ばーる ぼっこーね

Other

3	Okayama International Center	3	岡山国際交流センター
5	Okayama Digital Museum	5	岡山市デジタルミュージアム
7	Post Office	7	郵便局
10	I Plaza	10	アイプラザ
12	Central Post Office	12	中央郵便局
13	Kinokuniya (Cred Building)	13	紀伊國屋 (クレド岡山ビル)
14	Mitsui Sumitomo Bank	14	三井住友銀行
15	Okayama Symphony Hall; Maruzen	15	岡山シンフォニーホール; 丸善
17	Okayama Orient Museum	17	岡山オリエント美術館
18	Okayama Prefectural Museum of Art	18	岡山県立美術館
20	Korakuen	20	後楽園
21	Okayama Castle	21	岡山城

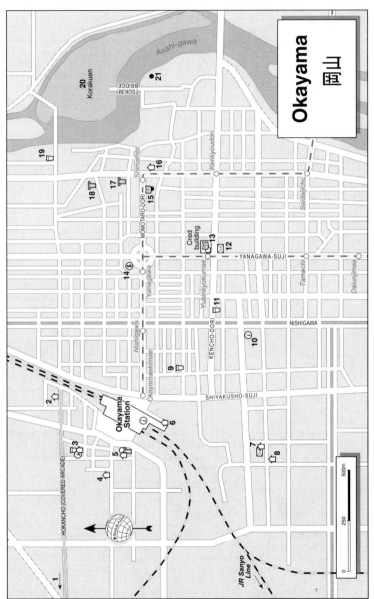

Okayama
岡山

HONSHU

Asahi-gawa

20 Korakuen

21
TSUKIMI BRIDGE

19

Kenkyoudon

Shiroshita
16

17
18

MOMOTARO-DORI

15

Cred building
13
12

YANAGAWA-SUJI

Yaragawa

14 $

Saidaijicho

Tamachi

Daiunjimae

Yubinkyokumae

11

NISHIGAWA

KENCHO-DORI

10

Nishigawa

9

Okayamaekimae

SHIYAKUSHO-SUJI

2

Okayama Station

6

3

5

4

7

8

HOKANCHO (COVERED ARCADE)

500m

250

0

1

JR Sanyo Line

⛩ **Hi-tech uniforms**
    The latest hi-tech Japanese primary-school uniforms made by an Okayama-based company come with a built-in global positioning transmitter. The product was launched amid growing concern that children are becoming victims of crime. Parents can keep track of their children's whereabouts via computer and can even contact a security firm to locate the child. The technology doesn't come cheap: each suit costs around ¥32,550, double the price of a regular school uniform.

east side. Find them on the far left-hand corner of the ground floor of the station concourse (as you stand inside the station).

Tourist information
The staff at the **tourist information desk** (☎ 086-222 2912, daily, 9am-6pm), by the station's east exit, speak a little English and can provide maps and a list of accommodation. They won't make hotel bookings, but will direct you to the NTA travel agency opposite the tourist information desk which will.

For more detailed information in English go to **Okayama International Center** (☎ 086-256 2914, 🖥 www.opief.or.jp, Tue-Sun, 9am-9pm, ground floor information counter 9am-5pm), a five-minute walk north-west from the station's west exit. The information counter has free internet access, CNN on TV, an information board and any number of brochures about places to visit in Okayama prefecture and the rest of Japan. Upstairs, there is a library (Tue-Sun 10am-7pm) with books, magazines and newspapers. *Okayama Insider* is published monthly by the International Center and has cinema/event listings.

Alternatively go to **I Plaza** (☎ 086-234 5882, Tue-Sun except 2nd Sun of the month, 10am-6pm), a ten-minute walk south-east from the station, which has an international exchange corner on the fourth floor. Here, they organize free Japanese culture classes and also arrange homestays.

Getting around
Okayama's tram network has a terminus in front of Okayama station. There's a flat fare of ¥100 for journeys within the central area, any further afield is ¥140. The nearest tram stop to Korakuen (see p256) is Shiroshita.

A limousine bus (¥680) takes 30 minutes from Okayama station to Okayama Airport, which handles mostly domestic flights.

Books
Maruzen, at Okayama Symphony Hall, has a selection of English books, as does **Kinokuniya**, on the 5th floor of Cred Okayama Building.

Where to stay
The JR-run *Hotel Granvia Okayama* (☎ 086-234 7000, 🖥 www.granvia-oka.co.jp; ¥13,860/S, ¥21,945/D/Tw) is an upmarket place right outside the east exit of the station. It's expensive even with a 10% discount to rail-pass holders. More luxurious still is the new *ANA Hotel Okayama* (☎ 086-898 1111, 🖥 www.anahotels.com; ¥13,860/S, ¥20,790/D/Tw), outside the redeveloped west exit of the station. It has plush rooms, facilities galore and a stylish ground-floor café/restaurant.

Also close to the west exit of the station and accessed directly from it is the 216-room *Toyoko Inn Okayama-eki Nishi-guchi-migi* (☎ 086-253 1045, 🖥 www.toyoko-inn.com; ¥6090/S, ¥7140/de luxe S, ¥8190/D/Tw).

Okayama City Hotel (☎ 086-221 0001, 🖥 www.okayama-cityhotel.co.jp; ¥7350/S, ¥12,600/Tw) is a good business-hotel option with surprisingly spacious rooms. It's a seven-minute walk from the east exit of the station. Opposite is *Mielparque* (☎ 086-223 8100, 🖥 www.mielparque.or.jp), one of a chain of hotels run by the Post Office (hence the post office flags out front and the small branch inside). Basic singles are ¥5000, though for ¥1000 more you get a much larger room. Basic twins go for ¥9546 or ¥16,000 if you want more space.

A good choice for the budget traveller is the new **Comfort Hotel Okayama** (☎ 086-801 9411, 🖥 www.choicehotels.com; ¥5800/S, ¥12,000/Tw), close to Korakuen. The rates include breakfast.

If you're looking for a Japanese inn, **Matsunoki Ryokan** (☎ 086-253 4111, 🖥 ht tp://ww3.tiki.ne.jp/~matunoki/english.htm; ¥5250/S, ¥8400/Tw) has tatami rooms with air con and attached toilet/bath. It's a friendly place that attracts a mix of Japanese and foreigners. Optional dinner (6-9pm) is ¥1300 and breakfast (7-9am) is ¥700. The ryokan is a couple of minutes' walk west from the station's west exit. Western-style rooms are also available. Check-in is from 3pm but guests can leave luggage earlier.

If in a fix, the **International Center** (☎ 086-256 2000, 🖥 www.opief.or.jp; ¥5600/S, ¥4000D/Tw and ¥3500/Tr per person) has a few rooms with attached bath and shared kitchen facilities. Check-in is 4-10pm and you're asked to be in by 11pm.

The accommodation at **Okayama-ken Seinen Kaikan Youth Hostel** (☎ 086-252 0651, 🖥 http://homepage3.nifty.com/okaya ma-yh; ¥2940/3570) is in shared tatami rooms that have seen better days. Optional breakfast is ¥525 and dinner ¥892. Take city bus No 5 from Okayama station and get off at the 'Seinenkaikan-mae' stop, then turn right on to the next street after the bus stop. The hostel is the building with the pink exterior.

Where to eat and drink

If you're at the station try **Azuma Zushi**, a branch of a popular sushi restaurant on the main station concourse. There is also a take-out counter. It's a good place to head if you want to try the local speciality, *barazushi* (platter of fresh local vegetables with seafood). Meals from ¥1000. Beneath the station is **Okayama Ichibangai**, an underground shopping mall, with a selection of cafés, restaurants and take-out bakeries. For lunch, a number of places do good-value all-you-can-eat buffets.

Outside the west exit of the station, on the second floor of the new complex which houses both ANA Hotel Okayama and Okayama Digital Museum, is a restaurant floor called **Lit Avenue** where you'll find a variety of Japanese and Western eateries. One of the nicest places is **Fukusa** (☎ 086-214 1293, 🖥 www.fukusa.biz, daily, 11am-3pm, 5:30-10pm), a modern Japanese restaurant with a mixture of tables and counter service and set lunches from ¥1200.

Heading into town, **Café Moni** does a sandwich-and-drink set for ¥850. **Skipper's** (Tue-Sun, 6pm-midnight) is a pub which serves Belgian Leffe beer, Guinness on tap as well as pizza, spaghetti, fish and chips (¥800), beef and Guinness stew (¥1100) and chilli con carne (¥850).

Ume no Hana (☎ 086-235 8655, 🖥 www.umenohana.co.jp, daily, 11am-3pm, 5-10pm), on the 21st floor of the Cred Building opposite the central post office, has fabulous tofu and a range of other Japanese dishes. Diners sit at tables in little tatami compartments affording views of the city below. Close to Korakuen, **Bar Boccone** (11:30am-late) has a pasta lunch with drink for ¥950 and a selection of cocktails from ¥500. The entrance is up a flight of stairs.

If visiting the International Center, **Café Fossette** is a small place, just to the right as you enter the building, that serves drinks and light snacks.

HIROSHIMA

For most visitors, the story of Hiroshima begins and ends with the dropping of the world's first atomic bomb at 8:15am on August 6th 1945. But it was the city's historical importance that made Hiroshima an obvious target to the American military.

The largest castle town in the Chugoku region throughout the Edo period, Hiroshima continued to be a centre of political and economic affairs right up to and beyond the Meiji Restoration of 1867 (see p39), when the city became the seat of the prefectural government. In the decades following the Meiji Restoration the city grew as a centre for heavy industry, while the nearby port of Ujina expanded to become a base for the Imperial Army.

The atomic bomb wiped out the military garrison in an instant but what is remembered is the human devastation – it's estimated that 140,000 had died as a direct result of the bombing by the end of 1945. Some feared it would be decades before grass would grow again, while others believed the scorched land would remain desolate for ever. Clocks and watches froze at 8:15am but time did not stand still after the blast. It only took 17 days to rebuild the railway between Hiroshima and Ujina, and only three for the first tram line to restart. Many survivors took heart in seeing the trams back in service so soon after the blast.

In the decades since 1945, Hiroshima has reinvented itself as a centre for world peace and now, as you pull into the station by shinkansen, what you see is a thriving city of shops, restaurants and open spaces.

What to see and do
The Peace Memorial Park area The park is on the west side of the city, sandwiched between the Honkawa and Motoyasu-gawa rivers. Before the A-bomb razed the city to the ground, this area was Hiroshima's main shopping and entertainment district. Now it is home to the **Peace Memorial Museum** (daily, 8:30am-6pm Mar-Nov, to 7pm in August, to 5pm Dec-Feb; ¥50), the one place everybody should visit when in Hiroshima. Divided into east and west exhibition halls, the first displays you see are two scale models of Hiroshima, before and after the explosion.

Just one second after detonation, the bomb created a fireball 280m in diameter – the aftermath and appalling effects of the A-Bomb are detailed in the west hall, where the most powerful exhibits are personal objects, such as a twisted pair of spectacles and a mangled bicycle frame. Don't leave the museum without stopping at the video booths, where some of the A-Bomb survivors – known as *hibakusha* – have recorded their own testimony of the day Hiroshima's sky turned black.

The Peace Park itself contains numerous memorial statues and peace monuments. Newest of all is **Hiroshima National Peace Memorial Hall for Atomic Bomb Victims** (same hours as the Peace Memorial Museum, free), opened in 2002 as a national repository for those who either perished in the blast or who died subsequently from the effects of radiation. Just across the river, and clearly visible from the tourist office, is the **A-Bomb Dome**, the burned-out shell of what was once the Hiroshima Prefectural Industrial Promotion Hall. A car park close by marks the actual hypocentre but the A-Bomb Dome is the only monument to be preserved as a reminder of the devastation.

The **Children's Peace Monument** is easily identifiable by the colourful paper cranes draped over it. The monument was erected in memory of Hanako Sasaki, a young girl who contracted leukaemia a decade after the bomb and who died in hospital before she could achieve her goal of making 1000 paper cranes.

The annual peace ceremony takes place in front of the **cenot**, neath which is a chest containing the names of all those claimed by atomic-bomb victims. By 2006 the list of names stood at more than 1.

Some of the monuments in the park are more unexpected. Near the tourist information centre, look out for the large stone, cut from Ben Nevis in Scotland and presented to the city as a symbol of goodwill and of the wish for reconciliation and world peace. The base of the **Korean A-Bomb Victims Monument** is a turtle because in Korean legend dead souls are carried to heaven on the back of a turtle. There are 2527 registered Korean victims but it's thought that as many as 20,000 were killed. For years the monument was only allowed to stand outside the Peace Park, on the other side of the river. It was finally allowed into the park in 1999.

Away from the Peace Park Try to fit in a visit to **Shukkeien** (daily, 9am-6pm, Oct-Mar 9am-5pm, ¥250), a beautiful Edo-period garden originally designed in 1620 by a feudal lord and located on the banks of Kyobashi-gawa. Next to Shukkeien is the **Prefectural Art Museum** (Tue-Sun 10am-6pm, to 8pm in July/Aug, ¥500) but it is really only of interest to fans of Japanese art. Another good place for an early evening stroll is **Chuo Park**, just west of the unremarkable **Hiroshima Castle** (daily, 9am-5:30pm, Oct-Mar 9am-4:30pm, ¥360), a 1958 concrete reconstruction of the 1589 original.

Finally, **Hiroshima City Transportation Museum** (Tue-Sun, 9am-5pm, ¥500) has interactive exhibits geared mostly towards children – the train simulator is the most popular. Serious trainspotters will find the place a bit gimmicky but there's just about enough here (old train posters, tickets, model engines and the like) to make the visit worthwhile. Pride of place in the museum goes to a huge model city, which is either a dream-like vision of how we will all be moving around in the future, or a futuristic urban nightmare, where the quaint idea of walking on foot has long since been abandoned. Outside, there are 'interesting bikes' and battery-powered cars (chargeable). Rail enthusiasts will enjoy the journey to the museum, by Astramline, Hiroshima's 'new transit system', as much as the place itself; take the Astramline from Hondori station in the city centre north to Chorakuji (¥390). The museum is next to the large Astramline office outside Chorakuji station.

PRACTICAL INFORMATION
Station guide
There are two sides to Hiroshima station: the south (for the city centre) and the shinkansen, also known as the 'Hotel Granvia', side; an underground passageway connects both.

On the south side, you'll find the unfortunately named Asse department store, with restaurants on the sixth floor and a food hall in the basement. The tram terminus is outside the south exit.

For coin lockers on the shinkansen side, head for the far right-hand corner (as you face the exit); all sizes including large ¥600 ones. At the south exit, the main bank of coin lockers (all sizes) is opposite the taxi rank outside. To find them, turn left as you exit the station and walk along the station building.

Rail buffs interested in collecting scale-model shinkansen trains and the like will be delighted to know that there is a shop to suit their tastes tucked away in a quiet corner of the second floor of the shinkansen side of the station.

Tourist information

There are **tourist information offices** on both sides of Hiroshima station. The one on the shinkansen side (daily, 9am-5:30pm, English spoken) is on the second floor by the shinkansen ticket barrier. Look for the large 'information' sign in yellow at the centre of the concourse. Staff will help with same-day hotel bookings in Hiroshima. On the south side, the office (☎ 082-261 1877, daily, 9am-5:30pm) is in a corner of the main JR ticket office. Ask for the 'Get

HIROSHIMA　広島

Where to stay

1	World Friendship Center	1	ワールドフレンドシップセンター
2	Ikawa Ryokan	2	いかわ旅館
4	Hiroshima International Youth House (Aster Plaza)	4	広島国際青年会館 (アステールプラザ)
6	Dormy Inn Hiroshima	6	ドーミーイン広島
7	Comfort Hotel Hiroshima	7	コンフォートホテル広島
15	Hiroshima Youth Hostel	15	広島ユースホステル
17	Rihga Royal Hotel Hiroshima	17	リーガロイヤルホテル広島
26	Hotel Active! Hiroshima	26	ホテルアクティブ！広島
28	Via Inn Hiroshima	28	ヴィアイン広島
29	Hotel Granvia Hiroshima	29	ホテルグランヴィア広島
30	Toyoko Inn Hiroshima-eki Shinkansen-guchi	30	東横イン 広島駅新幹線口
31	Hotel Zürich	31	ホテルチューリッヒ

Where to eat and drink

19	One Coin Bakery	19	ワンコインベーカリー
21	Andersen	21	アンデルセン
22	Pronto	22	プロント
24	Mario Espresso	24	マリオエスプレッソ
25	Okonomimura	25	お好み村
32	Giovanni	32	ジョヴァンニ
33	Lemongrass	33	レモングラス
34	Mozart	34	モーツァルト

Other

3	AquaNet Hiroshima (boat trips)	3	アクアネット広島
5	Central Post Office	5	中央郵便局
8	Hiroshima National Peace Memorial Hall for Atomic Bomb Victims	8	国立広島原爆死没者追悼平和 祈念館
9	Peace Memorial Museum	9	平和記念資料館
10	International Conference Center	10	国際会議場
11	Hiroshima City Tourist Association	11	広島市観光協会
12	Korean A Bomb Victims Monument	12	韓国人原爆犠牲者慰霊碑
13	Children's Peace Monument	13	原爆の子の像
14	A-Bomb Dome	14	原爆ドーム
16	Hiroshima City Transportation Museum	16	広島市交通科学館
18	Futaba (Futaba-Tosho Bookstore)	18	フタバ (フタバ図書)
20	AquaNet Hiroshima (boat trips)	20	アクアネット広島
23	Media Café Popeye	23	メディアカフェポパイ
27	Shukkeien/Prefectural Art Museum	27	縮景園/広島県立美術館

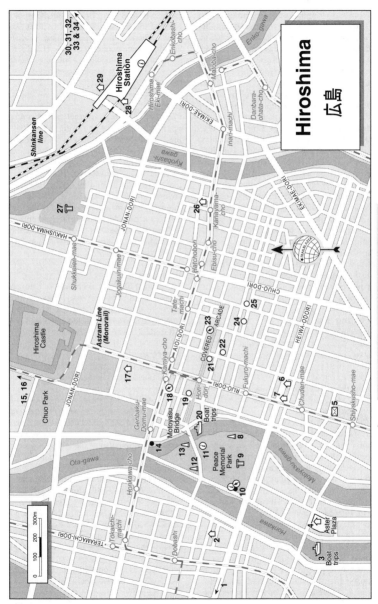

HONSHU

Hiroshima' English maps. The main tourist office in the city centre is **Hiroshima City Tourist Association** (☎ 082-247 6738, daily, Apr-Sep 9:30am-6/7pm, Oct-Mar 8:30am-5pm), in the Rest House on the edge of the Peace Park, just after you cross over Motoyasu Bridge.

If you're interested in visiting a Japanese home for a couple of hours, apply in person (with your passport) at the **International Exchange Lounge** (☎ 082-247 9715, ✉ golounge@pcf.city.hiroshima .jp, daily 10am-6pm Dec 1st-Apr 30th, 9am-7pm May 1st-Nov 30th), on the first floor of the International Conference Center in the Peace Memorial Park. Volunteer Peace Park guides can be arranged through the World Friendship Center (see opposite).

Two useful internet resources for information are Get Hiroshima (✉ www .gethiroshima.com) and Hiroshima Online (✉ www.hiroshimaonline.com); up-to-date listings of sights, hotels, restaurants, bars, cinemas and events in and around the city are provided.

Getting around
Hiroshima is one of Japan's best-known tram cities; provided the trams don't get stuck in traffic they are by far the best way of getting from the station to the downtown area. A one-day pass (¥600) is available from the tram terminal outside the south exit. Otherwise, individual tickets are ¥150 for any journey within the city centre. Alternatively, a ¥1000 pre-paid card gives ¥1100 worth of travel. Pick up a map of the tram network either from the tourist offices or from the ticket booth outside the station.

Rail-pass holders can get to the ferry port for the trip to Miyajima (see p268) for free; if you don't have a rail pass consider taking the tram from Hiroshima station to Hiroden Miyajima (¥270), or buying the two-day pass (see p268).

A less conventional way of seeing Hiroshima is by **pleasure boat**. Though there are no great views, you do get an alternative perspective on the city and the boats at least don't get snarled up in heavy traffic. There are two departure points: one

is close to Motoyasu Bridge which crosses into the Peace Park, the other (with fewer daily departures) is behind Aster Plaza). The 40-minute boat cruise costs ¥1200.

For further details, contact Aquanet Hiroshima (✉ www.aqua-net-h.co.jp; ☎ 082-240 5955).

Internet
Futaba is a 24-hour internet café charging ¥241 for 30 minutes of surfing (not including a compulsory membership fee of ¥100). Soft drinks are free and it's on the basement floor of the Futaba-tosho bookstore. Alternatively, **Media Café Popeye** is on the 4th floor of a building on the Hon-dori covered arcade. The charge is ¥250 for 30 minutes (free membership). There is free internet access at **Hiroshima Convention & Visitors Bureau** on the 3rd floor of the International Conference Center in the Peace Memorial Park.

Festivals
The annual **Peace Ceremony** is held on August 6th inside the Peace Park. In the evening, thousands of paper boats lit by candles are set afloat on the rivers and are left to drift towards the sea.

Where to stay
Book well in advance if planning to visit Hiroshima for the annual Peace Ceremony on August 6th.

Outside the shinkansen side of Hiroshima station is *Hotel Granvia Hiroshima* (☎ 082-262 1111, ✉ www.hgh .co.jp; ¥10,741/S, ¥20,212/Tw, ¥17,902/D), an upmarket member of the JR Hotel group. Despite being right next to the station it's a peaceful place with an impressive lobby, spacious rooms and a choice of restaurants.

Hotel Active! Hiroshima (☎ 082-212 0001, ✉ www.hotel-active.com; ¥6000/S, ¥9000/D/Tw) is a gem of a place – a design hotel at budget prices. You'll even find the words 'welcome home' on the bed drape! Check out the fireplace in the lobby – you need a double-take to see that the fire is actually an image on a plasma screen. The rooms are small but nicely furnished with flat-screen TVs. Nescafé coffee machines on each floor are a nice touch, as are the trouser presses. Breakfast is included. It's ideally located midway between the station and the Peace Park.

Toyoko Inn Hiroshima-eki Shinkansen-guchi (☎ 082-506 1045, 🖳 www.toyoko-inn.com, ¥6300/S, ¥8400/D /Tw) is close to the station (shinkansen side). Rates include a simple Japanese breakfast of onigiri, miso soup and coffee. Also near the station is ***Hotel Zürich*** (☎ 082-262 5111, 🖹 262 5126; ¥7500/S, ¥15,000/D, ¥16,000/Tw), a small, slightly eccentric business hotel a few minutes on foot from the shinkansen exit. It professes – by its name and the red-and-white flag outside – to be Swiss, but on the ground floor you'll find a German bakery/ cake shop-cum-café called Mozart and an informal Thai restaurant called Lemongrass. They only have a small number of rooms of varying sizes and decoration. Rates include breakfast.

Via Inn Hiroshima (☎ 082-264 5489, 🖳 www.viainn.com; ¥6825/S, ¥9030/Tw) is a business hotel bolted on to the end of the station building. It's accessed by turning right out of the south exit. There's a pleasant coffee shop (Café Di Espresso) on the ground floor. The entrance to the hotel is next to the Heart In convenience store.

Dormy Inn Hiroshima (☎ 082-240 1177, 🖳 in-hiroshima@dormy-hotels.com; ¥6300/S, ¥10,500/Tw) is close to the Peace Park and offers rooms which are a cut above the usual business hotel standard. A bonus is the hotel's own hot spring on the eighth floor. The in-house café/restaurant on the first floor is called 'Big Mamma'. Close by is ***Comfort Hotel Hiroshima*** (☎ 082-541 5555, 🖳 www.choicehotels.com; ¥6090/S), another good budget/mid-range choice.

The ***World Friendship Center*** (☎ 082-503 3191, 🖹 503 3179, 🖳 www.wfchiroshima.net, wfchiroshima@nifty.com) is a small house run by a very welcoming American couple. The centre, founded in 1965 to promote world peace, is non profit-making and has a couple of tatami rooms at ¥3500 per person (inc Western breakfast, served at 8am). They also have a living

room where they will let people sleep if desperate. It's a clean and tidy place with lots of maps and information. There's no curfew. Guests are asked to pay a deposit of ¥1000 for a key which gives you the freedom to come and go as you please. Their website has a very useful map and directions for finding the centre. If you're staying here, it's worth knowing that there's an ***okonomiyaki restaurant*** next door. The cheapest dishes are ¥400 and there is a Japanese-style sitting area at the back or you can eat directly at the grill. It closes at 8pm.

An upmarket choice in the downtown area is ***Rihga Royal Hotel Hiroshima*** (☎ 082-502 1121, 🖳 www.rihga-hiroshima.co .jp; ¥15,015/S, ¥23,100/Tw).

Ikawa Ryokan (☎ 082-231 5058, 🖹 231 5995, 🖳 ikawa1961@go.enjoy.ne.jp), a five- to ten-minute walk west of the Peace Park, is a small, modern Japanese inn with friendly owners. All rooms have toilet, air con and TV and some have attached bath. A single room with bath costs ¥5775 (or ¥4725 without); a room for two is ¥9450 with bath (or ¥8400 without). Breakfast (optional) is ¥735 and dinner ¥1365.

There's little to recommend about ***Hiroshima Youth Hostel*** (☎ 082-221 5354, 🖹 221 5377, 🖳 hyh@mint.ocn.ne.jp) except the rate it offers: ¥1770 (Apr-Jun and Oct-Nov) or ¥1940 (Jul-Sep and Dec-Mar). The 10pm curfew is inconvenient and accommodation is in very basic dorms. Another drawback is its location, 25 minutes by bus north of the station, which means you're reliant on public transport. From the station, take bus A, B or C from bus stop No 7 or 8 and get off at 'Ushita shinmachi-ichome', from where the hostel is a 10-minute walk uphill. Far better is ***Hiroshima International Youth House*** (☎ 082-247 8700, 🖹 246 5808), just south of the Peace Park and in Aster Plaza. The rooms are brightly decorated and an absolute steal for foreign guests who get special reduced rates of ¥3620 for a single and ¥3130 per person for two people sharing a twin. Facilities include a coin laundry and a reasonable restaurant – the only downside is a midnight curfew. Take bus No 24 from stop No 3 outside the south side

HONSHU

of Hiroshima station and get off at 'Kosei Nenkin Kaikan mae', from where it's one minute on foot to Aster Plaza.

Where to eat and drink

Hiroshima is known for *okonomiyaki* (savoury pancakes); the best place to try one is at **Okonomimura**, a building packed with three floors of small okonomiyaki places. Try *Sonia* (daily, 11:30am-2am) on the fourth floor (turn right as you exit the elevator and it's on the right-hand side). They'll give you chopsticks and a plate but the real way to eat it is straight off the griddle. If you're in or around Hiroshima station, the best place to try okonomiyaki is on the 2nd floor of the Asse department store. Here you'll find a row of okonomiyaki places, but the best (and hence the one with the longest queues at lunchtime) is *Reichan*. Seating is at tables or at the counter. A menu in English is available.

There are plenty of places to eat along the covered Hondori shopping arcade, one of the most popular being the enormous branch of *Andersen* (daily except 3rd Wed, 10am-8pm), which has a bakery, delicatessen, salad bar, restaurants and made-to-order sandwich counter. The pizzeria *Mario Espresso* (daily, 11am-10:30pm) is on three floors opposite a small park, a couple of minutes from Okonomimura. The

pizza is hand made and very popular but you can stop just for a drink on the first floor which opens out on to the street. Also in this area is a branch of *Pronto*, the coffee house by day that turns into a pub at night.

On the top floor of Rihga Royal Hotel, the ¥2500 all-you-can-eat lunchtime buffet is a feast and you get great views of the city. Don't overlook the *One Coin Bakery*, on a street that runs off from the Hondori shopping arcade. All the cakes, buns and rolls inside are ¥100 (actually ¥105 including consumption tax!), making this a good place to put together a cheap packed lunch.

Giovanni (11:30am-3pm, 5-11pm) is a run-of-the-mill Italian place, with a slightly sombre interior. The food (pasta, pizza and the like) is fine, and it's a good place to eat at if you're staying on the shinkansen side of the station and can't be bothered to head into the city centre. Pasta lunches cost from ¥945.

Lemongrass, a Thai restaurant on the ground floor of Hotel Zürich, does inexpensive lunch sets (from ¥840) and is reasonably authentic. The attached *Mozart* bakery is a good place to linger over a coffee and cake. There's another cake shop – also called *Mozart* – on the ground floor of the shinkansen side of the station. Both places sell exquisite cream cakes and chocolate éclairs.

Side trip to Miyajima

Three of the most compelling reasons for going to Miyajima are:
(1) Itsukushima Shrine, considered one of the top three scenic spots in Japan;
(2) the chance to visit somewhere that has no convenience stores or traffic lights;
(3) the ferry to the island is free for rail-pass holders.

From Hiroshima, take a local train eight stops westbound along the Sanyo line to Miyajima-guchi (25 mins). Local trains leave Hiroshima every ten minutes at peak times so just turn up and go! Alternatively tram No 2 takes just less than one hour from Hiroshima station to Miyajima-guchi and costs ¥270. The two-day pass (¥2000), which includes unlimited tram travel in Hiroshima, the ferry to/from Miyajima and the ropeway up Mt Misen (see box p270) is recommended.

At Miyajima-guchi, head out of the station and walk straight down the road to the ferry terminal. From here, JR Ferry services (daily, 6am-11pm, ¥340 return, free to rail-pass holders) take ten minutes to Miyajima and operate every 15 minutes at peak times and every 30-50 minutes at the beginning/ end of the day. JR shares the terminal with Matsudai Ferry, which runs an identical service, but rail passes are not valid on Matsudai ferries.

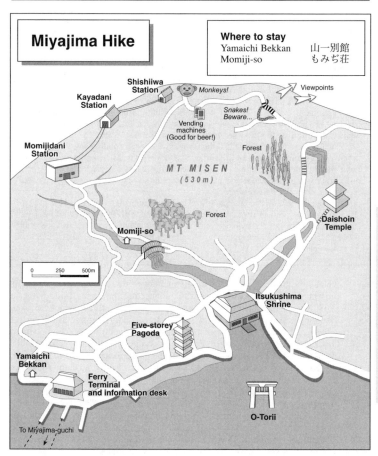

Miyajima Hike

Where to stay
Yamaichi Bekkan   山一別館
Momiji-so   もみぢ荘

Shishiiwa Station
Monkeys!
Kayadani Station
Viewpoints
Snakes! Beware...
Vending machines (Good for beer!)
Momijidani Station
Forest
M T M I S E N
(5 3 0 m)
Forest
Daishoin Temple
Momiji-so
0 250 500m
Itsukushima Shrine
Five-storey Pagoda
Yamaichi Bekkan
Ferry Terminal and information desk
O-Torii
To Miyajima-guchi

HONSHU

A **tourist information desk** (☎ 0829-44 2011, daily, Mar-Nov 9am-7pm, Dec-Feb 9am-6pm) is inside Miyajima ferry terminal. The office has maps and information and staff the can help book accommodation. FM radios (¥300) can be rented for a commentary in English but you may find you're spending more time trying to locate the nearest antenna than seeing any of the island. Rent A Cycle (daily, 8am-5pm, 2hrs/¥320, then ¥110/per hour) is available from the JR ticket office on Miyajima.

Be aware that there are deer everywhere where you get off the ferry, so be prepared to be chased if you are carrying food. Gluttons for punishment can even pay ¥200 for food to feed the deer and watch the chaos ensue!

Tour groups walk straight from the ferry terminal round to **Itsukushima Shrine** (6:30am-5/6pm, ¥300), which according to legend was founded in 593

Hiking Mt Misen (see map p269)

At 530m, Mt Misen is the highest peak on Miyajima; there are excellent hiking trails (or a cable car) which lead up to the summit. A good place to start the hike is **Daishoin Temple**, from where the 'Daishoin Course' winds its way uphill, passing by a number of picnic huts along the way. About a third of the way up the path becomes steep, though it's nothing really challenging (but pack water in the summer, as there's no river for over half the walk and no vending machine until you reach the top).

The route is easy to follow but stick to the path to avoid treading on any snakes. As you near the top there's the welcome sight of a vending machine (beer and soft drinks) and from the top there are great views out over the Inland Sea.

The monkeys here are wild and there's no guarantee of spotting any – every year a few visitors complain to the tourist office that they went up Mt Misen to see the monkeys and then demand a refund for the cable car ride when they can't find any. There are also deer at the top and if you are lucky you may see monkeys grooming the deer, especially if the latter are resting.

For those who have had enough of walking the location of the top cable car station is obvious. The cable car operates daily, 9am-5pm, ¥1000/1800 one-way/return. It is closed for safety checks twice a year, usually for about five days in June and December. From the bottom station, in Momijidani Park, it's an easy walk back to the ferry terminal.

when three goddesses were led to Miyajima by a crow. It was remodelled in its present structure, with long corridors connecting the main shrine halls, in 1168. Noh performances are occasionally staged at the shrine, which has even seen the occasional fashion show – the long corridors doubling as the perfect catwalk. The real attraction of the shrine is the vermilion **O-Torii** (Grand Gate), rising out of the sea (or, depending on the tide, sticking out of the silt) 200m from the main shrine. At high tide the gate appears to float in the water.

Yamaichi Bekkan (☎ 0829-44 0700, 🖳 www.gambo-ad.com; ¥6500/pp, no meals) only has a few rooms, all but one of which are Japanese style with attached toilet and bath, but the staff are welcoming. Another excellent bet is *Momiji-so* (☎ 0829-44 0077, 🖳 www.gambo-ad.com; ¥7000/pp no meals, ¥13,500/pp two meals), inside Momijidani Park and close to the cable car which runs up to Mt Misen (see box above). One reader agrees that Momiji-so is 'absolutely wonderful, the room and the food were fantastic ... the woman who ran it looked after us so well we called her mama-san'.

The cheapest place is back on the mainland at *Miyajima-guchi Youth Hostel* (☎/🖨 0829-56 1444, 🖳 ww4.et.tiki.ne.jp/~miyayh; ¥2730/pp; 30 beds), a small, old place very close to JR Miyajima-guchi station. Turn right on to the main road in front of the station and it's less than a minute down the road on the left. Accommodation is in plain bunk-bed dormitories or tatami rooms each sleeping four to six people.

Side trip to Yokogawa

Yokogawa is a minor place of pilgrimage for omnibus fans but is also interesting for its shitamachi (old town) district. It can be visited on your way to Miyajima (see p268), since local trains from Hiroshima travelling west along the Sanyo line also stop here (it's one stop from Hiroshima).

On February 5, 1905, Japan's first domestically manufactured omnibus went into service here, plying a 15-km route between Yokogawa and nearby Kabe. A newspaper of the time described the historic event: 'The time has at last matured for the arrival of the Yokogawa-Kabe Automobile Transportation Programme. At 3pm the day before yesterday an opening ceremony was held at the automobile boarding stand in front of Yokogawa station.'

The bus was manufactured in Japan using an American engine and parts, and passengers were charged a fare of 24 sen (by comparison, a horse-drawn carriage cost 15 sen). The maximum load was 12 passengers. Sadly, the tyres could not cope with the bumpy road conditions and the service was halted after just nine months. A replica of the original bus, painstakingly put together by a local club of omnibus enthusiasts from the only surviving photo of the original vehicle, is on display – encased in glass – in front of Yokogawa station. Unlike many old steam engines, which are left to gather dust on sidings in many parts of the country, this replica is kept gleaming.

A sign by the replica suggests that 'we intend to preserve this monument eternally as a symbol of the birthplace of Japan's first omnibus and as a force to breathe new life into the Yokogawa area in future'.

Aside from being the birthplace of the bus in Japan, Yokogawa is an interesting place to explore in its own right, with small restaurants, book shops and even an art house cinema in the station vicinity. No visit would be complete without a stop at *God Burger*, a grandly named hamburger joint close to the station. To find it, head out of the station on to the main street which runs parallel to the station building. Turn left on to this street and look out on your right for a small corner building with a green-tiled roof. The interior is nothing special – a counter with a few tables and chairs, and net curtains at the windows – but it's something of a Yokogawa institution and the burgers outclass those offered by McDonald's and the like. Try the Jumbo Royal God Burger (¥1100), the closest thing to heaven bar the calories.

Side trip to Kure

Another possible side trip by rail is to the sea-side town of Kure, just over 30 minutes south-east of Hiroshima on a rapid train on the JR Kure line. A five-minute walk from Kure station towards the coast is the **Yamato Museum** (Wed-Mon, 9am-5pm, ¥500), which displays a 1/10 reproduction of what was at one time the world's largest battleship. The *Yamato* was launched from Kure in 1941 but sank four years later during a suicide mission to attack the United States fleet on American-held Okinawa. On display are the handwritten wills of some of the 2475 sailors who perished on board. The museum is a bit short of written information in English, but a tape commentary is available.

MATSUE

'There seems to be a sense of divine magic in the very atmosphere, through all the luminous day, brooding over the vapoury land, over the ghostly blue of the flood – a sense of Shinto'.

Thus wrote Irishman Lafcadio Hearn of Matsue's Lake Shinji, which glistens out to your left as the train pulls into Matsue station. The seventh largest lake in Japan is unusual in that it's a combination of fresh and seawater, depending on the tide.

⛩ **Discounts for foreigners and foreign residents**
Foreign visitors as well as foreign residents are entitled to discounts off entry fees at a number of attractions in Matsue and the surrounding area. To receive the discount, visitors need to show their passport, while foreign residents must present their Alien Registration Card.

For full details, pick up a leaflet at the tourist information office outside the station or see 🖥 www.kankou.pref.shimane.jp/e/discounts/index.html.

Divided into north and south by Ohashi-gawa, Matsue well deserves its title 'city of water'. Matsue is an old castle town and the perfect place to break a journey along the San-in coast. Lafcadio Hearn (1850-1904) took up an English teaching appointment here in 1890; though he only lived in Matsue for a total of 15 months, his former residence is now one of the city's big draws. In his books Hearn often voiced his regret that Meiji-era Japan, in its rush to catch up on centuries of isolation from the outside world, was abandoning many of its ancient traditions. He would probably have been dismayed at the tourist industry that has grown up around his name. As well as the usual postcards, souvenir trinkets and T-shirts, more unusual Matsue souvenirs include Hearn chocolates and bottles of locally brewed Lafcadio Hearn beer.

What to see and do

Consider spending a couple of days in Matsue as this will give you a chance to see the city and fit in a trip to nearby Matsue-Onsen (see p274) or Izumo-Taisha shrine (see p278).

For a bird's-eye view of Matsue and – on a clear day – a stunning view of Lake Shinji, take the express elevator up to the 14th floor of the **San-In Godo Bank** headquarters (the tallest building in town) at 10 Uo-Machi, a 10- to 15-minute walk from the station. The lift is in a corner of the ground floor and only stops at the 14th floor. It's a bit hidden and there are no signs in English. If in doubt, ask bank staff to point you in the direction of the observation gallery (daily, 9am-5pm). On a clear day, you can see as far as Mt Daisen (1711m), over 50km away. Also, closer to home, there are great views of the castle. This is the perfect place to get your bearings when you arrive in Matsue – and best of all it's free!

Matsue Castle area The main city sights are all around Matsue Castle. From the station, take the Lakeline Bus to the castle and then walk between the sights described below. A **Universal Pass** (¥980) includes entry to the Lafcadio Hearn Memorial Museum, Buke-Yashiki samurai residence and Matsue Castle, and offers small discounts at a number of other sights. The pass is available at the entrance to all three places and is valid for three days, though you can only enter each property once.

The **Lafcadio Hearn Memorial Museum** (daily, Apr-Sep 8:30am-6:30pm, Oct-Mar 8:30am-5pm, ¥300 or ¥150 for foreign visitors) exhibits objects from Hearn's house and other items relating to his stay in Matsue. Unusual items include a pair of iron dumb bells and a trumpet shell which Hearn 'blew half for fun when he wanted his maid to bring him a light for his tobacco'. Look out also for the high desk Hearn used to compensate for his poor eyesight. Music by Enya plays softly as you walk around.

Next door, the **Lafcadio Hearn Former Residence** (daily, Mar-Nov 9am-5pm, Dec-Feb 9am-4:40pm, closed Dec 16th-Jan 1st, ¥250, 20% discount with Universal Pass) is now completely bare but there's a useful leaflet that describes how the rooms would have looked in Hearn's day. The small house looks out on to an even smaller Japanese garden that's similar to the one Hearn enjoyed when he lived in Kumamoto (see p404).

Further along the same street is **Buke Yashiki** (daily, Apr-Sept 8:30am-6:30pm, Oct-Mar 8:30am-5pm, ¥300 or ¥150 for foreign visitors), a samurai house built in 1730. Although you can't actually go into the house there is an outside path around the rooms which contain displays of samurai swords and artefacts used in daily life. If you go up the path behind the house you'll come to a small building where you can watch a film about Matsue's Drum Festival which takes places every November.

Matsue Castle (daily, April-Sep 8:30am-6:30pm, Oct-Mar 8:30am-5pm, ¥550 or ¥280 for foreign visitors) was built by the feudal lord Yoshiharu Horio in 1611, though what stands today is a 1950s reconstruction. Hearn often climbed the castle tower which he described as 'grotesquely complex in detail, looking somewhat like a huge pagoda'. On the ground floor of the donjon, the original dolphin and gargoyle-shaped roof tiles are displayed – these were too fragile to be used in the reconstruction. On other floors there are scale models of the castle and city over which it once presided, and photos of other well-known castles in Japan. But the best part of the climb is the tremendous view from the top-floor observation gallery over Matsue and Lake Shinji.

One hundred metres south of Matsue Castle, look out for the large, white, Western-style building that houses **Matsue Kyodokan (Regional Museum)** (daily, 8:30am-5pm, free). Inside there's a random assortment of odds and ends from the late samurai period to the present day, including a portable shrine, a Japan Olympic team blazer and various medals from the Tokyo 1964 Olympics.

Other areas Shimane Art Museum (🖳 www2.pref.shimane.jp/sam, Wed-Mon 10am-6:30pm, ¥300) is in a modern glass building on the banks of Lake Shinji. This is the place to head just before dusk to watch the sun set over the tiny tree-studded island in the lake. The museum building threatens to overshadow the collection of art and sculptures it houses, which include a few minor works by Monet and Gaugin, and a bronze cast of Rodin's 1897 *Monument to Victor Hugo*, which takes pride of place in the second floor entrance hall. Special exhibitions usually cost ¥1000 (or ¥500 for foreign visitors).

Karakoro kobo, in the former Bank of Japan building on the north side of Ohashi-gawa, houses temporary art exhibitions, a café, restaurant, art and craft shops. The word 'karakoro' comes, of course, from Lafcadio Hearn. It's said that when Hearn woke up after his first night in Matsue, he heard the noise of wooden geta shoes in the street outside his ryokan. To Hearn's ears, the noise each footstep made was 'kara, koro, kara, koro…'.

Finally, **Matsue Onsen** is the city's hot spring resort, on the banks of Lake Shinji close to Ichibata Railway's Matsue Shinjiko-Onsen station. The source of the spring is 1250m underground near the banks of the lake. At source, the water temperature is around 77°C, though it's cooled down by the time it reaches the bath houses of the lakeside hotels and ryokan. The best way of enjoying the area is to stay at one of the resort hotels by the lake (see pp276-7), most of which have their own hot spring with a lakeside view. If you can't afford this you can always soak your feet in the **Ashiyu** (foot bath) outside Matsue Shinjiko-Onsen station. It's open all hours (you'll even see people dipping their feet in for a warm soak in the early hours of the morning) and has a cover to protect both you and the water if it's raining. To reach the resort, take the Lakeline Bus from outside Matsue station.

PRACTICAL INFORMATION
Station guide
Matsue station has two exits; the north exit is the one for tourist information and the bus platforms. You'll find **coin lockers** of all sizes in a corner of the station concourse. As you leave the ticket barrier, on your left is the **JR ticket office** (daily, 5:15am-10:30pm) and in front of you a branch of **TiS travel agency** (Mon to Fri 10am-6pm, Sat/Sun 10am-5pm).

Also in the station is a branch of the *Little Mermaid bakery*, offering everything from cakes and buns to slices of pizza – perfect for a lakeside picnic. You'll also find a *UCC Coffee shop* serving simple pasta dishes (in the shopping mall which leads off behind you as you exit the ticket barrier) and a branch of *Mister Donut*.

Inside the station building are stalls selling various local products. This is a good place to seek out free nibbles, since the staff usually have samples to try (everything from locally made *castella* sponge cake to rice pudding!).

Tourist information
Matsue International Tourist Information Office (☎ 0852-21 4034, daily, 9am-6pm) is in the modern glass building right outside the north exit of the station. As you exit the ticket barrier, you'll see it immediately on your right. The staff here will assist with accommodation booking and can hand out city maps.

Various tours (see p276) can be booked here and passes purchased.

MATSUE 松江

Where to stay

7	Hotel Ichibata	7	ホテル一畑
10	Hotel Route Inn Matsue	10	ホテルルートイン松江
11	Matsue Lakeside Youth Hostel	11	松江レークサイドユースホステル
14	Matsue Tokyu Inn	14	松江東急イン
17	Toyoko Inn Matsue Ekimae	17	東横イン 松江駅前
21	Terazuya Ryokan	21	寺津屋旅館

Where to eat and drink

8	Coffee-kan	8	珈琲館
9	Hermitage	9	エルミタージュ
15	Casa Vecchia	15	カーサ ベッキア
16	Matsue Terrsa	16	松江テルサ
18	Kaba	18	かば

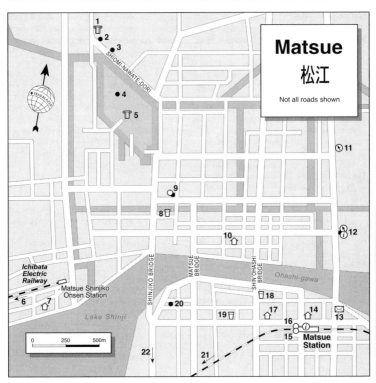

Where to eat and drink *(key continued from opposite)*
19 Shirokiya
22 Vecchio Rosso

19 白木屋
22 ベッキオロッソ

Other
1 Lafcadio Hearn Memorial Museum
2 Lafcadio Hearn Former Residence
3 Buke Yashiki
4 Matsue Castle
5 Matsue Kyodokan
9 Karakoro-kobo
11 Club Mont Blanc
12 Shimane International Center
13 Central Post Office
20 San-in Godo Bank
22 Shimane Art Museum

1 小泉八雲記念館
2 小泉八雲旧居
3 武家屋敷
4 松江城
5 松江郷土館
9 カラコロ工房
11 クラブモンブラン
12 島根国際センター
13 中央郵便局
20 山陰合同銀行
22 島根県立美術館

Getting around

The best way of seeing Matsue's sights is to hop on the retro tourist **Lakeline Bus** (daily, 8:40am-sunset Mar-Nov, 9am-4:40pm Dec-Feb) which runs in a loop around the city and stops outside the station. Single rides cost ¥200, or a one-day pass is ¥500 and this also entitles you to a discount (usually the group rate) at Matsue Castle, Hearn Memorial Museum, Buke Yashiki and Shimane Art Museum.

As the 'city of water', Matsue naturally enough offers opportunities for boat rides. First is a one-hour **Lake Shinji Boat Tour** (☎ 0852-24 3218, 🖳 www.hakuchou go.jp, daily Mar-Nov, 11am-5pm, ¥1300). There is also a daily sunset cruise (check with the tourist office for the exact times).

The **Horikawa Moat Tour** (☎ 0852-27 0417, daily March-Nov, 9am-4/5/6pm, Dec-Feb, 10am-3pm, ¥1200 or ¥800 for foreign visitors) is a 50-minute cruise around the moat of Matsue Castle. The boats have to pass under some very low bridges on their way round but this is Japan so a flick of the switch lowers the boat canopy and allows a safe passage underneath.

The Lakeline Bus plus Horikawa Moat Tour costs ¥1500; the Lakeline Bus plus Horikawa Moat Tour and Lake Shinji Boat Tour is ¥2500 and the Lakeline Bus plus a train journey on the private Ichibata Railway to Izumo Taisha (see p278) costs ¥1000. Finally, the 'Perfect Ticket' is a two-day pass which allows you to ride the Ichibata Railway, Lakeline Bus, Shiei city bus and Ichibata bus services for ¥2500.

Cycle rental is available from Nippon Rent a Car, across the street from the tourist information office, at a rate of ¥1000 per day. If you fancy a cycle along the banks of Lake Shinji it's worth knowing that the private Ichibata Railway transports cycles free of charge, so you can clock up the miles on your bike along the northern shore of the lake before jumping on a train back to Matsue Shinjiko-Onsen station.

Internet

Free internet access is available at **Shimane International Center** (🖳 www.sic-info .org, Mon to Fri, 8:30am-7pm, Sat 9am-5pm), on the second floor of Kunibiki Messe, a large building across the river, about ten minutes on foot north from the station. The centre also has a selection of English newspapers and magazines.

A further five minutes up the road (Route 485) from the International Center is a 24-hour internet café, **Club Mont Blanc** (🖳 http://club-montblanc.net/mat sue, ¥990/three hours, including free drinks). Go past the McDonald's drive-through on your right as you walk up the road from the International Center and you'll see it on your right.

Festivals

At the end of July/beginning of August is the Suigo-sai Festival, the highlight of which is a massive fireworks display over Lake Shinji.

The most raucous annual event is the Drum Festival on November 3rd.

Where to stay

Directly opposite the station is *Matsue Tokyu Inn* (☎ 0852-27 0109, 🖳 www .tokyuhotels.co.jp; ¥7875/S, ¥12,915/D, ¥14,910/Tw), a mid-range business hotel with two non-smoking floors. A new addition to the hotel scene in the station area is *Toyoko Inn Matsue Ekimae* (☎ 0852-60 1045, 🖳 www.toyoko-inn.com; ¥5040/S, ¥7770/D/Tw), to the left on the main road which runs parallel to the station. The rooms are spotless and the rates include a Japanese breakfast. *Hotel Route Inn Matsue* (☎ 0852-20 6211, 🖳 www.route-inn.co.jp; ¥4900/S, ¥10,000/D, ¥11,500/Tw) is a smart place a short walk north of the station across Ohashi-gawa.

Terazuya Ryokan (☎ 0852-21 3480, 🖳 www.mable.ne.jp/~terazuya) is a small family-run inn which has tatami rooms for ¥4000 per person, or ¥7000 with two meals. Dinner is a real feast and eaten with the family so there's a very homely atmosphere. Turn left out of the station and follow the train tracks round for about 10 minutes until you hit the ryokan on the left side. Alternatively, call for a lift from the station.

An alternative base is around Matsue-Onsen, where there is a mixture of Western hotels and ryokan.The top place to stay is *Hotel Ichibata* (☎ 0852-22 0188, 🖳 www .ichibata.co.jp/hotel). Ask for a room in the new annex – many of the rooms in the original building are dated and not worth the money. Some rooms, for which you'll pay more, have views over Lake Shinji. The cheapest twins without a view are ¥15,000.

You need to take the Ichibata Railway one stop from Matsue Shinjiko-Onsen station to Furue to reach *Matsue Lakeside Youth Hostel* (☎/🖷 0852-36 8620, 🖳 www .jyh.gr.jp/matsue; ¥2940 YH/HI mem, ¥3990 non-mem). Breakfast costs ¥630 and dinner ¥1050. The hostel is a 12-minute walk uphill from Furue station.

Where to eat and drink

Matsue is known in Japan for the 'seven delicacies of Lake Shinji'. Since the lake is a combination of fresh and sea water, the seven fish are an unusual mix: carp, eel, shrimp, *shijimi* clams, whitebait, bass and smelt.

The fish don't all appear in the same season so there are usually only two or three of the 'seven delicacies' on one plate but it's occasionally possible (for a lot of money) to eat all seven in one sitting. Ask at the tourist information office (see p274) for the best places to try the dish; wherever you go take a wallet full of cash.

Inside the station there are a few cafés and restaurants along 'New Orleans Walk'. On your left as you leave the north side of the station is Matsue Terrsa, a glass building which houses a café and restaurant. The ground floor *café* serves excellent coffee and cake in a corner of the impressive atrium. On the second floor is *Capricciosa* (daily, 11am-10pm), the popular Italian pizza and pasta chain.

A good alternative to Capricciosa is *Casa Vecchia* (daily, 11am-12 midnight). It's a cosy Italian place built into the side of

the station, next to the Terrsa building. The name is written in English.

In Shimane Art Museum is an upmarket Italian restaurant, *Vecchio Rosso* (Tue-Sun 10am-9pm, last orders 7:30pm). This place takes advantage of its lakeside location with floor-to-ceiling windows. It's a great place for watching the sunset over the lake. Dinner is expensive, with ¥3000 or ¥5000 courses, but lunch deals are more reasonable at ¥1500-2000, or there's a cheaper pasta lunch at ¥1250.

Shirokiya (daily 5pm-5am) is an izakaya-style food-and-drink place, a few minutes up the main road past Toyoko Inn. It's open until the early hours of the morning and they serve everything from basashi (raw horsemeat, see p408) to pizza and garlic bread, plus a good selection of beer and saké. You can even sing karaoke here in one of the backrooms. It's cheap, friendly and there's a chance of bumping into some of Matsue's resident gaijin. Look for the red sign with 'Shirokiya' written in white kanji above the entrance and the words 'Public house for enjoyable people' on the door.

Another watering hole frequented by Matsue's foreign residents is *Kaba*, a good place for late-night bar snacks (you can get pretty much whatever you want, even if it's a plate of chips!). It's across the street from a shrine, just before you reach Shin-Ohashi. The name is written in hiragana. It's usually still busy into the early hours of the morning.

The French café/restaurant *Hermitage* (Wed-Mon 11am-9pm, lunch 11:30am-2pm, dinner 5:30-9pm) is inside Karakoro kobo (see p273). The lunchtime menu (from ¥1000) usually includes soup and a choice of fish or meat as main course; the dinner is more pricey (from ¥3000).

Finally, a good place to stop for coffee is directly across the river from Karakoro kobo at *Coffee-kan*, where there are tables overlooking the river.

Side trip to Adachi Museum of Art

A short train and bus ride from Matsue is Adachi Museum of Art (🖳 www .adachi-museum.or.jp, daily, 9am-5/5:30pm, ¥2200 or ¥1100 for foreign visitors), considered one of the top cultural attractions in Japan, as famous for its stunning and immaculate landscaped gardens (which have won several awards and are frequently named the best in Japan) as for its collection of contemporary Japanese art. One reader commented: 'The food is expensive in the museum but there is a nice souvenir shop opposite the entrance with food for sale.'

To reach the museum, take a local or limited-express train from Matsue east towards Yonago (see p249) and get off at Yasugi. Local trains from Matsue take 25 mins and limited-express services take 15 mins. A free shuttle bus runs from outside Yasugi station to the museum seven times a day (see the website for the latest bus schedule).

Side trip to Izumo Taisha
Some 30km west of Matsue, at the foot of Yakumo Hill, is Izumo Taisha, a shrine complex known as the home of the god of marriage. Expect to see lots of happy couples, but also unhappy ones trying for a spiritual repair job. Lafcadio Hearn, who himself found love in Matsue when he married Setsu Koizumi, the daughter of a high-ranking samurai, visited Izumo Taisha twice and became the first foreigner to be allowed to enter the *honden* (inner shrine).

Izumo Taisha is accessible from Matsue Shinjiko-Onsen station via the private Ichibata Railway (55 mins, ¥750). Change trains at Kawato for the final leg to Izumo-Taisha-mae. To save money, rail-pass holders need to back-track along the JR San-in line from Matsue to Izumo-shi (see p248), and from there transfer on to the Ichibata Railway for the last part of the journey.

HONSHU

Tohoku (Northern Honshu) – route guide

INTRODUCTION

When Japanese TV programmes poke fun at rural life and local dialects, more often than not their targets are the 'country folk' of Tohoku. Some Japanese will only reluctantly venture into the region, fearing that the dialects they encounter will be so strong that they might as well be speaking a different language. Such is the power of television, but a trip around northern Honshu offers a rare chance in an overcrowded island to go off the beaten track.

In contrast to other parts of the country, Tohoku offers little in the way of famous temples or shrines. Volcanoes, lakes, mountains and rivers predominate,

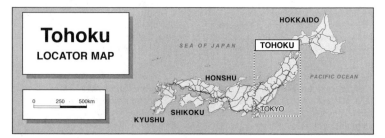

Tohoku
LOCATOR MAP

0   250   500km

HOKKAIDO

SEA OF JAPAN   TOHOKU

HONSHU   PACIFIC OCEAN

SHIKOKU   TOKYO

KYUSHU

Tohoku
RAIL ROUTES

HONSHU

❏ **Northern Tohoku Welcome Card**
If you're planning an extended tour around Tohoku it's worth downloading and printing off the Northern Tohoku Welcome Card (see box p53).

a geography which explains why northern Honshu lagged behind in the industrial race of the late 20th century. But, like many areas of Japan, traditional life – old farm-houses, small rural communities and local festivals – has not remained untouched by the modern age. The region is not without its large cities and industry. Yet more than enough remains of traditional Tohoku for the short-term visitor to experience something of what Japan's greatest haiku poet Matsuo Basho (1644-94) discovered, when he set off in the spring of 1689 on a five-month walking tour of the region: 'I had seen since my departure innu-merable examples of natural beauty which land and water, mountains and rivers, had produced in one accord.' (*The Narrow Road To The Deep North*, translated by Nobuyuki Yuasa, Penguin, 1966).

Rail access to the north is fast and efficient, thanks to the Tohoku shinkansen which extends as far as Hachinohe (to Shin-Aomori from 2010). Beyond this, running off to the east and west, is a network of local lines which are the best means of seeing Tohoku close up – the shinkansen is fast but due to the proliferation of tunnels the views are nearly always fleeting.

The following route travels in a loop around the region, starting with the journey north from Tokyo, on the eastern side of Tohoku to Aomori, on the northern tip of Honshu and the rail gateway to Hokkaido; then back towards Tokyo down the more off-the beaten track western side.

For details of JR East's regional rail passes, see p14.

Note: All JR East shinkansen and most limited express services were made entirely non-smoking in 2007. Smoking rooms are provided on the platforms at major stations along all four of the shinkansen routes operated by JR East.

TOKYO TO HACHINOHE

The bullet train from Tokyo to Hachinohe is called 'Hayate' ('Swift Wind'). All Hayate services are reserved seating only.

The 'Yamabiko' shinkansen runs from Tokyo to Morioka, the double-deck-er 'Max Yamabiko' to Sendai only, and the 'Nasuno' to Koriyama only. If trav-elling on from Hachinohe to Aomori/Hokkaido, the best bet is to pick up a Hakucho or Super-Hakucho LEX from Hachinohe (see p294).

Tokyo to Sendai   [Map 15, opposite; Map 16, p283; Table 12, p464]
Distances from Tokyo by shinkansen. Fastest journey time: 2 hours 50 minutes.

Tokyo (0km)   [see pp90-115]

Ueno (4km) Most trains call at Ueno (see p96), Tokyo's main terminal for the north. If joining the train here rather than at Tokyo, it's worth reserving seats because at certain times the non-reserved cars are full by the time the train leaves Tokyo.

Omiya (30km) Almost every service stops here. Omiya is so close to Tokyo it's impossible to see where one ends and the other begins. There's little incentive to stop so soon unless you're a Beatles fan and want to visit the **John Lennon Museum** (🖳 www.taisei.co.jp/museum, Wed-Mon, 11am-6pm, ¥1500). The museum opened on October 9th 2000, the day Lennon would have celebrated his 60th birthday. It's on the fourth and fifth floors of the Saitama Super Arena, centrepiece of a huge city redevelopment project. About 130 items are exhibited, including Lennon's first guitar, his trademark glasses, and clothes he and Yoko Ono wore on their frequent visits to the mountain resort of Karuizawa (see p135). From Omiya, change on to the Utsunomiya line and go one stop back (towards Tokyo) to Saitama Shin-Toshin, from where you should follow signs to the Super Arena (a three-minute walk).

October 14 is known in Japan as 'Railway Day'; on that day in 2007 a major new **Railway Museum** (🖳 www.railway-museum.jp for opening hours and entrance fee) opened, operated by JR-East. It is a paradise for trainspotters as it contains around 30 railway cars, train-cab simulators and scale models and train sets, as well as an early example of a city bus. The museum is one minute from Oonari, which is one stop from Omiya on the Saitama New Shuttle transit system.

Omiya is the last chance to change to the Asama shinkansen for Nagano (see p168). After Omiya, all Nasunos and some Yamabikos call at **Oyama (81km)**.

Utsunomiya (110km) All Nasunos and most Yamabikos stop here. The first ekiben, two rice balls and pickles wrapped in bamboo leaves, is said to have been sold at this station at the end of the 19th century. Change here for **Nikko** (see p114), a beautiful shrine and temple town. Nikko is 50 minutes by local train along the JR Nikko line.

After Utsunoyima all Nasunos and some Yamabikos call at **Nasu-Shiobara (158km)**.

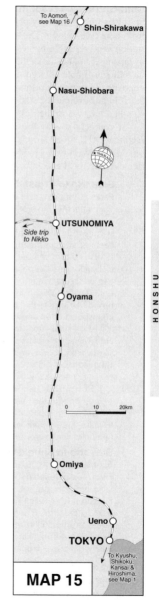

To Aomori, see Map 16 / Shin-Shirakawa

Nasu-Shiobara

UTSUNOMIYA

Side trip to Nikko

Oyama

0   10   20km

Omiya

Ueno

TOKYO

To Kyushu, Shikoku, Kansai & Hiroshima, see Map 1

MAP 15

HONSHU

Shin-Shirakawa (185km) All Nasuno and some Yamabikos stop here. Shin-Shirakawa is not a pretty place in itself, but some brief excursions can be made from here (see below). The tourist information office (daily, 8:30am-6pm) at the station is on the right-hand side next to the JR ticket office. It can provide maps in Japanese and bus timetables to British Hills. A small selection of coin lockers, including a couple of large-size ones, are on the left side of the station concourse, opposite the tourist information office. There is very little in the way of places to eat at in and around the station area, and the only convenience store is inside the station area, next to the ticket barrier. There's also an udon counter.

If you need to stay the night the best place is *Toyoko Inn Shin-Shirakawa Ekimae* (☎ 0248-23 1045, 🖳 www.toyoko-inn.com; ¥4620/S, ¥7140/D/Tw), outside the West exit. Good value, and the room price includes a simple curry-rice evening meal and Japanese breakfast (onigiri, miso soup and coffee).

Side trip to British Hills
Fancy a pint of warm ale? A game of croquet? Fish and chips? If that whets your appetite, consider a side trip from Shin-Shirakawa to **British Hills**, a recreation of life in Britain complete with country pub and manor house. The site, deep in the mountains of rural northern Japan, is primarily used by students of all ages wanting to immerse themselves in the English language and British culture without going to the trouble of buying an air ticket and flying to London. As the publicity puts it: 'British Hills is like a breath of fresh air, carried on the wind from the Middle Ages only to be reborn in woodland above Lake Hatori. More English than England itself, the genuine warmth and dignity of British Hills provides a gentle and comforting environment and the atmosphere of an almost forgotten age.'

It's actually not a bad place to stay, if you want to get away from it all while enjoying some creature comforts. Facilities include a swimming pool, Jacuzzi, sauna, tennis courts and snooker. The bedrooms are spacious if a little too faux-England (you can even spend the night in 'Her Majesty's Bedchamber'). For package rates, see 🖳 www.british-hills.co.jp or ☎ 0248-85 1313.

British Hills operates its own green shuttle bus service three times a day from outside the West exit of Shin-Shirakawa station to the resort. Alternatively a public bus operates twice a day (leaving Shin-Shirakawa at 9:25am and 1:40pm and returning at 11:40am and 3:45pm). Journey time is one hour. There is a flat fare of ¥500.

Side trip to Shirakawa
Komine-jo (daily, 10am-3pm), in Shirakawa itself, is a castle which is free to enter. It's particularly spectacular during the annual cherry-blossom viewing season and in August (August 8) for the summer festival when it forms the backdrop for a magnificent fireworks display. The castle is set in a park area, next to the attractive **Shirakawa Rose Garden** (daily, 9am-6:30pm, ¥300), home to some 6000 roses representing 300 varieties from around the world. From Shin-Shirakawa take the local Tohoku line one stop to Shirakawa, from where it's a five-minute walk north.

Soon after Shin-Shirakawa a brief succession of tunnels blocks out the view before opening up again and turning decidedly ugly with a sprawling city as the train approaches Koriyama.

Koriyama (227km) All Nasuno and almost all Yamabikos stop here. It's only after Koriyama, over 200km from Tokyo, that the views start to improve as the landscape becomes more rural, offering the first glimpses of what Tohoku has to offer. The view, however, is frequently blocked by tunnels.

Koriyama is a terminus for the Banetsu-sei line that runs some 190km across Honshu to Niigata (see p320).

Fukushima (273km) All the Yamabiko services stop here. Since the shinkansen line splits here some trains divide. If on a Max Yamabiko you should make sure you're in the right part of the train (if you have a seat reservation you will be); the Yamabiko part continues on to Sendai and Morioka, and the other part, the Tsubasa, branches off to Yamagata (see map p279) and beyond on the extension to **Shinjo (see p306; 421km)** via **Yonezawa (see below; 313km)**, **Takahata (see p285; 322km)** and **Yamagata (360km)**, the latter being a jumping-off point for the pilgrimage site of **Yamadera** (see p315), which can also be accessed as a side trip by rail from Sendai.

Side trip to Yonezawa and Takahata
The Tsubasa shinkansen's route offers some spectacular scenery, pine forests, rivers (and a few tunnels) but it does make you wonder why a shinkansen has been built here, since it's not exactly a teeming metropolis.

Yonezawa Although it's not worth going all the way to Shinjo, Yonezawa makes for a pleasant diversion by rail. The Tsubasa departs hourly though the times vary a bit and it takes about 35 minutes to Yonezawa It's only a small station with one exit. To your right as you exit the ticket barrier is the **JR ticket office** (daily, 6:30am-9:15pm) and adjacent View Plaza travel agency. A **tourist information desk** (daily, 8am-6pm) is to the left as you exit the ticket barrier. English maps are available. **Coin lockers** (including a few ¥500 ones) are to be found outside and to your left as you exit the sta-

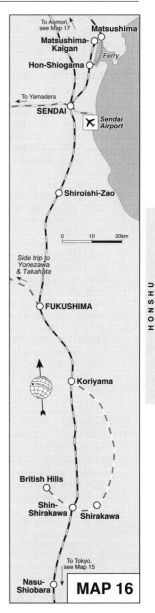

MAP 16

HONSHU

tion, at the end of the building and by the bus stops. Also here is an Eki Rent A Car booth, which also offers **cycle rental** (☎ 0238-22 8161, ¥500/4 hours, ¥1000/day).

Yonezawa is most associated with the Uesugi clan, generations of which ruled the area. Two of the most important sights, both worth visiting, are the Uesugi Mausoleum and Uesugi Shrine (the latter is usually busier than the first). They are a fair distance (the shrine is 2.3km, a 30-minute walk, and the mausoleum is 3.5km from the station), but a regular bus (¥200 per ride) runs in a loop around the town, stopping at both places. The tourist information desk can advise on the bus schedule. But you can save on the bus fare by getting here by train! Take a local JR Yonesaka line train from Yonezawa two stops to Nishi-Yonezawa, from where the mausoleum is ten minutes on foot.

Uesugi Mausoleum (¥200, English information sheet available), the last resting place for the feudal lords of the Uesugi clan, is set in a quiet residential part of town and surrounded by pine trees. Uesugi Shrine (free entry), on the site once occupied by Yonezawa Castle, is consecrated to Uesugi Kenshin (1530-78), the first feudal lord of the Uesugi clan. It burnt down in 1919 and was rebuilt four years later. The entrance is across a moat filled with koi (carp). Just before you head under the torii (gates) and into the **Uesugi shrine** precinct proper, look out on your left for a statue of Uesugi Yozan (1751-1822), a descendant of Kenshin. Next to it is a stone memorial upon which is written his motto in life: 'If there is the will, anything that can be imagined can be done'. It is reported that when John F Kennedy was asked about the politicians he admires, he mentioned Uesugi Yozan. Within the shrine precinct is the Keisho-den (Treasure House) (separate entry charge of ¥400) which contains swords, armour and other remnants of the Uesugi reign.

A good place to stay the night in Yonezawa is *Toyoko Inn Yonezawa Ekimae* (☎ 0238-22 2045, 💻 www.toyoko-inn.com; ¥4515/S, ¥7140/D/Tw), two minutes on foot from the station. Look for it on your left as you exit. The rates includes breakfast and internet access is free.

For food, there is not much inside the station beyond a noodle bar and convenience store. Yonezawa is famous for its beef which comes at a premium price. A meal could cost upwards of ¥10,000. A good place to try it which is not too expensive is *Toyokan*, a restaurant across the street from the station where Yonezawa beef is the only thing on the menu. The restaurant name is written in black kanji on the side of the building (on the right-hand corner of the main street which runs away from the station). Look for the picture of a black bull. The price varies depending on the cuts of meat/size of steak. The cheapest set menu (steak, rice, salad, soup and a small slice of melon) is ¥2800. It's a bit of a faded joint and could do with some renovation, but the food is good and the steaks are brought to your table still sizzling.

Rail fans might like to consider a further side trip from Yonezawa along the JR Yonesaka line to **Sakamachi** on the coast (from where you can connect with the route guide on p308). The trains are mostly local services, but twice a day there is a rapid service called 'Benibana', one of which runs all the way to Niigata (see p320). One reader commented: 'I did this line in the early spring when it was still snowy. It is a very scenic run, as it offers a good transition from Yonezawa in the mountains to Sakamachi near the coast.'

Takahata Takahata is unusual in that it is the only shinkansen station – and one of only a very small number of stations across the country – to have an onsen built into the station building. So if you fancy a soak in a tub less than a few steps from the train, this is where to get off. However, only a few Tsubasa services stop here, but local trains operate approximately hourly and take six minutes from Yonezawa. The entrance to the **bathhouse** (daily, 7am-9:40pm, ¥300) is immediately to your left as you leave the platform. Buy a ticket from the vending machine, hand it in at the desk and walk through the red curtain. On the other side are lockers where you can stow your clothes. Then just head through and prepare to soak! Takahata itself is a popular summer tourist destination with walking and cycle trails. **Cycle rental** (Apr to Nov, daily, 9am-5pm, ¥500) is available at the station. The JR-operated *Folkloro Takahata* (☎ 0238-57 5555, 🖹 57 5556), built into the station, offers spacious twins (from ¥12,600 to ¥14,070) and family rooms which sleep up to four (¥21,000-23,940). Rates depend on the season and get cheaper if you stay two or three nights. There is no discount for rail-pass holders.

There are several tunnels on the route between Fukushima and Sendai. After Fukushima some shinkansen stop at **Shiroishi-Zao (307km)**.

Sendai (352km)   [see p308]

Sendai to Ichinoseki by shinkansen   [Table 12, p464]
This is the fastest way to Ichinoseki (and further north to Hachinohe, Aomori and Hokkaido). After leaving Sendai the train dips into several tunnels, but otherwise the view of rural Japan to the left and right is superb. Most Hayate services run non-stop from Sendai to Morioka (see p292), but Yamabiko services stop at **Furukawa** and **Kurikoma-Kogen** before reaching Ichinoseki. If you choose to head north by either Hayate or Yamabiko shinkansen, pick up the route again from Ichinoseki, starting on p288.

Sendai to Ichinoseki via Matsushima
                        [see Map 17, p287; see tables 13 and 14, p465]
The following route goes off the beaten track and includes a stop at Matsushima Bay. Distances are by JR from Sendai. Fastest journey time: $1^3/4$ hours.

Sendai (0km) From Sendai, take the Umikaze rapid train on the JR Senseki Line (from platform 9). The train ride begins underground and then passes through an urban area.

Hon-Shiogama (16km) Shiogama is connected with Matsushima by a regular ferry service. The ferry is an alternative to taking the train to the next stop.

In the station, next to View Plaza travel agency, is a small **tourist information office** (daily, 10am-4pm). The staff don't speak English but can advise on ferry times. It's a 10-minute walk from the station to the Marine Gate Shiogama ferry terminal. Turn right on to the main road running parallel with the station. At the lights, turn right and go straight until you reach the terminal building. The new **Marine Gate building** (🖳 www.shiogama.co.jp) includes a selection of seafood restaurants with views overlooking the harbour, an observation platform and shops selling local foods and souvenirs. Tickets for the

ferry ride (50 mins) cost ¥1420. The boat tour goes past some of the many tiny islands that are a familiar sight along this coastline but the journey is marred by two forms of pollution; one is the chimney stacks and factories that occasionally rise up behind the islands, the other is the non-stop commentary in Japanese that pours out of speakers strategically placed around the boat.

Matsushima-Kaigan (23km) Confusingly, Matsushima has two rail stations, separated by a five-minute taxi ride (no bus). Trains do not connect the two stations since they are on different lines. Matsushima-Kaigan station is on the Senseki line and is the most convenient for the sights, being just five minutes on foot from Matsushima Bay. But the next part of the rail route begins at Matsushima station (see p288), which is on the Tohoku line.

Over 260 islands are scattered around Matsushima Bay; collectively they count as one of the top three scenic spots in Japan, along with Miyajima (see p268) and Amanohashidate. For centuries, poets have journeyed here in search of inspiration – indeed, the islands themselves are sometimes compared to verses of a poem. In the station there is even a small haiku box where travelling poets can deposit their own work. Matsuo Basho visited on his epic journey through the region and wrote that Matsushima was the 'most beautiful spot in the whole country of Japan'. He was reportedly left speechless by the beautiful scenery and abandoned plans to write a haiku in honour of his visit in 1689.

Matsushima Information Center (☎ 022-354 2263, daily, 10am-5pm, to 4:30pm in winter) is in a booth to the right as you exit Matsushima-Kaigan station. If you took the ferry from Shiogama to Matsushima you'll have arrived at the boat pier where there is a smaller tourist information desk (daily, 8:30am-5pm), but the staff here don't speak English.

A few of the islands just off the shore are linked by bridges to the mainland. The most popular is tiny **Godaidojima**, on which stands a hall containing five Buddhist statues which are put on view only once every 33 years (the last time was in 2006, so the next viewing won't be until 2039). Pleasant though it is, the tranquillity of the island is spoilt by the souvenir stalls set up along the approach to it. Much more relaxing is nearby **Fukurajima**, connected to the mainland via a long, red footbridge (¥200 to cross). This island has wooded paths free from souvenir stands and (almost) out of sight of any vending machines. From here, there are views to some of the other islands. Set just back from the port area is **Zuigan-ji** (daily, 8am-5pm, to 4pm in winter, ¥700), a Zen Buddhist temple built in 828 and later reconstructed by Date Masamune (see p308). On the right as you walk through the pine trees towards the temple entrance are some caves inside which monks used to train before the temple was built. Look out for the rail monument near the caves, a tall column flanked by railway wheels on pieces of track. It was built to remember those who died during the construction of the railways or in rail accidents.

If you didn't take the ferry from Shiogama to Matsushima and want to take a boat cruise around the bay, Matsushima Pleasure Boat, a kitsch tourist ferry, operates from Matsushima Port (¥1400). Departures are hourly in the summer (daily 9am-4pm).

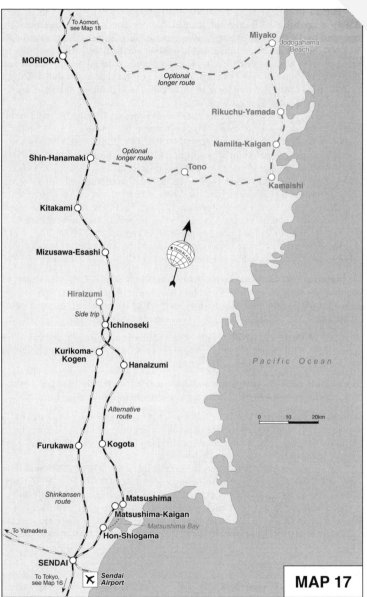

HONSHU

MAP 17

ernight stay, ***Folkloro Matsushima*** (☎ 022-353 3535, 🖷 353
...hind Matsushima-Kaigan station. The rooms in this pension,
... East, are Western style and feel very homely. Twin rooms cost
..., but better value if travelling in a group are the family rooms which can
sleep up to four adults for ¥21,000. Room rates are reduced on the second and
third nights. To reach the Folkloro, turn right on leaving Matsushima Kaigan
station, then sharp right under a short rail bridge and follow the road up for
about three minutes. It is on your left.

Alternatively, six stops along the Senseki line (two stops by rapid train)
from Matsushima-Kaigan brings you to **Nobiru**, from where it's a 15-minute
walk to ***Pila-Matsushima Youth Hostel*** (☎ 0225-88 2220, 🖷 88 3797, 🖳 www
.jyh.or.jp.english/touhoku/pila/inex.html, 🖳 matsushima@jyh.or.jp; ¥3360/
¥4360). It's a clean, modern hostel with good facilities and 100 beds in a choice
of Western and tatami rooms. Supper costs ¥1050 and breakfast ¥630. Online
booking is possible. Just off a road lined with pine trees and not far from Nobiru
Beach, the hostel is an excellent overnight base. Facilities include cycle rental
(3 hours/¥500) and tennis courts (rackets can be hired). Before setting out for
the hostel, pick up a map from the information centre (☎ 0225-88 2611, daily,
8:30am-5:30pm) in Nobiru station. From the station, cross the bridge and head
straight towards the beach. Look out for the 'JYH' sign along the way.

▲ **Matsushima (23km)** Transfer to Matsushima station for the next part of
the journey north along the Tohoku line (see Table 14, p465). This station is 30
minutes on foot from Matsushima-Kaigan (pick up a map from the tourist information desk outside the station) or a five-minute taxi ride.

Kogota (43km) About 20 minutes from Matsushima. Some trains terminate
here (Table 14 includes through services only), so you may have to change on
to another train for the rest of the journey to Ichinoseki.

Hanaizumi (79km) This rural town hit the headlines when the bones of a mountain buffalo thought to be 100 million years old were discovered here in 1956.

Ichinoseki (93km) The first major stop after Matsushima, Ichinoseki is a
transport hub and stop on the Tohoku shinkansen line and is divided by Iwai-
gawa (River Iwai). The main reason for stopping here is to take a side trip to the
temple town of Hiraizumi (see opposite).

An overhead passageway connects the shinkansen side of the station with
other JR lines. A small **tourist information counter** (☎ 0191-23 2350, daily,
9am-5:30pm) is next to the ticket barrier on the JR lines side. The staff do not
speak English but you can pick up leaflets on Ichinoseki and Hiraizumi.
There's little reason to overnight in Ichinoseki, especially since the temple
lodgings in nearby Hiraizumi are such an attractive option. Just in case you do,

---

(Opposite) This colourfully dressed woman is one of thousands who join the parade of
floats during Aomori's annual Nebuta no Sato (see p320). (Photo © Kazuo Udagawa).

Toyoko Inn Ichinoseki Ekimae (☎ 0191-31 1045, 🖳 www.toyoko-inn.com; ¥6090/S, ¥8190/D/Tw) is modern and has clean, comfortable Western-style rooms. It's on the right-hand side as you exit the station.

Side trip to Hiraizumi   [see Map 17, p287]

Eight kilometres north of Ichinoseki and reached in less than 10 minutes by local train along the Tohoku line (services operate hourly) is Hiraizumi. At first glance it's hard to believe that this rural town once boasted a population of over 100,000. In the 12th century it was a major centre of politics and culture, a period dominated by the wealthy Fujiwara family who ruled for four generations. Today, a couple of historic temples remain as a reminder of the place that once rivalled Kyoto in wealth and national influence.

Hiraizumi station is small with a few ¥300 **coin lockers**. A **tourist information office** (☎ 0191-46 2110, daily, 8:30am-5pm, to 4.30pm in winter) is in the small house with wooden doors to the right as you leave the station. Maps and local bus times are available. Next door is a small **Rent-a-Cycle booth** (2 hours ¥500, ¥200 for each additional hour; ¥1000 for a whole day). You receive a map with a recommended three-hour cycling trip around the town, including stops at both the temples described below.

The construction of **Chuson-ji** (daily, 8am-5pm Apr-Oct, 8:30am-4:30pm Nov-Mar, ¥800) began in 1124 and the temple compound once boasted over 300 buildings. Not all have made it into the 21st century but the temple is still an impressive sight. Allow a couple of hours to explore as many of the buildings as possible. There's no fee to enter the compound and there are plenty of places, including the Honden (main hall), that don't charge admission. The most important surviving building is the **Konjikido** (Golden Hall). Entry tickets allow access to the Konjikido as well as to a few other temple buildings, including the modern **Sankozo**, a treasure house with an attached ATM. If you go as far as is possible along the tree-lined avenue through the temple compound and then take a path off to the right, you'll reach **Hakusan Shrine**. After the opulence of Konjikido, the austerity of this Shinto shrine is a pleasant surprise. From a corner of the shrine area there are great views down below of plains typical of the Tohoku region. Also here is the temple's thatched-roof Noh stage (Noh is performed here on the evening of August 14th). Take an ordinary scheduled bus (¥140) or the tourist loop bus (¥130 per ride or ¥300 for a one-day pass) to Chuson-ji from Hiraizumi station. The tourist bus runs in a loop from the station to Chuson-ji, then on to Motsu-ji (see below), before returning to the station.

Motsu-ji (daily, 8:30am-5pm, to 4:30pm in winter, ¥500) was founded in 850 and is known today for its well-kept garden. The main reason for visiting here is to overnight at ***Motsu-ji Youth Hostel*** (☎ 0191-46 2331, 🖳 www.mot suji.or.jp, yado@motsuji.or.jp). As well as dormitory accommodation, private *shukubo* (temple lodging) rooms are available. Guests are welcome to take part in early morning zazen meditation sessions (July to September) with one of the

HONSHU

(Opposite) Top: The maple leaves in autumn are spectacular; Kyoto, Nikko, Miyajima and Koya-san are some of the most popular autumn 'leaves-viewing' destinations. (Photo © Bryn Thomas). **Bottom:** One of the many enormous illuminated floats pulled through the streets of Aomori during the Nebuta no Sato (see p320). (Photo © Kazuo Udagawa).

resident priests. Since this is a temple hostel you're also asked to keep strict hours; lights are switched out in the public rooms and the front door is locked promptly at 9pm. Rates are ¥4410/pp for a private room or ¥2940 for a hostel bed; breakfast costs ¥630. Guests are exempt from the temple/garden admission fee. Motsu-ji is a 10-minute walk up the main road that runs away from the station. The temple is on the left side of the road. The hostel is usually closed on Sundays, and for the New Year holiday (Jan 1st-3rd).

Ichinoseki to Hachinohe [Map 17, p287; Table 12, p464]

Distances from Ichinoseki. Fastest journey time: 1 hour 10 minutes.

Very few Hayate services from Tokyo to Hachinohe call at Ichinoseki. If you are joining the shinkansen at Ichinoseki and wish to travel to Hachinohe, you will probably have to first take a Yamabiko to Morioka (see p292) and change there onto a Hayate service for the final part of the journey.

Ichinoseki (0km) See p288.

Mizusawa-Esashi (25km) All Yamabiko shinkansen but very few Hayate stop at Mizusawa-Esashi, known for the 'Mizusawa Gourmet Festival' held in the autumn. During the event, the largest cast-iron pan in Japan is used to cook a soup which is shared out among festival-goers.

After Mizusawa-Esashi, all Yamabiko but very few Hayate call at **Kitakami (42km)**.

Shin-Hanamaki (55km) All Yamabiko and very few Hayate call at Shin-Hanamaki, a small city known for its hot springs and as the birthplace of the poet Kenji Miyazawa, who achieved popularity as a writer of children's stories, such as *Night on the Milky Way Train*.

The city's major annual event is the Hanamaki Festival held on the second weekend of September, when large floats and portable shrines are carried through the streets in time to music. On February 11th, Hanamaki Public Auditorium plays host to the 'All Japan Noodle Eating Contest', where contestants gorge on bowls of soba until they can eat no more.

Shin-Hanamaki is a major junction, with shinkansen running north and south, and conventional rail lines east and west. To reach Hanamaki city from Shin-Hanamaki, take a local train two stops west along the Kamaishi line to Hanamaki station. If you're interested in exploring the city, there are tourist offices in Shin-Hanamaki (☎ 0198-31 2244) and in front of Hanamaki (☎ 0198-24 1931) stations.

From Shin-Hanamaki, it's just 11 minutes to Morioka. If you're in a hurry to head further north, continue on the bullet train for the blink-and-you'll-miss-it ride to Morioka and pick up the next part of the route from p292. Alternatively, take the extended rail journey described opposite; it's very slow-going in parts but is one of the best ways of seeing traditional Tohoku close up. Although it's just about possible to complete this alternative route in one day, it's far better to break the journey by spending the night somewhere along the way.

Shin-Hanamaki–Tono–Kamaishi–Miyako– Morioka
Optional route [Map 17, p287; Table 15, p465]
From **Shin-Hanamaki (0km)**, pick up a local train or one of the Hamayuri
rapid trains (3/day) heading east along the Kamaishi line that runs through the
rice fields of the Tono Basin and over Sennin Pass, a total journey of 90km,
towards Kamaishi on the coast. This is Tohoku as you might imagine it, a landscape of green rice fields and occasional thatched cottages which are a long
way from the big cityscape of Sendai.

The first major stop is at **Tono (46km)**, which in the feudal era enjoyed
prosperity as a market and castle town thanks to its strategic location between
the plains and the coast. Today, most people know Tono as the location for a
series of folk tales contained in *The Legends of Tono*. Many of these legends
feature *kappa*, mischievous creatures that live in rivers and streams and are
instantly recognizable from the 'shell on their back, a dish on their head,
webbed hands and feet, and a sharp beak-like mouth'. Kappa stories were originally told to warn children of the dangers of playing near rivers.

Tono tourist information centre (☎ 0198-62 1333, daily, 8am-6pm) has
maps and also rents out bicycles; turn right as you leave the station and it's a
little further down on the right. There are a couple of museums within walking
distance of the station but to reach most of the sights, including **Tono
Furusato Village**, where a number of old farmhouses are preserved, you need
to rent a car – the tourist office can provide details.

Tono is a good place to break the journey, with an excellent accommodation deal in the JR-operated *Folkloro Tono* (☎ 0198-62 0700, 🖳 www.folk
loro.jp/tohno), a B&B pension immediately above the station. Rates vary
according to season but in July/August a family room (up to four adults) costs
¥23,100 on the first night, reduced to ¥18,900 on the second. In high season
twins start at ¥13,650, falling to ¥11,550 on the second night. Rates drop during the rest of the year. No discounts for rail-pass holders. Alternatively, the
homely and efficient *Tono Youth Hostel* (☎ 0198-62 8736, 🖳 www1.odn.ne
.jp/tono-yh/index-e.htm) is a bus ride away from Tono station; ask at tourist
information for times. The overnight charge is ¥3200/3800. Breakfast costs
¥550 and dinner ¥1050.

After Tono, the train begins to climb toward the Sennin Pass. It runs
through many tunnels before making its final descent into **Kamaishi (90km)**,
once a major centre for steel production in Tohoku and still home to the giant
Nippon Steel Works, right outside the station. The Kamaishi line terminates
here, so (on most trains) you will have to change here and continue north along
the Yamada line (local trains only) up the Rikuchu Coast to Miyako. Sit on the
right for sea views. It takes a while before you see the coast and the view is
sometimes obscured, but this section is still enjoyable. About 25 minutes after
leaving Kamaishi, look out for **Namiita Kaigan (108km)**. This is a very popular local beach – it's said that while tourists head for the much-hyped
Jodogahama Beach in Miyako (see below), locals prefer Namiita. Even if you
don't stop here, look out on the right-hand side for a great view from the train
down on to Namiita Beach. The coastal views disappear after **Rikuchu
Yamada (119km)** and trees tend to surround the track.

It's all change at **Miyako (146km)**, the nearest station to Jodogahama
Beach. According to legend, a Buddhist priest visited the beach more than 300

years ago and declared that it was 'just like paradise'. Don't buy too much of the publicity about the contrast between pine trees, blue ocean and white rock. The beach is fine as a place to go for a swim or to lounge around for a few hours but it's not worth seeking out just for its natural beauty. Buses to the beach run from outside Miyako station (20 mins, ¥210). Miyako TIC (daily, 9am-5pm) is in a booth to the right as you go out of the station; maps are available.

Suehirokan Youth Hostel (☎ 0193-62 1555, ▤ 62 3052) is two minutes on foot from Miyako station and has tatami rooms. To reach the hostel, head up the main road from the station to the first set of traffic lights. Turn right; the hostel is a few buildings along on the right. Look for the blue JYH sign at the entrance. The cost is ¥3045 (non-members pay a small supplement), and breakfast is ¥630 and dinner ¥1050. Miyako is known for its sushi; the best place to try some is at *Janome Sushi* (Thur-Tue, 10am-9pm). Janome is a couple of buildings up on the left-hand side along the main road that leads away from the station (look for 'Janome' written in English in small letters along the shop front). The set meals are good value and portions are large – try the salmon onigiri as a side order.

The final part of the journey continues inland along the Yamada line to **Morioka (248km)**. Only very infrequent local trains run on this route. The inland views are impressive for much of the time, though if you're taking the last, early evening service back to Morioka it's hard to resist nodding off as the train winds its slow way inland. By taking this optional route, you have now covered nearly 250km between Hanamaki and Morioka. By shinkansen, the distance is only 35km. The extra distance is worth it for the views.

Morioka (90km) The Yamabiko shinkansen terminates here, while Hayate services stop before continuing to Hachinohe. A branch line (the Komachi shinkansen) runs west from Morioka to Akita (see p294 and map p299).

Shinkansen services depart from the second floor of the station. Also on the second floor, behind glass doors on the station concourse, English-speaking staff at the **Northern Tohoku TIC** (☎ 0196-25 2090, daily, 8:30am-8pm) can help with accommodation bookings in Morioka, as well as provide more general information on sightseeing throughout the area.

The entrance to the private Iwate Ginga Railway (see below) is in a corner of the ground floor of the station. There are **coin lockers** in various corners of the station, including directly behind you as you enter Iwate Ginga Railway. There are also large ¥500 lockers in the passage between the North and South sides of the station.

The pre-shinkansen conventional railway line between Morioka and Hachinohe is now split between two private rail operators: the first part of the journey between Morioka and Metoki is operated by Iwate Ginga Railway, and Metoki to Hachinohe is in the hands of Aoi-Mori Railway. The total fare from Morioka to Hachinohe along this route is ¥2960; the service operates irregularly but approximately hourly taking about 90 minutes. Rail-pass holders and those in a hurry are advised to use the shinkansen line.

Morioka calls itself the 'castle town of Northern Japan' but only the stone wall ruins remain. Apart from a possible side trip to Lake Tazawa (see opposite), there's little reason to hang around in the city – unless you're passing through between August 1st and 4th, when **Sansa-odori** is held. Groups dressed in traditional costumes dance down the main street to the accompaniment of taiko drums and flutes. Festival stalls line the streets and there's a real street-party atmosphere. The best place to spend the night is at the friendly *Ryokan Kumagai* (☎ 0196-51 3020, 🖳 y-kuma@r-nac.ne.jp), an eight-minute walk from the station across Kitakami-gawa. Tatami rooms are ¥4700 for one, ¥8400 for two or ¥11,100 for three. Breakfast costs ¥800 and dinner ¥1500.

If you prefer a Western-style hotel, *Toyoko Inn Morioka Ekimae* (☎ 0196-25 1045, 🖳 www.toyoko-inn.com; ¥5460/S, ¥7140/D, ¥8190/Tw) is two min-utes on foot from the central station exit. As you exit the station, look for the tall building with 'HOTEL' written in blue neon above 'Toyoko Inn' in Japanese. More upmarket is the JR-run *Hotel Metropolitan Morioka* (☎ 0196-25 1211, 🖳 www.metro-morioka.co.jp; ¥8662/S, ¥16,747/D, ¥17,902/Tw), which also has a New Wing (not actually that new!), with more spacious (and more expensive) rooms (¥10,972/S, ¥18,480/D, ¥20,790/Tw). Rail-pass holders receive a 20% discount on rooms at both the original hotel and in the New Wing. Guests in the New Wing get access to the Central Fitness Club located in a building next door for ¥500/day. The New Wing is in a separate building a short walk from the station.

For a selection of **restaurants** under one roof, try the basement of Fesan department store, on the left of the main station exit. Here you'll find 'Delica Town' and 'Gourmet Town', full of places serving everything from tonkatsu to shabu-shabu. Morioka's most famous culinary export is wanko-soba, tradition-ally eaten in a competition where diners race to scoff the most noodles. One of the best – and most convenient – places to try this speciality is right outside the station, on the first floor of the white building across the street and directly above a branch of Mos Burger (look for the green Mos Burger sign). The entrance to *Azumaya* is via a flight of stairs directly behind Mos Burger. The restaurant is traditionally designed, with a choice of tatami tables or Western-style tables and chairs, and you can eat your fill for around ¥2500.

You can surf the internet at **Colon Internet and Comic Café** (daily, 10am-10pm), three minutes on foot up the main street from the station, next to and above a branch of the Daily Yamazaki convenience store. Daily Yamazaki has an in-store bakery and a café area with seats and tables. It also has a Post Office ATM where you can make cash withdrawals.

Side trip from Morioka [see Map 18, p299]
North-west of Morioka lies the volcanic peak of **Mt Iwate**. For a closer look, take a local train on the Tazawako line (approx 8/day) to Koiwai, from where a 10-minute bus ride takes you to **Koiwai Farm** (🖳 www.koiwai.co.jp/eng lish). The views are good but the farm itself is a tourist trap. However, rail enthusiasts may be impressed by the unusual *Steam Locomotive Hotel* (☎ 0196-92 4316, 🖳 www.koiwai.co.jp/makiba/stay/index.html) here; you can stay in the sleeping compartments of the D5168 train for ¥4200 or ¥6825 with two meals. Check-in is 3-8pm and check-out is by 10am.

Further along the line is **Tazawa-ko (Lake Tazawa)**. This is the deepest lake in Japan (423.4m) and is renowned for being a nearly perfect circle. It also attracts more than its fair share of legends, such as the following: 'Once upon a time, a village girl named Tatsuko drank the water of Lake Tazawa as instructed by the goddess Kannon, in order to make her wish of perpetual beauty come true. In the end, she was transformed into a dragon, whereupon she sank into the depths of the lake and was never seen again.'

Forty-minute boat tours on the lake cost ¥1170 (Apr-Nov). Tazawako station is also a stop on the shinkansen branch line from Morioka to Akita (take the Komachi shinkansen from Morioka; services operate hourly). The lake is a short bus ride (¥350) from the bus terminal opposite Tazawako station. The tourist information office (☎ 0187-43 2111, daily, 8:30am-6:30pm) in the station has some leaflets.

Iwate-Numakunai (121km) Some Hayate services make a brief stop here. You don't take this route for the views. It is almost exclusively tunnels so there is little to report in the way of sights. Every so often the train emerges from a tunnel but before you have time to take in the view it darts into another.

Ninohe (156km) Some Hayate stop here. 'Ichinohe' means the 'first door'. In medieval times, the northern part of Iwate and southern part of Aomori prefectures were divided into different political districts. Each district was known as a 'door', meaning the door or gateway to that district. So in this case 'Ninohe' means the 'second door'. The next 'door' to be found on the train line is the shinkansen terminus at Hachinohe (the eighth door).

The on-board recorded announcements as the train heads for Hachinohe fall on deaf ears, since they can hardly be heard over the noise of the train hurtling through tunnels.

Hachinohe (187km) This is currently the terminus for the shinkansen from Tokyo but from 2010 the line will be extended as far as Shin-Aomori (see the box on p296).

Hachinohe is an industrial and port city but not a major tourist centre. The reason for stopping here is to embark on an unusual side trip into the mountains to a small village where it's claimed Jesus Christ is buried (see box opposite).

Hachinohe is a modern station with the main concourse on the third floor. Shinkansen depart from platforms 11-14. Train spotters will love the 'South Bridge' waiting area as you come up from the shinkansen platforms. It overlooks the tracks and once the shinkansen line is extended you'll be able to see the trains speeding away into the distance. You can already see the track being built.

Hachinohe Tourism Information Plaza (☎ 0178-27 4243, 🖳 kanko@cit y.hachinohe.aomori.jp, daily 9am-7pm, some English spoken) is on the second floor of the station concourse (turn right as you leave the JR ticket barrier and head down the escalator. The entrance is on your left and **coin lockers** (with a few large ¥500) are behind you on your right. Don't bother with the 'Information Center' in the corner of the JR ticket office – they do not dispense tourist information. The **JR ticket office** (daily, 5:30am-10:50pm) and **View Plaza travel agency** are on the third-floor main concourse. **Toilets** are on the main concourse and look out for the unusual sign (for Japan): 'Request: this toilet is kept clean through tips. Thank you for your cooperation'.

⛩ **Jesus in Japan?**

The journey to the remote village of Shingo, deep in the mountains west of Hachinohe, certainly feels like a pilgrimage. There is no rail line and the only way of reaching the village is to take two buses. Your destination is the **Christ Park**, so called because locals claim that it contains the grave of none other than Jesus Christ. The story goes that instead of dying on the cross, Jesus escaped at the last minute, fled to Siberia, made his way to Alaska and finally boarded a boat bound for Japan, where he landed at the port of Hachinohe. He quickly found his way to the village of Herai (now called Shingo) where he married a Japanese woman called Miyuko, had three daughters and lived to 106. In his latter years, Christ is said to have travelled around Japan, 'endeavouring to save the common people, while observing the language, customs and manners of the various regions'. He is described in village records as being 'grey haired and rather bald with a ruddy complexion and high nose and [he] wore a coat with many folds, causing people to hold him in awe as a long-nosed goblin.'

The extraordinary story only came to light in 1935 when two graves were found in a bamboo thicket at the top of a small hill in the village. It wasn't until May 1936, when Christ's 'last will and testament' mysteriously turned up in the village, that the significance of these graves was revealed: one of the graves was Christ's, the other belonged to his brother, called Isukiri. Or rather, just his brother's ear. Supposedly Jesus managed to avoid crucifixion thanks to his brother who 'casually took Christ's place and died on his cross', allowing him to escape to Japan clutching one of Isukiri's ears along with some 'hair of the Virgin Mary'. Further 'proof' can be found down in the village: Herai, the ancient name of the village, is said to be a corruption of 'Hebrew' and a villager who died some years ago 'looked not like a Japanese, his eyes were blue like those of a foreigner'. Curiously, there has been little attempt to cash in on the story by turning the park into a tacky tourist trap. Indeed, there's so little publicity that it's almost as if the village is embarrassed by the legend and doesn't quite know what to do with its two graves up on the hill.

The Christ Park, which contains the two graves as well as a small museum (Thur-Tue, 9am-5pm) telling the story in Japanese and English, is open to the public. Take a Nanbu Bus from stop No 5 outside Hachinohe station to Gonohe (36 mins; ¥800). From Gonohe, connect with a bus that takes you direct to the Christ Park just outside Shingo Village (33 mins; ¥800). Tell the driver you want to get out at Kuristo-koen. The Tourist Information Plaza at Hachinohe station (see opposite) can advise on bus times and connections to/from Shingo; they also have an information sheet in English.

If you've arrived too late in Hachinohe to continue further north, there are a couple of overnight options. Most convenient, since it's built into the station, is the JR-operated *Hotel Mets Hachinohe* (☎ 0178-70 7700, 🖳 http://hotel.eki-net.com/mets; ¥6300/S, ¥12,600/Tw). Turn right as you exit the JR ticket barrier and the entrance is in the corner on the left. Take the lift to the reception on the fourth floor. If it's fully booked, a good alternative – and hardly much further to walk – is *Toyoko Inn Hachinohe Ekimae* (☎ 0178-27 1045, 🖳 www.toyoko-inn.com; ¥6090/S, ¥8190/D/Tw). It's across the street from Hotel Mets and visible on the left as you leave the station.

For a bite to eat there is a **soba/udon** counter on the main concourse (to the right as you exit the ticket barrier). Opposite the ticket barrier is a branch of View Plaza with an attached café. Alternatively there's a reasonably cheap revolving **sushi restaurant** opposite the lift which takes you to Hotel Mets. And if you take the escalator down to the east exit and turn left, you'll see a line of **yatai/izakaya-style places** which get packed out with businessmen at the end of the working day. Recommended.

Turn right as you leave the station to find '**Yew Tree Plaza**', a large building which houses in the main entrance one of the enormous floats from Hachinohe's annual **Sansha Taisai festival** (July 31-Aug 3). A video of the festival is also played on loop. On the first floor regional products are sold and there are more coin lockers. There's a restaurant on the second floor, which tends to be less busy than those in and immediately outside the station.

There is not much in the way of sights in the station vicinity. The nearest attraction is **Hachinohe City Museum** (Tue-Sun, 9am to 5pm, entry price depends on exhibition), a short bus-ride away. The tourist information office in the station can advise on what the current temporary exhibition is and provide bus times.

HACHINOHE TO AOMORI [Map 18, p299; Table 16, p466]

Distances by Hakucho or Super-Hakucho limited express from Hachinohe. Fastest journey time: 58 minutes.

Hachinohe (0km) For the first part of the journey, the view on both sides is blocked by a line of trees. When the view does open out, the countryside consists of wide green fields and hills, interrupted by small towns.

Misawa (21km) About five or six minutes after leaving Misawa look out on the right for the blue water of Lake Ogawara in the distance. It really is blink-and-you'll-miss-it, since for the most part trees block the view.

Noheji (51km) Noheji is a point of interchange for the JR Ominato line that runs part of the way up the Shimokita Peninsula.

Leaving Noheji, look out to the right for views over Mutsu Bay. It's frustrating at first, since thanks to the ever-present trees along the track you don't get a full view of the bay. It's not until just before the train approaches Aomori that the track gets close enough to the shore for a sweeping view of the bay. Look out for a beautiful pine-clad island that is impressive enough to make people look up from their newspapers.

Asamushi-Onsen (79km) Right outside the station is Yusa Asamushi, a modern building which contains a great **hot spring** (daily, 7am-9pm, ¥350)

🚉 Shinkansen – the next step

Originally the opening date for the shinkansen extension from Hachinohe to Shin-Aomori was expected to be 2012, but recent government funding decisions aim to open it in 2010. The extension between Hachinohe and Shin-Aomori contains what was – briefly – the world's longest tunnel. The Hakkoda Tunnel is 26.5km long and cost ¥66.7 billion during six and a half years of construction. But its claim to fame was short-lived, since it was soon eclipsed by the 34.6-km long Lötschberg Tunnel in Switzerland.

with views over Mutsu Bay. Small towels are sold but bring your own soap.
There is also a free foot bath right in front of the station.

Aomori (96km)   [see pp316-20]
It's a shame after the brief views of Mutsu Bay that the final approach into
Aomori is less impressive, with the usual city glut of concrete buildings. Look
out for the most famous landmark in Aomori, the triangular ASPAM building
(see p316), in the distance on your right as the train pulls into the station.

The Hakucho and Super-Hakucho LEXs continue on through the Seikan
Tunnel to Hokkaido. For details of the through journey, see p328.

AOMORI TO TOKYO VIA AKITA AND NIIGATA

The fastest way back to Tokyo is to take the Hakucho or Super-Hakucho LEX
south to Hachinohe, and from there pick up a Hayate shinkansen. However, the
route described below goes back to Tokyo via the western side of Tohoku. In
addition to this suggested route a summer-only alternative is included, via Lake
Towada by bus (see pp298-301), as well as a predominantly coastal route from
Aomori to Akita (see pp303-5) with magnificent views.

Aomori to Odate   [Map 18, p299; Table 17, p466]
Distances by JR from Aomori. Fastest journey time: 65 minutes.

There are two possible routes for this section of the journey. The first (described
below) is all by rail and includes a stop in the ancient town of Hirosaki. The second is a combination of JR bus and train, heading south from Aomori on a spectacular mountain route to Towada-ko (see p298), a caldera lake, but this is possible in a day only during the summer months.

Aomori (0km)   [see pp316-20]
From Aomori, take a train on the JR Ou line towards Akita – there are a few
limited expresses called either Inaho or Kamoshika.

The first part of the journey is through a residential area but gradually the
landscape opens up. The main sight from the train is Mt Iwaki, spiritual symbol
of the surrounding area. Look out for it in the distance to the right from about
20 minutes after Aomori.

Hirosaki (37km) Hirosaki flourished from the early 17th century as a castle
town of the Tsugaru feudal lords. The big festival of the year, **Neputa Matsuri**,
rivals Aomori's Nebuta Matsuri (see p320) and takes place at the same time,
August 1st-7th. There is a nightly procession through the town of colourful floats.

Turn immediately left as you leave the station and walk to the end of the
building to find **coin lockers** (up to ¥600 size). A **tourist information office** (☎
0172-32 0524, daily 8:45am-6pm, to 5pm in winter) is to the right as you go out
of the station. Staff here can provide you with maps and will help book same-
day accommodation. Alternatively, **Hirosaki Sightseeing Information Center**
(☎ 0172-37 5501, daily 9am-6pm, to 5pm in winter), in a modern building west
of the station opposite Hirosaki Park, offers similar services.

Top priority on a visit to Hirosaki should be given to **Fujita Memorial Japanese Garden (Fujita Kinen Teien)** (Tue-Sun, 9am-5pm, ¥300, closed .Nov 24th to mid-April), a typical Edo-period stroll garden built on two levels. From the upper level, Mt Iwaki can be seen in the distance. Across the street from the entrance to the garden is **Hirosaki Park**, inside which is the site of Hirosaki Castle, completed in 1611. The original five-storeyed castle tower was struck by lightning and burnt to the ground, so what stands today is a replacement three-storeyed tower that has been turned into a museum of samurai artefacts (daily, 9am-5pm, ¥300, closed Nov 24th-April 1st). To reach Fujita Kinen Teien and Hirosaki Park from the station, take the ¥100 tourist loop bus and get off at 'Shiyakusho-mae/Koen Iriguchi' (15 mins).

For accommodation, right outside the station is *City Hirosaki Hotel* (☎ 0172-37 0109, 🖳 www.city-hirosaki.co.jp), an upmarket member of the Tokyu Inn chain with a choice of restaurants and attached fitness club and indoor pool. The cheapest singles are ¥7875, with twins from ¥13,650. Rates rise during both Golden Week and Neputa Matsuri. *Hyper Hotel Hirosaki* (☎ 0172-31 5000, 🖳 www.hyperhotel.co.jp; ¥5040/S, ¥6090/D, ¥7140/Family room inc breakfast) has compact but comfortable rooms. Turn right out of the station and head straight up the main road for about 10 minutes. Keep going until you see Hirosaki Post Office on your left; the Hyper Hotel is just after this on your right.

The best budget choice is *Hirosaki Youth Hostel* (☎/🖹 0172-33 7066; ¥3045/4045, breakfast ¥630), in an old building out towards Hirosaki Park. From the station, take a bus (¥170) from stop No 6 and get off at 'Daigaku Byoin-mae', or take the ¥100 tourist bus to the same stop.

Alternative route (summer only): Aomori to Odate via Towada-ko (Lake Towada)

This route (see map opposite) is well served by JR buses from May to October, but during the winter months service is severely restricted because of heavy snow, making it impossible to complete the journey in a single day. The bus timetable is subject to change so, before planning your itinerary, call in at the tourist information office outside Aomori station (see p316). Staff here have up-to-date timetables and can advise on making connections.

Alternatively, if you wish to plan your journey before arriving in Aomori, call the JR Information Line (☎ 050-2016 1603) or JR Bus (☎ 0177-23 1621) for the latest timetable information in English. Reservations for the JR bus from Aomori to Lake Towada (free to rail-pass holders) should be made at the JR bus counter outside Aomori station. Without a rail pass the journey from Aomori to Towada-ko (Lake Towada, 3 hours) costs ¥3000. Pick up a JR bus from outside Aomori station bound for Towada Hills and get off at the **Moya Kogen** stop (40 mins). Along the way, you'll pass **Nebuta no Sato** (see p320). Walk back down the road from the Moya Kogen stop and look out for a small yellow house on your right, which is *Moya Kogen Youth Hostel* (☎ 0177-64 2888, 🖳 http://jyh.or.jp/english/touhoku/moyakoug/index.html, aomori@moya.jp; ¥3360/4360; 14 beds). This is a superb place to stay due to the peaceful location, clean tatami rooms and delicious meals; dinner costs ¥1050 and breakfast ¥630. The hostel's owner loves Ireland, so Irish cocktails, Guinness and Enya are optional extras.

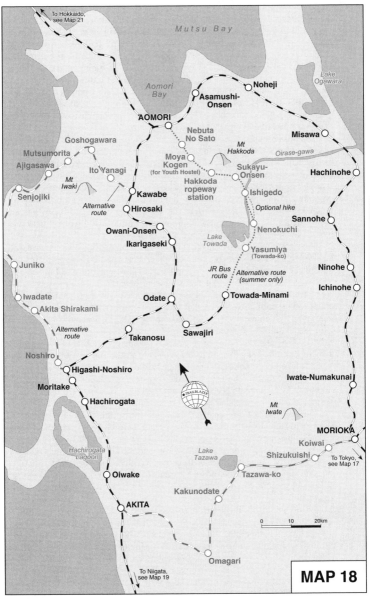

MAP 18

In the morning the owner will drop you at the bus stop in time to pick up the JR Bus to Towada-ko (Lake Towada). It's a $2^{1}/_{2}$-hour ride south to the lake. On the way, the bus calls first outside **Hakkoda Ropeway station** (30 mins from Moya Kogen), from where gondolas (daily, 9am-4:20pm, occasional closures, ¥1150 one-way, ¥1800 return) take 10 minutes to climb Mt Tamoyachidake (1326m). On a clear day, it's possible to see as far as Hokkaido. In winter this is a busy skiing area. The bus journey continues along the winding mountain road, stopping at a number of rural hot springs, the best known of which is **Sukayu-Onsen** (40 mins), famous for its mixed-bathing giant cypress-wood bath house (9am-5pm, ¥500) that can fit 1000 people – not that you'll see many of them through the steam.

It's possible to stay on the bus all the way to the lake but it's more fun to get off earlier at **Ishigedo** (1 hour 40 mins) from where an 8.9km hiking trail begins, following the course of Oirase-gawa to its source, Lake Towada. At the Ishigedo bus stop is a rest centre with toilets, a scale model of the path to the lake and a small snack bar where you can get noodles, ice cream and stock up on water. The path leads off from behind the rest area (it's very obvious). Ishigedo means 'huge slab of rock' – you'll see the rock supported by a tree at the trail start. According to the sign, an evil but beautiful woman who once lived here 'would kill travellers and steal their possessions'.

Assuming you survive this first obstacle the remaining 8.9km are unproblematic – the route is mostly sheltered under a canopy of trees and passes by a number of waterfalls. It's a very popular trail (I saw a group of businessmen walking in shirt and tie), but unless you're here during high season (July-August and again in October for the autumn leaves) there should be room to breathe. The only downside is that the path sometimes connects up with the main road, which means you have to compete with lorries and cars. Allow 2-3 hours to complete the hike.

The hike ends with a set of stone steps leading up to a bridge and your first view of Lake Towada, formed from a volcanic crater. You are now at the small lakeside resort of **Nenokuchi**, from where boat cruises (☎ 0176-75 2909; ¥1320) cross the lake to the main resort centre of **Yasumiya**. Alternatively, pick up the JR bus from Nenokuchi for the 20-minute ride to Yasumiya (in the timetable Yasumiya may just be called Lake Towada; either way it's the last stop).

The bus starts from outside Nenokuchi bus terminal (known as the 'JR House'), which also sells drinks and ice cream. You'll see it as you come off the hike. The bus terminates at Yasumiya JR bus terminal (also called 'JR House'). The lake is right in front of you and all around are hotels, restaurants and souvenir shops. Motor and paddle boats can be rented on the lake. The best-known lakeside sight is the **Statue of the Maidens** (known locally as 'two old women in the buff reaching out for each other'), created by Kotaro Takamura in 1953. Takamura's wife is said to have been the model for the statue, a 10-minute walk around the lake from the JR House. The temperature here can fall as low as -20°C in winter but because of its depth (327m), the lake never freezes.

To complete this route, pick up another JR Bus from the Yasumiya JR Bus terminal which runs to **Towada-Minami station** (64 mins; 4/day Apr 1st-Nov 10th), from where you can pick up a local train on the JR Hanawa line west to **Odate** (40 mins, 5/day). Along the way, the train will call at **Sawajiri**, an unremarkable place save for the fact that it is close to what is believed to be Japan's only major shrine dedicated to a dog. The story goes that during the Edo period a hunter named Sadaroku lost his way in heavy snow while hunting deep in the mountains and was arrested because he did not have his hunting licence with him. He told his faithful four-legged friend, who rushed back through the snow to his master's home.

The hunter's wife couldn't understand why the dog was barking and the household pet had to return to his master without the document he required. But the hunter repeated his urgent appeal, and the dog raced back home and barked again at the family shrine. His wife finally understood and fastened the licence securely to the dog's collar, all the while praying for her husband's safe return. The dog ran back to his master for the second time, but all was lost. The hunter had been executed. Legend has it that the dog died soon after, as if following his master. To this day on April 17 every year a ceremony to remember the hunter's dog is held at a special canine shrine located on the mountainside of Kuzuhara, near Sawajiri station.

From Odate, pick up the route starting on p302.

Owani-Onsen (49km) Only 10 minutes down the line by limited express, this is a popular stop for skiers in winter thanks to nearby Mt Ajara (709m), a mountain which even boasts its own ski shrine. It's pine-tree territory on both sides of the line between Owani-Onsen and Odate.

After Owani-Onsen a few trains stop at **Ikarigaseki (57km)**.

Odate (82km) This station is a terminus for the JR Hanawa line coming from Towada-Minami and Morioka.

Odate looks and feels a bit run down, and there's little reason to spend time here unless you're particularly interested in Akita dogs (see box below). Even then, the **Akita Inu Kaikan (Akita Dogs Center)** (daily, 9am-4pm, ¥100), a 20-minute bus ride from the station, is a very depressing place housing a small museum about the dogs. The only live specimen is the poor mutt stuck in a cage outside. It's thought that Akita dogs were bred from the Nara Period (710-794)

⛩ The legend of Hachiko

Hachiko was an Akita dog born in Odate in 1923 and brought to Tokyo by its owner, Eisaburo Ueno, the following year. A pet of unflinching loyalty, Hachiko bade his master goodbye every morning when he left for work and greeted him at the end of the day at Shibuya station. Such was the dog's devotion, that even after Ueno died in 1925 Hachiko continued to return every day for the next 11 years to the station and waited patiently for him.

The statue of Hachiko which stands today outside Shibuya station (see p94) is a popular local landmark and meeting place, but it's not the only monument to Japan's most famous dog. A similar but much less well-known statue stands outside Odate station. Anyone obsessed by the legend of Hachiko should not stop there: a 15-km journey (taxi only) south-west of Odate station will bring you to the house where Hachiko was born (look for the dog statue outside). Near the house stands a public toilet, the design of which was apparently 'inspired by the shape of Hachiko'. It has to be seen to be believed. The tourist information office at Odate station can give directions to the house.

when rivalry between feudal leaders and frequent battles meant that there was a great demand for personal guard dogs. In the early 20th century, dog fighting was a popular form of local entertainment.

Odate to Akita   [Map 18, p299; Table 17, p466]
Distances by JR from Odate. Fastest journey time: 1 hour 25 minutes.

Odate (0km) Join, or continue along, the JR Ou line towards Akita.

Takanosu (18km) Takanosu once won a place in the *Guinness Book of Records* by building the world's largest drum, measuring 3.71m in diameter, 4.32m in depth and weighing in at 3.5 tonnes.

Higashi-Noshiro (48km) The Ou line, which has been roughly following Yoneshiro-gawa towards the coast, turns south at this point on its way to Akita.

Hachirogata (75km) There is a major land reclamation area out to the right along this stretch of the journey. Although there's not a great deal to see, it's an amazing project on paper: Hachirogata Lagoon, once the second largest lake in Japan, was reclaimed and is now a vast expanse of rice paddies – an area equal in size to the space inside Tokyo's Yamanote line.

♦ Oiwake (91km) Limited expresses don't stop here but this is the nearest point of interchange for the local Oga line that heads west to the **Oga Peninsula** (27km, 40 mins). Oga is known for its Namahage Sedo Festival on December 31st, when men wearing demon costumes and masks, and wielding large kitchen knives and wooden buckets come down from nearby Mt Shinzan and invade the town. They knock on doors shouting the equivalent of 'Are there any cry babies in this house?' or, according to JNTO, 'Any good-for-nothing fellows around here?' – in short, threatening lazy children and adults to get their act together in time for the New Year.

Akita (104km) Akita is a large industrial city with a bright, modern rail station which was rebuilt when the Komachi shinkansen opened along the Tazawako line, linking Akita with Morioka (see p292). The main exit is on the west side of the station. Komachi shinkansen leave from platforms 11 and 12. **Coin lockers** (including a few ¥500) are in the waiting room adjacent to the JR ticket office on your right as you exit the main ticket barrier.

A **View Plaza travel agency** (Mon-Fri 10:30am-6pm, Sat/Sun 10:30am-5pm) is opposite the JR ticket office. The **tourist information office** (☎ 0188-32 7941, daily, 9am-7pm, English spoken) is directly opposite the ticket barrier. English maps are available. Topico department store is built into the west side of the station.

About the only reason for stopping in Akita is if you're passing through during the **Kanto Matsuri** between August 4th and 7th; men parade through the streets balancing bamboo poles topped with lanterns on their foreheads, shoulders, chins, heads and other parts of the body. During the rest of the year, the **Kanto Festival Center** (daily, 9:30am-4:30pm, ¥100) is the place to head to see a film of the action and a display of some of the lanterns and poles. At weekends from April to the end of October, volunteers demonstrate the astonishing pole-balancing act (visitors are welcome to join in). The centre is 20 minutes on foot west from the station.

Of limited interest is **Akarenga-kan Museum** (daily, 9:30am-4:30pm, ¥200), a striking white-and-red brick building which served as the headquarters of Akita Bank from 1912 until 1969. It is said to have survived several earthquakes. The teller windows on the ground floor are still there. Inside are some fine examples of Akita hachijo (naturally dyed silk fabric), lacquerware and dolls. It's a 20-minute walk across town, on the other side of the Asahi River.

A convenient upmarket choice for an overnight stay is the JR-run *Hotel Metropolitan Akita* (☎ 018-831 2222, 🖳 www.metro-akita.co.jp; ¥10,626/S, ¥18,480/Tw), right outside the west exit of the station. A cheaper option is *Toyoko Inn Akita-eki Higashi-guchi* (☎ 018-889 1045, 🖳 www.toyoko-inn.com; ¥6090/S, ¥8190/D/Tw), outside the east exit (turn left as you exit the main ticket barrier).

Another good place, offering a similar deal to Toyoko Inn, is *Hotel Alpha 1* (☎ 018-836 5800, 🖳 www.alpha-1.co.jp; ¥5600/S, ¥9800/D, ¥10,500/Tw), on your left as you take the west exit. It has a good adjacent restaurant. Look for the 'α-1' sign on the roof.

For food, the local speciality is *Inaniwa udon* (noodles) which you can try at *Sato Yosuke* on the basement floor of the Seibu department store outside the west exit. Menus cost from around ¥1000 and there's both tatami and table seating. For a quick caffeine fix, there's a branch of *Starbucks* on the ground floor of Hotel Metropolitan outside the station's west exit. Attached to Hotel Alpha 1 is *Karahashichaya*, which does a great buffet breakfast (6:30-9:30am), lunch (11:30am-2pm), tea-time cake sets (2-4:30pm) and dinner (5:30pm-12 midnight). It offers a variety of good-value Japanese meals.

You can surf the web at *Plaza 1*, an internet café on the second floor (main concourse level) of Topico department store inside Akita station. The charge is ¥200 for 30 minutes.

If in a hurry to return to Tokyo take the Komachi shinkansen that runs east to Morioka and from there on to Tokyo. The train travels 'backwards' as far as **Omagari**, the first stop after Akita – don't bother to turn the seats around, though, because the direction of the train reverses after leaving Omagari. Two places worth stopping at en route to Morioka (or visiting as day trips from Akita) are **Kakunodate**, a beautiful old town with a preserved samurai district, and **Tazawa-ko** (see p293), where you'll find the deepest lake in Japan.

Alternative route: Aomori to Akita via Senjojiki   [Map 18, p299]

At weekends and in holiday periods (New Year; Golden Week and late July to the end of September) Resort Shirakami (see box p304) trains operate on this route giving passengers the chance to hear live shamisen music and listen to traditional Japanese stories as they travel.

There are also on-board announcements (in Japanese only) at places of interest where the train conveniently slows down so that passengers have a chance to take in the scenery properly.

Shamisen players on a Resort
Shirakami train

The shamisen players and story tellers get on the train between Goshogawara and Mutsumorita.

The train slows down around Senjojiki (literally 'thousand tatami mat', so named because the flatness of the beach around here made a former emperor think it was as big as a thousand tatami mats) and between Juniko and Akita-Shirakami.

At Higashi-Noshiro the train changes direction; you then pass Hachirogata lagoon but scenically this is not as interesting as the coast line already passed.

At the time of writing the timetable was as follows: depart Aomori at 13.50 and arrive in Akita at 19:01 (from Akita the train departs at 08.26 and arrives in Aomori at 13.30).

The service operating in holiday periods operates between Hirosaki and Akita only; it departs Hirosaki at 16.09 and arrives in Akita at 20.42 (from Akita the service departs at 11.05 and arrives in Hirosaki at 15.50, however entertainment is not provided on this service). For up-to-date timetable information call the JR East infoline (see box p79).

Joyful Trains

It's a sad fact in Japan that many local railway lines are struggling to survive (see box p340), but JR-East has hit on an idea to both boost tourism in rural areas and at the same time maintain a transportation service for local communities. The solution is so-called 'Joyful Trains' (🖥 www.jreast.co.jp/train/joy ful/index.html).

The original Joyful Train went into service in 1997 under the name Resort Shirakami on the JR Gono line between Aomori and Akita. In fact, three tourist trains operate on this line: the orange Kumagera (woodpecker), which went into service in 2006, the green Buna (beech tree), which began operations in 2004, and the blue Aoike (blue pond), which started in 1997.

Each train has three carriages, the front and back ones have traditional seats but the middle carriage has a number of compartments seating four people in each. The seats in these can be pulled out so that passengers can sit as if sitting on the floor.

One reader describes the journey on a Joyful Train: 'I am not usually keen on touristy things like this, but the Resort Shirakami service on the local Gono Line was fantastic! In particular you get one of the best sunset views from the railway'.

There are similar Joyful Train services on other lines, including the Tsugaru line (see p328) and Uetsu line (see p305). Contact the JR-East Info Line (see box p79) for more details of these services.

Rail-pass holders can board Joyful Trains for free and there is no charge for seat reservations (but you must have a reservation!); when reserving a seat ask for Seat A to ensure a sea-side view. Without a rail pass, Aomori to Akita (or vice-versa) on the Resort Shirakami Joyful Train costs ¥4310 (basic fare) plus the seat-reservation fee (either ¥310 or ¥510 depending on the dates). Alternatively it may be worth considering a Gonosen pass (¥5000; valid for two days).

Akita to Niigata [Map 19, p306; Map 20, p307; Table 18, p467]
Distances by JR from Akita. Fastest journey time: $3^1/2$ hours.

Akita (0km) The next part of the route continues south towards Niigata along the Uetsu line on the Inaho LEX. Fifteen minutes after leaving Akita there are glimpses of the Japan Sea out on the right. These views last for another 15 minutes, before the line heads back towards more rice fields.

Limited expresses make brief stops at both **Ugo-Honjo (43km)** and **Nikaho (57km)** but the surrounding area is not particularly noteworthy.

♦ Konoura (63km) Unless you're on a local train you won't notice this stop but Konoura was the birthplace of Nobu Shirase, the first Japanese to set foot on Antarctica.

Kisakata (68km) The area around Kisakata station is not at all attractive so it's surprising to discover that up until the beginning of the 19th century the area was similar to Matsushima (see pp286-8), with tiny islands scattered along the coast. The islands disappeared for ever after a huge earthquake in 1804 pushed up the sea floor.

For the next 40km or so there are great views to the left of the mountains in Chokai Quasi National Park. The rail line skirts around the park, at the centre of which is Mt Chokai (2236m), a semi-dormant volcano known as the Mt Fuji of Akita. As the train moves into Yamagata prefecture, gradually the focus shifts towards the coast, with views out to sea on the right side.

Between Kisakata and Sakata the train stops at **Yuza (93km)**.

Although little more than a mile in width, this lagoon is not in the least inferior to Matsushima in charm and grace. There is, however, a remarkable difference between the two. Matsushima is a cheerful laughing beauty, while the charm of Kisakata is in the beauty of its weeping countenance.

Matsuo Basho, *The Narrow Road To The Deep North*, trans Nobuyuki Yuasa, Penguin, 1966

Sakata (105km) Sakata is a large port town at the mouth of Mogami-gawa. The area around the station is rather drab and depressing but Sakata does boast a good example of the classic **Japanese stroll garden**, worth a look if you haven't visited one before.

Only small ¥300 **coin lockers** are available at the station, though ask at the JR ticket counter and they may keep your bags for ¥410. The **tourist information office** (daily, 9am-5:30pm) is in the building to the right as you leave the station but the staff do not speak English and maps are in Japanese only.

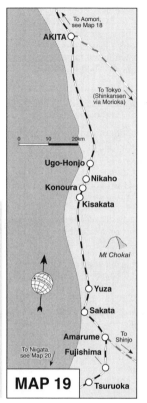

To Aomori,
see Map 18

AKITA

To Tokyo
(Shinkansen
via Morioka)

0   10   20km

Ugo-Honjo

Nikaho

Konoura

Kisakata

Mt Chokai

Yuza

Sakata

Amarume   To Shinjo

To Niigata,   **Fujishima**
see Map 20

MAP 19   **Tsuruoka**

Fortunately, the main sight is only a short walk from the station. Turn right on to the main road that runs along in front of the station. Go straight, past the A1 Hotel, until you see Daiei supermarket at a junction on your right. The entrance to **Homma Museum of Art** (🖳 www .homma-museum.or.jp, daily Mar-Oct 9am-5pm, Tue-Sun Nov-Feb, 9am-4:30pm, ¥700) is opposite Daiei.

The Homma family were one of the wealthiest in Japan thanks to rice production on their land, and they remained the most influential family in the area until WWII brought an end to their power. The museum is housed in an ugly 1960s concrete building and the exhibition changes periodically.

Far more interesting is the small Japanese garden and wooden guest house. Tea is served inside at tables overlooking the garden. A highlight of the garden used to be the 'borrowed' view of Mt Chokai in the distance; this has now been blocked out by karaoke signs and the Daiei supermarket outside.

Amarume (117km) Amarume is a stop on the Uetsu line and also a terminus for the Riku Saisen line running east to Shinjo. A quick way of returning to Tokyo from here would be to take a local train to **Shinjo** (50 mins), from where you can pick up the shinkansen which runs via Yamagata and Fukushima south to the capital. In 1960, a small oil and natural gas field was discovered beneath Amarume town and fossil fuels are still pumped out of the ground for local consumption.

♦ **Fujishima (126km)** Limited expresses don't stop here but it's worth noting that Fujishima is the venue for the annual National River Rope Crossing Tournament in August; contestants attempt to cross from one side of Fujishima-gawa to the other via a series of ropes. Anyone who falls in is, well, out.

Tsuruoka (132km) Tsuruoka station has small ¥300 **coin lockers** (in the waiting room). The staff at the **tourist information office** (☎ 0235-25 7678, daily, 9:30am-5:30pm), to the right as you go out of the station, don't speak English but will help book accommodation.

Most people who stop here are usually on their way to Haguro-san (Mt Haguro). The 414m mountain to the east of Tsuruoka is part of a chain known as **Dewa-Sanzan** (Three Mountains of Dewa), the other two being Gas-san and

Yudono-san. The mountains are considered to be the home of the *kami* (spirits), and pilgrims visit year-round to undertake spiritual cleansing: first to be climbed is Haguro-san (2446 steps), which represents birth, followed by Gassan, which represents death, and finally Yudono-san, representing the future or re-birth. The easiest to access, and possible as a day trip from Tsuruoka, is Haguro-san. Buses (operated by Shonai-Kotsu) take 45 minutes from Tsuruoka station to Haguro-san. Ask at tourist information for bus schedules.

Tsuruoka city has only a few sights, the most interesting of which is the **Chido Museum** (daily 9am-5pm, ¥620). There's an odd architectural mix of buildings here, including the former Tsuruoka Police station, a Western-style building from the late 19th century and the retirement residence of the former ruling Sakai lords. There's also a small Japanese garden. All signs inside are in Japanese, though a leaflet in English is available at the entrance. Take a bus from the station and get off at the Shiyakusho-mae stop (¥100), then keep following the road, past the park and look for the entrance on the right.

For accommodation, immediately opposite the station is *Tsuruoka Washington Hotel* (☎ 0235-25 0111, 🖳 www.tsuruoka-wh.com; ¥6000/S, ¥9500/D, ¥10,000/Tw). Alternatively try *Tsuruoka Youth Hostel* (see below).

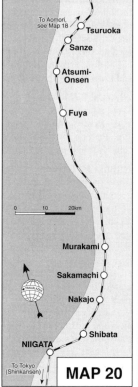

MAP 20

♦ **Sanze (149km)** Three stops from Tsuruoka by local train, alight here for *Tsuruoka Youth Hostel* (☎/🖹 0235-73 3205, 🖳 kryoma@mail.dewa.or.jp; ¥2625/3625). Call in advance for a pick up. The building is old and the bunk-bed dorms (that sleep four or five) are only adequate, but the staff are friendly and the meals good (breakfast ¥525, dinner ¥1050). Activities such as paragliding can be arranged. To continue the route take a local train to Atsumi-Onsen.

Atsumi-Onsen (162km) More than 1000 years ago, Atsumi served as a border checkpoint for travellers entering Tohoku. Sandwiched between mountains and the coast, Atsumi is nowadays a busy hot spring resort. According to legend, the spring in question was discovered by none other than Kobo Daishi, the priest who founded the Shingon sect of Buddhism and established its headquarters on Koya-san (see pp230-2).

After Atsumi-Onsen, some limited expresses call briefly at **Fuya (176km)**.

Murakami (212km) As far as Murakami the rail line runs along the coast, though views are limited due to the proliferation of tunnels (of various lengths) along this line. From here the train heads inland and after 15 minutes passes a major industrial complex. The views gradually deteriorate as the surrounding area becomes more built up on the final approach into Niigata.

Before arriving in Niigata, there are stops at **Sakamachi (224km)**, **Nakajo (233km)** and **Shibata (246km)**.

Niigata (273km)   [see pp320-6]
If not returning to Tokyo from here, Niigata also has direct rail connections with **Kanazawa**, just under four hours away by Hokuetsu LEX along the Hokuriku line. Pick up the route guide to Kanazawa from p142 as you pass Naoetsu (100 mins from Niigata).

Niigata to Tokyo
The fastest, though least scenic, way of returning to Tokyo from Niigata is by Joetsu shinkansen. The shinkansen line between Tokyo and Niigata is virtually all tunnels and the fastest journey time is 100 minutes; there is at least one service an hour. Single and double-decker trains (the Toki/Max Toki) run on this line; and it's worth reserving a seat on the upper deck of the latter for the snatches of mountain views in between the tunnels. However, these fill up quickly so book well ahead, or queue up early for a seat in the upper deck non-reserved cars.

If you have more time and are prepared to change trains you might consider the local Banetsu-sei line that runs inland from Niigata, via **Mikawa** (see p326) and the castle town of **Aizu-Wakamatsu**, to **Koriyama** (see p283) on the Tohoku shinkansen line. A good reason for doing this is that a **steam locomotive** operates between Niitsu and Aizu-Wakamatsu (Mar-Nov weekends only, daily during Aug). All seats are reserved so you'll need to book a place in advance at any JR travel agency (reservations are free to rail-pass holders). Tickets go on sale one month in advance and are often sold out within the day.

From Koriyama, you can complete the journey by jumping on a southbound shinkansen to Tokyo.

Tohoku (Northern Honshu) – city guides

SENDAI

Tohoku's largest city, Sendai (population: one million), is on the Pacific coast and shares the same latitude as Washington DC, USA, and the same longitude as Melbourne, Australia. The city was razed to the ground during WWII and consequently has few sights of historical interest. Sendai's history is dominated by the figure of Date Masamune (1567-1636), a feudal lord who earned the nickname 'one-eyed dragon' after he contracted smallpox during infancy and lost the sight in his right eye. Most visitors stop here briefly before heading on to Matsushima (see pp286-8), billed as one the top three scenic spots in Japan.

What to see and do

The best way of seeing the main sights is to take the **Loople Sendai**, a retro-style tourist bus in various colours that departs from platform No 15 of the bus pool outside the station (9am-4pm; half-hourly). A one-day pass costs ¥600 or individual tickets are ¥250, available from the driver or from the ticket office at the bus terminal. The loop runs one way around the city, with 11 stops en route. Show your pass at the entrance to paid attractions for a small discount (usually the group rate). There are announcements in English before each stop. Ring the bell to stop at each place. The following is a guide to the most interesting places along the way. A map at each bus stop shows the route to the place of interest.

At stop No 4, **Zuihoden** (daily, 9am-4:30pm, to 4pm in winter, ¥550) is a temple-style mausoleum of the Date family reconstructed in 1985. There are statues of Masamune Date, and Tadamune and Tsunamune Date in the mausoleum, though they're off limits to visitors. There's a pleasant wooded area you can wander around and a museum with statues, artefacts and video – but the only English is in the guide you receive at the entrance to the mausoleum.

Sendai City Museum (Tue-Sun, 9am-4:45pm, ¥400) at stop No 5 is more old fashioned than the hi-tech video show at Sendai Castle (see Stop No 6, below), but is very informative about the Date family with brief captions in English on most exhibits and an impressive scale model of the castle. A good pamphlet is available. There is a schedule of temporary exhibitions (an additional charge applies).

Stop No 6 is the site of the former **Sendai Castle**, also known as Aoba Castle, built on top of the 132m-high Aoba Hill in 1602 by Masamune Date. Destroyed in 1945, it has now been resurrected as a massive tourist arcade and includes a restaurant and modern shrine. The only reason for heading out here is the view over Sendai – an impressive view of an ordinary city. An exhibition hall (daily, 9am-5pm; ¥700) shows the history of the castle with a computer-generated reconstruction video, but it's not particularly informative and could easily be skipped.

Finally, stop No 8 is **Miyagi Museum of Art** (🖥 www.pref.miyagi.jp/bjiyutu/mmoa.old/indexe.html; Tue-Sun, 9:30am-5pm, ¥300; extra charges

---

⛩ Sendai Streetcar Museum

Rail fans might like to pay a visit to this museum, also known as Sendai City Train Museum (🖥 www.kotsu.city.sendai.jp/e/shiden.index.html; Tue-Sun, 10am-4pm; free), located close to Tomizawa subway station, the southern terminus of the Namboku subway line. The museum traces the history of streetcars in Sendai, which for half a century were the main form of local public transport in the city. The first four-wheeled wooden streetcar went into service in 1926 and at the height of its popularity was carrying in excess of 100,000 passengers a day. But the age of the automobile heralded the slow demise of the streetcar, which was finally taken out of service on March 31, 1976, almost exactly 50 years after it was inaugurated.

The museum exhibits some of the original carriages as well as a collection of mechanical parts, period photographs, tickets and signs. A free shuttle bus operates from outside the north exit of Tomizawa station to the museum.

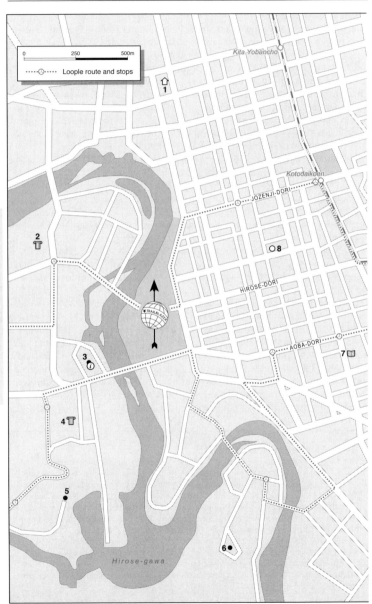

HONSHU

Where to stay

1	Bansuitei Ikoi-so Ryokan	1	晩翠いこい荘
9	Dormy Inn Sendai	9	ドーミーイン仙台
13	Roynet Hotel	13	ロイネットホテル
14	Sendai Chitose Youth Hostel	14	仙台千登勢ユースホステル
15	Hotel Metropolitan Sendai	15	ホテルモトロポリタン仙台
17	Hotel Monterey Sendai	17	ホテルモントレ仙台
19	Toyoko Inn Higashi-guchi No 1	19	東横イン 仙台東口I号館
20	Toyoko Inn Higashi-guchi No 2	20	東横イン 仙台東口II号館
22	Mielparque Sendai	22	メルパルク仙台
23	Holiday Inn Sendai	23	ホリデイイン仙台

[See p312 for continuation of key]

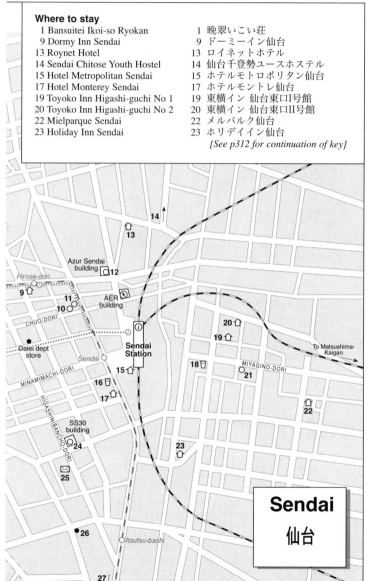

HONSHU

Sendai
仙台

SENDAI 仙台

Where to eat and drink *(key continued from p311)*

8	Ramen Kokugi-jo	8	ラーメン国技場
10	Capricciosa	10	カプリシヨーザ
11	Kirara-zushi	11	きらら寿司
12	Samba Samba; Mojadar; Miconos (Azur Sendai Bldg)	12	サンバサンバ; モジャダール; ミコノス (アジュール仙台ビル)
16	Pronto	16	プロント
18	Starbucks	18	スターバックス
21	Michel	21	ミッシェル
24	Restaurants (SS30 Building)	24	レストラン(SS30ビル)

Other

2	Miyagi Museum of Art	2	宮城県美術館
3	Sendai International Center	3	仙台国際センター
4	Sendai City Museum	4	仙台市博物館
5	Site of Sendai Castle	5	仙台城跡
6	Zuihoden	6	瑞鳳殿
7	Maruzen	7	丸善
16	Net U Internet	16	ネットU インターネット
25	Central Post Office	25	中央郵便局
26	Coin Laundry	26	オインランドリー
27	Sendai Streetcar Museum	27	仙台市電保存館

HONSHU

for temporary exhibitions), 500m north of Sendai City Museum. The main gallery exhibits the work of 20th-century local artists and some minor works of foreign artists, including three early figurative paintings by Kandinsky. If you have time to spare, there's a pleasant modern sculpture garden and café.

For **views of the city** and the Pacific Ocean pay a visit to the 31st-floor viewing terrace (daily, 10:30am-8pm; free) of the AER Building or, alternatively, head for the 30th-floor observation gallery (daily, 7am-11pm) of the SS30 Building where you get a great view of Sendai by day or night for free.

PRACTICAL INFORMATION
Station guide

There are east and west sides to Sendai station but the main exit into the city is on the west side. On the third floor is the central shinkansen entrance and main JR ticket office (daily, 5:30am-10:30pm). There are lockers all around the station, though these are mostly only small size. On the second floor is the central entrance for all other JR lines, including the Tohoku and Senseki Lines. Also on this floor is the tourist information office (see opposite) and a large View Plaza travel agency where rail-pass vouchers can be exchanged.

Heading out of the station from the second floor brings you to the overhead walkways that run above the central streets in front of the station. On the first floor (street level) there's a 'parcel storage' office (daily, 6am-11pm) where you can leave luggage for ¥410 per item per day (¥820 overnight); the office is at the right-side end of the station building.

There are plenty of places in the station for a snack – bakeries, cafés that do good-value morning sets as well as other deals and a couple of bars that fill up in the evenings with businessmen.

Tourist information

The **tourist information office** (☎ 022-222 4069, daily, 8:30am-8pm; English spoken) is located one floor down from the shinkansen level. Staff will not book accommodation (although they will call the youth hostel) but will direct you to the View Plaza travel agency on the same floor. The main JR ticket office is on the same level as the entrance to the shinkansen.

For more detailed information, contact **Sendai International Center** (English hotline ☎ 022-224 1919, 🖳 www.sira.or.jp/icenter/en, daily, 10am-8pm, closed occasionally). This place has a well-stocked library, foreign newspapers/magazines and travel brochures. The Loople Sendai tourist bus stops outside the centre (stop No 5).

Getting around

The best way of getting around is to take the **tourist loop bus**.

Sendai also has a network of buses and a **subway line** (see 🖳 www.kotsu.city.sendai.jp for timetables and fare). City centre subway fares are ¥200.

The Namboku subway line runs from Izumi city in the north through the city centre to the southern suburbs.

A second subway line, the Tozai line, is currently under construction and will cross the city from east to west. Full opening is not expected before 2014.

Sendai airport has connections with Hong Kong (Dragonair), Seoul (Asiana), Guam (Continental), Beijing and Shanghai (China Airlines) and Taipei (Eva). A limousine bus (¥910 one-way, 40 mins) operates between Sendai station and the airport.

Alternatively take the **Sendai Airport Transit rail link**; the non-stop express service runs from JR Sendai to the airport in just 17 minutes; the local stopping service takes 23 minutes.

Rail fans should note that the final part of the journey, from JR Natori station to the airport terminal, is on an elevated rail track. The train used on this line is a two-car electric set (type E721). The airport station is right alongside the terminal building.

Internet

Net U Internet is on the fifth floor of the AER building next to the station; you can surf the internet for free (10am-8pm; 30 mins per visit).

Festivals

Sendai's biggest annual event is the **Tanabata Matsuri** on August 6th-8th. Along the main streets and in the station, colourful paper streamers and decorations are hung from bamboo poles. One of the largest summer events in Tohoku, the festival attracts around two million visitors.

Where to stay

Next to the station is the JR-run *Hotel Metropolitan Sendai* (☎ 022-268 2525, 🖳 www.s-metro.stbl.co.jp), which has comfortable if not overly-luxurious rooms. Rack rates are ¥11,550 for a single and ¥20,790 for a twin but rail-pass holders receive a 20% discount.

A relatively new place offering rooms of a high standard is *Holiday Inn Sendai* (☎ 022-256 5111, 🖳 www.holiday-inn-sendai.jp; ¥10,972/S, ¥19,057/D, ¥20,212 /Tw, ¥23,677/Tr); it's a six-minute walk from the station's east exit.

Hotel Monterey Sendai (☎ 022-265 7110, 🖳 www.hotelmonterey.co.jp; ¥12,705/S, ¥20,790/Tw) is a good-value mid-range hotel with a European feel. Breakfast is an additional ¥1700. A one-day pass for the hotel's 17th-floor spa called Sala Terrena is ¥1515 for hotel guests. The Monterey is less than five minutes on foot from the central exit of Sendai station. Another budget option is *Dormy Inn Sendai* (☎ 022-715 7077, 🖳 www.dormy-hotels.com, ¥7980/S, ¥11,550/D, ¥13,650/Tw, Business suite/Japanese-style room ¥12,600 for two), about ten minutes on foot from the station, has both Western- and Japanese-style rooms. As an alternative to walking from the station, take the Nanboku subway line from Sendai station to Hirosedori, from where it's a minute on foot. Breakfast (¥840) is served in the adjacent 'Big Mamma' café. There's a washing machine (free)/dryer (¥100) on the second

HONSHU

floor and a public bath on the second floor (women 3-9pm, men 9:15pm-9am).

There are several branches of the popular Toyoko Inn (🖳 www.toyoko-inn.com) hotel chain in Sendai. Two are next to each other and close to the east exit of the station: *Toyoko Inn Sendai Higashi-guchi No 1* (☎ 022-256 1045) and *Toyoko Inn Sendai Higashi-guchi No 2* (☎ 022-298 1045) both offer singles at ¥5670, doubles at ¥7770 and twins at ¥8820.

A 10-minute walk north of the station is *Roynet Hotel* (☎ 022-722 0055, 🖳 dai-info@roynet.co.jp, 🖳 http://roynet .co.jp), a cut above the standard business hotel, with reasonably spacious singles going from ¥4980, doubles at ¥7950 and twins at ¥9990. Facilities include a coin laundry and 24-hour restaurant. You pay into a machine in the lobby, though human staff are also on hand.

Fifteen minutes on foot from the station's east exit is *Mielparque Sendai* (☎ 022-792 8111, 🖳 www.mielparque.co.jp; ¥6273/S, ¥10,910/Tw), part of the chain of hotels run by the post office (hence the post office in the lobby). The Western-style rooms have wide beds but small bathrooms; the Japanese-style rooms can accommodate two people for ¥12,728 or three for ¥16,364. The building is hard to miss as it looks as if a boat has been built into one side.

Bansuitei Ikoi-so Ryokan (☎ 022-222 7885, 🖷 223 2222, 🖳 www.ikoisouryokan .co.jp) is less than 10 minutes on foot from Kita Yobancho subway station, three stops from Sendai station. It has a smart wooden interior with tatami rooms – a big selling point is the common bath that turns into a Jacuzzi (which has, according to the owner, 'an ultrasonic massaging effect on your body recognized by the Health and Welfare Ministry'). A Japanese breakfast (¥840) and evening meals (¥1470) are available; ¥5500/pp no meals (¥5000/pp for two or three people sharing a room). The rate quoted is for bookings made online. A marginally cheaper rate is offered for reservations made by fax (!), which must be one of the few cases in the world where old technology offers a financial advantage. Pet lovers might like to know that this ryokan also offers a 'pet hotel', where dogs and cats can have their own air-conditioned room for ¥3000 per night. Take North Exit 2 at Kita Yobancho subway, turn right at the top of the steps that lead to street level, and walk for about eight minutes. The ryokan is on a quiet road off to the left, just before you reach Tohoku University Hospital.

Sendai Chitose Youth Hostel (☎ 022-222 6329, 🖳 chitose8@d4.dion.ne.jp; ¥3150/4150, breakfast ¥630, dinner ¥1050) is a good budget option with tatami rooms sleeping 2-4 people. In a residential area about 20 minutes on foot from the station (pick up a map from tourist information).

Where to eat and drink

Ramen Kokugi-jo (daily, 11am-2am) is a new place filled with informal restaurants selling all kinds of ramen, including varieties made famous in Sapporo, Kyushu and Shikoku. You'll find a host of different noodle options with dishes from ¥650. The adventurous holidaymaker might like to try the unusual ramen ice cream (¥250).

Turn right as you take the central shinkansen ticket exit and double-back on yourself to reach **Gyutan-dori** (Beef Tongue St) and **Sushi-dori**, a parade of beef-tongue and sushi restaurants. Grilled beef tongue, known as *gyutan-yaki*, is a Sendai delicacy. Another sushi place in the station which gets good reviews is *Heiroku-zushi*; it's on the basement (B1) level. A very cheap sushi place close to the station is *Kirara-zushi* (daily, 11am-2am), a conveyor-belt place where all the fish dishes are ¥90 each. You can fill up here without breaking the bank; it's very popular at lunchtime and in the early evening.

To your left as you take the main shinkansen ticket exit is an *organic juice bar* which serves ice-cold glasses of freshly squeezed vegetable and fruit juices such as carrot and cabbage.

If you're looking for a quick coffee and snack, head outside the station to find a *Pronto* café and coffee shop. Alternatively, there's a branch of *Starbucks* a couple of minutes from the east exit.

Also on the east side of the station, *Michel* (daily, 8am-10pm, early closing on Sun) is a boulangerie, patisserie and brasserie rolled into one. As well as simple food such as omelettes and sandwiches, they do a more elaborate four-course evening set menu including coffee for ¥2800. In the summer the doors are opened and you can sit at tables on the pavement-side terrace outside.

On the 20th floor of Azur Sendai building, a five-minute walk north of the station, are three restaurants under the same management: *Samba Samba* does Latin American food and has live music most nights, *Mojadar* mostly Indian and *Miconos* is Mediterranean; all three serve buffet lunches and are open for lunch 11:30am-2:30pm and in the evening from 5-11pm.

A popular student haunt is the pasta-and-pizza chain *Capricciosa* (daily, 11:30am-11pm) that specializes in enormous portions. It's on the second floor along the covered Clis Rd arcade.

On the 28th and 29th floors of the **SS30 Building** there are several restaurants – from sushi to tonkatsu – with views over the city.

Finally, look out across the city for branches of *Doutor Coffee* and *Pronto*, both of which are great for a quick breakfast. The steal Pronto has over Doutor is that in the evening the coffee shop turns into a pub, with beer on tap and well-priced spirits and cocktails. The transformation works surprisingly well and it's not as smoky as traditional Japanese bars.

Side trip to Yamadera

Some 50km west of Sendai lies Yamadera, a hillside temple founded in 860 by the priest Jikaku Daishi and considered to be of the holiest sights in northern Japan. The temple complex is within easy reach of Sendai, a 50-minute journey by 'rapid' train along the JR Senzan line to Yamadera station.

Once you pass the urban sprawl of Sendai city, the scenery begins to change. Unlike some rural rail routes that tend to be shut in by dense forest, along this line the views open up as the train weaves between the hills and passes from village to village. Yamadera station is small and has mostly ¥300 lockers. There's an overhead walkway from one side of the single-track line to the exit. There is no tourist information in the station but go to the ticket office and ask for a guide to Yamadera.

From the station, follow the signposted route up towards Yamadera (also known as Risshaku-ji), crossing Hoju Bridge. It's a two-minute walk to the entrance. Gates to the temple are open daily (8am-5pm) and admission costs ¥300. Give yourself an hour to climb 'about 1100' steps (it's easy to lose count). Getting to the top is like climbing a very long staircase: there's a handrail but some people buy wooden sticks to help with the climb. There are a few stalls on the way up selling soft drinks and the obligatory souvenirs.

The best views into the valley are from about two-thirds of the way up, at **Godai-do**, a temple built like a stage, which doubles as a useful viewing platform. Your goal at the top is **Okuno-in Temple**, which contains a large golden Buddha.

If you need somewhere to overnight, *Yamadera Pension* (☎ 0236-95 2134, ▤ 95 2240, ▣ yamadera@mmy.ne.jp) is immediately to the left as you leave the station. Don't make the mistake of going past it thinking it must be much further away! All the rooms are Western style with low beds; the staff are friendly and speak some English. It's popular and as there's not much else in Yamadera is often booked up in the summer. Expect to pay around ¥8000 for a room with attached bath/toilet and two meals.

AOMORI

The last major city before Hokkaido, Aomori is best known for its red apples, considered to be the best in Japan, and for Nebuta Matsuri, one of the major summer festivals in Tohoku. Summer is mild but in winter temperatures drop well below freezing and snow becomes a fact of life for months on end.

If visiting in the summer, look out for the phone boxes mounted well above street level with steps leading up to them. In winter, the steps – and sometimes much of the phone box – are buried in snow.

Up until just over a decade ago, all rail travellers bound for Hokkaido had no choice but to stop here in order to transfer on to a passenger ferry for the journey across the Tsugaru Straits. Even though it's possible to travel straight through Aomori by train, it's still worth stopping for at least a day, particularly to visit the museum where some of the summer festival floats are displayed year-round (see Side trip, p320).

What to see and do

A good place to begin a tour of Aomori is at **ASPAM** (Aomori Prefectural Center for Industry and Tourism, 🖥 www.aspm.or.jp), the large triangular building by the port 10 minutes on foot from the station. On the 13th floor there's an observation lounge and on the second floor a panorama theatre where Aomori prefecture is introduced on a 360° screen.

The observation lounge costs ¥400 and the panorama theatre ¥600; a combined ticket is ¥800. Show your Northern Tohoku Welcome Card (see box p53) at the information desk next to the ticket-vending machines on the first floor to receive 50% off these rates.

A five-minute walk from ASPAM, and visible across the water, is the **Memorial Ship** *Hakkoda Maru* (daily, 9am-6pm, ¥500), a former JR-operated ferry that ploughed the water between Aomori and Hakodate for 80 years until it was retired from service in 1987. You can climb aboard, look around and even put on a captain's jacket and cap and pose for photos. The ship has been preserved as it was, except that in the summer there's now a beer garden on the top deck.

Aomori Prefectural Museum (daily except Mon and occasional days, 9:30am-6pm, to 5pm in winter; ¥310) depicts the life of hunters and fishermen in Aomori from the Stone Age onward and has displays of wildlife found in the prefecture and a section devoted to Aomori apples.

There's only a limited amount of English on the signs but a good pamphlet is available. Take a city bus from stop No 4 or 5 outside the station and get off at the Honcho 5-chome stop.

PRACTICAL INFORMATION
Station guide

Aomori station is small with two sides, east and west. The main exit is on the east side. Note that the station will be rebuilt and renamed Shin-Aomori when it becomes the northern terminus for the shinkansen from Hachinohe in 2010.

As you leave the ticket barrier, the JR ticket office (daily, 5:30am-11pm) is on your right. The adjacent View Plaza (Mon-Fri, 10am-6pm, Sat/Sun to 5pm) is the place to make a reservation to stop at Tappi-kaitei station inside the Seikan Tunnel (see box p328).

There are a small number of **coin lockers** (including a couple of ¥500 ones) between the station and the entrance to Lovina department store. Otherwise there is a coin-locker room (daily, 5:30am-12 midnight) with lockers of all sizes on the left as you exit the station.

As you leave the main east exit of the station look out for the Auga shopping, restaurant and library building, though there's a branch of *Doutor Coffee* within the station.

Tourist information

A **tourist information desk** (☎ 0177-23 4670, daily, 9am-5:30pm) is in the bus-terminal office on the left as you exit the station. Staff can advise on accommodation and provide maps and travel information.

Another desk is on the ground floor of **ASPAM** (☎ 0177-34 2500, daily, 9am-10pm). Both places are staffed by English speakers.

Internet

On the 4th floor of the **Auga** Building across the street from the station you'll find computers offering internet access (daily, 10am-9pm; no charge for up to one hour). Enquire at the desk.

Alternatively, there's an internet café on the floor above *Cendrillon* (9:45am-8pm, last orders 7:30pm). The advantage here is that you can surf the web while tucking into a pastry and coffee bought from the patisserie below.

Books

A limited selection of run-of-the-mill American fiction as well as books in English about Japan are available at **Narita Honten**, a bookstore in the centre of town next to Cendrillon (see 'Internet' above).

Getting around

The centre of Aomori is walkable but there is also a network of city buses.

Festivals

Nebuta Matsuri (August 1st-7th) is one of the most popular festivals in Japan. Every night, giant, colourful floats are paraded through the city and on the evening of the final day, a fireworks festival is held in the port area.

The atmosphere of the city changes completely during the festival week. Thousands of visitors arrive from all over Japan, accommodation gets booked solid and even the plastic model of Colonel Sanders, outside the KFC along the main street, gets dressed up in a yukata and festival headgear for the occasion.

Foreign visitors to and residents of Aomori are invited not just to watch but to participate in the Nebuta festivities by dressing up in traditional costume free of charge. For more information contact ☎ 0177-77 5624 or 🖳 www.nebuta.or.jp/english/index-e.htm.

Where to stay

On a side street near the station is *Iroha Ryokan* (☎/🖷 0177-22 8689; ¥4000/pp, cash only), offering tatami rooms but no attached bath/toilet or meals. It's a small place and gets booked up quickly.

Convenient for the station is *Hotel Route Inn Aomori* (☎ 0177-31 3611, 🖳 www.route-inn.co.jp; ¥6000/S, ¥11,550/D, ¥12,600/Tw). It's clean, modern and very good value. The buffet breakfast costs ¥800.

Also near the station is *Toyoko Inn Aomori-eki Shomen-guchi* (☎ 017-735 1045, 🖳 www.toyoko-inn.com; ¥6090/S, ¥8190/D/Tw) which opened in 2007.

A popular upmarket choice is *Hotel JAL City* (☎ 0177-32 2580, 🖳 http://aomori.jalcity.co.jp; ¥9400/S, ¥12,700/D, ¥16,100/Tw), with an elegant lobby and large rooms, close to the ASPAM building.

Aomori Plaza Hotel (☎ 0177-75 4311, 🖳 www.imgnjp.com/ao_pla) has single rooms with wide beds for ¥5500 and twins at ¥10,000 including breakfast. It's a ten-minute walk up Shinmachi-dori from the station.

Hyper Hotel Aomori (☎ 0177-73 3000, 🖳 www.hyperhotel.co.jp) is similar but has an automated check-in (cash only). Regular rooms (¥5040) are singles but family rooms (¥6090) sleep two adults and a child. Rates include breakfast and there's also a coin laundry.

It's a 15- to 20-minute walk from the station up Shinmachi-dori. Look for the distinctive yellow/gold building with British, French and Australian flags flying outside the European façade.

Another popular budget option where the rate includes breakfast is *Super Hotel Aomori* (☎ 0177-23 9000, 🖳 www.super hotel.co.jp; ¥4980/S, ¥6980/D). It's a bit of a hike across town but worth the effort.

Where to eat and drink

For a quick packed lunch, the ground floor of the **Lovina** department store has a branch of the *Vie de France bakery* and attached *café*. You'll also find a branch of the tonkatsu-chain, Saboten, which offers sit-down meals and takeaway lunch boxes.

The basement of **Auga** (across the street from the station) has a fresh-fish market (5am-6:30pm). Sushi is naturally on offer at a couple of restaurants adjacent to the market area. Unsurprisingly there is an overwhelming smell of fish, so it's not a place to linger over a slow meal.

An all-you-can-eat buffet lunch (daily, 11:30am-2pm) is on offer at *Orie* on the ground floor inside the Post Office PaRuRu Plaza building; there is also a small post office branch here with an ATM. The ¥800 buffet deal (¥1000 at weekends) includes unlimited soft drinks, tea and coffee.

Masala Masala (Tue-Sun, 11:30am-3pm, 5-8pm), specializing in Indian curries, is tucked away on a quiet street a couple of minutes from the station. It has various set menus (¥600 to ¥1000+), depending on whether your dish comes with trimmings and side dishes or not. Take-away meals are also available. The curries are not overly spicy (they have to suit the Japanese palate!) and the place has a pleasant laid-back feel. Look for the yellow sign with red letters. It's a distinctive green and red building.

Saigon (daily, 11:30am-2:30pm, 5:30pm-midnight) is a small, wooden-table restaurant which does an excellent take on Vietnamese, Thai and Indonesian dishes. It's close to Hotel JAL City. The set lunch at ¥700 is recommended, as is the spicy Thai Red curry (¥750). The Vietnamese chicken curry is also good. It's easy to find because there's an English sign outside.

A branch of the Italian chain *Capricciosa*, serving full- and half-size portions of pizza and pasta, is 12 minutes on foot from the station's east exit along Shinmachi-dori. It's on the corner of a major junction; look for the red, white and green veranda.

There are several restaurants in the **ASPAM** building down by the port. On the 14th floor, *Quarterly* (lunch 11am-2pm) is a modern place serving a mix of European and Asian cuisine. Local ingredients are used wherever possible and – as the name of the place suggests – the menu changes according to the season. It describes itself as the 'best restaurant in Aomori' – it's certainly not the cheapest (lunch from ¥1500), but the food is good, as are the views. Don't leave without trying one of the desserts – the chocolate banana cake with vanilla ice cream is to die for.

On the 10th floor, *Nishimura*, a casual Japanese restaurant with low wooden tables, specializes in local fish dishes.

Close to ASPAM is *La Sera* (the restaurant inside Hotel JAL City), which does excellent-value set lunches with soup, salad bar, main course of the day, dessert and coffee for around ¥1000. It's open for lunch 11am-2:30pm, dinner 5:30-9pm and 'pub time' (beer on tap) 9-11pm.

For a decadent treat, try *Strauss*, on a side road close to Vivre department store. Downstairs is a cake shop, but upstairs is a very smart café where waitresses in 1920s-style black and white uniforms serve slices of rich cake and various coffees.

It's as near as you'll get to Vienna in Tohoku – the detail's there right down to the chandeliers and fireplace. There's no better place to escape a freezing Aomori winter than here with a hot chocolate and apple strudel.

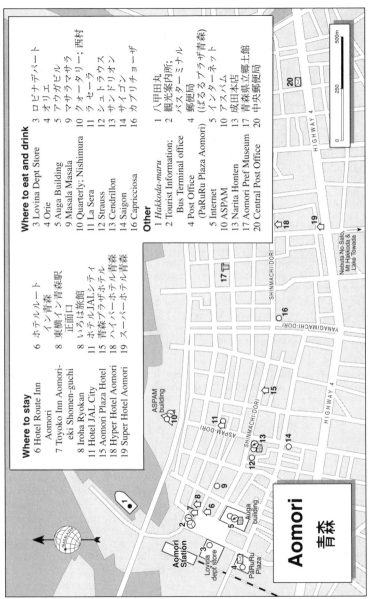

Aomori

青森

Where to stay

6 Hotel Route Inn Aomori — ホテルルート イン青森
7 Toyoko Inn Aomori-eki Shomen-guchi — 東横イン青森駅 正面口
8 Iroha Ryokan — いろは旅館
11 Hotel JAL City — ホテルJALシティ
15 Aomori Plaza Hotel — 青森プラザホテル
18 Hyper Hotel Aomori — ハイパーホテル青森
19 Super Hotel Aomori — スーパーホテル青森

Where to eat and drink

3 Lovina Dept Store — ロビナデパート
4 Orie — オリエ
5 Auga Building — アウガビル
9 Masala Masala — マサラマサラ
10 Quarterly; Nishimura — クォータリー; 西村
11 La Sera — ラ セーラ
12 Strauss — シュトラウス
13 Cendrillon — サンドリオン
14 Saigon — サイゴン
16 Capricciosa — カプリチョーザ

Other

1 Hakkoda-maru — 八甲田丸
2 Tourist Information; Bus Terminal office — 観光案内所; バスターミナル
4 Post Office (PaRuRu Plaza Aomori) — 郵便局 (ぱるるプラザ青森)
5 Internet — インターネット
10 ASPAM — アスパム
13 Narita Honten — 成田本店
17 Aomori Pref Museum — 青森県立郷土館
20 Central Post Office — 中央郵便局

HONSHU

Side trip from Aomori

Thirty minutes by bus (¥450) from Aomori station is **Nebuta no Sato** (🖳 www
.nebutanosato.co.jp, daily, 9am-5:30pm, until 8pm in summer, ¥630). The
route is operated by JR Bus and is free to rail-pass holders.

It's a huge indoor space displaying several of the colourful floats used in
Aomori's summer festival. Four times a day there's a show that introduces
some of the flavour of the festival, with performers on stage playing the flute
and drums, and visitors pulling one of the floats a few metres along inside the
hall. The floats are incredibly heavy; just pulling them along for a few metres
makes you wonder how participants manage to do it for two hours during the
festival.

The bus for Nebuta no Sato leaves from one of the stops outside Aomori
station (ask at the tourist information desk inside the bus terminal ticket office
for departure times). Get off at 'Nebuta no Sato Iriguchi'. A visit here can be
combined with the route from Aomori described on p298.

NIIGATA

Niigata is the largest city on the Japan Sea coast and was one of the first ports
to open to foreign trade when Japan reopened to the outside world in 1869 after
nearly 230 years of self-imposed seclusion.

Visitors are put off spending time here – most press on without delay to
nearby Sado Island – because it is a major industrial city. But it's difficult to
write the place off as just another identikit Japanese city when it's home to a
huge performing arts centre, a coastal area, quiet back streets and any number
of shopping and dining opportunities.

Winters here are cold (the average temperature in January is 2.1°C) but
summers tend to be hot and humid.

What to see and do

A good place to start is across Showa Ohashi bridge, on the other side of the city
to the station, at **Hakusan Park** inside which is **Hakusan Shrine**. A place of
worship for more than 400 years, the shrine is frequently visited by couples
seeking the support of a god of marriage enshrined here.

From the shrine walk through Hakusan Park, passing by the large lotus
pond. Though the park is not big, it's a welcome escape from the noise of the
city.

Also within the grounds of the park, but entered from a street just outside,
is **Enkikan** (daily except 1st and 3rd Mon, 9am-5pm, free), an old merchant
home that has been moved here and transformed into a house for traditional
Japanese arts such as tea ceremony and flower arranging (see p46). Though
modern, it's a beautiful example of a traditional Japanese house and there's no
charge to look around and enjoy the view of the lotus pond.

For ¥300 you'll be served a cup of Japanese tea in one of the tatami rooms.
To reach Hakusan Park, take the tourist shuttle bus operating on the 'Hakusan
Park' route. The park is the sixth stop from Niigata station.

⛩ Chuetsu earthquake

On October 23, 2004, Niigata was hit by a devastating earthquake, the worst to strike Japan since the Great Hanshin Quake of 1995 in the port city of Kobe (see p250). The Chuetsu Quake, as it became known, claimed the lives of 40 people, left some 3000 injured and thousands more homeless. It caused the first ever bullet-train accident, when eight of the ten carriages of a Joetsu shinkansen derailed near Nagaoka. No serious injuries were reported.

The 6.8-magnitude quake also killed more than a million *koi* (carp), which are widely bred in Niigata prefecture. Many of the breeding ponds were destroyed and a campaign was launched to raise funds to help save the surviving fish. Officials claimed that 40% of the koi stock perished in the quake. At one point a helicopter was even chartered to rescue some of the fish from damaged ponds cut off by road.

Walking through the park and leaving the other side you'll come to the **Prefectural Government Memorial Hall** (Tue-Sun, 9am-4:30pm, free) which dates back to 1883. Used as the prefectural parliament for 50 years it was apparently constructed in the same style as the Houses of Parliament in London, with Shinano-gawa in place of the Thames.

Around the walls of the assembly hall look out for some old photos of assembly delegates. It's interesting to note how the dress code has changed. In a group shot dated 1911 almost all the delegates are in traditional Japanese clothes. By 1931 the vast majority were in Western-style suits.

Leaving the hall, look out for the huge, modern building that is the **Performing Arts Center**, also known as **Ryutopia**. Opened in 1998, the total construction cost is speculated to have been in the region of ¥26,600,000,000. What the citizens of Niigata got for their money was an enormous concert hall, theatre and separate Noh stage. It's a world-class facility and attracts international orchestras, theatre troupes and singers.

Tickets can be purchased from the box office in the foyer, though you might want to check what's on with the English-speaking staff at the tourist office outside the station.

From here, it's an easy 10-minute walk to the central shopping area of **Furumachi**, where you'll find plenty of places for lunch. For a (free) bird's eye view of the city, the sea and on a clear day Sado Island, head for the 19th floor of the **Next 21 Building** (daily, 8am-11:30pm), a landmark that's easy to spot because it's shaped like a pencil.

Heading back towards the station, cross over Bandai Bridge and go straight. As you return towards the station, you'll see the **Rainbow Tower** (daily except 2nd Wed/Thur in March, June, Sept and Dec, 10am-6pm, 10am-9pm July/Aug; ¥450 or ¥400 with the one-day shuttle-bus pass), on your right after crossing Bandai Bridge. However, it's not worth the expense when you can get a free view from the Next 21 Building – or even better, from the 31st-floor free **observation gallery** inside Hotel Nikko Niigata (daily, 8am-10pm; see opposite), the

HONSHU

highest viewing point on the Japan Sea coast. The gallery is accessed via a dedicated express elevator from the first (ie ground) floor. On a clear day there are good views out towards Sado Island.

On the fifth floor of the Hotel Nikko Niigata building is **Niigata Bandaijima Art Museum** (☎ 025-290 6655, 🖥 www.lalanet.gr.jp/banbi, Tue-Sun, 10am-6pm; ¥300 or ¥240 with one-day shuttle-bus pass), a modern gallery space with a small permanent collection including a 1970 Andy Warhol painting. Temporary exhibitions incur additional charges. Take the shuttle bus operating on the 'Toki Messe' route. Hotel Nikko Niigata is the third stop from the station.

If the weather is cooperating, there can be no better way of seeing Niigata than on a relaxed cruise along the Shinano River. Ferries plough the water on a daily basis, stopping at various embarkation/disembarkation points along the way. Riding the full length of the **Shinanogawa Water Shuttle** (☎ 025-227 5200, 🖥 www.watershuttle.co.jp) takes just under one hour and costs ¥950 one-way. A sunset cruise departs daily from Toki Messe (site of the convention centre which includes Hotel Nikko Niigata) and costs ¥1500. Check the website or ask at the tourist information office for times.

Particularly in the summer, a good mini-escape from the city is down by the coast in the area around **Niigata City Aquarium**, also known as **Marinepia Nihonkai**. The aquarium (🖥 www.marinepia.or.jp, daily 9am-5pm, to 6pm late July to August, ¥1500 or ¥1200 with the one-day shuttle-bus pass) with its sea lions, penguins and dolphin shows (4/5 times per day) is mainly of interest to children but the seafront area is a good place for a stroll.

Near the aquarium are the Sea West restaurant/shopping blocks, numbered 1-3. *Popolo Gelateria* in Sea West 3 is open year-round and definitely worth seeking out as it serves probably the best hand-made ice cream anywhere in Japan. Down here, and with trees covering the concrete blocks behind, it's hard to believe you're in a major industrial city.

Finally, don't miss **Gokoku Shrine**, surrounded by pine trees, just a couple of minutes from the aquarium. It was built in 1945 to console the souls of the war dead.

To reach this area, take either of the tourist shuttle buses. Both services stop outside the aquarium. Instead of taking the bus back to the station, it's a very pleasant walk back into the city through quiet backstreets filled with old wooden houses and privately owned craft shops. It's a complete contrast to the bustling Furumachi shopping district.

PRACTICAL INFORMATION
Station guide

Niigata is the terminus for the Joetsu shinkansen to/from Tokyo. The station is divided into the shinkansen side and regular JR lines side. For the city centre, follow signs for the Bandai exit. A passageway connects both sides, though access is only via stairs/escalator. The shinkansen side has the most shops and restaurants. Coin lockers are available on both sides.

The main rail lines are the shinkansen line, the local Echigo line to Yoshida, the Shinetsu line to Nagano via Naoetsu, the Joetsu line to Ueno and the Uetsu line that runs north to Murakami and Akita.

Tourist information

A **tourist information centre** (☎ 025-241 7914, daily, 8:30am-5:15pm) is to the left as you take the main Bandai exit. The staff here speak English, have information about ferries to Sado Island and can book same-day city accommodation. Pick up a copy of the monthly *Niigata English Journal*, which contains restaurant reviews and listings for concerts, exhibitions and movies.

English speakers are also on hand at **Niigata International Friendship Centre**, also known as the International Exchange Foundation (☎ 025-225 2777, 🖳 www .pavc.ne.jp/~nigtief, daily except 4th Mon of month, 9am-9:30pm), in a modern building called CrossPal Niigata, 20 minutes on foot from the station. The centre is stocked with newspapers, has satellite TV and can supply excellent walking maps of the Bandai and Furumachi areas in Niigata.

Getting around

The central point for crossing over Shinano-gawa is Bandai Bridge. It's easy enough to walk around central Niigata but all city buses depart from the bus terminal outside the Bandai exit of the station. A flat fare of ¥180 operates within the city. There are also two tourist shuttle buses which operate on different circular routes around the city. Both services start and finish outside Niigata station. Individual tickets are ¥150 or a one-day pass costs ¥500. The one-day pass also offers small discounts at many tourist facilities in the city. An alternative means of transportation is the water shuttle (see opposite).

Niigata is a major international gateway for flights to/from Russia. Scheduled services operate to Vladivostok (for connections to the Trans-Siberian Railway) and a number of other destinations. A limousine bus to Niigata airport (¥350 one way) departs from bus stop No 11 at the bus terminal outside the station.

Internet

You can surf the web for up to 30 minutes a day free of charge at an internet café called **Internet Banana** (daily, 11am-7pm) inside the waiting room to your left as you leave

the Bandai ticket barrier (coming from the platforms). Registration is quite a complicated procedure; you need to sign in at the desk, will be given a 'Banana Passport', and will then be assigned a computer. This place is usually very busy and strict time limits are enforced. Open daily, but hours vary.

Festivals

Niigata Matsuri runs from August 7th to 9th. This started as a festival to pray for the prosperity of the port and growth of the city; it still involves a procession and folk dancing over Bandai Bridge (on the 8th) and ends with a huge fireworks display over Shinano-gawa on the evening of the 9th.

Where to stay

Five minutes on foot north of the station is *Dormy Inn Niigata* (☎ 025-247 7755, 🖳 www.hotespa.net/hotels.niigata, 🖳 in-niigata@dormy-hotels.com; ¥5775/S) and its newer annex. Both are good bets for basic business hotel accommodation. Clean, efficiently run and the hotel even boasts its own onsen. Breakfast is an additional ¥840.

A little further down Akashi-dori is another good budget place, *Super Hotel Niigata* (☎ 025-247 9000, 🖳 www.super-hotel.co.jp), where singles with continental breakfast go for ¥4980, doubles for ¥6980 and twins for ¥8800.

A new addition to the business-hotel scene is *Country Hotel Niigata* (☎ 025-229 3300, 🖳 www.niigata-c.jp; ¥6300/S, ¥11,000/Tw), on the other side of town past Shinano-gawa. If you can spare the extra yen, go for one of the 'deluxe singles' at ¥6800, which come with flat-screen TVs.

A new addition to the top end of the market is the luxury *Hotel Nikko Niigata* (☎ 025-241 0808, 🖳 www.hotelnikkoniigata.jp; ¥11,550/S, ¥18,480/D/Tw), opened as the centrepiece of a redeveloped harbour area which includes the Toki Messe international convention centre. The tallest hotel on the Japan Sea coast enjoys a superb waterfront location set back from the city centre. The rooms are spacious and there's a choice of restaurants.

Closer to the railway station is *Hotel Leopalace Niigata* (☎ 025-249 8100, 🖳

www.leopalacehotels.jp, niigata_hotel@leo
palace21.com; ¥7400/S, ¥12,000/D,
¥13,800/Tw), a good mid-range choice.

Opposite the Bandai exit of the station
is **Niigata Tokyu Inn** (☎ 025-243 0109, 🖳
www.tokyuhotels.co.jp), with singles from
¥6825, twins and doubles from ¥11,550.
Expect rates to fall by about ¥1000 between
December and the end of March. Some of
the rooms are women-only, with extra
amenities including humidifier, face lotion,
brush and hair band.

Even closer to the station is **Toyoko
Inn Niigata Ekimae** (☎ 025-241 1045, 🖳
www.toyoko-inn.com; ¥6090/S, ¥8610/D
/Tw), immediately on your right as you take
the Bandai exit. Reception is on the fourth
floor.

Where to eat and drink
On the shinkansen side of the station is the
PATIO restaurant/shopping area with
coffee shops, a bakery, a cheap revolving
sushi restaurant and a Chinese restaurant

NIIGATA　新潟

Where to stay

10 Country Hotel Niigata	10 カントリーホテル新潟
13 Hotel Nikko Niigata	13 ホテル日航新潟
17 Niigata Tokyu Inn	17 新潟東急イン
20 Toyoko Inn Niigata Ekimae	20 東横イン 新潟駅前
23 Hotel Leopalace Niigata	23 ホテルレオパレス新潟
24 Dormy Inn Niigata	24 ドーミーイン新潟
25 Super Hotel Niigata	25 スーパーホテル

Where to eat and drink

2 Popolo Gelateria	2 ポポロジェラテリア
7 Rivage	7 リヴァージュ
9 Essa	9 越佐
13 Serena	13 セリーナ
20 Royal Host	20 ロイヤルホスト
21 Immigrant's Café	21 イミグランツカフェ

Other

1 Niigata City Aquarium Marinepia Nihonkai	1 新潟市水族館/マリンピア日本海
3 Gokoku Shrine	3 護国神社
4 Hakusan Shrine/Park	4 白山神社/白山公園
5 Enkikan	5 燕喜館
6 Prefectural Govt Memorial Hall	6 県政記念館
7 Performing Arts Center/Ryutopia	7 新潟市民芸術文化会館
8 Next 21 Building	8 Next 21ビル
11 Niigata International Friendship; Center; CrossPal Niigata	11 新潟国際友好会館;（クロスパル新潟）
12 Shinanogawa Water Shuttle	12 信濃川ウォーターシャトル
13 Niigata Bandaijima Art Museum	13 新潟市万代島美術館
14 Niigata Ferry Terminal	14 新潟フェリーターミナル
15 Niigata Port International Passenger Terminal	15 新潟港国際旅館ターミナル
16 Rainbow Tower	16 レインボータワー
18 Tourist Information Center	18 観光案内センター
19 Internet Banana	19 インターネットバナナ
22 Central Post Office	22 中央郵便局

HONSHU

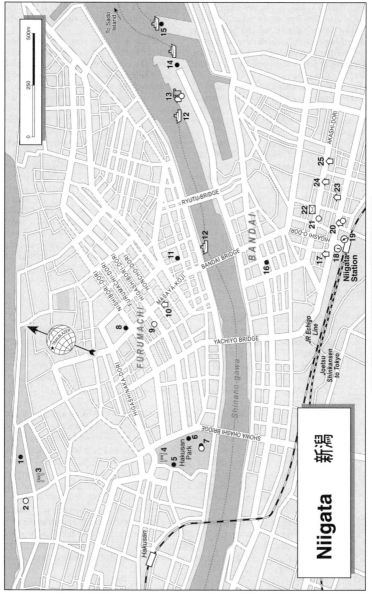

Niigata

新潟

To Sado Island

15
14
13
12

RYUTU-BRIDGE

25
24
23
22
21
20
19
Niigata Station

18
17
16

BANDAI

BANDAI BRIDGE

12
11

NISHIBORI-DORI
FURUMACHI-DORI
HIGASHIBORI-DORI
HONCHO-DORI

MASAYA-KOJI
10
9
8

AKASHI-DORI

HIGASHI-O-DORI

IWABLAZER

FURUMACHI

YACHIYO BRIDGE

Shinano-gawa

HIGASHINAKA-DORI

JR Echigo Line

Joetsu Shinkansen to Tokyo

SHOWA OHASHI BRIDGE

1
2
3
4
5
6
7

Hakusan Park

Hakusan

HONSHU

500m
250
0

that does a range of lunches from ¥650-800. If you're looking for casual family-restaurant-style dining, look no further than *Royal Host* (daily, 24-hour opening) on the ground floor to your right as you take the Bandai exit (in the same building as Toyoko Inn Niigata Ekimae).

An unusual dining experience is to be had at *Essa*, on a corner of the WITH building along Higashibori-dori (look for the moving crab on the wall outside). This is the place to go for seafood; you eat at the counter around a big pool where the staff go and fish your food so you know your meal is going to be fresh. It's pricey in the evenings but at lunchtime (11am-2pm) the ¥1200 set meal is a feast. The crab on the outside of the building is actually a sign for the crab restaurant on the eighth floor. For Essa, take the stairs down to the basement.

Rivage (daily 11:30am-2:30pm and 5-10pm) is a stylish restaurant on the third floor of the Performing Arts Center; it is a quiet place to go for lunch with tables overlooking Shinano-gawa – and is especially good in spring when the cherry blossoms

are out. A set lunch with starter, main course, small dessert and coffee costs ¥1200.

If you're in the harbour area it's worth taking in lunch at *Serena*, a modern all-day dining place on the third floor of Hotel Nikko Niigata where there are spectacular panoramic waterfront views through the bay windows. Buffet lunches and set meals are good value; lunch (11:30am-2pm) costs from ¥1800 and dinner (5:30-9pm) from ¥2500.

A popular haunt is *Immigrant's Café* (11am-3pm, 5pm-late), along Akashi-dori just across from the central post office, five minutes on foot from the station. It's popular with Niigata's foreign community as the staff (Japanese and foreign) all speak English. It offers a great selection of ethnic food (everything from oriental rack of lamb to Indonesian fried rice) and more predictable bar snacks in this split-level café, where most dishes are under ¥1000 and there are regular happy hours. For the menu and details of DJ nights and other events, see 🖥 www.immigrantscafe.com.

Side trips from Niigata

The most popular trip is to **Sado Island**, once a place of exile and now home to the world-famous Kodo drummers (🖥 www.kodo.or.jp). Ferries and jet foils depart from Niigata Port. The ferry crossing takes 2 hours 20 minutes (🖥 www.sadokisen.co.jp; ¥2060 one-way). The jet foil takes only one hour but is more expensive (¥5960 one-way, ¥10,730 return). To reach **Sado Ferry Terminal**, take a bus from stop No 6 outside the station and get off at Sado Kisen, the last stop.

An alternative side trip by rail could be made to **Mikawa**, some 46km from Niigata along the local Banetsu-sei line (you may need to change at Niitsu). Here, you can take a gentle boat cruise down Agano-gawa, the tenth longest river in Japan. Head out of Mikawa station and turn left on to the main road. Walk for about five minutes and the entrance for the boat cruise is on the right, just above the river. Cruises (¥2500, 50 mins) leave every hour on the hour from 9am to 4pm. There's a chance of seeing wild deer and monkeys along this scenic route, which is especially beautiful in winter when snow covers the mountains; the river itself doesn't freeze over, so cruises run year-round as long as the weather is reasonable. Free shuttle buses are provided at the end of the cruise (in Iwama), 13km further down Agano-gawa, to take you back to the start point, from where you can pick up the train. In winter call ahead (☎ 02549-92822) to check if cruises have been cancelled because of inclement weather.

PART 6: HOKKAIDO

Hokkaido – route guide

The northernmost of the major islands in the Japanese archipelago, Hokkaido represents one-fifth of the country's land mass but is inhabited by only one-twentieth of the total population. The island is the largest of Japan's 47 prefectures and is bordered by the Sea of Japan to the west, the Sea of Okhotsk to the north-east and the Pacific Ocean to the south.

Hokkaido is an island of stunning natural beauty, vast national parks with mountain ranges, volcanoes, forests, rivers, crashing waterfalls, wildlife ... and tourists. In the summer months, bikers, backpackers and cyclists descend on the island to feel what it is like to drive on the open road, unclogged by pollution, noise and urban development. Others come to escape the oppressive heat and humidity found elsewhere in Japan, to see cows, taste fresh Hokkaido milk, yoghurt and even Camembert-style cheese. In winter, when temperatures plummet and snow falls for months on end, skiers pour on to the slopes.

The bad news for the rail traveller is that parts of the Hokkaido network have closed in the last few decades. Spiralling costs, few passengers on remote lines and the difficulty of track maintenance in areas particularly exposed to the elements mean that some parts are no longer accessible by rail. But enough of the rail network remains to provide more than a glimpse of the spectacular natural environment.

You'll be travelling on mostly rural lines, so don't expect lightning-fast services, but few other places in Japan offer such breathtaking scenery from the train window.

INTRODUCTION

Aomori (see p316), on the tip of northern Honshu, is the rail gateway to Hokkaido. The route in this chapter follows a loop around Hokkaido, starting and finishing in Aomori. Three weeks would be enough to enjoy the island without feeling rushed.

For a shorter 'taste' of what the island has to offer, the line between Abashiri and Kushiro (see pp341-6) has some of the most impressive scenery. Since it's away from the major tourist areas, most visitors never make it this far but the views more than repay the distance and effort.

早稲の香や分け入る右は荒磯海

Through fragrant fields of early rice we went beside the wild Ariso Sea
(MATSUO BASHO)

⛩ **Tunnel vision**
The Seikan Tunnel (53.85km), under the Tsugaru Straits between Honshu and Hokkaido, is the longest underwater tunnel in the world. It was built as straight as possible in anticipation of the day (still some years away) that shinkansen trains would run through it. Though not recommended for claustrophobics, it's possible to go on a behind-the-scenes tour. If nothing else, there's the chance to make a call from public phones installed at the lowest point in Japan.

Coming from Aomori, the undersea stop is at **Tappi-Kaitei (64km)**. Here you are met by a guide who walks you through the service tunnel to a cable car which provides a scary journey up to the surface at Cape Tappi, the very tip of Honshu. There's a small tunnel museum here but there's also time to walk over to the cape from where there are great views of Hokkaido across the Tsugaru Straits. After a quick look around the museum, it's time to take the cable car back down to the underground station and pick up the train. Tickets for the cable car/tunnel museum are ¥2040 for adults, ¥1020 for children (rail passes are not valid).

A second stop in the tunnel, at **Yoshioka-Kaitei (87km)**, closed in 2006 to provide storage space for construction materials for the Hokkaido shinkansen.

Reservations to stop at Tappi-kaitei should be made in advance at Aomori or Hakodate stations since only a limited number of Hakucho LEX services stop there. Times vary depending on the time of year so check at any JR ticket office. Luggage can be stored in an underground locker for the duration of the tour. After the tour another Hakucho LEX picks you up from the underground station and continues on to Aomori or Hakodate.

AOMORI TO HAKODATE   [Map 21, p330; Table 16, p466]

Distances by JR from Aomori. Fastest journey time: 2 hours.

Aomori (0km)   [see pp316-20]

From Aomori, take the Hakucho or Super-Hakucho LEX along the Tsugaru Kaikyo line bound for Hakodate. The Green Car on these services has smart, wide blue leather seats with an in-seat laptop power supply. At the front of the carriage (in both classes) a graphic shows how far into the tunnel the train is. In the days before the Seikan Tunnel (see box above) the journey took 3 hours 40 minutes; it now takes just under two hours.

HOKKAIDO

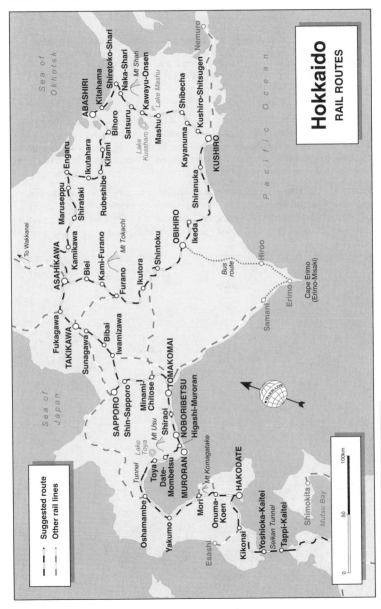

Hokkaido
RAIL ROUTES

Sea of Okhotsk

Pacific Ocean

Sea of Japan

Nemuro
Shiretoko-Shari
Kitahama
Naka-Shari
Mt Shari
ABASHIRI
Kawayu-Onsen
Bihoro
Lake Mashu
Satsuru
Shibecha
Engaru
Kitami
Mashu
Kushiro-Shitsugen
Ikutahara
Rubeshibe
Lake Kussharo
Maruseppu
Kayanuma
KUSHIRO
Shirataki
Kamikawa
Mt Tokachi
Shiranuka
Bihoro
Kami-Furano
Shintoku
ASAHIKAWA
Biei
OBIHIRO
Furano
Ikeda
Fukagawa
Ikutora
Iwamizawa
TAKIKAWA
Bibai
Sunagawa
Hiroo
Bus route
Cape Erimo (Erimo-Misaki)
Erimo
Minami-Chitose
Samani
SAPPORO
TOMAKOMAI
Shin-Sapporo
Shiraoi
Mt Usu
NOBORIBETSU
Higashi-Muroran
Lake Toya
Toya
Date-Mombetsu
MURORAN
Oshamambe
Mt Komagatake
Mori
HAKODATE
Yakumo
Onuma-Koen
Yoshioka-Kaitei
Shimokita
Seikan Tunnel
Kikonai
Tappi-Kaitei
Mutsu Bay
Esashi
Tunnel

To Wakkanai

- Suggested route
- Other rail lines

100km
50
0

HOKKAIDO

Leaving Aomori the line runs slightly inland from the coast on the journey
to Tsugaru Peninsula, so the views are better from the left side of the train,
where there are long stretches of rice fields. Towards the edge of the peninsula,
the train passes through several tunnels, easing passengers gently into the long
journey underground through the Seikan Tunnel.

Kikonai (119km) The first stop in Hokkaido after emerging from the tunnel,
unless you are on one of the few limited expresses which do not stop here.

Just as you begin to take in the Hokkaido scenery, the train abruptly plunges
into a series of tunnels. Once past these, sit on the right side for views over the

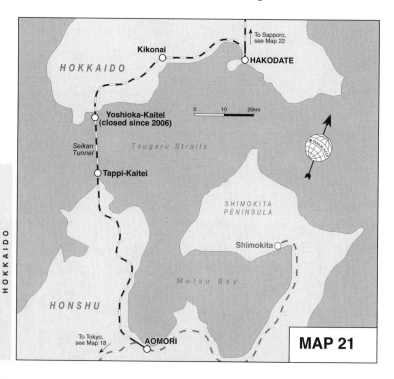

MAP 21

To Sapporo, see Map 22

To Tokyo, see Map 18

Tsugaru Straits and, in the distance, the tip of Shimokita Peninsula on Honshu. The train runs much closer to the coast than it does on the journey from Aomori and the views out to sea are superb. About 20 minutes before arriving in Hakodate you will see (or rather, should try to avoid) the large cement factory on the right that spoils the view.

Hakodate (160km) [see pp350-6]
Hakodate is the terminus for limited expresses from Aomori.

HAKODATE TO SAPPORO [Map 22, p333; Table 19, p467]

Distances by JR from Hakodate. Fastest journey time: 3 hours.

Hakodate (0km) The quickest way to Sapporo is along the Hakodate line on the Hokuto or slightly faster Super Hokuto LEX. The Green Car seating configuration is 1x2 and standard-class accommodation is 2x2. Free drinks in the Green Car are served in 'Twinkle Lady' cups.

Some trains stop at **Goryokaku (3km)**, see p351.

Onuma-Koen (27km) Not all limited expresses stop here. A few minutes before arriving at the station (around 20 minutes after leaving Hakodate), look out to the left for views of Lake Konuma, with its tiny islands scattered across the water.

One of the most beautiful, if foreboding, natural backdrops you're likely to come across in Japan is **Mt Komagatake**; it last erupted in a big way in 1640 when it killed more than 700 people. A minor eruption in 2000, which saw nearby areas covered in ash, proved that though Komagatake was dormant it is by no means extinct. There are hiking trails around the volcano, but you may prefer to admire the jagged peak from the safe distance of the lakes. Lake Onuma and two smaller lakes, Konuma and Junsainuma, were created when debris from an eruption of Komagatake settled as a natural dam.

To the right as you exit the small station (there are a few ¥400 coin lockers) is Onuma International Communication Plaza, a wooden building with a glass front, where there's a **tourist information counter** (☎ 0138-67 2170, 🖥 www .onumakouen.com, daily 8:30am-5pm) staffed by an English speaker.

Between April and November, motor boats, paddle boats (¥1000/30 mins) and canoes can be hired on the lakes. Alternatively, pleasure boats do 30-minute

⛩ **Japan's forgotten people**
   Hokkaido was colonized by the Japanese only in the middle of the 18th century; prior to that it was known as Ezo and was almost exclusively inhabited by the Ainu, an indigenous population who all but disappeared as more and more Japanese moved north from Honshu. In recent years there have been efforts to revive the Ainu culture and its traditions. But following decades when the Tokyo government barely acknowledged its existence it may now be too late to save one of the world's least-known aboriginal cultures; for more information on the Ainu, see the box on p366.

tours of Lake Onuma for ¥960. The best way of seeing the lakes and taking in the spectacular surrounding scenery is to hire a bike. There are rental places in the station area, the most obvious being Friendly Bear, opposite the station. Bikes cost ¥500 an hour or ¥1000 for the day. In winter the lakes freeze over and holes are cut in the ice for fishing.

Onuma Koen Youth Hostel (☎/📠 0138-67 4126, 🖥 http://homepage2.nifty .com/ONUMAKOEN-YH/English.htm) is a small, friendly hostel set back from Lake Onuma offering pension-style 2- and 3-bed rooms at ¥3300/4300 per person. Breakfast costs ¥630 and dinner ¥1050. The evening meal especially is a real feast. Cycles can be rented here for ¥500 per day. The only drawback is that the hostel is a good 30-minute walk from Onuma-Koen station, directly up the main road that runs alongside the lake. Alternatively, take a local train one stop back down the line towards Hakodate to Onuma station, from where you should change on to the Sawara line and go one stop to Ikeda-en station. At Ikeda-en, follow the grass path that leads off from the platform, rather than the overhead walkway. Turn left when you reach the surfaced path; at the end of that turn right and go straight until you see a wooden house on your left. Look for the JYH sign by the door.

If you prefer a more luxurious overnight stay, try *Crawford Inn Onuma* (☎ 0138-67 2964, 🖥 www.hopp.co.jp/crawford; from ¥9975/person including dinner and breakfast), a resort hotel three minutes on foot from Onuma-Koen station. Ask the tourist information office to point you in the right direction. Rail fans should note that this hotel is named after Joseph Crawford, a professor of engineering who introduced the technology used on American railways to Hokkaido in the 19th century.

For proximity to the station (right next to it!) *Station Hotel Asahiya* (☎ 0138-67 2654, 🖥 http://business2.plala.or.jp/asahiya, asahiyah@rainbow.plala .or.jp; ¥6300/S, ¥7600/Tw) can't be beaten. Rates rise slightly during the peak summer season. There's a reasonable in-house restaurant.

A 20-minute walk up the road from Onuma Koen Youth Hostel brings you to a viewing spot over the lake with Mt Komagatake reflected in the calm water. It's a great place to visit around dusk, when you can watch the sun set over the lake. If you're not eating at the hostel, try the *Lumber House* (Tue-Sun, 11am-7:30pm) in the log hut just a couple of minutes further up the road from the hostel. The speciality is steaks (steak with fries ¥2500) but hamburgers (¥800) and pizza (¥1000) are also served; Budweiser is on tap.

Mori (50km) As the train leaves Onuma-Koen, look right then left as the line passes between Lake Onuma (on the right) and the smaller Lake Konuma (on the left). It's a fleeting but superb last view of the two lakes. Soon enough, the line becomes enclosed by trees. Fittingly, it would seem, the next stop (not all limited expresses call here) is called Mori (forest). Just before the station the train passes right by the sea. Mori, despite its name, is actually situated on the coast. The sudden change from lakes and mountains to dense forest and coast is proof of the amazing scenic variety Hokkaido has to offer. The Hakodate-Onuma SL runs between Hakodate and here, for more details see box p78.

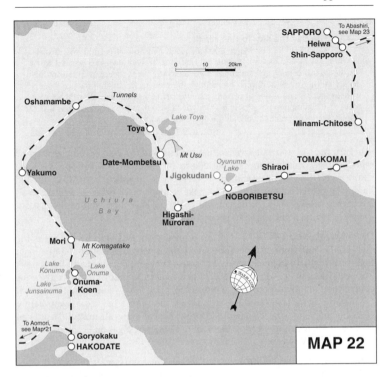

MAP 22

After leaving Mori the line begins to curve around Uchiura Bay. The track runs so close to the sea that you can see the different shades of blue in the water.

Yakumo (81km) Not all limited expresses stop here. The train runs further from the sea along this stretch of the line but look out to the left for views of the rolling green hills that are always featured on Japanese TV adverts for Hokkaido milk.

Oshamambe (112km) Not all limited expresses stop here. There is a long section of tunnels between Oshamambe and Toya, the next major stop along the line. About 15 minutes after the train leaves Oshamambe, just after emerging from another tunnel, look out to the right for a sweeping view around the bay (just before darting into yet another tunnel!).

From Oshamambe the train follows the Muroran line, not the Hakodate line (which branches off north from here) but you don't have to change trains.

Toya (154km) Not all limited expresses stop here. **Toya-ko** (Lake Toya) is a caldera lake formed by the collapse of a mountain following volcanic activity thousands of years ago. There was further activity in 2000 (see box p334).

⛩ **The day the sky turned black**
At 1:08pm on 31st March 2000 the resort area around Toya-ko was devastated when nearby **Mt Usu** erupted for the first time in more than two decades, spewing out clouds of rock and steam for several days. The whole area was covered in a thick film of grey dust, turning broad daylight into dark night. Ten thousand people were evacuated and it was to be three months before anyone was allowed back into the area. The eruption has left its mark to this day in the shape of a crater on a slope just above the resort centre but all the hotels are back in action.

Turn right as you exit Toya station for buses to the lake (¥320 one-way; 17 mins). Toya-ko lacks some of the charm of Onuma-Koen (see p331); huge resort hotels line the lake and spoil the scenery. In short, Toya-ko is just too much of a geared-up tourist resort to make it appealing. That said, the lake itself is worth a look and onsen fans might enjoy an afternoon wallowing in a hot spring or two in some of the larger resort hotels.

Date-Mombetsu (167km) Not all limited expresses stop here. This is the nearest the rail line gets to **Sobetsu**, a town which hosts an International Snowball Fight Tournament every February; for more details see 🖥 www.town .sobetsu.hokkaido.jp. Much more than just a bit of winter fun, this is a serious competition involving corporate sponsorship, prize money and a strict rule book.

After leaving Date-Mombetsu, the train runs along the coast again before entering more tunnels. Then, just to prove that it's not all unspoilt nature in Hokkaido, on the right there's a block of ugly factories, gas tanks, pipes and billowing chimney stacks.

Higashi-Muroran (190km) A branch line runs from here for 7km to the city of **Muroran**, known as a steel industry centre but of little interest to the tourist.

Noboribetsu (207km) Noboribetsu (🖥 www.noboribetsu-spa.jp/en) comes from the Ainu word 'Nupurupetsu', meaning 'a cloudy river tinged with white'. A bus ride from the station is a hot spring resort that draws water from **Jigokudani (Hell Valley)**, the centre of which is a volcanic crater where steam rises from the earth. It was only in 1858, when a businessman who was mining sulphur realized there was money to be made from tourism, that the first public bath house was opened using hot water from the crater. Since then tourism has taken off and the resort is now full of concrete hotel blocks and tourist attractions, such as a park full of caged brown bears, accessed by a cable car from the resort centre. Despite this, Jigokudani is worth seeing close up, as is bubbling **Oyunuma Lake**, and a visit here would not be complete without a trip to one of the hot springs in the resort.

From Noboribetsu station, buses run up to the terminal in the resort centre (¥330; 15 mins). Head up the road from the bus centre to find Noboribetsu Tourist Association (☎ 0143-84 3311, daily 9am-6pm), a couple of minutes up on the left-hand side. Staff can provide a useful English map and guide to the area. Keep walking up the main road, past the hotels, until you reach Jigokudani.

In 1924 the area was designated 'Noboribetsu Primeval Forest', a fitting description for the haunting landscape. Though you aren't allowed to walk around Hell Valley (not that you'd want to with the bubbling and smoke rising from the ground), there is a short promenade walk that most people take for a close-up view. There's a better walk up into the hills above Hell Valley and down to Oyunuma Lake, a volcanic bubbling swamp, where temperatures reach 130°C. Look for the sign pointing towards the 'mountain-ash observatory'. Head up the path and Oyunuma is about 15-20 minutes on foot.

Having seen the source there are plenty of opportunities to test out the water by taking a bath in one of the onsen hotels. The most popular, but also the most expensive, are the baths at ***Daiichi Takimotokan*** (🖳 www.takimotokan.co.jp/english/index.html, daily, 9am-5pm, ¥2000), the highlight of which is a rotemburo. This hotel is the last before Hell Valley; the onsen entrance is at the back of the building. For those interested in spending the night here room rates start from ¥10,000 per person including breakfast and a buffet supper. Less elaborate, but much better value, is **Sagiriyu** (daily, 7am-9:30pm, ¥390), the only municipal hot spring in the resort. Conveniently it's next door to the tourist office. The baths here are nothing fancy but it's a much more affordable option and you won't feel you have to spend all day in the water to get your money's worth. Look for the purple hanging curtain and wooden entrance, just before the tourist information office on the left side of the road heading up to Hell Valley.

As you leave, or arrive at, Noboribetsu station, you can't miss the enormous and kitsch European-style castle; this is **Noboribetsu Marine Park Nixe** (🖳 www.nixe.co.jp/englishinfo.htm; ¥2300), a large aquarium with dolphin, sealion and penguin shows.

◆ **Shiraoi (226km)** You'll need to catch a local train from Noboribetsu to reach Shiraoi, five stops along the line. Ten minutes on foot from the station is **Poroto Kotan** (🖳 www.porotokotan.jp, daily, 8am-5pm Apr to Oct; 8:30am-4:30pm Nov to Mar, ¥750), a reconstructed Ainu village; see the box on p366.

⛩ **Edo Wonderland**
    Edo Wonderland (☎ 0143-83 3311, 🖳 www.edo-trip.jp/en/index.html, Apr-Oct daily 9am-5pm, Nov-Mar Thur-Tue 10am-4pm; ¥2900), also known as **Noboribetsu Date Jidaimura**, is a reproduction Edo-period village and was rather fun. Of particular interest is the Ninja show involving a ninja sword duel, secret doors, a roped descent from the ceiling and a rather unconvincing earthquake scene. I also enjoyed the 'Scary Cat' house. It's like a house of fun but in each area you have to be careful of the cat; it appears behind secret panels, its giant furry paw descends from the ceiling and it even hides inside a giant bell ready to pounce! Beware of the cat! The Edo village is quite nice and comes complete with watchtower and Ninja house, and there were lots of costumed performers walking around.
                                                                    Andrew Picknell (UK)

Edo Wonderland is a ten-minute bus ride from Noboribetsu station (from JR Noboribetsu take a Donan Bus bound for Noboribetsu Onsen).

HOKKAIDO

To reach Poroto Kotan, turn left at the first set of lights in front of the station and go straight until the next lights. Turn left again, cross over the rail track and go straight until you see some shops on your right. Go past these, through a large souvenir shop, until you reach the entrance and ticket office. Apart from a few reconstructed huts and Ainu houses, where performances of Ainu dance and music are given, the most interesting part of the village is the Ainu Museum, which displays objects and garments used in daily Ainu life.

Tomakomai (248km) Tomakomai is a railway junction and has ferry connections with Tokyo, Sendai, Nagoya and Hachinohe (all of which are on Honshu). It's not a very attractive place; the factories that can be seen from the train belong to the Oji Paper Company. Paper is Tomakomai's biggest industry.

Space fans might like to make a stop here to visit the slightly incongruous **Space Station Mir Exhibition Hall** (💻 www.city.tomakomai.hokkaido.jp/kagaku, Tue-Sun, 9:30am-5pm; free), a 15-minute walk from the station's south exit (ask for a map at the tourist information office in the station). Mir was launched on 19th February 1986 and was taken out of service on March 23, 2001; it broke up during re-entry over the South Pacific Ocean. Now that Mir has gone forever, this small place (an annex to Tomakomai Science Museum) offers a fascinating insight into life on board the Soviet space station. You can walk around inside a genuine experimental prototype of Mir and see the shower facility, the 'private room' where astronauts slept standing up, cooking facilities, treadmill and the star attraction – at least if the Japanese visitors are anything to go by – the on-board toilet, which looks terrifying and involves lots of sucking and hydraulics. There are no English signs but the helpful staff will show you around.

Train buffs might prefer the more down-to-earth **steam engine** (C11 133) outside the exhibition hall. You can even climb on board and sit in the engine room.

Cycle rental (¥500/day plus ¥1000 deposit) is available from the helpful Tourist Information Office (English spoken, daily, 9am-6pm) inside the station. To find it, turn right as you exit the ticket barrier and it is on the lower level of the station concourse at the south exit. The JR ticket office (daily 7:15am-7:30pm) is immediately on your right as you exit the ticket barrier. A Twinkle Plaza travel agency (Mon-Fri 10am-6pm, Sat/Sun 10am-5pm) is adjacent. There is a row of coin lockers (including a few ¥500 ones) on the main station concourse to the left as you exit the ticket barrier.

Tomakomai is the starting point for the local **Hidaka line** which runs south along the coast towards Samani (3-3^1/$_2$ hours), the nearest rail station to Cape Erimo. It takes just over three hours to Samani, from where irregular buses (one hour, ¥1300) can be caught to the cape and on to Obihiro (see p346).

Toyoko Inn Tomakomai Ekimae (☎ 0144-32 1045, 💻 www.toyoko-inn.com; ¥6090/S, ¥8190/D/Tw) is to the right as you take the south exit, across the street from Daiei department store outside the station. ***Tomakomai New Station Hotel*** (☎ 0144-33 0333, 💻 http://tnshotel.fc2web.com; ¥6510/S, ¥10,550/T, ¥11,550/D) has its own fitness centre and pool (extra charge of ¥525). All rooms have separate toilet/bathroom and sink. Non-smokers should ask for a room on the 8th floor. Head out of Tomakomai station's south exit and look on your left for the building with a couple of white birds painted on the side. The hotel is one block back from the station.

The basement of Daiei, part of the SunPlaza complex outside the station, has a supermarket which sells lunch boxes and all kinds of Japanese food. There's a branch of *Seattle's Best Coffee* on the ground floor.

Minami-Chitose (275km) The penultimate limited express stop before Sapporo; change here for **Shin-Chitose Airport** (💻 www.new-chitose-airport .jp), three minutes away by local train. This is the nearest airport to Sapporo, handling both domestic and international flights.

Shin-Sapporo (308km) Some limited expresses make a brief stop here but stay on the train until the Sapporo terminus.

Only local trains call at **Heiwa (311km)**. It's appropriate that the rail station here should be called Heiwa (Peace) because this place is home to an unusual museum, the '**No More Hibakusha Kaikan**'; see p364.

Sapporo (319km)   [see pp356-65]

SAPPORO TO ASAHIKAWA   [Map 23, below; Table 20, p468]

Distances by JR from Sapporo. Fastest journey time: 80 minutes.

Sapporo (0km) From Sapporo, take the Lilac LEX or the slightly faster Super-White Arrow LEX on the Hakodate line to Asahikawa. Lilac trains do the journey in 90 minutes, the Super White Arrow in 80 minutes. The views from the train are less than spectacular as far as Iwamizawa, as it takes some time for the train to leave Hokkaido's capital behind.

Iwamizawa (41km) From here on, the familiar wide green spaces start to open up once more. Some trains stop at **Bibai (46km)** and **Sunagawa (64km)**.

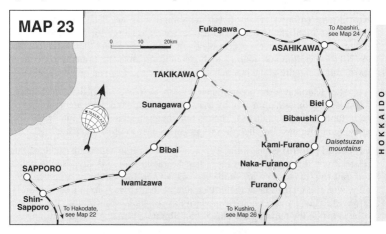

Takikawa (84km) The landscape is briefly interrupted by the small city of Takikawa, known throughout Hokkaido for its extremely heavy snowfall. The city plays host to an All Hokkaido Fancy Dress Tug-of-War Championship, held annually on the first Sunday in February. The Shibuki Festival, held on the first weekend in August, is worth experiencing if you are in the area at that time.

In 1980 the fossil of a manatee (large plant-eating aquatic mammal) was discovered here. The fossil is on display at the **Museum of Fine Arts and Natural History** (Tue-Sun, 10am-5pm, ¥600). To reach the museum from the station, turn left on to the main shopping street ('Bell Road'), walk up it for about five minutes and turn right when you reach the intersection with a branch of Mister Donut. Walk straight down this road for about ten minutes and turn left when you see the 'Kaihatsu Kyokan' (Hokkaido Development Center). Go straight and you'll see the red-brick entrance to the museum on your left.

About 10 minutes after leaving Takikawa, the train crosses Ishikari-gawa.

Fukagawa (107km) About 10 minutes after leaving Fukagawa there is a series of long tunnels.

Asahikawa (137km)   **[see pp365-70]**

ASAHIKAWA TO ABASHIRI   **[Map 24, opposite; Table 21, p468]**

Distances by JR from Asahikawa. Fastest journey time: 3 hrs 50 mins.

Asahikawa (0km) From Asahikawa, take the Okhotsk LEX that runs along the JR Sekihoku Line to Abashiri on the Sea of Okhotsk. This train originates in Sapporo. It's worth making a seat reservation as there are only a limited number of carriages. There's a Western-style toilet and trolley service on board.

All the clichés of Japan being a nation of no open space and houses packed together like rabbit hutches collapse on this stretch of the journey. The train travels slowly enough to see some of the tiny stations along the way.

Kamikawa (49km) Most tourists who alight here are heading to **Sounkyo-Onsen**, the highlight of which is a trip to Sounkyo Gorge for its waterfalls and rock formations. Neither is accessible by rail so it's necessary to transfer to a bus (¥770) for the 30-minute journey to the main resort area. Buses are timed to meet most trains; enquire at the bus ticket office to the right as you exit the station.

After Kamikawa the predominant scenery is forest, rather than open space. The track becomes hemmed in by trees on both sides and there are a number of semi-tunnels (with windows). There's one long tunnel about 15 minutes before arriving at Shirataki but then the countryside starts to open up again.

Shirataki (86km) Some limited expresses do not stop here but if you look out (even if you don't stop!), you'll see that Shirataki station is supposed to recall the railway of yesteryear, with a clock tower topped by a weathercock. However, the recreation of the golden age of the railways hasn't been entirely successful: as a concession to modern-day financial constraints, the station offices inside the building are closed and Shirataki remains unmanned.

Maruseppu (106km) Most limited express-es make a brief stop here.

Engaru (125km) Engaru used to be an impor-tant rail junction, with a line running up to Mombetsu on the east coast but as with so many lines JR Hokkaido no longer thought it was prof-itable so closed it. The train waits a few minutes here as everyone turns their seats around so as to continue facing the direction of travel.

Ikutahara (141km) Shortly after leaving Ikutahara (around 23 minutes after Engaru) the train heads into the Jomon Tunnel. The tunnel is very short but achieved notoriety some years ago when human bones (see box below) were discovered nearby.

Rubeshibe (162km) Nothing to stop for here but it's worth noting that Rubeshibe is home to one of the world's largest cuckoo clocks. In 2006 the town merged to become part of the city of Kitami.

From here to Kitami, the final major stop on the line to Abashiri, the wide plains seen during the early part of this journey return, with fields on either side of the track.

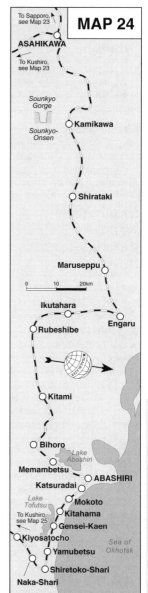

⛩ Human sacrifice?

It was once the practice in Japan, when a new bridge, tunnel or other major public works project was constructed, for an individual to be offered to the site as a human sacrifice.

One Hokkaido resident told me that when she was six or seven, human bones were found along the railway line at the Jomon Tunnel. The story goes that about 30 years before, a railway-man had been supervising the laying of addition-al track along the line. No doubt he had heard the stories concerning the ghosts that haunted the tunnel. Working alone late one evening he disap-peared mysteriously; it was only years later that his skeleton was discovered near the track deep in the tunnel. Locals claim that he'd been pushed by a ghost into the path of an approaching freight train, a sacrifice required because none had been made after the construction of the tunnel.

⛩ **The end of the line**
Kitami was until 2006 a point of interchange with the private 140-km Furusato Ginga line which ran south to Ikeda. Frequently threatened with closure, people living along this line lobbied hard to keep it open. But after years of uncertainty, the rail operator decided it was no longer financially viable and the final train ran on April 21, 2006. It was quite literally the end of the line for a stretch of track which had been in service for 95 years, but possibly not for ever – see box opposite.

Kitami (185km) During the last few kilometres before Kitami (see box above), the surroundings get a little more built up (for Hokkaido) and there's a long tunnel just before arriving at Kitami station.

A good overnight choice is ***Toyoko Inn Kitami Ekimae*** (☎ 0157-62 1045, 🖳 www.toyoko-inn.com; ¥6090/S, ¥8190/D/Tw June-Sept; ¥5040/S, ¥7140/D /Tw Oct-May), to the left across the street from the station as you exit.

Bihoro (210km) It's possible to rent a car here and head over the beautiful Bihoro Pass to Lake Kussharo and Kawayu-Onsen (see p343).

Memambetsu (222km) This station lies just at the edge of Lake Abashiri. From here, though the track looks as if it will run right by the lake, trees block out any view and it is only about four minutes before arriving in Abashiri that there is finally a glimpse (on the left) of the northern tip of the lake. Just in case you miss it, the conductor makes an announcement urging passengers to look out of the window and savour the fleeting view.

Abashiri (238km) Abashiri (🖳 www.abashiri.jp/tabinavi_en) is the terminus of the JR Sekihoku line from Asahikawa. In winter, people come here to see blocks of drift ice on the Sea of Okhotsk. Ornate, hand-crafted snow and ice sculptures are a highlight of the Drift Ice Festival in February.

Abashiri station is small but has some coin lockers (all sizes, but only a few ¥500 ones) in the space between the station building and the tourist information office. The staff at tourist information (☎ 0152-44 5849, daily, 9am-5pm), on your right as you exit the station, have maps and will help book accommodation.

The main sights are around Mt Tento; a bus runs on a loop around places of interest daily between 9:30am and 4pm. A one-day pass (¥900) is a good deal since it also gets you reductions on entry fees at the attractions mentioned below. The pass is available from the tourist office at the station. The bus departs from stop No 1, opposite the taxi rank in front of the station.

Taking the bus from Abashiri station, stop first at the former **Abashiri Prison** (Apr to Oct 8am-6pm; Nov to Mar, 9am-5pm, ¥1050), which during the freezing winters must have been a very bleak place in which to serve time. The prison relocated in 1984 and today visitors are allowed to wander around the rows of cells, the bathhouse (with waxwork models of tattooed inmates), and outhouse buildings.

Picking up the bus from outside the museum, the next stop is **Okhotsk Ryu-Hyo (Drift Ice) Museum** (Apr to Oct 8am-6pm, Nov to Mar 9am-4:30pm, closed Dec 29th to Jan 5th, ¥520), which has a 'Drift Ice Experience Room', where lumps of ice are supposed to show what the Sea of Okhotsk is like in the dead of winter. Of more interest are the views of Lake Abashiri and the Sea of Okhotsk from the lookout points on the third, fourth and fifth floors. Next pick up the bus or walk 800m to the **Hokkaido Museum of Northern Peoples** (Tue-Sun 9:30am-4:30pm, ¥300). This museum seems to attract fewer people than the other two, which is a pity since it's perhaps the best, with exhibits relating not just to the Ainu but to minorities across the northern hemisphere. The main exhibition hall displays everything from snow boots to a recreated winter home. TV screens show footage of events such as reindeer herding and hunting for fish by cutting holes through the ice. A pamphlet in English is available.

From January 20th to the first Sunday in April the bus also stops at the Aurora Terminal, from where the **Icebreaker Aurora** runs one-hour trips (¥3000) on the Sea of Okhotsk. 'Feeling the ice cracking beneath the ship's hull defies description,' reads the publicity. This trip is by far the best reason for paying a visit to Abashiri in the dead of winter.

To reach *Abashiri Ryuhyo-no-oka Youth Hostel* (☎/🖷 0152-43 8558, 🖳 www2.ocn.ne.jp/~ryuhyou, ikeda@seagreen.ocn.ne.jp; ¥3250/4250; 28 beds), take the bus to Okhotsk Aquarium, from stop No 1 in front of Abashiri station, and get off at the Meiji Iriguchi stop. A youth hostel sign points you up a road off the main road. Follow this road up for about 15 minutes. The hostel is a small, clean, friendly place, with mostly bunk-bed dorms and a good view over the Okhotsk Sea from outside.

ABASHIRI TO KUSHIRO   [Map 24, p339; Map 25, p343; Table 22, p468]

Distances by JR from Abashiri. Fastest journey time: $3^1/2$ hours.

Abashiri (0km) The next part of the journey has some of the most stunning scenery but is not for anyone in a hurry. Only local trains run along the single-track Senmo line that first heads east along the coast as far as Shiretoko-Shari, before turning south-west through Akan National Park towards the port town of Kushiro.

🏯 Is it a bus? Is it a train?

How about this for a novel form of transport? JR Hokkaido has introduced the first 'Dual Mode Vehicle' (DMV), a bus-like contraption which can operate on roads using conventional tyres but which, at the flick of a switch, turns into a train running on tracks with steel and rubber wheels.

The DMV entered service in 2007 on a trial basis on a tourist route from Hamako-Shimizu to Mokoto along the Senmo line on the north-east coast near Abashiri (see above), going one way on rail track (11 km) and then returning as a bus on the road (21 km). If the DMV proves successful it could serve as a model for other parts of the island. It's no secret that many rail routes on Hokkaido are unprofitable (see box opposite), but it's too early to say whether the DMV represents the future of public transport or whether it's just a quirky here-today-gone-tomorrow invention.

Katsuradai (1.5km) First stop after leaving Abashiri, there's a short tunnel immediately after leaving here. Emerging from the tunnel, there are great views out to the left of the Sea of Okhotsk.

Mokoto (9km) Mokoto station has a coffee shop with views out to sea, but a personal favourite is the coffee shop at the next stop.

Kitahama (12km) Although only a few minutes out of Abashiri, it really is worth stopping here briefly; there can be no better location to have a coffee than here facing the sea, especially in winter when the water becomes a sheet of ice. The old railway seats and battered suitcase make this the ultimate *café* for passing travellers. The menu includes toast, pasta, and a daily set lunch. The station's waiting room is worth seeing as it is covered with old railway tickets and business cards left by travellers. The café is open daily (except 2nd and 4th Sat), 10am to around 8pm.

After leaving Kitahama, look out to the right for views of Lake Tofutsu which, between November and April, becomes home to around 1000 Siberian swans.

Gensei-Kaen (17km) Gensei-Kaen station is a popular spot for viewing Lake Tofutsu.

Yamubetsu (26km) If it's not too foggy you should be able to see Shiretoko Peninsula on the left in the distance, though the view is blocked for much of the way by pine trees.

After Yamubetsu, there's a long stretch without any stations.

Shiretoko-Shari (37km) This is the nearest station to **Shiretoko Peninsula** and the point to connect up with buses that run part of the way along it. The peninsula is considered an idyllic retreat from the man-made world, an unspoilt territory inhabited by wild eagles, brown bears and the world's largest owls.

Turn left as you exit the station for Shari bus terminal (under the archway that reads 'Welcome to Shiretoko'). Most buses run from here along the peninsula to the bus terminal at Utoro (¥1490, 50 mins), from where it's about a ten-minute walk to the ferry terminal for tours of the peninsula. The longest ferry ride goes all the way around Cape Shiretoko (inaccessible by road) and back to Utoro for ¥6000 (225 mins; one a day). An alternative ferry ride that doesn't go as far is ¥2700 (90 mins; several daily). Note that in winter much of the peninsula is inaccessible.

Naka-Shari (42km) First station after Shiretoko-Shari; just after leaving here a large and unsightly factory looms into view on the right-hand side. This eyesore aside, the journey from here is one of the best parts of a rail route round Hokkaido. This is the only line on the island that actually runs through a national park, between Lake Kussharo and the smaller, but more mysterious, Lake Mashu. Neither lake is visible from the train, though there are good access points to both along the way.

Kiyosatocho (49km) After Kiyosatocho look out for the 1545m Mt Shari which, unless the summit is covered in cloud, should be visible out to the left.

Satsuru (57km) and Midori (65km)

There's a long stretch of line between these two stations in an area where trees very definitely outnumber people. Midori ('Green') station has a green roof and blue trees painted on the side, and is the last stop before Kawayu-Onsen in Akan National Park. The whole area, with the track surrounded by forest, is so lush and green that it is difficult to tell exactly where the national park officially begins. But about 10 minutes after leaving Midori the train passes through a tunnel. Emerging from this you are officially in Akan National Park.

Kawayu-Onsen (80km)

Built in 1936, the old station master's office has been turned into an excellent *café*. It's tempting to while away an afternoon right here but with such magnificent scenery so close to hand it would be a shame to miss out. Cycles can be rented for free (ask at the café) but they must be returned by 5pm. The station has no coin lockers but you should be able to leave stuff at the café.

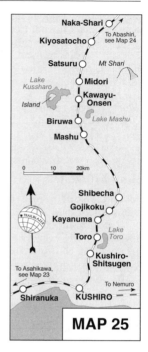

MAP 25

From the station, head up to the main road and turn right. Go straight until the first set of lights and turn left onto Route 391. A few minutes down this road, on the left-hand side, is the stunning **Mt Iwo**, still very much an active volcano. If you don't see it first, you'll almost certainly smell it. Smoke pours out from different places around the mountain and the sulphur turns the rock a bright yellow. Most people take a brief closer look at the smoke then rush back covering their mouths and noses.

Continue along the main road for another 2km until you reach the centre of Kawayu-Onsen. As you arrive in the centre, look for an orange Seicomart con-

---

Sumo in Hokkaido

Kawayu-Onsen was once the home of sumo wrestler **Taiho-san** who reached the rank of *yokozona*, sumo's highest honour, and claimed 32 tournament victories, twice winning six consecutive titles. Taiho-san is now a sumo trainer in Tokyo, but a small museum (daily, 9am-5pm; June to Sep 6:30am-9pm, ¥310) is close to EMC (see p344) in Kawayu-Onsen. On display are all 32 sumo tournament trophies won up to his retirement in 1971, along with photos and other memorabilia including one of the wrestler's oversize suits hanging next to more traditional sumo gear.

Taiho-san was born in Sakhalin (now part of Russia) but moved to Hokkaido and attended school in Kawayu-Onsen before leaving for Tokyo at the age of 16 to begin his sumo apprenticeship. Kawayu-Onsen's link with sumo explains why it is the venue for the annual Women's Sumo Championship.

H O K K A I D O

venience store on your right. Then look on the left for a sign pointing to **Kawayu Eco Museum Center** (EMC; Thur-Tue, May to Oct 8am-5pm; Nov to Apr 9am-4pm; free); this shows films of the area's wildlife, flora and fauna, has scale models of Akan National Park and free tea and coffee! Ask at the information desk for the *Let's walk around EMC* leaflet, with details of walks in the woods around the centre.

If not in a hurry, energetic cyclists might consider continuing on for a further 3km to **Lake Kussharo**, where Kussie – the local equivalent of Scotland's Loch Ness Monster – is said to live. Around the lake are a number of outdoor hot springs (some free) and summer activities on the lake include canoeing and kayaking. After the cycle tour head back to the station in time to pick up a train to Mashu, as Mashu-ko Youth Hostel (see below) is a good place to stay.

Biruwa (87km) This is more of a portakabin than a station.

Mashu (96km) A small station with a few ¥300 coin lockers by the exit. The tourist information office is open (daily 9am-5pm) in summer only.

Lake Mashu, 20km in circumference, is known as the lake 'of mystery and illusion'. No river flows in or out of the lake which is completely surrounded by trees. The only way of seeing the lake – if you are lucky and there isn't a blanket of fog over the water – is from elevated observation points. I arrived early in the morning but within 30 minutes the lake was completely swallowed up by mist. It's almost as if this mystical natural phenomenon becomes disgruntled by the unwanted attention, so cloaks itself in a mist to avoid the gaze of tourists. All the tour buses pull up at the Rest House, which has an observation platform but is also crammed full of souvenir stalls. If the weather is good, consider walking, hitching or taking the infrequent bus to the less crowded 'third observation platform' further along the road.

From Mashu-ko Youth Hostel (see below), it's a three-hour walk up the road that runs outside the hostel to the lake but it should be easy to hitch a lift with a fellow hosteller. Alternatively, a very infrequent bus stops right outside the hostel and goes to the first rest house (check times with hostel staff).

Mashu-ko Youth Hostel (☎ 015-482 3098, 💻 www.masyuko.co.jp; ¥3400/3900), situated on the way to the lake, is an ideal place to stay. Call ahead for a pick-up from the station. Meals are served in *The Great Bear*, the restaurant next to the hostel (dinner ¥1050, breakfast ¥630). Hostel staff organize summer and winter activities including cross-country skiing and canoeing (extra charge). Accommodation is in tatami or modern four-bed dorms and there is a coin laundry and internet access (¥10 per minute).

Mashu station lies just outside Akan National Park but the views from the train remain tremendous, with long gaps between isolated stations. The next major sight is Kushiro-Shitsugen National Park; it's a good idea to plan to spend a whole day on the journey between Mashu and the terminus at Kushiro.

Shibecha (121km) At the far end of the platform is a monument to an old steam locomotive that used to run along this line; you can ring the bell in memory of C1171.

Gojikoku (130km) This station is on the edge of the last national park before Kushiro, Kushiro-Shitsugen National Park. The park is mostly marshland, inhabited by Japanese cranes. Though not as well known as Akan National Park it still has some beautiful scenery.

Kayanuma (135km) A sign above the station name says that this is a 'station where Japanese cranes come'. During the mating season, between January and March, cranes perform elaborate mating dances on the snow-covered ground.

From here, there's a long stretch of track through marshland, so look out for swamp marshes on both sides.

Toro (142km) Bikes can be rented (¥700 per hour) from the coffee bar in this station. Ask the owner for a map of the area, which includes Lake Toro, the major lake in the marshlands area.

Two minutes on foot from Toro station is *Kushiro Shitsugen Toro Youth Hostel* (☎ 0154-87 2510, 🖥 www.youthhostel.or.jp/English/e_toro.htm, tohro@sip.or.jp, ¥3360/4360; 14 beds). It's a homely place and a good choice for an overnight stay if you're visiting nearby Kushiro (see below). Breakfast is ¥420 and dinner ¥840.

Kushiro-Shitsugen (152km) All the stations along this stretch of the line are tiny wooden buildings. There are plenty of hiking opportunities around Kushiro-Shitsugen. Views from the train remain impressive until about 10 minutes before Kushiro, where modern life begins to encroach on the unspoilt environment.

Kushiro (169km) Kushiro (🖥 www.kushiro-kankou.or.jp/english) is the terminus for the Senmo line from Abashiri and also a stop on the Nemuro line that runs east to Nemuro (see p346) and west to Obihiro and beyond. Facing the Pacific Ocean, Kushiro is the most easterly city in Japan. Turn left after the ticket barrier to find coin lockers (all sizes). The staff at the tourist information booth (☎ 0154-22 8294, daily, 9am-5:30pm) in the station do not speak English. On the concourse level you'll find a *Mister Donut* as well as a couple of noodle places. The horrendously kitsch chapel that sits incongruously outside the station is a fake, rented by couples in search of a white wedding. Kushiro was the first station in Japan to open a **Station Museum** (Tue-Sun, 10am-5pm, ¥100), which displays the work of local artist Eimatsu Sasaki.

Kushiro City Museum (Tue-Sun, 9:30am-5pm, ¥360) is 15 minutes by bus from the station. Here you can get an overview of the city and the Kushiro-Shitsugen marshland you have just travelled through. There are also exhibitions on Ainu traditions and on the Japanese crane (the feathered variety). Several buses go to the museum from the bus terminal to the left as you exit the station. Get off at Kagaku-kan-dori.

Fifteen minutes down the main road that leads from the station is **Fisherman's Wharf**, a large waterside shopping and restaurant complex popularly known as MOO. (MOO, I was told, stands for Marine Aqua Oasis. MAO was presumably deemed not capitalist enough for a Japanese shopping complex). As well as a fish market on the ground floor and various shops, cafés and restaurants on the second and third, Kushiro Fitness Center (daily 10am-9:30pm, Sun until 6:30pm; closed in winter on Thur) is on the fifth floor and has an indoor pool. While at MOO, don't forget to take a brief look at EGG (Ever Green Garden), a greenhouse tacked on to one end of the building.

The best accommodation in town is at *ANA Hotel Kushiro* (☎ 0154-31 4111, 🖳 www.anahotels.com; ¥9500/S, ¥19,000/Tw, ¥16,000/D), directly across the street from MOO. *Tokyu Inn* (☎ 0154-22 0109, 🖳 www.tokyuhotels .co.jp/en; ¥6930/S, ¥12,600/D/Tw) is just to the left across the street as you leave the station. The best youth-hostel choice is at nearby Toro (see p345).

From Kushiro, the Nemuro line extends east to its terminus in **Nemuro**, known for its locally caught crab and for the view of the Habomai Islands, currently disputed territory with Russia. The fastest train to Nemuro takes just over two hours; it's then a further 40 minutes by bus (¥1040 one-way) to the cape.

KUSHIRO TO SAPPORO & ASAHIKAWA
[Map 26, opposite; Map 23, p337]

Distances by JR from Kushiro. Fastest journey time: 4 hours.

Kushiro to Shintoku   [Map 26, opposite]
Kushiro (0km) From Kushiro, pick up the Super-Ozora LEX (bound for Sapporo), which has Western toilets and plenty of luggage space. The reserved-seat carriages are more comfortable than the older, non-reserved ones.

The first Super-Ozora leaves Kushiro at 7:39am, then further departures are at 8:39am, 11:17am, 1:25pm, 4:17pm, 6:42pm. Services from Sapporo leave at 7:03am, 9:04am, 11:51am, 1:58pm, 5:34pm and 6:58pm and arrive in Kushiro at 10:51am, 1.03pm, 3:42pm, 5.48pm, 9:13pm and 10:57pm respectively.

There are occasional glimpses of the Pacific Ocean during the first part of the journey. Some trains stop at **Shiranuka (27km)**.

Ikeda (104km) The first major stop after Kushiro. Five or six minutes after leaving Ikeda, the train crosses Tokachi-gawa.

Obihiro (128km) The Hidaka mountains lie to the south and west of Obihiro. There is little of interest in Obihiro itself, but in case you need to stay here the JAL/JR-operated *Hotel Nikko Northland Obihiro* (☎ 0155-24 1234, 🖳 www .jalhotels.com; ¥11,500/S, ¥14,500/D, ¥19,000/Tw; small discount for rail-pass holders) is right outside the station. The hotel has a shrine and a chapel for both Japanese- and Western-style weddings so look out for some happy couples. *Toyoko Inn Obihiro Ekimae* (☎ 0155-27 1045, 🖳 www.toyoko-inn.com; ¥6090/S, ¥8190/D/Tw) is also close by. Obihiro is famous for *butadon* (pork on rice, eaten in a bowl). The dish originated here and lots of restaurants serve it.

Obihiro is a distant access point for **Cape Erimo** (Erimo-Misaki), the southernmost point on Hokkaido. Tokachi buses run from the bus terminal outside Obihiro station to Hiroo (120 mins, ¥1830), part of the way along the coast to the cape. From Hiroo, a JR bus runs down to Erimo-Misaki (60 mins, ¥1510). The same bus continues around the cape up to Samani, where you can pick up

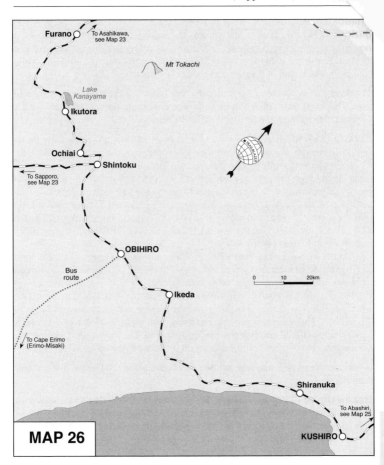

MAP 26

a local train on the JR Samani line that takes three hours to run up to Tomakomai (see p336).

Shintoku (172km) The town of Shintoku is famous for buckwheat soba (noodles) and you'll find buckwheat ice cream, buckwheat tea as well as buckwheat soba lunch deals in some of the restaurants. From here, the Super Ozora continues towards Sapporo along the Sekisho line.

▲ To follow the route described below, change here to a local train continuing along the Nemuro line to Furano. Stations along this line are spread out and there's a whole series of tunnels, one of the longest being about 25 minutes after leaving Shintoku.

..u to Asahikawa [Map 26, p347; Map 23, p337; Tables 23/24, pp468-9]

.ra (210km) Ikutora station was the setting for the movie *Poppoya*, a nostalgic story of a stationmaster who loses his young daughter, which grossed at least ¥3 billion at the box office. 'Poppoya' means railroad workers, while 'poppo' is the sound of a steam locomotive's whistle.

After leaving Ikutora, the train runs past Lake Kanayama on the right-hand side. The track then crosses the lake before entering a tunnel. After this, it's a pleasant ride through the hills and plains to Furano.

Furano (254km) Known in winter for its powder snow and in summer for its fields of lavender, Furano is one of the most popular tourist resorts in Hokkaido.

Lavender was introduced to Furano by a local farmer and it's now big business; lavender ice cream is available nearly everywhere and even the JR station has its name painted in purple above the entrance. The main attractions are lavender fields, dairy farms and cheese-making factories. Furano feels a little like the south of France and is probably of more interest to the domestic tourist. The official lavender-viewing season is July; during this month it's probably best to avoid Furano completely.

On the second floor of the white building across the street from the station is **Furano Information Center** (☎ 0167-23 3388, 🖳 www.furano-kankou .com/english/home.htm; daily, 9am-6pm) where there are a few leaflets in English. Furano has a bargain '*railway hotel*' – a disused coach next to the station where people can sleep on a thinly carpeted space for ¥700 a night (July to September). No bedding is provided so bring your own sleeping bag. Ask about staying here at the JR travel centre inside the station. The tourist office outside the station has a list of other accommodation in the area and can assist with bookings.

▲ Change trains here and take another local train along the Furano line towards Asahikawa.

Naka-Furano (262km) *Furano Youth Hostel* (☎/🖹 0167-44 4441, 🖳 www4 .ocn.ne.jp/~furanoyh/furano-yh-e.htm; ¥3360; 15 beds) is six minutes on foot behind this station. The rooms are all pension style. A simple breakfast and supper are included in the rate.

Leaving Furano, look out on both sides of the train. On your immediate left are low hills and fields but in the distance to the right are the more impressive peaks of the Daisetsuzan mountains.

Kami-Furano (269km) Three buses a day (dep 9:33am, 1:19pm and 4:31pm) run from here to two hot springs in Daisetsuzan National Park. The bus goes as far as Tokachi-dake-Onsen (¥500), but it's better to get off at **Fukiage-Onsen** (the stop is called Hakuginso). This is a completely natural (wild) hot spring where bathing is mixed and there are no admission fees. It's just there in the open for anybody to take a dip.

If mixed bathing in the wild is not your thing, just down the road from the spring is *Fukiage Onsen No Hakuginso* (☎ 0167-45 3251, 🖹 45 6634; no

English spoken), with a variety of segregated baths at different temperatures ᵻ well as a sauna and rotemburo affording views over the mountains. Buy a ticket (¥800) from the vending machine in the entrance lobby and hand it in at the desk. If you fancy a night in the mountains you can stay here, either in a tatami mat room or in bunk-bed dorms, for only ¥2600 per night.

For further information visit 🖳 www.furano.ne.jp/kamifurano/en.

Bibaushi (278km) There are opportunities here for cycling and walking. In addition, **Guide no Yamagoya**, in the wooden building across the street from the station, is an outdoor pursuits centre which arranges canoeing and rafting trips, and guided mountain bike rides out to Daisetsuzan National Park. From December to March, the main activity is cross-country skiing. Reductions on activities and equipment rental are offered to youth hostel guests (see below). This place also has a café, showers, coin lockers and laundry.

The bright white house right outside the tiny station is *Bibaushi Liberty Youth Hostel* (☎ 0166-95 2141, 🖳 www.biei.com/liberty; ¥3780/4380), where accommodation is mostly in four-bed dorms. The couple who run the hostel are really welcoming and it's small enough to feel very homely. The food is excellent (breakfast ¥630, dinner ¥1050).

Biei (285km) The building on your left outside the station is Shikino Johokan, the **tourist information centre** (☎ 0166-92 4378, daily, 8:30am-7pm May to Oct, 8:30am-5pm Nov to Apr). Luggage can be stored here for ¥300 per item. The counter on the ground floor is well stocked with leaflets and maps.

If descriptions of 'the greens of the rolling pastures, the delicate pinks of the potato flowers, the rusty yellows of the ripened seeds' appeal, Biei (🖳 www .eolas.co.jp/hokkaido/sikibiei/en) will be the perfect place to stop for an extended cycle ride (outside the snow season). The area is very hilly so be prepared for a bit of legwork, but your efforts will be rewarded with magnificent views.

Mountain and ordinary bikes can be hired from the *Rent A Cycle* (one hour ¥200, five hours ¥1000) place next to the tourist information centre. Luggage can be left at the shop and staff will give you a cycling tour map.

There are plenty of small cafés and private art galleries to explore in and around the hills above the station. *Biei Potato-no-Oka Youth Hostel* (☎ 0166-92 3255, 🖳 www.potatovillage.com; ¥5040/5590) is just over 4km from the station. If you call ahead, the hostel staff will pick you up from the station. Supper costs ¥1050 and breakfast ¥630.

From Biei, stay on the train for the rest of the journey along the Furano Line to Asahikawa.

Asahikawa (309km)   [see pp365-70]

ASAHIKAWA TO SAPPORO, SAPPORO TO HAKODATE, HAKODATE TO AOMORI

Follow the route starting on p337 in reverse.

Hokkaido – city guides

HAKODATE

The first major stop on a journey through Hokkaido, Hakodate is the third largest city on the island and was one of the first port cities in Japan to open to foreign trade in the 19th century. The first commercial treaty was signed with the USA in 1858, followed by similar agreements with Holland, Russia, Britain and France. Foreign consulates opened up near the port in order to oversee international trade, redbrick warehouses and churches were built, and many of the original buildings still stand as a reminder of the city's Western influence. Its proximity to Honshu means Hakodate gets packed out in the summer when tourists come to eat fresh crab and gaze down at the 'milky way floating in the ocean', a lyrical description of the night view of the city from the top of Mt Hakodate.

For up-to-date information in English on tourist facilities in and around Hakodate, see ▤ www.hakodate-kankou.com.

What to see and do

Outside the station's west exit is the busy **Morning Market**. Early in the morning the market-stall tanks are filled to bursting with fresh catches of crab and squid. Fruit (particularly musk melons) and vegetables are also big business. The market is up and running by 5am and most of the traders are packing up by midday, so get here as early as possible. Closed on Sundays in winter.

By the water behind the station is **Queen's Port Hakodate** (▤ www .queens-port.com), a complex which is home to a **Classic Car Museum** (Apr-Oct, daily 8am-10pm, Nov-Mar daily 9am-6pm, ¥1000). Heaven for automobile aficionados but a bit pricey for what it is. Also here is the entrance to **Memorial Ship *Mashumaru*** (Apr-Oct daily 8am-10pm, Nov-Mar daily 9am-6pm, ¥500). This old JR ferry plied the water between Aomori and Hakodate in the days before the Seikan Tunnel (see box p328). Similar to the preserved ship in Aomori (see p316), this one has a small museum and visitors can tour the bridge and radio control room, and even put on the captain's jacket and gloves. A combined ticket for the Memorial Ship and Classic Car Museum costs ¥1400.

Motomachi Motomachi is the the city's old quarter, where the former consulate buildings were located. The most interesting of the four main sights in this area is the **Museum of Northern Peoples**, housed in the former branch of the Bank of Japan. Displays include a collection of clothes and accessories worn by the Ainu as well as a number of ceremonial objects and everyday items such as a sled and fishing harpoons. Five minutes' walk uphill from the museum is the **Old British Consulate**, first opened in 1859. The building that stands today was constructed in 1913 and was used up to the closure of the consulate in 1934. Look out for the rusty 'Dieu et mon Droit' royal crest that used to hang on the consulate gate, and for the various kitsch models depicting life in Hakodate a century ago. One scene has the consul's wife 'teaching Western-style washing to the women of Hakodate'. The gift shop does a roaring trade in Beatrix Potter, Paddington Bear, shortbread biscuits and tea cups; hardly the image of 21st-century Britain the embassy in Tokyo is trying to promote.

A little further up from the consulate is the **Old Public Hall**, a large Western-style building completed in 1910, with a number of guest bedrooms and a large hall on the second floor that commands a great view of the harbour in the distance. Free concerts are held here occasionally between June and October. Finally, the least interesting is the **Museum of Literature**, which has displays on the life and works of novelists, poets and journalists who are connected with Hakodate. Individual tickets for any one of these costs ¥300, any two ¥500, any three ¥720 or all four ¥840. All are open daily 9am-7pm from April to October and 9am-5pm from November to March.

Other sights to look out for in the area are the **Motomachi Roman Catholic Church**, the **Hakodate Russian Orthodox Church** (Mon-Fri 10am-5pm, Sat 10am-4pm, Sun 1-4pm; ¥200) and **Hakodate Episcopal Church**. To reach Motomachi, take the tram from the station to Suehiro-cho.

Mt Hakodate, 334m above sea level, offers a panoramic view of the city. A ropeway (¥1160 return; times vary according to season) runs up to the top from Motomachi, or a walking path is open from spring to autumn. The cheapest way of reaching the summit is by bus from Hakodate station. Bus services (¥360 one-way, 20-25 mins) operate daily April 25th-November 14th and mostly in the evening, when the view is considered the most spectacular.

Side trips from Hakodate

For great sea views and crashing ocean waves, head out to **Cape Tachimachi**, the name of which is derived from words in Ainu meaning 'a rocky point where one waits for and catches fish'. Ride the tram from the station to the terminus at Yachigashira and then walk (uphill!) for about 15 minutes. Great views without having to pay for a cable-car ride!

About 4km north-east of Hakodate station is **Goryokaku**, the first Western-style fort in Japan. Built between 1857 and 1864 as a strategic location from which Hokkaido could be ruled, the fort is a pentagonal star shape (called 'the most beautiful star carved on earth'). Warriors from the fallen Tokugawa shogunate escaped from Honshu to Hakodate and occupied the fort in October 1868. Seven months later they gave themselves up to the Imperial Army, bringing Japan's feudal era to a dramatic end. At the main entrance is the 60m-high Goryokaku Tower (⌨ www.goryokaku-tower.co.jp, daily, Apr to Oct 8am-7pm, Nov to Mar, 9am-6pm, ¥840). It's a modern-day eyesore but does have an observation platform affording views over the fort and is the site of a son-et-lumière-style spectacular in the summer (see p353).

To reach Goryokaku take the tram to Goryokaku-Koen-mae and then walk north along the main road for about 10 minutes. Look for signs to the fort; you'll soon see the concrete tower in front of you.

H O K K A I D O

PRACTICAL INFORMATION
Station guide

Completely rebuilt in 2003, Hakodate station is bright, modern and serves as a welcoming gateway to the city. There is only one ticket barrier; it is on the same level as all the platforms (ie there are no lifts, escalators or underground passageways).

The main exit is the Central Exit. Take the West Exit for the Morning Market, which is to your right as you exit the ticket barrier.

Inside the station is a decent **bakery** and attached **café** on the ground floor (next to the coin lockers) as well as kiosks selling **ekiben** lunch boxes (specializing in crab).

One floor up (take the escalator from the station concourse) are a couple of places to grab a bite: *Waka* (10am-9pm) serves a range of typical Japanese dishes at reasonable prices (tempura set meal at ¥1000 or try the Waka special meal which includes a taste of everything at ¥1800).

There's also a Japanese curry house, *Hot Hot*, where the curry would be more accurately described as 'Bland Bland', but worth a look if you've grown accustomed to the mild gravy-like taste of Japanese curry. Prices start at ¥550; the seafood curry (¥600) is popular.

A **coin-locker room** (including large ¥700 lockers) is in the right-hand back corner of the station building as you prepare to leave the central exit.

Immediately to your left as you leave the ticket barrier are the **JR ticket office** and adjacent Twinkle Plaza **travel agency**. Both can handle rail-pass seat reservations.

For cash withdrawals, there is a Post Office **ATM** on the station concourse.

Tourist information

Hakodate Tourist Information desk (☎ 0138-23 5440, daily Apr to Oct 9am-7pm, Nov to March 9am-5pm, English spoken) is in the far corner of the Twinkle Plaza travel agency on the station concourse. Staff are used to dealing with foreign visitors and can provide plenty of information about the city and surrounding area.

An audio guide in English is available to rent on mini-disc, but at the time of writing there were no MD players for rental so the service is not very useful, unless you happen to have an MD player with you.

Internet

The **bakery café** inside the main station building (next to the coin-locker area) offers internet access at the rate of ¥500/hour. Otherwise try **Hot Web Café** (10am-8pm, ¥400/hour including soft drink), two minutes down the main shopping street which leads off from the station's central exit. It's just past Wako department store.

Books

A limited selection of English books is available on the 5th floor of **Boni Moriya** department store across the street from the station.

Getting around

Hakodate's **tram system** has been in operation since 1913 and it's still the best way of getting around the city. A one-day pass (¥1000, two days ¥1700) allows unlimited travel on all trams as well as city buses (except Hakodate Bus). If you only plan to take the tram, buy the ¥600 tram-only pass. The pass also covers the summer bus serv-

⛩ Karaoke tram

If you thought a tram was just a means of getting from A to B think again. In Hakodate it has become a night out in itself. Groups can hire a tram fully equipped with karaoke machine, flashing lights and microphones. Beer and snacks are allowed to get people in the mood for singing as the tram makes as many loops of the city as those on board can stand. Net curtains are installed to ensure passengers' anonymity.

ice to the top of Mt Hakodate. Purchase the pass either from the tourist information desk or from tram drivers.

A **shuttle bus** (¥300) operates between JR Hakodate and the city's airport. The bus leaves from/arrives at bus stop number 11 outside the station.

Festivals

In late July/early August an outdoor dramatic performance is staged at Goryokaku Fort (see p351). It's an astonishing theatrical event that tells the story of Hakodate using dry ice, fireworks, canons, motor boats, stampedes of horses, acrobatics, ballet, dance and an amateur cast of thousands.

A Frenchman had the idea for this when he visited Goryokaku and saw that the old fort was the perfect backdrop for a son-et-lumière-style spectacle.

Tickets can be purchased in advance (¥1800) or on the door (¥2000). Enquire at the tourist office.

Where to stay

The rates quoted below are for high season (June to Oct). Cheaper rooms are available outside of the peak season.

Most convenient for rail users is *Hotel Route Inn* (☎ 0138-21 4100, 🖳 www .route-inn.co.jp; ¥5200/S, ¥9500/Tw), right outside the station, to the left as you take the central exit. It has keenly priced, clean no-frills singles and twins. Breakfast is extra. Similar accommodation is to be had at either of the two Toyoko Inns (🖳 www .toyoko-inn.com) in town.

The first, *Toyoko Inn Hakodate Ekimae Asa-ichi* (☎ 0138-23 1045; ¥5880/S, ¥8190/D/Tw), is three minutes on foot from the station and located on the edge of the Morning Market, so you're perfectly placed for an early-morning walk around the stalls. It's also a good place to stay if in need of a haircut since there's a small hair salon attached offering bargain ¥1000, ten-minute cuts. Don't expect to have a long discussion about style.

The other, *Toyoko Inn Hakodate Daimon* (☎ 0138-24 1045; ¥6090/S,

¥8190/D/Tw), is a five-minute walk into town. Both offer the usual good-value singles with breakfast and high-speed internet access. The rate at Hakodate Daimon also includes a curry-rice supper (6:30-8pm).

Fitness Hotel 330 (☎ 0138-23 0330, 🖳 www.hotel330.co.jp; ¥7000/S, ¥12,000/ Tw), close to the station, has reasonably spacious rooms and a fitness club (additional charge).

Across the street is *Aqua Garden Hotel* (☎ 0138-23 2200, 🖳 www.aquagar denhotel.jp; ¥6500/S, ¥13,000/ Tw/D) with an internet corner in the lobby. The rooms are somewhat old-fashioned.

Near Horai-cho tram stop, *Hotel JAL City* (☎ 0138-24 2580, 🖳 http://hakodate .jalcity.co.jp; from ¥9240/S, ¥18,480/Tw) has small but upmarket rooms.

The nearest thing to a youth hostel is *Hakodate Youth Guest House* (☎ 0138-26 7892, 🖳 www 12.ocn.ne.jp/~hakodate, hako-ygh@cello.ocn.ne.jp; closed late Nov/early Dec, mid-Jan and mid-April), near Hotel JAL City. It's more like a pension than a hostel, with mostly twin Western-style rooms (no attached bath). The price ranges from ¥3800 (Oct 1 to June 30), to ¥4700 in summer; rates include a simple breakfast.

Where to eat

The morning market by the station is a good place to hunt around for an impromptu meal; you can be sure that the fish is fresh at the many restaurant stalls in the area.

Capricciosa (daily, 11:30am-10pm), on the second floor of Hotel JAL City, serves huge pizzas and pasta to a mostly young crowd. Hotel JAL City also has its own ground-floor restaurant, *Restaurant JAL City*, with lunch deals (the menu changes daily) from ¥1000.

Nearby is the *Jolly Jelly Fish Bar and Restaurant*. Look for the bright pink exterior and the name in English. Simple meals and beer on tap in an American pub-style atmosphere.

Hakodate Beer (daily, 11am-10pm) is a lively place where you can try various meat

Where to stay

10	Hakodate Youth Guest House	10	函館ユースゲストハウス
12	Hotel JAL City	12	ホテルJALシティ
17	Toyoko Inn Hakodate Ekimae Asa-ichi	17	東横イン函館駅前朝市
21	Hotel Route Inn	21	ホテル ルトイン
27	Fitness Hotel 330	27	フィットネスホテル３３０
28	Aqua Garden Hotel	28	アクアガーデン函館
29	Toyoko Inn Hakodate Daimon	29	東横イン函館大門

Where to eat and drink

5	Tao Tao	5	タオタオ
11	Jolly Jelly Fish	11	ジョリジェリフィッシュ

MOTOIZAKA SLOPE

Suehiro-cho

Hakodate Harbour

MOTOMACHI DISTRICT

HACHIMANZAKA SLOPE

Jujigai

Ropeway station for Mt Hakodate

YACHIZAKA SLOPE

GOKOKUJINJAZAKA SLOPE

Horai-cho

Aoyagi-cho

Hakodate

函館

HOKKAIDO

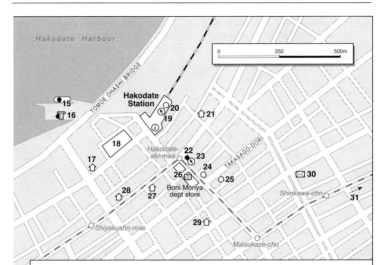

Where to eat and drink *(key continued from opposite)*

12 Capricciosa; Restaurant JAL City	12 カプリシヨーザ; レストランＪＡＬシティ
13 Lucky Pierrot	13 ラッキーピエロ
14 Hakodate Beer	14 函館ビール
20 Waka; Hot Hot	20 和華 ;ホットホット
24 Snaffle's	24 スナッフルス
25 Daimonyokocho	25 大門横丁

Other

1 Old Public Hall	1 旧函館区公会堂
2 Old British Consulate	2 旧イギリス領事館
3 Museum of Northern Peoples	3 北方民族資料館
4 Museum of Literature	4 文学館
6 Motomachi Roman Catholic Church	6 カトリック元町教会
7 Hakodate Russian Orthodox Church	7 函館ハリストス正教会
8 Hakodate Episcopal Church	8 函館聖ヨハネ教会
9 Yachigashira; Cape Tachimachi	9 営谷地頭; 立待岬
15 Memorial Ship *Mashumaru*	15 メモリアルシップ摩周丸

16 Queen's Port Hakodate;
    Classic Car Museum
	16 クィーンズポート函館;
	    クラシックカーミュージアム

18 Morning Market	18 朝市
19 Internet (bakery café)	19 インターネット (ベーカリーカフェ)
22 Wako (Dept Store)	22 Wako (デパート)
23 Hot Web Café	23 ホットウェブカフェ
26 Boni Moriya Dept Store	26 棒二森屋デパート
30 Central Post Office	30 中央郵便局
31 Goryokaku	31 五稜郭

HOKKAIDO

and seafood dishes and wash them down with locally brewed beers. In the summer, there's space to sit on a verandah outside.

In **Motomachi**, *Tao Tao* is a South-East Asian restaurant serving a range of Asian beers, soft drinks such as guava juice and great spicy food. It's open daily in summer from 12 noon to 11pm (in winter, Tue to Fri 5-11pm and Sat/Sun 12 noon-11pm).

Daimonyokocho is two rows of small informal shops serving everything from sushi to Asian cuisine. It's a very small area, less than five minutes on foot from the station, but a good place to look around for a bite to eat; dive into whichever place takes your fancy.

There are more than 20 stalls, most with counter or table service, and it's open in the evening from 6pm to late.

One of the best cake shops in town is *Snaffle's*, on the main street leading away from the station; it serves a great selection of cakes, buns and other sweet treats. They offer cake sets with tea/coffee.

There are several branches of the fast-food *Lucky Pierrot* hamburger and curry chain around town. The one most worth visiting, if only for the bizarre year-round Christmas décor, lies close to the Jujigai tram stop. It's easy to spot as it's the only building covered in Christmas trees and Santa Claus faces. Look out for the English sign 'Hamburger and Curry Restaurant. Santa Claus has come to Hakodate'. This place has to be seen to be believed. The burgers (from ¥350) are OK. They also serve a cheap ¥170 cup of coffee.

SAPPORO

The biggest city in Hokkaido (population: 1.86 million) and venue for the 1972 Winter Olympics, Sapporo is frequently voted the city where most Japanese would like to live. It certainly feels relaxed and cosmopolitan, with green parks, 19th- and 20th-century red-brick buildings and a thriving entertainment district. It's also one of the easiest cities to get around, thanks to the north–south grid layout. If you need a further incentive to spend a couple of days here, time your visit to coincide with one of the many summer and winter festivals, the most famous of which is the annual Snow Festival in February (see p362). Like the rest of Hokkaido, Sapporo receives a thick blanket of snow in the winter but summer is mild and provides the perfect opportunity for relaxing in the city's central Odori Park.

A good resource for online sightseeing information is 💻 www.welcome.city.sapporo.jp/english/index.html. An excellent guide in English (available in Kinokuniya bookstore, see p362) is the *Sapporo Guide Book* by Howard Tarnoff. It contains sightseeing tips as well as recommended restaurants and bars which have all been tried and tested by this local resident who shows a great love for the city. For more up-to-date information see 💻 www.xene.net, or get a copy of the bi-monthly *Xene*, see p359.

What to see and do

Free guided tours are offered at **Sapporo Beer Museum** (N7E9, 💻 www.sapporobeer.jp/english/guide/sapporo), on the site of a former working brewery (daily, 9am-4:30/5:30pm, free, reservations required by phone ☎ 011-731 4368 or 💻 museum@sapporobeer.jp). Guided tours are in Japanese only (tape in English available), but you're rushed around the different floors at such speed that there's barely time to take in any of the exhibits. If you're in need of a drink after the tour, walk over to Sapporo Beer Garden (see p363). To reach the museum and beer garden, take the bus which leaves from the south side of Seibu department store, outside the south exit of the station (stop is Sapporo Eki-mae).

Directly south of the station is **Odori Koen (Park)** which stretches for 1.5km through the centre of the city between West 1 and West 12. In summer, people come here to relax, play games and hang out. In the eastern corner of the park is the 147.2m-high **TV Tower** (daily, 9am-10pm in summer, 9.30am-9.30pm in winter, ¥700), built in 1957. It has an observatory that's not really high enough for exceptional views. (Much better is the 38th-floor observation platform inside the JR Tower at Sapporo station; see p358).

To the north of Odori Park is the former **Hokkaido Government Office Building** (daily, 8:45am-5pm, free), nicknamed 'Red Brick'. Built in 1888, it was gutted by fire and had to be completely rebuilt in 1911. Entrance is free, though not all the rooms inside are open to the public. One block south and slightly to the east is Sapporo's famous **Clock Tower** (Tue-Sun, 9am-5pm, ¥200). If you don't see the clock immediately, you'll no doubt see the tourists lining up at the official photograph point in front of it. The tower was constructed in 1878 but had to be redesigned when the clock that arrived from the USA was too big. Inside, the ground floor is used as an exhibition space and concerts are sometimes staged on the second floor.

West of the Hokkaido Government Building are the **Botanical Gardens** (Tue-Sun, Apr to Sep 9am-4pm; Oct to Nov 9am-3:30pm, ¥400), opened in 1886 and still the perfect place for a summer stroll. The ticket includes entry to a small Ainu museum in the grounds but there's a better museum devoted to preserving Ainu heritage and culture in **Kaderu 2.7** (N2 W7), across the street from the entrance to the gardens. On the seventh floor is a small **Ainu exhibition** (Mon-Sat, 9am-5pm, free) with items of Ainu clothing and equipment used in daily life. Pop into the office next door to pick up a leaflet.

Hokkaido Museum of Modern Art (N1 W17, Tue-Sun, 9:30am-5pm, ¥450) is worth a visit as they frequently have good temporary exhibitions of works from Japan and abroad.

Football and baseball fans might consider a guided tour of the 40,000-capacity **Sapporo Dome** (🖳 www.sapporo-dome.co.jp), a venue for the 2002 World Cup and home to local teams Consadole Sapporo (football) and Hokkaido Nippon-Ham Fighters (baseball).

The stadium is known for its grass pitch, which grows outside and is brought inside on a hi-tech cushion of air when matches are played. If you're not in town on a match day, you can watch the game on the website! Stadium tours (¥1000, ☎ 011-850 1020 for times) take in the stadium, bullpen, locker room and team director's room. An observatory (¥500) at the top of the dome is reached via an 'aerial escalator'. From 53m above the stadium ground level, you get a good view of the surrounding area. A combination ticket (stadium tour and observatory) costs ¥1200. Tickets for football matches (March to December; once or twice a month) and baseball games (April to October; six days each month) are available from travel agencies in the city as well as some

⛩ **Toilet in the sky**
Why not take a comfort break at the top of the city's highest building? The toilets at the JR Tower's 38th-floor observation room are 160 metres above street level and walled with glass. According to the designer, 'one is supposed to do it as if one is taking a leak into a river from the top of a bridge' – well, you can certainly imagine you are taking a leak onto the city below. The men's restroom has glass walls that afford an almost unobstructed view as long as weather permits. 'I tried to make men feel as if they were floating in the air while relieving themselves. I finally arrived at this uncompromising design,' revealed Junko Kobayashi, architect and director of the Japan Toilet Association.

convenience stores. Prices are ¥2700, ¥3200, ¥3700 and ¥4400 for football matches and ¥2200, ¥3500 and ¥4500 for baseball games. Concerts by international artists such as Billy Joel are also held here on an occasional basis. Take the Toho subway line to Fukuzumi station.

One hundred and sixty metres above the south exit of JR Sapporo station, the 38-storey landmark **JR Tower Sapporo** is a giant commercial complex; it houses a department store, hotel, spa and multiplex cinema. The top-floor observation platform (¥700) offers unparalleled views of the city and a possibly unique toilet experience (see box above). A special lift operates from the 6th to the 38th floor. Alternatively, if you don't want to pay just for the view, you could go for a drink in the revolving bar at the top of the Century Royal Hotel next to Sapporo station. You get the view for the price of a drink.

If you want to soak weary limbs at the end of a day of traipsing around the city, **Sky Resort Spa Pulau Bulan** (☎ 011-251 6366, daily, 11am-11pm, ¥2800, hotel guests ¥1500) boasts modern and minimalist hot spring facilities on the 22nd floor of JR Tower Hotel Nikko Sapporo (see p362). Take the lift from the ground-floor hotel lobby. Towels are provided. The spa is divided into men's and women's sections. Massage and spa-treatment packages are available (a 40-minute massage plus use of the spa is ¥6300). There are fantastic views and a variety of pools, Jacuzzis, a relaxation room and Finnish sauna. It's a great retreat from the noise of the station and city below.

In the evening, the place to head for an eyeful of Japan by night is the **Susukino** entertainment district. Susukino is (in)famous for its soaplands, but the streets are also packed with pachinko parlours, pubs and bars. Billed as the 'largest amusement area north of Tokyo', the area boasts between 4000 and 5000 bars and restaurants, all of which rely on the evening trade when the district is flooded by businessmen. Take the subway to Susukino.

PRACTICAL INFORMATION
Station guide
The station has two main exits: North and South; take the South exit for all the main sights, including Susukino, the Clock Tower, TV Tower and the Botanical Gardens. The station itself is divided into two halves, East and West, with JR ticket offices and Twinkle Plaza travel agencies on both sides. There are ticket barriers providing access to/from the platforms on both east and west sides. The best bet when leav-

ing a train and wanting to head for the centre of Sapporo (or for the tourist information office) is to leave the platform area and enter the station concourse via the west side. Coin lockers (including enormous ¥600 ones) are located in the passageway which connects the east and west sides of the station.

The station building is full of modern works of art which collectively form part of the JR Tower Art Guide – a full list of all the works of art, and where they are located, is on a board outside the entrance to Daimaru department store close to the south exit. All works of art are by Hokkaido-commissioned artists. The aim is to 'explore new possibilities of art for an urban public environment adjacent to a station'.

JR Hokkaido operates a **Visitors Information Desk** (daily, 8:30am-6:30pm), where rail passes can be exchanged, rail-pass holders can make seat reservations and you can buy a JR Hokkaido Pass (see p15), as well as the one-day Sapporo/Otaru Welcome Ticket (see p364). It's a separate counter (marked 'foreigner only') inside the main JR ticket office on the west side of the station. Of course you can also use any other JR ticket office or Twinkle Plaza to book tickets/make seat reservations.

The station is home to a flagship department store (**Daimaru**), another shopping mall and cinema complex, and a tower which houses the 350-room **JR Tower Hotel Nikko Sapporo** on the 23rd-34th floors (see p362). The **multiplex cinema** is on the 7th floor and is called Sapporo Cinema Frontier.

Tourist information

The **Tourist Information Corner** (☎ 011-209 5030, daily, 9am-5:30pm) is inside the JR Twinkle Plaza travel agency on the west side of the station concourse. You'll see it just before you take the south exit. Staff speak English, are well supplied with leaflets and maps, and can provide information/leaflets for other destinations in Hokkaido.

International Communication Plaza (N1 W3, ☎ 011-211 3678, daily 9am-5:30pm, 🖳 www.plaza-sapporo.or.jp) is in the city centre, on the third floor of the Sapporo MN Building across the street from the Clock Tower.

At either place, pick up a copy of the monthly *What's on in Sapporo?* and bi-monthly *Xene*, a magazine with listings for restaurants, bars and clubs.

Getting around

Sapporo has a modern subway system with three lines (Namboku, Tozai and Toho lines) that interconnect at Odori station, one stop south of Sapporo station. There is also a tram line. There is a minimum subway fare of ¥200. One-day subway passes (¥800) can be purchased from vending machines at subway stations. The 'common-use one-day card' (¥1000) is valid on the subway, tram and most buses.

Bikes can be rented from the **Rent A Cycle** (☎ 011-223 7662, daily, 8:30am-5pm, ¥1000/day) outlet at N2 E2.

Internet

On the ground (first) floor of the Sumitomo Seimei Building outside the south exit of Sapporo station (and directly above Paul's Café, see p363) is a 24-hour internet café called **i-Café** (N5, W5, ☎ 011-221 3440). Look for the green 'internet café' sign in English. Membership is free but you pay ¥200 for the first 30 minutes or ¥800 for three hours. Free snacks and soft drinks.

❑ Sapporo orientation

Thanks to Sapporo's grid system, it's easy to find your way almost anywhere in the city. Nearly all addresses include a grid reference, so a building at 'N3 W6', for example, is three blocks north and six blocks west of the grid apex on the eastern corner of Odori Koen in the city centre.

SAPPORO 札幌

Where to stay
 1 Hotel Sapporo Met's
 6 Toyoko Inn Sapporo-eki Kita-guchi
 7 JR Tower Hotel Nikko Sapporo
14 Nakamuraya Ryokan
18 R&B Hotel Sapporo
19 Sapporo Grand Hotel
25 Iceberg Hotel
26 Sapporo International YH
29 Toyoko Inn Sapporo Suskino-Minami
30 Hotel New Budget Sapporo
32 The Hamilton Sapporo

Where to eat and drink
 3 Sapporo Beer Garden
 9 Ramen restaurants (Esta Dept Store)
10 The Buffet (Daimaru Dept Store)
12 Paul's Café (Sumitomo Seimei Bldg)
20 Aji no Tokeidai
23 Aozora; Lilac (City Hall)

Other
 2 Sapporo Beer Museum
 4 Kura-no-yu
 5 Rent a cycle
 6 Central Post Office
 8 JR Tower Sapporo; Sky Resort
   Spa Pulau Bulau
 9 Esta Dept Store
11 Kinokuniya
12 i-Café
13 Botanical Gardens
15 Kaderu 2.7
16 Former Hokkaido Government
   Office Bldg
17 Kinko's (Onose Building)
21 International Communications Plaza
22 Clock Tower
24 TV Tower
27 Sapporo Dome
31 Odori Koen
33 Hokkaido Museum of Modern Art

 1 ホテルサッポロメッツ
 6 東横イン 札幌駅北口
 7 JRタワーホテル日航札幌
14 中村屋旅館
18 R＆Bホテル札幌
19 札幌グランドホテル
25 アイスバーグホテル
26 サッポロ国際ユースホステル
29 東横イン札幌すすきの南
30 ホテルニューバジェット札幌
32 ザ ハミルトン札幌

 3 札幌ビアガーデン
 9 エスタデパート
10 ザブッフェ (大丸デパート)
12 ポールズカフェ
20 味の時計台
23 あおぞら; ライラック (市役所)

 2 札幌ビア博物館
 4 蔵ノ湯
 5 レンタサイクル
 6 中央郵便局
 8 スカイリゾート;JRタワー札幌
   スパ プラウブラン
 9 エスタデパート
11 紀伊國屋
12 アイカフェ
13 植物園
15 かでる2.7
16 旧本庁舎

17 キンコーズ (小野瀬ビル)
21 国際プラザ
22 時計台
24 テレビタワー
27 札幌ドーム
31 大通り公園
33 北海道立近代美術館

There are internet terminals inside **Doutor Coffee** (N6 W3, Sapporo station north exit, daily 7am-10pm) and at a branch of **Kinko's** (N3 W3, 1F Onose Building, daily 8am-11pm). Most convenient of all, but not very relaxing, are the two internet terminals at the tourist information counter inside Twinkle Plaza. They are free to use but there is often a queue of people so you won't usually get more than a few minutes to check emails.

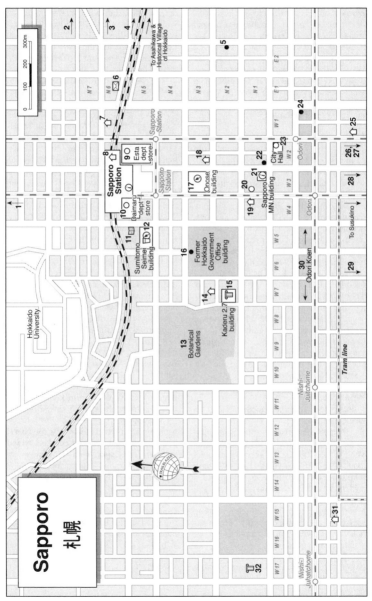

Sapporo
札幌

To Asahikawa &
Historical Village
of Hokkaido

0 100 200 300m

Hokkaido
University

Sapporo
Station

Sapporo Station

8

9 ○ Esta
dept
store

10 ○ Daimaru
dept store

11

Sumitomo
Seimei
building

12

16
Former
Hokkaido
Government
Office
building

13
Botanical
Gardens

14
15
Kaderu 2.7
building

17 ○ Onose
building

18

19 20
21 22
Sapporo
MN building

23
City
Hall

24

25

26
27

28

29

30
Odori Koen

31

32

Odori

To Susukino

Tram line

Nishi-
Juitchome

Nishi-
Juhatchome

HOKKAIDO

N 7 N 6 N 5 N 4 N 3 N 2 N 1 E 1 E 2

W 1 W 2 W 3 W 4 W 5 W 6 W 7 W 8 W 9 W 10 W 11 W 12 W 13 W 14 W 15 W 16 W 17

Books

A decent selection of English books, and small selection in German and French, are available on the second floor of **Kinokuniya** (N5 W5), next to the station. Walk through Daimaru department store, which is connected to the station, and you'll see Kinokuniya in front of you as you exit. There is a smaller bookstore on the 8th floor of **Daimaru** itself.

Festivals

The biggest event of the year is the **Yuki Matsuri** (Snow Festival) in February when tourists from around the country and the world flock to see the huge ice sculptures on display in Odori Koen. The **Yosakoi Soran Festival** in June brings together dance teams from all over Japan, who compete to win over the judges with their own interpretation of a dance rhythm that originated in Kochi (see p440). The festival dates back to 1991 when a student attended the Yosakoi Festival in Kochi and decided to organize a similar event in Sapporo. Thousands of dancers are now watched by a crowd of nearly two million.

In summer the **Pacific Music Festival** (July to August), originally started by Leonard Bernstein, brings together young musicians from all over the world who stage a series of concerts around the city. Some performances are free.

Where to stay

Most hotels offer reduced rates from October to May.

The plushest place in town is the 350-room *JR Tower Hotel Nikko Sapporo* (N5 W2, ☎ 011-251 2222, 💻 www.jr-tower .com; ¥16,170/S, ¥33,495/Tw). It's built onto the south side of the JR station and is part of a complex which also houses a department store and an 'observation spa' – a hot spring (see p358) with commanding views of downtown Sapporo. Rail-pass holders receive a moderate discount on standard room rates.

Nakamuraya Ryokan (N3 W7, ☎ 011-241 2111, 💻 www.nakamura-ya.com; ¥7350/S, ¥13,650/Tw, ¥18,900/Tr) is a typ-ical Japanese inn with tatami rooms (all with small attached bath/toilet). Breakfast is ¥1575 and dinner ¥3150. The ryokan is in the city centre, on the road between the Botanical Gardens and Hokkaido government buildings.

A couple of stops on the Nanboku subway line north of Sapporo station to Kita-Juhachijo station is *Hotel Sapporo Met's* (N17 W5, ☎ 011-726 5511, 💻 www.hotel mets.co.jp; ¥5250/S, ¥8930/Tw inc breakfast). For the price of a business hotel, you get a mini-apartment, including washing machine, tumble dryer and small kitchen area. *The Hamilton Sapporo* (S1 W15, ☎ 011-632 0080, 💻 www.the-hamilton.com; ¥8500/S, ¥13,500/Tw, ¥18,500/Tr) is a good mid-range choice in a quiet part of town. Take the Tozai subway line to Nishi Juhachi-chome station or the tram to Nishi-jugo stop, both are a minute from the hotel. *Hotel New Budget Sapporo* (S3 W6, ☎ 011-261 4953, 💻 www.newbudget.com; ¥5200/S, ¥8400/Tw inc breakfast) is a business hotel with automated check in (cash only).

Toyoko Inn (💻 www.toyoko-inn.com) has several branches in the city. Most convenient for the station is *Toyoko Inn Sapporo-eki Kita-guchi* (N6 W1, ☎ 011-728 1045; ¥7140/S, ¥9240/D/Tw). If you prefer to be closer to the nightlife, *Toyoko Inn Sapporo Susukino Minami* (S6 E2, ☎ 011-551 1045; ¥6930/S ¥9240/D/Tw) would be a better bet. Rooms are larger than average, with mini-kitchen areas which come with separate sink. Billed as 'condominium-style' rooms, with roomier bathrooms, this hotel would be a good bet if you're planning a few days in the city and want a bit more space without paying extra.

Another good budget bet is *R&B Hotel Sapporo* (N3 W2, ☎ 011-210 1515, 💻 www.randb.jp), where the single-only rate of ¥6720 includes a simple breakfast of croissants, coffee and orange juice. The rooms have wide beds and check-in is automated (with a key card). *Iceberg Hotel* (S2 W1, ☎ 011-290 3000, 💻 www.hyperhotel .co.jp/hoin/hotel_sapporo.html; ¥6090/S, ¥9240/D/Tw) is clean and well-located. Breakfast is included in the rate.

The best budget choice by far is *Sapporo International Youth Hostel* (☎ 011-825 3120, 🖳 www.youthhostel.or.jp/kokusai; ¥3800, breakfast ¥630). The family-size tatami rooms as well as the Western-style dorms (¥3200) are very comfortable and kept spotless. All rooms are equipped with individual lockers; in the basement there's a hot spring bath and coin laundry. From the station, take the Toho subway line to Gakuen-mae station and follow the signs for Exit No 2.

Where to eat

Check the latest issue of *Xene* (🖳 www.xene.net) for the newest restaurants and bars. There are plenty of places to eat in and around the redeveloped station area, including a selection of dedicated ramen restaurants on the 10th floor of *Esta*, the department store on the left as you take the south exit of the station.

Daimaru department store, built into the JR station building, has its own restaurant floor (the 8th floor) including sushi, tonkatsu, Italian, and an all-you-can-eat buffet restaurant called *The Buffet* which charges ¥1449 at lunch and ¥2079 for dinner, with soft-drink bar for an additional ¥210. In the store's basement there is a food court where you can pick up lunch boxes, fruit juices, pastries and the like.

A Sapporo speciality is *jingiskan* (Hokkaido lamb and vegetables grilled in a special pan), named after Genghis Khan and served in a pan shaped like a Mongolian hat. The best place to try jingiskan is *Sapporo Beer Garden* (N7 E9, daily, 11:30am-9pm) where there are various all-you-can-eat-and-drink deals (from ¥3100/pp for 100 minutes). In the summer, there's seating in the garden as well as in the large hall. The beer garden is close to Sapporo Beer Museum (see p356). During the winter, you can also try eating and drinking inside one of several **Snow Caves** (Feb 1-15, 12-9pm) at Sapporo Beer Garden. As the publicity says: 'Having hot dishes in the snow is definitely a unique experience.'

Another local speciality is Sapporo ramen, the broth of which is made from *miso* (fermented soybean paste) and is rich with garlic and butter. A popular place to try it is *Aji no Tokeidai*, which has several branches around the city. Closest to the station is the one opposite Sapporo Grand Hotel (N1 W4), on one of the main streets leading south from the station towards Odori Park. Sit at the counter and watch the chefs prepare your ramen. 'Miso ramen' (made, not surprisingly, with lots of miso) is recommended. The reasonable prices and large portions mean this place gets crowded at lunchtime.

Paul's Café (N5 W5, ☎ 011-231 7320, 🖳 www.mnc.to/~pauls, daily 11:30am-11pm) is an informal bar/restaurant near the station which serves authentic Belgian beer (on tap and in the bottle) and delicious roast chicken. As one Sapporo resident describes it: 'There are no traditional Japanese dishes but when tourists get tired of speaking Japanese or being ignored by shy Japanese people, this is a nice shelter to warm them up.' Paul the owner is proud of his roast chicken and Belgian pommes frites (¥1500), but he also does a variety of alternative dishes such as rabbit stew and beef stew. Lunch deals cost from ¥700. The café is in the basement of Sumitomo Seimei Building, which houses the Century Royal Hotel. Look for the hotel sign on the building to your right as you take the south exit of Sapporo station.

For a budget lunch, head for **City Hall** (N1 W2), where there are two café restaurants on the 18th and 19th floors that have good views as well as cheap food. *Aozora* on the 19th has simple meals such as chicken with rice or noodles for ¥500-600 and there's a similar menu at *Lilac* on the 18th.

Even cheaper is the *basement canteen*, where you buy a ticket from a vending machine (choose what you want from the plastic foods on display in the entrance and match up the kanji with the descriptions on the machine); take the ticket to one of the serving counters to collect your food. Prices start at around ¥300. If you arrive shortly before 12 noon, you'll be able to get a seat and witness the arrival of white-collar workers en masse.

HOKKAIDO

...ain bathing

'Those who like hot springs but are on a budget should consider a mini side-trip from Sapporo to **Kura-no-yu** (💻 www.kuranoyu.com), 'located just in front of Naebo station, the next station from Sapporo on the JR Chitose line ... What I was most surprised about was the price. It only costs ¥390. When you compare it to other hot springs in Sapporo, it is surprisingly reasonable. If you have time, try it!'

Mari Watanabe

Side trip from Sapporo

Though not accessible by rail, it's worth considering a trip to the **Historical Village of Hokkaido** (Tue-Sun 9:30am-5pm, April to Nov ¥830, Dec to March to 4.30pm and ¥680, 💻 www.kaitaku.or.jp) in Nopporo Forest Park in the suburbs of Sapporo, since the route is operated by JR Bus and is free to rail-pass holders. A large number of buildings from the Meiji and Taisho periods (mid-19th to early 20th century) have been restored and moved here. It's a very atmospheric place to wander around and there are explanations in English. The main entrance to the village is through the old Sapporo railway station, in use from 1908 to 1952.

Although the village is the main attraction of Nopporo Forest Park it's by no means the only reason for heading out here. Locals joke that tourists visit for the historical village, while residents head here for the 30km of trails through the forest. Pick up a map of the forest park from the tourist office in Sapporo; it has details of footpaths and distances along various routes.

Three buses a day run to the village from Sapporo station (60 mins). Alternatively, take the train to Shin-Sapporo, from where more buses go to the village. Buses leave from stop No 10 on the north side of the bus terminal outside Shin-Sapporo station.

Some of the return buses from the village continue on to Sapporo station after stopping at Shin-Sapporo, but it's quicker to take the train from Shin-Sapporo back to Sapporo.

See box p77 for details of **Otaru Transportation Museum**, a worthwhile side trip for rail enthusiasts. If travelling to Otaru without a rail pass, consider buying the **JR Hokkaido Sapporo–Otaru One-Day Welcome Pass** (¥1500), valid for journeys on all trains between Sapporo and Otaru, as well as the three subway lines in Sapporo. For more details, see 💻 www2.jrhokkaido.co.jp/global/english/travel/img/otaru_e.pdf.

The '**No More Hibakusha Kaikan**' museum in Heiwa is worth visiting: *Kaikan* means hall, and *Hibakusha* is the term used to refer to the victims of the atomic bomb attacks on Nagasaki and Hiroshima who are still alive. Hibakusha are scattered across Japan; a few hundred live in Hokkaido. It's a really small museum (Sun-Fri, 10am-4pm; free), the size of an ordinary house, and is owned by people who experienced the atomic bombs.

It's nothing like the scale of the museums in Hiroshima (see p262) or Nagasaki (see p397) but it's certainly worth a look if you haven't visited either of these places. Photos of the horrific injuries and burns sustained by victims minutes, hours, days and years after the atomic blasts are accompanied by paintings.

Local trains leave Sapporo (on the line to Shin-Sapporo) roughly three times an hour and take 12 minutes to Heiwa. The frequency is the same in the other direction.

To get to the museum head up the flight of steps at Heiwa station, turn right and walk all the way along the bridge to the end. Right in front of you as you leave the bridge is a red-brick building which has a copy of Hiroshima's A-Bomb Dome on the roof. Ring the bell to be let in.

ASAHIKAWA

Despite the backdrop of the Daisetsu mountain range, Asahikawa is not an attractive place by Hokkaido's standards. The second biggest city in Hokkaido after Sapporo serves mainly as a transport hub and a gateway to Daisetsuzan National Park (see p370).

What to see and do
Kawamura Kaneto Ainu Memorial Hall (daily, 8am-6pm in summer, 9am-5pm in winter, ¥500) is a very small museum with a few exhibits on Ainu traditions. The museum was founded by Kenichi Kawamura, an eighth generation Ainu who has campaigned for many years for greater recognition of Hokkaido's indigenous population (see box p366).

It's a ten-minute bus ride (bus No 24) from bus stop No 14 outside Seibu department store. Get off at Ainu Kinenkan-mae.

Check at the tourist information office if any good temporary exhibitions are showing at the otherwise missable **Asahikawa Museum of Art** (Tue-Sun, 10am-5pm, ¥100 for the permanent exhibition; additional charge for temporary exhibitions) located across town in a corner of Tokiwa Park – which is in itself a pleasant enough place to kill time. There are boating facilities on the lake in the summer.

The newest attraction in town is Asahikawa Science Center, or **Sci-pal** as it is known locally (Tue-Sun, 9:30am-5pm, ¥500), a lot more entertaining than its

---

⛩ **Racing with carthorses**
Apart from snow and ice, Asahikawa is known for a special type of horse race, unique to Hokkaido, known as *banba*. Horses, twice the weight of thoroughbreds (or so it is claimed), compete in a test of strength, racing to pull one-tonne sleighs and a driver around a track.

This unusual sport, which has its roots in France and Belgium, first appeared in Japan during the Meiji era when the pioneers who came to Hokkaido used horses to plough the fields. Today's race track includes a number of steep hills which the horse and driver have to negotiate. Unlike in a normal horse race, the winner is not the horse whose nose crosses the finishing line first. Both horse and attached sleigh must cross the line before the winner can be declared.

Racing takes place only on certain days each year so check details at the tourist information booth inside the station or call ☎ 0166-75 3100. Races take place outside the city at the race track in Kamui-cho.

⛩ The Ainu: fight for survival

When Kenichi Kawamura visited the National Museum of Natural History in Washington, USA, in April 1999, for an exhibition of Ainu artefacts, he was joined by the late Japanese prime minister, Keizo Obuchi. Kawamura overheard the prime minister enquire of another visitor to the museum, 'Are there still Ainu in Hokkaido?'

The Ainu have long been almost invisible to the outside world. In a speech to the United Nations in 1992, a representative of the Ainu people told how the Japanese government had "denied even our existence in its proud claim that Japan, alone in the world, is a 'mono-ethnic nation'". The Ainu originally populated parts of northern Honshu as well as Hokkaido, living in small communities of up to 10 families, fishing from the rivers and hunting bear – a sacred animal in Ainu tradition – in the forests.

There was never any question of land rights until the *wajin* (Japanese) moved further north, calling the Ainu 'dogs' (the Japanese word for dog is *inu*) and forcing them off their land. The only work that some could find was manual labour with logging companies – thus the Ainu found themselves in the extraordinary position of having to earn a living by destroying the very land on which they had lived.

In 1899, the Hokkaido Former Aborigine Protection Law was passed, giving the island's governor power to 'manage the communal assets of the Ainu people for their benefit', on the pretext that the Ainu were unable to manage these assets themselves. Almost a century was to pass until the law was repealed in 1997, replaced with a new act to promote Ainu culture and return assets that had been 'managed' by the prefectural government. Endless legal wrangles in court over the exact amount and how it should be paid suggest a quick resolution is unlikely.

There has been some attempt to revive Ainu traditions and in particular the Ainu language, now spoken by fewer than a dozen elderly people. Weekly Ainu language radio courses have started and storytellers are being trained to continue the Ainu oral tradition. In 1994, Shigeru Kayano became the first Ainu to win a seat in the Upper House of the Japanese Parliament, and in a landmark 1998 ruling a Hokkaido judge recognized the indigenous status of the Ainu people for the first time.

Kayano died in 2006, just short of his 80th birthday and not long before a picture book he wrote about the Ainu, *The Ainu and the Fox*, was published for the first time in English. Kayano wrote the story, based on an Ainu legend, in 1974 for elementary schoolchildren. During his lifetime he also compiled an Ainu-language dictionary and recorded folk tales. Nobody yet knows if all this was too little too late to save the Ainu from cultural extinction.

dry name suggests. Opened in 2005, the complex includes a state-of-the-art planetarium and interactive exhibits which give visitors the chance to experience zero gravity and feel what it is like to jump on the moon. Popular with children, Sci-pal set itself a target of 200,000 visitors in the first year, but surpassed this within two months.

Take bus No 82 from stop No 5 (across the street from the station). The bus goes to 'Minami Koko' but you should get out at the 'Kagakukan-mae' stop, right outside the building.

Asahiyama Zoo (Apr-Oct daily, 9:30am-5:15pm, ¥580, Nov-March Fri-Tue, 11am-2pm, ¥290) is Japan's northernmost zoo and is a good opportunity to see some of the animals native to Hokkaido, including the brown bear and red fox. An underwater tunnel gives access to the penguin tank. In the aquarium seals swim up through a tunnel into a large tank. The museum opened in 1967 but by the end of the 1990s was a very sorry affair; it hadn't been updated, was losing millions of yen in public money, and faced closure. Investment has led to a redesign of the enclosures, creating an environment tailored to each species. To reach the zoo, take an Asahikawa Denkikidou Bus (☎ 0166-23 3355) No 41 or 47 from stop No 5 outside Asahikawa station; the journey time is 35-40 minutes. A combination ticket (¥1800) gives entry to both Sci-pal and Asahiyama Zoo.

JR Hokkaido offers a special **Asahiyama Zoo Ticket** (⌨ www.jrhokkaido .co.jp/global; ¥5500), which includes the rail journey from Sapporo (unreserved seat on the limited express), bus journey from Asahikawa station to the zoo and entrance ticket (which also means you can walk straight in and don't have to queue up at the entrance). The ticket is valid for four days.

PRACTICAL INFORMATION
Station guide
Asahikawa is a major rail junction and it celebrates 110 years of connection to the rail network in 2008.

At the bottom of the stairs from the platforms up to the station concourse is an intercom that can be used to request assistance with getting up the stairs.

There is only one exit. Platform 1 is nearest the ticket barrier. For all other platforms you need to take the underground passageway. Local trains to Furano (see p348) and Biei (see p349) depart from platforms 6 and 7. On the ground floor is a soba/udon place, a non-descript restaurant, a branch of the *Lotteria* hamburger bar, a small bakery and a row of coin lockers (all sizes). There is a small branch **Post Office** (Mon-Fri 9am-6pm, Sat/Sun 9am-5pm) with **ATM** inside the station building.

Tourist information
The **Tourist Information Centre** (☎ 0166-22 6704, Wed-Mon, 9:30am-5pm) is in a corner at the end of the station building. Turn right as you exit the ticket barrier and go to the end, passing **coin lockers** as you go (all sizes, including ¥500 ones). Limited English is spoken, but English maps are available as is information on onward journeys to Asahidake (see p370), Furano and Biei. They also sell a decent assortment of local pottery and handicrafts and you can pick up a copy of the monthly English-language newsletter *Asahikawa Info*, with information on local events, concerts and film listings.

Festivals
In February (usually around 11th/ 12th), the city celebrates the **Asahikawa Winter Festival**. It's not as vast or commercial as Sapporo Snow Festival (see p362) but is just as impressive. The World Ice Sculpture Competition brings together international teams who compete to build giant sculptures in Tokiwa Park, about 15 minutes' walk north of the station. A fireworks display takes place on the opening night. For precise dates, contact the tourist office.

Where to stay
The JR-operated *Asahikawa Terminal Hotel* (☎ 0166-24 0111, ⌨ www.asahikawa -th.com; ¥7507/S, ¥13,282/D, ¥15,592/Tw) is right outside the station and is an ideal overnight base. The lobby is just a few steps from the ticket barrier. You might be able to get cheaper rooms by trying your luck on the day, when they will often include breakfast (otherwise this is an extra ¥1155). Rail-pass holders get the usual discount. There's a good Japanese restaurant on the sixth floor.

Toyoko Inn Asahikawa Ekimae (☎ 0166-27 1045, ⌨ www.toyoko-inn.com; ¥7140/S, ¥9240/D/Tw) is two minutes on foot from the station, as is *Hotel Route Inn Asahikawa Ekimae* (☎ 0166-21 5011,

ASAHIKAWA 旭川

Where to stay

10 Asahikawa Youth Hostel
11 Hotel Route Inn Asahikawa Ekimae
12 Asahikawa Terminal Hotel
14 Toyoko Inn Asahikawa Ekimae

10 旭川ユースホステル
11 ホテルルートイン 旭川駅前
12 旭川ターミナルホテル
14 東横イン 旭川駅前

Where to eat and drink

 3 Kimihiro
 4 Mister Donut
 5 Doutor Coffee
 6 Aji no Tokeidai
 7 McDonald's
 8 Baikoken
 9 Capricciosa
12 Orion (Esta Building)

 3 仁泰
 4 ミスタードーナッツ
 5 ドトールコヒ
 6 味の時計台
 7 マクドナルド
 8 梅光軒
 9 カプリチョーザ
12 オリオン (エスタビル)

Other

 1 Asahikawa Museum of Art
   (Tokiwa Park)
 2 Central Post Office
13 Post Office
15 Asahikawa Science Center (Sci-Pal)
16 Asahiyama Zoo

 1 旭川美術館 (常磐公園)

 2 中央郵便局
13 郵便局
15 旭川市科学館 (サイパル)
16 旭山動物園

⌨ www.route-inn.co.jp; from ¥5300/S, ¥9000/Tw).

Alternatively, take a 20-minute bus journey to *Asahikawa Youth Hostel* (☎ 0166-61 2800, 🖨 61 8886; ¥3360/4360). Most accommodation is in tatami dorms but there are a few twin rooms with attached bath/toilet. Excellent meals are served in the café; the huge breakfast (¥630) is especially recommended. In the winter you're perfectly placed to take advantage of the Inosawa ski slope next to the hostel. To reach the hostel take bus No 444 or 550 (¥200) from stop No 11, just along from Malsa department store, a couple of minutes from the station.

Where to eat

Sapporo ramen may be better known but Asahikawa is proud of its version, where the pork is stewed in shochu.

Along the main street that runs north from the station is a branch of the Sapporo ramen restaurant *Aji no Tokeidai* with a handy picture menu. Another good ramen place, *Baikoken* (11am-3:30pm, 5-8:30pm),

is in the basement of the Piaza building three minutes from the station. Popular with locals and crowded at lunchtime.

In the basement of the '**A.s.h.**' **building** is a branch of the Italian chain *Capricciosa*. Further up this street is *Kimihiro* (☎ 0166-26 8138, 11:30am-3pm, 5:30pm-12midnight), a casual Italian place with a decent selection of Italian wine. The imaginative menu goes beyond standard pizza fare. The entrance is up a flight of stairs, on the right hand side of the main street. Lunch deals for ¥950. Along this street you'll also find a variety of fast-food outlets, including *McDonald's*, *Doutor Coffee* and *Mister Donut*; all open daily.

On the fifth floor of the Esta building which includes Asahikawa Terminal Hotel there is a small selection of Japanese restaurants, including a ramen place. *Orion*, the casual café/restaurant in the lobby of Asahikawa Terminal Hotel, does afternoon cake sets (¥580) and best value of all is the 'daily lunch' set menu; for ¥740 you get soup, salad, bread, main course (changes daily) and coffee – a bargain.

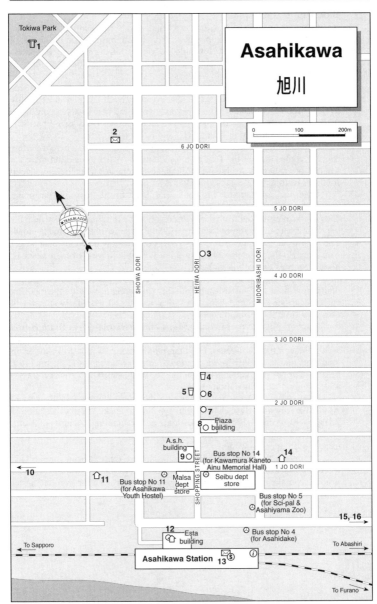

Asahikawa
旭川

Tokiwa Park
1

0   100   200m

2

6 JO DORI

5 JO DORI

TRAILBLAZER

SHOWA DORI

HEIWA DORI

MIDORIBASHI DORI

3

4 JO DORI

3 JO DORI

4

5   6

2 JO DORI

7

8 Piaza building

A.s.h. building
9

SHOPPING STREET

Bus stop No 14
(for Kawamura Kaneto
Ainu Memorial Hall)

14

1 JO DORI

10

11

Bus stop No 11
(for Asahikawa
Youth Hostel)

Malsa dept store

Seibu dept store

Bus stop No 5
(for Sci-pal &
Asahiyama Zoo)

15, 16

12 Esta building

Bus stop No 4
(for Asahidake)

To Sapporo

To Abashiri

Asahikawa Station 13

To Furano

HOKKAIDO

Side trip to Asahidake

An 80-minute bus ride from Asahikawa brings you to **Mt Asahi** or **Asahidake**, in Daisetsuzan National Park. Alpine flowers bloom in spring on the slopes of this, the highest mountain in Hokkaido. In winter, powder snow attracts skiers keen to take advantage of Japan's longest skiing season, from December to early May.

The bus runs to the resort of Asahidake-Onsen, stopping outside **Asahidake Ropeway** (🖳 www.asahidakeropeway.com; ¥2800 round trip July to Oct, ¥1800 Oct to June). The ropeway's operating hours vary according to the season but between July and September it operates daily 6am-7pm; it is closed for inspection May 16th to 31st and Nov 11th to 30th.

The ten-minute ropeway journey takes you up to 1600m, where it's a few degrees cooler than at the foot of the mountain. At the top station there's a small photo gallery of Asahidake through the seasons and a video show – good if you're waiting for a ropeway back down.

From the top station it's a gentle 1km walk to the main lookout point. Asahidake is similar in appearance to Mt Iwo in Kawayu-Onsen (see p343), with smoke pouring out from rock turned yellow by the sulphur. From here it's a further 2.6km to the summit which, at 2290m, is sometimes covered in cloud. The hike to the summit takes around two hours (allow a further hour to get back down to the top ropeway station); it's advisable to wear strong trainers or hiking boots as the path is rocky.

Before going up the mountain, pop in to the Asahidake Visitor Center (daily, 7am-6pm, to 5pm in winter), on the main street just before the ropeway entrance. Inside are some displays of local nature and wildlife; you can pick up a map from the reception desk.

The best place to overnight is at *Daisetsuzan Shirakaba-so Youth Hostel* (☎ 0166-97 2246, 🖹 97 2247, 🖳 www.jyh.or.jp/english; ¥3360/4360, breakfast ¥630, dinner ¥1050; 16 beds), less than five minutes on foot down the main road that leads up to the ropeway station. Camp-jo-mae bus stop, the final stop before the ropeway terminus, is right outside the hostel. The visitor centre has a list of other accommodation in the area.

From June to October, four buses a day run between Asahikawa and Asahidake ropeway. Buses leave from stop No 4 outside Asahikawa station at 9:10am, 10:45am, 1:10pm and 3:10pm, and return at 8:45am, 10:35am, 2:35pm and 5:05 pm (check times at the tourist information office). The service is less frequent in winter.

The bus is free from Asahikawa to Asahidake (except from June to Oct, when it costs ¥1000), and is also free for the return journey if you pick up a coupon from the ropeway station when you buy your ticket or from the hostel (otherwise it costs ¥1320).

PART 7: KYUSHU

Kyushu – route guide

Despite its modern-day reputation as something of a backwater, Kyushu's history has been more linked with the West than any of the other main islands. The port of Nagasaki, in particular, was the only place in the country where trading with the outside world was permitted during Japan's nearly 300 years of self-imposed isolation under the Tokugawa shogunate.

Today, the majority of visitors to Kyushu pause briefly in **Fukuoka** (see pp389-96), the island's capital, before making a beeline for **Nagasaki** (see pp396-403), the second city in Japan to be hit with an atomic bomb in 1945. But if you're prepared to devote more time to seeing the island, it really is worth travelling further south. Perhaps because of its relatively mild climate, Kyushu feels more relaxed and the people more laid back than on Honshu. This may also have something to do with the popularity of *shochu*, a strong spirit found in every bar that becomes even stronger and more popular the further south you go.

A trip down the west coast brings you to the shochu capital, **Kagoshima** (see pp409-15), sometimes described as the 'Naples of the East', and neighbouring **Sakurajima** (see p415), one of the world's most active volcanoes.

Over on the east coast, fans of water parks, flumes and a year-round tropical climate shouldn't miss a trip to the giant Ocean Dome in **Miyazaki** (see pp386-7). And right in the centre of the island, a perfect side trip by rail from either the east or west coasts, lies formidable **Mt Aso** (see pp387-8), where visitors can peer over the top of an active volcanic crater. Nagasaki can be seen in a couple of days but allow at least a week if you're travelling down either coast and planning to fit in a visit to Mt Aso as well.

Kyushu can be reached easily by rail from Honshu via the Tokaido and Sanyo shinkansen lines which run from Tokyo to the terminus in Hakata (for Fukuoka). Until 2004 that was as far south as you could go by bullet train but now the Kyushu shinkansen operates between Shin-Yatsushiro (see p380), halfway down the island's west coast, and the southern terminus of Kagoshima-chuo (see p382). The fastest journey time from Hakata to Kagoshima has thus been reduced from four to just over two hours. There are no Green cars on these shinkansen.

The second stage of this shinkansen, linking Shin-Yatsushiro with the Hakata terminus, is scheduled for completion in spring 2011. From then on, expect a lightning-fast travel time of a little over one

山
の
温
泉
や
裸
の
上
の
天
の
川

Hot spring in the mountains:
high above the naked bathers
the River of Heaven
(SHIKI MASAOKA)

⛩ **Swift as a swallow**
When JR Kyushu announced its new bullet-train service would take the name 'Tsubame' ('Swallow'), the company was thinking of the railway past as much as the future. The Tsubame first went into service more than 30 years before the Tokaido shinkansen was launched, running as a special express between Tokyo and Kobe in October 1930. This first incarnation of the Tsubame was pulled by a steam locomotive, but it heralded a new era in rail travel by cutting more than two hours off the journey time and arriving in Kobe less than nine hours after leaving Tokyo. In 1934 the Tsubame ran between Tokyo and Osaka in just eight hours, a record that remained unbroken for more than two decades.

The Tsubame has since gone through several incarnations, most recently as a limited express along Kyushu's west coast between Hakata and Kagoshima. Now in service as a bullet train, the Tsubame is an 800 series shinkansen, with a maximum speed of 260km/h.

hour between Hakata and Kagoshima. Beyond the shinkansen, JR Kyushu runs an efficient network that will take you just about anywhere and uses limited expresses on most of its lines. For details of JR Kyushu's rail pass, see p15.

SHIN-YAMAGUCHI TO HAKATA BY SHINKANSEN
[Map 27, p375; Table 3, pp458-60]

Distances from Tokyo by shinkansen. Fastest journey time: 45 minutes.

Shin-Yamaguchi (1027km) All Kodama, some Hikari and a few Nozomi stop here. Shin-Yamaguchi is a point of connection with the route guide around western Honshu.

⛩ **How to fillet a fugu**
Two stops west from Shin-Shimonoseki along the Sanyo line, right on the tip of Honshu, is Shimonoseki. This city is known for *fugu* (blow fish), the notorious fish that can kill when eaten if it is not correctly prepared; 70% of Japan's fugu is traded at a fish market in Shimonoseki. A unique method of bidding for fugu at the market involves the fisherman and buyer haggling over a price by grasping one another's fingers in a cloth bag.

At the restaurant table, fugu is served raw, as a fish jelly or deep fried. In a bid to ensure there are no foreign casualties the local government has produced step-by-step instructions in English on how to fillet a fugu. According to the manual, one should 'hit the fugu's head to knock it out', 'put the tip of the knife to the fugu's nostril and cut off the snout', 'scrape out the guts', 'take out the eyes' and 'chop the head'. If you can do or read all this without wincing, it's likely you could apply for a licence to prepare the fish; all would-be fugu masterchefs are required to have a licence before opening a restaurant serving fugu. This requirement should mean there is no risk to diners, though very occasionally reports of death-by-fugu creep into the national press. All the same, it's best not to think too much about the fugu swimming around above you as the shinkansen speeds through the underwater tunnel on its way to Kyushu.

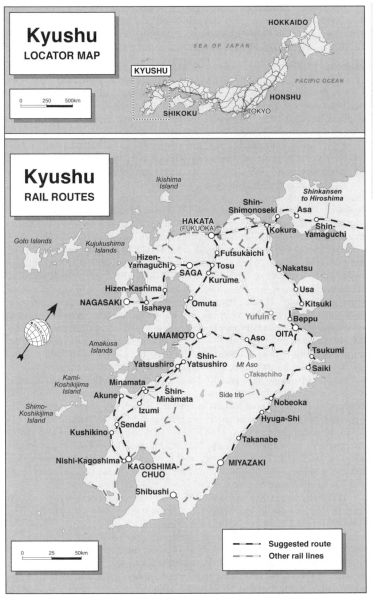

From here, continue on the shinkansen to Kokura, the first stop in Kyushu. Most Hikari run non-stop to Kokura but the Kodama stops twice at **Asa (1062km)** and then **Shin-Shimonoseki (1089km)** before heading into the tunnel for the journey through the narrow Kammon Straits to Kyushu.

Kokura (1108km) All services stop here. Heading out of the tunnel that connects Honshu with Kyushu, the train soon arrives at the sleek, modern Kokura station. Kokura made the American military's shortlist as the next A-Bomb target following the attack on Hiroshima, but cloud cover over the city on the morning of August 9th 1945 meant the plane carrying the bomb was forced to change direction and headed instead towards Nagasaki.

From Kokura, the shinkansen line continues on to Hakata/Fukuoka (see p389), and the Nippo line runs along the east coast towards Oita (p383) and Miyazaki (see p386). Regular trains to Hakata run on the Kagoshima line.

JR West runs the shinkansen tracks at Kokura, so if you're changing from the shinkansen follow the signs for 'JR Kyushu Lines'. The main station concourse, with a central plaza and large TV screen, is on the third floor. Since the station has been rebuilt there is good disabled access, with either lifts or ramps in addition to stairs/escalators to get from the concourse to street level.

The **tourist information counter** (☎ 093-531 9611, daily 9am-6pm) is on the main concourse. You are not guaranteed to find an English speaker, but they can provide you with an English map of Kokura and a copy of the Kitakyushu Welcome Card book (see box p53), which offers discounts to foreign tourists at some sights, shops, restaurants and hotels. There is another tourist information desk (daily 9am-6pm) hidden away in a corner on the floor below the central concourse which is usually less busy. From the main concourse, head towards the shinkansen entrance, next to which is an escalator that leads down to the north exit. Turn right at the bottom of the escalator and the office is in the corner. For cash withdrawals, the Post Office has an ATM on the main concourse, behind the entrance to the monorail. There are two JR ticket offices: one is to the left as you leave the shinkansen ticket barrier; the other larger one is on the main concourse. There are coin lockers behind the entrance to the monorail on the main station concourse, but only a very small number of ¥600 ones.

A 30-minute bus journey from Kokura will take you to **New Kitakyushu Airport** (🖳 www.kitaqair.jp), opened in 2006 on a man-made island off the Kyushu coast. It is the first airport in Japan able to operate 24 hours a day. Currently the only international flights are to/from Vladivostok (summer only) and Shanghai. Domestic routes include Tokyo and Nagoya.

Rail buffs might like to take a round trip on the **monorail** which departs from Kokura on an unspectacular 20-minute journey into the suburbs. The entrance and ticket desk is on the main concourse.

The nearest **internet café** to the station – Popeye – is on the first floor of Laforet Shopping Plaza to your right as you take the North exit.

Kokura is of limited appeal to the traveller. That said, with a couple of hours to spare, it's worth fitting in a trip to the **castle area**, a 15-minute walk from the south exit of Kokura station. Head up the main street, Heiwa-dori, turn right on

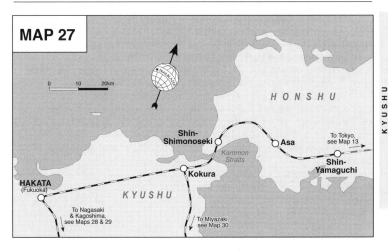

to Komonji-dori and cross the bridge. The entrance to the castle area is just past City Hall on your right. The castle itself (daily 9am-5pm, ¥350, discount for Welcome-card holders) is a 1990 reconstruction of the original 1602 building and now hosts a kitsch puppet show. The only reason to stop here would be for the views from the top floor but you get much better views (for free) from the top floor of City Hall.

It's better to skip the castle and head to the **Kokura Castle Japanese Garden** (daily, 9am-5pm, ¥300, discount for Welcome-card holders), the entrance to which is opposite the castle. An Edo-period home has been reconstructed overlooking a small Japanese garden, an unexpected oasis of calm in the middle of an industrial city. The only downside is the view of City Hall that looms overhead. For ¥500 extra, you'll be served a bowl of green tea and a Japanese sweetmeat by shuffling, kimono-clad women and you can briefly imagine yourself transported to a private house in Kyoto.

Having seen **City Hall** from the castle gardens (one of the most unfortunate examples of a 'borrowed view'), it's worth going in and taking the lift to the top, where there's an observation gallery (Mon-Fri, 8:45am-5pm). You can walk all the way around and get a bird's eye view of Kyushu's industrial heartland and of the shinkansen gliding away from Kokura back towards Honshu. Take the lift up to the 15th floor and then the stairs to the top. There are vending machines and chairs here, and a restaurant on the 15th floor that serves cheap pasta, ice cream parfaits and coffee.

Families flock to northern Kyushu to visit the **Space World** theme park (see 🖥 www.spaceworld.co.jp for opening times/latest prices and an attraction guide in English); it even has its own station (JR Space World) five stops from Kokura along the JR Kagoshima line. A one-day passport costs ¥3800 (¥300 discount with the Kitakyushu Welcome Card, see box p53).

The most convenient place to stay is ***Station Hotel Kokura*** (☎ 093-541 7111, 💻 www.station-hotel.com; from ¥6000/S, ¥11,000/Tw) built into the JR station building. A 10% discount off rack rates is offered to rail-pass holders. A good alternative would be ***Nishitetsu Inn Kokura*** (☎ 093-511 5454, 💻 www.n-inn.jp), three minutes from the South exit. It offers small singles for ¥6000 or slightly larger 'studio singles' with a sofa for ¥7000. Two people can share the studio single for ¥9000, or twins are ¥11,500. Some rooms have free internet-access points for laptops, but ask for these when making a reservation. A simple breakfast of toast, onigiri (rice balls), coffee and orange juice is included in the rate. The 190-room ***Toyoko Inn Kokura Eki Minami-guchi*** (☎ 093-511 1045, 💻 www.toyoko-inn.com; ¥6300/S, ¥8400/D/Tw) opened outside the station in 2007.

If you're looking for a bite to eat, Kokura's speciality is *yaki-udon* (similar to yakisoba, see p451, but the udon are fried). There are several places which serve this within walking distance of the station. One of the best is ***Ishin***, ten minutes on foot from the south exit. The tourist information counter can point you in the right direction. If you don't want to leave the station, try the 6th floor of AMU Plaza department store. There are several Japanese- and Western-style restaurants, including one, ***Masumasa Shokudo***, which serves yaki-udon.

From Kokura it's one more stop by shinkansen to Hakata/Fukuoka. If heading down the east coast (on the route starting on p382), change trains here rather than at Hakata, otherwise you'll have to backtrack.

Hakata/Fukuoka (1175km)   [see pp389-96]
It's mostly tunnels on the short journey between Kokura and Hakata; in the brief snatches of daylight it's surprising to see how lush and green the countryside is.

Hakata is the shinkansen terminus for the city of Fukuoka and a major transport hub for onward trips west to Nagasaki and south to Kumamoto and Kagoshima. Once the Kyushu shinkansen is completed Hakata will also be the starting point for JR Kyushu bullet-train journeys to Kumamoto and Kagoshima.

HAKATA TO NAGASAKI   [Map 28, opposite; Table 25, p469]

Distances by JR from Hakata. Fastest journey time: 2 hours.

Hakata (0km) A blueprint for an extension of the shinkansen line to Nagasaki was drawn up in 1973 – it still exists only on paper. For now, the fastest way is

---

❏ **Using the rail route guides**
The fastest point-to-point journey times are provided for each section of the route. Even though each route has been divided into different sections it may not be necessary to change trains as you go from one section to the next. Occasionally, however, it is essential to change train in order to complete the route described. Such instances are denoted by the following symbol ▲. Places which are served by local trains only are marked ◆. (**For more information see p449.**)

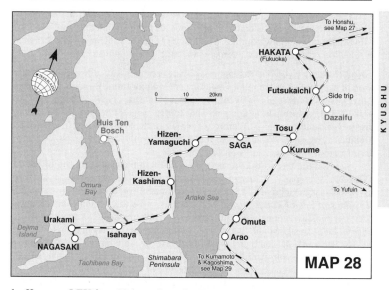

by Kamome LEX from Hakata along the JR Kagoshima line. The Kamome was introduced with great fanfare in 2000 under the slogan 'it's white, it's fast, it's beautiful' – well, it does have wooden floors and comfortable leather seats. Seating is 2x2 in ordinary cars and 1x2 in the Green Car.

Futsukaichi (14km) Some trains make a brief stop at this hot springs resort. Of more interest is Tenmangu Shrine, home to Sugawara Michizane, god of scholars and literature, in neighbouring Dazaifu. That's where you'll also find the new Kyushu National Museum (see p396).

From Futsukaichi, it's four minutes by bus to Nishitetsu Futsukaichi station, where a local train runs two stops to **Dazaifu**. If there are no buses, it's easy enough to walk between the two stations in about ten minutes. From Nishitetsu Futsukaichi, take a local train two stops to Dazaifu (rail passes are not accepted on the private Nishitetsu line). Train services run every 5-40 minutes (in both directions); services are most frequent during peak times. The **tourist information office** at Dazaifu station can provide a list of accommodation and a map. Cycles can also be rented here (¥200 per hour). ***B&B Guest House Dazaifu*** (☎/📠 092-922 8740, 🖳 ghdazaifu@hiz.bbiq.jp; ¥6000/person including breakfast), 1553-3 Dazaifu, is a 12-minute walk from Dazaifu station (pick up a map from tourist information).

Tosu (29km) Nothing particular to see here but Tosu is a major rail junction. From here, the Nagasaki line heads west towards Nagasaki; this is the route followed here. For details of the Kagoshima line south to Kumamoto and Kagoshima, see p379.

There are few facilities at Tosu station, apart from a small branch of the *Train D'Or* bakery and a convenience store. Exit the station and you'll see the 'Joyful Town' shopping complex a couple of minutes' walk away. Here, there's a selection of cafés and restaurants and a large department store.

Saga (54km) Everyone passes through Saga on their way to Nagasaki but few stop at this prefectural capital, venue for an **International Balloon Festival** in November. Sandwiched between the greater tourist draws of Nagasaki and Fukuoka, Saga offers little to the passing tourist. Saga prefecture is best known for its hand-made pottery, a centre for which is the small town of **Karatsu**, 80 minutes away on the local Karatsu line. Located on the coast, Karatsu was once a prosperous port town and a gateway to China.

Saga station has north and south exits and a **tourist information office** (☎ 0952-23 3975, daily, 8:30am-5/6pm) on the concourse. Also here is a *Train D'Or* bakery and a branch of *Mister Donut*. In case you decide to stay the night, *Toyoko Inn Saga Ekimae* (☎ 0952-23 1045, 🖳 www.toyoko-inn.com; ¥5040/S, ¥8190/Tw) is immediately to your right as you take the station's south exit. The rate includes breakfast and there is free laptop-internet access in rooms.

In Saga city, the main sight is **Kono Park**, inside which is the **Tea House Kakurintei** (Tue-Sun 9am-5pm, free), a reconstruction of the original built in 1846 by Lord Naomasa Nabeshima, 10th lord of the Saga Clan. It's small but has been faithfully reconstructed with a veranda commanding great views of the surrounding lake (and less impressive views of a concrete water tower). Green tea (¥300) is served.

Hizen-Yamaguchi (68km) This station is the junction for the Sasebo branch line. Travelling to Nagasaki there's no need to change trains because the Kamome LEX continues along the Nagasaki line.

Hizen-Kashima (83km) After Hizen-Kashima the line follows the coast, affording great views of the Ariake Sea on the left side. The train briefly comes to a halt along the coast to allow the train returning to Hakata to pass. The view is occasionally blotted out by the odd tunnel and gradually the train moves more inland before arriving at Isahaya.

Isahaya (129km) Isahaya is a gateway to **Shimabara Peninsula** which juts out east of Nagasaki into the Ariake Sea, with Mt Unzen at its centre. On a plateau south-west of Mt Unzen is the hot spring resort of **Unzen Jigoku**. Today, people visit for the scenery and the chance to bathe in the public spas but 350 years ago, during the time of religious persecution in Japan, 30 Christians were sent there for refusing to renounce their faith and were promptly thrown into the boiling hot springs. Unzen Jigoku is not accessible by rail. Buses to Unzen (90 mins; ¥1300 one-way) leave from the bus terminal directly opposite Isahaya station.

The private Shimabara Railway (JR passes not valid) runs from Isahaya around the peninsula, stopping at the port town of Shimabara on the eastern side. Turn right out of the JR station; the entrance to the Shimabara Railway is between Mister Donut and the Joyroad travel agency. Purchase tickets from the ticket machine in the JR station (Isahaya to Shimabara costs ¥1330).

For the last ten minutes of the journey to Nagasaki the train goes at full speed and there's one long tunnel about five minutes before arrival.

Urakami (152km) When it first opened in 1897, Urakami was Nagasaki station. But the growth of the downtown port area and land reclamation meant traffic shifted further away so a decision was made to construct a new Nagasaki station; in 1905 the station's name was changed to Urakami. The atomic bomb exploded at 11:02am on August 9th 1945 over this district; Urakami is the nearest JR stop to the A-Bomb Museum and Peace Park (see p397).

Nagasaki (154km)   [see pp396-403]

HAKATA TO KAGOSHIMA VIA KUMAMOTO
[Map 28, p377 & Map 29, p381; Table 26, p469]

Distances by JR from Hakata: a combination of limited express to Shin-Yatsushiro, then changing to the Tsubame (Swallow) shinkansen to Kagoshima-chuo. Fastest journey time: 2 hours 12 minutes.

Hakata (0km)   [Fukuoka/Hakata, see pp389-96]
The Relay-Tsubame LEX are silver trains with Western-style toilets, luggage racks in each carriage, and airline-style seats (a light above your seat and an individual footrest). The first carriage is the Green Car.

If you are travelling direct to Kagoshima, or anywhere between Shin-Yatsushiro and Kagoshima, you should buy tickets/pick up seat reservations for the whole journey before you leave Hakata because the services are scheduled to connect with each other so there would not be enough time to do that en route.

Tosu (29km) A major rail junction as tracks diverge: one line heading west to Nagasaki, the other, the Kagoshima line, continuing south to Kumamoto and Kagoshima. If heading to Nagasaki from Kumamoto or Kagoshima (or vice-versa), there's no need to backtrack all the way to Hakata since you can change trains here. Both Tsubame (for Kumamoto/Kagoshima) and Kamome (for Nagasaki) LEXs make brief stops here.

For information on Tosu and the route from Tosu to Nagasaki, see p377.

Kurume (36km) The area around Kurume is an unattractive mix of factories and industrial plants. Kurume station is the point of interchange for the Kyudai line that cuts across Kyushu (west to east), stopping briefly at the hot spring resort of **Yufuin** before terminating in **Oita** (see p383), a city on the east coast. The Yufu LEX runs three times a day in each direction: Kurume to Yufuin (99 mins); Yufuin to Oita (45 mins).

Omuta (69km) Omuta station is a run-down place but a few minutes out of here the train starts to speed through fields punctuated by villages and small towns as it heads towards the city of Kumamoto.

Kumamoto (118km)   [see pp404-9]
Kumamoto is a point of interchange for the scenic Hohi line which runs across
Kyushu to Oita on the east coast, via Mt Aso. For further details see pp387-8.

Shin-Yatsushiro (151km/0km) Change here from the Relay-Tsubame LEX
onto the Tsubame shinkansen to Kagoshima-chuo. If you are connecting immediately you'll find the bullet train on the platform opposite the one you've just
arrived at. Japanese efficiency even spreads to ensuring that you don't have to
walk far from one train carriage to the other: you will usually be seated in a
shinkansen carriage directly opposite the LEX carriage from which you disem-
bark. On-board announcements are
made in English, Chinese and Korean
as well as Japanese. The seating plan
on the Tsubame shinkansen is airline-
style 2x2 (seats can be turned around
so that small groups can face each
other). Cars 4-6 are non-reserved,
while 1-3 are for passengers with seat
reservations. There is no Green Car but
the carriages are comfortable with
wide reclining seats and attached mini
folding tables. It's frightening to think
how many trees were chopped down to make parts of the interior – including
the trendy shutter-style blinds at the windows – but the whole effect of
pinewood-meets-forest-fabric is apparently designed to make passengers 'feel
as if they are surrounded by trees'. To stay overnight in Shin-Yatsushiro, right
outside the station is *Toyoko Inn Shin-Yatsushiro Eki-mae* (☎ 0965-31 1045,
🖳 www.toyoko-inn.com; ¥5460/S, ¥8190/D/Tw), which opened in 2007.

> ❏ **The pre-shinkansen route**
> The section of pre-shinkansen rail-
> way line which runs between
> Yatsushiro and Sendai (see map,
> opposite) is now run by a private
> company, Hisatsu Orange Railway,
> and the fare between Yatsushiro and
> Sendai is ¥2550. JR rail passes are
> not valid on this route so it is best to
> take the bullet train.

Unfortunately nearly all the journey from Shin-Yatsushiro to Kagoshima-
chuo is through tunnels and there is very little to be had in the way of decent
views. The old JR line skirted Yatsushiro Bay and passengers enjoyed views out
to sea. Bullet-train passengers have to make do with speed and darkness but
they do get on-board comfort.

Shin-Minamata (43km) The station was constructed for the new shinkansen
and is connected to the Hisatsu Orange Railway (JR passed not accepted), on
your right as you exit. You'll need to connect to a local train on this railway line
if you're planning to visit the city of Minamata itself (see below). The fare from
Shin-Minamata to Minamata is ¥230. There are a few **coin lockers** of the ¥300/
¥400 variety in a corner of Shin-Minamata station. Outside, close to the
entrance to Hisatsu Orange Railway, is a **tourist shop** selling local products. No
English is spoken but the staff will provide you with an English map of the area.

The main point of going to **Minamata** is to visit the city's **Eco Park**, home
to Minamata Disease Museum (see box opposite; Tue-Sun 9am-5pm, free), the
adjacent Minamata Disease Archives (same times) and Minamata Memorial. In
the museum, headphones provide an English translations of the video panels.

❑ Minamata disease – fifty years on

In 2006 hundreds of people turned out in Minamata for a solemn ceremony to mark the 50th anniversary of the discovery of Minamata Disease.

In 1968, the Tokyo government had announced that a chemical company with a factory in Minamata was responsible for illegally dumping mercury waste into Minamata Bay. Although first discovered as far back as 1956, untreated mercury continued to pour into the sea for another decade. Thousands of local residents contracted what became known as Minamata Disease as a result of eating contaminated fish. As well as a number of fatalities, babies were born with severe mental and physical handicaps. A compensation agreement was signed in 1973 with Chisso Co Ltd, which finally admitted responsibility after years of attempted cover-up. The sludge in Minamata Bay was dealt with by dredging and through land reclamation (paid for by Kumamoto prefecture not Chisso), and the water is now some of the cleanest in the prefecture.

In what was seen as an unprecedented move, the then Prime Minister, Junichiro Koizumi, used the ceremony in 2006 to apologize for the government's tardy response to the disaster. But this was not enough for thousands of victims who, half a century on, are still fighting for compensation.

Buses run from Minamata station to the Eco Park's main entrance. A tourist information desk (daily, 9am-5pm, except Sun/Tues am) is at the station. Cycles can be rented at this station for ¥500 per day.

If you look carefully, for part of this stretch of the journey – when the train isn't speeding into tunnels – you can see the old JR track. Keep an eye out also for a brief glimpse of the sea to your right shortly before the train arrives. What you might also see – but only between November and March – are birds (see p382).

Izumi (59km) Some services call here briefly. It is a small station with connections to the

Hisatsu Orange Railway which runs along the old mainline. Izumi is home to 10,000 Siberian cranes during the winter months. It's a paradise for bird watchers and if you're here in season staff at the local products and information office opposite the station exit can advise on access to the **Crane Observation Centre** (daily Nov-March, 9am-5pm; ¥210). At the time of writing there were no direct buses to the bird-watching site. A taxi will set you back around ¥4500. In the summer months you can see the cranes come to life on the big screen at the Dome Theater inside the museum at **Crane Park Izumi** (daily Nov-Mar, Tue-Sun April-Oct, 9am-5pm; ¥310). The park is within walking distance from the station.

An alternative sightseeing spot, 20 minutes on foot from the station (maps available from the information office), is **Izumi-fumoto Bukeyashiki-ato**, an area of preserved Edo-period samurai residences. You can also get there by bike. Cycles can be rented from the station (¥300/3 hours) or from *Hotel Wing* (☎ 0996-63 8111). Staff at the local products and information office opposite Izumi station will call the hotel on your behalf. To find the hotel, take the escalator for the Hisatsu Orange railway and look for the 'W' sign on a white building to the left across from the railway track.

After Izumi, some services stop at **Sendai (92km)** before hurtling into tunnel after tunnel on the way to the **Kagoshima-chuo** terminal.

Kagoshima-chuo (138km) [see pp409-15]

Kagoshima-chuo station is the main rail terminal for the city of Kagoshima and the terminus for limited express trains from Hakata. Kagoshima station is one stop further along but it's small and you'll probably only pass through it if heading towards Miyazaki on the JR Nippo line (see below).

Alternative route back to Hakata

Instead of returning to Hakata the same way, it's possible to cut across Kyushu via the JR Nippo line (two hours by Kirishima LEX; services leave approximately every two hours) from Kagoshima-chuo to Miyazaki (see p386).

From Miyazaki, follow the route described below in reverse all the way up the east coast to Kokura (see p374). You can then take the shinkansen back to Honshu.

KOKURA TO MIYAZAKI
[Map 30, opposite; Map 31, p384; Table 27, p470]

Distances by JR from Kokura. Fastest journey time: 5 hours.

Note: Although it's possible to start a journey down the east coast of Kyushu from Hakata, you'll save a lot of time by taking the shinkansen one stop from Hakata back to Kokura and picking up a limited express from there.

Kokura (0km) Pick up a Nichirin LEX that runs straight down the east coast. This train is also known as the 'Red Express' but in truth the journey is anything but fast. From Kokura it takes just under five hours to Miyazaki. Another limited express, the Sonic, only goes as far as Oita but if you are on the 883 version you may like the fact that it has headrests that make you look like Mickey Mouse. Sit on the left side for views of the coast.

Nakatsu (52km) Located on the coast, this is one of a few brief stops that the Nichirin makes on the journey down the eastern side of Kyushu. If you're on the Sonic, the next stop is Beppu. If on the Nichirin, you'll make brief additional stops at **Yanagigaura (69km)**, **Usa (76km)** and **Kitsuki (99km)**.

Beppu (121km) Infamous as one of Japan's most garish hot spring resorts, the classic image of the rustic hot spring is shattered by the view as the train arrives in Beppu. It's a sprawling city and somewhere amongst the mass of concrete buildings lie hot springs that have to be seen to be believed – or simply avoided. Tacky, overly commercial, a tourist trap – all of these apply. But Beppu sweeps away criticism levelled at it with a confident, 'so what?'.

Oita (133km) A 'humanistic city with rich greeneries', according to the town guide given out at the **tourist information booth** (daily, 9am-5:30pm) at the station. Oita can certainly lay claim to being an international city since it's twinned with Austin, Texas (USA), Wuhan in China, and Abeiro in Portugal, and was also chosen as a host city for the 2002 Korea-Japan World Cup. The city's **Art Museum** (Tue-Sun 10am-5:30pm, price depends on exhibition) is ten minutes by bus from the station and has temporary exhibitions that change throughout the year. Check bus times and the museum schedule at the information booth.

Turn right after the ticket barrier and walk straight to find coin lockers (mostly ¥300 size but a few large ¥600 ones) at the very end of the concourse. For a snack in the station, the *Train D'Or* bakery is infinitely preferable to the fast-food joint *Lotteria*. *Mister Donut* is just outside and to the left as you exit the station.

The main reason for stopping in Oita is to connect up with the JR Hohi line that cuts across Kyushu to Kumamoto via the Mt Aso

MAP 31 To Kokura, see Map 30

Saiki

KYUSHU

Takachiho

Nobeoka

Side trip

Minami-Nobeoka

Hyuga-shi

0   10   20km

Takanabe

MIYAZAKI

tableland (see p387). Trains on this line depart from platform 6.

The Aso LEX runs along this line to **Mt Aso** (98km; 100 mins, 3/day) before terminating in **Kumamoto** (148km; 2 hours 40 mins). All other services are local and several changes of train are necessary.

The Yufu LEX runs three times a day in each direction: Oita to Yufuin (45 mins); Yufuin to Kurume (99 mins).

Continuing south from Oita, the Nichirin makes brief stops at **Usuki (169km)** and **Tsukumi (179km)**.

Saiki (198km) As you approach Saiki there are good views out to sea on the left side. The views become more spectacular as the train leaves the coast and begins to thread its way inland through the hills. One passenger I met on this train compared the landscape between Saiki and Nobeoka with that of Switzerland.

Nobeoka (256km) There is nothing to see in Nobeoka itself and you may well be disappointed that the verdant landscape enjoyed so far on the journey abruptly disappears as the train pulls in to the station. However, you can transfer here for the mountain railway to Takachiho (see opposite).

Nobeoka was put on the literary map by Japanese author Soseki Natsume, who mentions the place in his most famous novel, *Botchan*.

In the story, Koga, a quiet, well-mannered English teacher, is informed that he is to be transferred to a school in Nobeoka. His colleague, the novel's eponymous hero Botchan, later wonders why: 'It would have been different if he had been going to a fine place, like Tokyo, that had trams and trains. But Nobeoka, in Hyuga province? ... Nobeoka lies deep in the heart of the mountains, beyond range after range ... The very name sounded uncivilized. It made you imagine a place populated half by monkeys and half by men'.

But the novel is not all bad press for Nobeoka. Later, at a party to bid Koga farewell before he heads off into the unknown, the straightforward and outspoken maths teacher, Hotta, puts the record straight about the place: 'I know that Nobeoka is a remote, out of the way place, and that it may have some material disadvantages compared with here. But I have heard that it is a pastoral spot, where manners and customs are of the simplest and where both teachers and pupils are gentle and well-behaved, like the people of past ages.' (Excerpts from *Botchan*, translated by Alan Turney, Kodansha International, Tokyo, 1972, original text 1906).

To stay overnight in Nobeoka, *City Hotel Plaza Nobeoka* (☎ 0982-35 8888, 🖥 www.city-h.co.jp; ¥5040/S, ¥10,000/D/Tw) is to the left as you leave the station. Alternatively, a five-minute taxi ride away is the more upmarket *Hotel Merieges Nobeoka* (☎ 0982-32 6060, 🖥 www.merieges-n.co.jp; ¥7600/S, ¥12,100/D, ¥13,600/Tw). This place has a good Chinese restaurant and a rooftop beer garden (May-September only).

The short journey between Nobeoka and **Minami-Nobeoka (260km)** takes you through a mass of pipes that connect up the Asahi Kasei factories.

Side trip by rail to Takachiho
The main reason for stopping in Nobeoka is to take a trip on the private **Takachiho Railway** to the mountain town of Takachiho. Considered one of the most scenic mountain railways in Japan, the 80-minute, 50km journey is in a single carriage that winds its way slowly up into the mountains. Services operate 14 times a day in each direction but at irregular times. The first train from Nobeoka is at 6:16am and the last at 8:50pm; the first from Takachiho is at 5:33am and the last at 8:26pm.

Takachiho is known for *yokagura*, ancient dances which re-enact scenes from Japanese mythology. Traditionally, performances of yokagura take place in local people's homes and tend to last from early evening through to the following morning. Plenty of saké keeps everyone awake into the small hours. Tourists are welcome at these performances, which are organized at the weekend between November and February (call Takachiho Tourist Association on ☎ 0982-73 1213 for times). Alternatively, a one-hour version is performed nightly, at 8pm, at Takachiho Shrine in the centre of town (tickets ¥500 at the shrine).

A high priority is also a visit to **Takachiho Gorge**, formed by the gradual erosion of lava that once flowed from Mt Aso (see p388). You can rent a boat and row around the gorge (daily, 8:30am-5pm; 30 minutes ¥1500). There is no bus from the train station to the gorge – you have to take a bus to the bus centre and then hop on another one; a taxi would be quicker and not too expensive. For information on this and on accommodation contact Takachiho Tourist Association.

To get to Takachiho railway station in Nobeoka turn right out of the JR station. The one-way fare between Nobeoka and Takachiho is ¥1470.

Hyuga-shi (277km)
Hyuga has a number of beaches popular with local surfers but isn't really worth stopping at. There are, however, great views of the coast from the train.

Takanabe (314km)
The line between Hyuga and Takanabe is one of the most rewarding parts of the journey. There are fantastic views of the coastline on the left as the train runs for one stretch just a few metres from the shore.

Miyazaki (340km) 'Welcome to Vitamin Resort Miyazaki' proclaims a sign outside the station. Miyazaki is known for its long hours of sunshine and mild climate, making the city feel very relaxed.

Miyazaki's modern station is small and easy to find your way around. For food, there's a convenience store, *Mister Donut*, *Train d'Or* bakery and *KFC*. Inside the station, a **tourist information counter** (☎ 0985-22 6469) is open daily, 9am-7pm. A map is available and some staff speak a bit of English.

There's only one local speciality you should not leave Miyazaki without trying and that's *chicken nanban*, pieces of fried chicken served with a sweet and sour sauce. Many restaurants in Miyazaki have chicken nanban on the menu

⛩ **Paradise within a paradise**
Decades ago, when vacationing Japanese were not the world travellers they are today, Miyazaki was one of the most popular honeymoon spots in the country. As the demand for ever more exotic holidays increased, the number of visitors dwindled and it became the poor man's Hawaii. In a bid to recapture the tourist market the huge Seagaia Resort (🖥 www.seagaia.co.jp) was built and opened in the 1990s along the pine-tree clad Hitotsuba coast north-east of Miyazaki. The early years were a financial disaster and the resort nearly went bankrupt in 2001. But Seagaia has since been taken over and redeveloped by the Sheraton hotel group.

The big attraction is the enormous **Ocean Dome**, an indoor water paradise with an artificial beach at its centre. Body boards can be rented for surfing the artificial waves. Around this are flumes, roller coasters that dump you in water, ride-the-rapids simulators, whirlpools and water guns. Dubbed a 'paradise within a paradise', Ocean Dome is in the *Guinness Book of Records* as the 'world's largest indoor water park with a retractable roof' – the roof opens in fine weather to take advantage of Miyazaki's mild climate. Though it may seem bizarre to spend the day inside an artificial beach paradise just yards from the real Pacific Ocean, it's hard to find fault with Ocean Dome as a fun day out. One-day tickets cost ¥2500. Some attractions inside the dome are chargeable. The best deal is the 'attraction free' wrist band (¥1200) allowing unlimited use of all the attractions. The dome is open daily from 10am to (at least) 7pm, the hours vary depending on the season. Aside from the dome, other facilities at Seagaia Resort include a luxury spa with beauty-treatment facilities, bowling alley, a professional golf course designed by PGA star Tom Watson and a tennis club.

The most luxurious place to stay in Miyazaki – indeed, one of the top hotels in Japan – is the *Sheraton Grande Ocean Resort* (☎ 0985-21 1133, 🖥 sgocean@sea gaia.co.jp; ¥23,100/D/Tw). On the 43rd floor is an observation gallery which affords views of the ocean, coastline and Miyazaki city in the distance. Every guest room has an ocean view and hotel facilities include any number of restaurants and bars, a fully equipped fitness centre, spa and pool. Even if you don't stay here, it's worth stopping for an early-evening drink at the hotel's splendid Pacifica Cocktail Bar. The original shochu cocktails are the perfect antidote to a day at the water park. *Sun Hotel Phoenix* (☎ 0985-39 3131, 🖥 spfront@seagaia.co.jp; ¥15,800/Tw) is set amidst the pine forests along the Hitotsuba coast. Further information about both hotels is available from 🖥 www.seagaia.co.jp/english/hotel.

Buses run to the Seagaia Resort from outside the west exit of Miyazaki station (25 minutes). A free shuttle bus runs between Ocean Dome, the hotels and all other resort facilities.

but it's worth going to ***Taku-chan***, about a 20-minute walk from Miyazaki station. Grab a seat at the small counter and ask the friendly owners for the 'chicken nanban teishoku' (set meal).

To find Taku-chan, head up the main road in front of Miyazaki station (take the west exit) until you reach a major junction, with KFC on one corner. Turn left on to Tachibana-dori and head straight up this road until you see Hotel Big Man on your left. Taku-chan is just past the hotel on the opposite (right) side of the main road, before you reach the bridge which crosses Oyodo-gawa.

If you need to stay overnight, a good bet is ***Toyoko Inn Miyazaki Ekimae*** (☎ 0985-32 1045, 🖥 www.toyoko-inn.com, ¥5250/S, ¥7770/Tw), where the rate includes a Japanese breakfast. The hotel is just outside the station's West exit.

Miyazaki Airport (🖥 www.miyazaki-airport.co.jp) has one terminal which operates both domestic and international flights (at the time of writing the latter only Asiana Airlines to/from Seoul). The airport has its own railway station and is ten minutes from Miyazaki station on the JR Miyazaki-kuko line.

From Miyazaki, instead of retracing your steps, it's possible to connect up with the west coast rail route by taking a train along the JR Nippo line to Kagoshima (see p382) and then following the route (in reverse) from pp379-82.

Side trip from Kumamoto or Oita to Mt Aso   [Map 32, below]

A trip to the Aso Tableland with its spectacular mountain scenery and the chance to peer over the edge of a volcanic crater makes an excursion to the centre of Kyushu a highlight of any rail journey in Japan. An advantage of this journey is that it can be combined with a tour of both Kyushu's east and west coasts: from Kumamoto on the west side, follow this route to link up with Oita on the east coast. The following route runs **from Oita to Kumamoto**, so follow in reverse if starting from Kumamoto.

From Oita to Aso Very soon after leaving Oita (see pp383-4) on the JR Hohi line (also known as the Aso Kogen line) the train starts a gradual climb into the mountains and forest scenery takes over. As the train chugs down the single-track line there are long stretches where it passes small clusters of houses separated by fields and mountains. Heading towards Aso station, the craters that make up the Aso range should be visible in the distance.

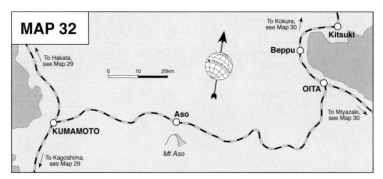

Mt Aso (98km from Oita/50km from Kumamoto) Mt Aso refers not to one particular mountain but to the whole caldera area and all five of its peaks, called Nakadake, Takadake, Nekodake, Kijimadake and Eboshidake. All of these are contained within the enormous outer crater that is the Aso tableland. The most accessible and impressive is Nakadake, the only active volcano, reached by a combination of bus and ropeway. If weather conditions allow you can peer over the edge of this volcanic crater and see the bubbling green liquid below. The last big eruption at Nakadake was in 1979, when a sudden explosion killed three and injured eleven. The ropeway to the crater is often closed because of sulphur gas, and sometimes when it is too foggy.

Aso station is the gateway to Aso National Park. The train only makes a very brief stop here, so be ready to jump off as soon as the doors open. After passing the ticket barrier, turn right for the **tourist information desk** (☎ 0967-34 0751, ✉ aso-info@aso.ne.jp, Thur-Mon 9am-5pm). The staff speak English and will help book accommodation. You can also store luggage here (9am-6pm, ¥300 per bag) if it won't fit into a coin locker. From the station, seven buses a day run up to Nakadake, taking 40 minutes to reach Asosan-nishi station (¥540). From Asosan-nishi, a ropeway (daily, 9am-5pm, every 8 mins, ¥410) completes the journey to the crater. Timetables are available from the information counter inside the station.

The ropeway deposits you just beneath the crater. It's an extraordinary experience to stand at the edge of the crater. Concrete bunkers have been built in the event of a sudden eruption; experts suggest that at the first sign of danger it's best to run backwards, looking at the crater, so as to dodge pieces of volcanic debris.

If the weather does not cooperate, **Aso Volcano Museum** (daily 9am-5pm, ¥840) displays footage of major eruptions and has real-time cameras for a close up of the crater without having to peer over the edge yourself. The museum is on the way to Asosan-nishi ropeway and the bus stops in front of it.

Aso Youth Hostel (☎ 0967-34 0804) offers the best budget accommodation in town – ¥3650 with meals or ¥2450 without. The manager has supplies of hiking route maps. Take the bus from the station bound for Asosan-nishi station; the hostel is the first stop along the route. Check-in is from 4 to 8pm and the front door is closed at 8pm. Right in front of Aso station is *Kokumin Shukusha Nakamura* (☎ 0967-34 0317), a small inn which charges ¥6800 with meals and ¥4500 without. The place boasts its own hot spring right next door, called **Yumenoyu** (daily, 10am-9:30pm), which is open to the public.

For a hearty meal you can't beat *Sanzoku Tabiji* (Thur-Mon, 11am-7:30pm). The set menus are huge and include mountain vegetables and wild potatoes. The staff do not speak English but are friendly. Head up the road from Aso station until you reach Route 57. Turn right on to this main road and the restaurant is a 10- to 15-minute walk along the road on the left.

From Aso to Kumamoto It's just under one hour along the Hohi line to Kumamoto; for the first half the train passes through the Aso valley and its rice fields. In the distance, the craters remain in view for a while after the train leaves Aso.

Kyushu – city guides

FUKUOKA/HAKATA

Fukuoka, literally 'happy hills', was one of the first parts of Japan to come into contact with foreign culture, due to its proximity to the Asian mainland. The city's JR station is called Hakata not Fukuoka, a confusion of names that dates back to the time when the city was divided into the merchants' district (Hakata) and the old castle town (Fukuoka).

At the weekend, people flock here from all over Kyushu and from further afield to take advantage of Fukuoka's abundant shopping and entertainment facilities. There are a good few cultural sights as well, making a stopover in Fukuoka an excellent introduction to the rest of the island.

What to see and do

If you only have time for one sight, make it **Fukuoka City Museum** (Tue-Sun 9:30am-5:30pm, ¥200). The museum traces the history of Fukuoka, right back to the Yayoi period when the introduction of rice farming led to sporadic fights between villages and the beginning of the age of warfare. The star exhibit is the gold seal of a Chinese Emperor, discovered on nearby Shikanoshima Island in 1784. Exhibits examine how and why Fukuoka has always been at the forefront of international exchange in Asia. The number of rusty daggers, spears and swords on display is visual proof that 'international exchange' has not always been harmonious.

Fukuoka's rapid modernization after the Meiji Restoration is also covered. This was the time when streets were paved, ¥1 taxis hit the streets, waterworks were built to improve sanitation and French-style cafés became the place for intellectuals to meet and discuss issues of the day. A typical café has been reconstructed, inside which you can see footage of what the city looked like at the start of the 20th century, before much of it was reduced to rubble in a 1945 American air raid.

There are bilingual signs on exhibits and headphones can be rented (free; bring your passport) for an English commentary. To reach the museum, take bus No 306 from the bus terminal outside Hakata station to 'Hakubutsukan kita-guchi' (¥220). This bus goes via Fukuoka Dome, Hawks Town and terminates outside Fukuoka Tower.

Fukuoka City Museum is in an area called Momochi, built on recently reclaimed land. Also in this area is **Fukuoka Dome**, opened in 1993 as a home for the Daiei Hawks, the city's professional baseball team. Backstage tours of the dome (which boasts the world's first retractable roof) and its locker rooms and practice areas operate daily (¥1000, hourly 9am-4pm) except when the stadium is in use. Though the dome is impressive, the tour is probably only of interest to die-hard baseball fans. Take bus No 306 from Hakata station and get off at the dome. Go up the stairs and walk around the building until you reach the Information Center between gates 7 and 8. Next to the dome is **Hawks Town**, a shopping and entertainment complex (see box below). The skyscraper beyond the dome is the 234m-high **Fukuoka Tower** (🖳 www.fukuokatower.co .jp, daily, 9:30am-10pm, to 9pm in winter, ¥800) which has a 123m-high observation deck open to the public. Entry is free if you can prove it is your birthday (give or take three days) on the day you visit. Built in 1989, the tower was designed to withstand earthquakes of up to seven on the Richter scale.

Ohori Koen is popular with joggers and skateboarders. As well as a boating lake the park is home to **Fukuoka Art Museum** (🖳 www.fukuoka-art-museum.jp; Tue-Sun 9:30am-5:30pm, Jul/Aug until 7:30pm; ¥200). The museum contains two floors of Western and Japanese art; on display are works by Salvador Dali and Andy Warhol. Next to the museum is a small **Japanese garden** (Tue-Sun 9am-5pm, ¥240), a pleasant place to stroll and avoid the joggers in the main park. Go by subway to Ohorikoen and take exit No 6.

Fukuoka Asian Art Museum (🖳 http://faam.city.fukuoka.jp.eng; Thur-Tue 10am-8pm, ¥200) is a modern gallery on the 7th floor of the Hakata Riverain complex. Artists in residence from across Asia display their own works and there is also a small permanent collection of contemporary Asian art. Take the subway to Nakasu-Kawabata.

If you need a break and a place to put your feet up, head for the **massage and foot reflexology** places on the 14th floor of the IMS building in Tenjin. This is a haven of calm and a million miles from the city-centre bustle below.

As an alternative to traipsing around the city sights, **a short excursion** that combines train and boat can be made from Hakata station. Take a local train on the JR Kagoshima line to Kashii (11 mins). Change on to a local train on the JR Kashii line and go to the terminus at Saitozaki (20 mins). This is a pleasant ride out along a narrow peninsula but the best part is the boat journey from the ferry terminal at Saitozaki back to Hakata Port (¥430 one-way). On this short ride there are great views of the skyline and bay area – Fukuoka Dome and Tower are two major landmarks to look out for. The boat ride is also a superb way of getting another perspective on the city.

⛩ **Fukuoka – shopping paradise**

Fukuoka is Kyushu's shopping capital and **Tenjin** (accessible by subway from Hakata) marks its centre. Wander just a little bit from here and you might find yourself in trendy **Daimyo**, a chic enclave of local stores and designer-label shops just west of Tenjin where you'd be lucky to find anyone aged over 30. Daimyo is an area of narrow streets filled with an eclectic mix of shops selling everything from snowboards to fashion haircuts. You'll know you've stumbled into Daimyo when you find stores with names like 'Garageland Seventies' and 'Modernize' – retro past meets the future.

Set away from all this is **Canal City**, a city within a city of shops, restaurants, food courts, thrill rides and a multiplex cinema. Finally, there's **Hawks Town**, next to Fukuoka Dome where you'll find more shops as well as a United Cinemas multiplex and bowling alleys, karaoke boxes and arcade games.

If you're not in town for Hakata Gion Yamakasa (see p394) it's worth paying a visit to **Hakata Machiya Folk Museum** (⌨ www.hakatamachiya.com, daily, 10am-6pm; ¥200), a regional cultural-heritage centre where you can watch a 20-minute film of the raucous highlights.

PRACTICAL INFORMATION
Station guide
A major redevelopment of Hakata station is due to be completed in 2011 when the Kyushu shinkansen starts running between Hakata and Shin-Yatsushiro. The following guide relates to the existing station.

Hakata station has two main exits: Hakata gate is the main exit for the city, while Chikushi gate (the shinkansen side) is the exit for JR Kyushu Hotel Fukuoka (see p395). If you take the Central Exit ticket barrier, the Hakata side of the station will be on your left, and the shinkansen side on your right.

The main bus terminal is on the right as you exit the Hakata gate. There are also separate entrances for the shinkansen (second floor) and the ordinary lines (ground floor concourse level). The entrance to the subway for downtown Fukuoka (Tenjin) and the airport is via an escalator in the middle of the concourse. There are several JR ticket desks on the main concourse – any of them can organize rail-pass seat reservations.

There are some coin lockers on the main concourse, but the best bet is to head out of the Hakata side of the station. Just outside you'll find a bank of coin lockers, including large ¥600 ones.

A branch of both *Mister Donut* and a *Train D'Or* bakery are on the main concourse level. One floor below, between the station and the subway, is the 'food market', full of cheap places to eat at ranging from Western-style family restaurants to fast food and okonomiyaki.

Don't confuse JR Hakata station with the private Nishitetsu Railway's Fukuoka station. Nishitetsu Fukuoka station is in Tenjin, the main shopping district.

Tourist information
The **Tourist Information Counter** (☎ 092-431 3003, ⌨ www.fukuoka-tourism.net, daily 9am-7pm) is a walk-up counter in the middle of the station concourse. Turn right as you leave the Central Exit ticket barrier. It's not the most relaxed of places since the concourse is busy, so it's not somewhere to linger for information.

Ask for a copy of the **Fukuoka Welcome Card** (see box p53) brochure, which offers discounts to foreign tourists on some sights, shops, restaurants and hotels. There is no card as such – the booklet doubles as the card. You just need to show it when requesting a discount.

An alternative source of tourist information is **Rainbow Plaza** (☎ 092-733 2220, ⌨ www.rainbowfia.or.jp, open daily except 3rd Tue 10am-8pm), on the 8th floor of the IMS Building in Tenjin. To reach the IMS building, ride the subway to Tenjin and take exit No 13. Here you'll find English-speaking staff, information on places throughout Kyushu and the rest of Japan, satellite TV, foreign newspapers, magazines and a noticeboard.

The staff at Rainbow Plaza produce the monthly *Rainbow* newsletter with cinema listings, details of special events and festivals. *Fukuoka Now!* is a free monthly booklet with reviews of new pubs, clubs, restaurants and shops. If you're planning a night out in the city, or some serious shopping, it's definitely worth a look. *Fukuoka on Foot* is a very well-researched booklet of city walking tours. Pick this up either from the tourist information counter or at Rainbow Plaza.

Finally, it's worth looking at ⌨ www .fukuoka-now.com before you arrive here: as well as reviews of the best sights, the site has extensive restaurant reviews and nightlife and cinema listings.

Getting around
The cheapest way of getting into the city centre is to take the **loop bus** (¥100 per ride), which departs from bus platform A

0   100   200   300m

★ TRAILBLAZER

2 Fukuoka Kokusai Center

Naka-gawa

3

4
SHOWA-DORI

Tenjin

10
IMS building

Nishitetsu-Fukuoka Station

11

Akasaka   MEIJI-DORI

Tenjin Bus Center

12
Daimaru dept store

5, 6, 7, 8, 9

DAIMYO

T E N J I N

Nishitetsu-Omuta line

Fukuoka / Hakata

福岡／博多

KYUSHU

Where to stay

14	Grand Hyatt Fukuoka	14	グランドハイヤット福岡
17	Hotel Skycourt Hakata	17	ホテルスカイコート博多
18	Toyoko Inn Hakata-guchi Ekimae	18	東横イン 博多口駅前
19	Nishitetsu Inn Hakata	19	西鉄イン博多
22	Comfort Hotel Hakata	22	コンフォートホテル博多
25	Roynet Hotel Hakata Ekimae	25	ロイネットホテル博多駅前
26	JR Kyushu Hotel Fukuoka	26	JR九州ホテル 福岡

Where to eat and drink

11	Mamma Mamma (IMS Bldg)	11	マンマ マンマ (イムズビル)
12	Daimaru Department Store	12	大丸デパート
15	Asian Kitchen (Canal City)	15	アジアンキッチン (キャナルシティ)
23	Ichiran	23	一蘭

Other

1	International Ferry Terminal	1	博多港国際ターミナル
2	Fukuoka Kokusai Center	2	福岡国際センター
3	Fukuoka Asian Art Museum (Hakata Riverain)	3	福岡アジア美術館 (博多リバーレイン)

[See p394 for continuation of key]

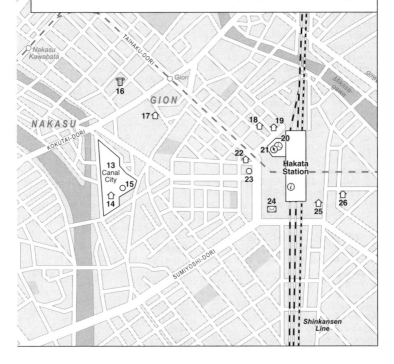

KYUSHU

FUKUOKA / HAKATA　福岡 / 博多

Other *(key continued from p393)*

4 Central Post Office	4 中央郵便局
5 Ohori Koen	5 大濠公園
6 Fukuoka Art Museum	6 福岡市美術館
7 Fukuoka Dome; Hawks Town	7 福岡ドーム；ホークスタウン
8 Fukuoka Tower	8 福岡タワー
9 Fukuoka City Museum	9 福岡市美術館
10 Kinokuniya (Tenjin Core)	10 紀伊國屋 (天神コア)
11 Rainbow Plaza (IMS Bldg)	11 レインボープラザ (イムズビル
13 Canal City	13 キャナルシティ
16 Hakata Machiya Folk Museum	16 「博多町屋」ふるさと館
20 Hakata Eki Transportation Center	20 博多駅交通センター
21 Popeye	21 メディアカフェポパイ
24 Post office	24 郵便局

outside the Hakata side of the station. On its way to Tenjin, the bus calls at the Canal City shopping/leisure complex (see p390). A handy English guide to the ¥100 loop bus system is available from the tourist-information desk at Hakata station.

Regular buses within Fukuoka city are operated by Nishitetsu Bus; the fare between Hakata station and Tenjin is ¥100. **Subway** fares are either ¥200 or ¥250. If unsure, buy a ¥200 ticket and use the 'fare adjustment' machine when you arrive at your destination station. A one-day subway pass is ¥600 and gives discounts on some attractions. Fukuoka's subway stations have good facilities for the disabled, with lifts at nearly every station from the platforms to the concourse.

Fukuoka Airport has three domestic terminals and an international terminal serving a number of destinations in Asia. The airport is connected to the city by subway – it's two stops to Hakata station (¥250). Free shuttle buses operate between the domestic and international terminals.

The **International Ferry Terminal** at Hakata Port has daily services to Pusan in South Korea. JR Kyushu (☎ 092-281 2315, 🖳 www.jrbeetle.co.jp) operates a high-speed jetfoil, the *Beetle II*, which zips between Hakata and Pusan in 2 hours 55 minutes (¥13,000 one-way or ¥24,000 return); online booking, up to three months

in advance, is possible. Rail passes are not accepted (the point is to encourage travel around Japan, not let you flee to Korea at JR's expense).

Alternatively, Camellia Line (☎ 092-262 2323, 🖳 www.camellia-line.co.jp) operates an overnight passenger ferry to Pusan. The cheapest option is the common tatami area (¥9000 one-way or ¥17,100 return). Private cabins are more expensive. From Hakata station, take bus No 11 or 19 for the port.

Internet
Popeye (☎ 092-432 8788, 🖳 www.media-cafe.ne.jp, ¥980 for 3 hours) is a 24-hour internet café on the 8th floor of the Hakata Eki Transportation Center (the large bus terminal), immediately to your right as you leave the Hakata side of the station. Alternatively you can surf the web/check email for up to 30 minutes free of charge at **Rainbow Plaza** (see p391).

Books
A branch of **Kinokuniya** is on the 6th and 7th floors of Tenjin Core with a selection of English books.

Festivals
The biggest annual event is **Hakata Gion Yamakasa** (July 1st-15th), the climax of which is a float race through the city; seven

teams carry their respective floats a distance of 5km.

The biggest sporting event is the **Kyushu Grand Sumo Basho**, the last tournament of the annual sumo calendar (see p44). It takes place in November at Fukuoka Kokusai Center.

Where to stay

Fukuoka has some world-class hotels at prices that would be impossible to find in Tokyo, as well as some cheap but clean business hotels.

Top of the range is *Grand Hyatt Fukuoka* (☎ 092-282 1234, 🖳 www.hyatt .com), in Canal City; it's *the* place to stay in Fukuoka if you can afford it. Large bathrooms feature a bath you can definitely sink into and separate shower – and a small TV screen you can watch while soaking in the tub. Hotel facilities include a gymnasium, swimming pool and saunas. Standard room rates start at ¥19,000 for a double, but ask about special offers or promotional packages.

Nishitetsu Inn Hakata (☎ 092-413 5454, 🖳 www.n-in.jp, ¥6900/S, ¥13,300/Tw) outside the Hakata exit is a large, spotless hotel offering a free simple breakfast, bright and modern rooms with desk space. The hotel boasts its own hot spring.

Rail-pass holders receive a 10% discount on room rates at *JR Kyushu Hotel Fukuoka* (☎ 092-413 8787, 🖳 fukuoka@ jrk-hotels.com) where the cheapest singles are ¥7500 and twins are ¥14,600. It's more luxurious than a standard business hotel with larger-than-average rooms; nice touches include refreshing towels offered to guests at the bijou check-in desk. It's very convenient for Hakata station, since the hotel is only a three-minute walk from the Chikushi Gate exit. Go straight up the main road from the exit and it's just past Hotel New Miyako.

Two budget business hotel choices in the station area are *Toyoko Inn Hakata-guchi Ekimae* (☎ 092-451 1045, 🖳 www .toyoko-inn.com, ¥5880/S, ¥8610/Tw) and *Comfort Hotel Hakata* (☎ 092-431 1211, 🖳 www.choice-hotels.jp, ¥6000/S, ¥12,000/Tw). On the shinkansen side of the station is *Roynet Hotel Hakata Ekimae* (☎ 092-433 0011, 🖳 www.roynet.jp/hakata, ¥10,000/S, ¥16,800/Tw) with an automated check-in.

One subway stop away from Hakata in Gion (exit 3) is *Hotel Skycourt Hakata* (☎ 092-262 4400, 🖳 www.skyc.jp/hakata.htm) which offers bog-standard business-hotel rooms from ¥4500 for a single and ¥8000 for a double.

Where to eat and drink

Hakata is associated with ramen: there are plenty of places around the station that serve up cheap bowls of the stringy yellow noodles but one popular place is *Ichiran* (daily, 10am-10pm) on basement level 2 of the black building opposite Hakata station (take the Hakata gate), next to the large red-brick building that houses Fukuoka City Bank. It's hidden away in a corner, so look out for the hanging red curtain with 'Ichiran' in black kanji. Buy a ticket (¥650) from the vending machine and take a seat. You'll then be given a sheet to fill out (ask for the English version), specifying exactly how spicy, how much garlic and what kind of vegetables you want in your ramen. There are branches of Ichiran in other parts of Fukuoka – look out for one in the basement of Canal City.

The big shopping and entertainment complexes are also good places to look for food. **Canal City** has a good selection of other restaurants, including *Asian Kitchen* on the fourth floor, where people queue in long lines at the weekend. The main eating area is on the basement level, where you'll find a selection of Japanese- and Western-style eateries.

If you're shopping in Tenjin, the basement of **Daimaru** department store has a good selection of food to take out. There are several restaurants on the 12th and 13th floors of the **IMS Building** in Tenjin. One of the best is *Mamma Mamma* (daily, 11am-4pm, 5-10pm), a buffet restaurant on the 12th floor. The all-you-can-eat lunch deal is ¥1500, rising to ¥2100 in the evening; terrific value and a great range of starters, main-course dishes and desserts.

Side trip by rail from Fukuoka/Hakata

Dazaifu (see p377), once the political heart of Kyushu and the town where the god of learning and literature is enshrined, is an easy day trip from Fukuoka but can equally well be visited en route to Nagasaki, Kumamoto or Kagoshima.

The splendid **Kyushu National Museum** (🖥 www.kyuhaku.com, Tue-Sun, 9:30am-5pm, ¥420), opened in 2005 and built in the shape of a blue wave, is one of only four in the country to be operated by the central government (the others are in Tokyo, Kyoto and Nara) and is the first national museum to be built in 100 years. The aim is to provide a 'new perspective on Japanese culture, in the context of Asian history'. Highlights include a historical document detailing two battles in the 13th century, known as Genko, in which Japan fought off attacks by the Mongolian empire ruled by Genghis Khan.

From Fukuoka, the most direct way is to take the private Nishitetsu-Omuta line (¥390, rail passes not accepted) from Nishitetsu-Fukuoka station in Tenjin (reach Tenjin by subway from Hakata, ¥200). The entrance to the station is in the large Mitsukoshi department store. Some trains run direct to Dazaifu, though you may have to change at Futsukaichi.

NAGASAKI

'I cannot think of a more beautiful place. There is a land-locked harbour; at the entrance are islands ... the ship winds up the harbour which is more like a very broad river, with hills on either side levelling down towards the extreme end where the town of Nagasaki stands.'

So wrote Elizabeth Alt, wife of William Alt, a 19th-century English merchant who lived and traded in Nagasaki. Nagasaki's history as a centre of international trade and its long period of contact with the West are still the reasons why tourists pour into the city, but it was the dropping of the second atomic bomb here on August 9th 1945 that ensured Nagasaki would become known throughout the world. More people were killed in this one blast than in all the bombing raids on Britain throughout WWII. Like Hiroshima, Nagasaki is now home to a Peace Park and A Bomb Museum, both of which record huge numbers of visitors every year.

For sightseeing purposes it's useful to consider Nagasaki as a city of two halves. North of the station, in the **Urakami district**, is the Atomic Bomb Museum and Peace Park. Down in the south, on the hills overlooking the harbour, is **Glover Garden**, full of 19th-century Western-style homes. One day would be just enough to visit both parts but it's preferable to allow a couple of days to do everything at a more relaxed pace and also include a tour of the central area including newly restored **Dejima**, the island enclave which was the only point of contact with the outside world during Japan's period of national seclusion (1641-1859).

What to see and do

A good start to a tour of Nagasaki would be to take **Mt Inasa Ropeway** (daily 9am-10pm Mar-Nov, 9am-9pm Dec-Feb, ¥700 one-way, ¥1200 return) for a panoramic view of the city. The best time to go is at night when the city is lit up; take a wide-angle lens with you. Look back over the dark hills for a strange and slightly eerie contrast to the bright lights that dazzle below. Take Nagasaki Bus No 3 or 4 from the station and get off at 'Ropeway-mae', or take tram No 1 or 3 two stops north from the station to Takara-machi. From here, follow the main road underneath the railway line and over Urakami-gawa. Cross the river, turn right and follow the road round until you see a shrine entrance on your left. Walk through the entrance gate and turn left to find the entrance to the ropeway.

Urakami district The atomic bomb dropped on Nagasaki at 11:02am on August 9th 1945 was meant for the city of Kokura (see p374). Poor visibility meant the plane carrying the bomb circled three times over Kokura before changing course for Nagasaki, where cloud also hampered visibility. A chance break in the clouds just after 11am sealed the city's destiny. It's estimated that over 70,000 (of a 240,000 population) were killed either instantly or in the period up to the end of 1945.

The bomb was intended for Nagasaki Shipyard but exploded instead over Urakami, a centre of Christian missionary work in Nagasaki since the latter half of the 16th century. As the bomb was dropped, a service was underway at Urakami Cathedral – all that's left today is a melted rosary on display in the A-Bomb Museum and one piece of the cathedral wall in the nearby Hypocenter Park. Today, Urakami is home to the Peace Park and Atomic Bomb Museum.

Nagasaki Atomic Bomb Museum (🖳 www.city.nagasaki.nagasaki.jp/na-bomb/museum; daily, 8:30am-5pm, ¥200) is a high priority, though the constant stream of school groups through the museum can be waring. What you want most is the chance to walk around quietly on your own – and that's the one luxury you're nearly always denied here. Passing through into the first hall, the scene immediately transforms to the precise moment that the bomb was dropped – a clock ticks and black and white images of the devastation appear on screens. As with the Peace Memorial Museum (see p262) in Hiroshima, the most memorable exhibits are individual objects, such as the glass bottles melted together from the heat of the blast and the burnt-out remains of a schoolgirl's lunchbox. Directly down the hill from the museum, and next to the main street, is the **Atomic Bomb Hypocenter**, marking the precise spot over which the A-bomb exploded.

The nearby **Peace Park** is filled with statues and memorials given to the city as a gesture of peace from all over the world – many are from former Eastern bloc countries. The centrepiece of the park is a giant Peace Statue, erected ten years after the bombing and now the backdrop for the annual peace ceremony held on August 9th. Throughout the year, visiting school parties hold their own peace ceremonies in front of the statue.

The nearest tram stop for the Peace Park and Atomic Bomb Museum is Matsuyama-machi, eight stops north of Nagasaki station on tram No 1 or 3.

Near Nagasaki station Nagasaki's importance as a historical centre for Christianity in Japan is most obviously seen at Oura Catholic Church below Glover Garden (see p398) and at the **Site of the 26 Christian Martyrs** in

Nishizaka-machi, a memorial to six Spanish missionaries and 20 Japanese Christians who were crucified here in 1597. It's a very simple memorial, a few minutes' walk east from the station, heading up the road to Nishizaka.

Very much off the tourist trail is **Oka Masaharu Memorial Peace Museum** (Tue-Sun 9am-5pm, ¥250). This peace museum focuses on Japan's actions before and during WWII in Korea, China, and South-east Asia. It's not an easy place to visit, some of the photos are shocking, but it provides a very different historical perspective to that offered at the 'official' A-Bomb Museum. The museum was founded in memory of the late Protestant Minister and peace activist, Oka Masaharu (1918-94), who devoted much of his life to relief efforts for Korean atomic bomb survivors in Japan. The signs are in Japanese and Korean but there's a pamphlet with some explanations in English; the photos that line the walls tell their own story. The museum receives few visitors and is not included in any of the tourist guides or brochures produced by the city. It's a little hard to find but follow the same road up to Nishizaka from the station as for the 'Site of the 26 Christian Martyrs'. The museum is just past this memorial.

Nagasaki Harbour area Glover Garden (⌨ www1.city.nagasaki.nagasaki .jp/glover; daily, 8am-6pm, ¥600), an area of Western-style houses built on a hill overlooking Nagasaki harbour, is usually swamped with visitors. The harbour views from the hillside repay the ticket cost, even if the houses are not overly exciting for Western visitors.

Best known of all the 19th-century residents was the man whom the garden is named after, Thomas Glover. Born in Scotland in 1838, Glover moved to Nagasaki in 1859, married a Japanese woman and involved himself in a number of key Japanese businesses, helping to set up the Japan Brewery Company in July 1885, predecessor to today's Kirin Brewery. Look out for the *kirin*, a mythical creature that sports a bushy moustache remarkably similar to Thomas Glover's, on cans and bottles of Kirin beer. Since the area was populated by merchants, it's appropriate that the management of Glover Garden has kept the financial spirit of Glover et al alive by selling Glover shortbread biscuits and the like.

On the way up to the Glover Garden entrance, look out for **Oura Catholic Church** (Mar-Nov 8am-6pm, Dec-Feb 8:30am-5pm, ¥300), built by French missionaries in 1864 and the oldest church in Japan.

⛩ Japan's first railway?
Though most history books conclude that the first railway line in Japan was built between Shimbashi and Yokohama, the estate of Thomas Glover begs to differ. In a corner of Glover's House a sign reveals that in 1865 the Scotsman purchased the 'Iron Duke', claimed to be Japan's first steam locomotive, and laid a 400m-long track in Nagasaki. He used Japanese coal to power the engine and opened the line up to an astonished public. It was not until 1872, seven years after the opening of this mini railway, that the Shimbashi–Yokohama line (see p92) opened for business.

An account of Thomas Glover's life can be found in Alexander McKay's *Scottish Samurai* (Edinburgh, Canongate Press, 1997).

To reach Glover Garden, take tram No 1 (bound for Shokakuji-shita) from Nagasaki station and change at Tsuki-machi. From here, change to tram No 5 and ride all the way to the terminus at Ishibashi.

Dejima From 1641 to 1859 the actual island of Dejima, just off Nagasaki, was Japan's sole point of contact with the outside world as the base for trade with the Dutch East India Company. A reconstruction of the Dutch enclave (daily, 9am-5pm, ¥500) opened in 2000 to mark the 400th anniversary of relations between Japan and the Netherlands. It has since been expanded with even more replicas of 19th-century buildings and an excellent museum recounting the story of the Dutch traders who were forced to live in isolation on the island.

The reconstruction will not be complete until 2010; the plan is to recreate Dejima's traditional fan-shape, surrounded by water on all sides. Many of the scheduled 25 buildings are already open to the public, some of which display objects found during ongoing excavation work.

Access and entry prices may change as Dejima expands, but at the time of writing parts of the complex were free to look around, while for the rest you needed to buy a ticket (¥500).

If you don't want to buy a ticket it's still worth visiting the free Dejima Theatre, a reconstructed warehouse which houses a mini-cinema telling the history of Dejima. English headphones are available. It's an informative and entertaining glimpse at what the place was like when the Dutch were trading here. Part of the film dwells on what sort of food the Dutch offered their hosts on special occasions (answer: steamed duck, sausage and castella cake). Castella is now a popular souvenir from Nagasaki.

There is also an obligatory gift shop, selling Dutch chocolate and cookies. Take tram No 1 three stops south from Nagasaki station to Dejima, which drops you right outside the reconstructed complex.

PRACTICAL INFORMATION
Station guide
Nagasaki station incorporates a hotel, department store and plaza under a giant canopy.

There is only one exit (Central Exit), on the same level as the platforms. Turn left after the ticket barrier, skirt around the travel agency and follow the station building round to the main coin locker area.

In front of you as you leave the platforms is AMU Plaza department store. On the fourth floor is a United Cinemas multiplex and the fifth floor has restaurants.

Tourist information
Nagasaki City TIC (095-823 3631, daily 8am-7pm Mar-Nov, 8am-5:30pm Nov-Feb) is inside the waiting room to your right as you exit the ticket barrier. The reasonably helpful staff dispense maps and hotel information. Pick up a useful guide to the city tram network.

For more detailed information, **Nagasaki Prefectural Tourist Federation** (☎ 095-826 9407, Mon-Sat 9am-5:30pm) is on the second floor of the Ken-ei Bus Center across the main road from the station. Use the overhead walkway to reach it. *The Nagasaki Beat*, a monthly newsletter with event listings, is available here.

Getting around
Nagasaki is known for its *chin chin densha*, old-fashioned **trams** that have been trundling around the city since 1915, and which are by far the best means of getting around.

KYUSHU

NAGASAKI 長崎

Where to stay
1	Minshuku Tanpopo	1	民宿たんぽぽ
4	Nagasaki Catholic Center YH	4	長崎カトリックセンター ユースホステル
6	Best Western Premier Hotel Nagasaki	6	ベストウェスタンプレミア ホテル長崎
10	Hotel Cuore Nagasaki Ekimae	10	ホテルクオーレ長崎駅前
11	JR Kyushu Hotel Nagasaki	11	JR九州ホテル長崎
13	Nagasaki Ebisu Youth Hostel	13	長崎ゑびすユースホステル
14	Toyoko Inn Nagasaki Ekimae	14	東横イン長崎駅前
17	Comfort Hotel Nagasaki	17	コンフォートホテル長崎
20	Hotel Belle View Nagasaki	20	ホテルベルビュー長崎
23	Holiday Inn Nagasaki	23	ホリデイインエクスプレス長崎
24	The Hamilton Nagasaki	24	ザハミルトン長崎

Where to eat and drink
11	AMU PLaza	11	アミュプラザ
16	Milan	16	ミラン
18	Coffee and Antique Nanbanjaiya	18	南蛮茶屋
19	Hamakatsu	19	浜勝
21	Dejima Wharf	21	出島ワーフ

Other
2	Peace Park	2	平和公園
3	Atomic Bomb Hypocenter	3	原爆落下中心地
5	Nagasaki Atomic Bomb Museum	5	長崎原爆資料館
7	Site of the 26 Christian Martyrs	7	日本２６聖人殉教地
8	Oka Masaharu Memorial Peace Museum	8	岡まさはる記念長崎平和資料館
9	Ken-ei Bus Center; Nagasaki Prefectural Tourism Federation	9	県営バスセンター; 長崎 県観光連盟
11	Kinko's (AMU Plaza)	11	キンコーズ
12	Central Post Office	12	中央郵便局
15	Ohato Ferry Terminal	15	大波止フェリーターミナル
21	Dejima Wharf	21	出島ワーフ
22	Dejima	22	出島
25	Dutch Hollander Slope	25	オランダ坂
26	Oura Catholic Church	26	大浦天主堂
27	Glover Garden	27	グラバー園

One-day tram passes (¥500) are available from tourist offices and some hotels but not on board the trams themselves. Individual rides cost ¥100, regardless of the length of journey, so work out how many trips you're likely to make in one day before purchasing the pass.

If you think you can manage to do most of the sights in Nagasaki in a day, it's worth considering the one-day Nagasaki Sightseeing Pass (¥1500, purchased from the TIC at Nagasaki station). The pass includes unlimited tram rides, as well as entry to Glover Garden, Oura Catholic Church, the Atomic Bomb Museum and a number of other attractions. Even if you just visit the attractions listed above and have more than five tram rides you'll save money.

KYUSHU

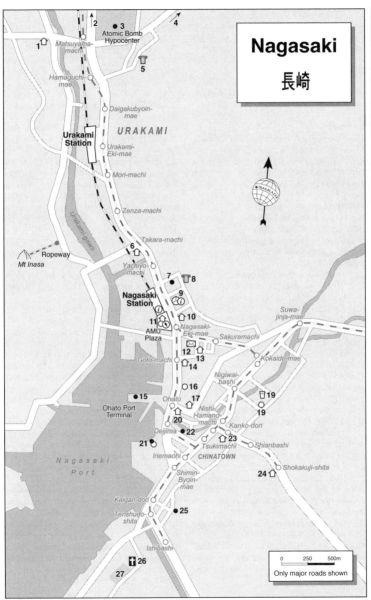

Nagasaki

長崎

1 · Matsuyama-machi

2

3 · Atomic Bomb Hypocenter

4

5

Hamaguchi-mae

Daigakubyoin-mae

URAKAMI

Urakami Station

Urakami-Eki-mae

Mori-machi

Zenza-machi

Takara-machi

Ropeway
Mt Inasa

Urakami-gawa

6

Yachiyo-machi

7 · 8

9

Nagasaki Station

10

11

AMU Plaza

Nagasaki-Eki-mae

Sakuramachi

Suwa-jinja-mae

Kokaido-mae

Goto-machi

12 · 13

14

Nigiwai-bashi

19

19

Ohato Port Terminal

15 ·

Ohato

16

17

Nishi-Hamano-machi

Kanko-dori

20

Deijima

22

23

Tsukimachi

Shianbashi

21

Iriemachi

CHINATOWN

24

Shokakuji-shita

Nagasaki Port

Shimin-Byoin-mae

Kaigan-dori

Tenshudo-shita

25 ·

Ishibashi

26

27

0   250   500m
Only major roads shown

Cycles (daily 9am-5pm, ¥600/4 hours with JR pass) can be rented from Nagasaki station. Buy a ticket from the JR ticket office (to your left as you exit the ticket barrier) and take it to the Eki Rent a Car counter round the corner.

The **shuttle bus** to Nagasaki Airport (domestic flights only) takes 60 minutes and costs ¥1200 from Nagasaki station.

Internet
The nearest place to the station is **Kinko's**, inside AMU Plaza. It's tucked away at the back of the ground floor, just behind a supermarket, and is open 24 hours on weekdays (Sat/Sun 8am-10pm).

Where to stay
For all the hotels in Nagasaki, except the business hotels, ask about special rates when booking as you'll usually be able to negotiate a discount (often they'll throw in breakfast).

JR Kyushu Hotel Nagasaki (☎ 095-832 8000, ⌨ nagasaki@jrk-hotels.com; ¥6900/S, ¥12,600/Tw) is built into the station complex. Rooms are good value.

Best Western Premier Hotel Nagasaki (☎ 095-821 1111, ⌨ www.bestwestern.co .jp/nagasaki; ¥15,000/S, ¥26,000/Tw) is a top-end hotel with a choice of restaurants and its own hot-spring facilities. The singles and twins are spacious and the more expensive rooms on the executive floor are even larger. There is also a ladies-only floor (ask for this when checking in). Internet-access points for laptops are in all rooms.

To reach the hotel, take the tram two stops north from the station to Takara-machi (look out for the hotel on your left as the train arrives in Nagasaki).

Two cheaper business-hotel options close to the station are the ever-reliable *Toyoko Inn Nagasaki Eki-mae* (☎ 095-825 1045, ⌨ www.toyoko-inn.com; ¥5460/S, ¥7560/Tw) and *Hotel Cuore Nagasaki Ekimae* (☎ 095-818 9000, 🖹 818 9006; ¥6300/S, ¥10,000/Tw). The latter, situated across the street from the station, offers the usual line in clean, no-frills singles and twins.

An alternative business hotel offering much the same deal, but closer to the port than to the station, is *Hotel Belle View Nagasaki* (☎ 095-826 5030, ⌨ www.hotel-belleview.com; ¥5800/S, ¥10,000/Tw), where the rate includes a simple breakfast.

Comfort Hotel Nagasaki (☎ 095-827 1111, 🖹 827 1154, ⌨ www.choicehotels .com; ¥5500/S, ¥8500/Tw) is terrific value; a simple breakfast is included.

Some of the rooms at *Holiday Inn Nagasaki* (☎ 095-828 1234, ⌨ www.hi-nag asaki.jp; ¥8950/S, ¥15,750/D, ¥16,800/Tw) are showing their age a bit, but this is still a clean, comfortable and convenient place to stay. There are more expensive 'luxury designer rooms' on the top floor. From the station, take tram No 1 and get off at Kanko-dori, right by the entrance to the Holiday Inn.

The Hamilton Nagasaki (☎ 095-824 1000, ⌨ www.hamilton-gr.jp/nagasaki; ¥9500/S, ¥18,000/Tw) is a smaller hotel further along the same road. Its theme is yesteryear Britain. The beds are wide and the rooms are a generous size.

If you prefer to be based closer to the Peace Park, *Minshuku Tanpopo* (☎ 095-861 6230, 🖹 864 0032) is a good choice. Tatami rooms with communal bath cost ¥4000 for one, ¥7000 for two or ¥10,500 for three people. It's close to Matsuyama tram stop but if you call in advance and arrive at JR Urakami station (last stop before Nagasaki, see p379) you should be able to arrange a free pick-up.

The small *Nagasaki-Ebisu Youth Hostel* (☎/🖹 095-824 3823, ⌨ www.jyh .or.jp; 10 beds) is a basic but cosy place five minutes from JR Nagasaki station. The rate is ¥2940 with breakfast an additional ¥525 and dinner ¥1050.

Alternatively try the 42-bed *Nagasaki Catholic Center*, part of which operates as a youth hostel (☎ 095-846 4246, 🖹 848 8310, ⌨ www.jyh.or.jp; ¥2700). The center is located in front of Urakami Cathedral (hence the hostel's selling point that guests can 'wake up to the sound of the cathedral bells'). The nearest rail station is JR Urakami. From the station, take a bus bound for Motohara and get off at the stop outside the Catholic Center.

Where to eat and drink
In the station area the obvious place to head is the fifth floor '**Gourmet World**' of AMU Plaza department store. Here you'll find a branch of the popular Italian pasta-and-pizza chain *Capricciosa*, a revolving sushi bar, a Chinese, and a flame-grilled steak restaurant. A *Train D'or* bakery is on the ground floor and there's a branch of fast-food joint *Royal Host* above it. Also inside AMU Plaza are branches of *KFC* and *Mister Donut*. To make your own lunch, the supermarket at the back of the ground floor of AMU Plaza does a range of takeaway meals such as sushi, tonkatsu and the like.

Popular with Nagasaki residents and visitors alike, *Hamakatsu* (daily 11am-10:30pm, last orders 10pm) is the place to eat tonkatsu. Seating is at tables or along the counter – or a take-out box of tonkatsu sandwiches costs ¥650. It's a five-minute walk north of Shianbashi tram station.

For a quiet drink surrounded by antiques, head for *Coffee and Antique*

Nanbanjaiya (open daily from around 12 noon-10pm), beyond the Kanko-dori arcade. Mellow music plays in the background in this 160-year-old wooden building. Go to the end of the covered arcade along Kanko-dori, cross the next road, go straight until you reach the convenience store (Daily Yamazaki), turn left, and look on the left-hand side for a red lampshade.

Another good area to look for food is **Dejima Wharf**, where there is a good selection of Western and Japanese restaurants. It's especially pleasant in the evening where you can sit and enjoy views of the harbour. You'll find a row of harbourside bars and cafés, including Chinese, Japanese and Italian. It's a good place to watch the sunset over a drink after a hard day of sightseeing in Nagasaki.

Milan, which despite its name is an Indian restaurant, is just past and on the same side of the road as the Toyoko Inn (see opposite). The cheapest lunch deal (11am-3pm) is the 'Service Lunch' at ¥714 which includes a curry, nan bread, rice, salad and lassi. Look for the sign in English above the entrance.

Side trip to Huis Ten Bosch
Huis Ten Bosch (⌨ www.huistenbosch.co.jp), the Dutch theme park overlooking Omura Bay north-east of Nagasaki, is one of Kyushu's most popular attractions for vacationing Japanese.

The idea for this bizarre re-creation of tulip fields and windmills in southern Japan came from Yoshikuni Kamichika, who visited Holland in 1979 and decided to build a city in Japan that would combine Dutch city planning with Japanese technology. The aim was to make the site a living, working, eco-friendly city 'to last 1000 years'. What you find is much more of a Disney resort, with hotels, rides and attractions, canals, shops that sell clogs and a cast of real Dutch who dress up in traditional costume and become walking photo opportunities. As one foreign resident in Nagasaki noted, Huis Ten Bosch can hardly be called authentic when the only grass to be had is in the green fields.

Plan to spend a full day at Huis Ten Bosch. A one-day passport allowing unlimited use of most attractions costs ¥4800 (12-17 years ¥3600 and 4-11 years ¥2600). Park operating hours vary according to the season, so check the website or at the tourist information office in Nagasaki station.

From Nagasaki take a train which runs along the Omura line to JR Huis Ten Bosch station (70 mins). Combined rail and one-day passport tickets are available from Nagasaki. Direct rail services also run from Hakata station in Fukuoka. The Huis Ten Bosch LEX takes 90 minutes from Hakata.

KYUSHU

KUMAMOTO

Halfway down the west side of Kyushu, Kumamoto once flourished as a castle town; today the (reconstructed) castle still rates as the city's biggest tourist draw. Probably Kumamoto's best-known resident was Miyamoto Musashi (1584-1645), an exceptional swordsman who wrote a book during the last years of his life in which he is said to have 'tempered his samurai way of thinking with more serene views of life'. His serenity did not stop him from being buried in full armour, clutching his sword. Miyamoto probably approved of the 'Kobori swimming technique', an unusual martial art originating in Kumamoto, which according to city publicity involved the 'art of swimming in the standing posture while attired in armour and helmet'.

What to see and do

Right in the centre of the city is **Kumamoto Castle** (daily, Apr-Oct 8:30am-5:30pm, Nov-Mar 8:30am-4:30pm, ¥500). Completed between 1601 and 1607, most of the structures that make up the fortifications were destroyed during the civil war of 1877. Extensive restoration was carried out in 2006 ahead of the castle's 400th anniversary in 2007. The construction (a 20th-century reconstruction) which exists today is as near as possible to what the original fortification must have looked like when it was completed in 1607. The castle is still an impressive sight, especially when lit up at night (until 11pm). Inside the donjon are displays on the civil war, the cultural history of the region and a scale model of the original castle. Enquire at the main gate ticket window about free guided tours of the castle in English. To reach the castle from the station, take the tram to 'Kumamotojo-mae' stop.

The trendiest art space in town is **Kumamoto Contemporary Art Museum** (🖳 www.camk.or.jp/english/index.html; Wed-Mon, 10am-8pm) on the third floor adjacent to Hotel Nikko Kumamoto. There is a free permanent collection and an entrance fee for temporary installations (check the schedule at the tourist-information desk at Kumamoto station). Avoid if possible staring for too long into Japanese avant-garde artist Yayoi Kusama's 'Infinity Mirrored Room'.

Flag-waving tour guides lead a constant stream of school parties around Kumamoto's other hot spot, **Suizen-ji Garden** (daily, 7am-6pm, ¥400), stopping briefly for a mass photo call in front of the main point of interest, a grass mound in the shape of Mt Fuji. Since it's much smaller than Kenrokuen (see p185) in Kanazawa, it's very hard to enjoy the park in tranquillity. Also in the grounds are **Izumi Shrine**, built in 1878 and a popular venue for New Year celebrations, and a **Noh theatre** (performances, lit by fire, are staged here during the summer festival, August 11th-13th). It's best to visit Suizen-ji as early as possible to avoid the crowds. Take the tram to 'Suizenji-Koen-mae' stop.

Behind Tsuruya department store in the city centre is the former home of Irish writer **Lafcadio Hearn**. Hearn is better known as a former resident of Matsue (see p273), from where he moved to Kumamoto in 1891. He lived in a house owned by a local samurai family, now in the middle of the downtown shopping area.

The house is very small but it's still worth spending ¥200 (Tue-Sun, 9:30am-4:30pm) to go inside, where panels in English tell the story of how Hearn was born on the Greek island of Levkas, lived in Dublin (Ireland), went to school in Durham (UK), travelled to the USA, worked as a reporter on the island of Martinique, and finally arrived in Yokohama in 1890 at the age of 40 on an assignment for *Harpers* magazine. He spent the rest of his life in Japan, where he lived in Matsue before spending three years in Kumamoto teaching English. Later Hearn moved to Kobe and in 1896 became a naturalized Japanese citizen. Koizumi Yakumo, as Hearn was called after his naturalization, died suddenly of a heart attack on 26th September 1904.

PRACTICAL INFORMATION
Station guide
Kumamoto station is south-west of the main city centre. On the second floor of the station is Fresta, a collection of shops and a few cheap restaurants, none of which is particularly recommended. On the ground floor is a **Train D'Or** bakery; just outside you'll find a **Mister Donut**, **Mos Burger** and an **udon shop**. For coin lockers (all sizes), exit the station and turn left. Also at the station is a branch post office and a convenience store.

Tourist information
The **tourist information counter** (☎ 096-352 3743, daily, 9am-5:30pm) in the station is usually staffed by an English speaker who can help book accommodation and provide a map.

Even better is the International Lounge, on the second floor of **Kumamoto International Association** (☎ 096-359 2121, 💻 www.kumamoto-if.or.jp, 9am-8pm Mon-Fri, 9am-7pm Sat-Sun, closed 2nd/4th Mon), which has CNN, internet terminals, newspapers and magazines. The lounge is air-conditioned and a great place to beat the heat in the summer. While here, pick up a copy of *Yoka*, a monthly newsletter that contains a calendar of events for Kumamoto prefecture.

For ¥500 you can also get your hands on an introductory primer in English to Miyamoto Musashi's classic 17th-century *Book of Five Rings*, which carries the subtitle 'Practical Wisdom for Everyday Life'.

Getting around
One-day passes (¥500) allow unlimited travel on the tram and Shiei Buses (mostly green) within the city centre. Passes are available from the tourist information counter at the station, or on board the trams themselves.

One of the trams, called the San Antonio after Kumamoto's sister city in the USA, has an on-board commentary in English and Japanese on the relationship between Kumamoto and San Antonio.

A tourist bus does a loop around town (8:30am-5pm, 2/hour, ¥130 flat fare), starting and finishing at the Transportation Center in the city centre, and includes a stop at the castle.

Internet
Internet access is available free of charge at Kumamoto International Association (see column opposite). Ask at the counter to use the computers.

Festivals
The biggest annual event is the **Hi-no-Kuni** ('country of fire') festival that takes place on August 11th-13th. Events include a fireworks display and late-night folk dancing.

Where to stay
Room rates in the station area are cheaper than in the centre near Kumamoto Castle and it's really not that much of a hassle to get into town – there are regular buses and trams from the station.

Best value in the station area by far is **JR Kyushu Hotel Kumamoto** (☎ 096-354 8000, 🖷 354 8012, 💻 kumamoto@jrk-hotels.com; ¥6900/S, ¥12,6000/Tw), immediately on your right as you exit the station. Rail-pass holders get a small discount. A more expensive option outside the station is

KYUSHU

Where to stay
1 JR Kyushu Hotel Kumamoto
2 Hotel New Otani Kumamoto
3 Komatsu-so
10 Ark Hotel Kumamoto
17 Hotel Nikko Kumamoto
18 Toyoko Inn Suidocho Dentei-mae
19 Suidocho Green Hotel
20 Suizen-ji Youth Hostel

1 JR九州ホテル 熊本
2 ホテルニューオオタニ熊本
3 小松荘
10 アークホテル熊本
17 ホテル日航熊本
18 東横イン 熊本水道町電停前
19 水道町グリーンホテル
20 水前寺ユースホステル

Where to eat and drink
1 Umaya
7 Mister Donut
11 Le Petit Paris
12 Aoyagi
13 Saint Etoile

1 うまや
7 ミスタードーナツ
11 ルプティパリ
12 青柳
13 サンエトワール

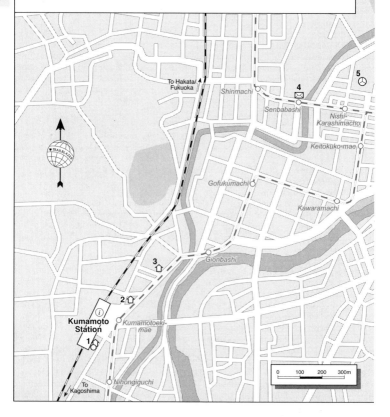

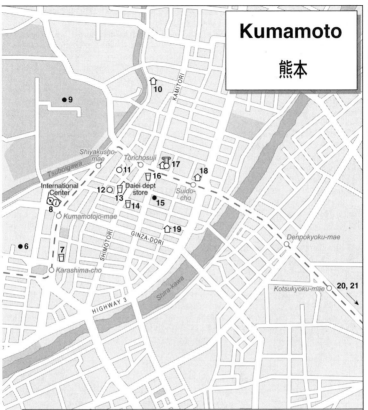

Where to eat and drink *(key continued from opposite)*

14 Swiss		14 スイス
16 Starbucks		16 スターバックス
17 Serena; Tao-Li		17 セリーナ; 桃李
21 Senri		21 泉里

Other

4 Central Post Office		4 中央郵便局
5 Kumamoto Transportation Center		5 熊本交通センター
6 Iwataya Department Store		6 岩田屋デパート
8 Kumamoto International Association		8 熊本国際協会
9 Kumamoto Castle		9 熊本城
15 Former Residence of Lafcadio Hearn		15 小泉八雲熊本旧居
17 Kumamoto Contemporary Art Museum		17 熊本市現代美術館
21 Suizen-ji Garden, Izumi Shrine		21 水前寺公園; 出水神社

Hotel New Otani Kumamoto (☎ 096-326 1111, 🖳 www.newotani.co.jp; ¥11,000/S, ¥18,000/Tw/D), which has all the facilities you'd expect of this top-class hotel chain.

A five-minute walk from the station is *Komatsu-so* (☎ 096-355 2634), a small minshuku that is homely if a bit run down. It's cheap at ¥3500/pp without meals, so at that price you can't really complain about the dust. It's an extra ¥700 for breakfast or add ¥2000 for breakfast and dinner.

Get on to the main road in front of the station, turn left and walk past Hotel New Otani; Komatsu-so is a little further down this road on the left. Look for the 'Welcome' sign. The entrance is up a narrow path.

It's advisable to book ahead at *Suizenji Youth Hostel* (☎ 096-371 9193, 📄 371 9218, 🖳 www.jyh.or.jp; ¥3045/4045) as they don't seem to like unannounced arrivals. There's a 10pm curfew.

From the station, take the tram to Misotenjin-mae, turn the first right, go to the end of this road, turn right again, then first left, and you'll see the hostel sign on the left-hand side.

For a cheap hotel bed in the downtown area try *Suidocho Green Hotel* (☎ 096-211 2222, 🖳 suidocho@greenhotels.co.jp;

¥6090/S, ¥8400/D). This business hotel has clean, compact singles.

Alternatively you'll find *Toyoko Inn Kumamoto Suido-cho Dentei-mae* (☎ 096-325 1045, 🖳 www.toyoko-inn.com; ¥6195/S, ¥8295/Tw) in front of the Suido-cho tram stop.

Going up in price is *Ark Hotel Kumamoto* (☎ 096-351 2222, 🖳 front@ kumamoto.ark-hotel.co.jp; ¥10,000/S, ¥16,000/Tw/D), with wide beds in fairly spacious rooms. Some twins have the option of a third child bed. It's situated just below the castle.

A more luxurious – and expensive – option is *Hotel Nikko Kumamoto* (☎ 096-211 1111, 🖳 www.nikko-kumamoto.co.jp; ¥16,170/S, ¥30,030/Tw), considered the best place to stay in town. It has larger-than-average rooms (some on the 10th floor with a view of Kumamoto Castle) and a choice of restaurants. Twins have a separate toilet and bathroom. Breakfast is available for ¥2000, but enquire when booking about special rates including breakfast. You're also ideally placed to visit the Contemporary Art Museum (see p404), since it's located on the 3rd and 4th floors of the hotel.

⛩ **Basashi – an acquired taste**

That evening I learned that raw horsemeat was a speciality of the area … I went to a little restaurant near Kumamoto station with my mind made up to try some. It was disappointingly stringy, and having come straight out of the refrigerator, was hard with bits of ice. I sat for a long time sipping beer, waiting for the horsemeat to thaw, while the only customer in the restaurant had a conversation with the owner.
Alan Booth, *The Roads to Sata*, Kodansha International, 1985

Kumamoto's big culinary draw doesn't sound the most appetizing of regional specialities; the main problem with *basashi* (raw horsemeat), however, is not so much the taste but that most places offering it are prohibitively expensive. You could easily spend around ¥10,000 per person by dining at a restaurant specializing in the stuff.

If you decide to try basashi it's best to buy some from a butcher and take it back to your ryokan or minshuku. If you ask, the butcher will prepare it ready to eat and probably include some soy sauce. I got a 'basashi take-out' from a butcher and took it back to the minshuku I was staying in. The owner gave me chopsticks (and more soy sauce), so I ended up trying Kumamoto's speciality at a fraction of the prices charged in basashi restaurants. Also, I did not have to wait for it to thaw and found it tasty and not stringy.

Where to eat and drink

Aside from the usual fast-food joints, the best place to eat in the immediate station vicinity is *Umaya* (7am-10/11pm), on your right as you exit the station and attached to JR Kyushu Hotel Kumamoto. Great-value set lunch menus are ¥720. You can sit at the counter – and have the food grilled in front of you – or at screened-off tables. It's a modern take on an izakaya.

In the city centre arcades there's a good selection of informal cafés and restaurants including the usual fast-food places. If you're looking for a lunchtime snack, you can do no better than *Swiss* (10am-11:30pm), a bakery/café serving simple meals and cake-and-coffee sets. It's on the Shimotori shopping arcade in the city centre.

Close by is a similar place, *Saint Etoile* (8:30am-9pm), which is also recommended. For a caffeine fix, there's a branch of *Starbucks* across the street from Hotel Nikko Kumamoto.

If you've a big appetite, it's worth considering the ¥2100 all-you-can-eat buffet lunch at *Serena* (11:30am-3pm), a brasserie-style restaurant on the 2nd floor of Hotel Nikko Kumamoto. On the same floor is an excellent Chinese restaurant,

Tao-Li (11:30am-2:30pm, 5-9:30pm), where the best deals are to be had at lunchtime.

For slightly more upscale dining try *Le Petit Paris* (☎ 096-359 5225, 11:30am-2:30pm, 6-10pm). Set lunch menus start at around ¥1300. It's a cosy place serving a variety of fish and meat dishes. It's on a quiet street in the centre of town and is a bit tricky to find: look out for a pink sign outside and a gold plaque at the foot of a set of stairs and go up them. If you get lost, the address is 3-12 Tetorihon-cho.

For more of a local flavour try *Aoyagi* (11:30am-10pm), a few steps from the Daiei department store; the sashimi is excellent. Expect to pay around ¥2000 per head. Look for the blue curtain hanging outside.

If you're visiting Suizen-ji Garden, *Senri* (11am-2:30pm, 5-10pm) has set lunches in private dining rooms starting at ¥2000. Ask for a room with a view on to the park. You can try *basashi* here (see box opposite) as part of the set lunch. Dinner courses are more expensive, starting at ¥4500, though you do get to view the park minus the tourists, since the restaurant stays open after the park closes for the day.

KAGOSHIMA

Known as the 'Naples of the Orient', Kagoshima is on the eastern side of the Satsuma Peninsula facing Kinko Bay. The island of Sakurajima (see p415), with its brooding volcano, lies just 4km away. The volcano's proximity means umbrellas are sometimes needed to keep off the dust/ash blown across to the mainland.

If Sakurajima dominates the skyline, historically it is the Shimazu family who have dominated the political map of Kagoshima. Successive generations of the family remained in power from 1185 through to the Meiji Restoration in 1871.

The southern gateway to Japan, Kagoshima was also the place where missionary Francis Xavier landed on 15th August 1549. As his ship approached the city, Xavier is said to have been filled with excitement on seeing what he thought was the cross of Jesus Christ, but which turned out to be the sign of the ruling Shimazu family. Little of Xavier's legacy is left today since the church he built was bombed during the Pacific War.

What to see and do

Apart from Sakurajima, Kagoshima's big draw is **Isoteien**, also known as Sanganen (daily 8:30am-5:30pm, ¥1500). It was constructed in 1660 as a residence for Mitsuhisa Shimazu, 19th lord of the Shimazu family. The layout of the garden takes full advantage of its Sakurajima backdrop. The ¥1500 ticket allows entry into the gardens and tea house, where there are short guided tours in Japanese before you are served a cup of green tea. Alternatively a ¥1000 ticket allows entry into the gardens only. To reach Isoteien take the tourist City View bus from Kagoshima-chuo station. The bus stops right outside the main entrance.

Either before or after visiting the garden take a quick look at adjacent **Tsurugane Shrine**, dedicated to the heads and family members of the Shimazu family who reigned over Kagoshima. One of the deities enshrined here is Princess Kameju. Born in 1571 as the third daughter of the 16th Shimazu Lord, Kameju became known as the guardian of female beauty. Legend has it that a woman who prays at the shrine will become even more beautiful.

Tickets for Isoteien are also valid for **Shoko Shuseikan Historical Museum**, on the site of the former factory used by the Shimazu family to manufacture iron and glassware. Inside, the history of the Shimazu family is told in great detail – there are plenty of signs in English. The museum is just across from the entrance to the garden.

The main attraction in the **Museum of the Meiji Restoration** (daily 9am-5/6pm, ¥300) is a 25-minute waxwork show, during which a model of Saigo Takamori (see box below) rises from the floor/grave and the story of his life is retold in dramatic fashion. The soundtrack is in Japanese only. Take the City View bus from Kagoshima-chuo station; the museum is the first stop on the route.

The best place for a bird's-eye view of Kagoshima and Sakurajima is from the Observatory on **Mt Shiroyama** which rises 107m above sea level. From the bus stop walk up past the stalls selling Saigo Takamori T-shirts and trinkets to the observation area, from where there's a great view of the city and of Sakurajima. The colour of the volcano is supposed to change seven times a day, so if it burns bright red and orange for too long, it's at least reassuring to know you're on high ground. Shiroyama itself consists almost entirely of volcanic

---

⛩ Saigo Takamori

It's impossible to walk very far around Kagoshima without seeing the name Saigo Takamori on the many statues and monuments around the city. Points of reference such as the 'Birthplace of Saigo', 'Statue of Saigo', 'House where Saigo was resuscitated', 'Cave where Saigo Takamori hid' and 'Place where Saigo Takamori died' can all be seen at one glance on a city map – laid out around town is the chronicle of one man's life, his journey from humble birth to a glorious if tragic death.

Saigo Takamori (1827-77) was born into a lower-class samurai family in the province of Satsuma (now Kagoshima), the eldest of seven children. In 1868 he became one of the leading figures in the battle to defeat the shogunate and restore power to the Meiji Emperor. It wasn't long before Saigo's loyalties were stretched between support for the new power base and his unerring allegiance to the large numbers of samurai in Satsuma who were being deprived of their status by Imperial edict.

His change of heart reached a dramatic climax in 1877 when Saigo gathered a 15,000 strong army and announced his intention to march on Tokyo. He never even got as far as Honshu and died on Mt Shiroyama in his native Kagoshima at 7am on 24th September 1877 after a defiant last stand against the government he had helped to found.

deposit and is famous as the death place of Saigo Takamori. Take the City View bus from Kagoshima-chuo station all the way to the observatory (the stop after the 'Cave where Saigo hid').

Kagoshima City Aquarium (🖳 www.ioworld.jp, daily, 9:30am-6pm, last entry 5pm, ¥1500), next to Sakurajima Ferry Terminal, is in the building with a roof that looks like a rough copy of the Sydney Opera House. Star attractions are the dolphins, though the 3D movie in which you can get wet without having to bring a change of clothes will keep children amused.

For a bird's eye view of Kagoshima without having to leave the area around Kagoshima-chuo station, head for the 6th floor of the **AMU Plaza** department store, where you'll find the entrance to the bright red Ferris wheel (daily, 10am-11pm; ¥600/person or ¥1800/4-seat gondola). The 6th floor is also home to a 10-screen multiplex cinema and games arcade.

PRACTICAL INFORMATION
Station guide
The terminus for the shinkansen from Shin-Yatsushiro is called Kagoshima-chuo. Kagoshima Station is where trains to Miyazaki and the east coast depart from. Coin lockers (all sizes) are easy to find on the main concourse. There is also the usual selection of food outlets.

Tourist information
The tourist information desk (daily 8:30am-6/7pm) is on the main station concourse. To find it, turn right as you exit the ticket barrier (coming from the platforms) and you'll find it by the East Gate exit. Staff can provide English maps of Kagoshima and Sakurajima (see p415) and assist with accommodation reservations.

Internet
Free internet access (30 minutes) is available at **Kagoshima International Exchange Plaza** (☎ 099-221 6620, 🖳 kia @po.synapse.ne.jp; Tue-Sun 9am-5pm), close to Suizokukanguchi tram stop. The plaza is part of Kagoshima Prefectural Citizens Exchange Center. As well as internet access, you'll find BBC World, newspapers, magazines, and an information/advice desk mainly geared to foreign residents.

Books
Kinokuniya on the 4th floor of AMU Plaza next to Kagoshima-chuo station has a small selection of English books and magazines. There's also a branch of HMV.

Getting around
Like Kumamoto, Kagoshima has a tram network which is by far the best way of getting around town. There is a flat rate of ¥160. One-day passes (¥600) allow you to board any tram, Shiei Bus, or the tourist City View bus, an old-fashioned bus that does a circuit of the main sights in just under one hour. Passes are available from the tourist information counter at Kagoshima-chuo station.

Kagoshima Airport (🖳 www/minc.ne .jp/kab) mostly domestic flights) is accessible by limousine bus (60 mins, ¥1200 one-way) from Kagoshima-chuo station.

Festivals
Two major festivals are the **Natsu Matsuri** (summer festival) at the end of July and **Ohara Matsuri** in early November.

Where to stay
JR Kyushu Hotel Kagoshima (☎ 099-213 8000, 🖹 213 8029, 🖳 kagoshima@jrk-hotels.com; ¥6500/S, ¥12,000/Tw) is the closest hotel you can get to the train platforms. Turn left as you exit the ticket barrier and follow the sign as you head towards the West Gate exit. The rooms are modern and brightly decorated and you're allowed to check in as early as 2pm (check-out is by 11am). Free high-speed **internet access** is available to guests in the lobby area.

Towards the centre of town, *Lexton Inn* (☎ 099-222 0505, 🖳 www.nisikawa .net/lexton/english/index.html; ¥7000/S, ¥12,600/Tw) has moderately spacious

KYUSHU

Where to stay
1 JR Kyushu Hotel Kagoshima
5 Lexton Inn Kagoshima
6 Kagoshima Plaza Hotel Tenmonkan
7 Toyoko Inn Kagoshima Tenmonkan No 2
12 Nakazono Ryokan
17 Shigetomiso

Where to eat and drink
1 AMU Food Cube
3 Daiei Department Store
8 Capricciosa
9 Häagen-Dazs
10 Noboru
13 Densuke

1 JR九州ホテル鹿児島
5 レクストンイン鹿児島
6 鹿児島プラザホテル天文館
7 東横イン 鹿児島天文館2
12 中園旅館
17 重富荘

1 アミュフォオドクブ
3 ダイエーデパート
8 カプリシヨーザ
9 ハーゲンダッツ
10 のぼる
13 でんすけ

[See p414 for continuation of key]

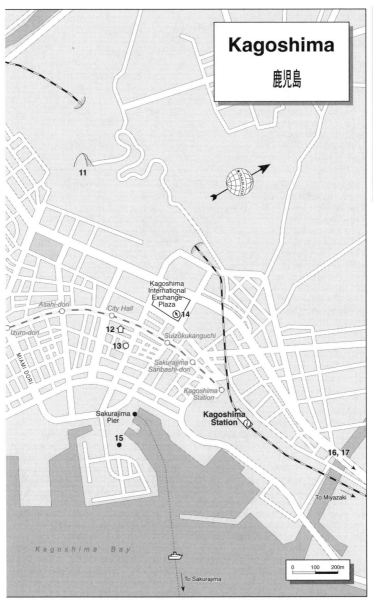

Kagoshima

鹿児島

11

Kagoshima
International
Exchange
Plaza
14

Asahi-dori
City Hall
Izuro-dori

12
Suizokukanguchi
13

MIAMI DORI
Sakurajima
Sanbashi-dori

Kagoshima
Station

Sakurajima
Pier

**Kagoshima
Station**

15

16, 17

To Miyazaki

Kagoshima Bay

0   100   200m

To Sakurajima

KYUSHU

KAGOSHIMA　鹿児島

Other (*key continued from p412*)

1 Kinokuniya (AMU Plaza Dept store)	1 紀伊國屋 　(アミュプラザデパート)
2 Central Post Office	2 中央郵便局
4 Museum of the Meiji Restoration	4 維新ふるさと館
11 Mt Shiroyama	11 白山
14 Internet (Kagoshima International 　Exchange Plaza)	14 インターネット (鹿児島 　県国際交流プラザ)
15 Kagoshima City Aquarium	15 鹿児島市水族館
16 Isoteien; Shoko Shuseikan 　Historical Museum	16 磯庭園; 尚古集成館

rooms with a minibar and hairdryer. There's also a coin laundry, Japanese restaurant and a very small tea room/coffee shop squeezed into a corner of the lobby.

Close by is *Kagoshima Plaza Hotel Tenmonkan* (☎ 099-222 3344, 🖹 222 9911, 🖳 www.kag-plaza.co.jp). There's a big column outside with 'business hotel' written on it. 'Standard singles' cost ¥6000, though the 'deluxe single' at ¥7000 is good value since you get a small sofa and a bit more breathing space. There are only a couple of twins at ¥11,000.

You can't fault *Toyoko Inn Kagoshima Tenmonkan No 2* (☎ 099-224 1045, 🖳 www.toyoko-inn.com; ¥6090/S, ¥8190/Tw), a relatively new addition to the nationwide chain of no-frills hotels with in-room internet access for laptops as well as a free breakfast. It's between Takamibaba and Tenmonkan-dori tram stops.

Nakazono Ryokan (☎ 099-226 5125, 🖹 226 5126, 🖳 shindon@satsuma.ne.jp) offers tatami rooms at ¥4000 for one, ¥8000 for two and ¥11,400 for three people sharing. Meals are not included but the owner is friendly and may well direct you to Densuke (see opposite), a popular izakaya just around the corner. All rooms have TV and telephone, though baths are communal (open 24 hours) and there's a coin laundry. Call ahead and, if he is free, Nakazono-san will collect you from the station.

Finally, top-of-the-range ryokan *Shigetomiso* (☎ 099-247 3155, 🖹 247 0960) deserves a mention for its location (close to Isoteien) and for its moment in

history when part of the James Bond film *You Only Live Twice* was shot there. Rates include two meals, though don't reckon on paying anything less than ¥20,000 per night to stay in one of the ryokan's eight rooms. Make a reservation through the tourist office if you don't speak Japanese. Originally built for Hisamitsu Shimazu, 29th feudal lord of the Kagoshima district, the ryokan commands great views of Sakurajima. If you do stay here it may be best not to mention Bond. When I enquired about Sean Connery's visit, the polite but firm response was: 'That was so long ago. Will it never be forgotten?'

Where to eat and drink

There's not much in Kagoshima-chuo station beyond a branch of *McDonald's* in the Friesta shopping area. A better bet is the vast **AMU Plaza Kagoshima**, a department store next to the station complex (take the East Gate exit). You can't miss it since it's the only building with a large red Ferris wheel (see p411) protruding from the roof. The 5th floor hosts an array of restaurants, while in the basement you'll find the *AMU Food Cube* (a food court serving everything from slices of pizza to curry, crêpes and freshly squeezed juices), a supermarket and stalls selling packed lunches.

Alternatively organize your own packed lunch at **Daiei** department store opposite the station. On the ground floor is a bakery and there's also a good range of hot and cold food to take out. A branch of *Mister Donut* is attached to Daiei.

Within the covered mall that leads off from Tenmonkan-dori tram stop are a number of casual eating places. A branch of the Italian chain *Capricciosa* is just off from the covered mall, between a KFC and a convenience store, and within the mall is a branch of *Häagen-Dazs*.

Noboru, a short walk south from Izuro-dori tram stop, is a small place with only one item on the menu: ramen. You can either sit at the counter downstairs or head upstairs to one of the small rooms. For ¥1000 you'll be served a huge bowl of ramen, together with large slices of *daikon* (Japanese radish) and cups of Japanese tea.

Finally, *Densuke* is an *izakaya* close to Nakazono Ryokan. Though Nakazono-san, the ryokan owner, describes Densuke as 'traditional', don't go there expecting kimono-clad staff and wailing shamisen music. This is above all a drinking place (Mon-Sat 5pm-late), where you can order up skewers of meat or fish to accompany your liquid refreshment.

Side trip to Sakurajima

Smoke, dust and ashes billowing out from Sakurajima are a common-enough sight in Kagoshima but the last major eruption was in 1946. The worst eruption of the 20th century was in 1914, when three million tonnes of lava buried eight villages and turned the island into a peninsula, completely filling a 400m-wide and 70m-deep sea.

Ferries (¥150, 13 mins) to Sakurajima depart 24 hours a day from the terminal next to Kagoshima Aquarium. JR Kyushu operates one-day bus tours around the island (¥4000) but rail passes are not accepted; tickets can be purchased from the JR ticket office at Kagoshima-chuo station. The bus starts and finishes at the station and includes stops around the city before heading to Sakurajima. Tours by Shiei Bus (☎ 099-257 2117; ¥1700, no reservations) start from Sakurajima Port and run twice a day with a two-hour tour of the island.

Your first port of call should be **Sakurajima Information Center** (☎ 099-293 2525) at the ferry terminal, where you can enquire about cycle rental (one hour ¥400, two hours ¥600, each additional hour ¥300) and car rental (¥5000 for two hours, plus ¥1000 for each additional hour). Signposted from the ferry terminal a couple of minutes along the main road by car is **Sakurajima Visitor Center** (☎ 099-293 2443, Tue-Sun 9am-5pm, free) which has a model of Sakurajima, an explanation of the ecosystem, displays of volcanic rock and footage of previous eruptions.

Just one main road circles the island; on the way round look out for observation points, lava fields and the *daikon* (giant radishes) that can grow up to 30kg in weight on the fertile slopes. One of the most enjoyable stops is at **Furusato-Onsen**, a seaside hot spring in *Furusato Kanko Hotel* (☎ 099-221 3111, 🖳 www.furukan.co.jp; Fri-Wed, 8:30am-5pm). Entering the hotel someone will direct you to the vending machine where you buy a ticket (¥1050), collect a yukata and head downstairs. It's easy to get lost in the corridors of the hotel, though staff are used to gaijin stumbling around, so eventually you'll open the door that leads outdoors and down some steps to the hot spring. Everyone has to wear their yukata in the water because the spring is part of a shrine. Located right by the sea, this ranks as one of the most impressive places to bathe in Japan. Room rates at the hotel are ¥15,000-30,000.

Sakurajima Youth Hostel (188-1 Yokoyama, ☎/🖹 099-293 2150) charges ¥2600 (no discount for YH/HI members). Breakfast costs ¥500 and dinner ¥700. It's about 10 minutes on foot uphill from the ferry terminal.

Shikoku – route guide

Shikoku ('Four Provinces') takes its name from the provinces into which the island was once divided. The old provinces of Sanuki, Tosa, Iyo and Awa are known today as the prefectures of Kagawa, Kochi, Ehime and Tokushima.

Predominantly rural, Shikoku has everything that the current image of Japan does not: wide open spaces, forests, rural villages and a dramatic natural landscape. However, the island is not just a provincial backwater. There's plenty to see and it's worth devoting at least a week to completing the loop route described below.

The route passes through all four prefectures and includes stops in the capital cities of three of them. Though a number of road bridges have opened in recent years, linking Shikoku with Honshu, the only entry/exit point by rail is across the Inland Sea via the Seto-Ohashi Bridge, opened in 1988.

This route starts in **Okayama**, taking the Marine Liner train across the bridge to **Takamatsu** (see pp430-7). From here the route heads south to **Kochi** (see pp437-42) via **Kotohira** (see p420). The route continues in a clockwise direction to **Uwajima** (see p424), known for its bull fights and sex museum, then on to **Matsuyama** (see p442-8), the largest city on the island and a good access point for a visit to Dogo-Onsen, Japan's oldest spa town. The last part of the journey covers the route from Matsuyama back towards Okayama on Honshu.

It's worth noting that though plenty can be accomplished on a rail tour of Shikoku, the more isolated parts of the island, including the two southern capes at Muroto and Ashizuri, can be reached only by infrequent buses or by hiring a car.

Most weekends between April and September (except in June due to the rainy season) open-air carriages are attached to some of the most scenic rail lines in Shikoku. These carriages are called 'Torocco' and carry an additional charge which is not covered by the rail pass. The routes change every year to take in a variety of railway lines, so check in advance (☎ 050-2016 1603).

One of the most popular Torocco services runs every year on the Yodo line between Kubokawa and Uwajima (see p424); an open-air carriage is attached between Tokawa and Ekawasaki. There is a charge of ¥310 and seat reservations should be made in advance from any JR ticket office.

冬
星
の
旅
青
鷺
は
番
な
り

Winter stars –
just two grey herons
as I journey by
(MINAKO KANEKO)

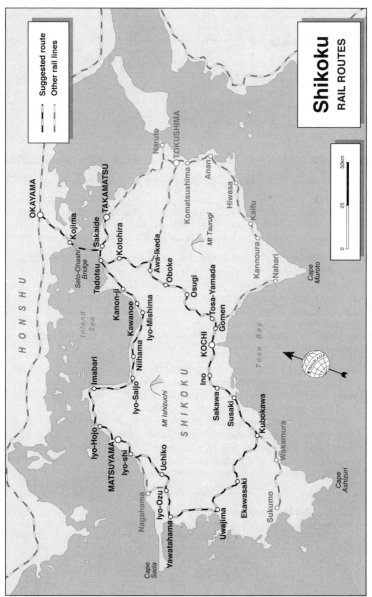

OKAYAMA TO TAKAMATSU [Map 33, p421; Table 28, p470]

Distances by JR from Okayama. Fastest journey time: 60 minutes.

Okayama (0km) [see pp256-61]
Take the Marine Liner rapid train along the Seto-Ohashi line, which runs direct to Takamatsu across the Seto-Ohashi Bridge. On its way to the bridge the train calls at **Senoo (8km), Hayashima (12km)** and **Chaya-machi (15km)**.

Kojima (28km)
Last stop on Honshu before the train crosses Seto-Ohashi. The bridge, or rather series of bridges, spans 9.4km and took nearly a decade to build, opening in 1988 with a construction bill of ¥1120 billion. The view from the train as it crosses the bridge is certainly impressive, though eclipsed by the scale and design of the bridge itself. However, one reader wrote that it was a 'disappointing journey because it was hard to see through the safety barriers'. The downside towards the end of the crossing is the view to the left of the huge Kawasaki factory.

Sakaide (51km)
First stop after crossing the bridge. Looking back towards Honshu, you'll see **Seto-Ohashi commemorative park**, where there's a museum and observation tower; outdoor concerts are held here occasionally. Change here if planning to visit Kokubun-ji (see opposite).

In the station are lockers up to ¥500, a convenience store with a few tables where you can sit and have a drink and, slightly hidden, a tourist information office (daily, 8am-7pm) where only Japanese is spoken. There are elevators between the concourse and platforms. Opposite one side of the station is the SATY shopping complex with a variety of restaurants.

❏ Using the rail route guides
The fastest point-to-point journey times are provided for each section of the route. Even though each route has been divided into different sections it may not be necessary to change trains as you go from one section to the next. Occasionally, however, it is essential to change train in order to complete the route described. Such instances are denoted by the following symbol ▲. Places which are served by local trains only are marked ♦. (**For more information see p449.**)

⛩ **Shikoku 88 temple pilgrimage**
Pilgrims who start out on the journey around Shikoku's 88 temple circuit are following in the steps of Kobo Daishi, the Buddhist saint who first walked around the island and who now lies in eternal meditation at Koya-san, home to the Shingon sect of Buddhism founded by him in the 9th century.

Most *henro* (pilgrims) visit Koya-san (see pp230-2) either before or after completing the Shikoku pilgrimage. It's not necessary to follow precisely in Kobo Daishi's steps by walking between the temples. There are no rules to prevent modern-day pilgrims taking a bus, taxi or private car. Indeed, many of the pilgrims you see in the temples today, dressed in traditional white and carrying sticks to help them along the way, have a minibus waiting in the car park ready to whisk them off to their next destination.

The pilgrimage does not have to be completed in one visit, so many make return trips to Shikoku over a number of years. Some, however, such as the Buddhist monks who walk the circuit for spiritual cleansing, do it the hard way.

♦ **Kokubu (60km)** Only local trains stop here; services operate approximately every 30 minutes from Sakaide (11 mins) and from Takamatsu (15 mins). It's a five-minute walk from the station to **Kokubun-ji**, the 80th temple on the Shikoku pilgrimage. If coming from Takamatsu cross the overhead bridge, exit the station and walk straight ahead to the main road that runs parallel with the rail track. Turn right and about three minutes down this road on the left is a sign pointing towards the temple. The entrance is just off the main road on the left. Despite the numbers of pilgrims, the temple remains a calm and tranquil place. To the right of the main temple, Japanese music plays, guiding you into a store where you can buy assorted lucky charms and various pieces of the pilgrim's outfit, including the white shirt and walking stick.

Takamatsu (72km) [see pp430-7]

TAKAMATSU TO KOCHI [Map 33 p421; Table 29, p470]

Distances by JR from Takamatsu. Fastest journey time: 130 minutes.

Takamatsu (0km) Pick up the Shimanto LEX heading south towards Kochi along the Dosan line.

Sakaide (22km) For details, see opposite.

Utazu (26km) For details, see p429.

Marugame (29km) For details, see p428.

Tadotsu (33km) For information see p428. The line splits here: the Yosan line heads west towards Matsuyama (see p442-8). The Shimanto LEX continues south along the Dosan line to Kochi.

Zentsu-ji (39km) Zentsu-ji is the birthplace of Kobo Daishi, the Buddhist priest who made a pilgrimage on foot around Shikoku (see box above). The

⛩ **Naked Festival**
The highlight of February's Hadaka Matsuri (Naked Festival) at Zentsu-ji is *fukubai*, the 'scrambling for good luck sticks'. Hundreds of young people, wearing only a loincloth, battle to grab hold of the sticks and ensure they enjoy good fortune for the rest of the year. A local guidebook suggests that, even though participants are wearing next to nothing, 'the fierce fights make participants steaming hot. Nakedness signifies innocence like a newborn baby, while the white of the loincloth represents the purity of its wearer.' Check with the tourist office in Takamatsu (see p434) for the exact date of the festival as it changes every year.

temple here is the 75th on the 88 temple circuit and one of the busiest because of its link with Daishi.

Inside the temple precincts are a 45m-high five-storeyed pagoda, completed in 1884 for the 1050th anniversary of Kobo Daishi's death, and Mie-do Hall, said to be the very spot where Kobo Daishi was born in 774. The temple is a 20-minute walk west along the main road which runs away from the station.

Kotohira (44km) Just one stop along the line from Zentsu-ji, Kotohira is home to an interesting shrine and is the ideal place to break your journey for a few hours on the way to Kochi. JR Kotohira station has a ticket office where you can make onward seat reservations and a small udon restaurant but the only coin lockers are small ones. Walk straight up the main road from the station to find the steps leading up to the shrine.

The shrine of Kotohira-gu is better known as **Kompira-san**, the affectionate name for the guardian deity of seafarers. Kompira-san rises up the slope of Mt Zozu ('elephant's head'); the reward for making it up the first 785 steps to the main shrine is a view over the valley below and out over the Inland Sea. From here, there are a further 583 steps to Okusha Shrine, the Inner Sanctuary. Along the way are stalls that sell walking sticks to assist with the ascent, as well as drinks and noodles.

The **Stone Steps Marathon** is held on the first Sunday of October; hundreds of participants race from the station up to the inner sanctuary and back, running up and down a total of 2736 steps.

Before or after making the ascent, drop in at **Kanamaru-za** (Wed-Mon 9am-4pm, ¥300), the oldest kabuki theatre in Japan. Take the road that leads left from the foot of the shrine steps and up a small hill. Built originally in 1835 the theatre later became a cinema before falling into a state of disrepair. Restored in 1976 you can now go behind the scenes, check out the backstage dressing rooms and wander underneath the stage itself. Kabuki is only staged here once a year, during the spring, when a parade of kabuki players announces that the playhouse will once again be used for performance.

If you continue up the road past the theatre, you'll reach the statue of Jinnojo Okubo in **Kotohira Park**. At the end of the 19th century, Okubo mooted the idea of linking Honshu and Shikoku with a bridge over the Seto Inland Sea – an idea that took another hundred years to be realized.

MAP 33

From Kotohira, trains continue along the Dosan line towards Kochi. Pick up the Shimanto or Nanpu LEX. Reservations are recommended as some trains run with fewer carriages making it a scramble for the non-reserved seats.

Awa-Ikeda (77km) This is an interchange station for the Tokushima line. Although not included on this route, the Tokushima line makes for an enjoyable side trip by rail, the slowest trains taking around two hours to wend their way alongside Yama-gawa towards Tokushima.

From Awa-Ikeda, the Dosan line continues south towards the area's big sight, **Oboke Gorge**. Unfortunately, many of the passengers who use the limited express train to commute to Kochi shut the curtains and sleep through some of the best views. If you don't want to miss out, reserve a window seat (both sides of the train have superb views).

Oboke (99km) Not all limited expresses stop here. If you're planning to visit the gorge, check that the train you plan to catch stops here.

The **gorge** – or 'canyon', as the Japanese signposts call it – is one of Shikoku's hidden highlights. The starting point for boat tours of the gorge is about 1km from the station. Walk up to Oboke Bridge above the station, cross it, turn right and go straight. A short walk brings you to 'Lapis Oboke', in a modern building overlooking the gorge. Inside is a café, souvenir shop and Museum of Rocks and Minerals (daily, 9am-5pm, ¥500). This is not an essential stop, so continue past until you hit another building further ahead that contains a restaurant and souvenir shop. The ticket office for the 30-minute boat tours (daily 9am-5pm or earlier if not busy, ¥1000) is inside. No rowing is required – all you have to do is sit back and admire the view.

If the weather is fine and you fancy something more adventurous, get off the limited express at Oboke and take a local train to **Tosa-Iwahara** (7 mins). Less than 100m from the station is **Happy Raft** (☎ 0887-75 0500, 💻 www.happyraft.com), which offers whitewater rafting and canyoning adventures on the Yoshino River from ¥6500 (half day)/¥12,500 (full day). Happy Raft is run by an Australian with years of whitewater-rafting experience around the world.

If you need to stay the night, a good choice is the homely *Pension Murata* (☎ 0887-75 0010, 💻 www.murata-p.jp), three minutes on foot from **Toyonaga** station, one stop further south by local train from Tosa-Iwahara. It's a cosy B&B-style place with a friendly owner who charges ¥7350 per night including two meals or ¥4725 without meals.

To continue your journey south from Tosa-Iwahara or Toyonaga, take a local train to Osugi (see below) and pick up the limited express for the final stretch of the journey to Kochi.

Osugi (120km) Not all limited expresses stop here. Osugi means 'big cedar'; the place is named after a nearby tree which some people claim is 3000 years old. Most of the next 5km are spent in tunnels.

Tosa-Yamada (144km) Tosa-Yamada is the nearest station to **Ryugado Cave** (💻 www.ryugadou.or.jp, daily, 8:30am-4:30/5pm, ¥1000), a 4km-long cave containing stalactites and stalagmites. Buses run out to the cave from here, or there's a bus service from Kochi station (check the times with tourist information in Kochi, see p440).

Gomen (149km) Last limited express stop before Kochi. Change here if you plan to visit Monet's Garden (see box opposite).

Kochi (160km)   [see pp437-42]

⛩ Borrowed from Belgium
One less well-known sight not far from Oboke Gorge is a copy of Brussels' best-known statue, Mannequin Pis (in Japanese, 'shoben kozo'). The naked boy is perched precariously on a clifftop looking down into the gorge, quietly relieving himself. The cliff-top vantage point is considered a place to prove your bravery. If you can stand next to the statue and look down at the gorge directly below, it's said that nobody will ever again question your courage.

♁ **Monet in Japan**

Shakespeare's home town was painstakingly recreated years ago in Japan, so it should not come as a surprise to discover that an attempt has been made to do the same for French impressionist Claude Monet (1840-1926), whose garden in Giverny has been faithfully copied and recreated almost blade by blade, lily by lily, in the small village of Kitagawa, accessed via the private Tosa-Kuroshio Railway (💻 www .tosakuro.co.jp) from Gomen.

Le jardin de Monet Marmottan au Village de Kitagawa (💻 www.kitagawa mura.net/monet, Wed-Mon, closed Jan/Feb, 10am-5pm, ¥700), to give the place its full French name, has been hugely popular since it opened to the public in 2000. If you've been to Giverny, it's still worth seeing the Japanese version and playing spot the difference. If you haven't seen the original, think of this as an opportunity to take a trip to France without leaving Shikoku.

To reach the garden change from the JR line at Gomen onto the private Tosa-Kuroshio Railway's Gomen-Nahari line and ride the train all the way to the terminus at Nahari (1 hour, ¥1040, rail passes not accepted). A shuttle bus (10 mins, ¥230) runs from Nahari and drops you off outside the main entrance.

KOCHI TO UWAJIMA [Map 34, p425; Table 30, p471]

Distances by JR from Kochi. Fastest journey time: 3 hours.

Kochi to Kubokawa

If you're in a hurry and want to skip the next (slow!) part of the journey from **Kochi** to **Matsuyama** via Uwajima, consider taking a direct JR bus between the two cities. Buses depart on the hour 7am-7pm (same schedule for buses departing from Matsuyama) and the journey time is 2¹/₂ hours. One-way costs ¥3500 but rail-pass holders travel free. You need to get a ticket from the bus centre ticket office, to the right as you exit Kochi station.

The timetable may change but at the time of writing buses departed from JR Kochi station at 9am, 10:50am, 1pm, 2pm, 4pm and 5:20pm, arriving at JR Matsuyama station at 11:30am, 1:20pm, 3:30pm, 4:30pm, 6:30pm and 7:50pm.

Kochi (0km) From Kochi, pick up the Nanpu LEX which continues along the Dosan line to Kubokawa, where you connect with the Yodo line that chugs slowly towards Uwajima.

Ino (11km) Ino has been a paper-making town for over a thousand years. Water from Niyodo-gawa is used to manufacture the paper. Ino is the terminus for one of Kochi's tram lines, so streetcar enthusiasts might consider a trip by tram between here and Kochi station.

Sakawa (28km) There are rice fields everywhere you look on this stretch of the journey. Kochi's mild weather and heavy rainfall means that it's the first place in Japan to harvest the year's crop of rice.

Susaki (42km) Approaching Susaki, and after the acres of rice fields spread out on either side of the rail line, it's something of a shock to come across factories, concrete buildings and industry; not the most attractive part of the journey. The next stop is at **Tosa-Kure (53km)**.

Kubokawa (72km) The JR Dosan line terminates here. From here, the private Tosa Kuroshio Railway runs further south to **Nakamura**, the nearest station to **Cape Ashizuri** (infrequent buses from Nakamura take 1 hour 40 mins to the cape and cost ¥1930). The JR Nanpu LEX continues along this private line, though rail-pass holders have to pay between Kubokawa and Nakamura.

▲ To follow the next part of this rail route, change trains here and connect up with the rural Yodo line, which runs along Shimanto-gawa before terminating in Uwajima. Pick up a Yodo line train from platform 4. If you don't have a rail pass take a ticket when boarding the train and pay the fare when you get off. No limited expresses run along this line.

Kubokawa to Uwajima   [Map 34, opposite; Table 31, p471]
The Yodo line is one of the most scenic and rural in Shikoku; most of the stops are barely stations – just places where the train pulls up, often on the edge of a field. In theory, since the line between Kubokawa and **Wakai** (5km; the first stop after Kubokawa) runs on private track, rail-pass holders should pay a ¥200 supplement. However, since nobody checks your ticket until you arrive in Uwajima, it seems that this additional fare is forgotten.

It takes around two hours for the train from Kubokawa to pull in to Uwajima, by which time the passengers will have probably changed several times. The train occasionally fills up with schoolchildren but then just as quickly empties again. For part of the way the line follows the course of Shimanto-gawa, claimed to be the 'last great virgin river in Japan'. No man-made dams have been built near it; unimpeded by mechanical barriers, the water is probably the clearest you'll see anywhere. Trout and *ayu* (sweetfish) are popular catches.

Even though the chugging of the train can be sleep-inducing, the scenery is worth staying awake for, as you'll see farmers working in the fields and storks in water-logged rice paddies. More often than not, the rail line has been cut between fields, so you can stare right down at the cauliflowers, cabbages and individual rice plants.

Between 22nd July and 31st August the torocco train operates on this line and an open-air carriage is added between **Tokawa (103km)** and **Ekawasaki (115km)**. After Ekawasaki the line leaves the Shimanto-gawa, which winds its way towards the Pacific Ocean and crosses into Ehime prefecture on its way to Uwajima.

Uwajima (150km) Uwajima station has platforms on the same level as the exit. Station staff have ramps to assist with boarding trains. You'll find a *Willie Winkie* bakery and convenience store at the station. Only small **coin lockers** are available but the staff at the ticket barrier may allow you to store large luggage for ¥410. The **tourist information office** (☎ 0895-22 3934, daily, 8:30am-5pm) – look for the red letters on white background – is on the street opposite the station. Pick up a map from here to locate the sights mentioned below.

As a staging post between Kochi and Matsuyama, Uwajima has a few attractions. Top of the bill is **Taga Shrine** and its **Sex Museum** (💻 www1.quolia.com/dekoboko, daily, 8am-5pm, ¥800). The museum is wall-to-wall penises, in various shapes and sizes, though the emphasis tends to be on the huge. The phallic models, pictures and works of art that leave nothing to the imagination are crammed into a three-floor building in one corner of the shrine. All the signs are in Japanese but it's not as if much explanation is needed.

Uwajima's other main attraction is **bull fighting**. The twist to this contest is that it's strictly bull against bull – no human risks getting hurt. Fights take place at the Municipal Bull Fighting Ring on the following dates: January 2nd, the first Sunday in April, July 24th, August 14th and the second Sunday in November (tickets cost ¥3000). At other times, a film of the fighting is shown (Mon-Fri, 8:30am-5pm, ¥500). The following extract from the promotional literature gives an idea of what to expect: 'Bouts between two bulls weighing nearly one tonne are quite dynamic. The bulls crash so hard against each other trying to push their opponent out that you may possibly hear the sound of their pant'.

If you need somewhere to stay, the JR-operated *Hotel Clement Uwajima* (☎ 0895-23 6111, 🖷 23 6666, 🖳 hotel@clement.shikoku.ne.jp; ¥6930/S, ¥11,550/D, ¥12,127/Tw) is immediately above the station – handy if you've got a lot of luggage. The rooms have modern furnishings, bilingual TV, and fridge. There are also a couple of spacious tatami rooms that are worth paying for if you can afford the ¥17,325 for two; 10% off all rates with the rail pass.

Uwajima Youth Hostel (☎ 0895-22 7177, 🖳 www2.odn.ne.jp/~cfm91130/eigo.htm, yasujiasada@mail.goo.ne.jp) has an enviable location up on a hill overlooking the town, but this also means that it's inconvenient to reach. There are no buses up to the hostel, so avoid a painful walk up by taking a taxi from the station. The hostel offers foreign visitors a special rate of ¥2100/night in dormitory accommodation. Breakfast costs ¥630 and dinner ¥1050.

Sirene, at the station, charges very reasonable prices. The menu is French/Western and the lunch courses are ¥800-1000 and the Sunday all-you-can-eat buffet lunch (11:30am-2pm) costs ¥1500. It's just inside the entrance to Hotel Clement. They sometimes serve Italian gelato from a stall outside.

UWAJIMA TO MATSUYAMA [Map 34, p425; Table 32, p471]

Distances by JR from Uwajima. Fastest journey time: 1^1/$_4$ hours.

Uwajima (0km) From Uwajima, pick up the Uwakai LEX which runs along the Yosan line to Matsuyama. The first stop is **Unomachi (20km)**.

Yawatahama (35km) Yawatahama is home to one of the region's largest fishing communities and is the nearest station to Cape Sada peninsula. The best way to reach the cape is to drive there (enquire about car-hire prices at the JR ticket counter). The 50km cape juts out a little further up the coast from Yawatahama. It's the longest and narrowest in Japan and at the tip is Cape Sada Lighthouse, from where there are good views of the Seto Inland Sea.

Iyo-Ozu (48km) From here the rail line divides, with a choice of either the **inland route**, which this guide follows (served by limited express or local train), or the **coastal route** (served by local trains only). If you're on a limited express and want to follow the coastal route, this is the last place you can change before the lines diverge. Taking the coastal route, the line follows Hijigawa out to sea, then heads slowly up the coast before converging with the inland line at Iyo-shi station; services operate roughly hourly and take approximately 70 minutes.

Uchiko (59km) There are elevators from platforms 1 and 2 down to street level. The station has small **coin lockers** only. In the square outside the station is a **steam locomotive** that ran on the Uchiko Line from 1969 to 1970, transporting cargo between Uchiko and Iyo-Ozu. Built in 1939, its accumulated mileage would be enough to circumnavigate the globe 33 times.

Between the Edo and Meiji periods, Uchiko prospered as a manufacturing centre for Japanese paper and wax. Today, Uchiko is known for the **Yokaichi Historical Area**, a street of old, preserved houses, some of which are open to the public as museums or upmarket coffee shops. From the station, walk along the road into town until you reach a junction where there's a branch of Iyo Bank. Turn left at this junction and walk uphill to find the old street.

Uchiko must have been wealthy because it even boasts its own kabuki theatre, **Uchiko-za** (daily, 9am-4:30pm, ¥300). Built in 1919, it is similar in design to the theatre at Kotohira (see p420), with a revolving stage. Look for signs to the theatre on your way into town from the station.

Iyo-shi (85km) This is the point at which the coastal and inland rail lines reconverge for the final part of the journey to Matsuyama.

Matsuyama (97km)   [see pp442-8]

As the train pulls in to Matsuyama, look out to the left for the silver Botchan Stadium. A location for city baseball games, the stadium is named after one of Matsuyama's most famous honorary citizens, the character from Soseki Natsume's novel of the same name. The character, Botchan, visited the Dogo-Onsen hot spring baths (see p448), still one of the city's biggest draws.

MATSUYAMA TO OKAYAMA
[Map 34, p425; Map 33, p421; Table 33, p471]

Distances by JR from Matsuyama. Fastest journey time: 2 hours 40 mins.

Matsuyama (0km) The final part of the journey around Shikoku; the Shiokaze LEX runs direct from here back to Okayama. If returning to Honshu, make sure you're sitting in cars 4-8, as cars 1-3 split off at Tadotsu and head to Takamatsu (if you have a seat reservation, you'll already be in the right part of the train).

Between Matsuyama and Iyo-Hojo, the line roughly parallels the main 196 trunk road but there are occasional views of the Inland Sea out to the left.

Iyo-Hojo (18km) Some limited expresses stop here.

About 20 minutes after Iyo-Hojo you should see, also out to the left, the Nishi-Seto Highway linking the island with Honshu.

Imabari (50km) Imabari is the starting point for the **Nishi-Seto Highway** which connects Shikoku with Honshu via a road bridge. Completed in 1999, the bridge uses six small islands as staging posts and runs across the Inland Sea to Onomichi. This is the third road bridge connecting Shikoku with Honshu. Imabari's other claim to fame is that it's the number one towel-producing city in Japan.

Iyo-Saijo (80km) If you happen to be passing this way around October 14th-17th, drop in on the town's annual festival. The highlight is a parade of portable shrines through the city on the morning of the 15th. Conveniently, Niihama (see p428) holds a festival at around the same time. On the way between the two stations, there's some mountain scenery out to the right.

S H I K O K U

⛩ **The Zenigata – a coin shape carved in the sand**
      There are a number of stories about how the Zenigata came to be in Kotohiki
Park (see Kanon-ji below). Some claim the coin is at least 350 years old, while others say it only dates back 130 years. However, the common consensus is that it was
completed in just one night by locals in 1633 as an unusual gift to the feudal lord of
the area, Ikoma Takatoshi, who was to arrive the next day on a tour of inspection.
Everybody knew that his lordship had to be pleased and a huge coin in the sand
seemed the perfect answer. Another theory is that the coin was and remains to this day
a UFO base (a Japanese version of crop circles?), while others attribute it to the mir-
acle-working of Kobo Daishi (see box p419). With a circumference of 345m, the
biggest mystery is why the design does not disappear in the rain or wind.
      Twice a year the coin is reshaped by a group of volunteers who have orders
shouted to them by one person commanding a bird's eye view. A two-day **Zenigata
Festival** is held around July 20th (Maritime Day), highlights of which include a fireworks display and dance contest in Kotohiki Park.

Niihama (91km) Expect **Niihama's Drum Festival** (October 16th-18th) to
be a noisy event. The drums that get paraded through the town weigh around
two tonnes each, and require 150 people to carry them.

      The limited express next calls at **Iyo-Mishima (116.8km)** and **Kawanoe
(122km)**, which is the last stop before the train crosses the border from Ehime
back to Kagawa prefecture.

Kanon-ji (138km) This is the best stop for Kotohiki Park, known for its massive and mysterious coin shape called **Zenigata** (see box above), carved about
2m deep in the sand. The park is a 20-minute walk north-west of the station,
across Saita-gawa.

Takuma (152km) Some limited expresses stop here. Between Takuma and
Tadotsu there are great views of the many tiny islands in the Inland Sea.

Tadotsu (162km) Tadotsu is a junction for the Yosan line between
Matsuyama and Takamatsu, and the Dosan line to Kochi. This is where the railway network on Shikoku began in 1889, when the first steam locomotive ran
15.5km from Marugame to Kotohira via Tadotsu.

      As soon as the Shiokaze LEX stops, a lightning-fast decoupling takes place,
allowing the front half (cars 4-8) to continue on to Okayama, while the remain-
der wait a couple of minutes before starting off for Takamatsu.

Marugame (166km) Marugame is a former castle town with a couple of
attractions. Take the south exit for **tourist information** (Mon-Fri 9:30am-6pm,
Sat-Sun 10am-5pm), just to the right as you exit the station. No English is spoken, but the place is well stocked with leaflets.

      Marugame Castle (daily 9am-4:30pm, closed Dec 25th-Feb 28th, ¥200)
was originally built in 1597 on a hill overlooking the city. Its design may not be

unusual but the mason who built the ramparts certainly was: legend records that he always worked naked.

The castle is about 15 minutes on foot down the main road which runs away from the south exit. There's no fee to visit the castle tower if you show the Kagawa Welcome Card (see box p53) at the entrance.

Right outside the station in a striking modern building is **Marugame Genichiro Inokuma Museum of Contemporary Art (MIMOCA)** (🖳 http://web.infoweb.ne.jp/MIMOCA, daily 10am-6pm, occasional holidays). The permanent exhibitions on the second floor display the works of Genichiro Inokuma (1902-93), who attended school in Marugame before heading off to Tokyo, Paris and New York (where he opened his own studio and stayed 20 years) before finally settling in Hawaii.

Tickets for the permanent galleries cost ¥300. The museum café on the third floor is a great place to relax and is much better than anywhere in the station for a drink and a quick snack. Earl Grey tea (¥450) and delicious homemade scones with jam (¥400) are on the menu.

Utazu (169km) Heading out of the station you can't miss **Gold Tower** (🖳 www.goldtower.co.jp, daily, 10am-10pm). It looks tacky from the outside and is even more so inside. It's a paradise for lovers of amusement arcades. Aside from electronic games, you'll find a bowling alley, karaoke booths, a children's play area and 'Wan Wan Land' – a small space where children can pet a selection of cute furry animals ('wan wan' is the Japanese equivalent of 'woof woof') in a controlled environment.

About the only thing worth doing here is to take the elevator to the top of the tower (¥840), where you'll find a 127-m-high observation gallery with views of the Seto-Ohashi Bridge.

On your way out, look out on the first floor for the world's only solid gold toilet and accompanying gold toilet slippers. In the kitsch stakes, this place really does rival Las Vegas and Graceland.

Utazu is the final stop in Shikoku before the train turns to cross the Seto-Ohashi Bridge bound for Okayama. If you're not returning to Honshu and haven't yet changed trains, this is the last chance to do so.

Kojima (187km) First stop back on Honshu, and the point where JR Shikoku staff are replaced by their counterparts from JR West.

Okayama (214km) [see pp256-61]

Shikoku – city guides

TAKAMATSU

Capital of Kagawa Prefecture for over a century and a former castle town, Takamatsu has recently transformed itself into a major business and tourism centre for the 21st century with the regeneration of the port area behind JR Takamatsu station. The hugely ambitious decade-long project to reclaim land dubbed 'Sunport Takamatsu' is still going on and has changed the face of the city beyond recognition. The skyline is dominated by the Symbol Tower, Shikoku's tallest building.

Kagawa may be the smallest prefecture in Japan but high-rise developments such as the Symbol Tower and the new Prefectural Office skyscraper suggest that it's probably not one of the poorest. The biggest attraction for tourists is Ritsurin Koen, a large park 2km south of the station area.

Takamatsu feels very international – you might be surprised to see how many foreigners there are in town – and has sister-city relations with a number of places around the world including Tours in France.

What to see and do

You can't miss the **Symbol Tower** (💻 www.symboltower.com), looming down on everything else in the station vicinity. It's on your left as you exit the station. Take the elevator up to the 30th-floor viewing platform (daily, 10am-8pm). On a cloudless day you'll get unparalleled views of the city and out over the Inland Sea. The best thing about this – apart from the views – is that it costs nothing!

Once you've got your bearings, and before you head into the city centre, consider taking a leisurely stroll out to the **Red Lighthouse**, located just beyond Mikayla restaurant (see p436). This is a popular place to hang out in the summer.

If you fancy a bird's-eye view while in the downtown area, head for the **Prefectural Office**, which has a free observatory on the top floor and is a good place to orientate yourself.

Tamamo Koen (daily, 8:30am-6pm in summer, 9am-5pm in winter, ¥150), by the harbour and next to Kotoden Takamatsu Chikko station, is a large park where Takamatsu Castle once stood.

Some of the original castle turrets remain but what makes the castle noteworthy is its unusual proximity to the sea. Originally built in 1590, waves crashed against the castle's northern ramparts up until 1900, when land was reclaimed to construct a new harbour.

An air raid on Takamatsu on 4th July 1945 killed more than 1300 people and destroyed over 18,000 buildings, including most of what remained of the castle. One reader commented that the remains are worth visiting 'to fill time but are otherwise not very exciting'.

Ritsurin Koen (daily, 8:30am-5pm; extended opening hours in summer, ¥400), Takamatsu's biggest draw, has a dramatic setting at the foot of Mt Shiun. One advantage Ritsurin has over other well-known Japanese parks is its size – the tour groups are there but there's much more space for them to spread out. There are plenty of narrow paths and observation points that give an impressive overview of the grounds which are divided into two: the Hokutei (northern garden) and Nantei (southern garden).

The 'wild ducks' in the duck pond are disappointingly tame – perhaps they realize they will no longer be shot as sport, which they were about 400 years ago when the gardens were part of the local feudal lord's villa residence. Look out for turtles along the paths, apparently oblivious to the hordes of tourists storming by.

Kikugetsu-tei ('moon-scooping cottage') is a restored teahouse where it's thought that moon-viewing parties were once held. The teahouse is sometimes open to the public for tea ceremony demonstrations (an extra ¥710 including tea and cake; check times with the tourist office).

Also within the park grounds is the small **Sanuki Folkcraft Museum** (free), containing a model portable shrine and various ceramics and masks. Animal lovers should avoid the zoo (an extra ¥600) in the park. To ensure you have as much peace as possible, go early but check opening times with the tourist office.

To get to the park take a local train from JR Takamatsu (on the Kotoku line towards Tokushima) two stops to Ritsurin-Koen Kitaguchi, just by the park's north gate. Alternatively, take the private Kotoden line from Takamatsu station to Ritsurin station (third stop, ¥150).

❏ The name's Bond-san

'Tiger Tanaka: *"Rule number one: never do anything yourself when someone else can do it for you."*
James Bond: *"And rule number two?"*
Tiger Tanaka: *"Rule number two: in Japan, men come first, women come second."*
James Bond: *"I just might retire here."'*

You Only Live Twice (Eon Productions, 1967)

James Bond is no stranger to Japan: Most of *You Only Live Twice*, starring Sean Connery opposite the characters Tiger Tanaka and Kissy Suzuki, was set and filmed in the country. But it may come as something of a surprise to discover that a small museum (💻 www.007museum.jp) devoted to Ian Fleming's British secret-service agent opened in 2005 on the island of Naoshima, a short ferry ride from Takamatsu.

The museum focuses on one of American author Raymond Benson's 007 novels, *The Man With the Red Tattoo* (Hodder & Stoughton, 2002), which was set in Japan, much of it on Naoshima itself. The museum displays information on Benson and other authors who have contributed to the Bond legacy, as well as memorabilia connected to the 007 franchise.

To reach the 007 – The Man With the Red Tattoo Museum, take a 50-minute ferry ride (¥960 return) from Takamatsu port (the entrance is across the street from the ANA Hotel Clement Takamatsu) to Naoshima. The ferry drops you off at Miyanoura port, from which the museum (free entry) is less than a minute on foot.

SHIKOKU

TAKAMATSU 高松

Where to stay

4	ANA Hotel Clement Takamatsu	4	ANAホテルクレメント高松
6	Hotel Fukuya	6	ホテル福屋
7	Toyoko Inn Takamatsu Hyogocho	7	東横イン 高松兵庫町
9	Rihga Hotel Zest Takamatsu	9	リガホテルゼスト高松
14	Wataya Ryokan	14	わたや旅館
19	Toyoko Inn Takamatsu Nakajincho	19	東横イン 高松中新町

Where to eat and drink

1	Mikayla	1	ミケイラ
2	Alice; Freshness Burger; Nakamura Komei; Szechwan (Symbol Tower)	2	アリス; フレッシュネスバーガー; 中村孝明; スーツァン
4	Bar Astro; Vent	4	バー　アストロ; ヴァン
11	City Hall	11	市役所
15	Doutor Coffee	15	ドトールコヒ
16	Zucca	16	ズッカ
17	Starbucks (Tenmaya dept store)	17	スターバックス; 天満屋デパート
18	Prem	18	プレム

Other

2	Symbol Tower	2	シンボルタワー
3	Ferry Terminal (to Megijima, Naoshima)	3	フェリーターミナル (女木島, 直島)
5	Tamamo Koen	5	玉藻公園
8	Post Office	8	郵便局
10	Takamatsu City Museum of Art	10	高松市美術館
12	I-PAL (Kagawa International Exchange Center)	12	アイアパル香川
13	Prefectural Office	13	県庁
20	Sanuki Folkcraft Museum	20	讃岐民芸館
21	Ritsurin Koen	21	栗林公園

Takamatsu City Museum of Art (Tue-Sun 9am-5pm, Fri until 7pm), housed in a modern building downtown, has a permanent collection (¥200) of mostly contemporary Japanese art that is worth a look. The galleries are small but exhibits are changed every few months. Temporary exhibitions (separate admission charge) are held on the second floor. The museum occasionally stages classical and folk music concerts.

Takamatsu is also an access point for some of the islands on the Inland Sea; check with the tourist office for ferry departure times and fares. The island of **Megijima**, also known as Onigashima, has a huge cave said to have been used as a pirate den. **Shodoshima** is much larger and is known as an island resort. Attractions here include a miniature version of the 88 temples on the Shikoku pilgrimage, useful for anyone in need of a fast-track spiritual cleansing. **Naoshima** is a place of pilgrimage for fans of James Bond (see box, p431) and home to an impressive art and cultural complex called **Benesse Art Site Naoshima** (🖳 www.naoshima-is.co.jp), the centrepiece of which is the superb

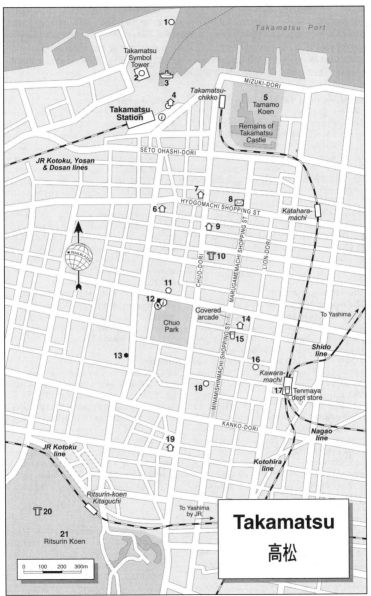

1 ○

Takamatsu
Symbol
Tower
2 3

*Takamatsu-
chikko*

MIZUKI-DORI

4

**Takamatsu
Station**

5
Tamamo Koen

Remains of
Takamatsu
Castle

SETO OHASHI-DORI

*JR Kotoku, Yosan
& Dosan lines*

7

HYOGOMACHI SHOPPING ST

8 ✉

*Katahara-
machi*

6

9

MARUGAMEMACHI SHOPPING ST

LION-DORI

TRAILBLAZER

CHUO-DORI

10

11

12

Chuo
Park

Covered
arcade

14

MINAMISHINMACHI SHOPPING ST

15

16

*Kawara-
machi*

*Shido
line*

To Yashima

13 ●

18

17 Tenmaya
dept store

KANKO-DORI

*Nagao
line*

19

*JR Kotoku
line*

*Kotohira
line*

*Ritsurin-koen
Kitaguchi*

To Yashima
by JR

20

21
Ritsurin Koen

0   100   200   300m

Takamatsu

高松

S H I K O K U

Benesse House (daily, 8am-9pm; ¥1000), a contemporary art museum designed by leading architect Tadao Ando. You can even stay the night here in super-swanky purpose-built rooms overlooking the Inland Sea. If you want to enjoy the place once the crowds have left for the day, check the website (💻 www. naoshima-is.co.jp/english/benessehouse/guestroom/index.html) for accommodation details, special offers and online booking.

PRACTICAL INFORMATION
Station guide
The station was completely rebuilt as part of the redevelopment of the port area. It has a spacious atrium interior as you exit the ticket barrier. Turn left on exiting the station for a branch of *Mister Donut*. Inside the station there are restaurants on the second floor.

Immediately to your left as you exit the ticket barrier are **coin lockers** (all sizes, including large ¥600 ones). To your right is the JR ticket office. Along the passageway to your right as you exit the ticket barrier you'll find a branch of the *Willie Winkie* bakery.

Tourist information
The **tourist information desk** (☎ 087-851 2009, daily, 9am-6pm) is in an office on the left side of the square in front of the main station exit. The helpful staff speak English and can advise on Takamatsu as well as trips to the outlying islands. They can also advise on accommodation in Takamatsu, but to book you have to ask at a separate desk (in the same room!).

Also of use is **I-PAL (Kagawa International Exchange Center)** (☎ 087-837 5901, 💻 www.i-pal.or.jp, Tue-Fri 9am-6pm, Sat/Sun 9am-5pm), in a corner of Chuo Park. Facilities here include newspapers, CNN, and free internet use. There's a library on the ground floor with a selection of English books, including a section of books on Japan. I-PAL also has copies of *TIA Info*, a newsletter in English with details of upcoming events and cinema listings. *Kagawa Journal* is a newsletter with articles written by foreign residents. Pick up the Kagawa Welcome Card (see box p53) from the tourist office at the station, from I-PAL, or print one off before you travel from 💻 www.21kagawa.com/visitor.

Getting around
As well as JR train services, the private **Kotoden Railway** (see box opposite) operates in and around Takamatsu. Though you may want to take a train to Ritsurin Koen, over on the other side of the city, the best way of seeing the city centre is on foot.

Cycles are available for rent outside the station. On the right side of the square (opposite the tourist information office) as you exit the station, take the stairs by the grey building down to the basement level for the cycle rental counter (¥100/day). It's very good value and you can drop off the cycles at a couple of other locations (the tourist information office has a map marked with the bicycle drop-off points).

Ferries to outlying islands Shodoshima and Naoshima, as well as to Kobe (see p250) and Osaka (see p116), depart from the Passenger Ship Pier across the street from ANA Hotel Clement Takamatsu.

Internet
I-PAL (see column opposite) has two computers offering free internet access. You're asked to sign in at the reception desk on the second floor and are expected to limit usage to 30 minutes (longer is OK if it's not busy).

Festivals
The biggest annual event is **Takamatsu Festival** (Aug 12th-14th), when thousands of people dance through the main streets (anyone is welcome to join in) and there's a fireworks finale.

Where to stay
Right outside the station, *ANA Hotel Clement Takamatsu* (☎ 087-811 1111, 💻 www.anaclement.com), centrepiece of the redeveloped port area, is dwarfed by the neighbouring Symbol Tower but is still a skyscraper by Takamatsu standards. It's

⛩ Kotoden – trainspotters' paradise
The private Kotoden rail company operates three lines around Takamatsu and Kagawa, with its main Kawara-machi station beneath Tenmaya department store in the city centre. Particularly among trainspotters – called *tetsudo maniaku* ('railway maniacs') in Japanese – Kotoden is known as a good place to photograph some of Japan's oldest trains still in service. The company has bought old rolling stock from cities such as Tokyo and Osaka and put them back into service on local lines. The oldest train dates back to 1925.

easily the most de luxe place to stay in town – with top-price room rates to match: singles from ¥12,474 to ¥16,170; doubles from ¥23,100 to ¥32,340 and twins from ¥24,255 to ¥40,425. Since the hotel is operated in association with JR-Shikoku, rail-pass holders receive a modest discount.

Away from the station area, there are two branches of the popular Toyoko Inn chain (🖥 www.toyoko-inn.com): the newer *Toyoko Inn Takamatsu Hyogocho* (☎ 087-821 1045; ¥6090/S, ¥8190/D/Tw), is five minutes on foot from the station. The original *Toyoko Inn Takamatsu Nakajincho* (☎ 087-831 1045; ¥5460/S, ¥8400/D/Tw) has a few de luxe single rooms at ¥6090, which are very spacious for the price and include a separate table-and-chair area.

Next to the lobby is a **barber shop** offering ten-minute haircuts for ¥1000. It is handy if you want a quick trim before checking in or out.

Hotel Fukuya (☎ 087-851 2365, 🖥 www.hotel-fukuya.com; ¥6720/S, ¥11,550/Tw) is 10-15 minutes from the station. The open-plan lobby is a welcome change from the tiny reception areas of most business hotels and rooms veer towards being spacious – the bathrooms remain tiny though. Even better are the tatami rooms at ¥12,705 for two people and ¥17,325 for three.

For a taste of luxury, head for *Rihga Hotel Zest Takamatsu* (☎ 087-822 3555, 🖥 www.rihga.com/kagawa). The rooms in the main building are nothing special (the smallest singles cost from ¥7854, twins from ¥17,325 and doubles from ¥15,015). More luxurious are the rooms in the newer annex, where a de luxe twin is ¥25,000. A

combination Western/tatami room that can sleep four also costs ¥25,000.

Wataya Ryokan (☎ 087-861 3806, 🖥 www.chuokai-kagawa.or.jp/wataya) has tatami rooms for ¥9000 per person including two meals. Located within the downtown shopping area, Wataya is good value if a touch gloomy.

Where to eat and drink
There are a few reasonable restaurants on the second floor of the station building. For more upscale dining try ANA Hotel Clement Takamatsu, which has a good-value ¥1500 all-you-can-eat buffet lunch in its informal brasserie café *Vent* (11:30am-2:30pm, 6-8:30pm). The evening buffet is a bit more expensive at ¥2541.

For take-out food, try the hotel's own bakery on the first floor and for a drink-with-a-view, try the 21st-floor *Bar Astro* (5pm-12am), where you can sip a range of cocktails (from ¥900) while admiring the sunset over the harbour area.

A few floors higher in the adjacent Symbol Tower is *Alice* (☎ 087-823 6088, 11:30am-9:30pm), a French restaurant where you pay for the stunning views as much as the excellent nouvelle cuisine (set menus from ¥3675).

One floor below is *Szechwan* (☎ 087-811 0477, 11am-3pm, 5-10pm), a good Chinese place, and *Nakamura Komei* (☎ 087-825-5656, 11am-4pm, 5-10pm), for Japanese food. Both have tables next to large bay windows. Inside the Maritime Plaza on the second floor you'll find a branch of fast-food joint *Freshness Burger* (10am-10pm), where all the burgers are made to order.

Mikayla (daily, 11am-12 midnight), part of Sunport Takamatsu, is out on the pier and has a terrace café which affords great views over the Inland Sea. The evening menu is a little pricey (from around ¥1500) but the food (pasta, salads, fish and meat dishes) is excellent. There are cheaper set deals in the afternoon (a pasta main course for ¥880) and the terrace is a great place to relax with a cocktail at sunset.

The glass entrance is easy to spot as the name, Mikayla, is written in English above the entrance. It's a five-minute walk from JR Takamatsu station.

In the city centre, try the 10th floor of **Tenmaya** department store, where there are several good restaurants, including places serving tonkatsu and Italian food; it's open until 10pm. A branch of *Starbucks* is on the ground floor beneath the Kotoden station and the main entrance to Tenmaya.

Zucca (Mon-Fri 11.30am-1.30pm, daily 6-11pm), a small Italian place on the second floor of a street off the covered arcade, dishes up a Japanese take on modern Italian cuisine from ¥950 for a main course.

Prem (daily, 11am-3pm, 5-10pm) is a decent Indian restaurant on a street off the covered arcade. The Indian chef dishes up authentic curries from ¥750. The lunch set menus are good value and there is also Kingfisher beer! Look for the 'Prem Indian restaurant' sign in English above the entrance.

Finally, for cheap food with a great view, try the canteen inside **City Hall**. It's on the 13th floor; though it's supposed to be for City Hall staff, it's open to anybody. Plastic models of the meals (from ¥450) make selection easy and you can get a window table with great views of Takamatsu. It's only open Monday-Friday for lunch and gets very busy between 12 noon and 1pm, when everyone takes their lunch break.

Side trips by rail from Takamatsu

To the north-east of Takamatsu lies **Yashima** ('roof-top island'), a plateau made of volcanic lava jutting out 5km into the Inland Sea. The plateau gained its place in national history as the site of a decisive battle between the Minamoto and Taira clans (see p37), both of which were vying to rule Japan in the 12th century. The plateau, accessed by cable car (daily, 8am-5:30pm, ¥1300 return), affords great views of the Inland Sea and is home to the 84th temple on the Shikoku pilgrimage, Yashima-ji. Below the plateau is **Shikoku Mura** (daily, 8:30am-4:30/5pm, ¥800), an open-air museum of traditional homes gathered from all over Shikoku.

After visiting Shikoku Mura the done thing is to stop for a bowl of *sanuki udon*, a traditional noodle dish, at *Waraya* (daily, last orders 6:30pm). The restaurant is in the building next to the water mill, by the entrance to Shikoku Mura. Alternatively, as you leave Shikoku Mura, look out for a traditional British-style building with red phone- and pillar-boxes outside. Inside is a *café* which serves tea and cakes; it's open daily, 9am-6pm.

Yashima can be reached from Takamatsu station by JR on the Kotoku line but it is more fun to travel on the private Kotoden line; this takes longer but drops you closer to the start of the cable car up to Yashima plateau. From Takamatsu-Chikko station (close to JR Takamatsu station) to Yashima, the fare is ¥310 (change at Kawara-machi station, beneath Tenmaya department store). As you exit Kotoden Yashima station you'll see the cable car going up the plateau. Shikoku Mura is a few minutes' walk east of the cable car entrance.

Families or anyone interested in seeing a Japanese amusement park close up should consider paying a visit to **New Reoma World** (🖳 www.newreoma

world.com, 10am-5pm, ¥1000), a 50-minute journey by private Kotoden railway into the Kagawa countryside from Takamatsu. Attractions include outdoor pools and a 50-metre Ferris wheel.

The park boasts its own hotel, ***Hotel Reoma No Mori*** (☎ 0877-86 5588, 🖳 www.reomanomori.com; ¥17,000/Tw). For years a loss-making enterprise, the park was renovated and reopened after a four-year hiatus in 2004. Access is via shuttle bus from Okada station on the private Kotoden line from Takamatsu-Chikko station (check times, fares and amusement-park opening hours at the tourist information office outside Takamatsu station).

KOCHI

Bordered in the north by the Shikoku mountain range and to the south by the Pacific Ocean, Kochi is known for its mild climate, long days of sunshine and relaxed, friendly atmosphere. The city definitely feels very laid-back and is a great place for anyone wanting to sample an unhurried and less frantic Japan.

What to see and do

Harimaya-bashi junction in the centre of Kochi is unusual in that it's a bridge that no longer has any water flowing under it. It remains a recognizable landmark and is the only point at which Kochi's two tram lines converge.

Two of the main sights that can be reached by tram are Kochi Castle in the downtown area, and Kochi Museum of Art which is about 20 minutes by tram from Kochi station. You can easily fit both into one day, or even half a day.

East of the city centre, Kochi's **Museum of Art** (Tue-Sun, 9am-5pm, ¥350) is housed in a modern building and is well organized, with large galleries for both regular and temporary exhibitions. The main collection is mostly expressionist works by both Japanese and Western artists. There's also a large hall used for films, concerts and theatre productions. Noh productions are staged here around twice a month; tickets are sometimes free. The museum prints a schedule of performance times (in Japanese only), which you should be able to pick up at Kochi station tourist information desk (see p440). The museum operates a small but attractive café called ***Villa Vitis***. From the station, take a tram or walk to Harimaya-bashi. From here, change for a tram heading for Gomen and get off at Kenritsu Bijutsukan-dori (Museum Rd).

A more recent addition to Kochi's museum scene is **Yokoyama Ryuichi Memorial Manga Museum** (🖳 www.bunkaplaza.or.jp/mangakan, Tue-Sun, 9am-7pm, ¥400). Opened in 2002, one year after the death of one of Japan's most famous cartoonists, the museum showcases Yokoyama's life and works. He was revered in Kochi itself – not just for his cartoons but for his work as a painter and sculptor. But he is perhaps best remembered for his comic-strip character 'Fuku-chan', who made his debut in a national newspaper in 1936 and was only retired in 1971 after a record-breaking 5534 appearances. The museum is worth a look if you're interested in the evolution of manga culture in Japan. Anybody obsessed by comics will be in heaven in the attached **manga library** (free entry).

SHIKOKU

Completed in 1611 by a feudal lord, **Kochi Castle** (daily 9am-5pm, ¥400), at the end of Otesuji-dori, is the city's big sight. Look out inside the castle for the huge, pointed lance made entirely of feathers. It's worth heading out here for the view of Kochi and the surrounding area from the top floor of the donjon.

Chikurin-ji (daily 7am-5pm; small museum 8:30am-5pm, ¥400), a stop on the Shikoku pilgrimage (see box p419), is accessible by bus from Kochi station or from the bus terminal next to Seibu department store. Take a bus marked 'Godaisan Chikurinji'.

If here on a Sunday, visit the **Weekly Market** on Otesuji-dori, the main street leading up to the castle. Stalls sell local produce, fruit and vegetables brought into Kochi from the surrounding countryside. Also worth a browse if you happen to be in town at the right time is the informal **Flea Market** that usually takes place on the second and fourth Sunday every month along Obisan-dori, which runs parallel to but a couple of blocks down from Otesuji-dori.

KOCHI 高知

Where to stay

1 Kochi Youth Hostel	1 高知ユースホステル
3 Comfort Hotel Kochi	3 コンフォートホテル高知駅前
4 Kochi Pacific Hotel	4 高知パシフィックホテル
5 Petit Hotel Kochi	5 プチホテル高知
6 Super Hotel Kochi	6 スーパーホテル高知
7 Tourist Inn Kochi	7 ツーリストイン高知
13 Bright Park Hotel	13 ブライトパークホテル
16 Tosa Bekkan	16 とさ別館
24 Hotel Nikko Kochi Asahi Royal	24 ホテル日航高知旭ロイヤル

Where to eat and drink

11 Hirome Market	11 ひろめ市場
12 Doutor Coffee	12 ドトールコヒ
14 Cadiz	14 カディス
17 Baffone	17 バッフォーネ
18 Tosahan	18 土佐藩
19 Daimaru Department Store	19 大丸デパート
20 Tosa Ichiba	20 土佐市場
23 Monte	23 モンテ
24 Angel View	24 エンジェルビュー

Other

2 Central Post Office	2 中央郵便局
8 Kochi Castle	8 高知城
9 Kochi International Association	9 高知国際交流協会
10 Akiyama Bicycle Rental	10 秋山自転車
15 Hot Station	15 ほっとステーション
21 Bus Terminal	21 バスターミナル
22 Kochi Museum of Art	22 高知県立美術館
23 Yokoyama Ryuichi Memorial Manga Museum	23 横山隆一記念まんが館

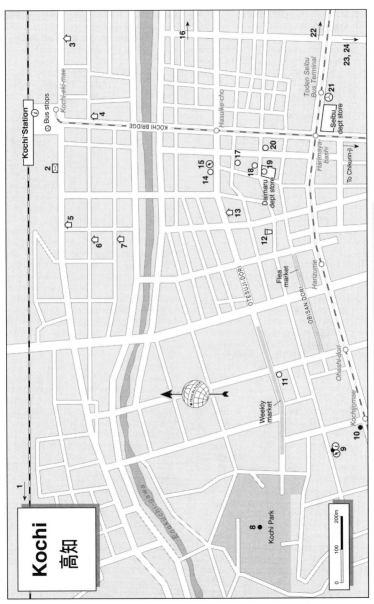

Kochi
高知

SHIKOKU

PRACTICAL INFORMATION
Station guide

Kochi station is showing its age and is in need of some renovation. The main area for **coin lockers** (all sizes, including ¥600 ones) is in a room to the left as you exit the station, close to the tourist information desk.

There is not much in the way of restaurants in the station vicinity. The *Willie Winkie bakery* (daily, 7am-7pm), to the right as you exit, has an attached café and does sandwich and drink sets. The bakery is part of the station building but has its own entrance. On the second floor of the station is a small department store and Japanese restaurant serving run-of-the-mill set meals.

JR buses to Matsuyama (see p442) depart from bus platforms to the right of the station exit. The tram terminus is on the main road that runs parallel to the front of the station.

Tourist information

Kochi's well-informed **tourist information counter** (☎ 088-882 1634, daily, 9am-8pm) is a walk-up booth to the left as you exit the station. It is staffed until 8pm, but after 5pm there is no guarantee of an English speaker (during the last three hours the office deals only with same-day hotel reservations). The staff are friendly and can advise on travel throughout Kochi prefecture as well as help with booking a room for the night in the city.

Another point of information is **Kochi International Association** (☎ 088-875 0022, 🖳 www.kochi-f.co.jp/kia/english, Mon-Sat 8:30am-5:15pm), in a small building opposite the castle park. It's on the second floor and has a selection of magazines and books. You might also enquire here about meeting up with volunteer guides – though, as ever, it's best to contact them ahead of your visit. You can also surf the web and check email free of charge.

Getting around

Kochi has an old but efficient tram system. There are two lines which intersect at Harimaya-bashi junction in the city centre. A flat fare of ¥100 is charged, or ¥180 if transferring between lines at Harimaya-bashi. A one-day pass costs ¥500, available from the bus centre ticket office at Kochi station. If changing tram lines at Harimaya-bashi, ask for a *norikae-kippu* which allows you to transfer without paying again.

Look out for the trams that have been brought from Germany, Portugal, Austria and Norway, each with a different design and interior layout.

There is no cycle rental at the station, but you can rent one from **Akiyama Bicycle Rental** in the centre of town (¥500/day).

Internet

Apart from the free internet access at Kochi International Association (see column opposite), a 24-hour internet café called **Hot Station** (¥105/15 mins) is on Otesuji-dori. You need to become a member, which can be done on the spot; the price includes unlimited soft drinks. They also do an all-night pass for ¥2080 if you don't have a bed for the night and are happy to slump in a reclining leather seat. Walk down the main street leading away from the station towards the centre of town, turn right when you see the Louis Vuitton shop on your right, and go straight on. It's just past Louis Vuitton on the right. It's on the 5th floor.

Festivals

Yosakoi Festival (August 9th-12th) is a high-energy dance event involving over 14,000 people divided into teams. One visitor a few years ago was so impressed by the event that he went home and launched a copycat festival in Sapporo (see p362). The one in Kochi, though, is the original and best.

Where to stay

Super Hotel Kochi (☎ 088-802 9000, 🖳 www.superhotel.co.jp; ¥4980/S) is part of the popular chain of no-frills business hotels where payment is by cash only using automated machines. The rate includes a simple breakfast of coffee, juice and bread. It's five minutes on foot south-west from the station and is a good budget choice.

If you want to stay near the station try *Comfort Hotel Kochi* (☎ 088-883 1441, 🖳

www.choicehotels.com; ¥5600/S, ¥9000/Tw); the hotel is part of the expanding US franchise chain, where all rooms have free internet access if you bring your laptop.

Petit Hotel Kochi (☎ 088-826 8156, 🖳 www.phk.jp; ¥5000/S, ¥9000/D), as its name suggests, is quite small, offering mostly singles and a few doubles (which are almost the same size as the singles). The rooms are certainly 'petit', but there is free internet access for those with laptops. The bright breakfast area opposite the reception desk offers breakfast for an additional ¥500: choose from the standard coffee and toast, the 'curry breakfast set' or the 'pizza breakfast set' (all the same price). The entrance is up a flight of stairs and there is no lift.

An alternative, close to both Super Hotel and Petit Hotel, is *Tourist Inn Kochi* (☎ 088-820 5151, 🖳 www.touristinn-kochi.jp; ¥4800/S, ¥7800/Tw), which offers the same kind of deal. Breakfast (¥500 Western-style, ¥900 Japanese-style) is extra.

A short way up the main road that heads away from the station towards the Harimaya-bashi crossing is *Kochi Pacific Hotel* (☎ 088-884 0777, 🖳 www.kochi-pacific.co.jp; ¥7700/S, ¥17,300/Tw). An upmarket business hotel (note the grandfather clock in the lobby), you pay for the space and the beds are wide. You can check in from 2pm, earlier than most business hotels allow.

Closer to the centre of town, handy if you want to investigate any of Kochi's many bars or visit the Sunday market, is *Bright Park Hotel* (☎ 088-823 4351, 🖳 www.brightparkhotel.co.jp; ¥6500/S, ¥10,000/D, ¥14,000/Tw). A good-standard business hotel, with a small coffee shop on the first floor.

If you're not on a budget, the best place to head is *Hotel Nikko Kochi Asahi Royal* (☎ 088-885 5111, 🖹 885 5115, 🖳 www.nikko.kochi.jp; ¥15,015/S, ¥25,410/D/Tw) overlooking the river and close to the Manga Museum (see p437).

The *Angel View* bar on the 22nd floor has great views and is the perfect place to sip a sunset cocktail.

Tosa Bekkan (☎ 088-883 5685, 🖹 884 9523) is a small Japanese inn which gets booked up quickly; per person rates without meals start at around ¥4500 (rates vary according to the season/whether the place is busy). There's a handy **coin laundry** right outside.

Finally, to reach *Kochi Youth Hostel* (☎ 088-823 0858, 🖳 www.kyh-sakenokuni.com; ¥2100; breakfast is ¥630 and dinner ¥1050; 25 beds), take a local train two stops west along the JR Dosan line to Engyoji-guchi station. The hostel is five minutes on foot from there.

Where to eat and drink

Freshly caught sea bream is popular and, according to one local gourmet guide, 'prepared so that it is still alive and in one piece before eating'. Less terrifying would be a bowl of *dorome*, tiny, clear fish that are the local speciality, available in many places including *Tosa Ichiba* (Tue-Sun, 11am-9:50pm), a popular local restaurant with a feast of plastic dishes to choose from in its window. They do reasonably priced set meals. There are seats at a counter as well as private tables with tatami seats (you don't have to sit cross-legged as there is space for your legs under the table!) which are closed off by shoji screens. Look for the picture of the whale on the sign outside.

Tosahan, directly opposite Daimaru department store, is similar to Tosa Ichiba. It's a very atmospheric place with low wooden tables. Check out the large fish tank on your way in. An extensive array of plastic food models are on display outside.

Baffone (daily, 12noon-11:30pm) is a small bistro that offers pasta lunches from ¥1000 and has a great selection of cheeses and wines, as well as coffee and cake in the afternoon. The menu changes regularly. It's a very authentic place, right down to the waiters in white. During the summer the seating area opens onto the street.

Cadiz (daily, 11:30am-3pm, 5pm-12midnight) is a Spanish/Mexican place with an all-wooden interior sprinkled with the odd cactus. The owner seems to have been keen to fit in as many flights of stairs as possible. Menus in English are available and the choice is what you'd expect: tacos, spicy fried potatoes, Spanish-style omelettes, burgers, pasta and pizza. There's a good selection of beers, wine and cocktails. The best deals as ever are at lunchtime, but this is also a good place for an evening meal if you want to linger over a drink or two. Look for the English 'Cadiz' sign over the entrance.

Hirome Market, in an indoor food mall open all year, is a good choice if you're looking for informal dining. For good coffee and sandwiches, try the branch of *Doutor Coffee* in the covered arcade, next to Toho cinema.

An Italian bistro called *Monte* (11:30am-9pm) is on the ground floor of the building housing the Manga Museum (see p437). Tables are set up outside in the summer. There is also a café on the 3rd floor, by the entrance to the museum, which offers simple dishes such as katsu-kare (pork cutlet and curry rice) and coffee/cake sets. It's a bright, open-plan place with large windows.

Finally, if you want to make your own lunch, the best place to head is the basement of *Daimaru* department store, where you can pick up whatever you need for a picnic.

Side trip from Kochi

It's possible but expensive to arrange a day's **whale watching** from Kochi. The people who once hunted whales have now turned to tourism to save them from a ban on whaling. To reach any of the points along the coast from where boats can be hired requires your own transport.

The tourist office at Kochi station (see p440) keeps a list of companies that organize whale watching and can advise on who to contact. Reservations must be made in advance; expect to pay around ¥5000 per person.

MATSUYAMA

Matsuyama, the largest city on the island, became prominent as a castle town in the 17th century. The castle and Dogo-Onsen, the oldest hot spring in Japan, are the city's main tourist draws. In recent years the city has benefited greatly from the opening of new road links with Honshu, in particular the Nishi-Seto Highway, which links nearby Imabari (see p427) with the main island. Matsuyama is keen to project itself as an international city and has established sister-city relations with Sacramento, California, and Freiburg, Germany.

What to see and do

Two priorities are Matsuyama Castle, perched on a hill in the city centre and accessible by ropeway, and nearby Dogo-Onsen (see p447). Both could be done in one day, but an overnight stay in either Matsuyama or neighbouring Dogo would be more relaxing.

Matsuyama Castle (daily, 9am-5pm, ¥350) is at the top of Katsuyama Hill in the city centre. Construction of the castle was completed in 1627 but has since suffered fates similar to those of other castles in Japan. Struck by lightning on New Year's Day 1784, the donjon burnt to the ground. The castle was reconstructed in 1854, only to suffer bomb damage during WWII.

Today, the castle is reached by taking either the ropeway or a cutesy chair lift (daily, 8:30am-5:30pm, ¥260 one-way, ¥500 return). It's difficult to imagine what the castle lords who occupied this fortification would have made of the sight of people gliding up the hill in moving chairs but it's safe to assume that as intruders they'd have been easy targets. You can avoid the expense of the ropeway by walking up the hill – even if you take the chair/ropeway, there's still a fair way to walk before you reach the donjon. The views from the top (132m above sea level) make the effort worthwhile and even eclipse the main purpose of the journey, which is to climb up inside the donjon. The constant flow of tour parties and school groups means the donjon's entrance becomes a bottle-neck – you just have to go with the flow until you eventually emerge at the exit. Back outside there's a great view of the city and surrounding area, with mountains on one side and the Inland Sea coastline on the other. The nearest tram stop for the ropeway up to the castle is Okaido.

The French-style building lower down the hill is **Bansui-so** (Tue-Sun, 9am-5pm) and was built in 1922 by a former feudal lord. Today it functions as an annex to the Prefectural Art Museum (see below). Entry to the ground floor is free but the second floor houses temporary exhibitions for which the charge varies. The nearest tram stop is Okaido.

A couple of minutes north of Minami-Horibata tram stop is **Ehime Prefectural Art Museum** (Tue-Sun, 9:40am-6pm, ¥500) which houses a permanent collection of Japanese and Western art alongside special exhibitions.

Popular with couples in search of a romantic view of Matsuyama is the **Ferris wheel**, an unmissable landmark (eyesore?) perched on top of Takashimaya department store, above Iyotetsu's Matsuyama-shi station. It's a recent edition to Matsuyama's skyline and worth a go for the views of the city (¥500/ride or ¥1000 to hire the whole four-seat gondola). The best time is at dusk as, if you time your trip correctly, you'll witness the sun setting over the city. Tickets are purchased from vending machines on the 9th floor; the last ride is at 9:30pm.

PRACTICAL INFORMATION
Station guide
Access to the platforms is by stairs only. However, if you walk to the end of platform No 1 (turning left after passing through the ticket barrier), you can cross over the tracks to the other platforms without having to use the stairs. The **JR ticket office** (daily, 5am-11pm) is combined with the travel agency. On the second floor of the station is a large souvenir shop.

As you exit the station, turn left for *Aunt Stella's Cookies*, which includes a café where you can have cake/biscuits and coffee. Turn right for *Willie Winkie bakery*.

There's an *udon/soba* place by the ticket barrier, and a *restaurant* on the second floor of the station building which does a variety of cheap set meals, but otherwise there's little in the way of places to eat.

Coin lockers (all sizes) are to the right of the station exit. Next to the locker room is a **Rent a Cycle office** (daily, 8:50am-6:30pm), where the daily rate is ¥300.

Tourist information
The **tourist information booth** (☎ 089-931 3914, daily 8:30am-5pm), to the left as you exit the ticket barrier, has maps but the staff may not speak much English.

A quirk of this place is that from 8:30am to 5pm it functions only as a tourist information office and cannot help with accommodation reservations. However, from 5 to 8:30pm hotel reservation staff take over and can provide help with hotel bookings but won't have all the detailed knowledge of the sights. So if you time your arrival for around 4:30pm you'll get the best of both worlds.

MATSUYAMA　松山

Where to stay

1	Terminal Hotel Matsuyama	1	ターミナルホテル松山
2	Hotel JAL City Matsuyama	2	ホテルJALシティ松山
8	ANA Hotel Matsuyama	8	全日航ホテル松山
10	Matsuyama Tokyu Inn	10	松山東急イン
15	Toyoko Inn Matsuyama Ichibancho	15	東横イン 松山一番町
16	Super Hotel Matsuyama	16	スーパーホテル松山
17	Matsuyama Downtown YH	17	松山ダウンタウンユースホステル
20	Matsuyama Youth Hostel	20	松山ユースホステル
21	Hotel Patio Dogo	21	ホテルパティオドウゴ
22	Yamatoya Honten	22	大和屋本店
24	Old England Dogo Yamanote Hotel	24	道後山の手ホテル

Where to eat and drink

2	La Terrazza	2	テラッツァ
5	Chibo (Takashimaya)	5	千房(高島屋)
8	Italo Provence	8	イタロプロヴァンス
9	Kanaizumi	9	かな泉
11	Starbucks; Shinonome	11	スターバックス; 東雲
13	Sushitoku	13	すし徳

Other

3	Ehime Prefectural Art Museum	3	愛媛県美術館
4	Matsuyama International Center	4	まつやま国際交流センター
5	Ferris wheel	5	大観覧車
6	Kinokuniya	6	紀伊國屋
7	Central Post Office	7	中央郵便局
12	Hot BB Station	12	ほっとBBステーション
14	Net Station	14	ネットステーション
18	Bansui-so	18	萬翠荘
19	Matsuyama Castle	19	松山城
23	Dogo Onsen	23	道後温泉
25	Ehime Prefectural International Center (EPIC)	25	愛媛県国際交流センター

Another tourist office is across the street from the tram terminus at Dogo-Onsen (see p448).

The staff at **Matsuyama International Center** (☎ 089-943 2025, 🖳 informic@ dokidoki.ne.jp, Tue-Sun, 9am-5:30pm) inside Matsuyama Gender Equality Center – known locally as COMS – can offer some advice in English but information is mostly geared to foreign residents. However, this place does offer internet access on the second floor (Tue-Sun, 9am-9pm, ¥100/hour). The centre is a short walk south-west of Minami-Horibata tram stop.

Ehime Prefectural International Center (☎ 089-917 5678, 🖳 www.epic .or.jp, Mon-Sat, 8:30am-5pm), known as **EPIC**, has free internet access and a selection of magazines in English.

From Matsuyama station, take a tram (15 mins) bound for Dogo-Onsen and get out at Minami-machi/Kenmin Bunka kaikan-mae.

At all these places, as well as in some hotels, you should be able to pick up a copy of *What's Going On?*, a monthly guide to events in Matsuyama.

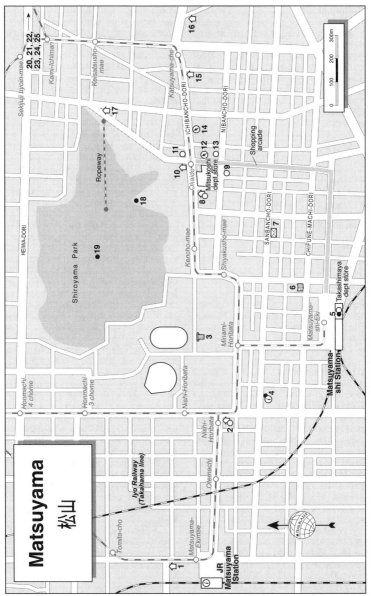

SHIKOKU

Getting around
The easiest way of travelling around Matsuyama is on one of its five tram lines – they're regular, cheap (¥150 flat fare) and go past all the major places in town. Enter at the back and pay as you leave at the front. A one-day pass costs ¥300 and can be bought from the tourist office at JR Matsuyama station or at Matsuyama Shi-eki station, the central tram terminal in the city centre.

Internet
In addition to the computer facilities listed on p444, **Hot BB Station** (24 hours, ¥450/hour) is on the third floor down the covered arcade as you walk away from the tram line. **Net Station** (24 hours, ¥300/30 mins) is on the main shopping road with the tram lines. Both offer the usual free drinks.

Books
Kinokuniya, close to Matsuyama Shi-eki station, stocks an assortment of English books on the fourth floor.

Festivals
The highlight of **Matsuyama Festival** (August 11th-13th) is a night-time parade of samba dancers. The event is kicked off by a fireworks display on August 10th.

Where to stay
As Shikoku's biggest city, Matsuyama is not short of top-class hotels. *ANA Hotel Matsuyama* (☎ 089-933 5511, 🖷 921 6053 🖳 www.anahotels.com/eng/hotels/my/index .html; ¥7500/S, ¥17,500/Tw/D) has the best location, opposite the castle and in the centre of town. The spacious rooms have wide-screen TV, mini bar and room service. Across the street is *Matsuyama Tokyu Inn* (☎ 089-941 0109, 🖳 www.tokyuhotels.co.jp; ¥7140/S, ¥15,750/D, ¥17,220/Tw), with a bright interior and smartly decorated rooms, some with views of Bansui-so (see p443).

Toyoko Inn Matsuyama Ichibancho (☎ 089-941 1045, 🖳 www.toyoko-inn.com; ¥5460/S, ¥8190/D/Tw) is in the city centre, close to Mitsukoshi department store. The rate includes breakfast and a curry rice supper. The Katsuyama-cho tram

stop is outside the hotel. About three minutes further along the road is *Super Hotel Matsuyama* (☎ 089-932 9000, 🖳 www .superhotel.co.jp; ¥4980/S including breakfast), a cash-only, no-frills business hotel.

Hotel JAL City Matsuyama (☎ 089-913 2580, 🖳 www.jalhotels.com; ¥9050/S, ¥18,480/D, ¥19,060/Tw) is within walking distance of the station and a cut above the standard business hotel.

The station area is not so convenient for sightseeing, though if you've got an early start and need to be close to the JR station, *Terminal Hotel Matsuyama* (☎ 089-947 5388, 🖳 www.th-matsuyama.jp) has functional single rooms for ¥5775 and a few twins at ¥10,500. Look for it to the left as you exit the station. Just by the entrance is a small coin laundry.

Matsuyama Youth Hostel (☎ 089-933 6366, 🖳 www.matsuyama-yh.com) is actually in the Dogo-Onsen area but the facilities and welcome make the trek out there worthwhile. Take tram No 5 to the Dogo-Onsen terminal and head for the steps that lead up to Isaniwa Shrine. Take the path to the right of these stairs and follow the 'Tsukasa View Hotel' signs along the way. The youth hostel is in an unmissable bright yellow building on the right before this hotel. A private room costs ¥3360 and a dormitory bed is ¥2625. Breakfast costs an additional ¥525 and dinner ¥1050.

The somewhat bizarre activities on offer to hostel guests include a spoon-bending course (¥300, minimum two people) and an opportunity to 'take a photograph of your 'aura'' (¥2500 for a photograph of 'your whole living body' and ¥1000 'for your fingers only').

Matsuyama Downtown Youth Hostel (☎ 089-986 8880, 🖷 934 3336, 🖳 www.aa .alpha-net.ne.jp/mdtownyh; ¥3200/4200) is at the bottom of the ropeway leading up to the castle. Breakfast costs an additional ¥500.

A few other places in the Dogo-Onsen area are *Hotel Patio Dogo* (☎ 089-941 4128, 🖳 www.patio-dogo.co.jp; ¥8610/S, ¥12,600/D, ¥14,700/Tw, see hotel website for possible discounts), offering Western-style accommodation right across from the bath house, and *Yamatoya Honten* (☎ 089-935 8880, 📄 935 8881), which is definitely the place to stay if you can afford it. It's all kimonos and shamisen music in this upmarket ryokan which even boasts its own Noh theatre. Most rooms are tatami style though there are some Western singles and twins. The hotel has its own hot spring. A twin room with two meals goes from ¥17,000. Room-only rates are available on request.

One of the newest places in Dogo is *Old England Dogo Yamanote Hotel* (☎ 089-998 2111, 🖥 www.dogo-yamanote .com; ¥11,550/S, ¥21,000/D, ¥23,100/Tw). Rates include breakfast; half-board is also available. This place exudes luxury and impresses from the moment you approach it, as bellboys compete to unburden you of your luggage and a line of smart receptionists stand behind the desk of the wood-panelled lobby. This is a place which tries and to some extent succeeds in recreating the atmosphere and décor of an English country house – so don't come here for an authentic Japanese experience. If you can't be bothered to walk around the corner to Dogo-Onsen hot spring, you can soak in the hotel's own spa. It's great for an unusual one-night escape.

Where to eat and drink

In *Sushitoku* (daily except 1st Wed, 10am-11pm) try to sit at the counter so that you can watch the staff rolling the fresh sushi.

ANA Hotel Matsuyama (see opposite) has a good choice of restaurants including *Italo Provence*, an Italian restaurant serving dishes from ¥2000.

Shinonome (11:30am-2pm, 5-9:30pm) serves a great range of Japanese dishes, including sushi and tempura. The tempura *teishoku* comes with all the trimmings, including a mini fresh-fruit dessert. To help you choose there are some food models on the side of the building; prices for the actual food start from around ¥1000. It's a little hard to find, on a corner opposite the covered arcade and across the street from the Tokyu Inn. The entrance, down a set of stairs, is next to a branch of *Starbucks*.

Chibo (11am-10pm), on the 9th floor of Takashimaya department store (the same floor as the Ferris wheel, see p443), is a branch of the famous okonomiyaki chain where the pancakes are fried up in front of you with your choice of topping/filling. Meals from ¥780.

Kanaizumi (11am-9pm) is on a side street round the back of Mitsukoshi department store. It specializes in udon and soba and offers a range of meals, such as tempura udon, from ¥700. Models of the food are outside. Look for the name written in black characters on a white sign above the entrance.

Alternatively, if you want to make your own packed lunch, try the basement floors of either Takashimaya or Mitsukoshi. Both sell a range of meals to take out and they're especially busy towards the end of the day, when prices are reduced. Takashimaya has two bakeries in its basement, *Andersen* and *Donq* – both sell cakes, sandwiches and sticky buns.

Side trip to Dogo-Onsen

Twenty minutes by tram from Matsuyama is the ancient spa town of Dogo. Today, Dogo is geared up to the tourist trade but a trip to the bath house is an excellent way to unwind after a day's sightseeing. Don't plan on doing any serious hiking after a trip to the baths though, since a visit here can leave you feeling extremely lethargic.

The hot spring dates back 3000 years and according to legend was discovered when a white heron put its injured leg into hot water flowing out of a crevice in some rocks. The main wooden bath house was built in 1894 and the cost of entry depends on the level of service you want. Tickets for the no-frills ground floor bath called Kami-no-yu (Water of the Gods) cost ¥400. For ¥800 you are given a yukata and served Japanese tea and a rice cracker afterwards on the second floor. The second floor also has its own bath, the more exclusive Tama-no-yu (Water of the Spirits), which costs ¥1200 including yukata, tea and rice cracker. Finally, to use the second floor bath and have a private room for changing and relaxing afterwards the charge is ¥1500. This includes Japanese tea and Botchan Dango, dumpling-shaped sweetmeats, that Soseki Natsume, author of *Botchan*, used to eat when he was a teacher at Matsuyama Junior High School. The private rooms have a balcony from where you can look down on people in their yukata and geta wandering around town. There are some signs in English inside, so there's no problem about making an onsen faux-pas such as stumbling into the wrong changing rooms. A towel can be hired for ¥50.

The bath house is open 6am-10pm (last entry 9pm), except the ground floor which is open until 11pm (last entry 10pm). Take a tram from Matsuyama station bound for Dogo-Onsen. The last stop on this line is the old-fashioned Dogo-Onsen terminal, a 1986 reconstruction of the original (1911) European-style building. From the tram station, walk through the covered shopping arcade, turning right when you reach a large modern bath house on your left. The main wooden bath house will be straight in front of you.

⛩ More than meals on wheels

One of Japan's leading convenience-store operators, Family Mart, has come up with a novel way of helping worried families keep tabs on elderly relatives living alone. If you order a prepared meal for home delivery to an elderly person, Family Mart delivery staff will – for no extra charge – check on the recipient's health and report back to you via an internet message. Family Mart said it was launching the service as a response to the growing number of old people in Japan. The latest statistics suggest that 3.86 million over-65s live alone.

(Opposite)
Row 1 left: Thunderbird LEXs run between Toyama and Kyoto/Osaka via Kanazawa.
Row 1 right: The Ocean Arrow, one of three trains on the route between Shingu and Kyoto.
Row 2 left: A local train on the JR Yonesaka line approaches Nishi-Yonezawa station.
Row 2 middle: Resort Shirakami, a Joyful Train (see box p304).
Row 2 right: A 500-series shinkansen.
Row 3 left: The Max Toki, a double-decker train on the Niigata to Tokyo route.
Row 3 right: The N700 shinkansen started operating between Tokyo and Hakata in 2007.
Row 4 left: A 700-series shinkansen passing through Atami station.
Row 4 right: The Haruka LEX operates to and from Kansai International Airport.
Row 5 left: The Tsubame shinkansen (see box p372) is an 800 series shinkansen.
Row 5 right: The Akita shinkansen Komachi runs from Morioka to Akita.

Photo credits: Row 1 © JR West; Row 2 left © Ramsey Zarifeh, Row 2 middle and right © Kazuo Udagawa; Row 3 left © JR East, Row 3 right © Central Japan Railway Company (JR Tokai); Row 4 left © Kazuo Udagawa, Row 4 right © JR West; Row 5 left © Ramsey Zarifeh, Row 5 right © Kazuo Udagawa.

APPENDIX A: USING THE RAIL ROUTE GUIDE

The route guides cover all four main islands. Each route has at least one point of connection with other routes described. Thus, if you are following the route round Western Honshu (see pp233-49) you will pass through Okayama (see p236), the starting point for the route guide around Shikoku (see pp418-29).

Each route guide begins with an introduction to the area, with information on regional highlights and suggested stopping-off points. Routes can be followed in reverse but in this case all points of interest from the train will be on the opposite side.

Though it's possible to travel every route by local train, it's assumed that most travellers will have a rail pass so will use the shinkansen and/or limited express (LEX) services. It is not possible to mention every station so, as a rule of thumb, only stops served by limited expresses (or by shinkansen if the route follows a shinkansen line) are included. Stations served solely by local trains are listed if they, or the area around them, are of particular interest. When a route includes a stop in a large town or city, a cross reference is given to that place's entry in the city guides section which appears immediately after the respective route guide.

The fastest point-to-point journey times are provided for each section of the route. Even though each route has been divided into different sections it may not be necessary to change trains as you go from one section to the next. Occasionally, however, it is essential to change train in order to complete the route described. Such instances are denoted by the following symbol ▲. Places which are served by local trains only are marked ◆.

🚉 Energetic soles

How's this for a brilliant energy-saving idea? In 2006 JR-East conducted an unusual power-generating experiment at the Marunouchi North exit of Tokyo station, one of the world's busiest thoroughfares. Special flooring was installed under ticket barriers in an attempt to absorb energy from the footsteps of the 700,000 commuters who pass through each day. Special gadgets converted the vibrations from each step into power. Sadly, the pilot project was not an unqualified success. While the hope had been that one day the footsteps of commuters would provide the power for information boards and lights inside the station, the reality was that – on the first day of testing the equipment – enough energy was generated only to light a 100-watt bulb for 36 seconds.

(Opposite) Lanterns are a common sight in Japan. The kind of lantern (*chochin*) in the photo is often seen in temple areas; the names of companies or individuals who have donated money to the temple are written on them. Chochin are also hung outside restaurants to make it easier for customers to find them, and are carried in festival parades to light the way. They are made from a frame of bamboo hoops covered in strong paper and have the advantage of being collapsible so they take up less space when not in use. (Photo © Kazuo Udagawa).

APPENDIX B: GLOSSARY

General

Basho sumo tournament

-bashi ..bridge

Bento lunch box

Bunraku puppetry

Conbini convenience store

Donjon the great tower or keep of a castle

-dori/odori ..street

-gawa ..river

Gaijin foreigner

Geisha person (usually a woman) trained to entertain at a party

Geta wooden clogs

Haiku poem of 17 syllables

Hiragana syllabary for writing Japanese words

Ikebana flower arranging

Izakaya Japanese-style pub/bar

-ji ..temple

-jo ..castle

Kaisoku rapid train

Kaiten-zushiya conveyor-belt sushi restaurant

Kami spirit/deity

Kanji Chinese characters used to write the Japanese language

Katakana syllabary for writing non-Japanese words

-ko ..lake

Koban police box

-koen park

Koto Japanese harp

Kyuko express train

Maiko trainee geisha

Manga comic

Meishi business card

Mikoshi portable shrine

Minshuku place to stay, similar to a B&B

Morning set/service a coffee shop's breakfast; usually coffee, boiled/fried egg and toast

Onsen hot spring resort

Rotemburo open-air hot spring bath

Ryokan Japanese-style hotel

Shamisen wood instrument covered in cat skin with three strings made of silk

Shinkansen super express or bullet train

Shohizei consumption tax (5%)

Shojin ryori vegetarian food served and eaten by priests in temples

Shokudo canteen, dining hall

Tokkyu limited express train

Torii gate at entrance to Shinto shrine

Yakuza Japanese mafia

-yama mountain

Yokozuna grand champion in sumo tournament

Yukata cotton garment worn as a dressing gown; also a summer kimono

Zazen Zen meditation

Food

Curry rice (kare raisu) A Japanese take on the Indian curry. The sauce is more like gravy than curry but it's a cheap filling meal.

Dango Dumpling-shaped sweetmeat or confection.

Donburi A bowl of rice topped with chicken and egg (*oyakodon*) or strips of beef (*gyudon*). These restaurants are easy to spot as the counter is usually full of businessmen and meal tickets are bought from vending machines at the entrance; a very cheap meal.

Kakigori Crushed ice served with different fruit flavours, similar to Slush Puppy.

Kani Crab, which is usually expensive and served in dedicated crab restaurants, instantly recognizable from the giant crab with moving pincers above the entrance.

Meron pan Melon-flavoured buns.

Miso soup Served with practically every Japanese dish, miso (soybean paste) is a staple ingredient in Japanese cuisine. In Nagano there's even a shop where you can try miso-flavoured ice cream (see p148).

Mochi A rice cake; a special type of mochi is eaten to celebrate New Year.

Nabe A kind of Japanese hot pot; chicken, beef, pork or seafood mixed with vegetables and cooked in a large pot at your table.

Natto Fermented soy beans. Foreigners are often asked if they like *natto*. Answering yes will shock your listener since gaijin are supposed not to like it.

Okonomiyaki Japanese savoury pancake with vegetables and meat, cooked on a grill and served in front of the customer.

Onigiri A popular convenience-store snack, onigiri are triangles of rice wrapped in a sheet of nori (seaweed) and containing fillings such as salmon, tuna or pickled plums.

Pocky A snack food, thin biscuit sticks which are covered in icing (in a variety of flavours) and are available in every convenience store.

Ramen Stringy yellow noodles, served in a soup/broth with vegetables. Originally imported from China, ramen is a popular late-night snack. Some restaurants offer 'challenge ramen' which is incredibly hot, but which you don't have to pay for if you can finish it without exploding. Also sold as 'cup ramen' in convenience stores.

Sashimi Slices of raw fish, the most common are tuna, eel, prawn and salmon roe; not to be confused with sushi, which is arranged on a bed of rice.

Shabu-shabu Thinly sliced beef cooked at your table with vegetables and served with a special sauce.

Soba Thin buckwheat noodles eaten hot in a soup/broth, or cold when the noodles are dipped into a separate sauce made from soy, mirin (rice wine for cooking) and saké.

Somen Noodles served cold and eaten only in the summer.

Sukiyaki Thinly sliced beef with vegetables grilled in a special iron pan at your table.

Sushi Slices of fresh fish (particularly prawn and tuna) on a bed of rice. The most common kind, on small, oval-shaped rice balls, is called nigiri-zushi. Add soy sauce (and wasabi) to taste and eat with a few slices of pickled ginger.

Takoyaki Pieces of octopus in batter; popular at summer festivals.

Tempura Prawns/fish and vegetables deep fried in batter; served with a dipping sauce.

Tofu Soybean curd, delicious when dipped in soy sauce.

Tonkatsu A pork cutlet, dipped in breadcrumbs and deep fried. Always served with a mountain of shredded cabbage, miso soup and rice (which can be refilled on demand). Also made with chicken.

Umeboshi Sour, pickled plums. Some restaurants have bowls of umeboshi on the table for diners to pick at before/after a meal.

Udon Wheat-flour noodles, much thicker than soba, served hot in a broth.

Unagi Eel, basted in soy and saké sauce, cooked over a charcoal fire and served on a bed of rice. Traditionally eaten in the summer as stamina food for beating the heat.

Wasabi Hot mustard, similar to horseradish, served with sushi and sashimi.

Yakisoba Pork mince and vegetables with fried soba; popular at summer festivals.

Yakitori Chunks of chicken (wing, leg, heart, liver) and/or vegetables (usually leeks and pepper) on a skewer, dipped in a sauce made from saké, mirin (rice wine for cooking), stock and soy sauce and cooked over a charcoal fire. Usually served along with mugs of cold draught beer in small Japanese bars called *izakaya*.

Drink

Asahi Superdry One of the top two beers in Japan (see also Kirin).

Calpis A milk-based soft drink popular with children. Its name was changed to 'Calpico' when launched overseas.

CC Lemon A fizzy drink which claims to have 'a hundred lemons' worth of Vitamin C' in every can.

Kirin Rivals Asahi Superdry for the title of 'nation's favourite beer'.

Pocari Sweat A well-known energy drink in a blue can.

Saké Often refers generally to alcoholic drinks, while 'Nihonshu' is more specifically what is known in the West as saké. Made from white rice, saké is served hot or cold. The saké served on New Year's Day is called o-toso.

Shochu A strong spirit popular in southern Japan (particularly Kyushu) and made from grain/potato. *Chulime* is shochu served with lime cordial.

Tea Cups of green tea are served free in nearly all Japanese restaurants. Earl Grey and English Breakfast are common in many hotels, while fruit and peppermint flavour tea infusions are also widely available.

Whiskey No karaoke bar would be without bottles of Suntory whiskey, the leading domestic brand. But really high-class establishments only serve imported Scotch (particularly Johnny Walker).

Yakult A 'lactic acid bacteria beverage' or, if you think it sounds more appealing, a fermented milk drink. Either way it is very popular in Japan.

APPENDIX C: USEFUL WORDS AND PHRASES

General words and phrases

Good morning	*ohaiyo gozaimasu*	Good evening	*konbanwa*
Good night	*oyasumi nasai*	Hello	*konnichiwa*
Please*	*dozo* or *kudasai*	Goodbye	*sayonara*
Thank you	*domo arigato*	Yes (see p67)	*hai*
(very much)	*(gozaimashita)*	No	*ie*
No thanks	*kekko desu*	Excuse me	*sumimasen*
I'm sorry	*gomen nasai*	I don't understand	*wakarimasen*

What's your name? — *O-namae wa nan desu-ka*
My name is .... — *Watashi wa .... desu*
Where do you live? — *Doko ni sunde imasu ka*
I'm from Britain/America/Canada/ Australia/New Zealand — *Igirisujin/Amerikajin/Kanadajin/ Australiajin/New Zealandjin desu*
Do you speak English? — *Anata wa eigo ga hanasemasu ka*
Please write it down for me — *Sore o kaite kudasai*
Could you repeat that please? — *Mo ichido itte kudasai*
How much does it cost? — *Ikura desu ka*

*Note: *kudasai* is used with a noun or when requesting/receiving something and *dozo* when giving something away.

Japanese hiragana script

a		i		u		e		o	
あ		い		う		え		お	
ka	ga	ki	gi	ku	gu	ke	ge	ko	go
か	が	き	ぎ	く	ぐ	け	げ	こ	ご
sa	za	shi	ji	su	zu	se	ze	so	zo
さ	ざ	し	じ	す	ず	せ	ぜ	そ	ぞ
ta	da	chi	ji	tsu	zu	te	de	to	do
た	だ	ち	ぢ	つ	づ	て	で	と	ど
na		ni		nu		ne		no	
な		に		ぬ		ね		の	
ha ba pa		hi bi pi		hu bu pu		he be pe		ho bo po	
は ば ひ		び ふぶ		へ べ ほ		ぼ べ ぺ		ほ ぼ ぼ	
ma		mi		mu		me		mo	
ま		み		む		め		も	
ya				yu				yo	
や				ゆ				よ	
ra		ri		ru		re		ro	
ら		り		る		れ		ろ	
wa				o				n	
わ				お				ん	

Numerals

1	ichi	一	11	ju-ichi	十一	21	ni-ju-ichi	二十一
2	ni	二	12	ju-ni	十二	22	ni-ju-ni	二十二
3	san	三	13	ju-san	十三	100	hyaku	百
4	shi/yon	四	14	ju-shi/yon	十四	101	hyaku-ichi	百一
5	go	五	15	ju-go	十五	200	ni-hyaku	二百
6	rokku	六	16	ju-rokku	十六	1000	sen	千
7	shichi/nana	七	17	ju-shichi/nana	十七	1001	sen-ichi	千一
8	hachi	八	18	ju-hachi	十八	2000	ni-sen	二千
9	kyu/ku	九	19	ju-kyu	十九	10,000	ichi-man	一万
10	ju	十	20	ni-ju	二十	20,000	ni-man	二万

Day/time

Monday	*getsuyobi*	Saturday	*doyobi*	morning	*asa*
Tuesday	*kayobi*	Sunday	*nichiyobi*	afternoon	*ogo*
Wednesday	*suiyobi*	today	*kyo*	evening	*yoru*
Thursday	*mokuyobi*	tomorrow	*ashita*	hour	*ji*
Friday	*kinyobi*	yesterday	*kino*	minute	*fun/pun*

Japanese katakana script

a		i		u		e		o	
ア		イ		ウ		エ		オ	
ka	ga	ki	gi	ku	gu	ke	ge	ko	go
カ	ガ	キ	ギ	ク	グ	ケ	ゲ	コ	ゴ
sa	za	shi	ji	su	zu	se	ze	so	zo
サ	ザ	シ	ジ	ス	ズ	セ	ゼ	ソ	ゾ
ta	da	chi	ji	tsu	zu	te	de	to	do
タ	ダ	チ	ヂ	ツ	ヅ	テ	デ	ト	ド
na		ni		nu		ne		no	
ナ		ニ		ヌ		ネ		ノ	
ha ba pa		hi bi pi		hu bu pu		he be pe		ho bo po	
ハ バ パ		ヒ ビ ピ		フ ブ プ		ヘ ベ ペ		ホ ボ ポ	
ma		mi		mu		me		mo	
マ		ミ		ム		メ		モ	
ya				yu				yo	
ヤ				ユ				ヨ	
ra		ri		ru		re		ro	
ラ		リ		ル		レ		ロ	
wa				o				n	
ワ				オ				ン	

Directions

North	*kita*	(Go) left	*hidari (itte)*
South	*minami*	(Go) right	*migi (itte)*
West	*nishi*	(Go) straight on	*massugu (itte)*
East	*higashi*		

Where is ...?   *... wa doko desu ka*

the train station	*Eki ...*	the ticket office	*Midori-no-madoguchi..*
the bus stop	*Basu noriba ...*	a tourist information office	*Kanko annaijo...*
the tram stop	*Romendensha noriba ...*	a toilet	*O-tearai* (polite)/
a taxi stand	*Takushi noriba ...*		*toire* (informal)

Railway vocabulary

Booking a ticket/making a reservation

adult	*otona*
child	*kodomo*
aisle (seat)	*tsuro (gawa no seki)*
berth	*shindai*
itinerary	*ryotei*
(railway) line	*sen*
no-smoking car	*kinen-sha*
refund	*haraimodoshi*
reserved seat	*shitei-seki*
reservation	*yoyaku*
seat	*seki*
sleeper train	*shindaisha*
ticket	*kippu*
ticket office	*midori-no-madoguchi*
(for seat reservations)	
timetable	*jikoku hyo*
transfer ticket	*norikae-kippu*
Travel Service Center	*ryoko senta*
unreserved seat	*jiyu-seki*

At the station

entrance	*iriguchi*
exit	*deguchi*
fare adjustment office	*ryokin seisanjo*
handicapped	*shintai no fujiyu*
platform	*platthomu*
station	*eki*
ticket gate/wicket	*kaisatsu-guchi*
underground/	*chikatetsu*
subway/metro	

On the train

departure	*shupatsu*
arrival	*tochaku*
buffet	*byuffé*
conductor	*shashosan*
Green car	*guriin-sha*
luggage	*nimotsu*
ordinary class	*futsu*
ordinary class coach	*futsu-sha*
railway lunchbox	*ekiben*

Railway phrases

How can I get to [Kyoto] from here?	*Koko kara [Kyoto] niwa made dousureba ikemasu ka*
I'd like to reserve a seat on the next train to [Kyoto]	*Tsugi no [Kyoto] iki ressha no zaseki o yoyaku shitai'n desu ga*
What time does the train to [Kyoto] leave?	*[Kyoto] iki ressha wa nan ji ni shupatsu shimasu ka*
Which platform does the train to [Kyoto] leave from?	*[Kyoto] iki no ressha wa dono homu kara shupatsu shimasu ka*
Excuse me, does this train go to [Kyoto]?	*Kono ressha wa [Kyoto] ni ikimasu ka*
Can you tell me where my seat is on this train?	*Kono ressha demo, watashi no seki o oshiete moraemasen ka*

Hotel

Hoteru

I'd like to book a single/ double/twin room	*Singuru/daburu/tuin no heya o yoyaku shitai'n desu ga*

I'd like a room but no meals	*Sudomari onegaishimasu*
Can I check-in please?	*Check-in onegaishimasu*
I'd like to check out please	*Check-out onegaishimasu*
Do you accept Amex/Visa card?	*Amekkusu/Viza kaado wa tsukaemasu ka*

Restaurant
	Resutoran
I'd like to make a reservation	*Shokuji no yoyaku o shitai'n desu ga*
Do you have a menu in English?	*Eigo no menyuu wa arimasu ka*
What is this?	*Kore wa nan desu ka*
I'd like this please	*Kore o kudasai*
What time does the restaurant open/close?	*Resutoran wa nan ji kara/nan ji made desu ka*

Useful kanji

male	男性	day	日	entrance	入口
female	女性	month	月	exit	出口
smoking	喫煙	year	年	north	北
non-smoking	禁煙	hour	時	south	南
reserved seat	指定席	minute	分	east	東
unreserved seat	自由席	second	秒	west	西

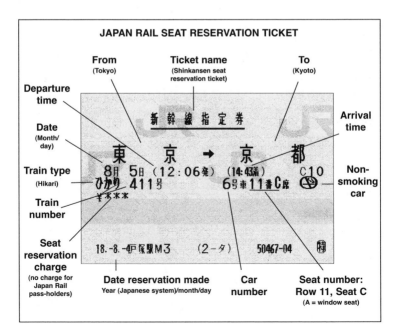

JAPAN RAIL SEAT RESERVATION TICKET

From (Tokyo) — Ticket name (Shinkansen seat reservation ticket) — To (Kyoto)

Departure time

Date (Month/day)

Arrival time

Train type (Hikari)

Train number

Non-smoking car

Seat reservation charge (no charge for Japan Rail pass-holders)

Date reservation made — Year (Japanese system)/month/day

Car number

Seat number: Row 11, Seat C (A = window seat)

APPENDIX D: TIMETABLES

THE JAPANESE RAILWAY TIMETABLE

Even though the summaries contained in this appendix will give you an idea of the services available, the Japanese Timetable (see p85) will always be the most up-to-date version so you may like to refer to one in order to check your plans.

How to use the Japanese Timetable

The route maps in the Japanese timetable use kanji to mark places so you need to know the kanji for where you are and where you want to go – a selection is provided below, or you can look at JNTO's *Tourist Map of Japan*. Find the route map which covers the area you are travelling in and then the places you want to travel between. Finally look for the number which appears immediately above or below it. This refers to the corresponding page in the timetable. For major services two numbers are given – one for each direction. Go to the relevant page. At the beginning of every timetable the names of all stops on a particular route appear in hiragana as well as kanji. Thus, even if you don't recognize the kanji, by using the hiragana syllabary on p452 you could work out the hiragana for eg Osaka. Working your way around the Japanese timetable can take time but it is ultimately rewarding and since the information contained in it is up to date it is by far the most reliable way of working out which train you need to catch.

English–Japanese place names

Abashiri	網走	Kubokawa	窪川	Okayama	岡山
Akita	秋田	Kumamoto	熊本	Osaka	大阪
Aomori	青森	Kushiro	釧路		
Asahikawa	旭川	Kyoto	京都	Sakurajima	桜島
Asakusa	浅草			Sapporo	札幌
Atami	熱海	Mt Aso	阿蘇山	Sendai	仙台
		Masuda	益田	Shinagawa	品川
Beppu	別府	Matsue	松江	Shinjuku	新宿
		Matsumoto	松本	Shin-Fuji	新富士
Furano	富良野	Matsushima	松島	Shin-Kobe	新神戸
Fukuoka	福岡	Matsuyama	松山	Shin-Osaka	新大阪
Hachinohe	八戸	Mishima	三島	Shin-Shimonoseki	
Hakata	博多	Miyazaki	宮崎		新下関
Hakodate	函館	Morioka	盛岡	Shin-Yamaguchi	
Hakone	箱根				新山口
Himeji	姫路	Nagasaki	長崎	Shin-Yatsushiro	新八代
Hiroshima	広島	Nagano	長野	Shin-Yokohama	新横浜
		Nagoya	名古屋	Shizuoka	静岡
Ichinoseki	一関	Nara	奈良		
		Narita Airport	成田空港	Takamatsu	高松
Kagoshima-chuo		Naoetsu	直江津	Takayama	高山
	鹿児島中央	Niigata	新潟	Tokyo	東京
Kamakura	鎌倉	Nikko	日光	Toyama	富山
Kanazawa	金沢	Noboribetsu	登別	Tsuwano	津和野
Kansai Airport					
	関西空港	Obihiro	帯広	Ueno	上野
Kobe	神戸	Odate	大館	Uwajima	宇和島
Kochi	高知	Odawara	小田原		
Kokura	小倉	Oita	大分	Yokohama	横浜

USING THE TIMETABLES IN THIS GUIDE

Timetables for shinkansen and limited express (LEX) services for most routes described in this book are provided below. Times for local/rapid trains are not included (except where they are the only option) even though these also operate on most routes.

The timetables below are included as an assistance to planning your trip but times should **always** be checked before heading to the station. Most services listed operate daily but weekend services can differ so checking is essential. It must also be noted that in most cases the timetables shown do not include all the services; nor in many cases are all the stops shown.

Table 1: Narita Airport to Tokyo via Narita Express (N'EX)

1a: Narita to Tokyo

Narita Airport	07:42	08:10	08:52	09:15	09:44	10:16[1]	13:43[2]
Airport Terminal 2	07:44	08:13	08:54	09:18	09:47	10:19	13:46
Tokyo	09:02[3]	09:27[3]	09:52[3]	10:14[3]	10:40[3]	11:10[3]	14:40[3]
Shinagawa	09:13	09:37		10:26	10:52	11:23	14:49
Shinjuku	09:26		10:15	10:36	11:04	11:31	
Ikebukuro	09:34		10:22			11:38	
Yokohama		09:57		10:46	11:12	11:44	15:08

[1] Hourly until 19:13 though subsequent times vary a bit.
[2] Hourly from 14:43 till 21:43 though subsequent times vary a bit.
[3] Trains divide at Tokyo – part goes to Shinagawa, Shibuya, Shinjuku, Ikebukuro and Omiya, the other part goes to Yokohama, Totsuka and Ofuna.

1b: Tokyo to Narita

Yokohama		06:26		07:26		09:30	13:00
Ikebukuro	06:00					09:33	13:04
Shinjuku	06:07	06:33	07:07		08:03	09:40	13:12
Shinagawa	06:13	06:47		07:48		09:50	13:20
Tokyo	06:30[4]	07:00[4]	07:30[4]	08:00[1, 4]	08:30[4]	10:03[2,4]	13:33[3,4]
Airport Terminal 2	07:26	07:52	08:34	09:01	09:26	10:53	14:25
Narita Airport	07:29	07:55	08:37	09:04	09:29	10:57	14:28

[1] Also at 09:00   [2] Hourly till 20:03 but subsequent times vary by up to 15 minutes.
[3] Hourly from 13:33 till 18:33 though subsequent times vary a bit.
[4] Trains join up at Tokyo – one part comes from Omiya, Ikebukuro, Shinjuku, Shibuya and Shinagawa; the other part comes from Ofuna, Totsuka and Yokohama.

Table 2: Kansai Airport to Shin-Osaka/Kyoto via Haruka LEX

	2a: Airport to Osaka/Kyoto				2b: Kyoto/Osaka to airport			
Kansai Airport	06:34[1]	07:55	08:46[2]	09:16[3]	▲ 07:11	07:42	08:54	10:04
Tennoji	07:17	08:42	09:22	09:50	│ 06:37	07:08	08:09	09:33
Shin-Osaka	07:38	09:05	09:38	10:07	│ 06:17	06:48	07:48	09:16
Kyoto	08:02	09:32	10:03	10:31	▼ 05:46[5]	06:22	07:16[5]	08:50[6]

[1] Also at 07:27; arr 09:03   [2] Hourly till 20:46   [3] Hourly till 22:16
[4] Also at 06:46   [5] Hourly till 20:15   [6] Hourly till 20:45

Note: For all services subsequent departure/arrival times vary by a few minutes from those given here.

Table 3: Tokyo to Hakata/Fukuoka by shinkansen

Note: The services listed below generally operate daily and hourly until approximately 20:00. The details given are accurate for the services shown but subsequent trains may not make all the same stops and some make additional stops. This therefore affects departure/arrival times.

In addition this list is only a sample of the services available: there are many more Nozomi services (see box opposite for details of some). Thus the table should be used as a guide only.

The JR pass is not valid for Nozomi services and it is not possible to pay a supplement to use them. If travelling without a rail pass, it's worth noting that all Nozomi services now have three non-reserved carriages (there is no longer a compulsory additional seat reservation charge for Nozomi trains).

> ❑ **The N700-series shinkansen**
> The N700 (see p76) entered service in 2007. It operates on four Nozomi services each way:
> No 99: dep Shinagawa 06:00, arr Hakata 10:45
> No 1: dep Tokyo 06:00 arr Hakata 10.50
> No 25: dep Tokyo 11.50 arr Hakata 16.52
> No163: dep Tokyo 21:20 arr Shin-Osaka 23:45
>
> In the other direction services are:
> No100: dep Shin-Osaka 06:00 arr Tokyo 08:26
> No 26: dep Hakata 12:28 arr Tokyo 17:30
> No 28: dep Hakata 12:50 arr Tokyo 18:06
> No52: dep Hakata 18:54 arr Tokyo 23:45

3a: Tokyo to Hakata/Fukuoka

	To Oka-yama (Hikari)	To Shin-Osaka (Hikari)	To Hakata (Nozomi)	To Shin-Osaka (Kodama)	To Nagoya (Kodama)
Tokyo	06:36	07:06	06:50	06:56	07:23
Shinagawa		07:14	06:58	07:04	07:30
Shin-Yokohama	06:53		07:10	07:16	07:45
Odawara	07:10			07:37	08:08
Atami				07:47	08:18
Mishima				08:00	08:28
Shin-Fuji				08:10	08:43
Shizuoka		08:14		08:25	08:58
Kakegawa				08:44	09:14
Hamamatsu		08:36		08:59	09:31
Toyohashi				09:18	09:51
Mikawa-Anjo				09:34	10:06
Nagoya	08:23	09:07	08:34	09:48	10:18
Gifu-Hashima	08:36			09:59	
Maibara	08:57			10:19	
Kyoto	09:21	09:45	09:12	10:41	
Shin-Osaka (arr)	09:36	09:59	09:27	10:56	
		Shin-Osaka to Hakata (Hikari)		**Shin-Osaka to Hiroshima (Kodama)**	**Okayama to Hakata (Kodama)**
Shin-Osaka (dep)	09:38	09:59	09:29	09:15	
Shin-Kobe	09:53	10:12	09:42	09:29	
Nishi-Akashi	10:03			09:40	
Himeji	10:20	10:29		10:01	
Aioi	10:30			10:13	
Okayama	10:46	10:51	10:15	10:32	09:21

Table 3a: *(cont'd)*

	Shin-Osaka to Hakata (Hikari)	Tokyo to Hakata (Nozomi)	Shin-Osaka to Hiroshima (Kodama)	Okayama to Hakata (Kodama)
Shin-Kurashiki			10:47	09:32
Fukuyama	11:09		11:02	09:45
Shin-Onomichi			11:21	09:56
Mihara			11:36	10:11
Higashi-Hiroshima			11:51	10:30
Hiroshima	11:34	10:52	12:03	11:04
Shin-Iwakuni				11:23
Tokuyama				11:37
Shin-Yamaguchi				11:57
Asa				12:12
Shin-Shimonoseki	12:18			12:30
Kokura	12:27	11:40		12:40
Hakata	12:44	11:57		13:01

3b: Hakata/Fukuoka to Tokyo (See Note opposite)

	To Tokyo (Nozomi)	To Shin-Osaka (Hikari)	To Shin-Osaka (Hikari)	Okayama to Tokyo (Hikari)	To Shin-Osaka (Kodama)
Hakata	06:23	07:35	07:59		09:14
Kokura	06:39	07:52	08:17		09:35
Shin-Shimonoseki					09:49
Asa					10:06
Shin-Yamaguchi	06:58				10:18
Tokuyama		08:21	08:36		10:39
Shin-Iwakuni					10:58
Hiroshima	07:30	08:45	09:10		11:34
Higashi-Hiroshima					11:47
Mihara					12:02
Shin-Onomichi					12:09
Fukuyama		09:11	09:35		12:18
Shin-Kurashiki					12:34
Okayama	08:06	09:29	09:52	07:33	12:46
Aioi				07:50	13:08
Himeji		09:50	10:14	08:02	13:25
Nishi-Akashi				08:14	13:38
Shin-Kobe	08:38	10:07	10:30	08:25	13:49
Shin-Osaka (arr)	08:51	10:20	10:44	08:40	14:04

		Nagoya to Tokyo (Kodama)	Shin-Osaka to Tokyo (Hikari)		Shin-Osaka to Tokyo (Kodama)
Shin-Osaka (dep)	08:53		08:19	08:43	08:23
Kyoto	09:09		08:35	09:00	08:39
Maibara				09:29	09:06
Gifu-Hashima				09:45	09:21
Nagoya	09:47	08:01	09:13	09:58	09:33
Mikawa-Anjo		08:14			09:47
Toyohashi		08:32			10:06
Hamamatsu		08:53	09:44		10:26

Table 3b: *(cont'd)*

	From Hakata (Nozomi)	From Nagoya (Kodama)	From Shin-Osaka (Hikari)	From Okayama (Hikari)	From Shin-Osaka (Kodama)
Kakegawa		09:05			10:40
Shizuoka		09:23	10:11		10:57
Shin-Fuji		09:41			11:10
Mishima		09:54			11:24
Atami		10:02	10:37		11:33
Odawara		10:17		11:09	11:47
Shin-Yokohama	11:10	10:34		11:26	12:03
Shinagawa	11:22	10:49	11:05		12:15
Tokyo	11:30	10:56	11:13	11:43	12:23

Table 4: Tokyo to Nagano by Asama shinkansen

Note: The services shown below are only a sample of the many on this route. During the day there are at least two an hour to/from Tokyo and one an hour to/from Ueno, thus the table should be used as a guide only. Only the main stops are shown.

4a: Tokyo to Nagano

Tokyo	07:52	08:40	09:48	10:44	12:24	13:04	14:44	16:24
Ueno	07:58	08:46	09:54	10:50	12:30	13:10	14:50	16:30
Omiya	08:18	09:06	10:14		12:50	13:30	15:10	16:50
Takasaki	08:53	09:31		11:40	13:15	13:58	15:35	
Karuizawa	09:15	09:48	10:53	12:02	13:37	14:15	15:57	17:28
Sakudaira	09:24	09:57	11:02	12:11	13:46	14:24		17:37
Ueda	09:34	10:07	11:12	12:21	13:56	14:34		17:47
Nagano	09:47	10:20	11:25	12:34	14:09	14:47	16:21	18:00

4b: Nagano to Tokyo

Nagano	08:49	10:08	11:09	13:02	13:45	15:26	16:17	17:41
Ueda	09:03		11:22	13:15	13:58	15:39	16:30	17:54
Sakudaira	09:14		11:33	13:26	14:09	15:50	16:41	18:03
Karuizawa	09:24		11:42	13:35	14:19	16:00	16:51	18:15
Takasaki			11:59	13:56		16:21	17:12	18:36
Omiya	10:06	11:08	12:26	14:26	15:06	16:46	17:46	19:06
Ueno	10:26		12:46	14:46	15:26	17:06	18:06	19:26
Tokyo	10:32	11:31	12:52	14:52	15:32	17:12	18:12	19:32

Table 5: Nagano to Nagoya via Matsumoto

	5a: Nagano to Nagoya				5b: Nagoya to Nagano			
Nagano	09:00	10:50	12:50	14:50	11:54	12:49	15:43	17:48
Shinonoi	09:08	10:58	12:58	14:58	11:44	12:41	15:35	17:40
Hijiri-Kogen				15:18				
Matsumoto	09:51	11:42	13:41	15:42	11:03	12:00	14:57	17:00
Shiojiri	10:01	11:52	13:51	15:52	10:51	11:50	14:46	16:50
Kiso-Fukushima	10:28	12:19	14:19	16:19	10:23	11:23	14:19	16:23
Nagiso			14:43	16:44		10:58		15:58
Nakatsugawa	11:05	12:56	14:56	16:56	09:47	10:47	13:44	15:47
Tajimi	11:32	13:23	15:23	17:23	09:22	10:22		15:22
Chikusa	11:49	13:40	15:40	17:40	09:06	10:06		15:06
Nagoya	11:56	13:47	15:47	17:48	09:00	10:00	13:00	15:00

Note: There is generally one through service an hour from both Nagano and Nagoya.

Table 6: Nagano to Toyama (and Kanazawa) via Naoetsu

	6a: Nagano to Naoetsu[1]		6b: Naoetsu to Toyama/Kanazawa)[2/3]				
			H	H	H	H	H
Nagano	08:11	Naoetsu	09:37	10:09	12:31	14:50	17:17
Toyono	08:24	Itoigawa	10:01	10:32	12:54	15:14	17:41
Kurohime	08:45	Tomari		10:52			17:59
Myoko-Kogen	08:54	Nyuzen					18:04
Sekiyama	09:01	Kurobe	10:29	11:01		15:41	18:13
Nihongi	09:09	Uozu	10:34	11:06	13:24	15:46	18:18
Arai	09:19	Namerikawa	10:40				
Takada	09:32	Toyama	10:53	11:22	13:41	16:03	18:34
Naoetsu	09:41	Takaoka	11:05	11:34	13:53	16:15	18:47
		Isurugi					18:57
		Tsubata					
		Kanazawa	11:31	12:00	14:18	16:40	19:15

	6c: Kanazawa/Toyama to Naoetsu[2/3]					6d: Naoetsu to Nagano[1]	
	H	H	H	H	H		
Kanazawa	07:09	10:35	13:16	14:14	17:17	Naoetsu	08:10
Tsubata		10:44				Takada	08:20
Isurugi	07:25	10:53				Arai	08:43
Takaoka	07:35	11:04	13:41	14:39	17:41	Nihongi	08:52
Toyama	07:47	11:16	13:49	14:51	17:53	Sekiyama	09:01
Namerikawa	07:59					Myoko-Kogen	09:10
Uozu	08:05	11:33	14:09	15:07	18:09	Kurohime	09:18
Kurobe		11:38	14:14		18:14	Toyono	09:38
Nyuzen	08:16				18:22	Nagano	09:50
Tomari							
Itoigawa	08:37	12:06	14:41	15:37	18:43		
Naoetsu	09:00	12:31	15:03	15:59	19:05		

H = Hokuetsu [1] There are no limited express services between Nagano and Naoetsu; the local service generally operates once an hour though at irregular times.
[2] The times shown are a sample of the almost hourly service (in each direction) between Naoetsu and Kanazawa.
[3] See Table 8 for details of other services between Toyama and Kanazawa.

Table 7: Toyama/Takayama to Nagoya[1, 2]

	7a: Toyama to Nagoya					7b: Nagoya to Toyama			
Toyama[1]	08:10	13:09	15:12	17:16	↑	12:18	14:46	16:47	18:51
Hida-Furukawa	09:23	14:23	16:24	18:27		11:09	13:36	15:35	17:36
Takayama	09:42	14:42	16:42	18:49		10:56	13:24	15:23	17:24
Gero	10:28	15:26	17:26	19:35		10:12	12:37	14:35	16:34
Mino-Ota	11:23	16:25	18:29	20:27		09:22	11:43	13:43	15:43
Gifu	11:47	16:47	18:48	20:47	↓	09:02	11:23	13:22	15:22
Nagoya	12:09	17:09	19:09	21:09	▼	08:43	11:03	13:03	15:03

[1] At the time of writing the Hida LEX, which operates between Toyama and Nagoya, was only running from Hida-Furukawa, while repairs to the track between Toyama and Hida-Furukawa are carried out. The line is scheduled to reopen in autumn 2007, after which you can follow the route as per the text on p146; the train times given for Toyama are from before the work started to give an idea of departure/arrival times. The times from Hida-Furukawa were accurate at the time of writing.

Before it reopens, the route between Toyama and Hida-Furukawa is as follows: From Toyama take a local train to Tsunogawa, then a replacement bus from there to Inotani (JR passes valid), followed by another local train from Inotani to Hida-Furukawa, from where you pick up the Hida LEX to Takayama (see p179) and Nagoya (see p159). All this makes the journey from Toyama much more time-consuming, particularly because the connections between local trains and the replacement bus service are not always ideal. For up-to-date times of the local trains/replacement bus service, ask at the JR ticket office in Toyama/Hida-Furukawa or call the JR Infoline ☎ 03-3423 0111.

[2] Services for Nagoya that start in Takayama (and vice versa) are not given but generally operate once an hour during the day; some of these services stop also at Kuguno, Hida-Osaka, Hida-Hagiwara, Hida-Kanayama, Shirakawaguchi, Unuma and Owari-Ichinomiya.

Table 8: Toyama to Osaka

	8a: Toyama to Osaka					8b: Osaka to Toyama			
Toyama	08:19	10:07[1]	14:13	16:07	▲	11:59	12:59	15:04	17:06
Takaoka	08:31	10:19	14:25	16:19	↑	11:46	12:47	14:51	16:53
Kanazawa	09:04	10:52		16:52		11:22	12:23	14:27	16:29
Komatsu		11:10	14:59	17:10				14:06	16:08
Kaga-Onsen		11:19	15:23	17:19			11:55	13:57	15:59
Awara-Onsen		11:30		17:30			11:44	13:47	15:48
Fukui	09:47	11:42	15:43	17:42		10:32	11:33	13:36	15:38
Sabae				17:50					15:28
Takefu		11:54		17:54				13:23	
Tsuruga		12:16		18:15			13:02	15:02	
Kyoto	11:09	13:09	17:07	19:08		09:10	10:10	12:10	14:10
Shin-Osaka	11:32	13:32	17:30	19:32		08:46	09:46	11:46	13:46
Osaka	11:37	13:37	17:34	19:37	▼	08:42	09:42	11:42[2]	13:42

[1] Also at 11:11, 12:07 and 13:11 [2] Hourly, at 42 mins past the hour, until 18:42. However, the stops and therefore departure/arrival times vary so it is essential to check.

Table 9: Nagoya to Shingu[1]

	9a: Nagoya to Shingu[2]					9b: Shingu to Nagoya[3]			
Nagoya	08:14	10:06	13:06	19:45	▲	09:34	12:18	16:18	20:40
Kuwana	08:32	10:24	13:24	20:03	↑	09:13	11:58	15:59	20:20
Yokkaichi	08:42	10:35	13:35	20:14		09:02	11:47	15:48	20:09
Suzuka	08:50	10:42	13:44	20:22		08:54	11:39	15:40	20:00
Tsu	09:02	10:57	13:57	20:35		08:41	11:27	15:27	19:48
Matsusaka	09:17	11:12	14:12	20:50		08:26	11:12	15:11	19:33
Taki	09:25	11:20	14:19	20:57		08:19	11:03	15:04	19:26
Misedani	09:46	11:42	14:41	21:19		07:57	10:40	14:41	19:04
Kii-Nagashima	10:14	12:09	15:09	21:46		07:30	10:13	14:14	18:37
Owase	10:35	12:32	15:30	22:07		07:08	09:51	13:51	18:15
Kumano-shi	11:02	13:02	15:57	22:34		06:41	09:24	13:23	17:48
Shingu	11:21	13:25	16:17	22:53	▼	06:22	09:04	13:03	17:28

[1] Rail-pass holders have to pay an additional fare (¥490) between Yokkaichi and Tsu.
[2] All trains apart from the 19:45 from Nagoya continue to Kii-Katsuura (see p202).
[3] All trains apart from the 06:22 start in Kii-Katsuura (see p202).

Table 10: Shingu to Shin-Osaka and Kyoto

	10a: Shingu to Kyoto				10b: Kyoto to Shingu			
	SK	SK	OA	SK	K	SK	OA	SK
Shingu	08:34	10:35	13:03	15:47	14:14	15:03	16:49	19:01
Kii-Katsuura	08:53	10:50	13:17	16:02	14:00	14:48	16:35	18:46
Taiji	08:59	10:56						18:40
Koza	09:16	11:14		16:29	13:38	14:23		18:23
Kushimoto	09:24	11:22	13:45	16:37	13:26	14:14	16:07	18:15
Susami	09:54	12:01	14:14	17:07	12:45	13:39	15:37	17:44
Tsubaki	10:07				12:31			17:31
Shirahama	10:30	12:34	14:33	17:34	12:22	13:19	15:14	17:19
Kii-Tanabe	10:41	12:45	14:44	17:45	12:12	13:07	15:04	17:07
Gobo	11:08	13:12	15:11	18:12	11:43	12:40	14:37	16:40
Wakayama	11:47	13:50	15:48	18:51	11:03	12:02	14:02	16:03
Hineno	12:05				10:44			15:44
Tennoji	12:29	14:29	16:29	19:34	10:20	11:20	13:20	15:20
Shin-Osaka	12:49	14:49	16:51	19:51	10:03	11:03	13:03	15:03
Kyoto			17:17	20:17	09:32	10:35	12:33	

SK = Super-Kuroshio   K = Kuroshio   OA = Ocean-Arrow
Note: not all stops are shown

Table 11: Shin-Yamaguchi to Yonago via Masuda and Matsue

	11a: Shin-Yamaguchi to Yonago				11b: Yonago to Shin-Yamaguchi			
Shin-Yamaguchi	08:51		13:02	17:00	15:07		18:43	10:13
Yuda-Onsen	09:02		13:14	17:11	14:58		18:33	10:03
Yamaguchi	09:07		13:17	17:15	14:54		18:30	10:00
Mitani	09:34		13:42	17:41	14:29		18:04	09:34
Tokusa	09:45		13:53	17:52	14:18		17:52	09:24
Tsuwano	09:58		14:06	18:05	14:06		17:39	09:11
Nichihara	10:08		14:16	18:15	13:55		17:29	09:01
Masuda	10:29		14:36	18:37	13:34		17:08	08:40[1]
Masuda	10:31	12:06	14:40	18:40	13:31	14:52	17:06	19:11
Mihomisumi	14:59		19:01		13:13		16:48	18:51
Hamada	11:05	12:40	15:14	19:17	12:57	14:19	16:31	18:36
Hashi	11:14		15:23		12:48		16:21	
Gotsu	11:22	12:55	15:31	19:32	12:37	14:04	16:14	18:19
Yunotsu			15:43	19:44			16:01	
Oda-Shi	11:49	13:25	16:04	20:01	12:10	13:37	15:45	17:47
Izumo-Shi	12:16	13:53	16:31	20:25	11:47	13:14	15:22	17:24
Shinji	12:27		16:49	20:36				17:10
Tamatsukuri-Onsen		14:13	16:58	20:46	11:25		15:03	16:58
Matsue	12:43	14:19	17:04	20:52	11:19		14:57	16:50
Yasugi	12:59	14:35	17:24	21:09	11:00	12:43	14:41	16:34
Yonago[2]	13:07	14:43	17:32	21:17	10:53	12:20	14:34	16:27
Kurayoshi		15:16	18:05		10:17	11:48	14:01	15:55
Tottori		15:43	18:31		09:49	11:21	13:34	15:21[3]

[1] The 08:40 from Masuda starts in Yonago at 05:52
[2] There are also LEX services from Yonago to Tottori at 12:17 arr 13:16 and 18:42 arr 19:43
[3] The 15:21 service from Tottori terminates at Masuda.

Table 12: Tokyo to Sendai, Morioka and Hachinohe by shinkansen

12a: Tokyo to Sendai/Morioka/Hachinohe

	HAY	HAY	HAY	HAY	Y	Y	MY	MY
Tokyo	08:56	09:56	10:56	11:56[1]	09:32	10:36[2]	09:24	10:08[3]
Ueno	09:02	10:02	11:02	12:02	09:38	10:42		10:14
Omiya	09:22	10:22	11:22	12:22	09:58	11:02	09:48	10:34
Utsunomiya					10:24	11:26		10:59
Koriyama					10:56	11:56		11:32
Fukushima					11:11	12:11	10:54	11:52
Sendai	10:38	11:38	12:38	13:38	11:42	12:42	11:24	12:20
Furukawa					11:56	12:56		
Kurikoma-Kogen					12:06	13:06		
Ichinoseki					12:15	13:15		
Mizusawa-Esashi					12:26	13:26		
Kitakami					12:34	13:34		
Shin-Hanamaki					12:42	13:42		
Morioka	11:26	12:26	13:26	14:26	12:53	13:53		
Iwate-Numakunai	11:39		13:39					
Ninohe	11:52	12:48	13:52					
Hachinohe	12:03	12:59	14:03	14:55				

HAY = Hayate   Y = Yamabiko   MY = Max-Yamabiko (double decker)

[1] hourly till 18:56 (see Table 16, p466, for details of some of the other Hayate services between Morioka and Hachinohe)
[2] hourly till 17:36   [3] hourly till 18:08

12b: Morioka/Sendai/Hachinohe to Tokyo

	HAY	HAY	HAY	HAY	Y	Y	MY	MY
Hachinohe	08:00	08:56	10:05	10:56[1]				
Ninohe	08:12	09:08		11:08				
Iwate-Numakunai		09:21		11:21				
Morioka	08:40	09:40	10:40	11:40	09:57	11:09[2]		
Shin-Hanamaki					10:10	11:21		
Kitakami					10:21	11:28		
Mizusawa-Esashi					10:30	11:37		
Ichinoseki					10:40	11:47		
Kurikoma-Kogen					10:49	11:56		
Furukawa					10:58	12:05		
Sendai	09:26	10:26	11:26	12:26	11:14	12:20	08:42	09:40[3]
Fukushima					11:37	12:47	09:13	10:17
Koriyama					11:56	13:03	09:29	10:33
Utsunomiya					12:30	13:32	10:01	11:05
Omiya	10:42	11:42	12:42	13:42	12:58	13:58	10:26	11:30
Ueno	11:02	12:02	13:02	14:02	13:18	14:18	10:46	11:50
Tokyo	11:08	12:08	13:08	14:08	13:24	14:24	10:52	11:56

HAY = Hayate   Y = Yamabiko   MY = Max-Yamabiko (double decker)

[1] approx hourly till 19:58 (see Table 16, p466, for details of some of the other Hayate services between Hachinohe and Morioka)
[2] approx hourly till 17:09   [3] hourly till 17:40

Note: The above is a selection of the many services on this route. Not all the stops are shown.

Table 13: Sendai to Matsushima-Kaigan

	13a: Sendai to M'shima-Kaigan		13b: M'shima-Kaigan to Sendai	
	Rapid[1]	Local[2]	Rapid[3]	Local[4]
Sendai	10:07	09:23	10:07	11:39
Hon-Shiogama	10:25	09:51	09:42	11:12
Matsushima-Kaigan	10:34	10:03	09:35	11:02

[1] Also at 11:07 and 12:07, thereafter at 58 minutes past the hour till 16:58.
[2] Hourly from 10:20 to 18:20.   [3] Hourly from 10:34 till 17:34   [4] Hourly till 18:02
Note: only the main stops are shown

Table 14: Matsushima to Ichinoseki

14a: Matsushima to Ichinoseki

Matsushima	08:26	09:24	11:04	13:08	15:07	17:04	18:06	19:20
Kogota	08:49	09:48	11:32	13:35	15:35	17:31	18:27	19:48
Hanaizumi	09:21	10:20	12:05	14:09	16:09	18:06	19:01	20:21
Ichinoseki	09:34	10:34	12:19	14:23	16:24	18:20	19:16	20:35

14b: Ichinoseki to Matsushima

Ichinoseki	08:00	10:56	12:49	14:52	16:43	17:55	19:00	19:54
Hanaizumi	08:15	11:10	13:03	15:06	16:58	18:10	19:15	20:08
Kogota	08:49	11:54	13:52	15:50	17:43	18:48	19:59	20:46
Matsushima	09:08	12:13	14:12	16:09	18:03	19:07	20:18	21:06

Table 15: (Morioka)–Hanamaki–Tono–Kamaishi–Miyako–Morioka

	15a: Hanamaki to Morioka				15b: Morioka to Hanamaki		
	R	R	R		R	R	R
(Morioka)	08:42	11:22	17:16		09:16	12:40	16:31
Hanamaki	09:12	11:53	17:46		08:42	12:05	15:56
Shin-Hanamaki	09:19	12:05	17:59		08:35	11:57	15:48
Tsuchizawa	09:31	12:12	18:05		08:28	11:50	15:41
Miyamori	09:44	12:25	18:19		08:14	11:36	15:27
Tono	10:11	12:48	18:43		07:53	11:12	15:03
Kosano	10:58	13:29	19:23		06:59	10:33	14:22
Kamaishi	11:04	13:35	19:29		06:55	10:28	14:17
	Lcl	Lcl			R	R	Lcl
Kamaishi	11:25	15:39	19:35		06:48	10:24	14:12
Namiita-Kaigan	11:55	16:04	20:04		06:23		13:44
Rikuchu-Yamada	12:10	16:26	20:21		06:07	09:51	13:29
Miyako	12:43	17:00	20:56		05:35	09:23	12:57
	Rpd	Lcl	Lcl		R	Lcl	Lcl
Miyako	09:17	15:49	18:11		12:48	15:47	18:53
Morioka	11:19	18:00	20:44		10:48	13:46	16:30
					Rpd	Rpd	Lcl

R = Rikuchu LEX, Lcl = local, Rpd = rapid

Table 16: Morioka to Aomori (and Hakodate)

16a: Morioka to Aomori (and Hakodate)

	HAY	HAY	HAY	HAY	HAY	HAY	HAY	HAY
Morioka	07:59	09:26	10:06	11:03	13:26	15:26	16:26	18:26
Iwate-Numakanai	08:13	09:39			13:39	15:39		
Ninohe	08:26	09:52	10:28		13:52	15:52		
Hachinohe	08:37	10:03	10:39	11:31	14:03	16:03	16:55	18:55
(change to LEX)	**SH**	**SH**	**H**	**SH**	**H**	**SH**	**SH**	**SH**
Hachinohe	08:52	10:15	10:50	12:16	14:15	16:14	17:07	19:02
Misawa	09:06	10:28	11:04	12:29	14:29	16:28	17:20	19:16
Noheji	09:24	10:45	11:22	12:46	14:47	16:45	17:37	19:33
Asamushi-Onsen	09:40			13:01	15:03	17:01	17:52	
Aomori	10:00	11:19	11:57	13:21	15:22	17:22	18:12	20:06
Hakodate	12:02	13:14	13:58	15:12	17:33	19:20	20:09	21:54

HAY = Hayate shinkansen   H = Hatsukari   SH = Super Hatsukari

Note: See Table 12 p464 for details of additional Hayate shinkansen services between Morioka and Hachinohe.

16b: (Hakodate and) Aomori to Morioka

	SH	SH	H	H	SH	SH	SH	H
Hakodate	07:00	08:48	10:40	11:28	12:53	13:54	15:42	16:51
Aomori	08:57	10:55	12:49	13:43	14:51	15:47	17:43	18:46
Asamushi-Onsen			13:02		15:04	15:59		18:58
Noheji	09:24	11:22	13:18	14:12	15:20	16:14	18:10	19:16
Misawa	09:41	11:39	13:36	14:30	15:37	16:31	18:27	19:34
Hachinohe	09:54	11:52	13:52	14:45	15:50	16:45	18:40	19:49
(change to shinkansen)	**HAY**	**HAY**	**HAY**	**HAY**	**HAY**	**HAY**	**HAY**	**HAY**
Hachinohe	10:05	12:05	14:04	14:56	16:05	16:56	18:56	19:58
Ninohe				15:08		17:08	19:08	20:11
Iwate-Numakanai				15:21		17:21	19:21	
Morioka	10:34	12:34	14:34	15:34	16:34	17:34	19:34	20:34

HAY = Hayate shinkansen   H = Hatsukari   SH = Super Hatsukari

Note: See Table 12 p464 for details of additional Hayate shinkansen services between Hachinohe and Morioka.

Table 17: Aomori to Odate (and Akita)

17a: Aomori to Odate & Akita

Aomori	06:07[1]	09:57	13:46	15:45
Hirosaki	06:39	10:27	14:16	16:16
Owani-Onsen		10:36	14:26	16:25
Ikarigaseki		10:44	14:34	16:33
Odate	07:11	11:02	14:54	16:51
Takanosu	07:26	11:17	15:09	17:05
Higashi-Noshiro	07:51	11:40	15:35	17:29
Hachirogata		12:04	16:00	17:52
Akita	08:51	12:28	16:24	18:17

17b: Akita & Odate to Aomori

Aomori	11:54	12:25	15:16	19:59
Hirosaki	11:12	11:50	14:46	19:28
Owani-Onsen		11:40	14:35	19:17
Ikarigaseki		11:33	14:28	19:10
Odate	10:31	11:15	14:10	18:52
Takanosu	10:13	10:53	13:56	18:38
Higashi-Noshiro	09:47	10:29	13:33	18:15
Hachirogata	09:15	10:07	13:08	17:52
Akita	08:46	09:41	12:43	17:30

[1] Continues to Niigata (see Table 18a).

The Tsugaru LEX also operates between (Hachinohe,) Aomori and Hirosaki approximately six times a day.

Table 18: Akita to Niigata

The services shown are the only direct services between Akita and Niigata; only the main stops are shown.

	18a: Akita to Niigata				18b: Niigata to Akita		
Akita	08:51[1]	12:49	16:34		12:11	16:15	19:28[2]
Kisakata	09:44	13:47	17:27		11:19	15:22	18:33
Sakata	10:31	14:22	18:00		10:48	14:51	18:02
Amarume	10:41	14:30	18:09		10:38	14:40	17:52
Tsuruoka	10:57	14:43	18:20		10:27	14:30	17:41
Atsumi-Onsen	11:18	15:03	18:39		10:07	14:09	17:20
Murakami	12:05	15:44	19:20		09:21	13:22	16:35
Niigata	12:59	16:32	20:07		08:33	12:34	15:48

[1] Comes from Aomori (see Table 17a).　　[2] Continues to Aomori (see Table 17b).

Table 19: Hakodate to Sapporo

19a: Hakodate to Sapporo

	SH	H	SH	SH	H	SH	H	SH
Hakodate	08:30	09:30	11:00	12:16	13:29	14:13	15:23	16:43
Goryokaku	08:34	09:34	11:04	12:21				
Onuma-Koen	08:49	09:53	11:20	12:36	13:49	14:30	15:43	
Mori	09:06		11:39		14:07	14:49	16:01	
Yakumo	09:25	10:30	11:57	13:08	14:28	15:07	16:22	
Oshamambe	09:43	10:49	12:15	13:26	14:47	15:26	16:43	
Toya	10:05	11:14	12:37	13:49	15:12	15:48	17:09	
Date-Mombetsu	10:15	11:25	12:47	13:59	15:23	15:57	17:19	
Higashi-Muroran	10:30	11:42	13:02	14:16	15:40	16:13	17:36	18:30
Noboribetsu	10:41	11:53	13:13	14:27	15:51	16:24	17:48	
Tomakomai	11:03	12:15	13:35	14:48	16:14	16:46	18:12	19:01
Minami-Chitose	11:19	12:31	13:50	15:03	16:29	17:01	18:28	19:16
Shin-Sapporo	11:39	12:50	14:09	15:22	16:50	17:20	18:50	19:35
Sapporo	11:47	12:59	14:17	15:31	16:58	17:29	18:59	19:43

19b: Sapporo to Hakodate

	H	SH	H	SH	SH	H	SH	SH
Sapporo	07:30	08:34	09:19	10:37	12:22	13:17	15:07	16:52
Shin-Sapporo	07:39	08:43	09:28	10:45	12:30	13:25	15:15	17:00
Minami-Chitose	08:00	09:04	09:47	11:05	12:48	13:45	15:34	17:19
Tomakomai	08:18	09:19	10:03	11:20	13:04	14:01	15:50	17:34
Noboribetsu	08:42	09:40	10:25	11:42	13:25	14:23	16:11	17:59
Higashi-Muroran	08:56	09:52	10:38	11:53	13:37	14:36	16:23	18:12
Date-Mombetsu	09:13	10:06	10:54		13:51	14:52	16:37	18:26
Toya	09:24	10:16	11:04	12:15	14:00	15:02	16:46	18:36
Oshamambe		10:39	11:30	12:39		15:28	17:10	18:59
Yakumo	10:11	10:57	11:49	12:56		15:47	17:28	19:17
Mori		11:15	12:10			16:08	17:46	19:35
Onuma-Koen	10:49	11:33	12:27	13:29	15:11	16:25	18:02	
Goryokaku						16:44	18:19	20:09
Hakodate	11:11	11:53	12:49	13:50	15:31	16:48	18:24	20:14

H = Hokuto　　　SH = Super Hokuto

Table 20: Sapporo to Asahikawa

	20a: Sapporo to Asahikawa		20b: Asahikawa to Sapporo	
	S	L	S	L
Sapporo	08:00[1]	09:30[2]	09:20	10:00
Iwamizawa	08:24	09:58	08:56	09:32
Bibai	08:34	10:08	08:46	09:21
Sunagawa	08:44	10:20	08:36	09:09
Takikawa	08:49	10:26	08:30	09:03
Fukagawa	09:02	10:40	08:18	08:49
Asahikawa	09:20	11:00	08:00[3]	08:30[4]

S = Super White Arrow   L = Lilac

[1] Hourly till 22:00   [2] Hourly till 19:30   [3] Hourly till 20:00   [4] Hourly till 18:30

Table 21: Asahikawa to Abashiri

	21a: Asahikawa to Abashiri				21b: Abashiri to Asahikawa			
Asahikawa	09:01	11:19	16:58	19:08	10:10	13:10	17:11	20:59
Kamikawa	09:42	12:01	17:48	19:50	09:25	12:31	16:32	20:20
Kitami	11:57	14:19	19:58	22:08	07:12	10:19	14:19	18:09
Bihoro	12:20	14:43	20:22	22:32	06:49	09:56	13:55	17:45
Abashiri	12:46	15:09	20:48	22:58	06:23	09:30	13:29	17:19

These services originate (and terminate) in Sapporo and are the only direct limited express services between Asahikawa and Abashiri. Times are given only for the stations where the route guide suggests stopping.

Table 22: Abashiri to Kushiro[1]

	22a: Abashiri to Kushiro				22b: Kushiro to Abashiri			
Abashiri	06:41	10:01	16:15	18:50	09:18	12:05	18:49	21:25
Kitahama	06:57	10:15	16:33	19:08	09:02	11:51	18:33	21:08
Shiretoko-Shari	07:27	10:46	17:30	19:36	08:34	11:25	18:06	20:43
Kawayu-Onsen	08:17	11:40	18:25	20:36	07:46	10:36	17:22	19:59
Mashu	08:37	11:55	18:47	20:55	07:29	10:21	17:05	19:42
Toro	09:36	12:48	19:36	21:48	06:34	09:36	16:19	18:52
Kushiro	10:07	13:19	20:06	22:19	05:59	09:05	15:48	18:19

[1] The services shown above are the only direct services between Abashiri and Kushiro; times are given only for the stations where the route guide suggests stopping.

See p346 for details of trains from Kushiro to Shintoku.

Table 23: Shintoku to Furano [All services shown are direct]

23a: Shintoku to Furano

Shintoku	05:51	07:58[1]	10:12[2]	11:32[2]	14:09[1]	19:20[2]	21:04[1]
Furano	07:19	09:41	11:32	13:03	15:45	20:33	22:29

[1] This service originates in Ikeda.   [2] This service originates in Obihiro.

23b: Furano to Shintoku

Furano	07:22[1]	09:15[1]	11:06[2]	16:44	19:10[1]	22:00
Shintoku	09:04	10:43	12:45	18:08	20:37	23:27

[1] This service continues to Obihiro.   [2] This service continues to Kushiro.

Table 24: Furano to Asahikawa

A steam train, SL Furano Biei, operates between Asahikawa months; check locally for details.

24a: Furano to Asahikawa

Furano	10:02	11:45	13:11	15:34	16:57	18:0			
Naka-Furano	10:12	11:52	13:22	15:47	17:07	18:1:			
Kami-Furano	10:22	11:59	13:33	15:57	17:21	18:21			
Bibaushi	10:32	12:15	13:42	16:10	17:31	18:30	19:39	21:08	
Biei	10:39	12:23	13:50	16:28	17:39	18:38	19:47	21:15	
Asahikawa	11:11	12:55	14:24	17:02	18:17	19:09	20:18	21:41	

[1] This service originates in Obihiro at 18:36 and departs Shintoku at 19:21 (see Shintoku to Furano opposite).

24b: Asahikawa to Furano

Asahikawa	09:29	11:30	13:37	15:25	16:30	17:46	18:34	20:38
Biei	10:02	12:08	14:16	16:01	17:03	18:20	19:13	21:15
Bibaushi	10:10	12:16	14:23	16:09	17:11	18:31	19:20	21:23
Kami-Furano	10:27	12:25	14:33	16:19	17:21	18:40	19:30	21:32
Naka-Furano	10:34	12:33	14:41	16:28	17:33	18:48	19:38	21:39
Furano	10:41	12:40	14:51	16:38	17:39	18:55	19:48	21:46

Table 25: Hakata/Fukuoka to Nagasaki

	25a: Hakata to Nagasaki			25b: Nagasaki to Hakata	
Hakata	10:02[1]	10:22[2]		09:20	11:00
Futsukaichi		10:34			10:50
Tosu	10:23	10:49		08:59	10:37
Saga	10:38	11:04		08:45	10:23
Hizen-Yamaguchi	10:47	11:15		08:35	10:12
Hizen-Kashima	10:58	11:25		08:25	09:57
Isahaya	11:33	12:09		07:49	09:10
Urakami	11:51	12:26		07:33	08:53
Nagasaki	11:54	12:29		07:30[3]	08:50[4]

Note: Services operate before and after the given times but not regularly. Even though the service operates twice-hourly departure/arrival times can vary by up to five minutes.
[1] Hourly till 21:02   [3] Hourly till 21:30
[2] Hourly till 18:22   [4] Hourly till 18:50

Table 26: Hakata/Fukuoka to Kagoshima-chuo (by LEX and shinkansen)

	26a: Hakata to Shin-Yatsushiro (LEX)			26b: Shin-Yatsushiro Hakata (LEX)	
Hakata	09:10[1]	09:30[2]		10:53	11:09
Tosu	09:30	09:51		10:33	10:46
Kurume	09:37	09:57		10:27	10:40
Omuta	09:56	10:20		10:03	10:20
Kumamoto	10:27	10:53		09:30	09:51
Shin-Yatsushiro	10:47	11:13		09:06[3]	09:26[4]

[1] Hourly till 21:10   [2] Hourly till 19:30   [3] Hourly till 19:06   [4] Hourly till 16:26
In both directions subsequent departure/arrival times sometimes vary by a few minutes.
Only the main stops are shown.   (Table 26 cont'd on p470)

_ont'd)

	26a: Shin-Yatsushiro to Kagoshima-chuo (shinkansen)		26b: Kagoshima-chuo to Shin-Yatsushiro (shinkansen)	
.ın-Yatsushiro	10:50[1]	11:16[2]	09:03	09:24
Shin-Minamata		11:30	08:49	
Izumi		11:38	08:42	
Sendai	11:17	11:50	08:30	08:58
Kagoshima-chuo	11:30	12:03	08:16[3]	08:45[4]

[1] hourly till 19:49 [2] hourly till 21:15 [3] hourly till 21:17 [4] hourly till 17:52
In both directions subsequent departure/arrival times sometimes vary by a few minutes.

Table 27: Kokura to Miyazaki

	27a: Kokura to Miyazaki				27b: Miyazaki to Kokura			
Kokura	10:48	12:46	14:46	16:46	12:32	15:31	16:32	19:06
Nakatsu	11:18	13:18	15:17	17:17	12:02	15:02	16:02	18:32
Beppu	11:56	13:56	15:55	17:56	11:22	14:23	15:23	17:43
Oita	12:10	14:10	16:09	18:11	11:12	14:10	15:11	17:34
Saiki	13:05	15:08	17:12	19:14	10:07	13:05	14:12	16:36
Nobeoka	14:05	16:04	18:15	20:12	09:09	12:07	13:11	15:35
Miyazaki	15:10	17:13	19:18	21:22	08:09	11:01	12:03	14:31

Services from Beppu/Oita to Miyazaki operate approximately once an hour and from Hakata/Kokura to Oita twice an hour. The same applies in the other direction.

Table 28: Okayama to Takamatsu

	28a: Okayama to Takamatsu		28b: Takamatsu to Okayama	
Okayama	09:04[1]	09:33[2]	09:16	09:45
Senoo		09:40	09:09	09:38
Hayashima	09:15		09:05	09:35
Chaya-machi	09:18	09:47	09:01	09:31
Kojima	09:28	09:56	08:53	09:23
Sakaide	09:43	10:10	08:37	09:08
Takamatsu	09:58	10:26	08:23[3]	08:53[4]

[1] Hourly till 19:14 [2] Hourly till 22:44 [3] Hourly till 21:13 [4] Hourly till 21:43
In both directions subsequent dep/arr times vary by up to ten minutes from those shown

Table 29: Takamatsu to Kochi

	29a: Takamatsu to Kochi				29b: Kochi to Takamatsu			
Takamatsu	08:08	09:10	12:10	20:17	11:06	17:11	20:41	21:36
Sakaide	08:23	09:26	12:24	20:30	10:53	16:56	20:27	21:22
Utazu		09:36	12:35	20:40	10:49	16:51	20:21	21:18
Marugame	08:29	09:39	12:38	20:43	10:43	16:45	20:15	21:12
Tadotsu	08:34	09:44	12:44	20:48	10:39	16:40	20:11	21:08
Zentsu-ji	08:39	09:49	12:49	20:53	10:34	16:34	20:05	21:03
Kotohira	08:44	09:53	12:54	21:01	10:29	16:29	20:00	20:58
Awa-Ikeda	09:16	10:21	13:22	21:25	10:06	16:06	19:33	20:35
Oboke	09:34	10:39	13:40	21:43	09:47	15:48	19:15	
Osugi	09:55	10:59		22:00			18:57	20:02
Tosa-Yamada	10:15	11:19	14:15	22:20	09:12	15:13	18:36	19:43
Gomen	10:19	11:23	14:19	22:24	09:07	15:08	18:32	19:38
Kochi	10:27	11:30	14:27	22:32	09:00	15:00	18:24	19:30

Table 30: Kochi to Kubokawa

	30a: Kochi to Kubokawa					30b: Kubokawa to Kochi			
Kochi	09:50	11:34	13:26	15:19		09:58	12:57	14:55	16:55
Ino	10:01	11:47	13:36	15:32		09:42	12:44		16:42
Sakawa	10:14	12:00	13:49	15:45		09:29	12:32	14:34	16:30
Susaki	10:31	12:20	14:02	15:58		09:17	12:19	14:21	16:17
Kubokawa	10:57	12:45	14:27	16:23		08:50	11:55	13:55	15:50

Not all stops are shown

Table 31: Kubokawa to Uwajima

	31a: Kubokawa to Uwajima					31b: Uwajima to Kubokawa			
Kubokawa	10:01	13:22	14:37	16:37		11:45	13:45	17:32	19:08
Tokawa	10:39	14:04	15:23	17:18		11:04	12:48	16:46	18:31
Ekawasaki	10:58	14:16	15:56	17:39		10:52	12:34	16:33	18:15
Uwajima	12:06	15:21	17:03	18:49		09:35	11:29	15:22	17:09

Table 32: Uwajima to Matsuyama

	32a: Uwajima to Matsuyama[1]					32b: Matsuyama to Uwajima			
Uwajima	08:32	09:51	12:47	14:51		09:26	10:22	11:27	12:37
Uno-machi	08:52	10:09	13:05	15:09		09:08	10:01	11:10	12:20
Yawatahama	09:06	10:21	13:20	15:24		08:57	09:49	10:58	12:04
Iyo-Ozu	09:18	10:33	13:32	15:37		08:44	09:37	10:45	11:51
Uchiko	09:30	10:46	13:41	15:47		08:34	09:28	10:35	11:41
Iyo-shi	09:48	11:02		16:03		08:14	09:08	10:19	11:25
Matsuyama	09:57	11:10	14:03	16:11		08:06	09:00	10:11	11:17[2]

[1] Services operate approximately hourly till 20:59 but at different times each hour.
[2] Hourly till 20:18 but not all trains stop at the stations shown and departure/arrival times vary by a few minutes.

Table 33: Matsuyama to Okayama

	33a: Matsuyama to Okayama								
Matsuyama	09:12	10:15	11:18	12:13	13:17	15:18	16:22	17:25
Iyo-Hojo	09:24							
Imabari	09:52	10:53	11:56	12:50	13:56	15:55	16:57	18:01
Iyo-Saijo	10:06	11:15	12:19	13:17	14:17	16:17	17:17	18:21
Niihama	10:22	11:23	12:26	13:25	14:25	16:25	17:25	18:29
Kanon-ji	10:57	11:57	13:00	14:00	14:57	16:58	17:58	19:01
Tadotsu	11:12	12:13	13:15	14:15	15:12	17:14	18:14	19:16
Marugame	11:16	12:16	13:19	14:19	15:16	17:17	18:17	19:20
Utazu	11:21	12:21	13:24	14:24	15:21	17:22	18:22	19:25
Kojima	11:36	12:36	13:37	14:37	15:36	17:36	18:36	19:38
Okayama	11:57	12:57	13:57	14:57	15:57	17:57	18:57	19:57

Note: Services divide at Utazu. The Shiokaze continues to Okayama but the other part of the train becomes the Ishizuchi and goes to Takamatsu. All services operate hourly but departure times vary by a few minutes.

Only the main stops are shown. *(Table 33 cont'd on p472)*

Table 33: *(cont'd)*

33b: Okayama to Matsuyama

Okayama	09:24	10:22	12:22	13:22	14:21	15:22	16:22	17:22
Kojima	09:46	10:46	12:45	13:45	14:45	15:45	16:45	17:45
Utazu	10:04	11:04	13:03	14:03	15:03	16:03	17:03	18:04
Marugame	10:08	11:08	13:07	14:06	15:06	16:07	17:06	18:08
Tadotsu	10:12	11:12	13:15	14:15	15:12	16:13	17:14	18:14
Kanon-ji	10:27	11:27	13:30	14:33	15:27	16:28	17:29	18:29
Niihama	10:58	11:59	14:01	15:07	15:58	17:00	18:00	19:02
Iyo-Saijo	11:06	12:07	14:09	15:15	16:06	17:08	18:21	19:19
Imabari	11:31	12:31	14:34	15:36	16:29	17:34	18:34	19:34
Iyo-Hojo					16:57	18:01	18:58	20:02
Matsuyama	12:05	13:07	15:10	16:14	17:09	18:13	19:11	20:14

Note: The Shiokaze from Okayama joins up with the Ishizuchi from Takamatsu at Utazu. Services from both places operate hourly though departure times vary by a few minutes.

Only the main stops are shown.

⛩ **High Steaks**

If you're dining on a budget, one place you may prefer to avoid in Tokyo is the Aragawa steak house (☎ 03-3591 8765, B1F, Hankyu Kotsusha Bldg, 3-9 Shimbashi 3-chome, Minato-ku) in Shimbashi, which according to forbes.com is officially the world's most expensive restaurant.

Aragawa serves Kobe beef, one of the best-known types of beef in Japan, with steak dishes going for a mere ¥50,000. Add on a starter and a glass or two of wine and you could easily be looking at a bill of ¥100,000 or more per person. The steak you get for your money is, apparently, tender and delicious: it's sourced from one particular farm in Hyogo prefecture, is cooked using a rare brand of charcoal called *binchotan*, and is seasoned with pepper and mustard.

INDEX

TRAILBLAZER GUIDES – TITLE LIST

For more information about Trailblazer, for where to find your nearest
stockist, for guidebook updates or for credit card mail order sales visit:

www.trailblazer-guides.com

Trans-Siberian Handbook *Bryn Thomas*
7th edn, 448pp, 60 maps, 40 colour photos
ISBN 978 1 873756 94 2, £13.99, US$19.95
First edition short-listed for the **Thomas Cook Guidebook Awards**.
New seventh edition of the most popular guide to the world's longest
rail journey. How to arrange a trip, plus a km-by-km guide to the
routes. Updated and expanded to include extra information on travelling independently in Russia. New mapping. '*The best guidebook is
Bryn Thomas's "Trans-Siberian Handbook"* **The Independent (UK)**

Siberian BAM Guide – rail, rivers & road
A Yates & N Zvegintzov, 2nd edn, 384pp, 22 colour photos
ISBN 978 1 873756 18 8, £13.99, US$23.95
Comprehensive guide to the BAM Zone in NE Siberia. Includes a km-
by-km guide to the 3400-km Baikal Amur Mainline (BAM) railway
which traverses east Siberia from the Pacific Ocean to Lake Baikal.
How to take the train and where to go in the BAM Zone, plus Lena
River and Kolyma Highway routes.
'*...an encyclopaedic companion.*' **The Independent**

Trans-Canada Rail Guide *Melissa Graham*
4th edn, 256pp, 35 maps, 30 colour photos
ISBN 978 1 905864 01 0, £11.99, US$19.95
New edition of this popular title. Comprehensive guide to Canada's
trans-continental railroad. Covers the entire route from coast to coast
with information for all budgets. Best sights, hotels and restaurants in
ten major stops including Quebec City, Montreal, Toronto, Winnipeg,
Jasper and Vancouver. '*Invaluable*' **The Daily Telegraph**

Australia by Rail *Colin Taylor*
5th edn, 304pp, 70 route maps & town plans, 30 colour photos
ISBN 978 1 873756 81 2, £12.99, US$21.95
Fifth edition of this long-running guide. With 65 strip maps covering all
rail routes in Australia, city guides (Sydney, Melbourne, Brisbane,
Adelaide, Perth, Darwin and Canberra), and now includes the new
Ghan line from Alice Springs to Darwin. '*Benefiting from Taylor's 30
years of travel on Australia's trains.*' **The Sunday Times**

Indian Rail Handbook *Nick Hill & Royston Ellis*   (Oct 2007)
1st edn, 256pp, 30 colour, 10 B&W photos, 80 maps
ISBN 978 1 873756 87 4, £12.99, US$19.95
India has the most comprehensive railway network in the world, with
almost all tourist attractions accessible by rail. For most visitors travel by
train is the preferred means of transport, the ideal way to see the coun-
try. This new book is a wholly inclusive guide for rail travellers in India.
● Fully-indexed **rail atlas** of 80 maps with all 7326 railway stations
● **Rail travel for all budgets** – from the luxury of the *Palace on
Wheels* to 2nd-class berths for budget-conscious travellers
● **Timetables, suggested itineraries** and how to book tickets
● **Special trains** and **railway history**

Due 2008 (in same format as *Indian Rail Handbook*):
China Rail Handbook *Nick Hill*
1st edn, 256pp, 30 colour, 10 B&W photos, 80 maps
ISBN 978 1 905864 05 8, £12.99, US$19.95

TREKKING GUIDES
Europe
Trekking in Corsica
Corsica Trekking – GR20
Dolomites Trekking – AV1 & AV2
Trekking in the Pyrenees
Scottish Highlands – The Hillwalking Guide
(and British Walking Series: see p477)
Africa
Kilimanjaro

South America
Inca Trail, Cusco & Machu Picchu
Australasia
New Zealand – The Great Walks
Asia
Trekking in the Annapurna Region
Trekking in the Everest Region
Trekking in Ladakh
Nepal Mountaineering Guide

The Inca Trail, Cusco & Machu Picchu *Richard Danbury*
3rd edition 320pp, 65 maps, 35 colour photos
ISBN 978-1-873756-86-7, £11.99, US$19.95
The **Inca Trail** from Cusco to Machu Picchu is South America's most pop-ular trek. Practical guide including detailed trail maps, plans of Inca sites, plus guides to Cusco and Machu Picchu. This expanded third edition includes new guides to the **Santa Teresa Trek** and the **Choquequirao Trek** as well as the **Vilcabamba Trail**. *'Danbury's research is thorough... you need this one'. **The Sunday Times***

Scottish Highlands – The Hillwalking Guide
Jim Manthorpe 1st edn 312pp, 86 maps 40 photos
ISBN 978-1-873756-84-3, £11.99, Can$26.95, US$19.95
This new guide covers 60 day-hikes in the following areas: ● Loch Lomond, the Trossachs and Southern Highlands ● Glen Coe and Ben Nevis ● Central Highlands ● Cairngorms and Eastern Highlands ● Western Highlands ● North-West Highlands ● The Far North ● The Islands. Plus: 3- to 4-day hikes linking some regions.

Trekking in the Pyrenees *Douglas Streatfeild-James*
3rd edition, 320pp, 97 maps, 60 colour photos
ISBN 978-1-873756-82-9, £11.99, Can$29.95, US$19.95
All the main trails along the France–Spain border including the GR10 (France) coast to coast trek and the GR11 (Spain) from Roncesvalles to Andorra, plus many shorter routes. 90 route maps include walking times and places to stay. *'Readily accessible, well-written '* **John Cleare**

New Zealand – The Great Walks *Alexander Stewart*
1st edn, 272pp, 60 maps, 40 colour photos
ISBN 978-1-873756-78-2, £11.99, Can$28.95, US$19.95
New Zealand is a wilderness paradise of incredibly beautiful land-scapes. There is no better way to experience it than on one of the nine designated Great Walks, the country's premier walking tracks which provide outstanding hiking opportunities for people at all levels of fit-ness. Also includes detailed guides to Auckland, Wellington, National Park Village, Taumaranui, Nelson, Queenstown, Te Anau and Oban.

Kilimanjaro: the trekking guide to Africa's highest mountain
Henry Stedman, 2nd edition, 320pp, 40 maps, 30 photos
ISBN 978-1-873756-97-1, £11.99, Can$24.95, US$19.95
At 19,340ft the world's tallest freestanding mountain, Kilimanjaro is one of the most popular destinations for hikers visiting Africa. It's possible to walk up to the summit: no technical skills are necessary. Includes town guides to Nairobi and Dar-Es-Salaam, excursions in the region and a detailed colour guide to flora and fauna. **Includes Mount Meru**.' *Stedman's won-derfully down-to-earth, practical guide to the mountain'.* **Longitude Books**

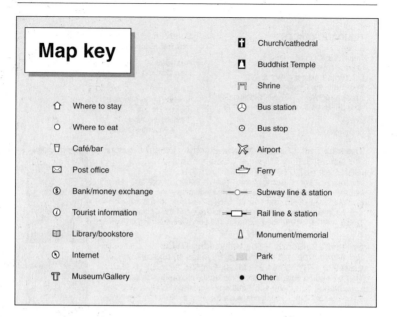

Map key

⇧	Where to stay	✝	Church/cathedral
O	Where to eat	卍	Buddhist Temple
⛾	Café/bar	🐦	Shrine
✉	Post office	⊘	Bus station
Ⓢ	Bank/money exchange	☉	Bus stop
ⓘ	Tourist information	✈	Airport
📖	Library/bookstore	⛴	Ferry
◑	Internet	—O—	Subway line & station
⊤	Museum/Gallery	▬□▬	Rail line & station
		Δ	Monument/memorial
			Park
		●	Other

(Opposite) Some typical Japanese dishes   [For more information see pp450-1]
Clockwise from top left
1: **Katsudon** – deep-fried breaded pork cutlet served on rice and covered with a soy sauce and egg based sauce.
2: **Sashimi** (raw fish) served with a shiso leaf, shredded daikon (radish) and wasabi.
3: **Sushi** – the main kinds are nigiri-zushi (on rice) and maki-zushi (wrapped in seaweed).
4: **Sanuki udon** (noodles) – a bowl of steaming hot noodles is the perfect way to warm up on a cold day.
5: **Unaju** – eel served on rice in a lacquerware box.
6: **Unagi** – eel grilling over charcoal.
7: **Tonkatsu** (deep-fried breaded pork cutlet) with shredded cabbage. Plastic models like this are often displayed in a restaurant's window to show customers what is available.
8: **Yakitori** – pieces of chicken on a bamboo stick cooked over a charcoal fire.

(Photo Nos 1, 3, 4, 5 and 8 © JNTO; No 6 © Wakayama Prefecture/© JNTO; Nos 2 and 7 © Kazuo Udagawa).

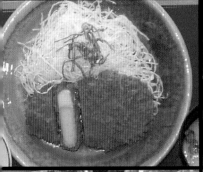

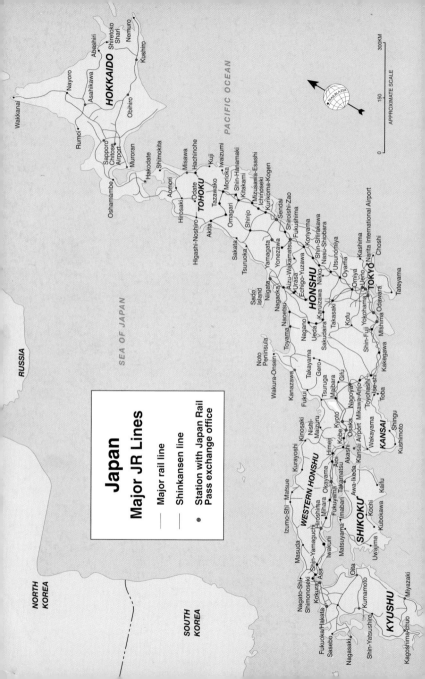